Jehovah's Witnesses:

Their Claims, Doctrinal Changes, and Prophetic Speculation. What Does the Record Show?

Edmond C. Gruss

Jehovah's Witnesses: Their Claims, Doctrinal Changes, and Prophetic Speculation. What Does the Record Show?
by Edmond C. Gruss

Printed in the United States of America
ISBN 1-931232-30-X

Xulon Press
11350 Random Hills Road
Suite 800
Fairfax, VA 22030
(703) 279-6511
XulonPress.com

Table of Contents

Acknowledgments

A study of this length and detail is only made possible because of the publications and contributions of many persons. All cannot be named here, but they are identified in the text and/or notes. Special thanks are given to these authors and publishers for permission to quote extensively from their publications: Carl Olof Jonsson, *The Gentile Times Reconsidered* (Commentary Press, 1998) and *The Sign of the Last Days—When?* (co-authored with Wolfgang Herbst) (Commentary Press, 1987); Raymond Franz, *Crisis of Conscience* (Commentary Press, 1992) and *In Search of Christian Freedom* (Commentary Press, 1991); and Dr. M. James Penton, *Apocalypse Delayed: The Story of Jehovah's Witnesses* (University of Toronto Press, 1997).

I also wish to thank Leonard Chretien and his wife, Marjorie, for their assistance in the research on Beth-Sarim and Beth-Shan, published in our book *Jehovah's Witnesses—Their Monuments to False Prophecy* and in the *Christian Research Journal* (1997), and for permission by editor Elliot Miller to use this material.

I am grateful to those whose experiences and testimonies are included in this book. I am also indebted to those I interviewed and the authors of numerous books, theses, dissertations, and articles, quoted in the text and listed in the endnotes, especially: Dr. Jerry Bergman, Robert Crompton, Dr. Melvin Curry, Dr. P. Gerhard Damsteegt, Duane Magnani, Jay Robert Nash, David Reed, Randall Watters, Timothy White, and Dr. Joseph Zygmunt.

Finally, I wish to thank Leonard Chretien, Dr. John Hotchkiss, Randall Watters, Duane Magnani, and Tom Freiling and the staff at Xulon Press, who reviewed the manuscript at various stages of completion, and Alex Odekerken for his computer assistance.

Publications and Other Information

Publications

The Watch Tower (Watchtower) publications quoted, or referred to in this study, will not include the place and publisher references in the notes. Each reference will include the date of publication the first time the source is cited. Material by other publishers will initially contain a complete entry.

The Golden Age magazine was published from October 1, 1919, to September 22, 1937. It was renamed *Consolation* in 1937 and *Awake!* on August 22, 1946, a title which is still current. In the notes these will be identified as *GA*, *Cons.*, and *Awake!*, respectively.

Zion's Watch Tower and Herald of Christ's Presence was first published in July 1879. It was renamed *The Watch Tower and Herald of Christ's Presence* on January 1, 1909, and *The Watchtower and Herald of Christ's Presence* on October 15, 1931. On January 1, 1939, it was changed to *The Watchtower and Herald of Christ's Kingdom*, and on March 1, 1939, *The Watchtower Announcing Jehovah's Kingdom*, which is still current. In 1919, the first forty years of the *Watch Tower* were reprinted in seven volumes of 6,622 pages, including an Index. References to page numbers for these years will be those found in the *Watch Tower Reprints* volumes. These are identified as *WTR* (*Watch Tower Reprints*), and all subsequent issues of the magazine to the present are designated *WT*.

With the exception of some articles in *The Golden Age* and *Consolation*, J. F. Rutherford wrote practically everything published while he was president. After his death, beginning with *The New World* (1942), books were published anonymously, but between 1942 and 1976, most were written by Frederick Franz. Other Watch Tower publications have also been anonymous, except for short "as told by" or "contributed by" articles.

The *New World Translation of the Holy Scriptures* (*NWT*) quoted is the revised edition of 1984, published by the Watchtower Bible and Tract Society of New York, Inc.

Watch Tower Presidents

Charles Taze Russell (1879-1916)
Joseph Franklin Rutherford (1917-42)
Nathan Homer Knorr (1942-77)
Frederick W. Franz (1977-92)
Milton G. Henschel (1993-2000)

A reorganization was announced in the January 15, 2001, *Watchtower* in which "certain members of the Governing Body of Jehovah's Witnesses who had been serving as directors and officers voluntarily stepped aside from the boards of directors of all the corporations used by 'the faithful and discreet slave' in the United States" (31). An earlier news release from the Jehovah's Witnesses Public Affairs Office was dated October 7, 2000.

Organization Names

The followers of C. T. Russell referred to themselves as Bible Students. This would change when the name Jehovah's witnesses (now Jehovah's Witnesses) was proposed by Rutherford and adopted in 1931. Those who did not follow Rutherford, and remained loyal to Russell's teachings, continued to use Bible Students. Witnesses was spelled with a lower case "w" until April 1976.

Russell incorporated Zion's Watch Tower Tract Society in 1884, which is now the Watch Tower Bible and Tract Society of Pennsylvania. People's Pulpit Association was the original name of the Watchtower Bible and Tract Society of New York, Inc., when it was established in Brooklyn in 1909. The International Bible Student's Association was chartered in 1914. Today, the Watch Tower Bible and Tract Society of Pennsylvania remains the official parent corporation over these and other corporations formed around the world.

Following the example of Raymond Franz and others, my references to the organization will use Watch Tower, Watch Tower Society, or Society.

Emphasis and Brackets

Unless otherwise noted, all **boldface type** found in quoted and non-quoted material is added for emphasis. Comments added to quotations are enclosed in **brackets** [ ]. Brackets which already appear in quotations will be noted.

Preface

My experience with the Jehovah's Witnesses began one day in 1940, when I was seven years old. A woman with a phonograph called on our home in Palms, California, and played a record of one of Watch Tower President Judge Rutherford's talks. My mother became interested in the urgent message. This initial contact turned into a ten-year period of hosting book studies in our home, studying the latest Watch Tower materials, attending congregational meetings at rented Kingdom halls, traveling to and working at assemblies, calling house-to-house and witnessing on street corners.

When I was eight years old, I accompanied my mother and other Witnesses to the national convention in St. Louis, Missouri. I remember receiving the new book *Children* which was released on "Children's Day," Sunday, August 10, 1941. The book further reinforced the belief that Armageddon was very near. It told the touching story of twenty-year-old John and eighteen-year-old Eunice. Although they loved each other very much, they agreed to postpone their marriage, reasoning: "Armageddon is surely near, and during that time the Lord will clean off the earth everything that offends and is disagreeable.... Our hope is that within a few years our marriage may be consummated and, by the Lord's grace, we shall have sweet children that will be an honor to the Lord. We can well defer our marriage until lasting peace comes to the earth" (366). As I write this, John and Eunice would now be in their late 70s.

When the September 15, 1941, *Watchtower* reported on the distribution of 15,000 copies of the book on "Children's Day," it stated: "Receiving the gift, the marching children clasped it to them, not a toy or plaything for idle pleasure, but the Lord's provided instrument for most effective work **in the remaining months before Armageddon**" (288). President Rutherford told the children: "It is your privilege between now and before the day school opens to spend six hours a day in taking the book *Children* to others." The *Watchtower* article then urges: "The parents should encourage their children to do this very thing, **if they would have them live**" (ibid.). I remember telling my friends and others how short the time was before Armageddon.

In 1950, at the age of seventeen, I accepted Jesus Christ as my personal Savior. I was like the Philippian jailer as he asked, "What must I do to be saved?" The answer came, "Believe on the Lord Jesus Christ, and thou shalt be saved" (Acts 16:31). Christ said: "Verily, verily, I say unto you, He that heareth my word, and believeth him that sent me, hath eternal life, and cometh not into judgment, but hath passed out of death into life" (John 5:24). I knew from that time onward that a change had come into my life. I also read in Ephesians 2:8-10 where works fit: "For by grace have ye been saved through faith; and that not of yourselves, *it is* the gift of God; not of works, that no man should glory. For we are his workmanship, created in Christ Jesus for good works, which God afore prepared that we should walk in them." (I read these and other passages from the *American Standard Version,* which the Watch Tower Society had reprinted.) Salvation came through faith in the finished work of Christ, not through an organization!

In the spring of 1971, I was checking the religion section of the card catalog in the Los Angeles Central library where I observed a man looking through the files under "Jehovah's Witnesses." I introduced myself and a conversation followed. He was looking for information on the Witnesses because his mentally gifted grandchildren were about to graduate from high school. They had been offered scholarships to college, but because of the nearness of Armageddon (1975), and Society warnings against higher education, they had turned them down to devote their efforts to field service before the end of this "system of things." I sent him information on the Witnesses, but I could not find anything current on their record of false prophecies. So I decided that I would write an article (a tract) on the issue. The more I investigated the matter, the longer the study became. It resulted in my book *The Jehovah's Witnesses and Prophetic Speculation* (1972, 2nd ed. Dec. 1975), with eight printings. The study looked back at the past Watch Tower Society failures and forward to the year 1975 (which also failed).

As I write this, many years have gone by since I wrote the *Speculation* book and much has been written exposing the doctrines and prophetic failures of the Witnesses. My interest in the subject has continued over the years with the collection of further historical information, examples of prophetic failure, erroneous interpretations, and doctrinal changes, far beyond what I put in the *Speculation* book. The present study is the result of those findings. It is my desire and prayer that the material will inform the reader. Beyond this, what is my motive in writing such a study? The answer is quite simple: **Truth.**

Introduction

The quantity of material available and the examples and details which could be included in surveying the subjects of this study are overwhelming, and in some cases an individual section or chapter could easily be expanded into an **entire book**. Because of this, the subjects or examples used must be selective and limited in their coverage, and many details must be omitted. As an example, note the potential for what might be included in a review of the doctrinal changes and new interpretations of second Watch Tower President Joseph F. Rutherford (1917-42). In his book *Merariism* (1938), Paul S. L. Johnson, "an able but eccentric colporteur ... perhaps [Watch Tower founder] Russell's best educated and most studious associate,"[1] discusses some of these changes. He says that he stopped reviewing Rutherford's writings in 1935 and notes some **140 times where his "supposed clarifications" were in "striking contradiction" to Russell's teachings.**[2] He then concludes: "If I would point out the details of errors coming under point (62) above—'misinterpreting thousands of verses properly interpreted by "that Servant" [Russell]'—**our list would swell into thousands of details**; for almost never does he allude to or quote a passage in an article on his pet views but he corrupts its sense. **Yet he says, he has not changed our Pastor's teachings, has only clarified them!**"[3] The point here is not whether Russell or Rutherford were right in their interpretations, but that Rutherford changed what had been taught for many years as **Scriptural truth**, revealed by God.

In their book *The Desolations of the Sanctuary* (1930), Bible Students Emil and Otto Sadlack, report on what they observed:

> **Now it happens frequently that the same point of doctrine was presented by the Society before 1918 totally different from the exposition given after 1918, and often in direct opposition to it.** Before 1918 it was said that the knowledge was from the Lord; this was expressly stated and with emphasis. Then when the new light came upon the same question after 1918, directly opposed to the first exposition, it was said again, and most emphatically called attention to with many words.... Be it noted that in the expositions before and after 1918 it is not the question simply of similar or related expositions, but often of **presentations totally opposed to each other.... Thinking Christians will put such questions as: "If the application given before 1918 was in truth from the Lord, why was it rejected after 1918 and replaced by an entirely new one?"**[4]

This concluding question is a very important one, and specific examples and details of what Johnson and the Sadlacks refer to are presented later in this book. As already indicated, this study must be selective, presenting examples which are typical of many others that might have been used. But, it might be asked: How many examples are necessary to make or prove a point? How many failed predictions, changes in God-given "due time" interpretations, dishonest or inept handling of sources, or misuses of Scripture, are necessary to question the credibility of the movement's claims? I believe the contents of this study are more than sufficient to settle the issue.

Organization

This study begins with a selection of statements and claims that relate to how the Watch Tower organization views itself and its publications, and how correct interpretations of Scripture and understanding of prophecy are accomplished. Are Watch Tower Society publications inspired? If not, what is an accurate understanding of the claims made? It is legitimate to look at the contents of these publications in the light of what is claimed for them, as well as the claims of the organization publishing them.

Next, several well-informed reviewers are quoted as they comment on the Witnesses' latest official history, *Jehovah's Witnesses—Proclaimers of God's Kingdom* (1993). Is this volume really candid as claimed? Does it always deal honestly with the history of the movement? Further insight into these questions is gained when the *Proclaimers* history is cited in the later chapters of this study.

It is necessary to look at William Miller (1782-1849) and the history of the Second Advent movement as a background to understanding the source of much of Charles Taze Russell's doctrinal system, especially his eschatology, which in some important particulars is still foundational to the Witnesses' teaching today. Can Russell's Bible Students movement be accurately described as another "Millerite offshoot"?

The major part of the study reviews and examines what has been taught by Russell and Watch Tower leadership since the 1870s, with special emphasis on their eschatology and prophetic speculation. What interpretations of prophecy have been taught and have any major predictions been fulfilled in the more than 120 years of the movement's history?

The twelve "Selected Quotations" sections, covering every year from 1876 to the present, drawn primarily from Watch Tower publications, are presented in chronological order and are usually arranged by decade. The quotations cited are typical examples of what was taught concerning end time events and prophetic speculations. These quotation sections are preceded or followed by chapters on specific doctrines or developments which relate to that period. In some cases they appear when a doctrine is "adjusted" or "clarified" because of "new light," or when it was rejected. For example, The Great Pyramid of Egypt is featured after the 1920s quotations because of its rejection in 1928. Rutherford's new identification of the "Great Multitude" as an earthly class (1935) follows the 1930s section. The "new light" on the "Superior Authorities" of Romans 13 (1962), the parable of the sheep and the goats (1995), and "this generation" of 1914 (1997) are all placed after the selected quotation sections for the decades of the 1960s and 1990s. Some subjects, which cover many years of the movement's history, are presented where thy seem to fit the best.

Because of its crucial importance to the organization's doctrines, claims, and authority, the Witnesses' teachings concerning 1914 is given the most extensive coverage. Several additional examples of doctrinal changes are reviewed in the last chapter before the conclusion.

The best way to get the overall picture of the study is to spend several minutes in reviewing the Table of Contents.

By design, there has been no attempt to deal with some of the major doctrines of Christianity, such as the Person and work of Christ—or some of the other doctrines important to the Jehovah's Witnesses, like blood transfusions—which have been adequately covered in other books.

Reviewing the Record

The April 1, 1972, *Watchtower* article, "They Shall Know that a Prophet Was Among Them," has often been quoted, where it is asked:

> So, does Jehovah have a prophet to help them, to warn them of dangers and to declare things to come? These questions can be answered in the affirmative. Who is this prophet?... This "prophet" was not one man, but was a body of men and women. It was a small group of footstep followers

of Jesus Christ, known at that time as International Bible Students. Today they are known as Jehovah's Christian witnesses.... **Of course, it is easy to say that this group acts as a "prophet" of God. It is another thing to prove it. The only way that this can be done is to review the record. What does it show?**[5]

The article goes on to review some of the "prophet's" publications beginning with World War I, the preaching of the "good news of God's kingdom," and the warning to Christendom of God's impending judgment. In the concluding portion of the article it is stated:

...Jehovah's witnesses today make their declaration of the good news of the kingdom **under angelic direction and support.** (Rev. 14:6, 7; Matt. 25:31, 32)[6] And since no word or work of Jehovah can fail, for he is God Almighty, the nations will see the fulfillment of what these witnesses say as **directed from heaven.** Yes, the time must come shortly that the nations will have to know that really a "prophet" of Jehovah was among them.[7]

As quoted above, "it is easy to say that this group acts as a 'prophet' of God," and that it preaches its message "under angelic direction and support," and as claimed elsewhere, that their understanding of prophecy and the interpretations of the Bible come from God.[8] Is the message proclaimed credible? Do the interpretations of Scripture and prophecy demonstrate God's direction, or merely the opinions of men? **What does the record show?**

Notes

1. M. James Penton, *Apocalypse Delayed* (2nd ed.; Toronto: University of Toronto Press, 1997), 40-41. Penton's book should be consulted for further information on Johnson. Under Johnson's leadership, the Laymen's Home Missionary Movement was established.
2. Paul S. L. Johnson, *Merariism* (Philadelphia: Paul S. L. Johnson, 1938), 373-77.
3. Ibid., 377.
4. Emil and Otto Sadlack, *The Desolations of the Sanctuary* (1st English ed.; Brooklyn: Pastoral Bible Institute, 1930), 147. The Sadlacks write that the Watch Tower Society under Rutherford's leadership "zealously persists in perverting every Bible doctrine. It lays its hand on everything. Every doctrine, be it ever so scriptural, must enter into the Society's laboratory, and from there it comes forth newly formed, torn, dislocated and deformed. 'Formerly we taught ... now we see'—this is now the Society's melody.... It declares with ever greater emphasis its new teachings as coming *from the Lord*, yes expressly states that the Lord is responsible (!) for it" (ibid., 167). Years later, Timothy White also wrote of Rutherford's handling of Russell's teachings: "These changes **had the effect of whittling away at all of Russell's ideas, until nothing resembling the 'divine plan' remained.** Whereas the Judge did not cease to teach the negative ones—that is that hell-fire, the trinity, the immortality of the soul, evolution, etc. were wrong—**he altered every important positive doctrine beyond recognition**" (Timothy White, *A People For His Name* [New York: Vantage Press, 1967], 220).
5. *WT*, 1 Apr 1972, 197. The article is found on pages 197-200.
6. See the chapter on the Parable of the Sheep and the Goats. The current Watch Tower teaching shifts the fulfillment of Matthew 25:31-32 to the future, after the tribulation.

1.

Watch Tower Claims, Progressive Revelation, and the Interpretation of Scripture

In his article, "The Watch Tower Society and Spiritual Authority," Ronald Frye, who was a Jehovah's Witness for 30 years, much of this in full-time pioneer service, concludes:

> The Watch Tower Bible and Tract Society of Pennsylvania is one of the most authoritarian religious organizations on earth. The fierce loyalty that Jehovah's Witnesses world-wide have towards it is based on the conviction that **it represents God's channel. This means that Jehovah God speaks to men only through this organization. Only those directing it possess God's holy spirit which communicates God's thoughts to men on earth.**[1]

Frye's statement is verified by the statements made in the Watch Tower publications quoted below.

The Watch Tower Society is God's Sole Channel, His Visible Organization

1917

Joseph F. Rutherford, after his election as President of the Watch Tower Bible and Tract Society stated:

"The WATCH TOWER BIBLE AND TRACT SOCIETY is the greatest corporation in the world, because **from the time of its organization until now the Lord has used it as his channel** through which to make known the glad tidings to many thousands..." (*WTR*, 15 Jan. 1917, 6033).

1919

"Is not the Watch Tower Bible and Tract Society **the one and only channel which the Lord has used** in dispensing his truth continually since the beginning of the harvest period?" (*WTR*, 1 Apr. 1919, 6414).

1940

"RESOLUTION ... We are in full accord with Jehovah's Word, the Bible, and **his explanation of the Bible which he is now revealing to us through his earthly channel**, the WATCH TOWER..." (*WT*, 1 July 1940, 207. Jefferson, Wisc. Company of JWs).

1943

"The food that the Lord's 'sheep' feed upon and that their feeders must serve to them is the spiritual food **provided by the great Life-giver, Jehovah. He gives it through his Good Shepherd, Christ Jesus.** Jehovah himself is the great 'Shepherd and Bishop of your Souls.' He sees to it that it is the **right food, in due season, and that it is served through his approved visible organization. The spiritual food served up during the past sixty years ... proves that the Society of Jehovah's consecrated people, as represented by the Watch Tower Bible and Tract Society, is God's approved visible organization**" (*WT*, 1 June 1943, 166).

1950

"He [Jehovah] has appointed Christ Jesus the Head of his visible organization and his associate interpreter for the organization, 'an interpreter, one among a thousand.' (Job 33:23) **So Jehovah's visible organization under Christ is a channel for bringing the divine interpretation of his Word to his devoted people**" (*WT*, 15 July 1950, 214).

1952

"The truths we are to publish are the ones provided through the **discreet-slave organization, not some personal opinions** contrary to what the slave has provided as timely food" (*WT*, 1 Feb. 1952, 79).

"Theocratic ones will appreciate **the Lord's visible organization** and not be so foolish as to pit against **Jehovah's channel** their own human reasoning and sentiment and personal feelings" (ibid., 80).

"**Jehovah has provided a channel**, the 'faithful and discreet slave class,' who are given spiritual 'food at the proper time,' and this spiritual food includes among other things **the understanding of the prophecies** in the course of their fulfillments. (Matt. 24:45, NW) **Jehovah's witnesses themselves are not nor can they be interpreters of prophecies. But as fast as the 'superior authorities' Jehovah God and Christ Jesus reveal the interpretations through their provided channel** that fast do God's people publish them..." (*WT*, 15 Apr. 1952, 253).

1957

"It is through his organization that God provides this light that the proverb says is the teaching or law of the mother. **If we are to walk in the light of truth we must recognize not only Jehovah God as our Father but his organization as our mother**" (*WT*, 1 May 1957, 274).

"Jehovah has established **a very definite channel of communication through which he deals with his people**.... Let us unmistakably identify **Jehovah's channel of communication for our day**, that we may continue in his favor.... It is vital that we appreciate this fact [God's selection] and **respond to the directions of the 'slave' as we would to the voice of God**, because it is His provision" (*WT*, 15 June 1957, 370).

1960

"In the first century it took the apostles and God's spirit to explain the deep things of God's Word. **As it operated through the Christian organization then, so it does today.... (1 Cor. 2:10) These deep things are being made known by the holy spirit through the theocratic organization of Jehovah's Witnesses.** As those who are responsible for supplying spiritual food for God's people diligently search the Scriptures for accurate knowledge, the spirit broadens their understanding little by little. Thus, in a gradual way, the light of understanding God's Word grows brighter and brighter as we draw closer to the divinely set date for Armageddon" (*WT*, 15 Feb. 1960, 104).

"The facts show that during this time [since 1919] and up to the present hour the 'slave' class has served as **God's sole collective channel** for the flow of Biblical truth to men on earth.... Abundant spiritual food and amazing details as to the doing of God's will have been flowing through this **unique channel actually as a miraculous evidence of the operation of holy spirit**" (*WT*, 15 July 1960, 439).

1967

"Evidences are now conclusive that Jesus Christ was enthroned in heaven in 1914 C.E. and that he accompanied Jehovah to his temple in 1918 C.E., when judgment began with the house of God. (1 Pet. 4:17) After cleansing those belonging to this house who were alive on earth, Jehovah poured out his spirit upon the them and assigned them the responsibility of **serving as his sole visible channel, through whom alone spiritual instruction was to come**. Those who recognize **Jehovah's visible theocratic organization**, therefore, must recognize and accept this appointment of the 'faithful and discrete slave' and be submissive to it" (*WT*, 1 Oct. 1967, 590).

"Therefore, in submitting to **Jehovah's visible theocratic organization**, we must be in full and complete agreement with every feature of its apostolic procedure and requirements" (ibid., 592).

1973

"Consider, too, the fact that **Jehovah's organization alone, in all the earth, is directed by God's holy spirit or active force** (Zech. 4:6). Only this **organization functions for Jehovah's purpose and to his praise. To it alone God's Sacred Word, the Bible, is not a sealed book**. Many persons of the world are very intelligent, capable of understanding complex matters. They can read the Holy Scriptures, but they cannot understand their deep meaning. **Yet God's people can comprehend such spiritual things**. Why? Not because of special intelligence on their part, but as the apostle Paul declared: 'For it is to us God has revealed them through his spirit, for the spirit searches into all things, even the deep things of God.' (1 Cor. 2:10)... How very much true Christians appreciate associating with **the only organization on earth that understands the 'deep things of God'**! Direction by God's spirit enables Jehovah's servants to have divine light in a world of spiritual darkness (2 Cor. 4:4)" (*WT*, 1 July 1973, 402).

1984

"Jesus said that upon his return he would find a 'faithful and discrete slave' providing spiritual food and that the 'slave' found so doing would be appointed over all the master's belongings.—Matthew 24:45-47.

"One Christian husband said: '**Jehovah's visible organization is a tremendously dependable source. Never once has it mislead me in any way.** Everything it has said has been based on God's Word and has been the best for me, for my family and for everyone I know. This builds tremendous faith as far as I am concerned'" (*WT*, 1 June 1984, 12).

1988

"When our heavenly Father, Jehovah God, speaks, whether through his Word, the Bible, or **through his earthly organization**, it is all the more important for us to listen and obey..." (*WT*, 1 Apr. 1988, 31).

1992

"*We will be impelled to serve Jehovah loyally with his organization if we remember that there is nowhere else to go for eternal life....* That organization still exists, and of it a longtime Witness of Jehovah said: 'If one thing has been most important to me, it has been the matter of keeping close to **God's visible organization....** How else can one get Jehovah's favor and blessing?' There is **nowhere else to go for divine favor and life eternal**" (*WT*, 15 Nov. 1992, 21).

1994

"It is obvious that we need help if we are to understand the Bible.... The fact is that we cannot understand the Bible on our own. We need help.... **Jehovah, through his organization**, however, has allowed his loyal servants to understand its meaning today" (*WT*, 1 Oct. 1994, 6).

"Jesus assured us that after his death and resurrection, he would **raise up a 'faithful and discreet slave' that would serve as his channel of communication....** All who want to understand the Bible should appreciate that the 'greatly diversified wisdom of God' can become known only through **Jehovah's channel of communication, the faithful and discreet slave**" (ibid, 8).

Jehovah's Prophet Today

1927

"'*I will raise them up a Prophet from among their brethren, like unto thee, and will put my words in his mouth; and he shall speak unto them all that I shall command him.*'—*Deuteronomy 18:18....* **He [Jehovah] has promised to raise up in their behalf a prophet of truth**, who really represents Jehovah and is ordained to be mediator between God and man. **He has put his words into the mouth of this prophet. By him he shall bring all the teachable out from under the deceptions of the evil one and his servants** and unto an accurate knowledge of the truth. **The Christ, Head and body, is this great Prophet and Mediator** like unto, yet greater than, Moses. **During the Christian era God has been gradually raising up this prophet. Soon membership in this mediatorial body will be complete**" ([*1928*] *Year Book*, 18 Sept.).

1959

"**Whom has God actually used as his prophet?** By the historical facts of the case Christendom is beaten back in defeat. Jehovah's witnesses are deeply grateful today that **the plain facts show that God has been pleased to use them**" (*WT*, 15 Jan. 1959, 40-41).

1971

"There is an additional way, among others, to determine whom Jehovah is using today. Bible prophecy, history written in advance, comes from God. (2 Pet. 1:20,21) He can foresee future conditions with total accuracy and keep his servants abreast of them.... These things Jehovah has made known to those who obey him as ruler: 'The Sovereign Lord Jehovah will not do a thing unless he has revealed his confidential matter to his servants the prophets.' (Amos 3:7) **In this century who has been correctly informed about the future?** the clergy? the political leaders? the economic heads? **Or has it been the witnesses of Jehovah?**" (*WT*, 1 Aug. 1971, 466.)

"Better it is to know now, rather than too late, that there is an **authentic prophetic class of Christians among us....** Concerning the message faithfully delivered by the Ezekiel class Jehovah positively states that it 'must come true.' He asseverates that those who wait undecided until it does 'come true' will also have to know that a prophet himself had proved to be in the midst of them.' (Ezekiel 33:33)... What is to be gained by hesitating and doubting to the end that **Jehovah can raise up and has raised up a genuine 'prophet'**

within our generation?" (*"The Nations Shall Know that I Am Jehovah"—How?*, 292.)

1972

"Yes. the time must come shortly that the nations will have to know that really **a 'prophet' of Jehovah was among them**" (*WT*, 1 Apr. 1972, 200).

1979

"For nearly 60 years now the Jeremiah class has faithfully spoken forth Jehovah's Word.... Unlike the clergy class, those of the **Jeremiah class have been sent by Jehovah to speak in his name.** Nevertheless, the clergy prophets also claim to speak in his name and, hence, to tell the Bible truth.... True, **the Jeremiah class back up their message by quoting the words, 'This is what Jehovah has said'**" (*WT*, 1 Sept. 1979, 29).

Are Watch Tower Leaders and Publications Inspired?

Watch Tower defenders quote many statements from their publications which deny inspiration or infallibility. But do these statements fully reflect the reality of organizational claims and actions? First, here are some statements which **deny inspiration or infallibility:**

"**We claim no** *new revelations*, for to our understanding the revelations of God to his saints are completed and finished by the records of John of Patmos. But while God's revelation in the sense of *utterance* ended eighteen hundred years ago, **yet revelation in the sense of understanding those utterances has continued down through the age**" (*WTR*, July 1882, 368).

"Nevertheless, **we are far from claiming any direct or plenary inspiration**. We believe, however, that there are many ways in which the Lord can guide those who are anxious to serve him, without directly inspiring or in any manner interfering with their free agency" (*WTR*, 15 July 1899, 2506).

"However, **we claim no infallibility**. We claim that there is no direct inspiration from God since the days of the apostles" (*WTR*, 1 Mar. 1916, 5867).

"It was never the thought of Pastor Russell that he was inspired, nor was it ever our thought respecting him" (*GA*, 13 Feb. 1924, 305).

"...For some years *The Watchtower* has been the means of communicating information to God's people. That does not mean that those who prepare the manuscript for *The Watchtower* are inspired..." (Rutherford, *Riches* [1936], 316).

"This pouring out of God's spirit upon the flesh of all his faithful anointed witnesses [Joel 2:28-29] **does not mean those now serving as Jehovah's witnesses are inspired. It does not mean that the writings in this magazine** *The Watchtower* **are inspired and infallible and without mistakes.** It does not mean that the president of the Watch Tower Bible and Tract Society is inspired and infallible, although enemies falsely charge us with believing so" (*WT*, 15 May 1947, 157).

"...Because it [Watch Tower Society] is **not infallible and has never claimed to be**, from time to time corrections are necessary" (*WT*, 15 Oct. 1954, 638)

"An official mouthpiece for this 'slave' class is the *Watchtower* magazine.... This magazine **makes no claim of inspiration** but is guided by the inspired principles and prophecies recorded in the sacred Bible due for progressive fulfillment today" (*WT*, 15 May 1955, 316).

"True, the brothers preparing these publications are **not infallible**. Their writings are **not inspired** as are those of Paul and the other Bible writers (2 Tim. 3:16). And so, at times, it has been necessary, as understanding became clearer, to correct views" (*WT*, 15 Feb. 1981, 19).

"The Governing Body consists of a group of anointed Christian men.... **They are not inspired by God and hence are not infallible**, but they rely on God's infallible Word as the highest authority on earth..." (*1986 Jehovah's Witnesses Unitedly Doing God's Will Worldwide* brochure, 26).

"Those who make up the one true Christian organization today **do not have angelic revelations or divine inspiration**" (*Jehovah's Witnesses—Proclaimers of God's Kingdom* [1993], 708).

The Rest of the Story

The Watch Tower's denial of inspiration and infallibility must be judged and understood in the light of additional claims and practices. The testimony of President Nathan H. Knorr in the *Moyle vs. Watchtower Bible and Tract Society* case (1943) is quoted:

Q. But you don't make any mention in the fore part of your Watch Tower that "We are not infallible and subject to correction and may make mistakes"?

A. **We have never claimed infallibility**.

Q. But you don't make any such statement, that you are subject to correction, in your Watch Tower papers, do you?

A. Not that I recall.

Q. **In fact, it is set forth directly as God's Word, isn't it?**

A. Yes, as His word.

Q. **Without any qualifications whatsoever?**

A. **That is right.**[2]

Raymond Franz, who had been involved for sixty years in the organization, nine of these as a member of the Governing Body, concludes:

> True, there is periodic acknowledgment in the publications that the writers are, after all, "imperfect men," and that the organization has "never claimed to be infallible." **In actual practice it works out quite differently**. One finds out that this only applies to the *past*, not to the *present*. While the organization must recognize that **it has changed a considerable number of its past teachings—which makes it evident that they were in error**—it does not feel moved to modesty by those errors, so as to remind its readers that what it *now* says may also suffer due to that same imperfection. To the contrary, **Jehovah's Witnesses are called on to take whatever is currently taught *as if it were* infallible.** In effect they are told, "You should accept everything published as absolute truth until such time as we may tell you it isn't."[3]

Franz comments further: "In place of 'inspired' information, the publications regularly speak of the organization as uniquely possessing *'revealed'* truth."[4] Ron Frye, former Jehovah's Witness traveling overseer, concludes that "the use of the term 'revealed' as opposed to claiming inspiration is a matter of semantics—a distinction that represents no difference—which is only called upon to explain away changes, contradictions and disappointments."[5] From his own experience, Frye further observes:

> The Society **does not claim to be inspired, but it speaks with the same degree of authority as though it were**. It demands that they be taken at face value **as though its leaders were inspired**—not even permitting people to question or have doubts or reservations about anything they teach. Then they beg off from responsibility when some doctrine has to be changed or corrected, or some prophecy goes unfulfilled.[6]

Prof. Jerry Bergman, a former Witness and author of many books and articles on the Witnesses, writes: **"Rutherford's writings were seen as almost inspired."** In a March 3, 1975, interview with Hayden C. Covington (who had served as head of the Society's legal department and briefly as Vice President), Bergman quotes him as saying "that 'God was writing through [Rutherford], and he was 'definitely inspired to do what he did.' Covington asserted that Rutherford had absolute power over the organization and the Board of Directors 'only rubberstamped his will and did nothing more and that's the way it should be.'"[7] Some evidence in support of Covington's statement concerning inspiration is found in a letter written by J. A. Bohnet, who became a member of the Society Board of Directors in 1917. It was published in the February 1, 1931, *Watchtower*:

> Careful readers of this book [*Light*, both volumes] can now plainly see why the Lord has kept secret his Revelation until now, and in his due time has made it so plain to his faithful remnant class.... **This book within itself conclusively proves that God directed its presentation**, and that its human author was not employing his own judgment and wisdom in its preparation. No human creature could have written *Light* unless the holy spirit of God operated on his mind, actuated his thoughts and guided its utterances. **It matters not whether Jehovah individually inspired the volume or had his representative Jesus do it.**
> **The evidence is that the work is of the Lord.** Brother Rutherford could not of himself have written this book. The wisdom therein is **beyond human. It is divine**.... *Light* carries witness in itself that **its presentations have divine origin. It is indeed divine revelation entrusted to human for portrayal**.... Brother Rutherford could not have improved on the book *Life* except by divine supervision.[8]

Timothy White was raised as a Jehovah's Witness and was an active member. After quoting some of Rutherford's writings in his book, *A People For His Name* (1967), he concludes: "Quotations could be multiplied, but these are enough to show that Rutherford certainly did believe that God, the angels or Christ were 'guiding, communicating, and motivating' his articles, and that this was a 'divine influence' on him. **He did, therefore, believe he was inspired**."[9] While Rutherford would deny that he was inspired, White writes: "But he could (and did always) claim that his articles were from God, and to disbelieve them was a mortal sin."[10] White's conclusion is confirmed in the April 1, 1986, *Watchtower*. In "Questions From Readers," it is asked: "Why have Jehovah's Witnesses been disfellowshipped (excommunicated) for apostasy some who still profess belief in God, the Bible, and Jesus Christ?" After the introductory discussion, the response is given:

> Approved association with Jehovah's Witnesses requires accepting the entire range of the true

teachings of the Bible, including those Scriptural **beliefs that are unique to Jehovah's Witnesses**. What do such beliefs include? ... That there is a 'faithful and discreet slave' upon earth today 'entrusted with all of Jesus' earthly interests,' which slave is associated with the Governing Body of Jehovah's Witnesses (Matthew 24:45-47). That 1914 marked the end of the Gentile Times and the establishment of the Kingdom of God in the heavens, as well as the time for Christ's foretold presence.... That Armageddon, referring to the battle of the great day of God almighty is near....[11]

It is clear that the Watch Tower Society's denial of inspiration and infallibility must be qualified in the light of additional claims and practices.

Claims for the *Watch Tower* and Other Publications

What has been claimed for the *Watch Tower* (*Watchtower*) and other Society publications? How have these been viewed over the years?

1890

"To many it [*Zion's Watch Tower*] may be said to be the only channel of communication between them and the remainder of the household of faith; to very many it is the **only channel** through which the voice of the Chief Shepherd is heard.... We are most firmly convinced that the TOWER is and has been **a chosen vessel in the Lord's hands for dispensing 'meat in due season,'** and we pray and labor that it may so continue to be used" (*WTR*, Jan. 1890, 1171).

1910

"If the six volumes of SCRIPTURE STUDIES are practically the Bible topically arranged, with Bible proof-texts given, we might not improperly name the volumes—**the Bible in an arranged form. That is to say, they are not merely comments on the Bible, but they are practically the Bible itself**.... Furthermore, not only do we find that people cannot see the divine plan in studying the Bible itself, but we see, also, that if anyone lays the SCRIPTURE STUDIES aside, even after he has used them, after he has become familiar with them, after he has read them for ten years—if he then lays them aside and ignores them and goes to the Bible alone, though he has understood his Bible for ten years, our experience shows that **within two years he goes into darkness**. On the other hand, if he had merely read the SCRIPTURE STUDIES with their references, and had not read a page of the Bible, as such, he **would be in the light at the end of the two years**, because he would have the light of the Scriptures" (*WTR*, 15 Sept. 1910, 4685).

1922

Letter to the *Watch Tower*: "We also desire to thank you for the blessed WATCH TOWER, laden with such wonderful and inspiring articles. Surely we have an abundance of evidence that **the Lord is still using the same channel in dispensing his truth and meat in due season!**" (*WT*, 1 Jan. 1922, 15).

1925

"Since he [Christ Jesus] commands what shall be done on earth we should have no difficulty in finding that he is directing his work. **THE WATCH TOWER is the medium of communication with the various ones who are watchmen and who love the Lord. The Lord has long used it for that purpose.** During the year just passed THE WATCH TOWER, we believe, has set forth some meat in due season sent from the Lord. Those who so believe study THE WATCH TOWER, not contenting themselves with giving a mere casual reading.... THE WATCH TOWER is therefore **the official organ for the church**, and every really consecrated and anointed child of God is interested in it" (*WT*, 1 Dec. 1925, 355).

"Satan is our worst enemy, and **we are his sole earthly foe**" (ibid., 356).

1926

Letter to the *Watch Tower*: "After coming into the 'truth' late in 1922 I occasionally have had some 'doubts and fears' as to the claim of **THE WATCH TOWER to being the 'channel' exclusively used of the Lord at this time.... Who could doubt** as THE WATCH TOWERS succeed each other, opening up the prophecies and giving accounts of the great work which is being done in the Name of the Lord!" (*WT*, 1 Oct. 1926, 303.)

1931

"*The Watchtower* recognizes the truth as belonging to Jehovah, and not to any creature. *The Watchtower* is not the instrument of any man or set of men, nor is it published according to the whims of men. **No man's opinion is expressed in** *The Watchtower*. **God feeds his own people...**" (*WT*, 1 Nov. 1931, 327).[12]

1932

"According to *Rotherham* the text says: 'The Sovereign Lord giveth the word....' 'The word,' or 'speech,' is a comprehensive form applied, not to only one specific message that the Lord gave ... but to the whole series or messages of truth which he gave and which he continues to give ever since the lightnings have been flashing from the temple and upon the record of his Word. **The expression 'the word,' therefore, includes every revelation of truth down to and including the book** *Vindication* **and whatsoever shall be revealed and published, by the Lord's grace, as long as the remnant is on earth**" (*WT*, 1 Apr. 1932, 101).

1933

"It has pleased the Lord to use *The Watchtower* as a means of conveying his message to his covenant people..." (Rutherford, *Preparation*, 113).

"As surely as Jehovah has an organization on the earth, just so surely he is feeding the members of that organization by the hand of Christ Jesus. The facts prove that **he uses the Watch Tower publications to bring these truths to the attention of his remnant**" (ibid., 176).

"To feed or teach his people **the Lord has used the Watch Tower publications**, and of this fact we have an abundance of proof. **No man** is given credit for the wonderful truths which **the Lord has revealed to his people through the Watch Tower publications**.... When we come together, instead of listening to the views of some man, why not have a study of some of the wonderful things which Jehovah has brought to the attention of his people and taught them through his chosen means of teaching? (*WT*, 1 Dec. 1933, 363.)

1934

"*The Watchtower* is not the teacher of God's people. *The Watchtower* **merely brings to the attention of God's people that which he has revealed**, and it is the privilege of each and every one of God's children to prove by the Word of God whether these things are from men or are from the Lord" (Rutherford, *Jehovah*, 191; *WT*, 1 May 1934, 131).

"It is announced with confidence that **the Lord uses the columns of** *The Watchtower* to transmit to the consecrated people things that **he reveals to them and provides for them to know.... There is no attempt on the part of** *The Watchtower* **to interpret prophecy, for the reason that no human creature can interpret prophecy....** Long centuries ago God caused holy men to write the prophecies, and **now it pleases him**

to unfold them that his faithful witnesses on earth at the present time may be assured that they are in the right way, and that their hope may be strong" (*1935 Yearbook*, 52).

1935

"Without a doubt the **Lord uses his angels to cause the truth to be published in** *The Watchtower,* and the faithful followers of Christ Jesus who hear and give heed to the message of truth from the Lord and render obedience thereto are thus a spectacle or theater to others, both men and angels, who observe that these faithful ones are maintaining their integrity toward God.... Certainly God guides his covenant people by **using the holy angels to convey his messages** to them" (*WT*, 1 Feb. 1935, 41).

"Jehovah has made the necessary arrangements within his organization to instruct his people, and we all recognize that **for some years** *The Watchtower* **has been the means of communicating information to God's people.** That does not mean that those who prepare the manuscript for *The Watchtower* are inspired, but rather it means that **the Lord through his angels sees to it that the information is given to his people in due time,** and he brings to pass the events in fulfillment of his prophecy and then invites those devoted to him to see the same. God through Christ Jesus feeds his people upon the food convenient for them, and gives it to them at the proper time. The angels of the Lord that accompany him at the temple judgment serve under his commandment, and the proof heretofore submitted through the Watch Tower publications shows conclusively that thus the Lord deals with his faithful ones on earth" (*WT*, 15 Aug. 1935, 246).

"*The Watchtower* magazine ... **is the channel used by the Lord for transmitting the unfolding of his prophecies** to those who are devoted to him and his kingdom. No human creature is entitled to any credit for what appears in *The Watchtower*" (*1936 Year Book*, 63).

1936

"*The Watchtower* is issued twice each month and brings to its readers the current report which **the Lord,** in the exercise of his loving-kindness, manifests in the unfolding of his prophecies to those who are devoted to him.... *The Watchtower* **being the means the Lord is pleased to use to transmit his message of truth to the people...**" (*1937 Year Book*, 82).

"Such is the reason why the Lord permits these truths to be published in *The Watchtower*. **What is said is not the opinion of man,** and no man is to be given credit therefor. The Lord has his own good way of informing and comforting his people. While the remnant need no man to teach them, it is the privilege of the remnant to be fed by Jehovah and Christ Jesus upon the food convenient for them in this day, and to that end the Lord causes understanding of the Scriptures and permits these to be published in *The Watchtower*" (*WT*, 1 Apr. 1936, 106).

"The Lord has graciously provided for the **publication of his message in the form of books,** that the people may be informed of the truth.... Those books **do not contain the opinion of any man**" (*Riches*, 353-54). All of Rutherford's 16 books from the *Harp of God* (1921) through *Riches* (1936) are listed and pictured (after the index).

1937

Letter to J. F. Rutherford: "I have been noting in *The Watchtower* the points you have been stressing of late concerning the criticism of the Society's publications by those in high positions and otherwise. I find myself in disagreement with all these criticisms, believing *The Watchtower* **to be Jehovah's mouthpiece upon the earth ever since its first publication, in 1879,** and I have been fed and nourished from its pages for the last forty years" (*WT*, 1 July 1937, 208).

1938

"The resolutions adopted by conventions of God's anointed people, booklets, magazines, and books published by them, contain the message of God's truth and are **from the Almighty God, Jehovah, and provided by him through Christ Jesus and his underofficers**.... These instruments being provided by Jehovah, and placed in the hand of the remnant, the remnant or 'servant' class is commanded to use the same" (*WT*, 1 May 1938, 143).

"It should be expected that **the Lord would have a means of communication to his people on the earth**, and he has clearly shown that the magazine called *The Watchtower* **is used for that purpose**" (*1939 Yearbook*, 85).

1939

"As his prophecies are made understandable by his grace the Lord uses the WATCH TOWER publications to make known the same. **Such publications do not attempt to express the opinion of any man**, but call attention to the prophecies and to the physical facts which God has brought to pass, and thus enable each one who is devoted to God to see and understand the meaning thereof. Those who now love God bear witness to the fact that since the year 1918 God has unfolded many of his prophecies which before could not be understood because not his due time" (*WT*, 15 June 1939, 182).

Rutherford stated in a discourse, "I hold in my hand a book which the publishers this day release to the people of good will. It is entitled *Salvation*. **It does not contain the theory or opinion or doctrine of any man**" (*Government and Peace*, 27 (1939)).

1942

"The Lord does not say to speak the words of wisdom of man, nor to be influenced or guided by the word of man. **Those who are convinced that *The Watchtower* is publishing the opinion or expression of a man should not waste time in looking at it at all**, because man's opinion proves nothing except when that opinion is based wholly upon the Word of God. Those who believe that **God uses *The Watchtower* as a means of communicating to his people**, or of calling their attention to his prophecies, should study *The Watchtower* with thankfulness of heart and give Jehovah God and Christ Jesus all the honor and credit and give neither honor nor credit to any man" (*WT*, 1 Jan. 1942, 5).

"Informed persons well acquainted with the **consistent contents** of *The Watchtower* agree that those who want to gain life in peace and happiness without end should read and study it together with the Bible and in company with other readers. This is not giving any credit to the magazine's publishers, but is due to the **great Author of the Bible with its truths and prophecies, and who now interprets its prophecies** by events in fulfillment and thereby enlightens the meek ones concerning the establishment of his Theocratic Government and its blessings and requirements for those who shall live. **He it is that makes possible the material that is published in the columns of this magazine** and who gives promise that it shall continue to publish the advancing truths as long as it continues to exist for the service of the interests of his Theocratic Government" (*WT*, 15 Jan. 1942, 31; *WT*, 15 Apr. 1943, 127).

"During the past twenty years he has equipped them with **his revealed Word in print** in the form of books, booklets, magazines, tracts and leaflets..." (*WT*, 1 July 1942, 203).

1943

In the *Moyle vs. WTBTS* trial, Watch Tower Vice President Frederick W. Franz was questioned by Moyle's attorney:

Q. Didn't you state that on October 15, 1931, the Watch Tower discontinued the naming of an editorial committee and then Jehovah God became the editor?

A. I didn't say Jehovah God became the editor. It was appreciated that **Jehovah God really is the One who is editing the paper**, and therefore the naming of an editorial committee was out of place.

Q. At any rate, **Jehovah God is now the editor of the paper, is that right?**

A. **He is today the editor of the paper.**

Q. How long has He been editor of the paper?

A. Since its inception [1879] he has been guiding it.

Q. Even before 1931?

A. Yes, sir.[13]

1950

"God, however, reveals the meaning of his Word only to those who are willing to seek, study and compare. This suggests the advantage of a **dependable Bible study aid. THE WATCHTOWER fulfills that need**. Since 1879 it has been published regularly for the benefit of sincere students of the Bible. Over that extended period of time *The Watchtower* has **consistently proved itself dependable**" (*NWT*, 1950 ed. ad in the back).

1954

Douglas Walsh Trial, Scotland, Society Secretary-Treasurer Grant Suiter's testimony:

Q. Isn't he [company servant] expected to familiarize himself with the publications of the Society?

A. He certainly is.

Q. Indeed can he in the view of Jehovah's Witnesses have an understanding of the Scriptures apart from the publications of Jehovah's Witnesses?

A. No.

Q. **Only by the publications can he have a right understanding of the Scriptures?**

A. **That is right.**[14]

1959

"...In many ways the evidence was beginning to accumulate that, of all the early voices heard, **Jehovah had chosen the publication we now call *The Watchtower* to be used as a channel** through which to bring to the world of mankind a revelation of the divine will and, through the words revealed in its columns, to begin a division of the world's population..." *Jehovah's Witnesses in the Divine Purpose*, 22).

1967

"**Since 1879** the *Watch Tower* magazine has been used by this collective group to dispense spiritual food regularly to those of this 'little flock' of true Christians" (*WT*, 1 Oct. 1967, 590).

1989

"...It is through the columns of *The Watchtower* that explanations of vital Scriptural truths have been provided for us by Jehovah's 'faithful and discreet slave.' *The Watchtower* is the principal instrument used by the 'slave' class for dispensing spiritual food" (*WT*, 15 Mar. 1989, 22).

1992

"**It is unlikely that someone who simply reads the Bible without taking advantage of divinely provided aids could discern the light.** That is why Jehovah God has provided the 'faithful and discreet slave,' foretold at Matthew 24:45-47. Today that 'slave' is represented by the Governing Body of Jehovah's Witnesses" (*WT*, 1 May 1992, 31).

How is the Correct Interpretation of Scripture and Prophecy Accomplished?

1922

"Keep in mind, then, that these truths **have not been brought forth by private interpretation, but that the Lord himself, acting through his duly appointed way, has done so**. Let all those, then, who insist on a private interpretation prove that they have occupied or now occupy a special position of servants of the Lord to interpret his Word; and failing in this proof, let them keep silent" (*WT*, 1 Dec. 1922, 376).

1931

"Today the children of Zion need no extraneous proof that **the spiritual food and understanding of the prophecies they have comes from God.** They know that no man or men could provide such food. No man or men on earth attempt to lay claim that any of these truths proceed from man. God has spread his table bountifully for his people, and the children of his woman feed thereat" (*WT*, 1 Nov. 1931, 328).

1932

"**Men do not interpret Scripture**; the church does not interpret Scripture; angels do no interpret Scripture; Christ Jesus himself does not interpret Scripture, except as that interpretation is given to Him of His Father (Rev. 1:1). **The only One who interprets Scripture, in the last analysis, is the One who gave it in the first place.** Obviously, until he furnishes the key to a passage it can never be unlocked.... **God reserves it to Himself to unfold them in His own good time...**" (*GA*, 17 Aug. 1932, 727).

1937

"Judge Rutherford shows where the well-known facts fit the Scriptures or where the Scriptures are fulfilled by the physical facts which God has caused to come to pass or to be made known in explanation of the Scriptures. Judge Rutherford merely records and calls these things to our attention, but **God by Christ Jesus is the interpretation-giver**" (*Model Study*, 10).

"**Then Jehovah straightway sent his Messenger, his Interpreter, Christ Jesus, to his temple.** The Interpreter being at the temple, it was time for him to gather unto himself his faithful ones in the temple and, gathering them, **to reveal to them the meaning of the prophecies....** Otherwise stated, the Greater Joseph at the temple **informs the remnant of the meaning of the prophecies of God**, and these in turn tell the meaning thereof to the Jonadabs or 'other sheep,' whom the Lord is gathering into the fold" (*WT*, 15 Feb. 1937, 53).

1941

"What is here said is not the opinion of man, nor man's interpretation of the Scriptures. **Jehovah's Word is the authority, and He is his own interpreter. The Scriptures cannot be properly interpreted by any man**" (Rutherford, *Theocracy*, 37).

1943

"...Christ Jesus, the Court's official mouthpiece of interpretation, reserves to himself that office as Head of Jehovah's 'faithful and wise servant' class. **He merely uses the 'servant' class to publish the interpretation after the Supreme Court by Christ Jesus reveals it**. How does the Lord God make known the interpretation? By causing the facts to come to pass visibly which are in fulfillment of the prophecy or dark saying or misunderstood scripture. Thereafter 'in due season' he calls such fulfillment or clarification of prophecy and scripture to the attention of his 'faithful and wise servant' class. Thereby he makes them responsible to make known the meaning of such scriptures to all members of the household of faith and to all persons of goodwill. **This constitutes giving them the 'meat in due season'**"(*WT*, 1 July 1943, 203).

1954

Frederick W. Franz answered questions asked by the Crown Counsellor in the Walsh case:

Q. Who is responsible for the interpretation in case of doubt, or in general, of scriptural writings for the guidance of Jehovah's Witnesses?

A. **We believe that Jehovah God who is the author and inspirer of the Bible is the one who makes the interpretations. He is his own interpreter. He does this by the use of his invisible active force, the Holy Spirit operating on the minds of his Witnesses upon this earth**, and he causes events to come to pass in the earth which are in fulfillment of his prophetic word and which, therefore, throw light upon the true significance of his word.

Q. That is very helpful, but it does not quite meet the point I was making. What I wanted you to tell me was whether you can say how the Biblical texts are authoritatively interpreted; who is the interpreter?

A. **The Jehovah God is the interpreter, but he guides his people upon this earth, and in this case the editorial committee of the Society, they study the Scriptures continually, and they examine and re-examine the evidence as it appears, and under this Divine guidance with the help of the Holy Spirit they arrive at the understanding of the Scripture.**

Q. Is that understanding promulgated to the Jehovah's Witnesses through the authority of the President and Directors of the Watch Tower Bible and Tract Society?

A. Yes. That is accepted as authoritative, and Jehovah's Witnesses throughout the world will refer to the publications of the Society as settling the issue in any discussion of these subjects.

Q. The authoritative publications are such as those to which you have been referred to, Nos. 15 and 16 of Process?

A. Yes.

Q. In addition may I take it that where in the periodical literature one finds an interpretation of Scriptural texts these also, being issued with the authority of the President and the Directors of the Watch Tower Bible and Tract Society, possess the same authoritative quality?

A. Yes. We take this position because **we cannot ascribe our interpretation of Scripture to any private individual**. As the Apostle Peter says in his Second General Letter to the Christians, Chapter One and verses 20 and 21, 'Knowing this first, that no prophecy of the scripture is of any private interpretation. For the prophecy came not in old time by the will of man; but holy men of God spake as they were moved by the Holy Ghost,' or Spirit.[15]

Testimony of Witness Douglas Walsh:

Q. Were you taught as to how the Scriptures were interpreted by Jehovah's Witnesses—by whom they were interpreted?

A. Yes.

Q. What were you taught in that regard?

A. **I was taught that interpretation came from the Most High God himself though Christ Jesus and by means of his Holy Spirit**, and his organization on earth would make known the truths of God's Word....

Q. How did Jehovah's Witnesses secure amongst themselves that interpretation? Through what means?

A. **By means of the Holy Spirit.**

Q. **Yes, but through which body of men did the Holy Spirit operate?**

A. **Through the Board of Directors of the Society.**

Q. And I take it through the Publications of the Society interpreting the Scriptures?

A. Yes.[16]

1981

"We all need help to understand the Bible, and **we cannot find the Scriptural guidance we need outside the 'faithful and discreet slave' organization**" (*WT*, 15 Feb. 1981, 19).

1982

"Today, a remnant of the 'faithful slave' is still alive on earth. Their duties include **receiving and passing on to all of Jehovah's earthly servants spiritual food at the proper time. They occupy a position similar to that of Paul and his co-laborers** when the apostle said of the wonderful truths God gives to his people. '**It is to us God has revealed them through his spirit**'" (**1 Corinthians 2:9, 10**) (*WT*, 1 June 1982, 17).

1984

"...Jehovah himself declared: 'The Sovereign Lord Jehovah will not do a thing unless he has revealed his confidential matter to his servants the prophets'—Amos 3:7. Does this ancient prophecy have meaning for us today? Yes, it has a powerful message for us! The inspired Word of God was compiled under divine direction, and it has been preserved down to 'the time of the end' for the benefit of God's people 'upon whom the ends of the systems of things have arrived.' **Its prophetic meaning is made known to us through 'the faithful and discreet slave**,' that group of anointed Christians whom the Master, Jesus Christ, is using now to provide spiritual **'food at the proper time'** for all of God's people'—Daniel 12:4; 1 Corinthians 10:11; Matthew 24:45-47" (*WT*, 1 July 1984, 8-9).

1990

"We have the opportunity to show love for our brothers who take the lead in the congregation or in connection with Jehovah's visible organization worldwide. This includes being loyal to the 'faithful and discreet slave' (Matthew 24:45-47). **Let us face the fact that no matter how much Bible reading we have done, we would never had learned the truth on our own**" (*WT*, 1 Dec. 1990, 19).

Progressive Revelation ("due time" light, "Present truth")

1880

"We have sometimes been accused by unbelievers for teaching that the true way to advance light was to displace the *truth* we learned yesterday by *new truth* learned today; but we utterly repudiate the absurd charge. **To *grow* in knowledge is to retain truth we have and add to our stock**" (*WTR*, July 1880, 119).

1881

"**A new view of truth never can contradict a former truth. 'New light' never extinguishes older 'light,'** but adds to it" (*WTR*, Feb. 1881, 188).

1910

"The Harvest the Due Time for a Clear Unfolding of the Truth." "So we believe that the thought for us to take in this connection is that it is because we are living in this particular time, in the ending of this age, that we are favored with such a **clear unfolding** of spiritual things.... The very ablest minds in the world have examined these subjects, but now, by God's grace, we have come to the place where **the vail is taken away and where we can see the real meaning of God's Word**—not merely one person can see it, but hundreds, thousands, see it" (*WTR*, 15 Sept. 1910, 4684-85).

1911

"No very clear understanding of the Bible was reached during all these centuries [past 400 years]. We account for this by supposing that **the Lord's due time for opening His Word to our understanding has only now come**.... Rather we should seek for dependent Bible study [Watch Tower publications], rather than for independent Bible study" (*WTR*, 15 Sept. 1911, 4885).

1916

"'Meat in due season' means the message of the kingdom to the church, **given at the time the Lord intended it should be given**" (*WTR*, 15 Dec. 1916, 6023).

1920

"'The Finished Mystery' merely calls attention to those things [rebuke of the unfaithful clergy] now, because **the time is due**" (*WT*, 15 June 1920, 186).

1921

"The Christian's meat in due season **is a proper explanation of the Scriptures as they become due to be understood**" (Rutherford, *The Harp of God*, 237—early editions).

1924

"The Bible could not be understood **until God's due time to have it understood. That due time is here now** because the time has come to establish his government. Now it is possible for even the children to understand the divine plan as set forth in the Bible" (Rutherford introduction, W. E. Van Amburgh, *The Way to Paradise*, iii).

1926

"... And with each edition [of *Studies in the Scriptures*] there was some change made by the author [Russell] because of **greater light**" (*WT*, 15 Apr. 1926, 116).

"True to his promise, **greater light has come to the church of God since 1918**.... It was in the year 1919 that **the Lord permitted the church to see for the first time** that Elijah pictured the work of the church prior to 1918 and that Elisha pictured the work of the church thereafter" (ibid., 117).

Is there new light "because a man or men are gifted with the powers of interpretation of the Scriptures? Emphatically, No.... In his own good way and time he gives interpretation to his church through the Head of the church, our beloved Lord Jesus Christ. It is God's light which shines upon his Word and which also gives a clearer vision to his anointed ones" (ibid., 118).

"...The Lord promised that the light should continue to shine unto the perfect day" (ibid., 119).

"...Many prophecies have had fulfillment since 1918. There is a reason for this. The reason is that it was in 1918 that the Lord came to his temple" (*WT*, 1 Sept. 1926, 259).

1927

Q. Why do Bible Students understand new things in the Bible which were never dreamed of one hundred years ago?

A. Because **it is now the due time for God** to reveal to the righteous many things which were heretofore hidden (*GA*, 20 June 1927, 637).

1928

"These same ones claim that *The Watch Tower* is out of accord with what the church learned twenty years ago and make this an excuse for their course of action in refusing to have any part in proclaiming the name of Jehovah. The fact is that *The Watch Tower* **has never deviated one jot or tittle from the fundamentals of the divine plan revealed to the church by the Lord, and as published in the** *Studies in the Scriptures*. From time to time God has given his people **more light and a clearer vision of his plan**, even as he promised. (Proverbs 4:18)" (*WT*, 1 Aug. 1928, 230).

1930

Concerning the book *Light*, in a letter to Rutherford: "But I wanted you to know that I thank God from the bottom of my heart for this **great illumination that has come to us from Jehovah**" (*WT*, 1 Nov. 1930, 335).

1935

"The testimony of Ezekiel's prophecy, [was] **sealed until the publication of these books** [*Vindication*, 3 vols.].... Since these studies were completed, God's object in writing the Scriptures, and the manner in which they are to be understood, are **clearly revealed**.... The work *Prophecy* was released. Never before has there been a book published that makes clear so much of the prophecies of the Bible as this book. Because **it is now God's due time to make clear His prophecies**, any unbiased student can now see much of the fulfillment thereof.... The work *Preservation* was released. Two of the most beautiful books of the Bible, Esther and Ruth, are **now due to be understood**" (*GA*, 10 Apr. 1935, 445).

"**If the present-day publications of the Watch Tower are the thoughts of a man or men, then no child of God should give heed to them.** On the other hand, if these publications are not the thoughts of creatures expressed, but contain the spiritual food which the Lord has provided for his people, a failure or refusal to study the same works detrimentally to those who thus fail or refuse to study. No one can today successfully withstand the assault of the enemy and prove his own faithfulness and integrity toward God who fails or refuses to feed upon **the spiritual food which God has provided for his people**" (*WT*, 15 Apr. 1935, 117).

"Prophecy he caused to be written so that it can be understood **only in God's due time**, and then by those who love him" (*WT*, 15 Oct. 1935, 316).

1936

"During the past few years **God has given to his people an understanding** of the prophecies of The Revelation, Ezekiel, Daniel, and Habakkuk, and many other prophecies" (*WT*, 15 Feb. 1936, 53).

Letter to J. F. Rutherford: "This continuous and wonderful unfolding of truth **no longer seems to be as flashes of light from the temple, but as a mighty, brilliant beam from the very throne of God himself**, lighting our pathway in this dark and pagan world" (*WT*, 15 May 1936, 159).

1937

"Every person now on earth and who is on the side of Jehovah and his kingdom is privileged to feed at the Lord's table and to learn of the **unfolding of prophecy, which is meat in due season** for him, and which is provided by the Lord for his comfort and hope" (*WT*, 1 Mar. 1937, 77).

"This shows why prophecy could **not be understood prior to 1918**" (*WT*, 15 Apr. 1937, 125).

"**Shortly after 1918** Jehovah began to make known to his servants the meaning of some of his prophecies" (*WT*, 1 Nov. 1937, 330).

1938

"The interpretation of prophecy, therefore, is not from man, but is from Jehovah; and Jehovah causes events to come to pass in fulfillment of the prophecy **in due time**" (*WT*, 1 May 1938, 143).

1939

"Jehovah reveals himself and his purpose to his people in **his own due time**. His prophecy, therefore, cannot be understood until it is **God's due time** for understanding it" (*WT*, 15 Oct. 1939, 317).

"**Prior to God's due time any attempted interpretation is merely a guess**" (ibid., 318).

1942

"These great truths Jehovah has hidden in his Word **until his due time** to vindicate his name; and **that time is now here**" (*WT*, 15 Jan. 1942, 29).

1952

"Jehovah's witnesses themselves are not nor can they be interpreters of prophecies. But as fast as the 'superior authorities' Jehovah God and Christ Jesus **reveal the interpretations through their provided channel**, that fast do God's people publish them the world over to strengthen the faith of all lovers of righteousness" (*WT*, 15 Feb. 1952, 253).

1960

"Down through the years the slavelike congregation has been feeding its true members faithfully and discreetly. From Pentecost, A.D. 33 up to this very present hour this has been lovingly and carefully performed. Yes, and these 'domestics' have been fed on **progressive spiritual food that keeps them abreast of the 'bright light that is getting lighter and lighter until the perfect day is firmly established'**" (*WT*, 15 July 1960, 435).

1964

"As Jehovah **revealed** his truths by means of the first-century Christian congregation so he does today by means of the present-day Christian congregation. Through this agency he is having carried out prophesying on an intensified and unparalleled scale. All this activity is not an accident. Jehovah is the one behind all of it. The abundance of spiritual food and the amazing details of Jehovah's purposes that have been **revealed** to Jehovah's anointed witnesses are clear evidence that they are the ones mentioned by Jesus when he foretold a 'faithful and discreet slave' class that would be used to dispense **God's progressive revelations** in these last days. Of this class Jesus said: 'Truly I say to you, He will appoint him over all his belongings.' —Matt. 24:47" (*WT*, 15 June 1964, 365).

1966

"Questions from Readers: 'At times there are changes in viewpoint on Biblical subjects discussed in the Watch Tower Society's publications. We speak of what we believe as 'the truth.' But does 'truth' change? ... We read at **Proverbs 4:18**: 'The path of the righteous ones is like the bright light that is getting lighter and lighter until the day is firmly established....' It is to be expected, then, that **at times there may be changes of viewpoint**. Our basic belief may be sound Scriptural truth, but there may be some details that we do not fully understand in the past. **In time, with the aid of Jehovah's spirit, we get those matters cleared up**" (*WT*, 1 Oct. 1966, 607-08).

Conclusion

In conclusion, there is no need to review the numerous confident declarations of Watch Tower authority, assertions of special Divine direction, and claims to Bible understanding through "due time" light. They are clear, but as stated earlier in this study, declarations, assertions, and claims such as these can be made by any organization, but are they supported by the record?

Notes

1. Ron Frye, *The Bible Examiner*, Sept.-Oct., 1982, 4.
2. *Watchtower Attorney Olin R. Moyle Sues Watchtower President Joseph F. Rutherford and Wins! (court transcript)*, 1474. This trial transcript is published as a bound volume by Witness Inc., P.O. Box 597, Clayton, CA 94517.
3. Raymond Franz, *In Search of Christian Freedom* (Atlanta: Commentary Press, 1991), 421.
4. Ibid., 422.
5. Frye, 23.
6. Ibid. From research and his own experience, Jerry Bergman writes: "Once questions are voiced, the questioner is all too often told that he or she is to accept whatever the Watchtower teaches, and is not to 'reason' on the word but simply, blindly and dogmatically, fully accept whatever is taught. Your reasoning, they stress, is 'human reason,' but the Watchtower's is 'God's reasoning'" (Jerry Bergman, "Why Jehovah's Witnesses Leave The Watchtower," *JW Research Journal*, Winter 1996, 31).
7. Jerry Bergman, *Jehovah's Witnesses and Kindred Groups* (New York: Garland Publishing Inc., 1984), xx. Brackets in original.
8. *WT*, 1 Feb. 1931, 47. Bohnet's picture is included in the *Proclaimers* book (79).
9. Timothy White, *A People For His Name* (New York: Vantage Press, 1967), 190.
10. Ibid.
11. *WT*, 1 Apr. 1986, 30-31.

12. The *Proclaimers* book (143) quotes this portion of the *Watchtower* article, but an ellipsis appears where the statement, "No man's opinion is expressed in *The Watchtower*" is made.
13. *Watchtower Attorney Olin R. Moyle Sues Watchtower*, 866.
14. Pursuer's Proof *Douglas Walsh vs. the Right Honorable James Laytham Clyde, M.P., P.C.,* Scottish Court of Sessions, Nov. 1954 (1958 ed.), 503. Douglas Walsh was a Jehovah's Witness congregational overseer.
15. Ibid., 22-24.
16. Ibid., 702-03.

2.

Jehovah's Witnesses— Proclaimers of God's Kingdom

The Watch Tower Bible and Tract Society has published two full-sized histories of the Jehovah's Witnesses. The first was *Jehovah's Witnesses in the Divine Purpose* (1959).[1] This was replaced in 1993 by *Jehovah's Witnesses—Proclaimers of God's Kingdom*. This is a very important book.

How has this new account been viewed? Author David Reed, an ex-Witness, describes the history as "a powerful propaganda tool aimed at immunizing JWs against exposes of the sect's false prophecies, doctrinal flip-flops, bizarre teachings, and other embarrassing skeletons in the Brooklyn headquarters' closet."[2] In his *'Proclaimers' Answered Page by Page*, Reed makes other observations. He states that the volume contains "revisions contradicting historical accounts printed earlier."[3] And later, he concludes:

> Although described in its Foreword as "objective" and "candid" ... [it] reads like a clever piece of propaganda.... Unlike history books which present matters in chronological order, this one covers JW history topically. The result is that the accounts of embarrassing episodes, when not omitted entirely, can be fragmented into less embarrassing bits and pieces related in different parts of the book. These bite-size fragments are easier to swallow than the whole truth presented clearly in one place.[4]

Reed sees the *Proclaimers* book as "obviously forged by the Watchtower Society as a powerful defensive weapon," but one which can be used by the non-Witness "to present to a JW the single, most devastating piece of evidence against the Watchtower Society's claim to be God's organization: **its blatant disregard for truth.**"[5]

Ken Raines, editor of the *JW Research Journal*, states:

> The *Proclaimers* book, while better written and even a little more "candid" than the Society's earlier history book, *Jehovah's Witnesses in the Divine Purpose*, published in 1959, has, I believe, serious omissions in its portrayal of their history. Despite endeavoring to present a "candid" and objective review of their history, it is still, like the earlier work, biased in its treatment and not very candid when dealing with certain aspects of their history.[6]

In his review of the *Proclaimers* book, Randall Watters, ex-Bethelite and editor of *Free Minds Journal*, writes:

> While generally well written, and well executed technically, much of the book is a collection of anecdotes and story fragments strung together with little apparent continuity. In the Society's usual fashion, the book gives few references for source material. This makes it difficult for a reader to check what has been said.... While there are a number of relatively candid discussions of material **that used to be covered up, much information has been left out** that could have presented a much clearer picture of their history. Likely the Society still wants to keep some of it hidden. In other cases information is presented in bits and pieces, so that the reader sees no continuity of thought. The casual reader will miss much.[7]

Author Carl Olof Jonsson, another ex-Witness, is also critical of the *Proclaimers* history, and rightly so, as he illustrates in his book *The Gentile Times Reconsidered*: "The book was introduced at the district assemblies of Jehovah's Witnesses that year as a 'candid look' at the history of the movement. The admissions, however, usually are contextually surrounded by a minimum of background information which, moreover, is so apologetically slanted and warped that it **often conceals more than it reveals.**"[8]

In the second edition of *Apocalypse Delayed*, under the heading, "The Continued Promotion of False History," Prof. M. James Penton concludes:

> Such behavior on the part of the governing body demonstrates that it is primarily interested in maintaining the authority of the Watch Tower organization by any means, including devious ones, even as it criticizes other religious movements for lacking moral integrity. So, too, does the **incredibly distorted history**, so called, that it continues to publish for the Witness faithful.... *Jehovah's Witnesses—Proclaimers of God's Kingdom.* According to the foreword, "The editors of this volume have endeavored to be objective and present a candid history." But if they have "endeavored to be objective"—which is more than doubtful—they have failed, and what has come to be known as the *Proclaimers* book is far from "candid."[9]

Penton goes on to present specific examples to support his critical statements.[10] In his annotated Bibliography entry on the *Proclaimers* book in *Apocalypse Delayed*, he writes:

> Obviously written and published to counter books written by ex-Witnesses, the *Proclaimers* book, as it is commonly known, does contain more information than *Jehovah's Witnesses in the Divine Purpose*. Still it is only a slight improvement over that work. It is **far more hagiographic propaganda than history**, and like *Jehovah's Witnesses in the Divine Purpose*, **it contains far too many sanitized accounts, omissions, half-truths, and outright falsehoods**. In addition, it is written in a way which makes it hard to bring information together on many important issues. **Anyone using it for scholarly purposes should recognize that it is little more than a bad piece of sectarian self-glorification.**[11]

The accuracy of these reviewers' statements is confirmed in the present study a number of times where the *Proclaimers* book is cited.

Notes

1. This was based on a 31-part series, "A Modern History of Jehovah's Witnesses," which began with the January 1, 1955, *Watchtower* and ended with the April 1, 1956, issue.
2. David Reed, *Comments from the Friends,* Spring 1994, 9.
3. David Reed, *'Proclaimers' Answered Page by Page* (Stoughton, Maine: Comments from the Friends, 1994), 3. A short review of the *Proclaimers* book by Reed was published in the *Christian Research Journal* (Spring/Summer 1994, 46).
4. Ibid., 4. Reed uses the 1925 failure as an example (*Proclaimers*, 78, 425, 632).
5. Ibid., 5.
6. Ken Raines, *JW Research Journal,* volume 1, number 1, Winter, 1994, 2.
7. *Notes on the new JW history book, Jehovah's Witnesses—Proclaimers of God's Kingdom*, 1. Watter's 17-page review is available from Free Minds, Inc., P.O. Box 3818, Manhattan Beach, CA 90266.
8. Carl Olof Jonsson, *The Gentile Times Reconsidered* (3rd ed.; Atlanta: Commentary Press, 1998), 67.
9. M. James Penton, *Apocalypse Delayed* (2nd ed.; Toronto: University of Toronto Press, 1997), 322.
10. Ibid., 322-24.
11. Ibid., 402.

3.

Russell's Bible
Students Movement—
A Millerite Offshoot

After looking at the historical evidence, researcher/author Carl Olof Jonsson concludes: "In all essential respects, therefore, Russell's Bible Student movement may be described as yet another offshoot of the Millerite movement."[1] A brief historical overview is helpful in establishing this connection and in determining where Russell acquired much of his theology. Some important developments in the movement are also reviewed.[2]

William Miller and the Great Disappointment

During the 1830s and the early 1840s, William Miller (1782-1849), a Baptist farmer-preacher, carried the message of Christ's Second Coming to thousands of Americans. Miller gave his first public lecture in August 1831, and in 1833 he published a 64-page booklet, *Evidences from Scripture and History of the Second Coming of Christ About the Year A.D. 1843, and of His Personal Reign of 1000 Years.*[3] In 1874, Isaac C. Wellcome observed: "It may be truthfully said that with his labors commenced effectively the proclamation of the Second Advent Message in this country, although others had taught it."[4] Multiplied thousands became part of the Second Advent movement in America.[5]

On January 1, 1843, Miller wrote: "I am fully convinced that sometime between March 21, 1843, and March 21, 1844, according to the Jewish mode of computation of time, Christ will come and bring all His saints with him; and that then he will reward every man as his work shall be."[6] When 1843 arrived, the missionary zeal of the movement became stronger than ever. Several adjustments were made in the chronology which shifted emphasis to 1844. So in the light of these refinements, when 1843 passed without the expected events being realized, expectations ran high for 1844.[7] The majority now looked to March 21, 1844, as the time for Christ's return. Just weeks before the March 21st date, Miller mentioned a possible delay, "If Christ comes, as we expect, we will sing the song of victory soon; if not, we will watch, and pray, and preach until he comes, for soon our time, and all prophetic days, will have been fulfilled."[8] When the limit of the time calculation was reached and Christ had not returned, Miller and his followers were extremely disappointed and troubled, and in May of 1844 Miller "publicly confessed his mistake as to a definite time, but reaffirmed his conviction that the end was near."[9]

This disappointment was explained by the use and interpretation of Habakkuk 2:3 as suggesting a delay: "'For the vision is yet for an appointed time, but at the end' [of the prophetic periods] 'it shall speak and not lie; though it tarry,' [beyond their apparent termination] 'wait for it; because' [when they are fulfilled] 'it will surely come, it will not tarry.'"[10] A short time later the failure was explained by the faithful who remained, as a purifying test.[11]

Another date was ultimately set by Millerite Samuel S. Snow—October 22, 1844 (Seventh Month movement—Jewish 7th month, tenth day). George Storrs, to whom Russell "felt a sense of indebtedness,"[12] a well-known and influential Second Adventist, supported Snow's calculations. He wrote an editorial in the September 24, 1844, issue of his *Bible Examiner* which expressed his faith: "I take up my pen with feelings such as I never before experienced. *Beyond a doubt*, in my mind, the tenth day of the seventh month will witness the revelation of our Lord Jesus Christ in the clouds of heaven."[13] Belief in the October 22, 1844, date became a popular movement; "meetings now multiplied; many gave up their secular business and congregated for the worship of God and the investigation of the Bible. Farmers left their crops unharvested; many seemed oblivious to worldly affairs."[14]

The failure of this date brought the second or Great Disappointment.[15] "From 1845 onward the majority of Adventists began to interpret this Disappointment as another failure in their time calculations. However, for a minority the mistake was not in the time setting but in the prediction of the nature of the event which was to take place on October 22, 1844." Many left the movement, the hopes of others still ran high that Christ would return shortly. This failure was also explained as a purifying test.[16] Hiram Edson came up with the interpretation of the Great Disappointment "that a mistake had been made in the *manner* in which the Adventists had expected Christ to come as the Bridegroom, but not in the predicted *time*."[17]

Miller, writing in 1845 concerning the Seventh Month movement and the Great Disappointment, acknowledged the failure and disappointment: "We expected the personal coming of Christ at that time; and now to contend that we were not mistaken is dishonest. We should never be ashamed frankly to confess all our errors." Miller rejected Edson's interpretation and stated: "**I have no confidence in any of the new theories that have grown out of that movement**, viz., that Christ then came as Bridegroom, that the door of mercy was closed, that there was no salvation for sinners, that the seventh trumpet then sounded, **or that it was a fulfillment of prophecy in any sense.**[18]

George Storrs, quoted above, who had been so sure of the Second Coming of Christ at that time, would later write:

> After having been convinced that we were mistaken with respect to definite time or exact time for the Second Advent of our Lord ... **I remain fixed, at present, in the belief that the *exact* time—day, hour, or year—for the Advent is not revealed in the Bible.** Those who think differently will still continue to make their figures, and give days, months and years, but time will probably show, as it has done again and again already, that they "labor in vain and spend their strength for naught."[19]

Putting this latest disappointment into perspective, historian Eric Anderson writes:

> William Miller and his followers began their schooling in failed prophecy long before the morning of October 23, 1844. Indeed, the history of the American "second advent awakening" is a history of recurring disappointment as well as a "blessed hope." It is possible to count **a dozen or more lesser disappointments before and after 1844**.... Before the "Great Disappointment," enthusiastic Adventists calculated other dates for the Second Coming, including February 10, February 15, and April 14, 1843, as well as the 1843 autumnal equinox, and March 21, 1844. After 1844 increasingly obscure "timists" found that Bible prophecy pointed to the Parousia in **1847** or **1851** or **1866** or **1873**.[20]

Jonathan Butler adds: "Some earmarked the end for October 23 at 6:00 P.M., others for October 24. There were high expectations for exactly a year after the Great Disappointment on October 22, **1845**, with **1846**, **1847**, and the seven-year point of **1851** also heating up the millenarianism."[21]

In my survey of this subject I found that a number of other years were proposed for Christ's Advent. These include: **1850, 1852, 1853, 1854, 1855, 1862, 1864, 1865, 1867, 1868, 1869, 1870, 1874, 1875, 1877, 1880, 1883, 1889, 1890-91, 1898-99.**[22] Not only were many new dates set, but after the 1844 Great Disappointment, "in 1855 prominent Second Adventist, J. P. Cowles, estimated there existed 'some **twenty-five divisions** of what was once the one Advent body.'"[23]

After noting the failed time prophecies of William Miller (1843, 1844), J. A. Bengel (1836), the English Irvingites (1835, 1838, 1864, 1866) and a Russian Mennonite group (1889, 1891), *Jehovah's Witnesses— Proclaimers of God's Kingdom* proposes an answer to the question as to why these disappointments occurred: "For the most part, because they **relied too much on men, and not enough on the Scriptures.**"[24] Were the new dates accepted and promoted by C. T. Russell and his associates, and his successors fulfilled? If not, how should they be viewed?

C. T. Russell and the Millerite-Second Adventist Connection

The *Proclaimers* book explains why the history of Charles Taze Russell is of importance to Jehovah's Witnesses today: "Because their **present understanding of Bible truths** and their activities can be traced back to the 1870's and the work of C. T. Russell and his associates...."[25] How did Russell identify many of "his associates"? "Looking back to 1871, we see that many of our company were what are known as Second Adventists...."[26]

Charles Taze Russell was born on February 16, 1852, in Old Allegheny (now a part of Pittsburgh), Pennsylvania. His parents were Presbyterians of Scotch-Irish descent. Little is known of Russell's childhood. His mother died when he was but nine years of age. He received his education in public schools and through private tutors.[27] Quoting Russell's own account as he explained it in the *Watch Tower*:

> Let me begin the narrative at the year 1868, when the Editor, having been a consecrated child of God for some years, and a member of the Congregational church and of the Y.M.C.A., began to be shaken in faith regarding many long-accepted doctrines. Brought up a Presbyterian, and indoctrinated from the Catechism, and being naturally of an inquiring mind, I fell a ready prey to the logic of infidelity as soon as I began to think for myself ["The doctrine of eternal torment of all mankind except the few elect became so abhorrent to him that at the age of seventeen he was a skeptic."][28]

> But that which at first threatened to be the utter shipwreck of faith in God and the Bible, was, under God's providence, overruled for good, and merely **wrecked my confidence in human creeds and systems of misinterpretation of the Bible**. Gradually I was led to see that though each of the creeds contained some elements of truth, they were, on the whole, misleading and contradictory of God's Word. Among other theories, **I stumbled upon Adventism**.[29]

It is ironic that Russell left orthodoxy at an early age because he had lost "confidence in human creeds and systems of misinterpretation of the Bible," only to borrow from contemporaries and to interpret Scripture himself, and as a result, constructed what proved to be yet another system of "misinterpretation of the Bible"—the passage of time proved Russell's predictions and many of his interpretations of the Bible wrong—either requiring "adjustments" or outright **rejection by his Watch Tower Society successors**.

Picking up Russell's account again—He recalls one evening in 1869, when "there, for the first time, I heard something of the views of Second Adventists, the preacher being Mr. Jonas Wendell [of the Advent Christian Church].... **Thus I confess indebtedness to Adventists as well as to other denominations.**"[30] But Russell could not accept the arguments of **his friend Jonas Wendell** and of other "Second Adventists who were expecting Christ in the flesh, and teaching that the world and all in it except Second Adventists would be burned up in 1873 or 1874...."[31]

In 1870 Wendell published a booklet, *The Present Truth; or, Meat in Due Season*, in which he affirmed the 1873 date:

> I must confess that it did appear to me that no other date could be found, in which all the periods would center, until within a few months; and now I am satisfied that **the year 1873 is the year in which the 2,300 days [years], the 1,335 days [years], and the 6,000 years end**. They come together in that year without the sound of a hammer; there is no passage of Scripture strained from its plain, literal meaning to reach this result. Some, I have no doubt, will continue harping upon the chronological mistakes of the people of God in other times, and who will adduce them as an argument why we should let the whole subject alone, and have nothing to do with it. **But I must confess, notwithstanding all past mistakes, my faith never was stronger in the angelic declaration, "The wise shall understand."**[32]

It is interesting to note that Jonas Wendell, who had been a follower of William Miller, had previously joined with Elder J. C. Bywater to publish *The Watchman* in 1850, a paper "started specially to advocate that the Lord would make his **second advent in 1850**."[33]

The 1869 contact with Wendell rekindled his interest "and in 1870, as an 18-year-old businessman in Allegheny, Pennsylvania, *Charles Taze Russell*, together with his father Joseph and some friends formed a class for Bible study. The group was formed as an outgrowth of Russell's contacts with some of the former Millerites ... especially Jonas Wendell, George Storrs, and George Stetson."[34] In his autobiography Russell states: "And here I gratefully mention assistance rendered by Brothers George Stetson and George Storrs.... The study of the Word of God with these dear brethren led step by step into greener pastures and brighter hopes for the world."[35]

George Storrs

George Storrs (1796-1879) was an important influence in Russell's life and according to Prof. Jerry Bergman, "C. T. Russell evidently met Storrs through Jonas Wendell in about 1869.... George Storrs conducted a personal Bible study with Charles Russell who adopted many, if not most, of his views."[36] Storr's monthly, *The Bible Examiner* also greatly influenced Russell and one of the first articles that Russell wrote, "Gentile Times: When Do They End?" was published in the October 1876 issue.

What were some of the specific areas in which Storrs influenced Russell? Prof. M. James Penton concludes:

> ...It is quite obvious that Storrs contributed much to the young Pennsylvanian's thinking. An Examination of the *Bible Examiner* indicates clearly that Russell learned the doctrines of the ransom atonement of Christ and the restitution of mankind to a paradise earth directly from Storrs and his associates plus, of course, the doctrine of conditionalism. It is evident, too, that the practice of celebrating the Memorial of the Lord's Supper once a year on the supposed date of the Jewish Passover, 14 Nisan, as is done by Jehovah's Witnesses today, was learned by Russell from

the editor of the *Bible Examiner*. Then, finally, Russell's negative feelings towards churches and religious organizations may have come directly from Storrs.[37]

One additional area of Storr's influence on Russell's belief system relates to the notion that the Great Pyramid of Egypt corroborates the Bible. It is significant that an article on the Great Pyramid by Piazzi Smyth was published in George Storr's *Bible Examiner* in the June 1876 issue, and in 1878 "Storrs published a series of major articles on the Great Pyramid and its prophetic significance in the *Herald of Life and the Coming Kingdom*."[38] It should also be noted that in 1877 Philadelphia pastor Joseph Seiss published *A Miracle in Stone: or the Great Pyramid of Egypt*.[39] "It is quite probable that Russell came to accept pyramidology because of the influence on him of such men as Dr. Joseph Seiss and George Storrs."[40] Russell's acceptance of pyramidology is important, because "what he did was to give a major historical-eschatological interpretation of the pyramid which he related to Barbour's system of biblical chronology and prophetic speculation. Accordingly, he came to teach that the Great Pyramid was the 'divine plan of the ages in stone.'"[41]

George Stetson

In addition to Russell's mention of the study of the Bible with George Stetson, the *Proclaimers* book identifies him as "an earnest student of the Bible and pastor of the Advent Christian Church in Edinboro, Pennsylvania."[42] Before this he had ministered in Pittsburgh and he also was a former Millerite.[43] In addition to the emphasis on the soon return of Christ, one of the major tenets of the Advent Christian Church was (and still is) a belief in conditional immortality a doctrine which Russell had also shared with Storrs and Wendell. As a pastor in the Advent Christian Church at that time it was not unusual that Stetson was a non-trinitarian (which obviously did not bother Russell).[44] Stetson requested that Russell preach his funeral sermon and a brief notice of his death and tribute to him was published in the November 1879 *Zion's Watch Tower*.[45]

Nelson H. Barbour

The *Proclaimers* book states that Nelson H. Barbour "had a profound effect on Russell's life" and "also caused his loyalty to Scriptural truth to be put to the test."[46] To find the source of Russell's time chronology, including 1914, one must briefly review the history of Nelson H. Barbour. When Barbour joined the Millerite movement in 1843, he was 19 years old. He "lost his religion" with the October 22, 1844, failure and went to Australia that year and became a miner. In 1859, he left Australia to return to America by way of England. His interest in reading the Bible again was stimulated when a chaplain on the ship "proposed a systematic reading of the prophecies," to which he assented. In his reading he thought that he discovered a 30-year error in Miller's system—the 1335 days of Daniel 12 would then end in 1873. Barbour's chronological view was based on William Miller's, with a 30-year tarrying period added. While in London he went to the British Museum library and found Christopher Bowen's chronology in Elliott's *Horae Apocalypticae* which he believed also confirmed the 1873 date, because using Bowen's data, 6,000 years since Adam's creation also ended in that year.[47] Barbour explains: "It was surprising that prophetic periods once thought to point to 1843, now marked 1873 so clearly. But here was a chronology, not made for the occasion, as too many have been, which pointed with *steadfast finger* to 1873, in spite of every effort to make it end in 1866 [Elliott's position]."[48]

In the United States, "From 1868 onward he began to preach and publish his findings" and a number of his articles on chronology appeared in "the two leading papers of the Advent Christian Association."[49] In 1870 he published *Evidences for the Coming of the Lord in 1873; or the Midnight Cry*, and in 1873 he started his own monthly magazine: *The Midnight Cry, and Herald of the Morning*. "When the target year of 1873 had nearly passed, Barbour advanced the time of the second advent to the autumn of 1874."[50] When Christ did not appear, Barbour and those of like belief were dumbfounded: "They had examined the time-prophecies that had seemingly passed unfulfilled, and had been unable to find any flaw, and had begun to wonder whether the *time* was right and their *expectations* wrong...."[51] The explanation that Barbour accepted came through Adventist B. W. Keith who saw the rendering "presence" instead of "coming" in Matthew 24:27, 37, 39 in *The Emphatic Diaglott*.[52] This solved the problem—but an invisible presence did not satisfy most of the *Midnight Cry, and Herald of the Morning* subscribers, and 15,000 readers quickly dropped to about 200.[53]

In the September 1875 issue of Barbour's monthly, retitled *Herald of the Morning*, the dates (in addition to 1874), which would later become familiar to Russell's followers, were already published by Nelson Barbour: "I believe that though the gospel dispensation will end in 1878, the Jews will not be restored to Palestine until 1881; and that the 'times of the Gentiles,' viz. their seven prophetic times, of 2520, or twice 1260 years, which began where God gave all, into the hands of Nebuchadnezzar, 606 B.C.; did not end until A.D. 1914; or 40 years from this."[54] As Jonsson and others have documented, Nelson Barbour did not originate this interpretation which applied the year-day principle to the "seven times" of Daniel 4 as a period of 2,520 years—it was John Aquila Brown in *The Even Tide*, published in England in 1823. And "his calculation for the 2,520 years, and his having based these on Daniel chapter 4, have since played a key role in certain modern interpretations of those Gentile times."[55]

C. T. Russell and Nelson H. Barbour: A Short-lived Union

Russell explains how he became acquainted with Nelson H. Barbour: "It was about January 1, 1876, that my attention was specially drawn to the subject of prophetic time, as it relates to these doctrines and hopes."[56] He had received a copy of Barbour's *Herald of the Morning*, and found the invisible Second Coming view set forth in agreement with his. In addition, Barbour had concluded that Christ's invisible presence occurred in 1873-74. Russell explains his thinking at the time: "Here was a new thought: Could it be that the *time prophecies* which I had so long despised, because of their misuse by Adventists, were really meant to indicate when the Lord would be *invisibly present* to set up his kingdom—a thing which I clearly saw could be known in no other way? ... Could it be that these *time* arguments, which I had passed by as unworthy of attention, really contained an important truth which they had misapplied?"[57]

Russell wrote to Barbour asking him about the proofs for the 1874 Second Presence and the harvest period to follow. "The answer showed that my surmise had been correct, viz.: that the *time arguments*, chronology, etc. were the same as used by Second Adventists in 1873, and explained how Mr. Barbour and Mr. J. H. Paton, of Michigan, a co-worker with him, had been regular Second Adventists up to that time...."[58] Russell relates: "... I paid Mr. Barbour's expenses to come to see me at Philadelphia ... to show me fully and Scripturally, if he could, that the prophecies indicated 1874 as the date at which the Lord's *presence* and 'the harvest' began. He came, and **the evidence satisfied me**."[59] Beyond a doubt, Barbour convinced Russell that his chronology was right, for in his *The Object and Manner of Our Lord's Return* (1877) Russell tells the reader: "(Those interested in knowing the **evidences as to the time**, I would refer to Dr. N. H. Barbour, editor of the 'Herald of the Morning,' Rochester, N.Y.) **I simply add that I am deeply impressed, and think, not without good scriptural evidence, that the Master is come and is now inspecting the guests to the marriage**."[60]

In 1876, convinced that the invisible presence of Christ had begun in 1874 and that the harvest period was underway, Russell became an Assistant Editor (with J. H. Paton) of Barbour's *Herald of the Morning* and he provided funds for the publication of *Three Worlds* (1877).[61] This book concludes with "WM. MILLER'S DREAM," and its appearance here is explained:

We publish the following because it has been so perfectly fulfilled. Every position on the prophecies held by Bro. Miller has been attacked during the "tarrying of the Bridegroom," and while the "virgins all slumbered and slept." And yet **every one of those applications have of necessity again been incorporated in** *these present arguments*, and the casket [filled with jewels, diamonds, precious stones, gold and silver coins], enlarged and rearranged, does indeed "shine brighter than before."[62]

Russell also accepted Barbour's theory published in *The Three Worlds* that a 3½-year harvest period (1874-1878) was underway, during which time the last call for the "little flock" (Church) was to be given. Translation of the Bride of Christ would take place in 1878. Russell explains: "Coming to the spring of 1878 ... we naturally and not unreasonably expected some change of condition, and all were more or less disappointed when nothing supernatural occurred."[63] Russell concluded that 1878 was a marked year after all because it was the year in which **the resurrection of the dead in Christ occurred**, and the Bride of Christ members who would die after this time would join them at death.[64] Barbour did not accept this view and after his denial of "the doctrine of the atonement" Russell "withdrew entirely from the *Herald of the Morning* and from further fellowship with Mr. B. [Barbour]."[65] In Russell's account, "The Spring of 1878 proved far from a blessing to Mr. Barbour and to many under his influence. Rejecting the plain, simple solution presented above, Mr. B. [Barbour] seemed to feel that he must of necessity get up something new to divert attention from the failure of the living saints to be caught up en masse."[66] According to Russell, Barbour and co-laborer A. P. Adams "went out of the light into the outer darkness of the world **on the subjects once so clearly seen—namely, the time and manner of the Lord's presence**; and since then they have been **expecting Christ in the flesh** every Spring or Fall and twisting the prophecies accordingly."[67]

How did Nelson Barbour view Paton and Russell? Looking back, in the March 1898 *Herald of the Morning*, he writes:

Of the leaders of the various factions who found themselves out of the movement, after the midnight cry [1874]; Eld. J. H. Paton, became interested in 1873-74, mainly by reading the papers I sent to him; and finally by hearing my lectures on these subjects; though he was an adventist before that. C. T. Russell first became slightly interested by reading the HERALD OF THE MORNING, in 1875, but did not identify himself with the movement until the autumn and winter of 1876-7, through listening to lectures which I delivered during the Centennial, at St. George's Hall Phila., and in other places. Both men left the movement in 1878. C. T. Russell then, having been in the movement about eighteen months; felt competent to start a paper of his own. **Since which he has remained faithful to just what he learned from me, prior to the "midnight," while we "all slumbered and slept." Namely, that Christ came as king, in 1878; and believes it because of the time arguments, as he then learned them from me.**[68]

New Publications and a New Organization

In 1879, Russell began the publication of *Zion's Watch Tower* with the assistance of John H. Paton (1843-1922), who had become Russell's good friend and who sided with him when he left Barbour. Paton is listed as a "regular contributor" in its first issue and he wrote more than fifty articles for the magazine until he and Russell parted in 1881. Under Russell's direction, Paton also wrote *The Day Dawn* (1880), a book to replace *Three Worlds*.[69] While Paton is given little attention in the *Proclaimers* history, Bergman concludes that Paton was "probably one of the most influential Bible Students" who "supplied much of the impetus for the early Watchtower movement, and was highly influential in formulating the doctrine of the early Watch Tower

Society."[70] Paton's "work left an important mark on the Society, especially its chronology which concludes we are in the last days and basic theology, much of which is still accepted even today."[71]

Barbour's chronology had also featured the year 1881. Would Russell continue to follow Barbour's prophetic time scheme? What was expected for 1881? Reexamination brought "new light"—the 3-year harvest period was extended to 7 years (to 1881).[72] An article in the *Watch Tower* by A.D. Jones, "How Long, O Lord?" answers the question, "How soon will our change be?" Jones writes: "...While we would not attempt to prove our change at any particular time, yet we propose looking at some of the evidences which *seem* to show the **translation or change from the natural to the spiritual condition, due this side or by the fall of our year 1881....** We shall now present what we adduce from the types and prophetic points as seeming to indicate **the translation of the saints and closing of the doors to the high calling by 1881."[73]** Russell's article in the December 1880 *Watch Tower* showed he agreed with Jones.[74] Yet, in the May 1881 *Watch Tower*, Russell writes: "The WATCH TOWER **never claimed** *that the body of Christ* **will be changed to spiritual beings this year**. There is *such a change* due sometime. We have not attempted to say when, but have repeatedly said that it could not take place *before* the fall of 1881."[75] Russell taught that 1881 was the year when the harvest of the "little flock," the Bride of Christ would end—and the door would be shut. It was explained in the May 1881 *Watch Tower*: "...The *favor* which ends this fall, is that of entering the *Bride company*. We believe the *door of favor* is now open and any who consecrate *all* and give up *all*, can come in to the wedding and become members of the Bride, but that with this year the company will be reckoned *complete* and the *door to that high calling* (not the door of mercy) closed forever."[76] Although the living saints did not experience their change in 1881—one thing was sure—the door of opportunity mentioned above was shut!—at least for the present. Defectors would make room for new Bride replacements.[77] Hope for a soon "translation" was still alive. Missionary activity continued to reach the "great company" (those not Bride members).

In 1884 Zion's Watch Tower Tract Society (currently known as Watch Tower Bible and Tract Society of Pennsylvania) was incorporated by Russell, and in 1886 Russell published *The Divine Plan of the Ages*, the first volume of the *Millennial Dawn* (retitled *Studies in the Scriptures*) series. Robert Crompton writes:

> The first volume of *Studies in the Scriptures*, despite the claim to originality, ... **is a reworking of a modified dispensationalism expounded by Russell's early associate, Nelson H. Barbour**, a former associate of Miller, in his book, *Three Worlds....* In *The Divine Plan of the Ages*, Russell expounded a version of dispensationalism which had its origins within the millennialist circles with which he was first associated.[78]

In *The Divine Plan of the Ages* and in the second of the series, *The Time Is at Hand* (1889), M. James Penton concludes: "Russell restated almost in its entirety the eschatology contained in *Three Worlds*."[79]

The last important date in Barbour's prophetic scheme was 1914. In chapter 4 of *The Time Is at Hand*, "The Times of the Gentiles," Russell writes, "In this chapter we present the Bible evidence proving that the full end of the times of the Gentiles, *i.e.*, the full end of their lease of dominion, will be reached in A.D. 1914; and that that date will be the farthest limit of the rule of imperfect men."[80] Needless to say, predictions for 1914 also failed, as it is shown elsewhere in this study.

Miller, Barbour and Russell in God's Plan

The Witnesses' *Proclaimers* history does mention William Miller—that he predicted Christ's visible return in 1843 and 1844, that "Russell had been critical of those who had set various dates for the Lord's return, such as William Miller and some Second Adventist groups," that wrong dates had "caused many followers of

William Miller and various Adventist groups to lose faith."[81] The earlier history, *Jehovah's Witnesses in the Divine Purpose* (1959), mentions Miller only once: "He predicted the return of Christ Jesus visibly and bodily in 1843 or 1844. But his view was completely opposed to God's purpose as revealed in the Bible."[82] N. H. Barbour is often mentioned in the *Proclaimers* book, but there is no reference to **how Russell viewed Barbour in prophecy.**[83]

How did **Russell** view William Miller and N. H. Barbour in his interpretation of the meaning of the parable of "The Ten Virgins" in Matthew 25:1-13 and in his other writings? How did Russell fit in?

In Russell's interpretation of the passage, he writes:

> While we are neither "Millerites" nor "Adventists," yet we believe that this **much of this parable met its fulfillment in 1843 and 1844, when William Miller and others**, Bible in hand, walked out by faith on its statements, expecting Jesus at that time.... The disappointment of that company of Christians (which was composed of many of the best Christians from all denominations) all are well aware of, but it was foretold in the parable: "While the Bridegroom *tarried* they all slumbered and slept...." As the former movement in the parable had been represented by Miller and others, so to this second movement we give a similar application. **A brother, Barbour of Rochester, was we believe, the chosen vessel of God through whom the "Midnight Cry" issued to the sleeping virgins of Christ, announcing a discrepancy of thirty years in some of Miller's calculations**, and giving a rearrangement of the same argument (and some additional), **proving that the *night* of the parable was thirty years long, and that the morning was in 1873, and the Bridegroom due in the morning in 1874.**
>
> We do not here give the time arguments or proofs.... We merely notice here that Bible chronology, first dug from Scripture by **Bowen of England, which show clearly and positively that the 6,000 years from Adam ended in 1873**, and consequently that there the morning of the Millennial day (the seventh thousand) began, in which a variety of things are due. The establishment of the kingdom of Christ, the binding of Satan, the restitution of all things, and the blessing of all the families of the earth, are all due.... If these movements were of God, and if Bros. Miller and Barbour were his instruments, then that "Midnight Cry," based on the prophetic and other statements and evidences, was correct, and the "Bridegroom *came*" in 1874. **We believe that Midnight Cry was of God, and was fulfilled by the Bridgroom's coming, not because Bros. Miller and Barbour claimed it, but because the Word of God supports it.**[84]

In his *Thy Kingdom Come* (1891), Russell credits the Millerite movement as

> **the beginning of the *right* understanding of Daniel's visions, and at the right time to fit the prophecy. Mr. Miller's application of the three and a half times (1260 years) was practically the same as that we have just given**, but he made the mistake of not starting the 1290 and 1335 periods at the same point. Had he done so he would have been right. On the contrary, **he started them thirty years sooner**—about 509 instead of 539, which ended the 1335 days in 1844, instead of 1874. It was, nevertheless, the ***beginning* of the right understanding of the prophecy**; for after all, the 1260 period, which he saw correctly, was the key; and the preaching of this truth (even though in combination with errors, and misapplications, and false inferences) had the effect of separating and purifying "many," and at the very time the Lord had foretold.[85]

Years after Russell's death, the February 15, 1925, *Watch Tower* declares:

No doubt **Mr. Miller was correct in locating 1844 as a Bible date. But he expected too much**. 1874 was also easily located. 1878 was also a marked date, and one which caused Brother Russell a severe trial until he corrected his expectations, as noted in his "Harvest Siftings," of April 1894, now out of print.[86]

"...In the fulfillment of God's prophecy **no individual among God's covenant people is or will be identified**. It would be contrary to the Scriptures to single out some individual and say that such individual is fulfilling prophecy" (Rutherford, "Prophecy," *WT*, 15 Apr. 1937, 124).

To complete the succession, according to *The Finished Mystery* (1917): "Pastor Russell took the place of Mr. Barbour who became unfaithful and upon whom was fulfilled the prophecies of Matt. 24:48-51 and Zech. 11:15-17."[87] Further details are provided later in this volume:

> **In 1878 the stewardship of the things of God, the teaching of Bible truths, was taken from the clergy, unfaithful to their agelong stewardship, and given to Pastor Russell.** In the interim, until 1881, the new steward was setting the things in order, getting the truths of the Bible in logical and Scriptural form for presentation.... Then, **in 1881, he became God's watchman for all Christendom**, and began his gigantic work of witness.... The function of watchman was not given until 1881.... Faithfulness in individual watching during a trial period of seven years **was rewarded by the bestowal of the office of the greatest servant whom the Church of God has had since the Apostle Paul**.... Pastor Russell's warning to Christendom, **coming direct from God**, has been of the imminent collapse of the present "Christian" civilization in a welter of war, revolution and anarchy, to be succeeded by the early establishment of the Kingdom of God. In all his warnings he claimed no originality. He said that he could never have written his books himself. **It all came from God, through the enlightenment of the Holy Spirit.**[88]

It is interesting that when George Storrs died in 1879, "A number of Storrs' followers felt that the 'mantle' was passed from Storrs to Russell in that Russell's magazine began just as *The Bible Examiner* was ending."[89]

An Insightful Admission

In a discussion on "this generation" (Matt. 24:34) in a Governing Body session in 1979, Raymond Franz recalls:

> At the discussion's end, with the exception of a few members, the Body members indicated that they felt that 1914 and the teaching about "this generation" tied to it should continue to be stressed. The Writing Committee Coordinator, **Lyman Swingle, commented**, "All right, if that is what you want to do. But at least you know that **as far as 1914 is concerned, Jehovah's Witnesses got the whole thing—lock, stock and barrel—from the Second Adventists.**"[90]

A Significant Observation

What is the importance of Russell's Millerite-Adventist roots to the longevity of his movement? Joseph

Zygmunt concludes:

> It probably would have remained a purely local sectarian group rather then, as it came to be, the launching ground for a trans-local sectarian movement, **were it not for Russell's continued contacts and developing relations with certain Adventist preachers, once active in the old Millerite movement and now seeking to revive some of its ideas in revised form.** Besides suggesting many general doctrinal notions which eventually came to be incorporated in the belief-system of his group, **the more direct importance of these contacts derived from their influencing Russell to espouse the view that the Second Coming was imminent, and that, in fact, it was already in process.** It was the injection of chiliasm of this short-term variety into the developing belief-system that was mainly instrumental in extending the scope of the Allegheny sect into a translocal movement. The conviction that **Christ had come back to earth in 1874**, was now (1876) invisibly present, and would be completing the "harvest work" by 1878, after which he would establish his Kingdom, imparted the activating note of urgency required to launch a broader evangelistic enterprise.[91]

The Millerite-Adventist Connection: Additional Observations

The statements which follow are made by researchers who have thoroughly investigated Russell and the Bible Students movement. Jerry Bergman writes: "None of Russell's doctrines were original, and most of them were openly accepted (or at least commonly discussed) by the Millerites and the early Adventists, especially the Second Adventists."[92]

Joseph Zigmunt concludes:

> Despite the rifts which emerged, it seems quite clear that Russell's contacts and associations with "unassimilated" Adventists played a decisive role in furthering the movement's passage beyond the Allegheny congregational phase. In fact, it is doubtful whether the Allegheny group would have developed very much beyond a local Bible cult had it not been for this structuring and energizing influence. Jonas Wendell, George Storrs, George Stetson, N. H. Barbour, J. H. Paton, B. W. Keith, H. B. Rice—**had all been associated with the Millerite movement** and, though remaining on the margins of the main Adventist groups, had continued preaching the imminent coming of Christ.... Worthy of note is Russell's permissiveness and almost deferential attitude toward these early Adventist associated in matters of doctrine. While he insisted that the public representations of "present truth" include, or at least be consistent with, his own views concerning election, hellfire, future probation, and atonement, which his Adventist associates seemed at first willing to accept, Russell delegated much of the responsibility for doctrinal formation to the latter.[93]

Zygmunt further observes that many of the early *Watch Tower* articles "sought to relate the present group to the older Millerite movement."[94] "The appeals, the proof-texts, the imagery that permeated the early articles drew copiously upon standard Adventist themes."[95]

David and M. James Penton conclude:

> Although Russell never regarded himself as a Second Adventist, many of the persons who influenced him in a major way were [all had been involved with William Miller].... **So while he rejected the name, in fact Russell was basically an Adventist in the Second Adventist tradition....**[96] The Bible Students were all, in one way or other, the heirs of William Miller as such

had long tried to calculate the time of Christ's parousia or second advent from Daniel, the Revelation, and other prophetic books of the Bible.[97]

M. James Penton observes: "Although almost all of the major figures who influenced Russell were Adventists, and his doctrinal system was certainly Adventist, like George Storrs, **he rejected denominational labels**."[98] Melvin Curry asks a very important question: "Why did Russell continually disclaim dependence on the Adventists?" He concludes:

> First ... He did not want to be identified with the remnant of Miller's followers who taught that the earth will be burned up and that the wicked will suffer eternal torment; second, **so that he and the Bible Students might convincingly argue that they represented a genuine non-sectarian restoration of primitive Christianity**; and third, **that Russell himself might appear to be an independent theologian who had rediscovered the Divine Plan of the Ages**. It remains true, nevertheless, that Russell's entire theological structure is permeated with Adventist terminology; with the Adventist emphasis on types, antitypes, and parallel dispensations; and in particular, his doctrines of Christ's invisible presence, the ransom, election, restitution, conditionalism, and universalism were all taught by various Adventist preachers.[99]

Carl Olof Jonsson found that Russell was in contact with some Adventist groups and "established close connections with certain of their ministers and read some of their papers, including George Storr's *Bible Examiner*. Gradually, he and his associates took over many of their central teachings," and as quoted earlier, **"In all essential respects, therefore, Russell's Bible Student movement may be described as yet another offshoot of the Millerite movement**."[100] This conclusion is fully verified by the material presented in this chapter.

Notes

1. Carl Olof Jonsson, *The Gentile Times Reconsidered* (3rd ed.; Atlanta: Commentary Press, 1998), 43.
2. For a more detailed treatment of this period see: Carl Olof Jonsson, *The Gentile Times Reconsidered* (3rd ed.; Atlanta: Commentary Press, 1998), chapter 1, 312-14; M. James Penton, *Apocalypse Delayed* (2nd ed.; Toronto: University of Toronto Press, 1997), chapter 1. Robert Crompton, *Counting the Days to Armageddon*. Cambridge: James Clark & Co., 1996. Clyde E. Hewitt, *Midnight and Morning: An Account of the Adventist Awakening and the founding of the Advent Christian Denomination 1831-1860*. Charlotte, N.C.: Venture Books, 1983. Joseph Zygmunt, *Jehovah's Witnesses: A Study of Symbolic and Structural Elements in the Development and Institutionalization of a Sectarian Movement*. Unpublished Ph.D. diss., University of Chicago, 1967.
3. P. Gerhard Damsteegt, *Foundations of the Seventh-Day Adventist Message and Mission* (Grand Rapids: Wm. B. Eerdmans, 1977), 14.
4. Isaac C. Wellcome, *History of the Second Advent Message and Mission, Doctrine and People* (Yarmouth, Maine: Isaac C. Wellcome, 1874), 41.
5. In 1845, Miller wrote: "In nearly a thousand places Advent congregations have been raised up, numbering, as near as I can estimate, some fifty thousand believers" (*William Miller's Apology and Defence*, in *Advent Tracts*, vol. II [Boston: J. V. Himes, n.d.], 22). For a brief study on developments in Great Britain see: Louis Billington, "The Millerite Adventists in Great Britain 1840-1850," in *The Disappointed*, eds. Roland L. Numbers and Jonathan M. Butler (Bloomington, Ind: Indiana

University Press, 1987), 59-77.

6. Damsteegt, 37-38.

7. Ibid., 89-91.

8. Ibid., 93.

9. Clyde E. Hewitt, *Midnight and Morning* (Charlotte, NC: Venture Books, 1983), 105.

10. Damsteegt, 93. Brackets in original.

11. Ibid.

12. *Jehovah's Witnesses Proclaimers of God's Kingdom* (1993), 46. George Storrs (1796-1879) was a able Methodist preacher who left the church in 1840. He began the publication of the *Bible Examiner* in 1843 which continued until 1880. He joined Miller's movement in 1842 and is identified as a prominent Millerite spokesman. "Storrs had one distinctive view of theology which sometimes prevented him from having the closest fellowship with other Millerite ministers," he rejected eternal punishment and believed that the unsaved would be annihilated (Francis D. Nichol, *The Midnight Cry* [Takoma Park: Review and Herald Publishing Assoc., 1944], 191-92). "He was an able expositor of prophecy, being equally effective as a writer or preacher. He had a highly prominent part in the seventh-month movement, stressing the parable of the ten virgins in connection with the return of the bridegroom" (LeRoy E. Froom, *The Prophetic Faith of Our Fathers*, IV, 808). Damsteegt says Storrs "was one of the most vigorous advocates of the Seventh Month movement but one of the first to reject it after the second disappointment" (P. Gerard Damsteegt, Foundations of the Seventh-Day Adventist Message and Mission [Grand Rapids: Wm. B. Eerdmans, 1977], 83. See also 96-98).

13. Wellcome, 358.

14. Ibid., 359.

15. Damsteegt, 99.

16. Ibid., 103-04.

17. Ibid., 117. In answer to prayer Edson explains: "Heaven seemed open to my view, and I saw distinctly and clearly that instead of our High Priest coming out of the Most Holy of the heavenly sanctuary to come to this earth on the tenth day of the seventh month, at the end of 2300 days, that He for the first time entered on that day the second apartment of that sanctuary; and that He had a work to perform in the Most Holy before coming to this earth" (ibid). In 1855 the group led by Hiram Edson would merge with two other groups of Millerites to establish what would be officially named the Seventh-Day Adventist Church in 1860.

18. *William Miller's Apology and Defence*, 28.

19. Wellcome, 370.

20. Eric Anderson "The Millerite Use of Prophecy: A Case of a 'Striking Fulfillment,'" in *The Disappointed*, eds. Ronald L. Numbers and Jonathan M. Butler (Bloomington, Ind.: Indiana University Press, 1987), 78.

21. Jonathan M. Butler, "The Making of a New Order: Millerism and the Origins of Seventh-Day Adventism," in *The Disappointed*, 199.

22. Dates for Christ's Second Coming **before** 1843 had also been set. For example, George N. H. Peters' *The Theocratic Kingdom*, vol. 3 (New York: Funk and Wagnals, 1884), includes the following: 1532, 1656, 1666, 1694, 1716, 1717, 1776, 1785, 1786, 1789, 1793-94, 1796, 1798, 1800, 1816, 1836 (99).

23. Jonsson, 42.

24. *Proclaimers*, 40.

25. Ibid., 42.

26. *WTR*, Feb. 1881, 188.

27. *WTR*, 1 Dec. 1916, 5997.

28. "Biography," Russell, *The Divine Plan of the Ages* (1927 ed.), 1.

29. *WTR*, 15 July 1906, 3821.

30. Ibid.

31. *Zion's Watch Tower* (Extra Edition), 25 Apr. 1894, 97; *WT*, 15 July 1906, 3822. The 1873 date for Christ's return was accepted by many Second Adventists, "especially within the Advent Christian Church, with which Barbour evidently associated for a number of years. One reason for this readiness to accept the 1873 date was that it was not new to them. As Barbour points out in his *Evidences* ... (pp. 33, 34), Miller himself had mentioned 1873 after the 1843 failure.... The increasing interest in the date caused the Advent Christian Church to arrange a special conference, February 6 to 11, 1872, in Wooster, Mass, for the examination of the time of the Lord's return and especially the 1873 date. Many preachers, including Barbour, participated in the discussions. As reported in the *Advent Christian Times* of March 12, 1872, 'The point on which there seemed to be any general unanimity was the ending of the thirteen hundred and thirty-five years in 1873'" (Jonsson, 45, footnote 41). Isaac Wellcome questions whether Miller ever mentioned the 1873 date attributed to him by Barbour and others by quoting Miller's own statements (Wellcome, 270-75).

32. Jonas Wendell, *The Present Truth; or Meat in Due Season* (Edenboro, Pa.: Jonas Wendell, 1870), 35-36. The brackets in the quote are Wendell's.

33. Wellcome, 585. Welcome states that Jonas Wendell became a convert to the Second Advent message under the preaching of Mrs. L. M. Stoddard in 1842-43 (ibid., 305-06).

34. Jonsson, 47.

35. Clayton J. Woodworth and George H. Fisher, *The Finished Mystery* (1917), 179; *WT*, 15 July 1906, 3821.

36. Jerry Bergman, *Jehovah's Witnesses and Kindred Groups: A Historical Compendium and Bibliography* (New York: Garland, 1984), 58.

37. Penton, 16-17.

38. David J. Penton and M. James Penton, "A Case of Science, Pseudo-Science and Religion-Pyramidology in the Adventist-Bible Student Tradition," http://www.geocities.com/Athens/Parthenon/1697/pyramid.html, accessed 14 Aug, 1998, 6-7. In 1877 Piazzi Smyth published his book *Miracle of the Ages: The Great Pyramid* (London: Dalby, Isbister and Co.).

39. The book by Seiss was obviously a popular one. The copy I acquired indicated that it was the "fourteenth edition enlarged" (Philadelphia: Porter and Coats, 1877).

40. D. Penton and M. Penton, 7.

41. Ibid. See also Russell's *They Kingdom Come* (1891), Chapter X: "The Testimony of God's Stone Witness and Prophet, the Great Pyramid in Egypt."

42. *Proclaimers*, 45.

43. D. Penton and M. Penton, 7.

44. Penton, 343, n64. That many Advent Christian pastors were not Trinitarian at this time was verified in my conversations with two representatives of the Advent Christian General Conference.

45. *Proclaimers*, 45.

46. Ibid., 46.

47. Jonsson, 44-45; Nelson H. Barbour, *Evidences for the Coming of the Lord in 1873; or the Midnight Cry* (2nd ed.; Rochester, N.Y.: Nelson H. Barbour, 1871), 32-33.

48. Barbour, 33.

49. Jonsson, 45. According to Wayne A. Scriven, "N. H. Barbour had been a member of the Advent Christian Church for a number of years prior to 1874" (*Date Setting in America for the Second Coming of Christ During the Late Nineteenth and Early Twentieth Century* [unpublished MA thesis, SDA Theological Seminary, 1947], 29). Scriven also says Barbour was a member of the Advent Christian Conference of Michigan between 1860-70 (ibid., 48).

50. Jonsson, 45. Note the exact duplication of the Millerite Seven Month movement date in Barbour's chronology with a 30-year "correction"—1844 to 1874: "...**The Seventh Month movement ... predicted the Second Advent to occur on October 22, 1844, the 10th day of the seventh month** of the Jewish Karaite year" (Damsteegt, 100). "...Christ must complete the atonement and *come out* on **the 10th day of the seventh month ... October 22, 1874.... We are compelled to believe that Christ left the Holy Place, on the 10th day of the seventh month occurring in October 1874**" (Barbour, *The Three Worlds*, 105).

51. *Zion's Watch Tower*, 25 Apr. 1894, 98-99.

52. Ibid., 99. There is some question whether Keith was at this point just a "reader" of *The Midnight Cry, and Herald of the Morning*—renamed *Herald of the Morning* in June 1875 (*WT*, 3822; Penton, 18; Jonsson, 46). The *Proclaimers* book refers to him as "an associate of Barbour" (46). In the three issues of the *Herald of the Morning* examined, B. W. Keith had contributed two articles (Aug. and Sept. 1878) and one presented him as a speaker—along with Paton and Russell (July 1878, 2). Raymond Franz refers to Keith as "a Second Adventist contributor to Barbour's magazine" (*Crisis of Conscience*, 147). After Russell departed from the *Herald*, Keith is listed in the first issue of *Zion's Watch Tower* as one of the "regular contributors" (July 1879, 3) and his articles appear there from 1879 to 1882.

53. Jonsson, 46-47.

54. Ibid, 47 n48, 48. The *Proclaimers* book also acknowledges that it was Barbour who "pointed *to 1914 as marking the end of Gentile Times*" (134). Russell would not place the same emphasis on 1881 concerning the Jews as Barbour. But in the May 1880 *Watch Tower,* J. H. Paton writes: "The only change we can see as taking place three and one-half years after the cross, was in the condition of the *nominal* Jewish church and the gospel turning to the Gentiles. **A corresponding change in 1881** would affect the condition of the nominal Christian church and **the gospel turning in some special sense to the Jews again**" (*WTR*, May 1880, 103).

55. Jonsson, 34-36. See Jonsson (32-40) for further details.

56. *WTR*, 15 July 1906, 3822.

57. Ibid. In his article, "The Theory of Christ's *Parousia* as an 'Invisible Presence,'" Carl Olof Jonsson concludes that Russell's invisible presence of Christ view was probably taken from Lutheran pastor Dr. Joseph Seiss, a fact Russell wanted to conceal. The "views and arguments, presented by Seiss ... were identical to those of Charles published years later. It is quite obvious that Russell did not originate his view of Christ's invisible coming and presence himself but took it from others, and although it cannot be established with absolute certainty, the available evidence strongly indicates that he plagiarized the ideas of Dr. Seiss on this matter" (*The Bible Examiner*, Jan.-Feb. 1983, 15).

58. Ibid.

59. Ibid.

60. Russell, *The Object and Manner of Our Lord's Return* (Rochester, N.Y.: Office of Herald of the Morning, 1877), 62.

61. Concerning authorship of *The Three Worlds*, Russell states: "... As I was enabled to give some time and thought to its preparation it was issued by us both jointly, both names appearing on its title page—though it was mainly written by Mr. Barbour" (*WTR*, 15 July 1906, 3822).

62. N. H. Barbour and C. T. Russell, *Three Worlds, and the Harvest of This World* (Rochester, N.Y.), 189.

63. *WTR*, Feb. 1881, 189.

64. Ibid.

65. Ibid. Penton explains that "what Barbour did deny was the doctrine of *substitutionary* atonement and the significance of Christ's death. To the end of his life Barbour continued to use the terms 'ransom' and 'atonement'" (Penton, *Apocalypse Delayed*, 342 n45).

66. *WTR*, 15 July 1906, 3823. Beginning with the 1878 disappointment Barbour writes: "In August, 1878, a new supply of oil made our lamps begin to shine as they had never shown before; and during the next 3½ years, the faith once delivered to the saints, complete, as we now hold it; was restored; at the same time, **the time arguments were all re-adjusted**; and our pathway, made luminous.... From August, '78, to the spring of '82, during 3½ years, **nearly every doctrine we had ever believed**, beginning with that of Vicarious punishment as the basis of atonement, as began to be investigated in the August, '78 paper, **had to be renounced**" ("Parable of the Ten Virgins," *Herald of the Morning*, Mar. 1898, 359). As one example of a rejected doctrine, Barbour asks: "Is there any proof that six thousand years was to be the measure of present human institutions; or that the seventh thousand would be the millennium? ... There is not one particle of direct or indirect evidence in Scripture to support it" (ibid., 369).

67. *WTR*, 3824.

68. Nelson H. Barbour, *Herald of the Morning*, Mar. 1898, 368.

69. *WTR*, 3824.

70. Bergman, 60.

71. Ibid, 61.

72. *WTR*, Feb. 1881, 189; May 1881, 224-25.

73. *WTR*, Jan. 1881, 180.

74. *WTR*, Dec. 1880, 172.

75. *WTR*, May 1881, 224.

76. Ibid.

77. The door was wide open in 1909 when Russell speculated that possibly 30,000 (of 40,000 members) had defected since 1881 (*WTR*, 1 Jan. 1909, 4303-04).

78. Robert Crompton, *Counting the Days to Armageddon* (Cambridge: James Clarke & Co., 1996), 31.

79. M. James Penton, "The Eschatology of Jehovah's Witnesses: A Short, Critical Analysis," in *The Coming Kingdom*, M. Darrol Bryant and Donald W. Dayton (eds.) (Barrytown, N.Y.: International Religions Foundation, Inc., 1983), 179.

80. Russell, *The Time Is at Hand* (1889), 76-77.

81. *Proclaimers*, 40, 60, 62.

82. *Jehovah's Witnesses in the Divine Purpose*, 13.

83. *Proclaimers*, 46-48, 120, 131, 133-35, 575, 619-20, 718.

84. *WTR*, Oct.-Nov. 1881, 288.

85. Russell, *Thy Kingdom Come*, 86-87.

86. *WT*, 15 Feb. 1925, 57.

87. *The Finished Mystery*, 54. "The Lord Jesus, in his great prophetic statement in Matthew 24:45-47, made known the fact that at the end of the age, He ... should have a special servant ... to give meat in due season ... Pastor Russell is that servant" (*WTR*, 1 Nov. 1917, 323-24).

88. *The Finished Mystery*, 386-87.

89. Bergman, 59.

90. Raymond Franz, *Crisis of Conscience* (2nd ed.; Atlanta: Commentary Press, 1992), 216.

91. Zygmunt, 723.

92. Bergman, 53.

93. Zygmunt, 216-17.

94. Ibid., 218.

95. Ibid., 219.

96. D. Penton and M. Penton, 7.

97. Ibid., 9.

98. Penton, "The Eschatology of Jehovah's Witnesses," 203, n 4.

99. Melvin Dotson Curry, Jr., "Jehovah's Witnesses: The Effects of Millennarianism on the Maintenance of a Religious Sect." Ph.D. diss.; Florida State University, Tallahassee, Fla., 1980, 131.

100. Jonsson, 43.

4.

Selected Quotations from Publications Associated With C. T. Russell and Watch Tower Publications for the Years 1876-1889

1876

"...The seven times will end in A.D. 1914; **when Jerusalem shall be delivered forever**, and the Jew say of the Deliverer, 'Lo, this is our God, we have waited for Him and He will save us.' **When Gentile Governments shall have been dashed to pieces; when God shall have poured out his fury upon the nations and they acknowledge him King of Kings and Lord of Lords** (Russell, "Gentile Times: When Do They End?" *Bible Examiner*, Oct. 1876, 27).[1]

1877

"The writer believes that we are now living under the sounding of the *Seventh* [trumpet],[2] that it has **been sounding for more than thirty years**, and continues during the time of trouble, and until the Kingdom of the Lord is Universal Empire" (Russell, *The Object and Manner of Our Lord's Return*, 46).

"(Those interested in knowing the evidences as to the time, I [Russell] would refer to Dr. N. H. Barbour, editor of the 'Herald of the Morning,' Rochester, N.Y.) I simply add that I am deeply impressed, and think, not without good scriptural evidence, **that the Master is come [in 1874] and is now inspecting the guests to the marriage**.... Even the outward signs seen by the world seem to point to the fact that a great dispensational change may be near. From their stand-point **the last century would seem to be the 'day of [God's] preparation'**" (ibid., 62. Brackets in original in this paragraph).

The title page of *Three Worlds, and the Harvest of This World* reads in part: "...WITH THE EVIDENCES THAT WE ARE NOW IN THE 'TIME OF HARVEST,' OR CLOSING WORK OF THE GOSPEL AGE."

"THE END OF THIS WORLD; that is, the end of the *gospel*, and **beginning of the *millennial* age is nearer than most men suppose; indeed we have already entered the transition period**, which is to be a 'time of trouble, such as never was since there was a nation' (Dan. 12:1)" (N. H. Barbour and C. T. Russell, *Three Worlds*, 17).[3]

"The nations are perplexed, and are preparing for a terrible struggle; huge engines of war are being multiplied by land and sea; millions of men are under arms, and still their numbers are increased, while the people are becoming desperate and alarmed. When the struggle begins, **as soon it must**, a ball will be set in motion before which **'all the kingdoms of the world, that are upon the face of the earth, shall be thrown down;'** and, according to Scripture, one wild scene of desolation and terror will result" (ibid., 19).[95]

"Although there is no direct evidence that at the end of six thousand years from the creation of Adam, the 'second' Adam should begin the new creation, or restitution of all things; still there is much *indirect* evidence.... The mass of evidence which synchronizes with **the fact that the six thousand years are already ended, is absolutely startling**, to one who will take the trouble to investigate" (ibid., 67).

"One evening spent with Bible, paper and pencil ... will enable you to master the whole subject, and measure for yourself, the six thousand years to their termination in 1873; and having done this, **you will be able to understand all the evidences which prove that we are now in the midst of the greatest changes this world has ever experienced since men were upon the earth**.... If you have the spirit of a little child, you will please get a piece of paper, your Bible and pencil, and begin with Gen. 5:3. **Let me urge you, a few months and 'The harvest will be passed, the summer ended'**" (ibid., 68).

"... And this **forty years [1874-1914] upon which we have now entered is to be such 'a time of trouble as never was since there was a nation.'** And during this forty years, the kingdom of God is to set up, (but not in the flesh, 'the natural first and afterwards the spiritual'), the Jews are to be restored, the Gentile kingdoms broken in pieces 'like a potter's vessel,' and the kingdoms of this world become the kingdoms of our Lord and his Christ, and the judgment age introduced" (ibid., 83).

"And as we journey on a little further, **deliverance may come any time between this ["Seventh month" of 1874] and the end of the 'harvest,' in 1878**" (ibid., 124).

"The seven prophetic times of the Gentiles, or 2520 years ... reach from B.C. 606 to A.D. 1914, or *forty years* beyond 1874. **And the time of trouble, conquest of the nations, and events connected with the day of wrath, have only ample time, during the balance of this forty years, for their fulfillment**" (ibid, 189).

1878

"**There can be no doubt but that a time of trouble, such as the world has never yet experienced, is approaching**, and that it is the immediate precursor of the millennial age. And to this agree both the chronology, the prophetic periods, and the signs of the times. **Just what we are expecting in the next thirty-seven years**, is, **first** the gathering of the spiritual element of the churches into the light of present truth; a sanctifying or *separating* work, by which the church is to get the victory over the world.... **Second**, the translation, or glorification of the chosen bride of Christ. **Third**, the return of the Jews to Palestine, in the midst of the overturning of Gentile governments, falling of thrones, etc. **Fourth**, the battle of the great day [Armageddon]. **Fifth**, the ushering of the millennium" (N. H. Barbour, *Herald of the Morning*, July 1878 vol. 7, #1, 2).

"What a short time since **our expectations of translation failed of realization**, doubtless all who understood the foundation upon which these hopes were based felt somewhat disappointed; yet we did not for a moment feel cast down. We realized that what God had so plainly declared must some time have a fulfillment.... Did our disappointment prove that we were in error as to the time—our chronology wrong? The Bible chronology taught us that the 6000 years from Adam were full in the fall of 1873" (C. T. Russell, "The Prospect," ibid., 11).

1879

"This is the first number of the first volume of 'ZION'S WATCH TOWER,' and it may not be amiss to state the object of its publication. That we are living 'in the last days'—'the day of the Lord'—'the end' of the Gospel age, and consequently, in the dawn of the 'new' age, are facts not only discernible by the close student of the Word, led by the spirit, but the *outward signs* recognizable by the *world* bear the same testimony..."

(*WTR*, July 1879, 3).

"'But, If I go away, I will come again,' *cannot* refer to a spiritual coming *again*, because, spiritually, He never went away, as He said, 'Lo, I am with you alway, ever to the end of the world' [age]. **Therefore, Jesus taught His** *second* **PERSONAL** *coming*" (ibid., 4. Brackets in original).

"As most of our readers are aware, we believe that the Word of God furnishes us with **indubitable proof** that we are *now* living in this 'Day of the Lord'; that it began in 1873, and is a day of forty years duration..." (*WTR*, Sept. 1879, 26).

1880

"Our claim is that the *period* is revealed, *during* which Christ comes, the living generation will be judged, the dead in Christ raised, the living changed, the nations overwhelmed in a time of trouble, the Jews restored, and the whole church of Christ glorified, ready for the glorious millennial reign; but that we are left without definite time to the change or translation expected. We believe that period is one of forty years and commenced in 1874, and will reach to 1914. This period is the time for the disposal of the church and nations as now existing, and is in that sense the harvest. It is the time of exaltation of both Jewish and gospel churches to their position for millennial work, and hence is the day-dawn" (J. H. Paton, *Day Dawn*, 79-80).[4]

"We have, from a Bible standpoint, good reasons for fixing upon **A.D. 1914**, as a limit of the times of the Gentiles, and as **the date from which Jerusalem, freed from her long bondage, will become 'a praise in all the earth.'** As a means to the breaking in pieces and removal of the Gentile powers, the kingdom of God is to be set up, as we have seen. This fact locates the coming of Christ and the exaltation of the saints, some by resurrection, and some by translation, **long enough before 1914 to give time for the subjugation of earth's kingdoms, before the full time expires. This gives ground for expecting the foretold time of trouble, between now and 1914, during which Daniel's people are to be delivered**" (ibid., 109-10).

"We believe, for reasons not yet given, that Christ took the first step of the second advent—leaving the most holy place—in the Autumn of **1844**; that He tarried thirty years, and took the second step in the Autumn of **1874**.... The equality of these dispensations, with the law of correspondence between them, is our reason for believing that **Christ entered upon the office of King in the Spring of 1878**" (ibid., 204).

"...We understand there will be upon *christendom*, so called, a period of 33 years of trouble—making with the preceding 7 years the 40 years of trouble or 'Day of wrath' ending with the times of the Gentiles **in 1914, when the kingdom of God** [soon to be *set up* in power] **will have broken in pieces and consumed all earthly kingdoms**" (*WTR*, Aug. 1880, 124. Brackets in original).

"We need not here repeat the evidences that the **'seventh trump' began its sounding A.D. 1840**, and will continue until the end of the time of trouble, and the end of "The times of the Gentiles,' A.D. 1914..." (*WTR*, Nov. 1880, 152).[5]

"Soon, probably by, possibly before, the fall of **1881, we shall be changed**, born of the spirit [of which we are now begotten] into the glorious likeness of our Head" (*WTR*, Dec. 1880, 166. Brackets in original).

1881

"'How soon will our change come?' ... In the article concerning our change, in [the] December paper, we expressed the opinion that it was nearer than many supposed, and while we would not attempt to prove our change at any particular time, yet we propose looking at some of the evidences which *seem* to **show the translation or change from the natural to the spiritual condition, due this side or by the fall of our year 1881**" (*WTR*, Jan. 1881, 180).

"We now have taken prophetic measurements and allegories together, five different points seeming to teach the **resurrection of the dead in Christ and change of the living between the fall of 1874 and 1881.**

Two or more witnesses are enough to prove any case, as a rule, and certainly God has given us abundant evidence" (ibid., 181-82).

"Well, 1873 came, the end of 6,000 years, and yet no *burning* of the earth, &c. But prophecies were found which pointed positively to **1874 as the time when Jesus was due to be present, and the resurrection of Daniel was also due** as proved by the ending of jubilee cycles and the 1335 days of Dan. xii" (*WTR*, Feb. 1881, 188).

"...We do not expect Jesus to come this year, nor any other year, for we believe that all the *time* prophecies (bearing upon Jesus coming) **ended at and before the fall of 1874**, and that *He came there*, and the second advent is now in progress and will continue during the entire Millennial age. We believe that his presence will be *revealed* to the *eyes of man's understandings* gradually during this 'Day of the Lord,' (forty years—from 1874 to 1914).... The *favor* which ends this fall, is that of entering the *Bride company*.... With this year the company will be reckoned *complete* and the *door to that high calling* (not the door of mercy) **closed forever**" (*WTR*, May 1881, 224).

"We continually meet with this difficulty in referring to the present year, 1881. ... Since all know we expect the Saints to be *changed* from human to spiritual being, and since we frequently refer to October of the present year as the terminus of the prophetic parallel, some readers have supposed that we expect the *change* at that time. This is not the case; **we look to October of this year, as the limit of favor ... of opportunity to become a member of the Bride of Christ and partaker of his** *Divine Nature*" (*WTR*, July-Aug. 1881, 247).

"The seven years ... ended October 3d, 1881. ... If our application of Scripture be correct, the *favor* has now ended, and in the language of the parable, **'the door was shut'**; and to those who have never fully consecrated and sacrificed self to God, **we cannot any longer hold out the great prize of our high calling**, viz.; **to be members of the Bride of Christ**, joint heirs of Glory, Honor, and Immortality" (*WTR*, Oct.-Nov. 1881, 289).

1882

"... Some time ago we took the position that it was *more* **than probable that the 'dead in Christ' were raised, or were then being raised**, and we yet believe that the position was a true one.... The **nominal churches** not having been *true* witnesses were given up by him, **spewed out of his mouth in the spring of 1878....** **Jesus was due to enter on his Kingly office in the spring of 1878....** The nominal churches have been spewed out of his mouth, they are in darkness, and know not that Jesus has entered on his reign as King.... We shall soon enter on our reign with him and his armies" (*WTR*, Mar. 1882, 328).

"... In 1876 ... we showed that God's special *favor* was due to pass away from the *nominal* Gospel church though it would still continue to *really* consecrated individuals: and that **the favor would return again in some form, to the Jew in 1878** as foretold by Paul and the Prophets" (*WTR*, June 1882, 356-57).

"Very shortly now, this mystery of God, this company of divinely-begotten sons [the church] will be FINISHED—completed.... **We believe that we are just on the eve of the finishing of this church**, or mystery" (*WTR*, July 1892, 369).

1883

"**The day of the Lord, in the beginning of which we are now living**, is everywhere throughout the Scriptures referred to as a time of special trouble—beginning first on the Church.... The day of the Lord is the day when Jesus takes to himself his kingly power.... Since our Lord and King *has come*, the light of truth has been shining as never before" (*WTR*, Jan. 1883, 430).

1884

"When we and others called attention in 1876 and 1877 to the *presence* **of the Lord, and showed that it was taught by the revelations of God's word, we found few ready to believe our report**, and many said, 'Where is the promise of His presence?' The only answer we could then give them was, that they should examine the Scriptural evidences offered. But soon outward evidences appeared which corroborate the Scriptures!" (*WTR*, June 1884, 621).

1885

"In October, 1883, the question was asked through the TOWER; 'Are there any other papers than the TOWER which teach, as it does, **that Jesus is now present?**' And the answer was given: 'We know of no other which teaches the *personal presence* of Christ Jesus' etc." (*WTR*, Mar. 1885, 735).

"The substance of things hoped for is about to be revealed; the dark night of sin and suffering is far, far spent; **the glorious morn of heavenly glory is about to break upon the world**, and the little flock that have kept the testimony of Jesus and shared with him in sufferings and temptations, are going to take the kingdom, and will be associated with Christ in the work of restitution that shall perfect forever the nations of the renovated earth" (*WTR*, Dec. 1885, 811).

1886

"The outlook at the opening of the New Year has some very encouraging features. The outward evidences are that the **marshalling of the hosts for the battle of the great day of God Almighty, is in progress while the skirmishing is commencing.... The** *time* **is come for Messiah to take dominion of earth and to overthrow the oppressors and corrupters of the earth,** (Rev. 19:15 and 11:17, 18) preparatory to the establishment of everlasting peace upon the only firm foundation of righteousness and truth" (*WTR*, Jan. 1886, 817).

1887

"**Matters are rapidly shaping themselves for the great physical struggle of the 'Battle of the great day of God Almighty.'** In Europe all the great men and many of the little ones are full of fear and anxiety, looking after those things coming upon the earth—seeking to read the future and desiring to shape their course accordingly" (*WTR*, Feb. 1887, 898).

"*The time is short....* **The establishing of an earthly home and the rearing of an earthly family, which is generally regarded as the principal business of life, should not be the ambition of the saints.** The injunction to increase and multiply and fill the earth, was given to the natural man, but not to the little flock, the new creatures, partakers of the divine nature" (ibid., 901).[6]

1888

"But the appointed work of the Gospel age, as shown in the Scriptures, has been going on and is **almost accomplished**, just as intended and foretold. The Word has gone forth as a *witness* to all nations; and **the end of the 'harvest' is here....** The little flock is almost complete, and should now lift up their heads and rejoice, knowing that their redemption draweth nigh, and that their prayer—'*Thy Kingdom come*, thy will be done on earth as in heaven'—**is about to be fully answered**" (*WTR*, Dec. 1888, 1079).

1889

"...We present the Bible evidence proving that the full end of the times of the Gentiles, *i.e.*, the full end of their lease of dominion, will be reached in A.D. 1914; and that **that date will be the farthest limit of the**

rule of imperfect man" (Russell, *The Time is at Hand*, 76-77).

"True, it is expecting great things to claim, as we do, that **within the coming twenty-six years all present governments will be overthrown and dissolved**; but we are living in a special and peculiar time, the 'Day of Jehovah,' on which matters culminate quickly..." (ibid., 98-99).

"In view of this strong Bible evidence concerning the Times of the Gentiles, we consider it an established truth that the **final end of the kingdoms of this world, and the full establishment of the Kingdom of God [in the earth], will be accomplished by the end of A.D. 1914**" (ibid., 99—1906 ed.). (The 1907 ed. reads "**at** the end of A.D. 1914," and another reads: "**near** the end of A.D. 1915" (1912, 1920, 1925 eds.)).

"...The setting up of the Kingdom of God is already begun, that it is pointed out in prophecy as due to begin the exercise of power in A. D. 1878, and that **the 'battle of the great day of God Almighty' (Rev. 16:14), which will end in A.D. 1914** [the 1912 edition reads "A.D. 1915"] **with the complete overthrow of earth's present rulership, is already commenced**. The gathering of the armies is plainly visible from the standpoint of God's Word" (ibid., 101).

"...The forty years of the Gospel age harvest will end October, 1914, and that likewise **the overthrow of 'Christendom,' so-called, must be expected to immediately follow.** 'In one hour' judgment shall come upon her.—Rev. 18:10, 17, 19**"** (ibid., 245). [*The Finished Mystery* explains the "one hour" as "in the one year 1917-1918..." "one short year, 1917-1918..." (282, 285)].

Notes

1. The *1975 Yearbook* makes reference to this article and then quotes only the words: "The seven times will end in A.D. 1914." The paragraph concludes: "True to such calculations, 1914 did mark the end of those times and the **birth of God's kingdom in heaven** with Christ Jesus as King. Just think of it! Jehovah granted his people that knowledge nearly four decades before those times expired" (37). This is a disingenuous use of Russell's statement.

2. This interpretation was carried over from Second Adventism: "... In **1844** when the trumpet of the seventh angel began to sound..." (P. Gerard Damsteegt, *Foundations of the Seventh-Day Adventist Message and Mission* (Grand Rapids: Wm. B. Eerdmans, 1977), 216. See also: 43, 123, 131. *The Finished Mystery* (1917), identifies "the seventh angel" as "Pastor Russell" and says the trumpet "has been symbolically sounding since October, **1874**, and will continue to the end of the Millennium" (180). *Revelation—Its Grand Climax At Hand!* (1988), presents yet another interpretation: "When the **sounding of the seven trumpets got under way in 1922**, the Bible Students' convention at Cedar Point, Ohio, featured a talk by the president of the Watch Tower Society, J. F. Rutherford, based on the scripture 'The kingdom of heaven is at hand.'(Matthew 4:17, *King James Version*).... The **trumpet blast of the seventh angel** was reflected in highlights of the Bible Students' convention in Detroit, Michigan, **July 30–August 6, 1928**" (172). The *Revelation* book presents the "Highlights of Jehovah's Trumpetlike Judgment Proclamations" for 1922-1928 (173).

3. *Three Worlds*, was jointly published by Barbour and Russell, with Barbour as the primary writer. Russell provided the funds (*WTR*, 3822). Barbour was a Second Adventist who published the *Herald of the Morning* of which Russell was assistant editor. For further details on N. H. Barbour and *Three Worlds* see: M. James Penton, *Apocalypse Delayed* (2nd ed.; Toronto: University of Toronto Press, 1997), 18-24. *Three Worlds* is "a very important work. In fact, it contains within it most of the ideas that Russell and those in association with him were to promulgate during the next nearly forty years" (ibid., 22).

4. Russell explains the publication of *Day Dawn*: "The book, *The Three Worlds*, having been for some time out

of print, it seemed as if another edition of that, or else a new book covering the same features, should be gotten out. Mr. Paton agreed to get it ready for press, and Mr. [A. D.] Jones offered to pay all the expenses incidental to its printing and binding and to give Mr. Paton as many copies of the book as he could sell, as remuneration for his time spent in preparing the matter, provided I would agree to advertise it liberally and gratuitously in the TOWER..." (*WT*, 15 July 1906, 3824). After Russell and Paton separated, Paton published a revised edition of *Day Dawn* in 1882—one which Russell could not endorse (ibid.).

5. The 1840 date is connected with the Millerite movement and Josiah Litch (Damsteegt, 43-44). "The first Millerite experiment in prophetic time-setting which occurred in 1840, set a pattern for all the rest" (Eric Anderson, "The Millerite Use of Prophecy," *The Disappointed*, edited by Ronald L. Numbers and Jonathan M. Butler [Bloomington: Indiana University Press, 1983), 1987], 78-80). It was acquired by Russell from Nelson Barbour: "The sixth trumpet ended in August, 1840, and the seventh began to sound" (*Three Worlds*, 142). (See note 2 above.)

6. The **1987** "district Assemblies of JWs told Witnesses it was **better not to have children**, because the end is near, and you can be more effective with making new converts than raising them in the truth" (*Bethel Ministries*, Sept.-Oct. 1987). And the next year they were told: "Now as never before, 'the time left is reduced.' Yes, only a limited time remains for Jehovah's people to finish the work he has given them to do.... That work must be accomplished before the end comes. It is, therefore, appropriate for Christians to ask themselves how **getting married or, if married, having children** will affect their share of the vital work" (*WT*, 1 Mar. 1988, 21).

5.

Selected Quotations
from Watch Tower Publications
for the Years 1890-1899

1890

"It is astonishing with what rapidity matters are shaping themselves for the great time of trouble predicted in the Scriptures. When, some fourteen years ago, we presented the Scriptural declaration **that the Millennium of peace and blessing would be introduced by forty years of trouble, beginning slightly in 1874 and increasing until social chaos should prevail in 1914**—few believed, some scoffed..." (*WTR*, Oct. 1890, 1243).

1891

"The '**Time of the End,' a period of one hundred and fifteen (115) years, from A.D. 1799 to A.D. 1914, is particularly marked in the Scriptures**. 'The Day of His Preparation' is another name given to the same period..." (Russell, *Thy Kingdom Come*, 23).

"[Chapter 12 of Daniel] produces three periods of time, 1260, 1290 and 1335 prophetic days, which corroborate and establish the lesson of chapter xi, that the beginning of the Time of the End was in the year 1799" (ibid., 24).

"Thus it will be seen that the separating work of the 'Miller movement' had its beginning at the time foretold—at the end of the 1290 days [days=1290 years from A.D. 539], 1829" (ibid., 88).

"... Note how these rays of testimony unitedly and harmoniously blend, clearly revealing the blessed fact, not that the Lord is coming, nor that he will soon come; **but that he has come; that he is now present, a spiritual king, establishing a spiritual empire**, in the harvest or end of the Gospel age, which laps upon the now dawning Millennial age" (ibid., 124-25).

"And with the end of A.D. **1914, what God calls Babylon, and what men call Christendom, will have passed away**, as already shown from prophecy" (ibid., 153).

"That the **deliverance of the saints must take place some time before 1914** is manifest, since the deliverance of fleshly Israel, as we shall see, is appointed to take place at that time.... **Just how long before 1914 the last living members of the body of Christ will be glorified**, we are not directly informed; but it certainly will not be until their work in the flesh is done; nor can we reasonably presume that they will long remain after that work is accomplished" (ibid., 228).

"... In the **spring of 1878 all the holy apostles and other 'overcomers' of the Gospel age who slept in Jesus were raised as spirit beings**, like unto the Lord their Master. And while we, therefore, conclude that their resurrection is now an accomplished fact, and hence that they, as well as the Lord, **are present in the earth, the fact that we do not see them is no obstacle to faith when we remember that, like their Lord, they are now spirit beings, and, like him, invisible to men**" (ibid., 234).

"In view of all the evidences presented in this and the preceding volumes of this work, we have no hesitancy in proclaiming to the Lord's loyal and faithful people, his beloved Zion, this glorious intelligence: 'Thy God reigneth!' **The oft-repeated prayer of the Church has been answered: the Kingdom of God has indeed come**. In the days of the present kings of the earth, before their lease of dominion expires, **it is being set up. The dead in Christ are even now raised** and exalted with our Lord and Head" (ibid., 301).

"Wonderful truths are these!—The Kingdom of God in process of setting up; the **Lord Jesus and the risen saints already here and engaged in the great harvest work**, with whom we also, as members of that honored body, as the 'feet of him,' though still in the flesh, are permitted to be co-workers..." (ibid., 302).

"We have marked, too, the fixed dates to which the Prophet Daniel calls attention. The **2,300 days** point to **1846** as the time when God's sanctuary would be cleansed of the defiling errors and principles of Papacy.... We have noted the fulfillment of the **1,260 days** ... and the beginning there, in **1799**, of the Time of the End. We have seen how the **1,290** days marked the beginning of the understanding of the mysteries of prophecy in the year **1829**, culminating in the great movement of **1844** known as the Second-Advent movement, when, according to the Lord's prediction, the wise virgins went forth to meet the Bridegroom, thirty years prior to his actual coming.... We have marked with special delight the **1,335 days**, pointing, as they do, to **1874** as the exact date of our Lord's return..." (ibid., 305-06).

"...This date, **1910, indicated by the Pyramid, seems to harmonize well with the dates furnished by the Bible**. It is but **four years** before the full close of the time of trouble which ends the Gentile times; and when we remember the Lord's words—that the overcomers shall be accounted worthy to escape the severest of the trouble coming upon the world, we may well **accept as correct the testimony of the Great Pyramid, that the last members of the 'body' or 'bride' of Christ will have been tested and accepted and will have passed beyond the vail before the close of A. D. 1910**" (ibid., 363-64, early editions only). Later editions (the one used here was 1925) were changed to read: "It is but a **few years** before the full close of the time of trouble which ends the Gentile times; and when we remember the Lord's words—that the overcomers shall be accounted worthy to escape the severest of the trouble upon the world we may understand the reference to be to the anarchous trouble which will follow October 1914; but a **trouble chiefly upon the Church may be expected about 1910 A.D.**" (ibid., 363-64).

1892

"...There is a great time of trouble ahead of the present comparative calm in the world—a trouble which will embroil all nations, overthrow all existing institutions, civil, social and religious, bring about a universal reign of anarchy and terror, and prostrate humanity in the very dust of despair, thus to make them ready to appreciate the power that will bring order out of that confusion and institute the new rule of righteousness. **All this, the Scriptures show us, is to come to pass before the year 1915...**" (*WTR*, 15 Jan. 1892, 1354).

"The date of the **close of that 'battle' is definitely marked in Scripture as October, 1914. It is already in progress, its beginning dating from October, 1874....** In many respects the convictions of the world's great generals coincide with the predictions of God's Word. Then 'Woe to the man or nation who starts the next war in Europe; for it will be a war of *extermination*.' It will be abetted not only by national animosities, but also by social grievances, ambitions and animosities, and if not brought to an end by the establishment of God's kingdom in the hands of his elect and then glorified Church, it would exterminate the race—Matt. 24:22" (ibid., 1355).

"And when its [ecclesiasticism's] present power of superstitious reverence is broken, and its authority no longer binds men in subjection to the civil powers by the false doctrine of the divine right of kings, the fate of the civil powers will not long tremble in the balances, and the ever-darkening war cloud will burst in all its destructive fury. **This culmination we do not expect, however, before about 1905...**" (ibid., 1356).

"...The final overthrow of present governments will be at the same time as the fall of ecclesiasticism, and will be **followed by from five to seven years of socialism and anarchy, to end with 1914 by the establishment of Christ's Millennial government**" (*WTR*, 1 Aug. 1892, 1434),

1893

"The question comes from many quarters: 'Brother Russell, are you not possibly mistaken by a few years in your calculations, since you expect, upon Scriptural authority, that the **great trouble will all be over by A.D. 1915**, and that in its severity it will probably not reach us before A.D. 1906 to 1908?'... We answer, No; we think there is no mistake" (*WTR*, 1 and 15 Sept. 1893, 1581).

"**A great storm is near at hand**. Though one many not know exactly when it will break forth, it seems reasonable to suppose that it cannot be *more* than **twelve or fourteen years yet future** [1905 or 1907]. As the harvesters in the natural field often find it necessary to withdraw, as the clouds get very dark and the winds blow, so the reapers in this harvest may by and by be compelled to cease their active service.

Some may be inclined to think that the harvest work is largely done; but **probably the larger portion of this work is to be done in the coming six or eight years** [1899 or 1901]" *(Zion's Watch Tower*, 1-15 July, 1893, 194.[1]

1894

"Worldly people not only see the great 'battle' approaching, but they see that **the skirmishing is already beginning** all along the line—in every civilized country and on every imaginable issue" (*WTR*, 1 Jan. 1894, 1605).

"CAN IT BE DELAYED UNTIL 1914? Now, in view of recent labor troubles and threatened anarchy, our readers are writing to know if there may not be a mistake in the 1914 date. They say that they do not see how present conditions can hold out so long under the strain. We see no reason for changing the figures— nor could we change them if we would. They are, we believe, **God's dates**, not ours. But bear in mind that **the end of 1914 is not the date for the** *beginning*, **but for the** *end* **of the time of trouble**" (*WTR*, 15 July 1894, 1677).

"But, says one, twenty years is a short time in which to close up all the kingdoms and other governments; all the denominational isms and religious oligarchies and all the other evils of 6,000 years. I reply, It is long enough.... The stone is rolling; the hill is steepening; the impetus becomes terrible very soon, and **twenty years will amply suffice to destroy old things and fit the earth for the new:**—Dan. 2:34" (*WTR*, 15 Sept. 1894, 1705).

1895

"God forbid that any of those at present rejoicing in the truth should thus fall away, **now when the kingdom and its glory are so near**" (*WTR*, 1 Apr. 1895, 1797).

"Thus we see that the trend is the same in the monarchies of Europe as in this Republic. By inspiration the great Apostle Paul gave still a clearer and truer picture of nominal Christendom, saying: 'In the last days perilous times shall come. For men shall be lovers of their own selves [selfish], covetous, boastful, proud, blasphemers, disobedient to parents, unthankful, unholy, without natural affection, trucebreakers, false accusers, incontinent, fierce, despisers of those that are good, traitors, heady, high-minded, lovers of pleasure more than lovers of God, having a form of godliness, but denying the power thereof: *from such turn away*.'—**2 Tim.**

3:1-5" (*WTR*, 1 Oct. 1895, 1870. Brackets in original).

1896

"Whenever the *general* European war occurs [not for ten years, we feel quite confident], we may feel tolerably sure that **its outcome will be world-wide anarchy**, accompanied eventually by all the horrors of the French Revolution—worse by far than those perpetrated recently in Turkey. Of that time the prophet declares every man's hand shall be against his neighbor; and our Lord says that unless those days should be shortened (by the setting up of the elect in the kingdom) there shall be no flesh saved" (*WTR*, 1 Jan. 1896, 1912).

"The Psalmist prophetically taking a standpoint of observation of the future from his day declared, 'The Lord reigneth, let the earth rejoice; let the multitude of isles be glad thereof.' As has been shown, this began to be true **in 1878, when our returned Lord Jesus took unto himself his great power**. Yet not until **1915, when his kingdom will be fully set up and established in the earth**, will his glorious reign be fully manifested and recognized" (*WTR*, 1 Jan. 1896, 1913).

1897

"Her [Christendom] destruction **will be fully accomplished** by the end of the appointed 'Times of the Gentiles'—**1915**. Events are rapidly progressing toward such a crisis and termination" (Russell, *The Battle of Armageddon*, retitled *The Day of Vengeance*, 111).

"But now we are in the end of this Gospel age, and the Kingdom is being established or set up. Our Lord, the appointed King, is now present, since October **1874**, A. D., according to the testimony of the prophets, to those who have ears to hear it: and the **formal inauguration of his kingly office dates from April 1878, A.D.**..." (ibid., 621).

"...The Kingdom of God must first be set up before its influence and work will result in the **complete destruction of 'the powers that be' of 'this present evil world'**—political, financial, ecclesiastical—**by the close** ["about the close," 1918 ed.] **of the 'Times of the Gentiles**,' October A.D. 1914" (ibid., 622).

1898

"Only now—**since 1878**—is their **[Israel's]** measure of chastisement coming to its full, so that we may fulfill the words of the Lord through the prophet Isaiah,' Comfort ye, comfort ye my people, saith your God...'" (*WTR*, 15 Apr., 1898, 2296).

"At that point in time **[1878]** therefore, we believe on the strength of the testimony of the Scriptures, **our Lord assumed the office of King**, which he still holds, and will continue to exercise until he shall have overthrown present institutions, falsely called Christian institutions, dashing them 'in pieces as a potter's vessel,' in a great time of trouble..." (*WTR*, 1 May 1898, 2301).

"For twenty-three years past we have been calling attention to Isaiah 40:1, 2,—showing that it became applicable in April, 1878, and that within forty years (**before 1915**) the prophesied divine favor beginning by **regathering Israel** from all lands 'into their own land,' would be an accomplished fact" (*WTR*, 1 Oct. 1898, 2361).

1899

"As pointed out in these columns as long ago as 1880, 'Christendom,' since 1878, is passing through the sifting and testing of the close or 'harvest' time of the Gospel age, foretold by the apostles: a sifting which is to result in the fall of many in nominal Spiritual Israel" (*WTR*, 15 Apr. 1899, 2450).

"Claiming, as we do, that **we are now living in the closing days of the Gospel age**, it is quite proper that we should look about us to see whether or not present conditions correspond to the Apostle's inspired descriptions of what must be expected in the last days of this age [2 Tim. 3:1-5] ... a description of the condition of 'Christendom'" (*WTR*, 1 May 1899, 2459).[2]

"Having satisfied ourselves respecting the fulfillment of the Apostle's charges against 'Christendom' and having found his **predictions fully corroborated** by facts well witnessed to..." (ibid., 2463).

Notes

1. The first two sentences of this statement are quoted in *Jehovah's Witnesses in the Divine Purpose* (1959), 52. The article, "Harvest Work Before the Storm," was dropped from the *WT Reprints*.
2. Each of the vices of 2 Timothy 3:1-5 is reviewed and found to be fulfilled at that time.

6.

Who is "that Faithful and Wise Servant"?

Who is that "faithful and wise servant" ("faithful and discreet slave" *NWT*) of Matthew 24:45-47? "In 1881, Brother Russell himself had expressed the view that the 'servant' was made up of the entire body of faithful spirit-anointed Christians."[1] This was presented in the October-November 1881 *Zion's Watch Tower*.[2] In 1895,[3] "Brother Russell's wife publicly expressed the idea that Russell himself was the faithful and wise servant. The view that ... came to be generally held by the Bible Students for some 30 years."[4]

"Particularly following his death [October 31, 1916], *The Watch Tower* itself set forth this view for a number of years."[5] This statement from *Jehovah's Witnesses—Proclaimers of God's Kingdom* is more candid than that in the *1975 Yearbook* which says that "the idea adopted by many was that C. T. Russell himself was the 'faithful and wise servant"—which separates the promotion of the doctrine from the Society or the *Watch Tower*.[6] The interpretation, still held today, that "the faithful and wise servant" was not Russell (an individual), but the anointed class, came with the publication of Rutherford's article: "Servant—Good or Evil?" in the February 15, 1927, *Watch Tower*.[7] This **return to the earlier position** is viewed by Jehovah's Witnesses as an example of progressive light.[8]

The importance of this interpretation of Matthew 24:45-47 is explained by former Governing Body member Raymond Franz:

> In their calls for loyalty and submission, no other portion of Scripture is so frequently appealed to by the Governing Body of Jehovah's Witnesses.... Their claims of organizational authority rests not only upon their interpretation of this parabolic statement of Jesus Christ, but more especially upon *the way they make use of that interpretation*. It is employed primarily to support the concept of a *centralized administrative authority*, exercising extensive control over all members of the Christian congregation (understood by Witnesses as applying only to themselves).[9]

The following chronological survey provides an overview of the positions taken and the claims made over the years. Was the removal of Russell as "the faithful and wise servant" an easy and legitimate "adjustment" in the light of statements published by the Watch Tower Society before 1927?

1896 "New light"

Russell argued: "In our examination of this text [Matt. 24:45-47] we seem to have treated the term 'that

53

servant' as though the Spirit had erred in saying 'that servant' when it meant servants (plural), and we have applied it to *all true* servants of God. Since then we have been met from various quarters with objections to so general an application, and the suggestion that it would be wrong to allow modesty or any other consideration, good or bad, to warp our judgment in the exposition of the inspired Word; to which proposition we agree" (*WTR*, 1 Mar. 1896, 1946).

1904

In his discussion of "that servant," Russell said:

"The implication seems to be that when the right time should come for understanding the parable, it would be clearly set forth: that at the time of the parable's fulfillment the Lord would **appoint a servant in the household** to bring these matters to the attention of all the servants, and that certain responsibilities would rest upon such a one respecting the dispatch of his duties" (*WTR*, 15 Apr. 1904, 3355).

"There would be no violation of principle, however, in supposing that the Lord at the time indicated would **specially use one member of his church as the channel** or instrument though which he would send the appropriate messages, spiritual nourishment appropriate at that time; because in various times of the past the Lord has used individuals in such a manner" (ibid., 3356).

1906

"No, the truths I present, as **God's mouthpiece**, were not revealed in visions or dreams, nor by God's audible voice, nor all at once, but gradually, especially since 1870, and particularly since 1880. Neither is this clear unfolding of truth due to any human ingenuity or acuteness of perception, but to the simple fact that God's due time has come; and **if I did not speak**, and no other agent could be found, the very stones would cry out" (*WTR*, 15 July 1906, 3821).

1911

"...We have FAITH that the Lord has returned, that HE is the CHIEF REAPER in this 'Harvest,' that HE has been supervising the work, for now about thirty-seven years, and that **HE has placed Pastor Russell in charge of the work this side the vail**. We are glad therefore to recognize him as 'that servant,' spoken of by the Lord; glad to recognize that the work he is doing is **the work the Lord appointed him to do**.... Many have thought what a grand thing it would have been to have made one of the convention tours with the Apostle Paul. Well, this was considered an opportunity of traveling with a **'Paul'**—one who is doing a work in this end of the Gospel age, similar to the work the Apostle did at the beginning of the age" (Foreword of the *1911 Convention Report*).[10]

Russell died October 31, 1916.

1916

"He [Russell] was not the founder of a new religion, and never made such claim. He revived the great truths taught by Jesus and the apostles, and turned the light of the twentieth century upon these. He made no claim of a special revelation from God, but held that **it was God's due time for the Bible to be understood; and that, being fully consecrated to the Lord and his service, he was permitted to understand it**" (*WTR*, 1 Dec. 1916, 5997).

"Thousands of the readers of Pastor Russell's writings believe that he filled the office of 'that faithful and wise servant," and that his great work was giving to the household of faith meat in due season. His modesty and humility precluded him from openly claiming this title, but he **admitted as much in private conversation**" (ibid., 5998).

"The Lord Jesus promised that at his second coming, which should be invisible to human eyes, **he would have one wise and faithful servant** whom he would make ruler over all his goods to give meat to the household of faith in due season. **Christians throughout the world who are familiar with the work of Pastor Russell readily recognize that he has been that wise and faithful servant of the Lord**" (From J. F. Rutherford "Oration at [the] Evening Service" of C. T. Russell's funeral. *WTR*, 1 Dec. 1916, 6012).

1917

In a letter to the "Brethren" after his election as Society president, Rutherford writes: "**All of us realize** the peculiar relationship that our dear Brother Russell bore to the church as **'that servant'**" (*WTR*, 15 Jan. 1917, 6035).

"All the 'feet members' who are now engaged in proclaiming this precious message, received their enlightenment by partaking of the 'food' which the Lord sent through his chosen servant. THE WATCH TOWER **unhesitatingly proclaims Brother Russell as 'that faithful and wise servant'**" (*WT*, 1 Mar. 1917, 6049).

"We never understood the Plan of God until he was pleased to give it to us through **the interpretations of his Servant—our dear Brother Russell.** If we would maintain our faith and increase it, it would seem absolutely essential that we abide by the food the Lord has supplied, and we are certain that we can be a greater help to the dear brethren everywhere if we confine ourselves to the spiritual food provided of the Lord through this channel. **To search for spiritual food elsewhere is equivalent to saying that the Lord did not provide that which is sufficient through His chosen servant**, and upon careful consideration we know that none of the fully consecrated would want to say this" (Rutherford letter, *WTR*, 15 Apr. 1917, 6075).

"The great drama of the Gospel age opened with the Apostle Paul as the chief messenger, or angel, to the church. It closes with Pastor Russell as the seventh, and last, messenger to the church militant. For the other five epochs of the church the Lord provided messengers.... **The two most prominent messengers, however, are the first and the last—St. Paul and Pastor Russell....** The Lord Jesus, in his great prophetic statement in Matthew 24:45-47, made known the fact that at the end of the age he would be present and would have a special servant ... to give meat in due season.... **Pastor Russell is the servant promised to the church** in the closing days of its earthly pilgrimage. Many are perceiving more and more each day that he was chosen of the Lord to perform a great work" (*WTR*, 1 Nov. 1917, 6159).

"Recognizing Brother Russell as **the Lord's messenger to the Laodicean church and as the Lord's chosen servant** for the period of the harvest, coupled with his strong personality, his kind and loving manner, all of the Lord's people of the present time who knew him were led to more or less lean upon him.... It was the thought of many that his entering the kingdom marked the end of the work" (*WT*, 1 Dec. 1917, 6181).

1918

"Where a brother gives an interpretation of a Scripture which differs from that given by Brother Russell, and Brother Russell's interpretation seems reasonable and in harmony with the plan of God, then we believe it is a safe rule to follow Brother Russell's interpretation, for the reason that **he is the servant of the church**, so constituted by the Lord for the Laodicean period; and therefore **we should expect the Lord to teach us through him**" (*WTR*, 15 Feb. 1918, 51).

On this matter of identifying the "faithful and wise servant" ("faithful and discreet slave" *NWT*), how reliable is this statement from the November 1, 1993, *Watchtower*? "**Since 1919 it has been clear** that 'the faithful and discreet slave' is the anointed remnant" (8).[11]

1920

"**No one in present truth for a moment doubts** that Brother Russell filled the office of the 'faithful and wise servant, whom his Lord hath made ruler over his household, to give meat in due season.' (Matthew 24:45)" (*WT*, 1 Apr. 1920, 100).

"**The Society, in regular session, by an overwhelming majority vote, expressed its will in substance thus: Brother Russell filled the office of 'that servant' and has finished his work.** While here, acting under the supervision of the Lord, he organized the Society and left it as his successor to continue the work yet to be done..." (ibid., 101).

1921

"**Without a doubt Pastor Russell filled the office** for which the Lord provided and about which he spoke, and was therefore that **wise and faithful servant**, ministering to the household of faith meat in due season" (Rutherford, *The Harp of God* [1921 ed.], 239, para. 420). **This was dropped in later editions**, e.g., 1928.

"Clearly, then, the Lord foretold an office that would be filled by **a man**. We believe that almost all, if not quite all, the readers of THE WATCH TOWER will agree that the man whom the Lord chose to fill that office was that modest, humble, and faithful servant, **Brother Russell**" (*WT*, 1 May 1921, 135).

1922

"It must be conceded, then, that at the end of the world, at the 'time of the end,' during the presence of the Lord, during the harvest, he would have in the earth a servant who would be faithful and wise. The physical facts show that Brother Russell met every one of these requirements. This prophetic utterance [Matt. 24:45,46], then, has been fulfilled. Therefore fulfilled prophecy, or physical facts, and the circumstantial evidence are conclusive proofs that **Brother Russell filled the office of that faithful and wise servant**" (*WT*, 1 Mar., 1922, 74).

"Jesus clearly indicated that during his second presence he would have amongst the church a faithful and wise servant, through whom he would give to the household of faith meat in due season. The **evidence is overwhelming** concerning the Lord's second presence, the time of the harvest, and **that the office of 'that servant' has been filled by Brother Russell**. This is not man-worship by any means.... Above all, Brother Russell was, the Lord's servant. **Then to repudiate him and his work is equivalent to a repudiation of the Lord...**" (*WT*, 1 May 1922, 132).

"**Satan** has attempted by many attacks upon this fact to break it down; to cause the Lord's people to believe: (1) that Brother Russell was *not* the only channel by which the Lord would lead his people...." (*WT*, 15 Sept. 1922, 279).

"...**Satan** would have such cast away much that the Lord has provided for his people and has brought forth upon his table through his wise and faithful steward.... **He [Satan] would cause them ... to deny, of course, that Brother Russell filled the office of the wise and faithful steward...**" (*WT*, 1 Dec. 1922, 374).

"Whom has the Lord used to thus serve the church meat in due season? Every one who desires to state the facts must answer that he used Charles Taze Russell" (Ibid, 376).

"This passage [Luke 12:42-44] has been under much notice during the past forty years because of **a very**

apparent fulfillment. There are some who loudly dispute a fulfillment in any man; but **those who have seen, held, and taught present truth,** most assuredly have believed that our late beloved leader, Brother Russell, held that position of steward. And this we most certainly hold, both as a **fact and as a necessity of faith**" (*WT*, 15 Dec. 1922, 396).

1923

"We believe that all who are now rejoicing in present truth will concede that **Brother Russell faithfully filled the office of special servant of the Lord;** and that he was made ruler over all the Lord's goods.... Often when asked by others, Who is that faithful and wise servant?—Brother Russell would reply: 'Some say I am; while others say the Society is.' Both statements were true; for Brother **Russell was in fact the Society in a most absolute sense, in this, that he directed the policy and course of the Society without regard to any other person on earth**" (*WT*, 1 Mar. 1923, 68).

"How true the Apostle's picture [Eph. 4:14] to the experiences of some in this Gospel age harvest! **Many there are who once accepted Brother Russell as that servant.** But overlooking his faithful and wise ministry and the Lord's effective use of him, **they later stultified themselves by denying that he was the one chosen of God to fill the office of 'wise and faithful servant'**" (*WT*, 1 Sept. 1923, 260).

"A denial or reversal of formerly held truths is naturally suggested to those having a morbid desire for novelty. Instead of dispelling the doubt by a reexamination of Brother Russell's writings, an endeavor is made to prove the *new* views and ideas to be *Scripturally* correct" (ibid., 261).

1924-1927

A "Biography of Pastor Russell" was added to *The Divine Plan of the Ages* (1886) and published in the special editions of 1924, 1925, 1926 and 1927.[12] The following quote is taken from the 1927 edition:

> ...Jesus said: "Who then is a faithful and wise servant, whom his Lord hath made ruler over his household, to give them meat in due season? Blessed is that servant, whom his Lord, when he cometh, shall find so doing. Verily I say unto you, that he shall make him ruler over all his goods." Thousands of the readers of Pastor Russell's writings believe that **he filled the office of "that faithful and wise servant,"** and that his great work was giving to the household of faith meat in due season. His modesty and humility precluded him from openly claiming this title, but **he admitted as much in private conversation** [Biography, 7].

After looking at the various titles applied to Russell ("faithful and wise servant," "Laodicean Messenger," and "man with the inkhorn" in Ezekiel 9), M. James Penton concludes: "In effect, to the Bible Students, Pastor Charles Taze Russell became God's spokesman, his channel, dispensing spiritual food in a way that no other could."[13]

The Watch Tower publications quoted above may be briefly summarized: It was God's due time for the parable's fulfillment and to identify the **individual** who would be selected as the "faithful and wise servant" of Matthew 24:45-46. The Lord appointed Russell to that position. The *Watch Tower* and its readers in present truth accepted this interpretation as true, without doubt or hesitation. Russell himself acknowledged his calling. To question that Russell was "That Servant," one must deny the overwhelming evidence. Only Satan would be behind such a denial, a denial of fact and of a "necessity of faith." Those who now reject what they once believed are foolish.

A Cult?

Should the Watch Tower Society in these expressions concerning Russell as "That Servant" be viewed as a cult according to the following characteristic of a cult set forth in the February 15, 1994, *Watchtower*? "It is precisely because of this close adherence to Bible teachings that the **veneration and idolization of human leaders so characteristic of cults** today is not found among Jehovah's Witnesses."[14] But was this not true in the past?

"Old Light" Becomes "New Light"

In spite of all of the foregoing affirmations of Russell's position, the subsequent denial that Russell was the "faithful and wise servant" took place under Rutherford's leadership. Although Russell died in 1916, being recognized as "That Servant" meant that Rutherford could not have complete control or change major teachings until that doctrine was challenged. This challenge would begin in 1926, and in 1927 it would become a direct attack, contradicting much of what had been claimed and taught as truth, even by Rutherford, for over 30 years.

In his article in the February 15, 1927, *Watch Tower*, Rutherford argues that the Matthew 24:45-46 text **could not be understood and applied until 1918**, when Christ came to his temple, and that it **could not find fulfillment in an individual**:

> The scriptures heretofore cited prove beyond a question of a doubt that God's chosen Servant whom he approves and in whom he delights is **The Christ**; that The Christ consists of Jesus and the faithful members of his body.... The inference must now be drawn that when the Lord comes to his temple he finds a **faithful and wise Servant class**.... The irresistible conclusion is that "the faithful and wise servant" mentioned by the Lord is a *class*, made up of those whom he finds faithful at the time he comes to his temple.... (*WT*, 15 Feb. 1927, 55).

> Some have claimed that the scripture, "The faithful and wise servant," specifically applies to Brother Russell. **He never made that claim himself.** That Brother Russell was greatly used of the Lord no one can doubt who knew him.... To say that "that faithful and wise servant" specifically applies to one individual and to none other would imply that a large proportion of the body members of Christ could not be classed either as faithful or wise (ibid., 56).[15]

1937

"Aside from Jesus Christ **no individual** is foretold or foreshadowed in the selection and development of the members of God's organization. It necessarily follows that in the fulfillment of God's prophecy **no individual** among God's covenant people is or will be identified. **It would be contrary to the Scriptures to single out some individual and say that such individual is fulfilling prophecy**" (*WT*, 15 Apr. 1937, 124).

1943

"Whom do the facts of our day prove to be that 'faithful and wise servant?' Aside from Christ Jesus, divine prophecy foretells **no individual man**.... The expression 'faithful and wise servant' **does not picture any man or individual** on earth now, but means the faithful remnant of Jehovah's witnesses who are begotten of His spirit and gathered into a unity unto Him and His service" (*WT*, 1 July 1943, 203).

1959

"The insistence that Russell had been 'that servant' led many to regard Russell in what amounted actually to **creature worship**. They believed that all the truth God had seen fit to reveal to his people had been revealed to Russell, and now nothing more could be brought forth because 'that servant' was dead" (*Jehovah's Witnesses in the Divine Purpose*, 69).

1981

"Rather, the record that the 'faithful and discreet slave' organization has made for the past more than 100 years forces us to the conclusion that Peter expressed when Jesus asked if his apostles also wanted to leave him, namely, 'Whom shall we go away to?' (John 6:66-69). No question about it. We all need help to understand the Bible, and **we cannot find the Scriptural guidance we need outside the 'faithful and discreet slave' organization**" (*WT*, 15 Feb. 1981, 19).

1984

"Jesus said that upon his return he would find a 'faithful and discrete slave' providing spiritual food and that the 'slave' found so doing would be appointed over all the master's belongings.—Matthew 24:45-47. One Christian husband said: **'Jehovah's visible organization is a tremendously dependable source. Never once has it mislead me in any way.** Everything it has said has been based on God's Word and has been the best for me, for my family and for everyone I know. This builds tremendous faith as far as I am concerned'" (*WT*, 1 June 1984, 12).

1992

"It is unlikely that someone who simply reads the Bible without taking advantage of divinely provided aids could discern the light. That is why Jehovah God has provided 'the faithful and discreet slave,' foretold at Matthew 24:45-47. **Today, that 'slave' is represented by the Governing Body of Jehovah's Witnesses**" (*WT*, 1 May 1992, 31).

═══════════

"Does the claim in the first sentence above sound familiar? Isn't this basically what Russell said about his publications which are no longer printed by the Watch Tower Society?" (*WTR*, 15 Sept. 1910, 4685).

What has been observed in this chapter is the movement away from a **cult of personality** (Russell) to a **cult of organization**.

Notes

1. *Jehovah's Witnesses—Proclaimers of God's Kingdom* (1993), 626.
2. *WTR*, Oct.-Nov. 1881, 291. "We believe that every member of this body of Christ is engaged in the blessed work, either directly or indirectly, of giving meat in due season to the household of faith. 'Who then is that *faithful and wise servant* whom his Lord hath made ruler over his household,' to give them meat in due season? Is it not that 'little flock' of consecrated servants who are *faithfully* carrying out their consecration vows—the body of Christ—and is not the whole body individually and collectively, giving the meat in due season to the household of faith—the great company of believers? (291). *God's Kingdom of a Thousand Years Has Approached* (1973) quotes this statement and concludes: "From this it is clearly seen that the editor and publisher [C. T. Russell] of *Zion's Watch Tower* disavowed any claim

to being individually, in his person, 'that faithful and wise servant.' He never did claim to be such" (346). It is true that in 1881 Russell denied that the "faithful and wise servant" was an individual, but this was not his final view as the *Proclaimers* (1993) history would later admit. Even *God's Kingdom of a Thousand Years Has Approached* in a footnotes directs the reader to *The Battle of Armageddon* (1897), 613. When the page cited is read, it is obvious that Russell had changed his view.

3. *WTR*, 15 July 1906, 3811; 1 Oct. 1909, 4482.

4. *Proclaimers*, 143.

5. Ibid., 626.

6. *1975 Yearbook* (1974), 88.

7. *WT*, 15 Feb 1927, 51-57. The *Proclaimers* book states: "This understanding was reaffirmed by the Bible Students in 1927" (626). Rutherford had already discussed the "servant class" before 1927 (*WT*, 15 Aug. 1926, 243-49).

8. *Proclaimers*, 626.

9. Raymond Franz, *In Search of Christian Freedom* (Atlanta: Commentary Press, 1991), 125. Franz devotes an entire chapter of his book to objections to the Watch Tower's claims: "The Faithful and Discreet Slave" (125-78). The Witnesses' misinterpretation of Matthew 24:45-47 passage is also covered by Robert M. Bowman, Jr., in *Understanding Jehovah's Witnesses* (Grand Rapids: Baker Book House, 1991), 58-61.

10. Photocopy in Duane Magnani's *Who is the Faithful and Wise Servant?* (3rd ed.; Clayton, Calif.: Witness Inc., 1984), 64.

11. But in contradiction to this the *Proclaimers* book (1993) states that "particularly following his death, *The Watch Tower* itself set forth this view [that Russell was "that Servant"] for a number of years" (626).

12. Magnani, 29-30.

13. M. James Penton, *Apocalypse Delayed* (2nd ed.; Toronto: University of Toronto Press, 1997), 34.

14. *WT*, 15 Feb. 1994, 7.

15. How was the transition from Russell as authority to the organization under Rutherford's absolute control accomplished? In his dissertation, Joseph Zygmunt explains. The process went through several stages: The first stage was the "'canonization' of Russell following his death. This involved the open acknowledgment and elaboration of his charismatic status by linking Russell as a symbolic figure more firmly and fully to the supernatural sphere.... Deference was shown to his image, and his written and oral declarations were invoked as a source of authority and guidance" (932).

   "The second stage involved attempts to collectivize Russell's charisma by transferring large portions of it to the movement as a whole. It was not that each individual member was a 'prophet' but rather that the *collective body of believers* had the supernatural status which had been attributed to Russell" (ibid.). This as Zygmunt states, was "not entirely new," but what was significant was "that the very same honorific titles which had come to be conferred upon Russell by way of defining his special status were now taken from him and conferred upon the group as a whole" (ibid.).

   "The third stage involved more forthright and systematic efforts at the explicit 'decanonization' of Russell. His symbolic status as an authority figure was severely downgraded. Those who continued to exalt and to defer to his image were accused of 'creature worship.' Some of his teachings were attacked as erroneous and unscriptural, and some of the organizational arrangements instituted by him were criticized and rejected as 'ecclesiastical' remnants" (932-33).

   The fourth stage saw "the charisma which had previously been 'collectivized' ... invested not in any particular person nor in any particular office but rather in ... the organizational structure which exercised control over the movement as a whole, the 'Brooklyn Office' or the 'Society Headquarters....'

Great exertions were made to weave the organizational concept of the 'Theocracy' into the group's identity design, an important final step in the stabilization and institutionalization of the movement's authority system" ("Jehovah's Witnesses: A Study of Symbolic and Structural Elements in the Development of a Sectarian Movement" [Ph.D. diss., University of Chicago, 1967], 933).

7.

Selected Quotations from Watch Tower Publications for the Years 1900-1914

1900

"And just so now, the collapse of *nominal* Christianity, 'Christendom' or 'Babylon,' is not to be expected until A.D. 1914, though fallen from favor since 1878. The **collapse will be sudden and awful** when it does come: and while only a few realize the *fallen-from-grace* condition of Babylon in the present, none will be ignorant of her collapse when it comes" (*WTR*, 1 Jan. 1900, 2553).

"The **time is short**; the harvest work is great; the laborers are few; our time is consecrated; we must labor while it is called day, knowing that a night cometh wherein no man can work" (*WTR*, 1 Aug. 1900, 2675).

1901

"The culmination of the trouble in October, 1914, is clearly marked in the Scriptures; and we are bound therefore to expect a beginning of that *severe* trouble **not later than 1910—with severe spasms** between now and then. Should the severe trouble come in 1910 we may infer that it will be preceded by a period of gradual financial and social disturbances, similar to those of the past, and leading on toward the condition of desperation then, or sooner, to be reached" (*WTR*, 15 Sept. 1901, 2876).

"The arming and drilling and building of ships will continue until the people of Europe are thoroughly awakened, when they will refuse to be bought and taxed, and a **revolution in favor of Socialism** shall ensue—resulting, however, in **Anarchy**, as the Scriptures indicate, preparing the way for Christ's Millennial Kingdom" (*WTR*, 1 Dec. 1901, 2914).

1902

"The time for lifting up our heads in glory **is nearing**, too, and already the Master directs that seeing (with the eye of faith) the evidences of their approach, we may lift up our heads and rejoice, knowing that our redemption draweth nigh" (*WTR*, 1 Jan. 1902, 2936).

"Hence the watchers may reckon that Gentile rule will terminate and Immanuel's rule be fully set up in 2,520 years from the time the Lord removed the diadem from Zedekiah.... And measuring this period, we find that 2,520 years will expire with the close of the year **1914 A.D., and consequently that by that time Gentile rule will be no more**, while God's kingdom will then hold sway" (*WTR*, 15 Mar. 1902, 2977).

"Take another line of prophecy: we find that the 1,260 days, and the 1,290 days, and the 1,335, so particularly set forth in Daniel's prophecy, and corroborated in Revelation, **have had fulfillments—the 1,260 days ending in 1799, the 1,290 days ending in 1829 and the 1,335 days ending in 1874.** Our friends known as 'Second Adventists' were wont to use these 'days of Daniel,' and once applied them as we do here: but they abandoned them after 1874 passed and they failed to see Jesus with their natural eyesight.... The fault is not with the days nor with their application as above; but with the wrong things expected" (ibid., 2978).

"...Since 1878 the fully consecrated of the Lord's people, those who are completely 'dead with him,' will not *sleep in death*, as has been necessary with all the preceding members of the body of Christ throughout the Gospel age; it means that **from 1878, onward, the dead, who die in the Lord, will in the moment of dying experience their 'change...**" (*WTR*, 15 Mar. 1902, 2982).

"**Those who have studied the plan of the ages and its times and seasons know that this is due to be accomplished by the year 1915**—only 12 or 13 years from the present time. Then will the words of this prophecy [Psalm 24:1-4] be fulfilled—'The earth is the Lord's and the fullness thereof; the world, and they that dwell therein; for he hath founded it upon [instead of] the seas, and established it upon [in place of] the floods—Verses 1, 2.... That is, the present earth, or social organization, and the present heavens, or ruling powers, will have passed away, and the **new earth will be established upon the ruins of the old**" (*WTR*, 1 Dec. 1902, 3113. Brackets in original.).

1903

"So far as the Scriptures guide us, **we expect the climax of the great time of anarchous trouble in October, 1914**. Our opinion is that so great a trouble would necessarily last in violent form **at least three or four years** before reaching that climax. Hence, **we expect strenuous times by or before October, 1910**. Reasoning backward from 1910 A.D. we are bound to assume that the conditions leading up to such violence as we then expect would include great financial depression, which probably would last some years before reaching so disheartening a stage. We could not, therefore, expect that **depression to begin later than, say, 1908**" (*WTR*, 1 Feb. 1903, 3141).

"It will be vain for Zionists to hope to establish an *independent* government in Palestine.... Palestine will be 'trodden down of the Gentiles, until the times of the Gentiles be filled full'—viz., **October, 1914, A.D. By that time the heavenly kingdom will be in power and the ancient worthies—Abraham, Isaac and Jacob, and all the holy prophets—will be resurrected** and constitute the earthly representatives of the spiritual and invisible kingdom of Christ and his bride—the Gospel church" (*WTR*, 1 Oct. 1903, 3249).

"Soon this work of the church, of announcing the kingdom and calling upon men everywhere to repent and reform, will be at an end, and the kingdom will be introduced with power and great glory" (*WTR*, 15 Dec. 1903, 3293).

1904

"According to our expectations the stress of the **great time of trouble** will be on us soon, somewhere **between 1910 and 1912—culminating** with the end of the 'Times of the Gentiles,' October **1914**. The beginning of the severity of the time of trouble is not distinctly marked in the Scriptures, and it is rather conjectural. We infer that so great a trouble, so world-wide a catastrophe, could scarcely be accomplished in less that three years, and that if it lasted much more than three years 'no flesh would be saved'" (Russell, *The New Creation*, 579).

"**UNIVERSAL ANARCHY—JUST BEFORE OR AFTER October, 1914 A.D.**" "What seems at first glance the veriest trifle and wholly unrelated to the matter, has changed our conviction respecting the time when universal anarchy may be expected in accord with the prophetic numbers. We now expect that the anarchistic culmination of the great time of trouble which will precede the Millennial blessings **will be after October, 1914, A.D.—very speedily thereafter**, in our opinion—'in one hour,' 'suddenly'.... Our forty years' harvest, ending October, 1914 A.D., should not be expected to include the awful period of anarchy which the Scriptures point out to be the fate of Christendom" (*WTR*, 1 July 1904, 3389).

A letter to Russell asks: "If the 'Times of the Gentiles' can be changed as suggested in the July TOWER, so that the **anarchy will follow 1914 A.D., instead of preceding it**, might not similar changes be made in respect to all the various lines of prophetic time-proof set forth in MILLENNIAL DAWN, Vols. II and III?"

Answer: "You are entirely in error. Not a figure, not a date, not a prophecy is in any sense or degree affected by the article to which you refer. Indeed the harmony and unity of the whole is the more fully demonstrated.... The harmony of the prophetic periods is one of the strongest proofs of the correctness of our Bible chronology. ... **To change the chronology even one year would destroy all this harmony...**" (*WTR*, 15 Aug. 1904, 3415).

When a letter to Russell questioned his view of the "Gentile Times," he responded: "The brother errs in supposing that we have changed our view of 'Gentile Times.' Those 'times' or years are 2520, with a definite beginning in B.C. 606, and a definite ending, A.D. 1914. **We know of no reason for changing a figure: to do so would spoil the harmonies and parallels so conspicuous between the Jewish and Gospel ages. The only '*change*' in view is that the anarchy to follow the ending of these 'times' will not shorten them**; and that the forty year 'harvest' of the church will be complete and not be interfered with by the worldwide anarchy to follow it" (*WTR*, 1 Oct. 1904, 3437).

1905

"**Shortly**, as soon as 'the very elect,' the church, the 'bride' of Christ, shall have been selected and prepared by the trials and disciplines of this present evil world, and been glorified and united to her Lord, the Redeemer, then the next great step in the divine program for the uplift of the world will begin. Then, for the thousand years of Christ's Messianic reign..." (*WTR*, 1 Mar. 1905, 3517).

"DEAR BROTHER RUSSELL: The Lord has enabled me to see another remarkable confirmation of the Parallel Dispensations, teaching that **1914 A.D. is the date when Christendom will lose its crown, will be finally overthrown**, and when he, 'whose right it is,' will take his power and reign" (*WTR*, 15 June 1905, 3574). [The Dr. John Edgar material is reproduced 3574-75, and is followed by a second letter of further confirmation, 3575-79.]

"Let us remember to expect various outbreaks at intervals, but that the **general collapse of all governments in anarchy is not to be expected before the close of 1914 A.D.**... We have every confidence that the end of the 'times of the Gentiles,' in Oct. 1914, will find **Socialism not only fully developed but changed to Anarchism**, as the Word implies" (*WTR*, 1 Dec. 1905, 3671).

1906

"The thief-like work of taking the church is already in progress; by and by it will be all completed, and **shortly thereafter—1915—the kingdoms of this world, with all of their associated institutions, will go down in a climax of trouble** such as the world has never known, because after gathering his bride class the Lord will execute judgments upon Babylon" (*WTR*, 1 June 1906, 3784).

"The 'times of restitution of all things'... are, we believe the Scriptures to teach, **just at the door. Soon the last members of true body of Christ will have finished their course**, and then, with their glorious Head and all the other members of the body, they will shine forth as the sun for the blessing of the entire redeemed race" (*Old Theology Quarterly*, July 1906, 4).

"...Thirty years ago we were preaching the **regathering of natural Israel to Palestine before A. D. 1914.**

Others mocked, and even orthodox Jews assured us that they did not expect such things for several centuries" (*WTR*, 15 Sept. 1906, 3855).

"To our understanding the wise virgins have been entering into the marriage since the autumn of 1878, A. D., and are still entering in—passing beyond the vail, changed in a moment.... **Soon the entire first resurrection will be complete, the last member being changed**. Then and there the door will be shut and no more will be permitted to enter" (*WTR*, 1 Oct. 1906, 3868-69).

"Thus, in their due time, matters are shaping around for the **termination of Gentile rule in anarchy by the appointed time—October, 1914**, when their lease or permit will expire" (*WTR*, 1 Dec. 1906, 3898).

1907

"ZION'S WATCH TOWER AND HERALD OF CHRIST'S PRESENCE was founded in 1879, and the 'voice' therefrom, to the true Israel of God, announced that the **second advent of our Lord, as the deliverer of the world, had already taken place**—that he was *present* but invisible, a spirit being.... He was present for the purpose of establishing his kingdom and delivering his saints and the whole groaning creation from the bondage of corruption—as many as will obey him" (*WTR*, 15 Sept. 1907, 4058).

"A dear Brother inquires, Can we feel absolutely sure that the Chronology set forth in the DAWN-STUDIES is correct?—that the harvest began in A.D. 1874 and will end in A.D. 1914 in a world-wide trouble which will overthrow all present institutions and be followed by the reign of righteousness of the King of Glory and his bride, the church? We answer, as we have frequently done before in the DAWNS and TOWERS and orally and by letter, that we have never claimed that they were *knowledge*, nor based upon indisputable evidence, facts, knowledge; our claim has always been that they are based on *faith*.... We remind you again that the weak points of chronology are supplemented by the various prophecies which interlace with it in so remarkable a manner **that** *faith* **in the chronology almost becomes** *knowledge* **that it is correct**.... But let us suppose a case far from our expectations: suppose that A.D. 1915 should pass with the world's affairs all serene and with evidence that **the 'very elect' had not all been 'changed' and without the restoration of natural Israel to favor under the New Covenant** (Rom. 11:12, 15). What then? **Would not that prove our chronology wrong? Yes, surely!** And would not that prove a keen disappointment? Indeed it would! **It would work irreparable wreck to the parallel dispensations and Israel's double, and to the Jubilee calculations, and to the prophecy of the 2,300 days of Daniel, and to the epoch called 'Gentile Times,' and to the 1,260, 1,290, and 1,335 days, the latter of which marking the beginning of the 'harvest' so well fulfilled its prediction.... None of these would be available longer. What a blow that would be!** One of the strings of our 'harp' would be quite broken!" (*WTR*, 1 Oct. 1907, 4067).

"THE APPROACHING BATTLE" "The Bible forewarns us respecting the character of the great trouble-time everyone sees is approaching rapidly. It tells us it will be different from any trouble of the past" (ibid., 4074).

1908

"...**During 1915, according to the Bible, we expect that anarchy will gain the upper hand of control** throughout Christendom, overthrowing present institutions, civil and religious, financial and social, and in a general way plunging the poor world into the most awful trouble it has ever experienced..." (*WTR*, 1 Jan. 1908, 4110).

"The **final spasm, which we look for in 1915**, will give birth to the new dispensation of peace and blessing, the Millennial reign of Messiah..." (ibid., 4111).

1909

"And these 2,520 years we believe will expire with October, **1914**; at that time we believe the Gentile lease of power will expire, and that **the God of heaven will set up His Kingdom in Israel**" (Russell, "The Times of the Gentiles," in *Convention Report Sermons*, 44).

"…The great Messiah, Head and members, in glory will set up the long-promised kingdom of God. Its blessing will come **first to natural Israel for their restitutional uplifting, and subsequently will extend through Israel to 'all the families of the earth**….' The Christian sees with the eye of faith glory, honor and immortality and a share with the Redeemer in the privileges of the Millennial kingdom, which is **shortly** to bless the world with a reign of righteousness, in fulfillment of the Lord's prayer. 'Thy kingdom come. Thy will be done on earth as it is done in heaven'" (*WTR*, 15 Oct. 1909, 4501).

1910

"We merely reviewed this Great Witness [Great Pyramid] to the Lord of hosts and recalled to mind **its testimony**…. We again noted with admiration the exactness of the construction of this wonderful 'pillar in the land of Egypt'" (*WTR*, 1 June 1910, 4621).

"True, we have said, and still say, that we believe the time is near when insurance companies, with all the other arrangements of our present civilization, will be overwhelmed in the great time of trouble foretold by the Prophet Daniel (12:1). It is equally true that we anticipate that the **climax of trouble is not farther away than 1915**" (*WTR*, 15 Oct. 1910, 4699).

"By a system of deductions based upon the prophecies of old, the pastor [Russell] declared that the return of the kingdom of the Jews might occur at so near a period as the year **1914. Persecutions would be over and peace and universal happiness would triumph**" (*WTR*, 15 Oct. 1910, 4701).

"The nearer we get to the grand consummation of our hopes, the more swiftly do the years go by, and the more interesting and meaningful do they become to us. If we realize our hopes, **four more years will see the 'elect' little flock of God all gathered; and the world's time of trouble begun**, in which brethren of the 'great company' will share and wash their robes in the blood of the lamb" (*WTR*, 15 Dec. 1910, 4726).

C. T. Russell wrote a number of articles for the *Overland Monthly* magazine beginning in 1909 and continuing until his death in 1916. These were collected in *What Pastor Russell Wrote for the Overland Monthly* by the Chicago Bible Students:

"The image [Dan. 2] has stood nearly as long as was Divinely intended—seven symbolic times or years— 2520 literal years, expiring in October, 1914. What will happen then? Let the prophecy continue to tell its story to a consummation. It tells that the glorious image of autocracy and worldly empire, which God has permitted to be in the hands of the Gentiles, **will fall a mass of ruins at the end of the Gentile times— 1915 A.D.** It tells that the God of Heaven, who gave over the dominion of earth for 'Seven Times' to the Gentile governments of this image, purposes that **at the close of those 'Seven Times' he will wipe them out of existence**" ("God's Chosen People Chastened 'Seven Times,' A Period of 2520 Years," in *What Pastor Russell Wrote for the Overland Monthly*, 82).

1911

"Suppose that our chronological calculations (never set forth as infallible) should prove to be fallible and in error. Our conclusion would merely be that **the error could not be very great**. Outward signs of restitution multiplying on every hand tell us that the rising of the Sun of Righteousness is near at hand…. The stress along the lines of social, political and financial affairs all indicate that the great time of trouble and anarchy with which this age will end **cannot be far off—cannot lie much, if any, beyond October, 1914. And if** that date pass it would merely prove that our chronology, our 'alarm clock,' went off a little before the time" (*WTR*, 1 Jan. 1911, 4737).

"Our readers know that for some years we have been expecting this Age to close with an awful time of trouble, and we expect it to break out with suddenness and force **not long after October, 1914,** which, so far as we can understand the Scriptures, is the date at which the Times of the Gentiles—the lease of earth's dominions to the Gentiles—will expire; the time, therefore, when **Messiah's kingdom will be due to begin its exercise of power, which the Scriptures declare will dash the nations in pieces as a potter's vessel. By that time we think the Scriptures indicate that the church will be complete and will have passed beyond the second veil...**" (*WTR*, 15 May 1911, 4822).

"Noting these parallels, we find 1874 as the beginning of this 'harvest' and the gathering together of the 'elect' from the four winds of heaven; 1878 as the time when Babylon was formally rejected, Laodicea spewed out—the time from which it is stated, 'Babylon is fallen, is fallen'.... **October, 1914, will witness the full end of Babylon, 'as a great millstone cast into the sea,' utterly destroyed as a system....** Our understanding is that the open or general 'call' of this age to kingdom honors [Bride of Christ] **ceased in October, 1881**" (*WTR*, 15 June 1911, 4842).

"If any be disposed to dispute these figures [Gentile Times ending in 1914] we need have no quarrel, but simply say that any **difference in the calculations must of necessity be but small—possibly one year, possibly twenty years**—but in so long a period how trifling would be such a variation" (*WTR*, 1 Aug. 1911, 4867).

———

A letter to the *Brooklyn Daily Eagle* from a former Bible Student in England, says in part: "Very many have gone so far as to sell up their homes over here, expecting to die before 1914 (at the latest), and many others have so arranged their affairs as to last till that date only" (*Brooklyn Daily Eagle*, 26 Dec. 1911, photocopy in Duane Magnani's *Cruel and Unusual Punishment*, 203).

———

1912

Under the heading, "TO MARRY OR NOT TO MARRY," "We are asked to publish the below letter respecting marriage, in the hope that it may be helpful to some considering the subject.... 'A single person, when consecrating, agrees to give up more time to the Lord than can a married one. Realizing this, would it be right for me to take back some of the time which I have given to the Lord and give it to some one else? Would I be pleasing to the Lord by so doing?'" (*WTR*, 15 Jan. 1912, 4959).

"'**The time is so short! It is not so much the years now, but we count the time in weeks and days**; as was mentioned at the Mountain Lake Convention, **it is only about one hundred and fifty weeks until the last member of the little flock shall have passed beyond the second veil**, and some of this time has since passed....' Let each one be fully persuaded in his own mind" (ibid. 4960).

"If it is true, as we believe, that the forty years 'harvest' of this age began in 1874, the implication is that **the trials of the church are nearly at an end**; that the faithful will soon be gathered to the heavenly garner. By the glorious 'change' he will cause them to 'shine forth as the sun in the kingdom of their Father,' for the scattering of the world's dark night and the ushering in of the new day. **Messiah's day is to bring glorious opportunities for earthly blessing to Israel, and to all the families of the earth through Israel**. If our hopes be true, then they mean a blessing, not for the church alone, but for the entire groaning creation..." (*WTR*, 1 May 1912, 5018).

"The lease of power to the Gentiles may end in October, 1914, or in October 1915. And the period of intense strife and anarchy 'such as never was since there was a nation' may be the final ending of the Gentile Times or the beginning of Messiah's reign.... Finally, let us remember that we did not consecrate either to October, 1914, nor to October, 1915, or to any other date, but 'unto death.' If for any reason the Lord has permitted us to miscalculate the prophecies, the signs of the times assure us that **the miscalculations cannot be very great**" (*WTR*, 1 Dec. 1912, 5142).

1913

"**THE MILLENNIUM HAS COME!** We must look in another direction, if we would rightly understand and properly appreciate the meaning of the wonderful inventions of our day. They are coming to us because we are living in the dawning of a new dispensation! They are the foregleams of an Epoch so wonderful as to be beyond our most vivid imagination.... **Everything is getting ready for the Millennium! Not only is it coming, but it is here!** We are not, indeed, enjoying its full blessings yet; but what we are enjoying is a foretaste of them" (*WTR*, 1 Jan. 1913, 5153).

"Indeed, **as respects the date 1914**, which we have emphasized, and respecting which we have repeatedly expressed our faith, our conviction—even respecting this date we have never knowingly spoken in infallible terms.... **We see no reason for disparaging the date and convictions associated with it**.... This is the good tidings of God's grace in Christ—whether the completion of the church shall be accomplished before 1914 or not" (*WTR*, 1 June 1913, 5249).

"Therefore the Scriptures indicate that a great time of trouble similar to that which came upon the Jewish nation **will now come upon all Christendom. The experiences of Israel in the year 70 will be paralleled in the experiences of the year 1915**" (*WTR*, 15 June 1913, 5256).

"We are waiting for the time to come when the government of the world will be turned over to Messiah. We cannot say that it may not be **either October, 1914, or October 1915. It is possible that we might be out of the correct reckoning on the subject a number of years. We cannot say with certainty. We do not know. It is a matter of faith, and not knowledge.** 'We walk by faith, not by sight'" (*WTR*, 15 Oct. 1913, 5328).

These and other statements show a reversal as compared with earlier statements by Russell. For example, writing in 1894 concerning the 1914 date:

> We see no reason for changing the figures—nor could we change them if we would. They are, we believe, **God's dates, not ours.** But bear in mind that the end of 1914 is not the date for the *beginning*, but for the *end* of the time of trouble" (*WTR*, 15 July 1894, 1677).

Russell's Preparation For Prophetic Failure

In his doctoral study, Melvin D. Curry, Jr., presents an insightful summary of Russell's provision for the failure of his 1914 predictions, based upon *Watch Tower* articles:

> Russell used a number of devices to negate in advance the effect of prophetic failure. **First**, he denied that he was inspired and argued that his predictions were based on faith and were therefore not infallible, however, he still contended that the Biblical evidence is so strong "that faith in the chronology almost becomes knowledge." **Second**, he affirmed that his failure to predict accurately the events of 1914 "would merely prove that our chronology, our 'alarm clock,' went off a little before the time, and that the error could not be very great." For example, he conceded that

the Gentile Times "may end in October 1914, or in October 1915." **Third**, he narrowed the predictions so that they were restricted to non-empirical supernatural events, such as, the expiration of "the lease of power granted to the Gentile nations" and the end of "the harvest period of the Gospel age." **Fourth**, in 1904 he reversed the sequence of events expected to occur and contended that "world-wide anarchy" would follow the ending of the Gentile Times in 1914 rather than precede it. **Fifth**, he changed his prediction that the collapse of Christendom would be "sudden and awful" to a denial that the nations "will all fall to pieces in that year." Instead, he claimed that "the earthly phase of the kingdom will be established later than 1914; this left a period of time after the expiration of the Gentile lease for the fall of the nations and the gradual establishment of the kingdom on earth." **Finally**, he likened his possible chronological error to other Biblical uncertainties [such as the precise date of creation].[1]

A number of statements made by Russell during 1914, and also in 1915 and 1916, in reference to Armageddon and the establishment of Messiah's Kingdom, are significant. Here are some published in 1914.

1914

"From every point of view the Year 1914 seems big with possibilities.... So far as our judgment goes, the Year 1914 is the last one of what the Bible terms 'Gentile Times'—the period in which God has allowed the nations of the earth to do their best to rule the world. The end of their 'times' marks the date for the beginning of Messiah's kingdom, which the Bible declares is to ushered in with a great time of trouble, just such as we see impending. As already pointed out, **we are by no means confident that this year, 1914, will witness as radical and swift changes of dispensation as we had expected**. It is beyond the power of our imagination to picture an accomplishment in one year of all that the Scriptures seem to imply should be expected before the reign of peace is ushered in" (*WTR*, 1 Jan. 1914, 5373).

"We may not read the time features with the same absolute certainty as doctrinal features.... We are still walking by faith and not by sight. We are, however, not faithless and unbelieving, but faithful and waiting. If later it should be demonstrated that the church is not glorified by October, 1914, we shall try to feel content with whatever the Lord's will may be. We believe that very many who are running the race for the prize will be able to thank God for the chronology, even if it should prove not accurate to the year, or even out of the way several years. We believe that the chronology is a blessing. If it should wake us a few minutes earlier or a few hours earlier in the morning than we would otherwise have waked, well and good! ... **If in the Lord's providence the time should come twenty-five years later, then that would be our will.** If October, 1915, should pass [without the predicted events fulfilled], ... we would say that evidently we have been out somewhere in our reckoning.... **Have we been expecting the wrong thing at the right time?** The Lord's will might permit this. Our expectation as a church is that our change is near. Nothing of restitution blessings can come to the world until after the church has been glorified" (*WTR*, 1 Jan. 1914, 5374).

"There is **absolutely no ground for Bible students to question that the consummation of this Gospel age is now even at the door,** and that it will end as the Scriptures foretell in a great time of trouble such as never was since there was a nation. We see the participants in this great crisis banding themselves together.... The great crisis, the great clash, symbolically represented as a fire, that will consume the ecclesiastical heavens and the social earth, is **very near**.... We remind our readers here that in these columns and in the six volumes of STUDIES IN THE SCRIPTURES we have set forth everything appertaining to the times and seasons in a **tentative form**; that is to say, not with positiveness, not with the claim that we knew, but merely with the suggestion that 'thus and so' seems to be the teaching of the Bible.... **The chronology still seems strong as ever to the Editor.** He sees nothing to alter or amend. Nevertheless, the Editor wishes to put all

THE WATCH TOWER readers on notice, as he already has done twice this year, that to his judgment it now seem unreasonable to expect during the present year all that he had anticipated, as suggested previously.... This does not prove the chronology wrong, nor does it prove that the Times of the Gentiles do not end with this year" (*WTR*, 1 May 1914, 5450).

When asked by a reader if *Studies in the Scriptures* would be distributed after October 1914, Russell replied:

[Paragraph heading: "Kingdom of God Soon to Be established on Earth"] "It is our thought that these books will be on sale and read for years in the future, provided the Gospel age and its work continue.... We have not attempted to say that these views are infallible, but have stated the processes of reasoning and figuring, leaving to each reader the duty and privilege of reading, thinking and figuring for himself. That will be an interesting matter a hundred years from now; and if he can figure or reason better, he will still be interested in what we have presented. In any event, **we think that the consummation cannot be long deferred**" (*WTR*, 1 July 1914, 5496).

"To my [Russell's] understanding, **the Bible teaches that Jesus has been present in the world since 1874**. In other words, His Second Advent then began.... They [Bible Students] understand the Bible to teach that this Parousia will continue for a thousand years; but that the Epiphania, or manifestation to the world, will be due in forty years from the time the Presence began. For this reason **they are looking very interestedly to see what the present war will bring**. And do we not see everywhere signs of unrest, a time of trouble brewing? **It looks as though this year would mark the beginning of the 'flaming fire' of judgments upon the world which will mark the closing of this Age and the inauguration of the New Dispensation of Messiah's kingdom**.... The transition may be painful, yet it will be blessed, marking the overthrow of Satan's empire and the reign of sin and death and the inauguration of Messiah's Kingdom and its reign of righteousness and life eternal (*The Bible Student's Monthly*, Vol 6, No. 1, 1-2). [Paragraph heading: "Kingdom of God Soon to Be Established on Earth"]: "And from the Prophets we learn that **this Kingdom is soon to be established in the earth**..." (ibid., 3).

"But Socialism is, we believe, the main factor in the war now raging and which will be earth's greatest and most terrible war—**and probably the last**.... But after the shock of battle—What? Such a war as is now progressing **will surely bring no great victory to any single nation or to any combination of nations**.... The great Armageddon battle of the Scriptures will have been only partially fought. The remnants of armies, returning to their homes sour and discouraged with defeat or costly victory, will be war-sick and mad against their rulers who led to the carnage. **Then the great Armageddon of the Bible may be expected**. Every man's hand will be against his neighbor. Various factions and parties will proclaim panaceas, and will endeavor to force them upon the public. As a result, foretold in prophecy, 'there shall be a time of trouble, such as never was since there was a nation,' Daniel 12:1." The shaking process will continue, the Apostle tells us, until Messiah's unshakable kingdom shall assert itself and take control of earth's affairs" (*WTR*, 15 Aug. 1914, 5516).

"Our thought is that this war will so weaken all the nations, so impoverish them, as to make them ready for anarchy the which the Bible portrays. The disbanding of the troops and the returning of them to their homes, disappointed, dissatisfied and angry with the kings, rulers, nobles, **will result in the anarchy which will doubtless prevail throughout Europe—and extend to every nation**, as the Bible predicts... While it is possible that **Armageddon may begin next Spring**, yet it is purely speculation to attempt to say just when. We see, however, that there are parallels between the close of the Jewish age and this Gospel age. These parallels seem to **point to the year just before us—particularly the early months**" (*WTR*, 1 Sept. 1914, 5526-27).

"The present war will weaken the nations, not only of their life-blood, but also of their wealth; and it will demonstrate the inefficiency of all Gentile kingdoms to bring to the world peace, righteousness, satisfactory government. But Messiah's Kingdom, **which will then be inaugurated**, will be 'the desire of all nations.' **This war and the anarchy of Armageddon, which will follow it**, will prove conclusively the great need of Divine intervention in human affairs.—Hag. 2:7" ("Distress of Nations With Perplexity," 4 Oct. 1914, *Pastor Russell's Sermons* [1917], 418-19).

"The war will proceed and will eventuate in **no glorious victory for any nation**, but in the horrible mutilation and impoverishment of all. **Next will follow the awful Armageddon of anarchy**" (*WTR*, 15 Oct. 1914, 5554).

"Should we expect that the Lord would reveal himself the very moment the Gentile times end? The Bible declaration is that he shall be revealed in 'flaming fire.' Just how long after the Gentile times close will be the revealment in 'flaming fire' we do not know. Seemingly, **following this great war will come the greatest 'earthquake' that ever occurred—a revolution that will involve all the civilized nations** (Revelation 16:18). Then Socialism may loom up, but will be short-lived and develop into anarchy" (*WTR*, 1 Nov. 1914, 5567).

"The treading down of the Jews has stopped. All over the world the Jews are now free—even in Russia.... Where are the Jews being trodden down now? Where are they being subjected to scorn? At present they are receiving no persecution whatever. We believe that **the treading down of Jerusalem has ceased, because the time for the Gentiles to tread down Israel has ended**.... Some one may ask, Since the fulfillment of the various time prophecies demonstrates that God's methods of operating are slow, **may it not be that the kingdom will not be ushered in for five, ten or even twenty-five years?** Our reply is, **we are not a prophet**; we merely believe that we have come to the place where the Gentile times have ended. If the Lord has five years more for us here, we shall be very glad to be on this side of the veil.... If the Lord has even one more year for us as good as the past year has been, what more can we ask?" (ibid., 5568).

"But **we cannot be far from our change**; and we advise that all of the Lord's people live day by day just as though this was the last day on this side of the veil, and that tonight or tomorrow would usher us into the glorious things beyond the veil" (ibid., 5569).

"While we are not certain that all the dire calamities of the day of the Lord will befall the earth **within the next eleven months, nevertheless, there seems to be a sufficient possibility of this to warrant us in making certain provisions against the distress of that time**—in the interest of our families, our friends, and our neighbors. We recommend those having dry, clean cellars, or other places suitable and well-ventilated, to lay in a good stock of life's necessities; for instance, a large supply of coal, of rice, dried peas, dried beans, rolled oats, wheat, barley, sugar, molasses, fish, etc.... Do not sound a trumpet before you, telling of your provision, intentions, etc..." (ibid., 5572).

Headline in *The Bible Students Monthly*: "DISTRESS OF NATIONS PRECEDING ARMAGEDDON—Pastor Russell Declares Present War will Eventuate in No Marked Victory for Either Side—Then 'Armageddon'" (Vol. 6, No. 5)

"This war, and the anarchy of Armageddon, which will follow it, will prove conclusively the need for Divine interposition in human affairs.... And when the war is ended, these nations, sorrowful and famine-stricken, will be greatly angered at their rulers. Then will come the determination for something like Socialism. This the government will endeavor to put down, and to some extent they will succeed. **Then will follow the great explosion—the Armageddon of the Scriptures**. Then will be the Time of Trouble, immediately preceding the Messianic Kingdom, which will inaugurate the long-promised Peace on Earth" (*The Bible Students Monthly*, vol. 6, #5, 1914, published in *Harvest Gleanings*, vol. 1, 676).

Pastor Russell's sermons were published in the *New York Times*. Here are two excerpts from 1914:

For 2,500 years God, through the Bible Prophets, has been telling his people about this great war [World War I] and concerning the more terrible Armageddon which will follow it.... The war will proceed and will eventuate in no glorious victory for any nation, but in the horrible mutilation and impoverishment of all. **Next will follow the Armageddon of anarchy.** For forty years I have been proclaiming this very war and **its glorious outcome**... (Russell, *New York Times*, 5 Oct. 1914, 8).

Few of the awakening ones realize that the **present war** is permitted for the weakening of the nations, preparatory to the **utter collapse of the Present Order of Things—and the ushering in of the New Order**—the Reign of Righteousness, under Messiah's Kingdom (Russell, *New York Times*, 14 Dec. 1914, 6).

Notes

1. Melvin Dotson Curry, Jr., "Jehovah's Witnesses: The Effects of Millennarianism on the Maintenance of a Religious Sect" (Ph.D. diss.; Florida State University, Tallahassee, Fla., 1980), 157-59. *WTR*, 4067, 4737, 5142, 4751, 3437, 4751, 5496. Some examples from the *Watch Tower Reprints* which illustrate Curry's point: **1907** "If our chronology is not reliable we have no idea where we are nor when the morning will come.... If, therefore, dearly beloved, it should turn out that our chronology is all wrong, we may conclude that with it we have had much advantage everyway" (4067-68). **1912** "Finally, let us remember that we did not consecrate either to October, 1914, nor to October, 1915, or to any other date, but 'unto death'" (5142). **1913** "The date 1914 is not an arbitrary date; it is merely what the chronology of the Scriptures seems to teach. We have never said positively that the Scriptures do so teach—that the Jewish favor will begin exactly at that time, or that the Gentile times will end exactly at that time. We say that according to the best chronological reckoning of which we are capable, it is approximately that time—whether it be October, 1914, or later" (5328). "The fact is that, notwithstanding the strength of our position and our hope that it may be true, it is nevertheless of faith and not of knowledge.... We must admit that there are possibilities of our having made a mistake in respect to the chronology, even though we do not see where any mistake has been made in calculating the seven times of the Gentiles as expiring about October 1, 1914.... Whether within one year or within ten of twenty years, the things which we are expecting will surely be accomplished" (5348). **1914** "...We are by no means confident that this year, 1914, will witness as radical and swift changes of dispensations as we have expected" (5373). "...Time is not so definitely stated in the Scriptures as are the basic doctrines" (5374). "...It is possible that the Gentile Times might close without world-wide trouble immediately..." (5502). "...We might expect the transition to run on a good many years" (5567).

TWENTY TIME-PROOFS

THAT THE REIGN OF EVIL WILL CEASE AND THE EARTHLY PHASE OF THE KINGDOM OF GOD BE ESTABLISHED IN 1914-1915.

Gen. 15:9 The ages of the animals offered by Abraham aggregated eleven years, which applied prophetically, on the scale of a year for a day, equal 3960 years, the length of time from the date of the Abrahamic Covenant, 2045 B.C. to A.D. 1915 ....Z' 07-79

Isa. 40:2 One of the prophecies showing that the Jewish and Gospel Ages would be of equal length and that the Gospel Age would end therefore in 1914 ....B219

Jer. 16:18 Another of the prophecies showing that the Jewish and Gospel ages would be of equal length and that the latter would end in 1914 ....B218

Zech. 9:12 Another of the prophecies showing that the Jewish and Gospel ages would be of equal length and that the latter would end in 1914 ....B218

Num. 9:11 The fact that Christ was slain at the full of the moon (symbol of Israel under the Law Covenant), typified that it was the turning point between two equal periods of Jewish history. This foreshadows Israel's rehabilitation in A.D. 1915 ....Z' 98-68

Gen. 25:24 The fact that Esau, type of Fleshly Israel, and Jacob, type of Spiritual Israel, were twins, typified that the length of the Jewish and Gospel Ages would be equal. This would bring the full end of the Gospel Age in A.D. 1914 ....Z' 94-63

Lev. 26:18 The Jewish people were promised, under certain conditions, a special chastisement of "Seven times" otherwise called "The times of the Gentiles". These "Seven Times", or 2520 literal years, began with the overthrow of Israel's typical kingdom in the days of Zedekiah, 606 B.C. and will therefore end in A.D. 1914 ....B87

Dan. 4:16 Nebuchadnezzar's seven years of insanity, typified the Times of the Gentiles, 2520 years, ending in 1914 ....B95, 97

2 Chr. 36:22 The decree of Cyrus, 536 B.C., 605 years prior to Israel's complete overthrow as a people, typifies Christendom's overthrow in 1914, 605 years after the transfer of the Papal residence from Rome to Avignon ....Z' 05-183

Ezra 4:24 Ezra's resumption of work upon the temple, 521 B.C. 500 years prior to Israel's complete overthrow, typified Christendom's overthrow in 1914, 500 years after the publication of Marsiglio's *Defensor Pacis.* ....Z '05-183

Ezra 6:15 Completion of rebuilding of the temple, 517 B.C., 586 years prior to Israel's overthrow, typified Christendom's overthrow in 1914, 586 years after the death of Marsiglio ....Z' 05-183

Ezra 7:7 Dedication of the temple, 467 B.C., 536 years prior to Israel's overthrow, typified Christendom's overthrow in 1914, 536 years after the schism in the papacy, when two popes were on the throne at one time; Wycliffe's turning point ....Z' 05-182

Neh. 2:8 Nehemiah's commission, 454 B.C., 523 years prior to Israel's overthrow, typified Christendom's overthrow in 1914, 523 years after Huss became acquainted with Wycliffe's works and continued the Reformation ....Z' 05-182

Dan. 9:25 The point 405 B.C., 474 years prior to Israel's overthrow, marked by Daniel's setting apart of the "seven weeks" from the "sixty and two weeks", typified Christendom's overthrow in 1914, 474 years after the invention of printing ....Z '05-182

1 Ki. 12:16 The division of the kingdom of Israel into the ten-tribe and the two-tribe Kingdoms, 393 years prior to Zedekiah's overthrow, foreshadows Christendom's overthrow in 1914, 393 years after Luther's excommunication ....Z '05-179

2 Ki. 20:1 The sickness of Hezekiah, 125 years before Zedekiah's overthrow, foreshadows Christendom's overthrow in 1914, 125 years after the French Revolution ....Z '05-179

2 Chron. 33:15 Manasseh's reformation, 68 years before Zedekiah's overthrow, foreshadows Christendom's overthrow in 1914, 68 years after the formation of the Evangelical Alliance ....Z '05-180

2 Chr. 34:3 The beginning of Josiah's seeking after God, 45 years before Zedekiah's overthrow, foreshadows Christendom's overthrow in 1914, 45 years after the editor of ZION'S WATCH TOWER began the search for what is now "Present Truth" ....Z '05-180

2 Ki. 22:3 The finding of the book of the law by Josiah, 35 years before Zedekiah's overthrow, foreshadows Christendom's overthrow in 1914, 35 years after the founding of ZION'S WATCH TOWER ....Z '05-180

Ezek. 21:25 The overthrow of Zedekiah, 3520 years after the fall in the garden of Eden, foreshadows the complete wiping out of the fall 3520 years later in the year 2914 A.D., and since the Millennium is a period of a thousand years duration this proves that the Millennium proper begins with the close of the year 1914 ....Z '04-343

8.

Twenty Time-Proofs

The "Twenty Time Proofs"—"**That the Reign of Evil Will Cease and the Earthly Phase of the Kingdom of God Be Established in 1914-1915**"—were published in the *Berean Bible Teachers' Manual* (1907, 1908 eds.).[1] These "proofs," as indicated by the references at the end of each of them, were all originally published in Watch Tower materials—various issues of *Zion's Watch Tower* (Z) and volume 2 of Russell's *Studies in the Scriptures: The Time is at Hand* (B).[2]

Time proof one is an interesting example of a "due time" understanding which was sent to Russell. He obviously thought it credible enough to publish it in the March 1, 1907, *Watch Tower*. The sender, George Matthews, writes:

> The other day, having read the 15th chapter of Genesis, the 9th verse seemed to suggest that the years mentioned had some meaning, and, doing a little figuring, here is the result. In the 8th verse Abraham asked some proof that he should inherit the land promised him in the seventh verse. In verse 9 the Lord said to Abraham, "Take me an heifer three years old, and a she goat three years old, and a ram three years old, a turtle dove and a young pigeon." Now a bird is usually considered young up to one year old. So I figured three years each for the heifer, goat and ram—nine years—and one year each for the birds, eleven years in all. Eleven prophetic years of 360 days each equals 3,960. A day for a year gives us 3,960 years. On page 42, Vol. II of the DAWN [Russell's *The Time is at Hand*] we have the chronology as follows: ... Total ... 2045 years. 2045 taken from the 3960 years leaves 1915 years from A.D. 1, which seems to be the proof Abraham asked of the Lord whereby he should know that he would inherit the land. This seems at least to be a remarkable coincidence.[3]

That this material was taken seriously is not only shown by its initial appearance in the *Watch Tower* and later in the *Berean Bible Teachers' Manual*, but by its being cited again in the October 15, 1917, *Watch Tower*:

> **We need not suppose that Abraham perceived any symbolic meaning hidden away in the ages of the victims selected. This is one of the things "hidden from the ages and generations," but now made known unto us by the Spirit.** The three beasts were each three years of age; the two birds were young birds. We quote the Biblical comment on Genesis 15:9—"A bird is usually considered young up to one year old. Figuring thus, the ages of the animals represent 11 years. Eleven prophetic years of 360 literal years each equal 3,960 years, the time from the giv-

ing of this covenant to Abraham till the year 1915, when he will inherit the land." The method here used in obtaining the period elapsing from the giving of the covenant till Abraham should inherit the land **is sound and in accord with other symbolisms under which God hid or covered information until due time for it to be known. The period of 3,960 years seems a well fixed chronological period.**[4]

However, since Abraham did not inherit the land in 1915 as predicted, the 2,045 B.C. date for the giving of the covenant in this article was changed to "2,035 B.C. 2,035 plus 1,925 equals 3,960. Accordingly Abraham should enter upon the actual possession of his promised inheritance in the year 1925 A.D."[5]— which also was not fulfilled.

It is obvious that the "Time Proofs" were wrong—the "earthly phase of the Kingdom of God" was not "established in 1914-1915"—and most of these "proofs" are no longer accepted by the Jehovah's Witnesses.

Notes

1. Page 482. Part I of the *Manual* (481 pp.) was compiled by C. J. Woodworth who became editor of *The Golden Age* (renamed *Consolation*) from 1919-1946. He also was co-author of *The Finished Mystery* (1917). The "Time Proofs" were removed in later copies of the *Manual*. The *Manual*, as republished by the Chicago Bible Students, includes the "Time Proofs."
2. In addition to those "Time Proofs" written by Russell, the one on Genesis 15:9 was submitted by George Matthews in a letter to the *Watch Tower* (*WTR*, 1 Mar. 1907, 3957). The 11 "Time "Proofs" from the June 15, 1905, *Watch Tower* (*WTR*, 3574-79) are presented in "Remarkable Chronological Parallels," by John Edgar. The "Time Proof" from the November 15, 1904, *Watch Tower* (*WTR*, 3459-60) was submitted by "three different brethren" (ibid., 3459).
3. *WTR*, 1 Mar. 1907, 3957.
4. *WTR*, 15 Oct. 1917, 6157.
5. Ibid.

9.

The Jehovah's Witnesses and 1914

Of the doctrines believed by the Jehovah's Witnesses, few have been so vigorously promoted and defended as the claim that in 1914, the "times of the Gentiles" or the "appointed times of the nations" ended, God's Kingdom by Jesus Christ was set up in heaven, and the "time of the end" began. This belief is the basis for further significant claims and doctrines. This chapter deals with two issues: (1) the crucial significance of 1914, and (2) how the Jehovah's Witnesses argue in establishing that date.

The Crucial Significance of 1914

How crucial is the Witnesses' 1914 date to the Watch Tower Society and its claims? In his book *Crisis of Conscience*, Raymond Franz, former Governing Body member, writes:

> 1914 is a pivotal date on which **a major portion of the doctrinal and authority structure of Jehovah's Witnesses rests** [associated doctrines are reviewed].... To weaken belief in the significance of the foundation date of 1914 **would weaken the whole doctrinal superstructure ... that rests on it**. It would also **weaken the claim of special authority** for those acting as the official spokesman group for the 'faithful and discreet slave' class. To *remove* that date as having such significance **could mean the virtual collapse of all the doctrinal and authority structure founded on it**. That is how crucial it is.[1]

Ex-Bethelite Randall Watters also explains how important 1914 is to the Witnesses:

> Most Jehovah's Witnesses do not realize the critical significance of the date 1914 **on their entire organizational structure and doctrine**.... The Governing Body has explained to the Witnesses that when Christ returned in 1914, there was a "cleansing of the organization" for 3½ years, culminating in Christ judging the organization and finally choosing it in 1918 as his "faithful & discreet slave" to instruct mankind of God's truths in these last days. This was also the year of the invisible "rapture," where deceased Witnesses (supposedly including the "early Christians") were resurrected and ascended to heaven. They arrive at this by interpreting the 3½ years of Revelation 11:11 as applying to this time period, counting from the pivotal date of 1914. **So, the whole concept of "God's Organization" is dependent on the accuracy of the date 1914.**

Yet that is not all. The choosing of another "class" of Christians, those who would live on earth but not be born again or anointed by the Holy Spirit, was also based on this pivotal date of 1914 [1935, Great Crowd].... Now we are in a position to see the real importance of the date 1914. If it is wrong, then so is 1918 and 1935. If 1914 is wrong, Christ did not return invisibly. If 1918 is wrong, Christ did not appoint the Watchtower as his special prophet. **If 1935 is wrong, there are no class distinctions—all Christians are the same, all must be born again** (John 3:3,5,7), all must take the bread and the wine (John 6:53,54) and all must have Christ as their mediator, not a man-made organization (1 Tim. 2:5).[2]

Carl Olof Jonsson, former Witness pioneer and author of *The Gentile Times Reconsidered,* writes:

It is not just a question of an erroneous chronology that has to be corrected. **The unique claims of the Watch Tower movement are closely connected with the year 1914.**

If the leaders of the Watch Tower organization would admit that Christ's kingdom *was not* set up in 1914 and that Christ *did not* come invisibly that year, they would also have to admit that Christ *did not* make any specific inspection of the Christian denominations at that time and *did not* appoint the members of the Russellite movement "over his domestics" in 1919. Then they would have to admit that their claim of being God's sole "channel" and "mouthpiece" on earth *is false,* and that for almost a whole century they have appeared on the world scene *in a false role with a false message.*

So much of the movement's identity is "invested" in the 1914 date that it would be a tremendous step to admit that the sophisticated system of prophetic explanations infused into that date is **nothing but a figment of the imagination.**[3]

Several statements from the *Watchtower* magazine relating to the subject are pertinent here. The April 15, 1984, issue claims: "The fulfillment of Jesus' sign since 1914 points back to that date as being the correct one to which Bible chronology had pointed forward. Yes, **1914 is indeed a focal point of Bible prophecy!**"[4] The January 1, 1983, *Watchtower* states: "Properly, then, the ending of the Gentile Times in the later half of 1914 still stands on a historical basis as one the **fundamental Kingdom truths to which we must hold today.**"[5] This "truth" is so fundamental that a Witnesses' hope of eternal life depends on it. A Witness who would not accept Watch Tower teachings on this point would be disfellowshipped.

In "Questions from Readers" in the April 1, 1986, *Watchtower,* it is asked, "Why have Jehovah's Witnesses disfellowshipped (excommunicated) for apostasy some who still profess belief in God, the Bible, and Jesus Christ?" The response:

Approved association with Jehovah's Witnesses requires accepting the entire range of the true teachings of the Bible, including those Scriptural beliefs that are unique to Jehovah's Witnesses. What do such beliefs include? ... **That there is a 'faithful and discreet slave' upon earth today** 'entrusted with all of Jesus' earthly interests,' which slave is associated with the Governing Body of Jehovah's Witnesses (Matthew 24:45-47). **That 1914 marked the end of the Gentile Times and the establishment of the Kingdom of God in the heavens,** as well as the time of Christ's foretold presence.... That **Armageddon,** referring to the battle of the great day of God Almighty **is near....**[6]

While other teachings are given, it should be noted that all those quoted above for "approved association with Jehovah's Witnesses" are in some way connected with the 1914 date. The May 1, 1981, *Watchtower* makes it clear that because of 1914, the message of the Witnesses is a different "gospel":

> Let the honest-hearted person compare the kind of preaching of the gospel of the Kingdom done by the religious systems of Christendom during all the centuries with that done by Jehovah's Witnesses since the end of World War I in 1918. **They are not one and the same kind. That of Jehovah's Witnesses is really "gospel," or "good news," as of God's heavenly kingdom that was established by the enthronement of his Son Jesus Christ at the end of the Gentile Times in 1914.**[7]

What does Paul say about a different kind of "good news"?

> However, even if we or an angel out of heaven were to declare to YOU as good news something beyond what we declared to YOU as good news, let him be accursed. As we have said above, I also now say again, Whoever it is that is declaring to YOU as good news something beyond what YOU accepted, let him be accursed [Gal. 1:8-9, [*NWT*].

The crucial importance of 1914 to the Jehovah's Witnesses has been adequately illustrated in the statements above. How was this date determined?

Jehovah's Witnesses' Arguments for 1914

Presented here is a summary of Jehovah's Witnesses' arguments establishing their prophetic program of Christ's second coming and the "time of the end" and its termination.

The Witnesses predicted the significance of 1914 many years before. According to the April 1, 1984, *Watchtower*:

> ...The *Watch Tower* magazine as far back as December of 1879 pointed to 1914 as a marked date in regard to Bible prophecy. And the March 1880 issue of the *Watch Tower* linked God's Kingdom rule with the ending of what Jesus Christ referred to as "the appointed times of the nations," or "the times of the Gentiles" (Luke 21:24; *Authorized Version*). That *Watch Tower* said: "The Times of the Gentiles extend to 1914, and the heavenly kingdom will not have full sway till then."[8]

And as further confirmation of the 1914 prediction, the following "evidence" has often been cited: "In its August 30, 1914, issue, the New York newspaper *The World* drew attention to the remarkable fact that the International Bible Students Association (Jehovah's Witnesses) had pointed to 1914 as a marked date in Bible prophecy."[9]

The Witnesses' book *Reasoning From the Scriptures* (1985) summarizes their arguments in support of 1914:

> **Why do Jehovah's Witnesses say that God's Kingdom was established in 1914?** *Two lines of evidence point to that year:* (1) Bible chronology and (2) the events since 1914 in fulfillment of prophecy.... *Read Daniel 4:1-17.* Verses 20-37 show that this prophecy had a fulfillment upon Nebuchadnezzar. But it also has a larger fulfillment.... The prophetic dream, then, points to the time when Jehovah would give rulership over mankind to his own Son. *What was to happen in the meantime?* Rulership over mankind, as represented by the tree and its rootstock, would have

the heart of a beast" (Dan. 4:16). The history of mankind would be dominated by governments that displayed the characteristics of wild beasts.... As Jesus showed in his prophecy pointing to the conclusion of the system of things, Jerusalem would be "trampled on by the nations, until the appointed times of the nations" were fulfilled (Luke 21:24).... *For how long would such governments be permitted to exercise this control before Jehovah gave the Kingdom to Jesus Christ?* Daniel 4:16 says "seven times" ("seven years").... The Bible shows that in calculating prophetic time, a day is counted as a year (Ezek. 4:6; Num. 14:34). How many "days," then, are involved? Revelation 11:2,3 clearly states that 42 months (3½ years) in that prophecy are counted as 1,260 days. Seven years would be twice that, or 2,520 days. Applying the "day for a year" rule would result in 2,520 years.

When did the counting of "seven times" begin? After Zedekiah, the last king in the typical Kingdom of God, was removed from the throne in Jerusalem by the Babylonians. (Ezek. 21:25-27) Finally, by early October of 607 B.C.E. the last vestige of Jewish sovereignty was gone....

How, then, is the time calculated down to 1914? Counting 2,520 years from early October of 607 B.C.E. brings us to early October of 1914 C.E.... *What happened at that time?* Jehovah entrusted rulership over mankind to his own Son, Jesus Christ, glorified in the heavens—Dan. 7:13, 14.[10]

The second evidence presented by the Witnesses that "the last days" began in 1914 is fulfilled prophecy. "The Bible describes events and conditions that mark this significant time period. 'The sign' is a composite one made up of many evidences; thus its fulfillment requires that all aspects of the sign be clearly evident during one generation."[11] These aspects include: world wars, famines, great earthquakes, pestilences, increased lawlessness, and preaching of the "good news," to name a few.[12]

In the following chapters each major part of the Witnesses' system and claims will be examined to determine if they are valid.

Notes

1. Raymond Franz, *Crisis of Conscience* (2nd ed.; Atlanta: Commentary Press, 1992), 139.
2. *The Watchtower Bible & Tract Society—The Critical Years 1965-1985* (Manhattan Beach, Calif.: Randall Watters, n.d.), 2.
3. Carl Olof Jonsson, *The Gentile Times Reconsidered* (3rd ed.; Atlanta: Commentary Press, 1998), 274-75.
4. *WT*, 15 Apr. 1984, 6.
5. *WT*, 1 Jan. 1983, 12.
6. *WT*, 1 Apr. 1986, 30-31.
7. *WT*, 1 May 1981, 17.
8. *WT*, 1 Apr. 1984, 6.
9. Ibid., 5.
10. *Reasoning From the Scriptures* (1985), 95-96.
11. Ibid., 234.
12. Ibid., 234-38.

10.

What Was Predicted for 1914?

Watch Tower writers have frequently stated that the Bible Students (now known as Jehovah's Witnesses) successfully predicted that 1914 was to be a pivotal year in Bible prophecy. According to them, this successful prediction was verified even by an outside publication, *The World Magazine*, and this advance knowledge clearly demonstrates they were directed by God's holy spirit (God's "active force"). This chapter will examine: (1) The March 1880 *Watch Tower* and 1914, (2) what Russell predicted for 1914, (3) *The World Magazine* citations in Watch Tower publications, and (4) the claim that advance knowledge concerning 1914 is evidence of God's direction by his holy spirit.

The March 1880 Watch Tower and 1914

This short excerpt from the 1880 *Watch Tower* has been quoted numerous times[1] in Watch Tower publications as proof of a special insight into prophecy:

> In the "Watchtower" magazine of March, 1880, they said: "**The Times of the Gentiles extend to 1914, and the heavenly kingdom will not have full sway till then.**" Of all people, only the witnesses pointed to 1914 as the year for **God's kingdom to be fully set up in heaven**.[2]

Sometimes an earlier date for the 1914 prediction was mentioned. For example, the book *"Your Will Be Done on Earth"* (1958) states: "...From 1877 onward, Jehovah's dedicated people of his 'sanctuary' class were openly declaring in their publications that the Gentile times or 'appointed times of the nations' would end in 1914. In that year the kingdom of God was to be **fully established in the heavens** to see that His will should be done on earth."[3] And in a similar statement in *Man's Salvation Out of World's Distress at Hand!* (1975), we read: "Furthermore, the remnant of spiritual Israel had for decades, yes, since the year 1876, been looking forward to the ending of the Times of the Gentiles in the autumn of 1914. They were expecting God's Messianic kingdom to be **fully established in the heavens** by then and also for the remnant of spiritual Israel to be glorified with Jesus Christ in the heavenly kingdom at that time."[4] These quotations all have one thing in common: the claim that the 1914 was predicted as the year "for God's kingdom to be **fully set up in heaven**," or "established **in the heavens**."

Did Russell and his Bible Students expect and teach that the kingdom of God would be "fully set up in heaven" in 1914? In his book on the Jehovah's Witnesses, Alan Rogerson disagrees: "Despite what the Witnesses say, however, Russell *did not* **believe that 1914 marked the establishment of the Kingdom of**

God in heaven (for that had happened in 1878) and he certainly did not believe that 1914 would be followed by another generation of conflict without any intervention by God."[5] Can this be documented? Russell's statements are clear: "The year **1878** being thus indicated as the date when the Lord began to take unto himself his great power, it is reasonable to conclude that **there the setting up of the Kingdom began**.... Our Lord, the appointed King, is now present, since October 1874 A.D., ... and **the formal inauguration of his kingly office dates from April, 1878 A.D.**...[6] "Be not surprised, then, when in subsequent chapters we present proofs that the **setting up of the Kingdom of God is already begun**, that it is pointed out in prophecy as due to **begin the exercise of power in A.D. 1878**, and that the 'battle of the great day of God Almighty' (Rev. 16:14) which will end in A.D. 1914 with the complete overthrow of earth's present rulership, is already commenced."[7]

A reading of the March 1880 *Watch Tower* reveals two significant things: (1) The quotation as cited in Watch Tower publications is not complete, but an ellipsis is not used. (2) When the entire statement is read in context, the kingdom spoken of was to established in or on **the earth** (not "set up in heaven") in 1914! The complete sentence reads:

> "The Times of the Gentiles" extend to 1914, and the heavenly kingdom will not have fully sway till then, **but as a "Stone" the kingdom of God is set up "*in the days* of these (ten gentile) kings," and by consuming them it becomes a universal kingdom—a "great mountain and fills the whole earth."**[8]

This is in agreement with what Pastor Russell wrote when he stated that the consummation of the "time of the end" would see "the full establishment of the Kingdom of God **in the earth at A.D. 1914**, the terminus of the Times of the Gentiles."[9] "Not until the full end of Gentile Times (October, A.D. 1914) should we expect the earthly phase of God's Kingdom...[10] "The beginning of the **earthly phase of the Kingdom in the end of A. D. 1914** will, we understand, consist wholly of the resurrected holy ones of olden time...."[11]

The December 1, 1984, *Watchtower* quotes the identical portion of the 1880 *Watch Tower*, and while the next paragraph is more candid, it still obscures what was taught at that time: "Admittedly, it was thought that the **establishment of the Kingdom in the heavens would mean the immediate destruction of earthly kingdoms** and that the anointed Christians would be 'caught away' to join deceased anointed Christians due to be resurrected at the time of Christ's presence (2 Thessalonians 2:1)."[12]

What Russell Predicted for 1914

Very few Jehovah's Witnesses have read the predictions of Watch Tower founder Russell that he taught would be realized in 1914, or shortly thereafter. What was expected to occur at the end of the "Times of the Gentiles"?

Jehovah's Witnesses—Proclaimers of God's Kingdom states that "in 1889 the entire **fourth chapter** of Volume II of *Millennial Dawn* (later called *Studies in the Scriptures*) was devoted to the discussion of 'The Times of the Gentiles.' But what would the end of the Gentile Times mean? The Bible Students were not completely sure what would happen."[13] It is significant that in the *Proclaimers* discussion, there is **not one direct quotation** from the material itself. What was predicted for the end of the "Times of the Gentiles" in **chapter four** of Russell's book, *The Time Is at Hand*?

Times of the Gentiles.

In this chapter we present the Bible evidence proving that the full end of the times of the Gentiles, *i.e.*, the full end of their lease of dominion, will be reached in A.D. 1914; and that that date will be the farthest limit of the rule of imperfect men. And be it observed, that if this is shown to be a fact firmly established by the Scriptures, it will prove:

Firstly, That at that date the Kingdom of God, for which our Lord taught us to pray, saying, "Thy Kingdom come," will obtain full, universal control, and that it will then be "set up," or firmly established, in the earth, on the ruins of present institutions.

Secondly, It will prove that he whose right it is thus to take the dominion will then be present as earth's new Ruler; and not only so, but it will also prove that he will be present for a considerable period before that date; because the overthrow of these Gentile governments is directly caused by his dashing them to pieces as a potter's vessel (Psa. 2:9; Rev. 2:27), and establishing in their stead his own righteous government.

Thirdly, It will prove that some time before the end of A.D. 1914 the last member of the divinely recognized Church of Christ, the "royal priesthood," "the body of Christ," will be glorified with the Head; because every member is to reign with Christ, being a joint-heir with him of the Kingdom, and it cannot be fully "set up" without every member.

Fourthly, It will prove that from that time forward Jerusalem shall no longer be trodden down of the Gentiles, but shall arise from the dust of divine disfavor, to honor; because the "Times of the Gentiles" will be fulfilled or completed.

Fifthly, It will prove that by that date, or sooner, Israel's blindness will begin to be turned away; because their "blindness in part" was to continue only "*until* the fulness of the Gentiles be come in" (Rom. 11:25), or, in other words, until the full number from among the Gentiles, who are to be members of the body or bride of Christ, would be fully selected.

Sixthly, It will prove that the great "time of trouble such as never was since there was a nation," will reach its culmination in a world-wide reign of anarchy; and then men will learn to be still, and to know that Jehovah is God and that he will be exalted in the earth. (Psa. 46:10) The condition of things spoken of in symbolic language as raging waves of the sea, melting earth, falling mountains and burning heavens will then pass away, and the "new heavens and new earth" with their peaceful blessings will begin to be recognized by trouble-tossed humanity. But the Lord's Anointed and his rightful and righteous authority will first be recognized by a company of God's children while passing through the great tribulation—the class represented by *m* and *t* on the Chart of the Ages (see also pages 235 to 239, Vol. I.); afterward, just at its close, by fleshly Israel; and ultimately by mankind in general.

Seventhly, It will prove that *before that date* God's Kingdom, organized in power, will be in the earth and then smite and crush the Gentile image (Dan. 2:34)—and fully consume the power of these kings. Its own power and dominion will be established as fast as by its varied influences and agencies it crushes and scatters the "powers that be"—civil and ecclesiastical—iron and clay.[14]

As 1914 came and passed, Russell and his followers could legitimately salvage only the date from his predictions—all else had failed. Certainly 1914 was not "the farthest limit of the rule of imperfect man," and God's kingdom had not been "established in the earth," nor had the kingdoms of the world been destroyed. There was no evidence that the last member of the church had been glorified (8,661 members still claimed to be of the anointed in the year 2000!). Natural Israel's blindness had not begun to be turned away, Jerusalem was not restored to honor, universal anarchy was not realized, etc.

But what about the beginning of World War I in 1914? Carl Olof Jonsson responds: "... Although there were a number of predictions in the Watch Tower publications as to what would take place in 1914, *none of them came close to a prediction of the outbreak of a world war in that year.*"[15]

After reviewing Russell's predictions in *The Time Is at Hand* and its treatment in the *Proclaimers* book, Jonsson makes some pertinent and accurate observations:

> What does the Society's new history book do with the pretentious claims and the very positive language that originally encapsulated these predictions? **They are totally smoothed over or concealed.**... Although some of the predictions are briefly mentioned, the Society carefully avoids terming them "predictions" or "prophecies." Russell and his associates never "predicted" or "foretold" anything, never claimed to present "proof" or "established truth." They just "thought," "suggested," "expected," and "earnestly hoped" that this or that "might" happen, but they "were not completely sure." **Thus the predictions are wrapped up in language that completely masks the true nature of the aggressive doomsday message proclaimed** to the world by the International Bible Students for over a quarter of a century before 1914. **Disguising the presumptuous predictions in such vague and unassuming words and phrases, of course, makes it easier to "humbly" concede that these failed.**[16]

Raymond Franz, after looking at these same predictions, concludes: "Few Jehovah's Witnesses today have any concept of the magnitude of the claims made for that year [1914] or the fact that **not a single one of the original seven points was fulfilled as stated**. Those expectations now receive only the briefest of mention in the Society's publications; some are totally passed over."[17] And Robert Crompton adds: "Whereas future generations of Watch Tower adherents came to regard Russell's predictions as greatly successful, he and his contemporaries faced considerable difficulty when trying to interpret current affairs in the light of what they had expected...."[18]

In spite of the evidence of total failure, a response to a critic in the February 13, 1924, *Golden Age* claims: **"It is not at all true that our 'expectations concerning this date [1914] failed of realization.'** Others now admit for that date all that we ever claimed for it."[19] No specifics are cited.

The World Magazine Citations

Watch Tower publications have often supported their claim that Pastor Russell successfully predicted the beginning of World War I in 1914, by citing an article in the August 30, 1914, magazine section of *The World*, a leading New York newspaper.[20] It is significant that both of the Witness-published histories of the movement mention this article, obviously viewing it as an important testimony. The most recent citation, in *Jehovah's Witnesses—Proclaimers of God's Kingdom* (1993), is very short, extracting only two sentences from the article: "The terrific war outbreak in Europe has fulfilled an extraordinary prophecy.... 'Look out for 1914!' has been the cry of the hundreds of travelling evangelists, who, representing this strange creed [associated with Russell], have gone up and down the country enunciating the doctrine that 'the Kingdom of God is at hand.'"[21] This brief quotation omits *The World Magazine* article headline: "END OF ALL KINGDOMS IN 1914."

Jehovah's Witnesses in the Divine Purpose (1959) reproduces a much longer portion of the article. A knowledgeable reader can therefore conclude that the claim is **not true** that the war's outbreak "has fulfilled an extraordinary prophecy."[22] Russell's teachings quoted in the article speak of the "Time of Trouble," the proclamation "that the Day of Wrath prophesied in the Bible would dawn in 1914," and "that the final end of the kingdoms of this world and the full establishment of the Kingdom of God" would be realized then, or shortly thereafter.[23] To be fulfilled, Armageddon would have to be fought.

With knowledge of Russell's predictions for 1914, and after examining the *World Magazine* article, Carl Olof Jonsson and Wolfgang Herbst conclude:

> Pretending that Russell's predictions came true, the Watch Tower Society has often quoted *The World Magazine* of August 30, 1914.... In an article headed, 'End of all Kingdoms in 1914' in that magazine it was claimed that 'The terrific war outbreak in Europe has fulfilled an extraordinary prophecy.' Then Pastor Russell's publications are copiously quoted, and this in a way that gives a reader the impression that Russell had foreseen the war.... In reality, the predictions of Russell quoted in the article referred to the 'great trouble,' the 'battle of Armageddon,' the 'end of all kingdoms' and the establishment of God's Kingdom on earth. *None of these events was fulfilled in 1914*, as Russell had predicted. On the other hand, what *did* come, the world war, could not be found among Russell's prophecies.[24]

A further examination of *The World Magazine* article and other Watch Tower sources establishes beyond doubt that Russell's predictions failed:

1. It is obvious that the headline, "END OF ALL KINGDOMS IN 1914," in reference to Russell's prediction, was not realized in that year or thereafter. Russell's statement in *The Time Is at Hand* is quoted in the article: "'In view of this strong Bible evidence,' Rev. Russell wrote in 1889, 'we consider it an established truth that the final end of the kingdoms of this world and the full establishment of the Kingdom of God will be accomplished by the end of A.D. 1914.'"[25] This obvious failure produced the following Witness explanation:

> Now, as factual evidences began to appear to verify the conclusions they had reached by Bible study, they were certain that October 1, 1914, brought a **legal end** to the 2,520 years of Jehovah's tolerance of the sovereignty assumed by the Gentile nations over the earth; **that legally the "end of all nations" had come in 1914**.... It was not to be expected that the clergy of Christendom would accept the evidences of the **legal "end of all nations."**[26]

No one could successfully argue that *The World Magazine* featured the headline, "END OF ALL KINGDOMS IN 1914," because of a prediction "that legally the 'end of all nations'" would be realized in that year!

2. What was Russell's view of Armageddon "and who would constitute the 'army of the Lord'"? The article writer explains that Russell "did not declare it as an absolute certainty, but reasoned that the great army which was to destroy the nations was the very army already being recruited by them in order to perpetuate their national lives."[27] In further explanation, Russell's *The Battle of Armageddon* was cited in the *World* article, where he quotes Joel 2:2-11 and explains its meaning:

> The Lord, by his overruling providence, will take a general change of this **great army of discontents—patriots, reformers, socialists, moralists, anarchists, ignorants and hopeless**—and use their hopes, fears, follies and selfishness, according to his divine wisdom, to work out his own grand purposes in the overthrow of present insti-

tutions, and for the preparation of man for the Kingdom of Righteousness. For this reason only it is termed "The *Lord's* great army."[28]

But, according to Rutherford's later "due time" commentary on Joel's prophecy, published in his book *Religion* (1940), Russell's interpretation of Joel **could not have been fulfilled in 1914**: "The prophecy of Joel specifically relates to religion and its final end.... The complete fulfillment of the prophecy of Joel **began to take place after A.D. 1918**, the date when Christ Jesus appeared at the temple of Jehovah for judgment...."[29] Joel's prophecy then is reinterpreted as applying to the period during Rutherford's presidency, and Joel 2:2-11 **represents God's "strange work," the witnessing activity of the Jehovah's Witnesses "locust army"** and Satan's opposition to it during the years prior to the judgment of Armageddon.[30]

3. In the following two paragraphs from *The World Magazine* article, the bold print indicates what was **not quoted** in any of the Watch Tower publications that cited it:

    > **Two years ago he wrote: "For forty years the Armageddon forces have been mustering for both sides of the great conflict. Strikes, lockouts and riots have been merely incidental skirmishes as the belligerents cross each other's paths. The lines of battle are daily becoming more distinctly marked. Nevertheless, Armageddon cannot yet be fought. Gentile Times have still two years to run."**

    > And in 1914 comes the war, the war which everybody dreaded but which everybody thought could not really happen. Reverend Russell is not saying, "I told you so;" and he is not revising the prophecies to suit the current history. He and his students are content to wait—to wait until October, which they figure to be the real end of 1914. **By that time, it is believed, the realignment will have taken place; the troops will have deserted their former banners and will have plunged into the universal war of classes; the nations will be tumbling headlong into anarchy; our whole social fabric will topple; our most cherished institutions will fall to rise no more. The United States will be no exception. And in some ways, may suffer worse than Europe.**[31]

    Note what was expected for the "real end of 1914." Were these predictions fulfilled?

4. What else did Russell teach that was mentioned in the article but was not fulfilled or was later rejected by Watch Tower Society leadership? "So the year 1914 is heralded not only as a time of trouble but as **the beginning of the great millennium.**"[32] "Every period in the world's history was examined by this scholar [Russell], and they all brought him to the same conclusion. They also convinced him that the **second coming of Christ, a spiritual presence, occurred in October, 1874, just six thousand years from the day that Adam was expelled from paradise.**"[33]

In conclusion, *The World Magazine* article, which stated that "the terrific war outbreak in Europe has fulfilled an extraordinary prophecy," cannot be used to support the Society's claim that Russell accurately predicted the beginning of World War I. Rather, it should be seen as another proof of prophetic failure.

Was 1914 as a Marked Year Evidence of God's Direction?

Over the years, Watch Tower publications have connected their prediction that 1914 was a marked year with a special insight or standing with God, as the following statements from *The Watchtower* illustrate. The August 1, 1971, magazine asks: "How could Jehovah's witnesses have known so far in advance what world leaders themselves did not know? Only by God's **holy spirit** making such prophetic truths known to them."[34] This claim was made again in the July 1, 1973, issue: "...*Zion's Watch Tower* of March 1880 had declared: 'The Times of the Gentiles' extend to 1914, and the heavenly kingdom will not have full sway till then.' Only God by his **holy spirit** could have revealed this to those early Bible students so far in advance."[35] The April 1, 1984, issue asks: "But how could they have had advance knowledge of such a momentous event? Not because of extraordinary human wisdom. No, but because they have **prayerfully studied the Scriptures**, heeded God's prophetic word and paid more than usual attention to what God's Son foretold (2 Peter 1:19; Hebrews 1:1, 2; 2:1)"[36] And finally, the October 15, 1990, magazine claims: "For 38 years prior to 1914, the Bible Students, as Jehovah's Witnesses were then called, pointed to that date as the year when the Gentile Times would end. **What outstanding proof that is that they were truly servants of Jehovah!** Yet, like first century servants of God, they also had some wrong expectations."[37]

Can the Bible Students be accurately identified as "holy spirit" led and as being prayerful students of Bible prophecy just because they predicted that 1914 would be a marked year in God's program? Is their prediction proof "that they were truly servants of Jehovah"? If so, what should be said of others who also saw 1914 as a significant year? It wasn't until recently that Watch Tower publications acknowledged this.

The *Awake!* magazine of November 8, 1994, points out that even before the 1879 *Zion's Watch Tower*, articles were published designating 1914 as a significant year: "in the middle of the 19th century—other students of the Bible had hinted that 1914 was possibly a year marked in Bible prophecy." A footnote explains:

> In 1844, a British clergyman, **E. B. Elliott**, drew attention to 1914 as a possible date for the end of the 'seven times' of Daniel chapter 4. In 1849, **Robert Seeley**, of London, dealt with the subject in like manner. **Joseph Seiss**, of the United States, pointed to 1914 as a significant date in Bible chronology in a publication edited about 1870. In 1875, **Nelson H. Barbour** wrote in his magazine *Herald of the Morning* that 1914 marked the end of a period that Jesus called the "appointed times of the nations."—Luke 21:24.[38]

A similar point is made in *Jehovah's Witnesses—Proclaimers of God's Kingdom* (1993), adding John A. Brown.[39] What both of these Watch Tower sources do not tell the reader is that, except for Barbour, Russell's mentor, the others

> *used a chronology that dated the desolation of Jerusalem to 588 or 587 B.C.E.* (not 606 B.C.E. as in Russell's writings).
>
> Although all of them based their calculations on chronologies that were **rejected** by Russell and his followers, the Society claims that these expositors "could see that 1914 was clearly marked by Bible prophecy." How they "could see" this "clearly" by using chronologies that the Society still holds to be false is certainly puzzling.[40]

It was Nelson H. Barbour who met with C. T. Russell in 1876 and who convinced him of Christ's invisible presence since 1874. "It is apparent that during these meetings Russell accepted not only the 1874 date but *all* of Barbour's time calculations, including his calculation of the Gentile times."[41]

Some Others Who Made Predictions

In his discussion of the "Signs of the Times," **Mormon Apostle** Bruce R. McConkie begins his discussion: "In every age the Lord sends forth clearly discernible *signs* and *warnings* so that those who are spiritually inclined can know of his hand-dealings with men."[42] Before listing them, McConkie writes: "By the power of the Holy Ghost the faithful saints are able to discern the signs of the times, signs preparatory to and part of this final great dispensation...."[43] Later, he relates that the spirit of inspiration rested upon Mormon President Wilford Woodruff. On June 24, 1894, he said: "'Calamities and troubles are increasing in the earth, and there is a meaning to these things.... Great changes are at our doors. The next 20 years will see mighty changes among the nations of the earth' (*Discourses of Wilford Woodruff*, p. 230). It is interesting to note that almost 20 years later to the day, June 28, 1914, the Archduke Ferdinand of Austria was assassinated, thus initiating the first World War."[44]

In his book, *Our Near Future: A Message to All the Governments and People of Earth* (1896), William A. Redding explains:

> ..."Gentile times" will end, 1896 A.D.; but the governments of earth will be permitted to stand and dwindle downward eighteen years longer ... and this makes their final end and disappearing from earth occur 1914 A.D., as eighteen years added to 1896 makes 1914, which is just 2520 years from 606 B.C.... The present order of things will be made desolate and its *total* destruction will occur by 1915 A.D."[45]

J. Bernard Nicklin makes reference to two books that he had acquired before World War I:

> *The Approaching End of the Age* by Dr. Grattan Guinness, published in 1878, and *Christ is Coming* by T. H. Salmon. From these we had gathered that the "Times of the Gentiles," a long period of 2520 years, would begin to expire in an epoch commencing about 1914-1915.... Salmon had suggested it would see war on a grand scale. "It appears probable that some time between now [1910] and 1914," he wrote (p. 99), "the nations will be at war." Thus, in the summer of 1914, when the Great War began, it certainly seemed that the outcome of the researches of these scholars had been proved correct by events.[46]

Nichlin also refers to David Davidson, author of *The Great Pyramid: Its Divine Message*, who on the basis of Great Pyramid measurements fixed the date of August 4-5, 1914, which marked "Britain's entry into World War I."[47] It should also be remembered that Russell taught that the Great Pyramid of Gizeh (later identified as a "monument of demonism")[48] verified the 1914 date. In his *Thy Kingdom Come* (1891), Russell writes: "Thus the Pyramid witnesses that the close of 1914 will be the beginning of the time of trouble such as was not since there was a nation—no, nor ever shall be afterward."[49]

In 1887, Blanton Duncan published *The Near Approach of Christ's Second Advent,* which gave his interpretation of the time-prophecies of Daniel and the end of "times of the Gentiles." Duncan "arrived at the date 1913-1914, believing that to be the time when some wonderful event would take place, and that the event would doubtless be the second coming of Christ."[50]

Andrew N. Dugger, Church of God (Seventh Day) minister, became editor of *The Bible Advocate* in 1914. He explained how his father, Andrew F. Dugger, concluded "years before" "that a great war would break out sometime between 1912 and 1914." This was based on his father's interpretation of Leviticus 26:27-28 and the "seven times" mentioned there. He also concluded that in 1914 with the restoration of "the Jewish state would end what Jesus called the 'times of the Gentiles.' ... With their passing, Duggar believed

Jesus' return could not be far behind."[51]

One might ask, should German Chancellor (1871-90) Otto von Bismarck (without a Bible formula) be viewed as also having special prophetic insight when he predicted a short time before his death in 1898: "If there is ever another war in Europe, it will come out of some damned silly thing in the Balkans"? This prediction was fulfilled by the assassination of Archduke Franz Ferdinand, Austrian heir apparent, by Serbian nationalist Gavrilo Princip, in Sarajevo, on June 28, 1914.[52]

And finally, how can 1914 be used as a proof of special insight or standing with God when the events predicted by Russell were 100 percent **unfulfilled?**

Notes

1. Each of these *Watchtowers* quote the identical portion of the March 1880 *Watch Tower:* 1 May 1952, 260-61; 1 Aug. 1971, 468; 1 July 1973, 402; 1 Apr. 1984, 6, 16; 15 Apr. 1984, 3; 1 Dec. 1984, 16. It also appears in *Awake!*, 22 Oct. 1989, 20.
2. *From Paradise Lost to Paradise Regained* (1958), 170.
3. *"You Will Be Done on Earth"* (1958), 268.
4. *Man's Salvation Out of World's Distress at Hand!* (1975), 136.
5. Alan Rogerson, *Millions Now Living Will Never Die* (London: Constable, 1969), 20-21.
6. Russell, *Thy Kingdom Come* (1891), 234; Russell, *The Battle of Armageddon* (1897), 621.
7. Russell, *The Time Is at Hand* (1889), 101.
8. *WTR*, March 1880, 82.
9. Russell, *Thy Kingdom Come*, 126. In later printings the words "at A.D. 1914" would be changed to "after 1914."
10. Russell, *The Battle of Armageddon*, 624.
11. Ibid., 625.
12. *WT*, 1 Dec. 1984, 17.
13. *Jehovah's Witnesses—Proclaimers of God's Kingdom* (1993), 135.
14. Russell, *The Time Is at Hand*, 76-78.
15. Carl Olof Jonsson, *The Gentile Times Reconsidered* (3rd ed.; Atlanta Commentary Press, 1998), 63.
16. Ibid., 70-71.
17. Raymond Franz, *Crisis of Conscience* (2nd ed.; Atlanta: Commentary Press, 1992), 155.
18. Robert Crompton, *Counting the Days to Armageddon* (Cambridge: James Clarke & Co., 1996), 83.
19. *GA*, 13 Feb. 1924, 306. In the response it is interesting that the *Golden Age* writer stated earlier: "We cannot undertake here to quote at any considerable length from Pastor Russell's writings **as to his expectations regarding 1914**"—who then quotes briefly from the January 1881 *Watch Tower*, which claims that the Jewish and Gospel ages are parallel (30 A.D.–70 A.D., 1874-1914). Why not just list the seven predictions in *The Time Is at Hand* (76-78) as a test of Russell's predictions as to their success or failure?
20. Without an exhaustive search it was found that *The World Magazine* article was cited 22 times in Watch Tower publications: *WT*: 15 Aug 1989, 13; 1 Apr. 1984, 5; 15 June 1974, 355; 15 Sept. 1971, 560; 1 Aug. 1971, 468; 1 Feb. 1969, 71; 15 Feb. 1967, 110; 15 Oct. 1961, 631; 15 July 1960, 433; 1 Jan. 1955, 8; 15 Mar. 1955, 173; 1 May 1952, 260. *Awake!*: 8 May 1981, 7; 8 Apr. 1975, 15; 8 Oct. 1973, 17; 8 Apr. 1972, 20; 8 Oct. 1968, 12. *Jehovah's Witnesses—Proclaimers of God's Kingdom* (1993), 60; *Insight on the Scriptures*, vol. 1 (1988), 135; *Revelation—Its Grand Climax*

at Hand! (1988), 105. *Aid to Bible Understanding* (1971), 96; *Jehovah's Witnesses in the Divine Purpose* (1959), 54-55.

21. *Proclaimers*, 60.
22. *Jehovah's Witnesses in the Divine Purpose* (1959), 54-55.
23. Ibid.
24. Carl Olof Jonsson and Wolfgang Herbst, *The Sign of the Last Days—When?* (Atlanta: Commentary Press, 1987), 133.
25. *The World Magazine*, 4, quoting *The Time Is at Hand*, 99. On page 101 Russell writes: "Be not surprised, then, when in subsequent chapters we present proofs that the setting up of the Kingdom of God is already begun ... and that the 'battle of the great day of God Almighty' (Rev. 16:14), which will end in A.D. 1914 with the complete overthrow of earth's present rulership, is already commenced."
26. *Jehovah's Witnesses in the Divine Purpose*, 55.
27. *World Magazine*, 4.
28. Ibid., quoting *The Battle of Armageddon*, 550. Russell made some other predictions in this book which did not materialize: The combined religious power of Christendom will be utterly futile against the rising tide of anarchy when the dread crisis is reached [in 1914]" (552).... "While the time of trouble and distress of this day of the Lord will be first and specially upon Christendom, and eventually upon all nations, the final blast, we are informed by the Prophet Ezekiel (38:8-12), will be upon the people of Israel regathered in Palestine.... All men are witnesses to the fact that such a gathering of Israel to Palestine is begun..." (552-53).

  "...The final conflict of the battle of the great day will be in the land of Palestine" (354).... In the midst of the trouble God will reveal himself as Israel's defender as in ancient times, when his favor was with them nationally" (555).
29. Rutherford, *Religion* (1940), 111-12.
30. See *Religion*, 168-203 for Rutherford's commentary on Joel 2:2-11; *WT*, 15 July 1939, 211-19 and *WT*, 1 Aug. 1939, 228-32. See also the *WT*, 15 July 1979, 16-17, for a brief interpretation of the Joel 2:1-11 passage.
31. *World Magazine*, 17.
32. Ibid.
33. Ibid. The 1874 date was changed to 1914 and the six thousand years was changed to end in 1975.
34. *WT*, 1 Aug. 1971, 468.
35. *WT*, 1 July 1973, 402.
36. *WT*, 1 Apr. 1984, 16.
37. *WT*, 15 Oct. 1990, 19. "C. T. Russell wrote an article entitled 'Gentile Times: When Do They End?,' which was published in the magazine *Bible Examiner*, October 1876. On page 27 the article said: 'The seven times will end in A.D. 1914'" (ibid.).
38. *Awake!*, 8 Nov. 1994, 10.
39. *Proclaimers*, 134. See Jonsson's *The Gentile Times Reconsidered* for a review of J. A. Brown's views and his influence on apocalyptic thought (32-36) and how the *Proclaimers* book distorts Brown's position (67-69).
40. Jonsson, 69-70.
41. Ibid., 49. In recounting the meetings with Barbour, Russell wrote: "...I had much to learn from him concerning time..." *(WTR*, 15 July 1906, 3822).
42. Bruce McConkie, *Mormon Doctrine* (2nd ed.; Salt Lake City: Bookcraft, 1966), 715.
43. Ibid., 716.

44. Ibid., 728.

45. William A. Redding, *Our Near Future* (Peekskill-on-Hudson, N.Y.: Ernest Loomis & Co., 1896), 25, 29-30.

46. J. Bernard Nicklin, *Signposts of History* (Merrimac, Mass.: Destiny Publishers, 1956), 19. Guinness had proposed not one, but many terminal dates in God's prophetic scheme. According to Jonsson, the most important "were 1915, 1917, 1923 and 1934" (Jonsson, 236).

47. Ibid., 64.

48. *WT*, 15 Nov. 1955, 697.

49. *Thy Kingdom Come* (1891, 1903 ed.), 342; *WT*, 15 Oct. 1913, 5336.

50. Blanton Duncan, *The Near Approach of Christ's Second Advent* (Louisville, Ky.: Bradley and Gilbert, 1887), 15, in Wayne A. Scriven, "Date-Setting in America for the Second Coming of Christ During the Late Nineteenth and Early Twentieth Century" (M.A. Thesis, Seventh-Day Adventist Theological Seminary, 1947), 66-67.

51. Ralph G. Orr, "How Anglo-Israelism Entered Seventh-Day Churches of God" (paper presented to the Conference on Faith and History, So. Calif. Chapter, March 26, 1999), 22-23. The formula followed by Dugger was: the "seven times" of the Leviticus text equal seven years of 360 days; the 2,520 days equal 2,520 years; the chastisement of the Jews "began to climax with Nebuchnezzar's first siege of Jerusalem," which he dated "606 B.C. He next calculated 2,520 years forward and came to 1914 (ibid). Russell also used this same argument based on the "seven times" of Leviticus 26:28 (*WTR*, 15 Oct. 1909, 4497; 1 Aug. 1911, 4867; 1 Nov. 1914, 5564).

52. This was "said to Herr Ballen 'towards the end of [Bismarck's] life,' and related by Ballen to Winston S. Churchill a fortnight before World War I. See *Hansard*, Vol. 413, col. 84)" (*The Oxford Dictionary of Quotations* (3rd ed.; New York: Oxford University Press, 1979), 84).

11.

The "Seven Times" of Daniel 4:16

This chapter deals briefly with two questions: (1) Does Nebuchadnezzar's "seven times" experience have a larger fulfillment, and (2) are the "seven times" actually seven years in length? Each question is important to the Witnesses' prophetic scheme. If Nebuchadnezzar's experience does not relate to the "times of the Gentiles" (or "appointed times of the nations" *NWT*), and the "seven times" cannot be shown to be seven years, the dating system for 1914 is gone, without further arguments needed.

Do the "Seven Times" Have a Larger Fulfillment?

Daniel 4:4-27 gives the account of Nebuchanezzar's dream and its interpretation. Jehovah's Witnesses claim that Nebuchadnezzar's period of madness (vv. 25, 33) had a larger fulfillment and symbolized the Gentile nations who would have dominion during the "appointed times of the nations." The "seven times" (vv. 16, 23, 25, 32) were literal in Nebuchadnezzar's experience, and they say that by comparison with Revelation 12:6, 14, the "seven times" of Daniel are to be understood as 2,520 days, which are to be converted into years, which ran out in 1914.

In answer, there is no good reason to accept such an interpretation. But beyond this, there are some pertinent questions and observations that should be stated:

1. Where in the Bible does one find that Nebuchadnezzar's dream has any connection with the "times of the Gentiles" (Luke 21:24)? After examining the Witnesses' claim, Carl Olof Jonsson concludes:

   > In Daniel 4 and Luke 21 the word "times" is explicitly applied to two quite different periods—the "seven times" to the period of Nebuchadnezzar's madness, and the "times of the Gentiles" to the period of the trampling down of Jerusalem—and the two periods may be equalized only by giving them greater application beyond that given in the texts themselves. Therefore, the supposed connection between the "times of the Gentiles" at Luke 21:24 and the "seven times" at Daniel 4:16, 23, 25, and 32 **appears to be no more than a conjecture.**[1]

2. How could Nebuchadnezzar picture Gentile dominion or rule during his "seven times" of madness, **when he was not ruling?** Daniel's interpretation of the dream is clear at this point: "And you they will be driving away from men, and with the beasts of the field your dwelling will come to be, ... and seven times themselves will pass over you, until you know that the Most High is Ruler in the kingdom of mankind...." (4:25 *NWT*). The fulfillment which began twelve months later is stated in verse 33.

3. The dream, its interpretation, its fulfillment, and the restoration sequence of Nebuchadnezzar are all that are required for an understanding of the passage. Any attempt to give a future prophetic fulfillment to this portion of Scripture is nothing more than an assumption.[2]

4. Using the "seven times" as seven years formula, there is no objective evidence that the "times of the Gentiles" were terminated in 1914.

Are the "seven times" seven years?

While the Jehovah's Witnesses and even non-Witness commentators have interpreted the meaning of "seven times" in Daniel 4:16 as being "seven years," many prominent Bible scholars do not agree. For example:

Exegete Carl F. Keil writes: "Whether these times are to be understood as years, months, or weeks, is not said, and **cannot at all be determined**."[3]

Professor of Old Testament Edward J. Young comments: "This is to be done until *seven times* (or periods of time, the length not being stated) *pass over him*. Since the length of the times is not stated, **we are not warranted in identifying the duration in terms of years**."[4]

> The Aramaic word means a fixed and definite period of time. But I do not see how it is possible to determine the length of such a period. All that is meant is that seven such periods must pass before the king's reason returns to him. **Possibly *years* are intended but this is by no means certain**.... The positive teaching of this vs. is simply that for a definite period of time, **the exact length of which is not stated**, Neb. will be deprived of his reason.[5]

In his answer to critics concerning Daniel's account of Nebuchadnezzar's period of madness and the meaning of "seven times," Old Testament scholar Robert Dick Wilson, writes:

> That translation of "seven years" **is possible, but not necessarily correct**. The word rendered "years" is not the ordinary word for year (*shana*), but a word which means a fixed or appointed time (`*iddan* or `*adan*). It seems to be a word of Babylonian origin, meaning "fixed time," and is equivalent often to the Greek *kairos*.... To be sure, the old version of the Seventy renders this passage by "seven years"; but the version of Theodotion has "seven seasons" (*kairoi*), the Latin Vulgate has *tempora*, and the Arabic has "times" (`*azminatin*).[6]

In his article on Nebuchadnezzar in *The New Bible Dictionary*, Assyriologist Donald J. Wiseman views the "seven times" of his madness as "seven **months**,"[7] and in his commentary on Daniel, John E. Goldingay translates: "seven periods are to pass by for him" (end note: "not 'years'....")[8]

Old Testament professor J. Barton Payne concludes: "The duration of the *seven times* **is uncertain**. The unit of measure might be months, or seasons, or years, though **seven full years would be the more difficult to integrate into the known historical situation**."[9]

Researcher Carl Olof Jonsson comments on the difficulty alluded to by Payne. On the basis of the **documented activities of Nebuchadnezzar's rule** (presented by Jonsson),[10] "it is difficult to find a period of seven years within his reign of 43 years when he was absent from his throne or inactive as ruler."[11] This does not question Daniel's account of Nebuchanezzar's madness, but does argue that the "seven times" **were a time period of less than seven years**.[12]

Notes

1. Carl Olof Jonsson, *The Gentile Times Reconsidered* (3rd ed.; Atlanta: Commentary Press, 1998), 244.

2. The treatment in the Witnesses' *"All Scripture Is Inspired of God and Beneficial"* (1963) illustrates the point that the "tree vision" requires no additional fulfillment and is included for our instruction (140, 142). That Daniel 4 is of larger prophetic significance and Nebuchanezzar's "seven times" prefigures the duration of years (2,520) of the "times of the Gentiles" is found in writings of some writers in the **nineteenth century** and was not unique when Russell accepted the theory. The book *Three World's* (1877) written primarily by Barbour (with Russell on the title page) sees the "seven times" as seven prophetic years, which represent 2,520 years, which "is the measure of the 'times of the Gentiles'" (81). Russell accepted the view that this passage had prophetic significance from N. H. Barbour.

   Of all the commentaries examined I did not find one twentieth century writer who either held to or even mentioned the interpretation of the "tree vision" found in Watch Tower publications. Nineteenth century writers who set forth the position include: H. Grattan Guiness, *The Approaching End of the Age* (first published 1878); R. C. Shimeall, *The Second Coming of Christ* (1873); E. B. Elliott, *Horae Apocalypticae* (1851).

3. C. F. Keil and F. Delitzsch, *Commentary on the Old Testament*, C. F. Keil, *Ezekiel, Daniel* (Grand Rapids: Wm. B. Eerdmans, n.d.), 153.

4. Edward J. Young, "Daniel," *The New Bible Commentary* (2nd ed.; Grand Rapids: Wm. B. Eerdmans, 1954), 673.

5. Edward J. Young, *The Prophecy of Daniel: A Commentary* (Grand Rapids: Wm. B. Eerdmans, 1949), 105.

6. Robert Dick Wilson, *Studies in the Book of Daniel* (New York: G. P. Putnam's Sons, 1917), 289.

7. Donald J. Wiseman, "Nebuchadnezzar," *The New Bible Dictionary* (Grand Rapids: Wm. B. Eerdmans, 1962), 873.

8. John E. Goldingay, *Word Bible Commentary*, vol. 30 Daniel (Dallas: Word Books, 1989), 78, 81.

9. Barton Payne, *Encyclopedia of Biblical Prophecy* (Grand Rapids: Baker Books, 1973), 377.

10. Jonsson, 254.

11. Ibid., 253.

12. For a more detailed discussion of the "seven times" question see Jonsson, 253-56; Young, *The Prophecy of Daniel*, 105.

12.

The Year-Day Theory
(Principle)

In the Witnesses' interpretation, the 2,520 days (based on Daniel's "seven times" and Revelation's 3½ times or "time, and times and half a time") were converted into years and the extent of the "times of the nations" was calculated (607 B.C. + 2,520 years = A.D. 1914). The arithmetic is simple, but is the year-day theory or principle valid? What is the origin of the year-day principle? Carl Olof Jonsson found that "the use of the year-day principle was relatively common among Jewish sources from early centuries," but Cistercian Abbot Joachim of Floris (Fiore) (c. 1130-1202)

> was probably the first *Christian* expositor to apply the year-day principle to the different time periods of Daniel and Revelation. This was pointed out during the last century by *Charles Maitland*, a leading opponent of the idea, in a number of works and articles. Joachim's works initiated a new tradition of interpretation, a tradition in which the "year-day principle" was the very basis of prophetic interpretations. During the following centuries, innumerable dates were fixed for Christ's second advent, most of them built upon the year-day principle.[1]

The year-day principle was very popular among interpreters of prophecy in the nineteenth century. For example, in *Hints on the Interpretation of Prophecy* (1842), Prof. Moses Stuart observes:

> It is a *singular fact* THAT THE GREAT MASS OF INTERPRETERS in the English and American world have, for many years, been wont to understand the *days* designated in Daniel and the Apocalypse as the *representatives or symbols of years*. I have found it difficult to trace the origin of this GENERAL, *I might say* ALMOST UNIVERSAL, CUSTOM.... For a long time these principles have been so current among the expositors of the English and American world that scarcely a serious attempt to vindicate them has of late been made. They have been regarded as *so plain*, and so well *fortified* against *all objections*, that *most expositors* have deemed it quite useless even to attempt to defend them."[2]

In 1818, after a two-year study of the Bible, William Miller, a New England Baptist farmer, applied the year-day principle and established a date for the return of Christ and other end-time events. Various dates were set in 1843 and 1844, and later Miller frankly admitted that he was wrong. It was from the Second

Adventists, who had predicted that the world would end in 1873-1874, specifically Nelson H. Barbour and John H. Paton, that Russell adopted the system which incorporated the year-day principle.[3]

English Biblical scholar Samuel P. Tregelles (1813-1875) decisively refuted this theory in his book *Remarks on the Prophetic Visions in the Book of Daniel*, first published in 1852.[4] A more recent extensive examination of the history of the year-day principle and its problems is found in Carl Olof Jonsson's *The Gentile Times Reconsidered* (1998).[5] It is interesting to learn that former Millerite George Storrs, named several times in the *Proclaimers* book as Russell's mentor and friend, came to regard "**the year-day theory as nonsense. In an** article in *Herald of Life and the Coming Kingdom* of 2 October 1867, he congratulates his old adversary Dr. Josiah Litch for abandoning the theory."[6] N. H. Barbour reported that when he contacted Fitch in 1860, whom he regarded as "one of God's mighty men" in the Millerite movement, "Bro. Fitch, in a very kind but positive manner, informed him that **all these prophetic periods were literal days, still in the future, and hence to listen would be a waste of time.**"[7]

The year-day theory must establish its validity on a Scriptural foundation to be true. Several lines of argument may be used to demonstrate that it is not valid. Numbers 14:33-34 and Ezekiel 4:5-6 are interpreted to mean that "with God each day counts for a year." Numbers 14:33-34 simply states that because of sin Israel was to suffer "by the number of the days that YOU spied out the land, forty days, a day for a year, you will answer for YOUR errors forty years..." (*NWT*). On this passage, Milton S. Terry (1840-1914) concludes: "Here then is certainly no ground upon which to base the universal proposition that, in prophetic designations of time, a day means a year. The passage is exceptional and explicit, and the words are used in a strictly literal sense; the days evidently mean days, and the years mean years."[8] And so with Ezekiel 4:5-6: "The days of his prostration were literal days, and they were typical of years, as is explicitly stated. But to derive from this symbolico-typical action of Ezekiel a hermeneutical principle or law of universal application, namely, that days in prophecy mean years, would be a most unwarrantable procedure."[9] Terry's comments were written while Russell was still alive, and since that time Rutherford and other Watch Tower writers have **also denied the universal application of the year-day theory in prophecy**, as will be further examined below.

Another argument against the year-day principle is that those who have utilized it and made predictions concerning the Second Coming of Christ and other end time events have failed. Terry expands the point:

> We have lived to see his [William Miller's] theories thoroughly exploded, and yet there have not been wanting others who have adopted his hermeneutical principles, and made A.D. 1866 and A.D. 1870 [and 1873, 74 and many other dates] as the "time of the end." A theory which is so destitute of scriptural analogy and support ... and presumes to rest on such a slender showing of divine authority, is on those grounds alone to be suspected; but when it has again and again proved to be false and misleading in its application, we may safely reject it, as furnishing no valid principle or rule in a true science of hermeneutics.[10]

In his book *Counting the Days to Armageddon* (1996), Robert Crompton explains that he was raised by Witness parents who became involved in the movement during the mid-1940s. He served as a special pioneer in the early 1960s until he "began to have some serious doubts about Watch Tower doctrine." One of his concerns was with the arbitrary application of the year-day principle, which the Watch Tower Society followed in the "seven times" of Daniel 4 and in Daniel's "seventy weeks" in chapter 9. "However, it is not followed for the interpretation of certain periods which occupy an apparently secondary place in the overall system, namely, the 1,260 days, 1,290 days, and 1,335 days of Daniel 12 and the 2,300 days of Daniel 8."[11]

Upon investigation, he discovered that Watch Tower Society founder Pastor Russell

> **had expounded a system of interpretation of prophecy which was very different from present Watch Tower teaching**. As a loyal Witness, I had always supposed that the development of doctrine had proceeded by the gradual addition of detail, together with minor corrections, to an underlying structure which remained unchanged. In fact, this was not at all the pattern which I discovered; **rather, one system had apparently been replaced by another which was, in some significant respects, less detailed and exhibited less internal consistency.**[12]

In agreement with Crompton, reviewing what happened to the year-day principle since Russell's death, Jonsson writes:

> This concept is no longer accepted as a *general principle* by the Watch Tower Society. **It was taken over by Pastor Russell from the Second Adventists**, but was abandoned by the Society's second president, J. F. Rutherford, in the 1920's and early 1930's. The 2,300 evenings and mornings (Daniel 8:14), and the 1,260, 1,290, and 1,335 days (Daniel 12:7, 11, 12; Revelation 11:2, 3, 12:6,14), earlier held to be as many *years*, have since then been interpreted to mean *days* only.[13]

Jonsson concludes: "To apply the year-day principle to the 'seven times' of Daniel 4, then, is evidently **quite arbitrary**, and this is especially true if those doing the applying no longer apply that principle to other prophetic periods."[14]

The following quotations illustrate the point that days were viewed as year-days by Russell, but were later viewed differently:

> Take another line of prophecy: we find that the 1,260 days, and the 1,290 days, and the 1,335 days, so particularly set forth in Daniel's prophecy, and corroborated in Revelation, **have had fulfillments;—the 1,260 days ending in 1799, the 1,290 days ending in 1829 and the 1,335 days ending in 1874.** Our friends known as "Second Adventists" were wont to use these "days of Daniel," and once applied them as we do here: but they abandoned them after 1874 passed and they failed to see Jesus with their natural eyesight.... **The fault is not with the days nor with their application as above; but with the wrong things expected.**[15]

In Rutherford's *The Harp of God* (1921 and 1928 editions), in agreement with Russell, he applies the year-day principle to the 1,260 days (which end 1799) and 1,335 days (which end 1874).[16] But the year after the 1928 edition was published, Rutherford followed in the footsteps of the Second Adventists (referred to by Russell) and changed his interpretation to **literal days**: "The 1260-day period ended in **April, 1918**. The 1290-day period ended **September, 1922**,"[17] and the 1,335-day period ended in **May, 1926**.[18]

The 2,300 days of Daniel 8:14—Another Example

The 2,300 days of Daniel 8:14 is another example where Watch Tower publications used the year-day principle in interpreting Scripture and subsequently dropped its application. The verse states: "Until two thousand three hundred days, then shall the sanctuary be cleansed." In 1891, Russell explained:

> In the examination of this period of time the student is at once struck with the fact that **literal days cannot be meant**; because 2300 literal days would be less than eight years, and yet the

prophecy evidently covers all the long period of the defiling of the Sanctuary and the treading down of the truth.[19]

...The **autumn of 1846, marks the end of the vision of the 2300 days, and the date when the Sanctuary was due to be cleansed.** This prophecy being fulfilled, we should expect, in this as in other cases of fulfilled prophecy, to find the facts proving its fulfillment clearly set forth on the pages of history....[20]

And, as though God would arrange that thereafter there should always be a class representing his Sanctuary cleansed, kept separate from the various sects, this very year **1846** witnessed the organization of Protestant sects into one great system, called *The Evangelical Alliance.*[21]

The 2,300 days point to **1846 as the time when God's sanctuary would be cleansed of the defiling errors and principles of Papacy**; and we have noted the cleansing there accomplished.[22]

That the 2300 days terminated in 1846 was still taught by Russell in 1914:

Another prophetic period mentioned by the Prophet Daniel was the 2300 days. This period was to mark certain things, and at the expiration of these days the sanctuary was to be cleansed. This work of cleansing the true church, the sanctuary class, from the defilements of the dark ages culminated, we believe, **in 1846, the time of the fulfillment of the 2300 days.**[23]

In 1933, Rutherford's interpretation of the 2300 days changed radically:

It would therefore be **entirely foreign to the prophecy to conclude that the cleansing of the sanctuary took place in A.D. 1846** by the formation of the Evangelical Alliance, which alliance was part of the **Devil's organization.**[24]

2300 DAYS According to the proof set forth in the December 15 (1929) *Watchtower,* the **'days,' or time clearly appear to be literal, and not symbolic**; hence the reader is referred to that *Watchtower* for the proof that the 'days of Daniel' **are literal** and are to be calculated as such, and **are not symbolic.**[25]

Beginning to count from the *transgression* resulting by reason of the League of Nations, and the giving of notice, which must **begin May 25, 1926**, the twenty-three hundred days, or six years, four months, and twenty days, would **end October 15, 1932.**[26]

...What, then, took place at the end of the twenty-three-hundred-day period? *The Watchtower,* issues of August 15 and September 1, 1932, brought before God's people the Scriptural proof that **the office of "elective elder,"** chosen or selected by vote of creatures, does not Scripturally exist, and that therefore **the selection of elders by such means should end.**[27]

In Rutherford's booklet *World Recovery* (1934), this explanation was affirmed again, and he claimed that "within the past few months **the Lord has made clear the meaning of the cleansing of the sanctuary.**

(Daniel 8:13, 14)."[28]

Writing in 1958, F. W. Franz gives the same dates for the 2300 days (May 25, 1926, to October 15, 1932), and asks: "How was Jehovah's 'sanctuary' cleansed, vindicated or restored to its rightful state by that date?" He explains that it was accomplished by a resolution on October 5, 1932 (published in the October 15 *Watchtower*), that "called for a cleansing of the congregational organization, a restoring of it to the rightful state of Jehovah's sanctuary class. How? By the **ridding of the organization of 'elective elders'** [elected by democratic vote]...."[29]

Jehovah's Witnesses in the Divine Purpose (1959) attributes the "cleansing" notification to God Himself:

> ...The announcement in the *Watch Tower* magazine of October 15, 1932, at the exact end of the time period mentioned in Daniel's prophecy, was the **official notification made by Jehovah through his visible channel of communication** that his sanctuary had been cleansed and had been restored to its rightful state as regards the **elimination of this democratic procedure in electing elders**.[30]

After the foregoing specific application and dates of the 2300 days were attributed to Jehovah by Rutherford and his successors, one wonders about that claim after reading a **radically new** and detailed interpretation in the December 1, 1971, *Watchtower*.[31] While it is identified as a "clarification of beliefs,"[32] in actuality it is a **completely new interpretation**. The previous understandings of fulfilled prophecy are not even mentioned. The new view is summarized in this quotation from the *1975 Yearbook*:

> Though Jehovah's people did not then realize it, what they did organizationally **in 1944** evidently had Biblical significance. Daniel's prophecy had foretold that for **2,300** "evenings and mornings," or days, a symbolic 'small horn' (the Anglo-American World Power) would trample Jehovah's theocratic 'holy place' as represented by Jesus' anointed followers on earth (Dan. 8:9-14). **This occurred during World War II.** At the beginning of the foretold 2,300 days the two-part article "Organization" appeared in *The Watchtower* (June 1 and June 15, 1938)....
>
> If counted from **June 1, 1938,** the 2,300 days extended to **October 8, 1944.** Or, if reckoned from **June 15, 1938,** they ended on **October 22, 1944.** At the end of that period, **theocratic organization again was emphasized** by the organizational talks and adjustments at the convention and annual meeting of September 30 to October 2, 1944 ... and in articles on theocratic organization published in *The Watchtower* of October 15 ... and November 1, 1944....[33]

Raymond Franz sees this kind of interpretation as illustrating "the fallacy of **provincialism**"—"the organization's depicting itself as the central figure of various Bible prophecies."[34] As shown by this and other examples, it is obvious that Watch Tower interpretations are subject to change at will to serve organizational purposes.

In conclusion, from a study of its history and the record of its application and failure, the year-day principle is not a valid approach to the interpretation of prophecy.

Notes

1. Carl Olof Jonsson, *The Gentile Times Reconsidered* (3rd ed.; Atlanta: Commentary Press, 1998), 27-28. An informative history of Joachim is found in Marjorie Reeves', *Joachim of Fiore and the Prophetic*

Future. New York: Harper & Row, 1976. Some sources have the name Jochim of **Flora**. Reeves says **Fiore** is the proper spelling (Preface).

2. Isaac C. Wellcome, *History of the Second Advent Message and Mission, Doctrine and People* (Yarmouth, Maine: Isaac C. Wellcome, 1874), 460-61, quoting *Hints*.

3. *WTR*, 15 July 1906, 3822.

4. Samuel P. Tregelles, *Remarks on the Prophetic Visions in the Book of Daniel* (6th ed.; London: Samuel Baxter and Sons, 1883), 112-27. The section is titled "Note on the 'Year-Day' System." A short article by Roy L. Aldrich, "Can the End of the Age be Computed by the Year-Day Theory?" was published in the April 1958 issue of *Bibliotheca Sacra*, 159-65. Aldrich concludes his article with the statement: "It is time that the year-day theory was recognized for what it is—a principle of error, the use of which contradicts the clear teaching of Christ that the time of His coming is secret" (165).

5. Jonsson, chapter 1; 251-53.

6. M. James Penton, *Apocalypse Delayed* (2nd ed.; Toronto: University of Toronto Press, 1997), 341 n27.

7. Nelson H. Barbour, *Evidences for the Coming of the Lord in 1873: or the Midnight Cry* (2nd ed.; Rochester, NY: Nelson H. Barbour, 1871), 34. In 1867, Fitch "published a **rejection of the prophetic day-literal year formula** as a general principle of hermeneutics. Noting that the standard proof texts were unrelated to the issue of prophecy, he concluded that the 2,300 days were literal days. 'The burden of proof ... that some other rule has been given rests on those who maintain the year-day theory, not on those who reject the theory'" (Eric Anderson, "The Millerite Use of Prophecy," in *The Disappointed* edited by Roland L. Numbers and Jonathan M. Butler [Bloomington: Indiana University Press, 1987], 81). The chapter deals with "A Case of a 'Striking Fulfillment'"—the predicted fall of the Ottoman Turks on August 11, 1840, by Josiah Litch employing the year-day principle—a principle which he later rejected.

8. Milton S. Terry, *Biblical Hermeneutics* (2nd ed.; Grand Rapids: Zondervan, n.d.), 387.

9. Ibid. Terry cites a number of Scripture references that do not support the year-day view. For example, are the "seven days" and "forty days and forty nights" of Genesis 7:4 to be understood as years? Should Jonah's prophecy (Jonah 3:4) announcing the judgment of Nineveh be interpreted as symbolizing forty years? Should the sixty-five years of Isaiah 7:8; the three years of Isaiah 16:14 and the seventy years of Jeremiah 25:12 be multiplied by 360 and then converted into years to get the proper understanding? The year-day theory cannot be supported by the only possible understanding of other prophecies, that which Terry calls, "the analogy of prophetic scriptures (ibid., 387-88).

10. Ibid., 389-90.

11. Robert Crompton, *Counting the Days to Armageddon: Jehovah's Witnesses and the Second Coming of Christ* (Cambridge: James Clark & Co., 1996), 9.

12. Ibid.

13. Jonsson, 251-52.

14. Ibid., 252.

15. *WT*, 15 Mar. 1902, 2978.

16. Rutherford, *The Harp of God* (1921 ed.), 229-30; (1928 ed.), 234-35.

17. *WT*, 15 Dec. 1929, 377.

18. The statement in the December 15, 1929, *Watchtower* is not as clear as this one: "The feast, beginning in 1922, later reached that state of blessedness spoken of by the prophet, to wit, 'Blessed is he that waiteth, and cometh to the thousand three hundred and five and thirty days [the year 1926]" (*WT*, 15 Oct. 1935, 312).

19. Russell, *Thy Kingdom Come* (1891), 105.

20. Ibid., 108.
21. Ibid., 119.
22. Ibid., 305-06. It is of interest that in 1878, when Russell was an assistant editor of N. H. Barbour's *Herald of the Morning*, we read: "The first point, that of **1843-44**, is marked by the **ending of the 2300 days** of Dan. 8:14..." (Sept. 1878, 48). The front cover also states, "2300 days ended in 1843-4."
23. *WTR*, 1 Nov. 1914, 5565.
24. *WT*, 15 July 1933, 212.
25. Ibid., 212-13.
26. Ibid., 214.
27. Ibid., 215.
28. Rutherford, *World Recovery* (1934), 55.
29. *"Your Will Be Done on Earth,"* 214-15.
30. *Jehovah's Witnesses in the Divine Purpose* (1959), 127. The end of the democratic election of elders also resulted in "the *complete elimination of elder bodies*, these being restored only some 40 years later in the 1970s; this elimination of elder bodies opened the way for the centralizing of all administrative authority in Brooklyn headquarters" (Raymond Franz, *In Search of Christian Freedom* [Atlanta Commentary Press, 1991], 442).
31. *WT*, 1 Dec. 1971, 724-28.
32. *Watch Tower Publications Index 1930-1985* (1986), 228.
33. *1975 Yearbook* (1974), 247. The September 15, 1982, *Watchtower* presents this same new interpretation of Daniel 8:14 (16-17).
34. Franz, 441. For example *Our Incoming World Government—God's Kingdom* (1977), 121-47; "The Days of Daniel," *WT*, 15 Dec. 1929, 371-77.

13.

Did Jerusalem Fall to Nebuchadnezzar in 607 B.C.?

How reliable is the Witnesses' date of 607 B.C. (they use B.C.E—before common era) for the fall of Jerusalem and the beginning of the "Times of the Gentiles"? Much has been written on the subject, **establishing beyond a doubt that the Witnesses' position is absolutely wrong**. Rather than to present a detailed answer to the 607 B.C. claim, which has been done by others,[1] the experiences of three dedicated Witnesses who researched the subject and their conclusions are reviewed. That these investigations were done at different times and in different places, without contact among them, makes their conclusions very significant.

Max Hatton

In the early 1960s, Max Hatton and his wife were dedicated and zealous Jehovah's Witnesses in Australia who moved from Western Australia to Melbourne, where "the need was greater." It wasn't long before Max was challenged by Geoff Rogerson, a Seventh-day Adventist, to examine the Watch Tower chronology.[2] Hatton writes:

> ...I used every moment I could spare from my busy programme as a dedicated "Witness" to defend the Watch Tower position. I was sure the Society would be right, and I believed that truth could stand a thorough investigation.... I exchanged literally hundreds of pages of correspondence on the subject with Geoff in a determined effort to follow the matter through.... On several occasions I wrote to the headquarters of the Society in Brooklyn, New York, begging help with the problems I was discovering.[3]

A letter received from Brooklyn, dated May 15, 1963, stated that "the headquarters staff was too busy preparing for an assembly to undertake the extensive research that would be required to answer my letter."[4] Hatton also wrote letters to experts in Bible chronology:

> For three years I desperately tried to support the Watch Tower teaching, but as I studied and gathered more information during that time, I realized that the situation became more hopeless....[5] I found the evidence overwhelming. I discovered that there is not another period of ancient history

where there is more positive evidence for the accepted chronology (the Society refers to it as "secular chronology") than the period of the Neo-Babylonian Empire....[6] Archeology, history, astronomy, and the Bible evidence were all so inextricably bound together, it became impossible to support the Watch Tower contentions.[7]

When the new book, *"Babylon the Great Has Fallen!" God's Kingdom Rules!* was published in 1963, Hatton anticipated that there would be answers to his problems. But after checking some pertinent material in the book, he concluded: "However, instead it only confirmed what I was being forced to admit, the Society was in error, and not facing up to it honestly."[8] (See the endnote for confirmation.)

Hatton continues: "I tried desperately to undermine all the accruing facts that were overwhelming the Society's position that I supported. After battling for three hard years I began to experience feelings of despair and guilt, realizing that I was trying to defend a false position, and an organization that was not being honest with me, or its faithful people."[9]

After attending a lecture conducted by The Australian Institute of Archaeology, where he heard of the "Adda-Guppi Stele" discovered in 1956, he explains its significance and the decision the evidence required him to make:

> The Chronological details provided on this monument from the period of the Neo-Babylonian kings confirms exactly the accepted chronology for the period and denies emphatically the Watch Tower expansion of it. That night I made my decision. I knew I could not deny the obvious any longer! I decided I could no longer teach or witness from home to home such error. In all honesty I would have to resign my positions with the Watch Tower Society. Immediately my feelings of guilt and despair were gone. My struggles were over. Truth at last had triumphed.[10]

Raymond Franz

In his book *Crisis of Conscience*, Raymond Franz recounts his experience with researching the subject of "Chronology" for the Witnesses' Bible dictionary entitled *Aid to Bible Understanding*, completed in 1971. After briefly reviewing the Witness teachings on "The Gentile Times," he mentioned the year 607 B.C., accepted by the Witnesses as the starting date for the "Gentile Times," which they claim ended in 1914. "I knew that the 607 B.C.E. date seemed to be peculiar to our publications but did not really know why."[11] He explains what happened in his investigation:

> Months of research were spent on this one subject of "Chronology" and it resulted in the longest article in the *Aid* publication. Much of the time was spent endeavoring to find some proof, some backing in history, for the 607 B.C.E. date so crucial to our calculations for 1914. Charles Ploeger, a member of the headquarters staff, was at the time serving as a secretary for me and he searched through the libraries of the New York city area for anything that might substantiate that date historically.
>
> **We found absolutely nothing in support of 607 B.C.E. All historians pointed to a date twenty years later.** Before preparing the *Aid* material on "Archaeology" I had not realized that the number of baked-clay cuneiform tablets found in the Mesopotamia area and dating back to the time of ancient Babylon numbered into the tens of thousands. In all of these there was nothing to indicate that the period of the Neo-Babylonian Empire ... was of the necessary length to fit our 607 B.C.E. date for the destruction of Jerusalem. Everything pointed to a period twenty years shorter than our published chronology claimed. Though I found this disquieting, **I wanted to**

believe our chronology was right in spite of all of the evidence to the contrary. Thus, in preparing the material for the *Aid* book, much of the time and space was spent in trying to weaken the credibility of the archeological and historical evidence that would make erroneous our 607 B.C.E. date and give a different starting point for our calculations and therefore an ending date different from 1914.[12]

Franz next mentions a visit he and Ploeger made to Prof. Abraham Sachs of Brown University, an ancient cuneiform text specialist, to see if any evidence of error could be found in the astronomical data. He found no support for the 607 B.C.E. date. "Again, like an attorney faced with evidence he cannot overcome, my effort was to discredit or weaken confidence in the witnesses from ancient times who presented such evidence, the evidence of historical texts relating to the Neo-Babylonian Empire. The arguments I presented were honest ones, but I know their intent was to **uphold a date for which there was no historical support.**"[13]

In 1979, during a discussion of 1914 and "this generation," in a meeting of the Governing Body, Franz writes: "In the course of the session, I pointed out that the Society's 607 B.C.E. date had no historical evidence whatsoever for support."[14]

In recounting this meeting, Franz mentioned that he had copied some material from Carl Olof Jonsson's study on the "Gentile Times," which Jonsson had sent to the Society that same year. "Each member of the Body received a copy. Aside from an incidental comment, they did not see fit to discuss the material."[15] Who was Carl Olof Jonsson? What did his study present?

Carl Olof Jonsson

Carl Olof Jonsson was a well-educated and dedicated Swedish Jehovah's Witness.[16] He recounts his experience in the Introduction of his book, *The Gentile Times Reconsidered*. In 1968, Jonsson was a full-time pioneer. He was conducting a Bible study with a man who challenged him "to prove the date the Watch Tower Society had chosen for the desolation of Jerusalem by the Babylonians, that is 607 B.C.E."[17] The man stated that this was not in agreement with historians who dated the same event in 587 or 586. He promised the man he would investigate the matter. Jonsson explains what happened: "As a result, I undertook a research that turned out to be far more extensive and thoroughgoing than I had expected. It continued periodically for several years, from 1968 until the end of 1975. By then the growing burden of evidence against the 607 B.C.E. date forced me reluctantly to conclude that the Watch Tower Society was wrong."[18]

He shared and discussed his findings with some of his "research-minded" Witness friends, and when they could not refute his data, he decided to prepare a systematic presentation to send to the Governing Body in Brooklyn. The treatise was completed and sent in 1977.[19]

He continues: "In 1977 I began to correspond with the Governing Body concerning my research. It soon became very evident that they were unable to refute the evidence produced. In fact, there was not even an attempt made to do so until February 28, 1980. In the meantime, however, I was repeatedly cautioned not to reveal my findings to others."[20] He received letters from Watch Tower headquarters, which led him to believe that in due time his treatise would be given careful attention and evaluation. He concluded that Society officials "seemed prepared to examine the data presented to them honestly and objectively."[21] But this was not to be the case.

On September 2, 1978, Jonsson was asked to appear before two Watch Tower representatives in Sweden, who informed him that the Brooklyn brothers were very concerned about his study and that he should not tell others about what he had written. He was also told "that the Society did not need or want individual Jehovah's Witnesses to become involved in research of this kind."[22] He resigned as an elder and from his other responsibilities, explaining his reasoning in a letter to the other elders in his local congregation. It became widely known in Sweden that he had rejected the Society's chronology and others joined him. What happened next?

> We were publicly characterized in the most negative terms as "rebellious," "presumptuous," "false prophets," "small prophets who have worked out their own little chronology," and "heretics." We were called "dangerous elements in the congregations," "evil slaves," "blasphemers," as well as "immoral, lawless ones." Privately, some of our Witness brothers, including a number of the Watch Tower Society's traveling representatives, also intimated that we were "demon-possessed," that we had flooded the Society with criticism" and that we "should have been disfellowshipped long ago." These are just a few examples of the widespread defamation, one that has gone on ever since, although no names, for obvious legal reasons, have even been mentioned publicly.[23]

After further correspondence with Brooklyn, and a visit from the coordinator of work in Sweden, the long awaited (almost three years) response to his treatise was received. Jonsson writes:

> The argumentation presented, however, turned out to be largely a repetition of earlier arguments found in various places in the Watch Tower Society's literature, *arguments which had already been demonstrated in the treatise to be unsatisfactory.* In a letter dated March 31, 1980, I answered their arguments and added two new lines of evidence against the 607 B.C.E. date. Thus the Society not only failed to defend its position successfully, but the evidence against also became considerably stronger.[24]

An attempt by the Society to uphold its position in the Appendix of *"Let Your Kingdom Come"* (1981) "added nothing new to the earlier arguments," says Jonsson, "and to anyone who has carefully studied the subject of ancient chronology, it appears to be no more than a feeble attempt to save an untenable position by concealing facts.... The contents of the Watch Tower Society's 'Appendix,' however, finally convinced me that *the leaders of this organization were clearly not prepared to let facts interfere with traditional fundamental doctrines.*"[25]

In the third edition of *The Gentile Times Reconsidered* (1998), Jonsson presents a detailed examination of the "Appendix." In his summary he writes:

> ...The Watch Tower Society in its "Appendix" to *"Let Your Kingdom Come"* does not give a fair presentation of the evidence against their 607 B.C.E. date:

(1) Its writers misrepresent *historical evidence* by omitting from their discussion nearly half of the evidence presented in the first edition of this work ... and by giving some of the other lines of evidence only a biased and distorted presentation. They erroneously indicate that priests and kings might have altered historical documents (chronicles, royal inscriptions, etc.) from the Neo-Babylonian era, in spite of the fact that all available evidence shows the opposite to be true.

(2) They misrepresent *authorities on ancient historiography* by quoting them out of context and attributing to them views and doubts they do not have.

(3) They misrepresent *ancient writers....*

(4)   Finally, they misrepresent *biblical evidence* by concealing the fact that the most direct understanding of the passages dealing with the seventy years shows them to be a period of Neo-Babylonian rule, not the period of Jerusalem's desolation. This understanding is in good agreement with the historical evidence, but in glaring conflict with the application given to it by the Watch Tower Society. It is truly distressing to discover that individuals, upon whose spiritual guidance millions rely, deal so carelessly and dishonestly with facts. Their "Appendix" to "Let Your Kingdom Come" in defense of their chronology is nothing but yet one more cleaver exercise in the art of concealing truth. It may be asked why the leaders of an organization that constantly emphasizes its interest in "the Truth" in reality find it necessary to suppress the truth and even oppose it? The obvious reason is that they have no other choice, *as long as they insist that their organization was appointed in the year 1919 as God's sole channel and mouthpiece on earth*. If the 607 B.C.E.—1914 C.E. calculation is abandoned, this claim will fall. Then these leaders will have to admit, at least tacitly, that their organization for the past hundred years has appeared on the world scene in a false role with a false message. When occasionally the questioning of the 607 B.C.E. date has been commented upon in the Watch Tower publications in recent years, the sole defense has been a reference to the "Appendix" of 1981....[26]

As the Society's "Appendix" contains only a series of failed attempts to undermine the evidence *against* the 607 B.C.E. date, and as the only "convincing evidence" presented *in support of* the date is a reference to "yet undiscovered material," the Watch Tower writers evidently trust that the majority of the Witnesses are completely unaware of the actual facts. And the leaders of the Watch Tower Society want it kept that way.... The leaders of the Watch Tower Society evidently fear that if Witnesses are allowed to be exposed to these facts, they might discover that **the basis of the prophetic claims of the movement is nothing but a groundless, unbiblical and unhistorical chronological speculation.**[27]

In the third revised and expanded edition of *The Gentile Times Reconsidered* (1998), Jonsson further demolishes the 607 B.C.E. date required for the Witnesses 1914 scheme, presenting **fourteen** (formerly seven) lines of evidence against it.[28] Jonsson's departure from the Jehovah's Witnesses would require great personal loss, but in 1982, after 26 years as a dedicated active member, he was ready to leave. He writes:

It was quite clear to me that this would mean a complete break with the whole social world I had been a part of during all those years. The rules of the Watch Tower Society require Jehovah's Witnesses to cut off all contacts with those who break with the organization, whether this break occurs by excommunication or by a voluntary resignation. I knew that I would lose virtually all my friends, but also my relatives within the organization (of which there were over seventy, including a brother and two sisters with their families, cousins and their families, and so on). I would be regarded and treated as "dead"....[29]

In May 1982, Jonsson received a summons to appear before a "judicial committee." Since its members did not show any interest in his treatise on the Witnesses' chronology, or to allow discussion of it, he did not attend the meeting. He was disfellowshipped on June 9, 1982.[30] The following statement in the introduction to Jonsson's original typewritten treatise, sent to the Governing Body in 1977, was not taken seriously—as it should have been:

Truth is all-important. Convictions not founded upon facts are often worthless, and sometimes dangerous. Why cling to them if they are obviously wrong? Faith and zeal are not virtues in themselves. Without accurate knowledge they can lead us far astray—Rom. 10:2.

Notes

1. The definitive study and refutation of the Witnesses' position is by Carl Olof Jonsson, *The Gentile Times Reconsidered*. 3rd ed.; Atlanta: Commentary Press, 1998. Another brief study is William MacCarty, *1914 and Christ's Second Coming*. Washington, D.C.: Review and Herald, 1975.
2. Max Hatton, "Defending Watch Tower Chronology," *Witness* (Apr.-May-June, 1976), 4.
3. Ibid.
4. Ibid.
5. Ibid.
6. Ibid., 5.
7. Ibid. "Thus each item of evidence corresponded with the generally accepted chronology, but conflicted with the Watch Tower arrangement" (ibid.).
8. Ibid., 6. Using the Witnesses' *"Babylon the Great Has Fallen!" God's Kingdom Rules!* (1963) one can show that 607 B.C. (or B.C.E.) cannot be the date for the fall of Jerusalem and the beginning of "times of the Gentiles." Follow the directions below:

   (1) On page 184 (second paragraph) of the *"Babylon the Great Has Fallen!"* book, figure **backwards** from the reign of **Nabonidus which lasted 17 years (539-556 B.C)**. You will notice that the length of his reign is not given in the *Babylon* book, but it does state that he "had a fairly glorious reign till Babylon fell in 539 B.C." The Watch Tower publication, *Insight on the Scriptures* vol. 2 (1988), in its article on "Nabonidus," states: "Last supreme monarch of the Babylonian Empire; father of Belshazzar. On the basis of cuneiform texts he is believed to have ruled some 17 years (556-539 B.C.E.)" (457). There is no question concerning the length of Nabonidus' reign: "That Nabonidus was the king of Babylon when Cyrus conquered Babylonia in 539 B.C.E. is clearly shown by the *Nabonidus Chronicle* (B.M. 35382). The chronicle evidently dated this event to the 'seventeenth year' of Nabonidus, but as was pointed out earlier, this portion of the chronicle is damaged and the year is illegible. Nonetheless, **a whole group of economic texts has been found that provides chronological interlocking connections between Nabonidus' seventeenth year and the reign of Cyrus**" (Jonsson, 135-36). See Jonsson's book for further details on this (336-39). **539-556 B.C.**

   (2) From the 556 B.C. date, continue figuring *backwards* using the figures in the *Babylon* book: **Labashi-Marduk** ("within nine months he had his throat cut by an assassin") His reign may have been only two months (Richard A. Parker and Waldo H. Dubberstein, *Babyonian Chronology: 626 B.C.-A.D. 75* [Providence: Brown University Press, 1956], 13). **556 B.C. Neriglissar** ("reigned for four years") **556-560 B.C. Evil-merodach** "after reigning but two years ... was murdered") **560-562 B.C.** So Evil-Merodach succeeded his father Nebuchadnezzar in **562 B.C.**

   (3) On page 183 of the *Babylon* book it is stated that Nebuchadnezzar's "oldest son was named Evil-Merodach, who was to become his father's immediate successor.... **Amel-Marduk (Evil-Merodach)** as the oldest son succeeded Nebuchadnezzar to Babylon's throne in **581 B.C.**"
   581 B.C.
   Note the gap between 562 B.C. and 581 B.C.

   (4) According to fully confirmed non-Witness chronology, **Nebuchadnezzar's** reign was 605-562. This

fits with the figures in the *Babylon* book and eliminates the time gap. Expert chronologer, Edwin R. Thiele concludes: "Among all ancient historical dates none is more solidly established than is 605 as the year when Nebuchadnezzar began his rule in Babylon…" (Edwin R. Thiele, "Jehovah's Witnesses and the Dates of the Babylonian Captivity," *The Ministry*, Feb. 1976, 10). In contrast, the Witnesses' dates for Nebuchadnezzar's reign are 624-581 B.C.E. (*Aid to Bible Understanding* [1971], 1212) or 624-582 B.C.E.) *Insight on the Scriptures*, vol. 2, 480).

(5) Since Scripture states that Jerusalem was destroyed in Nebuchadnezzar's 19th year (2 Kings 25:8-10; Jer. 52:12-14), **this requires the date 587/586**—not the Witnesses' 607 B.C. Without the 607 B.C. starting date, the 1914 year for the end of the "times of the Gentiles" cannot be sustained. "The reason for uncertainty among scholars as to whether Jerusalem was desolated in 587 or 586 B.C.E. stems from the Bible, not extra-biblical sources. All scholars agree in dating Nebuchadnezzar's eighteenth regnal year to 587-86 B.C.E. (Nisan to Nisan). The Bible dates the desolation to Nebuchadnezzar's *nineteenth* regnal year at 2 Kings 25:8 and Jeremiah 52:12, … but to his eighteenth year at Jeremiah 52:29. This discrepancy may be solved if a nonaccession year system is postulated for the kings of Judah" (Jonsson, 293).

9. Hatton, 7.
10. Ibid. For a detailed discussion of the *Adad-guppi' inscription* and its significance see: Jonsson's, *The Gentile Times Reconsidered* (3rd ed.), 113-16, 125-26, 330-32.
11. Raymond Franz, *Crisis of Conscience* (2nd ed.; Atlanta: Commentary Press, 1992), 25.
12. Ibid., 25-26.
13. Ibid., 26.
14. Ibid., 215.
15. Ibid., 214.
16. M. James Penton, *Apocalypse Delayed* (2nd ed.; Toronto: University of Toronto Press, 1997), 107.
17. Jonsson, 7.
18. Ibid. In a letter dated April 26, 1999, Jonsson says that by 1975 "I had spent about seven years on studying the Neo-Babylonian chronology, and I knew that the Society's Gentile Times chronology was wrong, and thus also their prophetic claims. Yet, I continued as an elder for another three years, as I thought it was possible to convince the Watchtower Society's leadership about their errors. As it turned out, this was a rather naive hope."
19. Ibid.
20. Ibid.
21. Ibid., 8.
22. Ibid., 10.
23. Ibid., 10-11.
24. Ibid., 12-13.
25. Ibid., 13.
26. See for example: *WT*, 1 Nov. 1986, 6; *WT*, 15 Mar. 1989, 22.
27. Jonsson, 304-06.
28. Ibid., chapters 3 and 4. The 14 lines of evidence are summarized on 147-52, 186-90.
29. Ibid., 16-17.
30. Ibid., 17-18.

14.

Jerusalem and the End of the "Appointed Times of the Nations" ("Times of the Gentiles") —Literal or Symbolic?

Luke 21:24 speaks of the city of Jerusalem being "trampled on by the nations, until the appointed times of the nations ['times of the Gentiles'] be fulfilled" (*NWT*). Russell held to a literal interpretation, for he predicted that from 1914 "forward **Jerusalem shall no longer be trodden down of the Gentiles**, but shall rise from the dust of divine disfavor, to honor...."[1] Fulfillment of the prophecy was claimed in the November 1, 1914, *Watch Tower*: "The **treading down of the Jews has stopped**. All over the world the Jews are now free—even in Russia.... We believe that the **treading down of Jerusalem has ceased**, because the time for the Gentiles to tread down Israel has ended."[2]

In answering a critic who questioned this claim, pointing out that "Palestine continues under Gentile rule," the February 13, 1924, *Golden Age* published this response: "The Lord said that Jerusalem would be trodden down of the Gentiles until the Times of the Gentiles should be fulfilled; but he did not say that the very day that the Times of the Gentiles ended the Gentile nations would all be thrown upon the scrap heap at one and the same instant."[3] In *Deliverance* (1926), Rutherford writes: "Other further testimony was given by Jesus, corroborating what he had previously said and further showing that the world has ended and that his kingdom has come. 'And Jerusalem shall be trodden down of the Gentiles, until the times of the Gentiles be fulfilled' (Luke 21:24). **Jerusalem here undoubtedly refers to the Jewish people**, because the text distinguishes them from Gentiles."[4] In his book *Comfort For the Jews* (1925) and repeated in *Life* (1929), after reviewing how the end of the "Times of the Gentiles" in 1914 was calculated, Rutherford writes: "If this calculation is correct, and it must be, then something should have occurred in 1914 to mark **the end of God's favor to the Gentiles and something to indicate shortly thereafter that God's favor was returning to the Jew. We find it even so.**"[5] But this interpretation could not be maintained because Jerusalem continued to be "trodden down of the Gentiles." As with other failed predictions, a new interpretation was needed.

While teaching the literal fall of Jerusalem and the overthrow of Zedekiah as the beginning of this period, the new Watch Tower interpretation by Rutherford no longer viewed its conclusion as relating to earthly Jerusalem as it was once taught. This is how it is currently explained in the February 1, 1985, *Watchtower*.

Well, then, in that year [1914], did old Jerusalem cease to be trampled on by non-Jewish, or Gentile, nations? **No.... How, then, can we say that the Gentile Times ended in 1914? Because in that year the government of the great King Jehovah was born in heaven.**[6] ...Happily for the Jewish Christians then, and for all Christians since, there is another Jerusalem, a more exalted one, "heavenly Jerusalem."—Hebrews 12:22.

In line with this fact, Jesus' prophecy recorded in Luke 21:24 **began with an application to earthly Jerusalem but must end with reference to "heavenly Jerusalem."** Yes, for "heavenly Jerusalem" has replaced earthly Jerusalem as "the city of the great King" Jehovah God. There, in that celestial "city," was the place for "the great King" Jehovah to install his glorified Son Jesus Christ at the end of the Gentile Times in 1914.[7]

But, as Robert Crompton points out:

> This interpretation of the events implies **a radical change** in what is meant by the end of the "times of the Gentiles." The end of 2,520 years during which the typical kingdom of God was "trodden down of the Gentiles" (Luke 21:24), was marked, **not by the re-establishment of an earthly, Jewish kingdom, but by the inauguration of the great heavenly antitype. The new teaching obviously called for a reappraisal of the place of the Jewish people in the divine plan.**[8]

And as Carl Olof Jonsson observes, "this relocation of the 'downtrodden Jerusalem' from earth to heaven created other questions ... which never have been satisfactorily answered."[9] What are these questions? Space limitations do not allow for a discussion of them here, but the questions are covered in Jonsson's *The Gentile Times Reconsidered,* in which he summarizes his findings.[10] The Witnesses' view, quoted above,

> was shown to be contradicted by several texts in the Bible, which unequivocally establish that **Christ's universal kingdom was set up at his resurrection and exaltation,** when he also began to rule "in the midst of his enemies."
>
> Finally, the claim that Satan was hurled down from heaven in 1914 was examined and found to be biblically untenable. **The Bible clearly shows that the "fall of Satan" was occasioned by Christ's death and resurrection.** Thus, a number of events that the Watch Tower Society claims to have taken place in 1914 **are actually shown by the Bible to have occurred at Christ's death, resurrection, and exaltation.**[11]

In conclusion, the prediction that 1914 would see the end of the "trodding down of Jerusalem" literally, as taught by Russell, was not realized, and the reinterpretation of the prophecy, with a heavenly fulfillment in 1914, resulted in a view that contradicts Scripture.

Notes

1. Russell, *The Time Is at Hand* (1889), 77. N. H. Barbour and Russell's *Three Worlds* (1877) presents a literal interpretation of Luke 21:24: "...There are Scriptures which appear to make the return of the Jews to begin with the living Jews of this generation who are called '*a remnant*,' and after their return **Jerusalem is surrounded, the city is taken,** and one-half go into captivity, (see Zech. 14), then the

Lord interferes and saves them. And yet 'Jerusalem must be trodden down of the Gentiles, until the times of the Gentiles are fulfilled;' hence, trodden down until A.D. 1914, when the day of wrath will be passed, and the resurrection and return of the 'whole house of Israel' due" (165-66).

2. *WTR*, 1 Nov. 1914, 5568.
3. *GA*, 13 Feb. 1924, 307.
4. Rutherford, *Deliverance* (1926), 241, or 253 in later editions.
5. Rutherford, *Comfort For the Jews* (1925), 59; Rutherford, *Life* (1929), 130.
6. *WT*, 1 Feb. 1985, 11.
7. Ibid., 12.
8. Robert Crompton, *Counting the Days to Armageddon* (Cambridge: James Clarke & Co., 1996), 109.
9. Carl Olof Jonsson, *The Gentile Times Reconsidered* (3rd ed.; Atlanta: Commentary Press, 1998), 260.
10. Ibid., 258-74.
11. Ibid., 274. Some of the passages of Scripture which show that through Christ's death, resurrection, and exaltation Christ's ruling authority was already universal, and nothing could be added in 1914 are: Ps. 110: 1-2; Luke 22:69; Matt. 26:64; 28:18; John 12:31; 1 Cor. 15:24-25; Eph. 1:20-23; Col. 2:10; Heb. 1:3, 13; 1 Pet. 3:22; Rev. 1:5; 3:21.

15.

The Jehovah's Witnesses
and World War I

World War I is crucial to support the Jehovah's Witnesses' claim that Russell and the Bible Students, as they were then known, predicted that 1914 was to be a marked year. The *Watch Tower Publications Indexes* (1930-85, 1986-1990) list many articles and quotations that show the importance of World War I in Witness thought. One could easily write an entire book on the use and misuse by Watch Tower writers of the sources they cite and the arguments and claims they make.[1]

Watch Tower publications claim that the period before 1914 was one of peace and security which was suddenly brought to an end by the outbreak of World War I. They claim a knowledge of this coming event and its characteristics which were not possessed by others. In support of these claims, they cite Bible chronology and they quote well-known persons such as former English Prime Minister Harold Macmillan and German Chancellor Konrad Adenaur. They have also quoted the observations of lay persons such as George Hannan. The following statements are typical:

> From Bible chronology, Jehovah's witnesses as far back as 1877 pointed to the year 1914 as one of great significance.... The momentous year of 1914 came, and with it World War I, the most widespread upheaval in history up to that time. It brought unprecedented slaughter, famine, pestilence and overthrow of governments. **The world did not expect such horrible events as took place. But Jehovah's witnesses did expect such things... How could Jehovah's witnesses have known so far in advance what world leaders themselves did not know?** Only by God's holy spirit making such prophetic truths known to them (*WT*, 1 Aug. 1971, 468).

> In a recent lecture, **Harold Macmillan**, former British Prime Minister, recalled the world of his youth. During the age of Queen Victoria, people looked forward to "automatic progress," he said. "Everything would get better and better." Instead, **"suddenly, unexpectedly**, one morning in 1914 the whole thing came to and end."

> Average citizens made similar observations. "**Nobody expected World War I**," points out **George Hannan**, an American who was born in 1899. "It was a tremendous shock. People had been saying that the world had become too civilized for war. But **world war came out of nowhere, like a bolt from the blue**"(*Awake!*, May 8, 1981, 5-6).

> More than 50 years after 1914, German statesman **Konrad Adenauer** reflected: "Thoughts and pictures come to my mind,... thoughts from before the year 1914 when there was **real peace,**

quiet and security on this earth—a time when we didn't know fear.... Security and quiet have disappeared from the lives of men since 1914 (*WT*, 1 May 1982, 14).

Are the decades before 1914 accurately described in the above statements? Is it true that "nobody expected World War I"? Was peace suddenly shattered by a war that came without any warning?

It should be noted that many articles dealing with military preparation and war were published in the *Watch Tower* magazine **before** 1914. In addition to Russell's observations based on what was taking place, these articles often quoted the statements of contemporary writers and journalists, as well as governmental and military leaders. Do these observations and statements support the Watch Tower Society's position as set forth above?

Excerpts From *Watch Tower* Articles

1882

"Truly it has been said, 'Europe is a huge standing camp.' '**All Europe stands ready for war**'" (*WTR*, June 1882, 362).

1887

War possible next Summer: "In view of the recognized policy of Russia in connection with Turkey, this speech [by German Chancellor Bismarck] is significant as preparing the way for all of the great powers of Europe hitherto opposed to it, to give their consent to such an arrangement, or by declaring themselves opposed to it, to involve themselves in war to protect Turkey. **This all looks as though next Summer would see a war on foot which might engage every nation of Europe**" (*WTR*, Feb. 1887, 899).

1889

Europe's armies "must soon be called into action." "...Remember, that **at no period of the world's history** were there ever, as today, armies numbering eleven millions of men, thoroughly equipped and trained, ready at a moment's call to rush to battle, armed with weapons of carnage, a hundred fold more dreadful and destructive than were ever before known, which make them **equal to a hundred millions in former times**. Remember too, that **these eleven millions must soon be called into action**, if for no other reason than that the great expense of their maintenance is rapidly bankrupting these various kingdoms of Christ(?)" (*WTR*, Jan.-Feb. 1889, 1094).

1891

Von Moltke: the next war will be "fierce and protracted." "Count von Moltke, Germany's greatest general in modern times, whose death has lately been announced, in a recent speech before the Reichstag **left no one in ignorance as to his views of the next European war. The powers of Europe, he declared, 'are armed as they never have been armed before....** In his opinion such a war would be both **fierce and protracted**" (*WTR*, May 1891, 1304).

1892

War possible in 1892 or 1893—Russell: "trouble is yet nearly fifteen years future." "...The daily papers and the weeklies and monthlies, religious and secular, are **continually discussing the prospects of war in Europe**. They note the grievances and ambitions of the various nations and **predict that war is inevitable** at no distant day, that it **may begin at any moment** between some of the great powers, and that the prospects are that it **will eventually involve them all**.... For several years past thoughtful observers has said, War cannot be kept off much longer: it must come soon—'next spring,' 'next summer,' 'next fall,' etc....

These rumors of impending European wars, and the desire to judge whether observation would tend to confirm the divine revelation that **the intensity of the great predicted trouble is yet nearly fifteen years future**, formed no small part or our motive in visiting Europe during the past summer.... **As for war, it is the talk of everybody in Germany, Austria, Russia, Italy and France.** And all seemed agreed that if it did not break out this fall it would surely come by next spring. All seem ready for what they consider the inevitable" *(WTR,* 15 Jan. 1892, 1354).

1894

The coming war will be a world war. "Take the war shadow first. Have armaments been decreasing? On the contrary, Europe, the east, everything within the sphere anciently ruled by Rome ... **is filled as never before with armed men.** All nations, with feverish haste, are **increasing their armaments....** Within two years Bismarck and Gladstone, the most experienced and sagacious living statesmen, have said that the situation does not admit of a peaceful solution, that **the world is hastening toward the war of wars**, the outcome of which no man can predict. This is also the expressed opinion of that singular man whose only position is that of Paris correspondent of the *London Times*, but whose wisdom, judgment and prudence are such that he is consulted by every cabinet and trusted by every sovereign—De Blowitz. And **all are agreed that the war, when it comes, must involve the earth**" (*WTR*, 15 Jan. 1894, 1612).

War possible in 1894. "Washington Diplomats and others are calling attention to the fact that **European armies were increased fully one hundred thousand men** during 1893. They assert that the **long feared, general European war involving all nations** is sure to begin during 1894.... All this looks probable; but *we* nevertheless do not expect a general war, the *great* trouble of Scripture, for some years yet" (*WTR*, 1 Feb. 1894, 1619).

Europe under a war cloud—when will it burst forth? From the *London Daily Telegram*: "Of course, one chief and obvious reason for this [unsatisfactory state of European affairs] is that **armed peace** which weighs upon Europe like a nightmare, and has **turned the whole Continent into a standing camp....** The possession of these prodigious means of mutual destruction is a constant temptation to use them, and some day, it is to be feared, the **pent-up forces of this war-cloud will burst forth**. The world has not yet invented a better clearing-house for its international cheques than the ghastly and costly Temple of War" (*WTR*, 15 Mar. 1894, 1632-33).

1896

War possible in 1896; Russell said not for 10 years. "Turkey has long been known as 'the sick man' amongst nations; and the Great Powers of Europe, all anxious to get hold of his possessions, fear each other.... The situation is greatly strained every way. If it results in war, the Turks will make a stern resistance, and after their fall, Russia, with her army already on the spot, will be unwilling to let go, especially as she now has the French navy for an ally on the sea. **This would be likely to involve all Europe, and perhaps Japan, in a war such as was not since there was a nation.** But while the outlook is threatening, and **many consider it sure that such a general European war will break out during this year**, we do not share their fear. Turkey may be still further dismembered, or even entirely cut up, but the *general* European war will certainly not come for several years yet; **not for ten years**, we feel quite confident" (*WTR*, 1 Jan. 1896, 1911-12).

Major wars narrowly averted in 1896. "During the short space of this year, 1896, **several immense wars have narrowly been averted**—between Russia and Japan, between Turkey and the combined powers of Europe, between Great Britain and the United States, between Great Britain and Germany and between the

United States and Spain, backed possibly by France; besides a number of smaller affairs" (*WTR*, 1 Apr. 1896, 1953).

1900

"The War Spirit Growing." "**For years Germany, France, Italy, Austria and Russia have had military fever, as is well known**; and now the same has spread in virulent form to Great Britain and her colonies and to the United States" (*WTR*, 1 June 1900, 2641).

1901

Wars, preparations for war, peace is not secure. "The view ten years ago showed a placid, smiling river; now we see the boiling rapids of a torrent plunging toward what abyss no one knows. **War has followed by war with swift succession**.... What the next stroke will be, who can say?—*Springfield Republican*. Lord Salisbury said of threatened wars: '**These wars come upon us absolutely unannounced and with terrible rapidity**. The war cloud rises in the horizon with a **rapidity that obviates all calculation**, and, it may be, a month or two months after the first warning you receive, you find you are engaged in, or in prospect of a war on which your very existence is staked.' ... Prof. Andrews, ex-president of Brown University, says: '**No well-informed person in Europe seems to believe that peace is destined to endure very long**. On all hands people are preparing for war'" (*WTR*, 15 Feb. 1901, 2768).

"**NATIONAL PREPARATION FOR WAR.**" "We clip the following from a Pittsburgh daily, which shows that the Hague Peace Conference of 1899 is not taken very seriously by any of the nations." The article is quoted and it concludes, "Verily, **the wings of the angel of peace are not to be spread over the ocean during the early years of the new century**" (*WTR*, 15 Mar. 1901, 2783).

"As our readers are aware, we credit the prosperity of the world during the past three years very **largely to their wars**, which have put hundreds of millions of dollars into circulation among the people..." (*WTR*, 15 Sept. 1901, 2875).

1903

War fought in the Balkans—war might involve all of Europe. A Philadelphia *Ledger* correspondent writes: "As far back as ten years ago de Blowitz held that in the **course of a generation** Europe would be a congerie of bankrupt states; that all the national debts in Europe would be repudiated, with the exception of Britain's, and that vast social changes, **involving bloody wars and reigns of terror, would come to pass in many countries**" (*WTR*, 15 Mar. 1903, 3162).

"Yet **statesmen especially are fearful of war**—fearful, too, that despite their desire to avoid it something may enkindle the blaze which may **involve all Europe**" (*WTR*, 1 Apr. 1903, 3169).

"Present appearances are that **war has started in earnest in the Balkans**, and no human being can say where it will end" (*WTR*, 15 Sept. 1903, 3242).

1904

The Russo-Japanese war could lead to a world war. "The present outlook is that the success of the Japanese over the Russians thus early in their war will prolong the conflict and quite probably draw into it many other civilized nations.... Ever the United States may become involved, improbable as that may at present appear. If the Great Powers of Europe become involved, as above suggested, it would be very difficult for this nation to remain neutral.... Another reason why **we incline to expect a general war** is, that at present the nations are so strong that a successful **anarchous uprising against them would be little short of a miracle.** But such a general war would increase taxation and breed general discontent alarmingly and quickly, causing the seeds of Socialist propaganda to shoot up and blossom and bring forth red-handed anarchy speedily" (*WTR*, 1 Mar. 1904, 3327).

1907

"**WAR FEARED; NO WORLD'S FAIR IN 1913.**" Reported in the *Toledo News-Bee*: "Opposition of Kaiser William is expected to cause the abandonment of the proposal to hold an international exposition in Berlin in 1913. Most significant, however, is the reason on which the German war lord bases his objection. The **emperor believes the possibility of Germany being drawn into a European war before the time set for the exposition** is too great for the nation to take the risk involved in arranging an international exposition" (*WTR*, 1 July 1907, 4018).

1909

"**DANGER SIGNS OF A GREAT WAR.**" Quotes then follow from the *London Daily Mail, London Spectator, Chicago Tribune* (*WTR*, 1 May 1909, 4383-84).

"ARMAGEDDON." "... Peace treaties became fashionable, and a week rarely passed without an account of some happy pact between the very nations now most desperately bent on **preparing for the great Battle of Armageddon** and some one of the nations whom their warlords and captains of the military industry pretended to suspect or fear." *Dallas Morning News* (*WTR*, 1 June 1909, 4403).

Belligerent mood worldwide, preparations for war. An article by C. E. Jefferson and published by the American Association for International Conciliation is quoted: "The future historian of the first decade of the twentieth century will be puzzled. He will find that **the world at the opening of the century was in an extraordinary belligerent mood**, and that the mood was **well-nigh universal, dominating the New World as well as the Old, the Orient no less than the Occident**. He will find that **preparations for war**, especially among the nations which confessed allegiance to the Prince of Peace, were carried forward with tremendous energy and enthusiasm, and that the air was filled with prophetic voices, picturing national calamities and predicting **bloody and world embracing conflicts**" (*WTR*, 15 June 1909, 4411).

"**All the great nations are today facing deficits, caused in every case by the military and naval experts**. Into what a tangle the finances of Russia and Japan have been brought by militarists is known by everybody. Germany has, in a single generation, increased her national debt from eighteen million dollars to more than one billion dollars.... Financial experts confess that France is approaching the limit of her sources of revenue. Her deficit is created by her army and navy. The British government is always seeking for new devices by means of which to fill a depleted treasury.... Italy has for years staggered on the verge of bankruptcy because she carries and overgrown army on her back. Even our own rich republic faces this year a deficit ... largely due to the one hundred and thirty millions we are spending on our navy" (ibid., 4413-14).

War between Germany and Britain possible in 1912. "Lord Northcliffe, owner of the *London Times*, in an interview at Winnepeg, Manitoba, **predicted war between Germany and Great Britain**. He said in the Krupp works alone 100,000 mean are working night and day and on Sundays, preparing for war.... He said some observers think such a **war might begin by 1912**" (*WTR*, 1 Dec. 1909, 4523).

1910

War between Britain and Germany possible within two years. "A German war scare makes some fearful and some belligerent.... The **argument advanced is that war should be declared against Germany speedily, while the British navy is so much stronger of the two**.... Meantime the British and the Germans are improvising their treasuries with war preparations, and latterly Austria has become bent on being a sea power, and is also building dreadnoughts. With the amount of zeal everywhere manifested to serve King

Money it **would not at all surprise us if there should be a cruel and dreadful war between the two great 'Christian' nations, Great Britain and Germany, within two years**" (*WTR*, 1 Jan. 1910, 4539).

1911

Preparations for war. "The situation in Europe is still worse. Does not this **preparation of the so-called Christian nations of the world to destroy one another** prove to us that there is a mistake—that the term Christian has been misapplied to them? Nor can we say that there is no danger, for only fear could lead to such **costly preparations for war**" (*WTR*, 1 Apr. 1911, 4795-96).

1914

War. "The long expected shaking of the social earth is, we believe, already in progress. **The great war for which Europe has been drilling its troops, preparing it treasuries and armaments, is shaking every nation in the world**, financially, socially, politically. Strong as the nations feel themselves to be, all tremble in dread at the results of the conflict now in progress" (*WTR*, 15 Aug. 1914, 5516).

The Secular Press: *The New York Times*.

What was being reported in the secular press in the years just before 1914 relative to the preparations for war and its likelihood? Was this period seen as one of peace and security? Here are some excerpts from *The New York Times*.

1910. Lloyd-George, British Chancellor of the Exchequer is quoted: "But I must admit that the **increase in expenditures, not only in this country but in every land under the sun, is due to ... the mad and insane competition in armaments between the various countries of the world**. The countries of the world are spending annually 450,000,000 [$2,250,000,000] upon this machinery of destruction.... All nations seem to be infected with an epidemic of prodigality in that respect which seems to be **sweeping over the world and sweeping to destruction**. We take the lead in that expenditure" (*New York Times*, 16 Oct. 1910, 12).

1911. "**In the Balkans war is inevitable**. It must be, because some of the Continental newspapers frequently say so. The Turks are preparing to crush the Albanians, the Montenegrins will interfere, and then, bang!—**Austria, Russia, Germany, Italy, France, and Great Britain will be involved in the fracas.** As for the Moroccan dispute, it can never be settled except by force of arms. **This will make another fine war, in which all the Powers will take part.**... On this side of the Atlantic, however, **rumors of war are plentiful. The Summer of 1911 seems to be one long nightmare for the advocates of peace.**... The people who have been trying to believe that war has been finally suppressed must find the incidents of the Summer of 1911 rather disturbing to their theories. Universal peace is most desirable, but the hot weather is not wholly responsible for this **new set of war rumors**" (*New York Times*, 10 July 1911, 6).

1912. "WAR TALK IN PEACE FORUM." **"Ex-Senator Towne Finds That the World Is in a Mood to Fight."** "Charles A. Towne, former United States Senator from Minnesota, startled a well-attended meeting of the International Peace Forum at the Fifth Avenue Baptist Church last night by stating that **the immediate future of the world 'was big with possibilities of war**....' As it is, Germany and England are in exceedingly sensitive relations just now, and so are Japan and the United States.... 'The world is in a solemn situation just now, and the next great war must never happen'" (*New York Times*, 4 Mar. 1912, 6).

"CANNOT SEE END TO WARS." "Speakers at Military Order Dinner **Have No Faith in Universal Peace**." "All the agitation in the cause of universal peace hasn't convinced the members of the Military Order of Foreign Wars that armies and battleships are to be thrown into the discard.... Capt. Louis S. Van Duzer, Commander of the Brooklyn Naval Yard, said he didn't look for the millennium tomorrow and was heartily applauded" (*New York Times*, 13 Dec. 1912, 10).

"ROOSEVELT ADVISES READINESS FOR WAR." "Country Must Be Better Prepared Than It Was for the Past Conflicts, He Says." "A warning that **the United States must be prepared for immediate war** and far better prepared than the country has been for past wars was the feature of the address by Theodore Roosevelt this afternoon at a conference of the Military Historical Society of Massachusetts" (*New York Times*, 29 Dec. 1912, 4).

1913. "BILLION A YEAR TO ENFORCE PEACE.... ALL EUROPE REINFORCING." "One thousand million dollars is the amount spent by the world annually on armaments in order to maintain peace, according to the estimate of Senator Gervais, a leading authority on military matters, who has just published a striking article dealing with the **stupendous growth of armies and navies in Europe**. 'At the very moment when all nations profess the strongest aspirations toward universal peace,' he says, '**Europe is in a perfect frenzy over military preparations**.' He points out that aside from the Balkan trouble and the new French and German army laws, which summon 1,500,000 men to the flag yearly, **all Parliaments are confronted with projects from military reorganization and reinforcement**" (*New York Times*, 5 Oct. 1913, IV, 3).

The October 11, 1914, *New York Times* published a book review of a condensed version of German Gen. Friedrich von Bernhardi's book *How Germany Makes War*, which had been written over two years before and translated and published in England in 1913. His earlier book, *Germany and the Next War* (1911), is also mentioned. What did Bernhardi say in his latest book? The reviewer writes: "Gen. Bernhardi takes his frank stand that Germany must be prepared to the top notch of efficiency for war, because **she will have to make war to get what she wants**." Bernhardi writes that because of Germany's rapidly growing population,

> we need to enlarge our colonial possessions.... **With every move of our foreign policy today we have to face European war against superior enemies**.... It is impossible to change the partition of the earth as it now exists in our favor by diplomatic artifices. If we wish to gain the position in the world that is due us, **we must rely on our sword, renounce all weakly visions of peace**, and eye the dangers surrounding us with resolute and unflinching courage.[2]

Observations by Historians and Other Scholars

The following quotations are a representative sample of observations made by historians and other experts on the years leading up to World War I. How did they see the period?

"**The war had been long expected**. 'The Great European war begins,' wrote *The Times* [London] on August 7, as if to allude to something **much talked of, before that date.... Europe had had, for a generation, the smell of gunpowder in all its transactions**" (Hugh Thomas, *A History of the World* [New York: Harper & Row Publ., 1979], 466).

"The **threat of continental war had haunted Europe for 40 years before the coming of World War I**. Preceding this global conflict, diplomatic tensions and insecurities had led the European states to create self-protective networks that appeared to guarantee peace. In reality, these alignments indicated where each nation would stand when World War I erupted" (*The Twentieth Century Almanac* [New York: World

Almanac Publications, 1985], 72).

"A clear indication of what was to come was given in a work published in 1898 by I. S. Block, a Warsaw banker, which made a pretty accurate forecast of the nature of total war. **He clearly had in mind that a great war could not be long delayed**. He argued that in the event of large-scale war in Europe a stalemate between the armed forces of the contending nations was inevitable—due to technical development of weapons, and to the harnessing of all political and economic forces of powerful states to war.... Bloch's warnings were largely put aside by military commanders in Europe because he was not a professional soldier..." (Viscount Montgomery, *A History of Warfare* [New York: The World Publishing Co., 1968], 459).

"In Germany as in England the topic of coming conflict between the two countries was fashionable, fomented by the Navy League's slogans, 'The Coming War!' 'England the Foe' 'England's Plan to Fall on Us in 1911' and the Pan-German accompaniment, 'To Germany belongs the world!' **In every country as the air thickened with talk of war**, the instinct of patriotism swelled" (Barbara W. Tuchman, *The Proud Tower: A Portrait of the World Before the War 1890-1914* [New York: The Macmillan Co., 1966], 445).

In 1911, General Friedrich von Bernhardi published *Germany and the Next War,* which countered Norman Angell's *The Great Illusion*. Three of the chapter titles: "The Right to Make War," "The Duty to Make War," and "World Power or Downfall" summarize his position. "It was 'unthinkable,' he wrote, that Germany and France could ever negotiate their problems. **'France must be so completely crushed that she can never cross our path again'**; **'she must be annihilated** once and for all as a great power'" (Barbara W. Tuchman, *The Guns of August* [New York: Macmillan Co., 1962], 11).

Concerning Count Alfred von Schlieffen, Chief of the German General Staff from 1891-1906: **"Believing that war was a certainty** and that Germany must enter it under conditions that gave her the most promise of success, Schlieffen determined not to allow the Belgian difficulty to stand in Germany's way" (ibid., 17).

"Never had the European states maintained such huge armies in peacetime as at the beginning of the twentieth century. One, two, or even three years of compulsory military service for all young men became the rule. In 1914 each of the Continental Great Powers had not only a huge standing army but millions of trained reserves among the civilian population. **Few people wanted war; all but a few sensational writers preferred peace in Europe, but many took it for granted that war would come some day.** In the last years before 1914 **the idea that war was bound to break out sooner or later** probably made some statesmen, in some countries, more willing to unleash it" (R. R. Palmer and Joel Colton, *A History of the Modern World Since 1815* [8th ed.; New York: McGraw-Hill, Inc., 1995], 695-96).

"Germany was entirely prepared for war with France and Russia. She had long realized that the maintenance of her continental hegemony might lead to a conflict of arms, and **since 1912 had been putting herself in condition to carry on the war on both of her frontiers**" (Charles Seymour, *The Diplomatic Background of the War 1870-1914* [New Haven: Yale University Press, 1916], 272).

"But **although war was staved off, it continued to impend**; for the relations of States continued to be as they were before. Thus the Serbian minister in London reports as early as September 1911, a conversation held with M. Cambon [French Ambassador], which he sums up as follows: 'France is conscious that in any case the **war will be forced upon her**. But France together with her allies is of the opinion that the **war must be postponed to a more distant period, i.e., 1914-1915**, even at the cost of greater sacrifice" (G. Lowes Dickinson, *The International Anarchy, 1904-1914* [New York: The Century Co., 1926], 211).

"Although few wanted war, almost everyone had come to expect it, and preparations proceeded accordingly. **'I only meet people who assure me that an early war with Germany is certain, in fact, inevitable,'** the Belgian envoy reported from Paris in 1913. **'People regret it, but they accept it.' This resignation prevailed all over Europe**" (Andreas Dorpalen, *Europe in the 20th Century* [New York: The Macmillan Co., 1968], 10).

"**The great states of Europe had never been so powerfully prepared for war in human and material resources as in 1914**. And this was a natural result of the policy which they had pursued. In spite of lip-service rendered in theory and practice to international law, each had tended, partly unconsciously, to organize itself upon a basis of absolute power, and to worship its own collective image. The idea of European solidarity was no longer seen with even the deceptive clearness of a mirage. Thus the period has been well named by the author of a poignant book 'the international anarchy'" (C. R. M. F. Cruttwell, *A History of the Great War* 1914-1918 [2nd ed.; Oxford: Clarendon Press, 1936], 1).

"Thus it came about that the nineteenth century, and in particular its last three decades, intensified and universalized the principal of universal service" (ibid., 2).

"It is true to say that the growth of insecurity corresponded with the growth of armaments. Therefore, while peoples did not envisage war, they did not clearly embrace peace; their desire was rather for security, an impossible ideal, given the unrestricted sovereignty of the state-system.... And the natural result of these crises [in the decade before 1914] was to **intensify military preparation and to influence national hatreds**. So the vicious circle went round" (ibid., 3).

"In Russia and in France military development was the order of the day. **There were many who looked upon the general war as inevitable**; the Dual Alliance must get ready and must omit no step which might increase its diplomatic and military weight.... **Europe thus prepared for war** and, as William Graham Sumner used to say, 'What you prepared for you get.' It is true that in 1913 the immediate danger seemed to pass. ... But as the British Premier later wrote, the diplomats were conscious that they 'were skating on the thinnest of ice and that the peace of Europe was at the mercy of a chapter of unforeseen and unforeseeable accidents.' Like Roosevelt, House was convinced that **a European war must necessarily attain such proportions that every part of the world would be touched**, and that it was both the duty and the interest of the United States to do all in its power to avert it" (Charles Seymour, *The Intimate Papers of Colonel House*, vol. 1 [New York: Houghton Mifflin, 1926], 238).

"In a sense, there was no inevitability about the spread of war after Sarajevo, but by 1914 alliance systems had their own logic, the rivalries were fixed, and the antagonism of nations came for the depths of their past, from part of their collective consciousness. Contemporaries might believe war could be put off a year or two; it would come in the end. **War had conquered men's minds before it ever broke out**" (Marc Ferro, trans. Nicole Stone (*The Great War 1914-1918* [London: Routledge & Kegan Paul, 1973], 25).

"Illusions were virtually universal—only the 'wild' H. G. Wells, the designer, Albert Robida, the Russian theorist, Ivan Bloch, appreciated that the war would be industrialized, with millions of deaths and entire nations mobilized. **Works on war became so numerous after 1906 that they provoked a whole subsidiary literature**, a great army of critics. When war came, these were still attempting to make something out of the phenomenon" (Ibid., 27).

"**The British for their part had been preparing since 1911 for a possible landing on the coast of Jutland**; latterly they had decided to send their expeditionary force to the main armies' chief front—they would set up a strong-point in Antwerp, attach their forces to the French left at Maubeuge. They were prepared to go to war if necessary" (ibid., 28).

"**There were few doubts about war—whether it would come or how it would be fought. Men wondered only as to the occasion for it, whether it should be now or later**" (ibid., 32-33).

"That a clash should come in these circumstances may easily, in retrospect, be seen as no more than natural, not to say **inevitable. Preparations for war were indeed mounting on all sides, and it is an easy game to collect quotations** from the Kaiser, Conrad, Sazonov, or Lord Fisher, not to mention a bevy of others, **that prove the war was expected—nay, planned**...." (Rene' Albrecht-Carrie, *A Diplomatic History of Europe Since the Congress of Vienna* [New York: Harper and Row, Publishers, 1958], 294).

"It had been building up, this war that few men wanted, more and more rapidly since 1900. **There had been crisis after crisis**.... By the beginning of that fateful summer of 1914, Colonel Edward M. House, who was President Wilson's confidant and advisor declared: '**It only needs a spark to set the whole thing off**'" (Hanson W. Baldwin, *World War I: An Outline History* [New York: Harper & Row, 1962], 16).

"**Four times within ten years the Central Powers had challenged the governments of the Entente: Tangier, 1904; Bosnia, 1908; Agadir, 1911; Serbia, 1913**. Each time the Teutonic allies had sought gains which were legitimate according to the standards of power politics, but the main result had invariably been to arouse one or more of the Entente powers to the necessity of tightening their union and preparing for the future. **Soon Germany's authority would have to be exerted with finality or it would cease to exist**.... To the conservatives and nationalists in Germany **this belief meant that war was inevitable. In March 1914, Colonel Frobenius published Germany's *Hour of Destiny*, a book which soon ran into twelve editions in which he urged Germany to take aggressive action before Russia and France completed their preparations**. On April 19, 1914, the executive committee of the Pan-German League proclaimed that 'France and Russia are preparing for the decisive struggle with Germany and Austria-Hungary and they intend to strike at the first favorable opportunity.' On May 12, 1914, Moltke wrote to Conrad that 'if we delay any longer the chances of success will be diminished'" (D. F. Fleming, *The Origins and Legacies of World War I* [London: George Allen and Unwin Ltd, 1969], 140).

"**By the spring of 1914 the joint work of the French and British General Staffs was complete to the last billet of every battalion**, even to the places where they were to drink their coffee..." (Barbara W. Tuchman, *The Guns of August* [New York: The Macmillan Co., 1962], 55).

The Statements by Harold Macmillan and Konrad Adenauer

What can be said of the reminiscences of Harold Macmillan and Konrad Adenauer as quoted in Watch Tower publications? Internationally known historian Barbara W. Tuchman puts such memories of the past into perspective in the Foreword of her book, *The Proud Tower: A Portrait of the World Before the War 1890-1914*. Her research for the book changed her preconceptions:

> The period was not a Golden Age or *Belle Epoque* except to a thin crust of the privileged class. It was not a time exclusively of confidence, innocence, comfort, stability, security and peace. All these qualities were certainly present.... Our misconception lies in assuming that doubt and fear, ferment, protest, violence and hate were not equally present. **We have been misled by the people of the time themselves who, in looking back across the gulf of the War, see that earlier half of their lives misted over by a lovely sunset haze of peace and security**. It did not seem so golden when they were in the midst of it. Their memories and their nostalgia have conditioned our view of the pre-war era but I can offer the reader a rule based on adequate research: all statements of how lovely it was in that era made by persons contemporary with it will be found to have been made after 1914. A phenomenon of such extended malignance as the Great War does not come out of a Golden Age.[3]

These conclusions are also supported by the numerous quotations already cited above. What about Macmillan's statement that "Suddenly, unexpectedly, one morning in 1914 the whole thing came to an end"? This is not an unusual comment on the commencement of a war. The February 1, 1901, *Watch Tower* (cited above) quoted British statesman Lord Salisbury who said of threatened wars: "**These wars come upon us absolutely unannounced and with terrible rapidity**. The war cloud rises in the horizon with a **rapidity that obviates all calculation**, and, it may be, a month or two months after the first warning you receive, you find you are engaged in, or in prospect of a war on which your very existence is staked."[4]

What about Konrad Adenauer's (1876-1967) reference to the time "before the year 1914 when there was real peace, quiet and security on this earth"? This may have been how he remembered this pre-war period, but was this accurate? "It is true that *Europe* had experienced one of its longest peace periods before 1914.... *But this held true only of Europe....* The stark fact is that, for the rest of the world, frequent wars raged practically everywhere before 1914."[5] To document this last statement, one might consult the table of "World Major Wars, 1816-1965" by Singer and Small. This shows that for the period from the end of the Franco-Prussian war (1871) to the beginning of World War I there were **28 wars**.[6] This information, combined with the numerous quotations above, show that Adenaeur's appraisal of the pre-1914 period was wrong.

George Hannan

In his observations on the war in the May 8, 1981, *Awake!*, George Hannan was not identified as a prominent Jehovah's Witness. In his testimony in the January 15, 1970, *Watchtower*, "Waiting on Jehovah with Endurance," he informs the reader that he had already spent 47 years in service at Brooklyn headquarters.[7] The observations made by Hannan as a 15-year-old American farm boy beginning his first year of high school, that "nobody expected World War I," etc., while in agreement with the Watch Tower Society's view provides no support for their position.[8]

Conclusion

It is obvious from the foregoing review that Watch Tower claims as cited earlier are not credible.

Notes

1. For some examples of the writers, scholars and publications cited and often misused in Watch Tower publications, see: Carl Olof Jonsson and Wolfgang Herbst, *The "Sign" of the Last Days—When?* (Atlanta: Commentary Press, 1987), chapter 5: "Some Remarkable Facts About Wars."
2. "The New York Times Review of Books," Autumn Book Number, Section 5, 421.
3. Barbara Tuchman, *The Proud Tower: A Portrait of the World Before the War 1890-1914* (New York: The Macmillan Co., 1966), xiii-xiv.
4. *WTR*, 1 Feb. 1901, 2768. Lord Salisbury was foreign minister under Benjamin Disraeli and was present at the Congress of Berlin (1878). He served as Prime Minister (1885-86, 1886-92, 1985-1902. He died in 1903.
5. Jonsson and Herbst, 135.
6. Francis A. Beer, *Peace Against War* (San Francisco: W. H. Freeman and Co., 1981), 27-28.
7. *Awake!*, 15 Jan. 1970, 56-61.
8. Ibid., 57. Hannan's traveling and speaking for the Watch Tower Society are reported in: *WT*, 15 July 1945, 220-22; *WT*, 15 Jan. 1952, 59-60. The May 8, 1981, *Awake!* article also used statements made by three other long-time Jehovah's Witnesses: Ewart Chitty, Maxwell Friend, and John Booth (6). Their testimonies are found in the *Watchtower:* Chitty (15 Feb. 1963, 118-20), Friend (15 Apr. 1967, 249-55), Booth (15 Sept. 1983, 21-27).

16.

"The Sign" of Christ's Presence in 1914 and "the Last Days"

As the Witnesses' second major part of the argument that Christ's presence and "the last days" began in 1914, they cite the events viewed as fulfilling prophecy since that year. It is explained: "The Bible describes events and conditions that mark this significant time period. 'The sign' is a composite one made up of many evidences; thus its fulfillment requires that all aspects of the sign be clearly in evidence during one generation."[1] Typical of many other statements, the May 1, 1952, *Watchtower* claims: "**At no time in previous history have all these things occurred at once to comprise a composite sign as has been the case since 1914.**"[2] And the February 15, 1994, *Watchtower* adds: "Informed people acknowledge that **the composite sign** foretold at Matthew 24:7-14 and Revelation 6:2-8 has been **manifest since the first outbreak of world war in 1914.**"[3]

Watch Tower publications have presented variations of "the sign" numerous times in their publications, or in some cases featured just one of its aspects. An example of this is "Wars A Sign of What?" in the April 1, 1983, *Watchtower*, the first issue of a series.[4] Upon examination, it is possible to divide the features of "The sign," as currently viewed, into two broad categories: those relating to the Witness movement since 1914, and those relating to the conditions in the world that are viewed as peculiarly characteristic of the "last days." The latter category is usually featured in the literature for public consumption and would include such features as world wars, famines, pestilences, earthquakes, and increasing lawlessness. Is it as clear as the Witnesses claim: "The 'last days' contain their own pattern of marks or happenings. These form a positive 'fingerprint' that cannot belong to any other time period"?[5] As a preliminary response to the Witnesses' position, the following statement by Carl Olof Jonsson and Wolfgang Herbst should be considered:

> What of the argument that "every feature of the sign would have to be *observed by one generation*"? Does that single out the generation of 1914—or any generation of this century—as unique in this respect? By no means. Anyone who undertakes an honest and careful investigation of the matter will soon discover that it is practically impossible to find *one* generation during the past 2,000 years that *has not* observed the combined different features of the supposed "composite sign"![6]

The authors back up their contention in their book, *The "Sign" of the Last Days—When?* (1987), from which this statement is taken. While **many Christians do believe that these are "the last days,"** the question is, do these "signs" support the Witnesses' claim that the "the last days" and Christ's "presence" **began in 1914?**

The signs cited by Witnesses to verify their interpretation of prophecy have been featured in numerous articles and in various combinations in Watch Tower publications. The following representative selection, "Twenty-Four Features of the Sign," is found in the March 1, 1993, *Watchtower*.[7]

1. Unprecedented Warfare—Matthew 24:6,7; Revelation 6:4

It should be noted that the sign being identified as "unprecedented warfare" goes beyond what the Matthew passage actually says. It simply reads, "YOU are going to hear of wars and reports of wars.... For nation will rise against nation and kingdom against kingdom..."(*NWT*).

Under the heading "WARS AND RUMORS OF WARS," the *Watch Tower* of March 1, 1904, presents Russell's scenario of what was seen concerning war before 1914:

> In using the above words (Matt. 24:6) our Lord indicated by their connection that the mere fact of war should prove nothing to his people respecting the consummation of the age. They were to be otherwise guided in their discernment of the signs of the times.... **Our expectations respecting a war have been realized**. We based that expectation not on any private information, nor on prophecy, but upon the thought that unless war intervened to prolong the commercial prosperity of Christendom a great financial depression would be sure to come speedily; and because we could not see time enough for such a depression and a recovery from it and a subsequent depression, all before October, 1914, when prophecy teaches us to expect the great climax of earth's troubles.... **The present outlook is that the success of the Japanese over the Russians thus early in the war will prolong the conflict and quite probably draw into it many other civilized nations.**[8]

Russell then presents a possible scenario of the involvement of other nations: Great Britain, Turkey, France, Germany, and even the United States. But the war here is connected with the Russo-Japanese war of 1904-05.[9]

Randall Watters points out that the April 1, 1983, *Watchtower* asks the question, "Are We Living in the Last Days?" (p. 3)

> and referred to the frequency of wars as a proof of such, quoting Quincy Wright in *A Study of War* [p. 6]. Yet what they failed to mention was that Wright himself produces evidence of the following:

> 1. The turning point regarding wars is not 1914, but 1942.
> 2. The frequency of wars actually decreased after 1914.
> 3. Although 1914 was the first world war, the evidence shows that all the major powers in the world fought general wars since 1600.[10]

In their book *The Wages of War 1816-1965: A Statistical Handbook*, professors J. David Singer and Melvin Small look at the trends in the incidence of wars and conclude:

> **Is war on the increase as many scholars as well as laymen of our generation have been inclined to believe? The answer would seem to be a very unambiguous negative**. Whether we look at the number of wars, their severity or their magnitude, **there is no significant trend**

upward or down over the past 150 years. Even if we examine their intensities, we find that later wars are by and large no different from those of earlier periods, Likewise, even if we differentiate among different types of war, there seems to be no appreciable change in their frequency, when we control for their statistical probability as a function of the number of national units available to fight in these types of war. That is, the number of interstate wars per decade has risen no faster than the number of nations in the interstate system...."[11]

Political science professor John Mueller observes: "On May 15, 1984, the major countries of the developed world had managed to remain at peace with each other **for the longest continuous stretch of time since the days of the Roman Empire**."[12] And now (Summer 2001) more than 17 years may be added. More recently, an article in the August 22, 1999, *Los Angeles Times* reported:

> Since the fall of the Soviet Union, it is commonly believed, interethnic and religious wars have dramatically increased. **There is just one problem with this picture: It does not reflect reality**. No matter how you count it—number of deaths, number of new outbreaks of violence or severity of violence—the evidence shows **a steady downward trend in conflicts since the early 1990s**. Peacemaking is prevailing over war-making.[13]

2. Earthquakes—Matthew 24:7; Mark 13:8

"Earthquakes in one place after another" (*NWT*). The following quotations are typical of the many statements and claims repeatedly made concerning earthquakes in Watch Tower publications in support of the 1914 date. The September 15, 1924, Watch Tower claims: "There have been more literal earthquakes since 1914 than known in all the history of man...."[14] The May 1, 1933, issue agrees: "There have been more earthquakes experienced since 1914 than ever before in the history of man."[15] *From Paradise Lost to Paradise Regained* (1958) states: "Since 1914 earthquakes have been great. At Mark 13:8 the Son of God said: 'There will be earthquakes in one place after another.' True it is: **since 1914** earthquakes have occurred more often than ever before."[16]

The front cover of the February 22, 1977, *Awake!* features the article title: "Earthquake Alert! What Should You Do?" The article itself is followed by another: "'There Will be Great Earthquakes'" (Luke 21:11), which concludes:

> Interestingly, for a period of 1,059 years (856 to 1914 C.E.), reliable sources list **only 24 major earthquakes**, with 1,972,952 fatalities. But compare that with the accompanying *partial list* citing 43 instances of earthquakes, in which 1,579,209 persons died during just the 62 years from 1915 to 1976 C.E.... **The dramatic upsurge in earthquake activity since 1914 helps to prove that we are living in the time of Jesus' presence**. These mighty temblors fulfill his prophecy: "There will be great earthquakes."[17]

In the popular book, *You Can Live Forever in Paradise on Earth* (1982), next to a graphic picture of earthquake devastation, is a similar statement: "From 1914 until now, there have been many more major earthquakes than in any other like period in recorded history. For over 1,000 years, from the year 856 C.E. to 1914, **there were only 24 major earthquakes**, causing some 1,973,000 deaths. But in the 63 years from 1915 to 1978, a total of some 1,600,000 persons died in 43 great earthquakes."[18]

Are Watch Tower Claims Credible?

Do Watch Tower publications present a credible case for these and similar claims? In their chapter, "Earthquakes and Historical Facts," in *The "Sign" of the Last Days—When?*, authors Jonsson and Herbst ask the question raised by the Watch Tower Society material: "Is our planet Earth shaking with greater frequency and intensity than ever before in human history?"[19] After a careful examination of a number of the statements and claims concerning earthquakes in Society publications, what did they conclude?

> Quotations taken out of context and given a different, slanted meaning; biased selection of figures and data; misuse of and even fabrication of statistics that are then presented as though coming from an outside, neutral source—these are the methods employed by the Watch Tower publications to support the claim that the number of earthquakes and of quake victims has soared since 1914. How is it that persons considered as devout and respectable men resort to such methods?[20]

> We have seen, one by one, the different claims of the Watch Tower Society demolished by historical facts: that the period A.D. 856-1914 saw only 24 major earthquakes, that the great earthquakes of the past occurred "years, even centuries, apart," that history records only five "superquakes" from the time of Christ to 1914, and that no single generation before 1914 can equal the one following that year with respect to earthquake victims. Is it really possible that the writers of the Watch Tower publications are so ignorant of past earthquakes—or are they trying to conceal the truth about them from their readers? We prefer to believe that they *primarily* have been ignorant of the facts. But if so, it is extremely remarkable that an organization claiming authorization by Jesus Christ to interpret the signs of the times seems to take so little interest in verifying that its interpretations and statistics are in line with historical reality.[21]

They conclude their study on earthquakes with the following statement:

> **...There is no evidence whatsoever in support of the claim ... that earthquake activity is markedly different in our century compared with earlier centuries. All information available points to the contrary**. The shifting, twisting, uncoordinated claims of the Watch Tower Society and their juggling of facts and figures in an effort to prove that an increase has occurred have been revealed above as fraudulent—hopefully not deliberately so, but as a result of remarkably poor research, superficial analysis and wishful thinking.[22]

For anyone interested in reading the details of the Watch Tower Society's unfounded position, with a strong rebuttal to their claims, one should read the chapter, "Earthquakes and Historical Facts," in *The "Sign" of the Last Days—When?* and also Appendix A, which reproduces "Correspondence with Seismologists."[23]

Watchtower: **"Earthquakes a Sign of the End."** To illustrate by specific examples what is referred to by Jonsson and Herbst, three are taken from *The Watchtower* article, "Earthquakes A Sign of the End?" in the May 15, 1983, issue:

1. *Watchtower:* "Some seismologists believe that the earth is now in an active earthquake period. For example, Professor Keiiti Aki of the Department of Earth and Planetary Sciences at the Massachusetts Institute of Technology speaks of 'the apparent surge in intensity and frequency of major earthquakes during the last one hundred years,' though stating that the period from 1500 to 1700 was as active."[24]

Response: In reality, when Aki's letter (dated September 30, 1982) to the Watchtower Society is read, it is obvious that his position was misrepresented. What he actually said was: "The **apparent** surge in intensity and frequency of major earthquakes during the last one hundred years is, **in all probability, due to the improved recording of earthquakes and the increased vulnerability of human society to earthquake damage**."[25]

In a letter to Jonsson and Herbst (dated September 5, 1985), Aki writes: "I feel strongly that the seismicity has been **stationary for thousands of years**. I was trying to convince Jehovah's Witnesses about the **stationarity of seismicity** using the data obtained in China from the period 1500 through 1700, but they put only weak emphasis in the published statement."[26]

2. *Watchtower:* In the Italian journal *Il Piccolo*, of October 8, 1978, Geo Malagoli observed: "Our generation lives in a dangerous period of high seismic activity, as statistics show. In fact, during a period of 1,059 years (from 856 to 1914) reliable sources list only 24 major earthquakes causing 1,973,000 deaths. However, [in] recent disasters, we find that 1,600,000 persons have died in only 63 years, as a result of 43 earthquakes which occurred from 1915 to 1978. This dramatic increase further goes to emphasize another accepted fact—our generation is an unfortunate one in many ways."[27]

Response: If the words of this statement sound familiar to the reader, it is because they are basically a repetition of what was published in the February 22, 1977, *Awake!* quoted above. And as Jonsson and Herbst observe: "And from now on this Geo Malagoli began to appear in the Watch Tower publications, time and again, every time the subject of earthquakes was brought up for discussion—elevated to the position of a neutral, impartial earthquake authority!"[28]

And in conclusion on this point, they write:

Thus we find that the Watch Tower Society's principal, yes, its sole seemingly "neutral" and "impartial" proof that earthquake activity has increased since 1914 is an Italian writer, who—undoubtedly in good faith—borrowed his "information" right out of the *Awake!* magazine. That "information" on seismic activity in the past, is, in turn, completely erroneous and has nothing to do with actual historical evidence. The fact that the Society, time and again, has presented this false information—seemingly from a neutral source—in order to "prove" its interpretation of the "sign" since 1914, should induce every honest reader of its publications to ask if this society is genuinely deserving of his or her confidence in its remarkable claims.[29]

What about the statistics from the *Awake!* article repeated in *Il Piccolo* by Malagoli? Jonsson and Herbst write: "The statement that 'reliable sources list only 24 major earthquakes for the 1,059 years from 856 to 1914' is so far from the truth that it is almost impossible to understand how anyone with even an elementary knowledge of the subject could make such a statement. *The fact is that reliable sources list literally thousands of destructive earthquakes during this period!*"[30] Yet, the Witness author of the book, *You Can Live Forever in Paradise on Earth* (1982), quoted above, could write: "For over 1,000 years, from the year 856 C.E. to 1914, there were only 24 major earthquakes, causing some 1,973,000 deaths."[31] The interested reader can quickly and easily check on the statements of Jonsson and Herbst and those in Watch Tower publications on this point by perusing the "Significant Earthquakes Listed Chronologically" chapter in the *Catalog of*

Significant Earthquakes 2150 B.C.-1991 A.D., available in many public libraries.[32]

In an obvious later attempt to escape the "only 24 major earthquakes" claim, the book *Reasoning from the Scriptures* (1985) asks the question, "Has there actually been a significant number of major earthquakes since 1914?" The pre-1914 time period was changed from 856 A.D. to the 2,000 years before 1914. The criteria of selection was that the earthquake "measured 7.5 or more on the Richter scale, or that resulted in destruction of five million dollars (U.S.) or more in property, or that caused 100 or more deaths."[33] (The Watch Tower criteria for selection exceeded those for "significant earthquakes" in the *Catalog*.)[34] The *Reasoning* book continues: "It was calculated that there had been 856 of such earthquakes during the 2,000 years before 1914. The same tabulation showed that *in just 69 years* following 1914 there were 605 such quakes. That means that, in comparison with the previous 2,000 years, the average per year has been **20 times as great since 1914**."[35]

Jonsson and Herbst comment: "Although this is a step in the right direction, this figure is a far cry from the actual truth. The arguments based on this new figure are as deceptive as those based on the earlier figures."[36] They sent letters to a number of recognized seismologists and asked about the "20 times" increase claim. "All of them rejected the claim and none of them thought that our century is in any way unique with respect to the number of great earthquakes."[37] One of these responses was written by Waverly J. Person, Chief of the National Earthquake and Information Service, dated October 8, 1985: "Our records do not show any significant increase in great earthquakes. Enclosed is a list of all magnitude 8.0 or greater earthquakes we have on file."[38]

Dr. Person's list presents these earthquakes from 1897 onward and is summarized by Jonsson and Herbst as follows.[39]

17-year period	No. of great earthquakes	Annual average
1897-1913	49	2.9
1914-1930	28	1.6
1931-1947	28	1.6
1948-1964	14	0.8
1965-1981	10	0.6

3. *Watchtower*: The article presents an "incomplete list" of "Some Major Earthquakes Between 1914 and 1982. Some 18 earthquake locations and the number of deaths resulting from each are listed. While the total of deaths is not given, when added, it is 1,570,900.[40]

Response: Watch Tower publications have published other earthquake lists with their death tolls, but as Jonsson and Herbst point out: "Interestingly, the death figures in these lists also seem to change from one list to [the] next, and they differ with authoritative reports in several instances."[41] This is illustrated by comparing the May 15, 1983, *Watchtower* list with the one in the February 22, 1977, *Awake!* on six earthquakes: China (1920), Turkey (1939), India (1950), Iran (1962), Nicaragua (1972) and China (1976). The 1983 list raises the figures by almost 200,000 deaths.[42] How is this to be explained? Different sources sometimes do give different information: "But the Watch Tower Society's listings reveal a clear tendency to choose always the *highest*, not the most *reliable*, figures in these works, evidently in an attempt to present earthquakes of the twentieth century as being as 'great' as possible, while the tendency to *reduce* the numbers and size of the earthquakes *before* 1914 is equally apparent. This is not an honest, objective use of data."[43]

Of special interest is the great earthquake in China in 1976. The February 22, 1977, *Awake!* places the number of deaths at **655,235** and the May 15, 1983, *Watchtower* places them at **800,000**. This earthquake "in reality claimed **242,000** lives according to figures released by the Chinese authorities! This lower figure is now generally believed by seismologists to be the correct one."[44] The July 15, 1991, *Watchtower* even quoted, without questioning, the October 19, 1989, *Yorkshire Post*, which says of the 1976 quake: "China suffered the worst quake in its modern history. At least **240,000** died when the northeastern city of Tangshan was almost completely leveled...."[45]

The foregoing examples are typical of many others which are covered by Jonsson and Herbst and clearly show the Watch Tower arguments are not objective or tenable.

Some Additional Observations

What have others written about the claimed increase of earthquake activity during the 20th century? In his article, "Earthquakes," in *Natural History* (December 1969), Charles F. Richter (after whom the "Richter scale" is named) makes some important observations pertinent here:

One notices with some amusement that certain religious groups have picked this rather unfortunate time to insist that the number of earthquakes is increasing. In part they are misled by the increasing number of small earthquakes that are being catalogued and listed by newer, more sensitive stations throughout the world. **It is worth remarking that the number of great earthquakes [magnitude 8] from 1896 to 1906 (about twenty-five) was greater than in any ten-year interval since.**[46]

In his article "Earthquakes in These Last Days," geologist Steven A. Austin explains why the uninformed often reach wrong conclusions concerning the history of earthquake activity:

Some people have supposed that earthquake frequency and intensity have been increasing significantly in recent years, and that this is fulfilling prophecy. This is an illusion caused lately by more frequent detection of earthquakes (more seismographs with greater sensitivity). The illusion is also promoted by the fact that earthquakes inflict greater damage on today's larger, urbanized populations, and, therefore, make the news more often. Since good seismographs went into operation late in the 1890's, **no steady trend suggesting increased frequency or intensity has been demonstrated.**[47]

In a second article, "Twentieth-Century Earthquakes: Confronting An Urban Legend," Austin again examines the claim that earthquakes have been on the increase this century. He presents some significant information:

Excellent global summaries of the frequency of large earthquakes have been prepared by the NEIC [National Earthquake Information Center].... These include the "killer quakes" which cause most of the fatalities. The frequency of this century's "major" (magnitude 7.0-7.9) and "great" (magnitude 8.0 and higher) earthquakes is summarized in figure 1.... The global earthquake frequency data can be used to argue just the opposite of the popular urban legend; **earth-**

quake frequency through the century appears to indicate overall a slight decrease. From the data in figure 1 we note 1,093 big earthquakes for the first half of the century (1900 to 1949). That is an average of 22 big earthquakes per year. For the nearly completed second half of the century (1950-1996) we note just 850 big earthquakes. That is an average of just 18 per year. When 1998 and 1999 are completed, it is likely that the second half of the century will have about 900 big earthquakes—nearly 200 less than the first half. Thus, the 30-year cyclic pattern appears to be modulated around a slightly-declining trend.[48]

The article on "Famous Earthquakes" in *Magill's Survey of Science* explains:

There are a few misconceptions about great earthquakes. After a newsworthy earthquake, **people often wonder if earthquakes are becoming unusually frequent. The reverse has been true in the twentieth century**: There are about two earthquakes per year of magnitude 8 on the average, in contrast to an annual average of eight during the years 1896-1907. One apparent pattern is real, however: Great killer earthquakes are becoming more common. **The reason is demographic rather than geologic.** Many seismically active regions are in underdeveloped nations where populations, especially in cities, are growing explosively and where construction standards are often poor. The population at risk from earthquakes is steadily increasing.[49]

The *Catalog of Significant Earthquakes 2150 B.C-1991 A.D.* cautions:

...It is misleading to use the numbers of significant earthquakes in that publication to suggest statistically that there has been an increase in worldwide seismic activity since 1900 or for any other period.... In summary, using the data in *Catalog of Significant Earthquakes, 2150 B.C.–1991 A.D.* to suggest that there has been an increase in worldwide earthquake activity **is misleading and erroneous**.[50]

In spite of this testimony from experts in the field, The January 15, 1987, *Watchtower* states:

Many seismologists believe that earthquakes are no greater or more frequent now than they were in the past. Conversely, **others conclude that our generation has experienced earthquakes more frequently than did previous ones. Based on available records, the 20th century does significantly overshadow the past in seismic activity.** Publications of the Watch Tower Society have repeatedly called attention to this, highlighting the Biblical significance of earthquakes occurring since 1914.* [*See "Earthquakes—A Sign of the End?" in *The Watchtower* of May 15, 1983.][51]

The first part of the sentence in the above statement has already been adequately documented. Who are those who "conclude that our generation has experienced earthquakes more frequently than did previous ones"? No one is named in the article, and the reference to the May 15, 1983, *Watchtower* article (discussed above) quotes Geo Malagoli (who drew his "expert" knowledge of the subject from the *Awake!* magazine) and Professor Keiiti Aki (whose position was misrepresented in the article). Aki's true position, and the statements by the authorities quoted earlier, answer the *Watchtower* claim. In another attempt to prove their position, the April 22, 1995, *Awake!* cites Matthew 24:7, "Earthquakes, in one place after another," and states: "During this century, earthquakes measuring from 7.5 to 8.3 on the Richter scale have been experienced in

Chile, China, India, Iran, Italy, Japan, Peru, and Turkey."[52]

This is true—but **a number of the earthquakes of this magnitude in these same countries occurred in the years before 1914**—between 1900 and 1913: **Chile** (1906, 1909); **China** (1902, 1906); **India** (1905, 1908, 1909, 1911); **Iran** (1909); **Italy** (1905, 1908);[53] **Japan** (1900, 1901, 1904, 1905, 1906, 1908, 1909, 1910, 1911); **Peru** (1906, 1907, 1908, 1912, 1913); and **Turkey** (1912).[54]

Other countries could be added which make the same point. For example: **Greece** (1903, 1904, 1905); the area of the former **USSR** (1900, 1901, 1902, 1904, 1905, 1906, 1907, 1908, 1911, 1913); **Philippines** (1901, 1903, 1907, 1908, 1911, 1913; **Mexico** (1900, 1902, 1903, 1906, 1907, 1908, 1909, 1911, 1912; **Indonesia** (1903, 1905, 1907, 1908, 1909, 1910, 1913).[55]

And finally, the September 15, 1998, *Watchtower* claims: "During the last 2,500 years, **only nine earthquakes** have each killed over 100,000 people. Four of these quakes occurred since 1914."[56] I sent this statement (without identifying the source) in a letter to the National Geophysical Data Center in Boulder, Colorado, asking about its accuracy. The letter in response dated July 6, 1999, states: "There were **24 events** from [A.D.] 115 to today that have caused deaths over 100,000. Of these events, from 1920 to 1976 there were four events causing deaths over 100,000. I don't know why someone might have counted nine events, unless they considered many of these events as duplicates [which does not fit the data]." The letter is accompanied by a full-page printout of documentation. Earthquakes prove nothing concerning 1914.

Russell's "Earthquakes in Prophecy" Sermon

Pastor Russell spoke to an overflow crowd at Thomas' Orchestra Hall in Chicago on January 20, 1907, on the topic, "Earthquakes in Prophecy." His text was Luke 21:11: "And there shall be great earthquakes in divers places and famines and pestilences; and fearful sights and great signs shall there be from heaven." In his message he said:

> About a year and a half ago an earthquake destroyed eighteen villages in Cambria, Italy, with a loss of thousands of human lives. A little later another earthquake sent a monster tidal wave over the city of Esmeralda and swallowed up four small islands off the coast of Port Limones. Next came the earthquake in the Island of Formosa, Japan, destroying thousands. A short interval and San Francisco and other adjacent cities were almost demolished and other thousands of lives sacrificed. Then another destroyed Valaparaiso and killed many. Since then Sweden and Great Britain report slight tremors, which scientific instruments indicate must have been of great severity somewhere. Now we have the Kingston [Jamaica] disaster.[57]

> The New York *Tribune* remarks: "The last year and a half will probably go down in history as one of the most disastrous periods of earthquake activity in the records of the human race." Our opinion is to the contrary, that much more violent and much more destructive disturbances **are just ahead of us**: and our opinion is based upon the testimony of the Scriptures. **The recent prevalence of earthquakes properly draws our attention to the Scriptures and what they have to say on the subject. Our text is from the Master's own lips** [Luke 21:11: "and there shall be great earthquakes in divers places"]—**a part of his description of the trouble that would come upon the world in the close of this age, preparatory to the inauguration of the Millennial age**.... It is far from our thought than an earthquake is of itself a sign of the end of the age.... But ... we have pointed out in our "Studies in the Scriptures" various lines of prophecy which converge upon the present time, clearly marking the period between 1875 and 1915 as the harvest time of this Gospel age, in which the elect are to be gathered ... ultimately to experience the

change of resurrection and glorification to the spiritual, heavenly nature. And that shortly thereafter the new dispensation will begin, the Millennial Kingdom....[58]

After reviewing earthquake activity and results mentioned earlier, Russell concludes: "...All these things appeal to us as being incidental **corroborations of the prophecies that show that we are getting close to the great time of trouble**. True, there may be a lull for a time, but we have confidence that our Lord's prophecy of our text has a meaning, and that the time for its fulfillment must be very close."[59] It is obvious that the prophecy concerning earthquakes was viewed by Russell as already in the process of fulfillment **before** 1914.

Conclusion

So much more could be examined and documented, but when the evidence on earthquakes is examined, the twentieth century since 1914 is not unique. Earthquake statistics do not support the Watch Tower claims and the 1914 date.

3. Food shortages—famine Matthew 24:7; Mark 13:8 — "There will be food shortages [famines]" (*NWT*).

4. Pestilences—Luke 21:11; Revelation 6:8

While famines and pestilences are listed as two separate features in Watch Tower publications, they will be reviewed together here as they are joined in Luke 21:11 ("pestilences and food shortages" *NWT*). The following statistics on famine, pestilence and related deaths during the nineteenth century and through 1913, unless otherwise noted, are selected from *Darkest Hours* (1977) by Jay Robert Nash.[60]

1810 – China – "First great famine of century in this country." Deaths: "millions."

1811 – China – "Second great famine." Deaths: "millions."

1812-1813 – India – "Country devastated by famine, locusts, plague of rats & masses of starved immigrants." Deaths: "millions."

1816-1817 – Ireland – "Severe famine swept country." Deaths: "737,000."

1826-1837 – Europe – "Cholera epidemic killed 900,000 in 1831, continent scourged for years." Deaths: "millions."

1833 – India – "...Underwent a famine in 1833 that took the lives of more than 200,000 persons, a conservative estimate by most standards."[61]

1837-1838 – India – "Lack of rain caused absolute drought in the northwest." Deaths: "800,000."

1840-1862 – The World "Epidemic of cholera infected the earth for 2 decades." Deaths: "millions."

1845-50 – Ireland – "For four years, beginning in 1845, the potato crop in Ireland was destroyed by blight (as it was throughout Europe). Since potatoes were the staple food of the Irish people, famine set in along with typhoid, typhus and scurvy killing 1,029,552...."[62]

1846 – China – "Third great famine to cripple country this century." Deaths: "millions."

1849 – China "**Famines in the first-half of this century took over 45 million lives.**" Deaths: "millions."

1863-1875 – The World "Cholera epidemic continued for a decade: over 300,000 victims died in 1866 in Eastern Europe." Deaths: "millions."

1866 – India – "... More than 1.5 million persons died of starvation and subsequent diseases"[63]

1876-77 – India – "The Great Famine of 1876-77 was the most extensive on record and took a record number of six million lives.... Coupled to this [famine] was widespread cholera, which took more than half the lives lost."[64]

1877-78 – China – "Details of this mammoth disaster are sketchy to this day, yet it has been reliably determined that between 9.5 and 13 million people perished in northern and central China during the years 1877-78.... More than 70 million Chinese were affected by the famine."[65]

The April 15, 1983, *Watchtower* mentions this same famine: "And it is true that history is full of accounts of famine from away back in the days of Abraham and Joseph up to the **greatest recorded famine of all time**, the one that struck China between 1878 and 1879.... Estimates of the number of Chinese who died in that famine vary from 9 to 13 million."[66]

1889-1890 The World "Influenza epidemic affected 40% of the earth's population." Deaths: "millions."

1892-1894 China "Drought brought great famine." Deaths: "1,000,000"

1893-1894 – The World "Cholera epidemic spread everywhere." Deaths: "millions." The May 1, 1895, *Zion's Watch Tower* reports that the English newspaper "The London *Spectator*, after telling of the ravages of influenza during the past winter doubling the death rate, suggests that the world is resting in a fancied security as to safety from plagues such as have visited the world in the past...." Then it comments: "The Scriptures indicate that pestilences, as well as physical convulsions, will mingle with anarchy in making up the sum of the great trouble approaching, which will be a judgment from the Almighty...."[67]

1896-97 – India – "Drought caused famine & widespread disease." Deaths: "5,000,000." The *Watch Tower* of February 15, 1897, reports:

> **We are living in a day when history is being made as never before.** Before us lies an account from the Chicago *Times-Herald*, stating ... the secretary of the Bureau of the Associated Charities of that city declared that there are 8,000 families in Chicago actually starving to death.... Another account is from Louisiana, of which Congressman Boatman declares that there are one hundred thousand destitute people in the Northern part of the state on account of the failure of crops in that vicinity. The London *Chronicle* sums up **a total of eighty-four millions of the population of India affected by the famine**.... And the famine has recently been supplemented by the Bubonic plague, which is making terrible ravages.[68]

1898 – India – "Scarcity of food for two years, the failure of major crops and an almost total absence of rain reduced great tracts of India to rampant famine during 1898.... The death toll of this Indian famine topped one million."[69]

1899-1900 – India – "Drought caused millions to starve with millions more dead from disease which followed." Deaths: "1,250,000."

1899-1901 – India – "Famine of long duration." Deaths: "1,000,000."

In his book, *The Geopolitics of Hunger*, Josue' de Castro estimates that during the nineteenth century "some **one hundred million" Chinese died of starvation**, and in India **"twenty million people died of hunger** in the last thirty years of the century...."[70]

In the article on "Famine" in *Collier's Encyclopedia*, one reads that "during the latter half of the 19th century six serious famines occurred in Russia, accounting for more than half the notable famines of that period in the world outside of India."[71]

According to the November 15, 1901, *Zion's Watch Tower*: "Phenomenal conditions have given American farmers great prosperity—at the expense of millions in India and Russia, who have suffered from famine."[72]

1903 (Jan.-Aug.) – India – "Plague throughout wide area." Deaths: "600,000."

1904 – India – "Plague in Bombay, Bengal, the N.W. provinces and the Punjab" Deaths: "1,000,000."

1905 – India – "Plague" as in the above areas Deaths: "500,000."

1906 – India – "Plague throughout country." Deaths: "356,700."

1907 – India – "Plague continued in country." Deaths: 1,316,000.

1910-1913 – China and India – "Bubonic Plague ravaged both countries for great duration." Deaths: "millions."

The July 1, 1911, *Watch Tower* reported: "Harrowing reports come from both China and India. Eighty-eight thousand four hundred and ninety-eight are said to have died in India in February.... In Northern China the plague has been gradually progressing since early December [1910]. And it is said that not one who was taken the disease has, thus far, recovered."[73]

1911 – Russia – "This famine climaxed ones of 1891 & 1906, 30 million people were affected but no accurate statistics of dead."

Some Conclusions by Jonsson and Herbst

What about famine and pestilence in the twentieth century—**since 1914**? Have these become worse? In their book, *The "Sign" of the Last Days—When?*, Carl Olof Jonsson and Wolfgang Herbst, after an extensive review of the evidence on famine and pestilence, state some conclusions pertinent here.[74]

> Even if it is true that statistics are incomplete, there is enough information preserved to demonstrate that the **number of famines has *decreased* in our century** compared with earlier centuries! This will become apparent in the following survey of past famines in China, India, Europe, and other parts of the world.[75]

> Our examination of famines in the three greatest population centers on earth [China, India, and Europe], with a combined population of *more than half of mankind*, thus shows a remarkable development: from having been the most famine-plagued areas on earth, our twentieth century has seen these centers gradually freed almost completely from the scourge of famine! This phenomenal *decrease* of famines in these countries is more than enough to show that **any claimed *increase* in famines in this century, or since 1914 in particular, simply has no foundation in fact**.[76]

> The evidence brought to light during our investigation can lead to only one conclusion, namely, that on a world basis **famines have *decreased*, and decreased *very conspicuously*, in this twentieth century**, including the period since 1914.[77]

> Faced with the hard evidence that famine and hunger were unquestionably greater in past centuries than today, those who write material designed to excite a sense of impending doom often resort to the discussion, not of what *has* happened or *is* happening, but of what *might* happen.[78]

> Today, in this last quarter of the twentieth century, people still become ill and people still die. But only a small fraction die from pestilence, fewer than ever before in known history. Despite the dire forebodings and frightening scenes dramatically drawn by some authors and religious sources, the facts show that the health picture in our century is, not darker, but measurably brighter for mankind as a whole.[79]

Finally, in agreement with the above, David Beckmann and Arthur Simon, current president and founding president of Bread for the World, write: "In the developing countries, the proportion of the **population that is hungry has decreased over the last 25 years** from one-third to one-fifth. And even though the population of those countries grew substantially, **fewer people are hungry now than in 1970.**"[80]

Notes

1. *Reasoning from the Scriptures* (1985), 234.
2. *WT*, 1 May 1952, 276.
3. *WT*, 15 Feb., 1994, 12.
4. All are 1983 *WT*:

   April 1: "Wars A Sign of What?"
   April 15: "Famine What Does It Mean?"
   May 1: "Disease A Sign of the Last Days?"
   May 15: "Earthquakes A Sign of the End?"
   June 1: "Increasing Lawlessness A Sign of What?"
   June 15: "Disobedience to Parents A Sign of the Last Days?"
   July 1: "Pleasure Put in God's Place—Why?"
   July 15: "Fear A Sign of the End?
5. *You Can Live Forever in Paradise on Earth* (1982), 149.
6. Carl Olof Jonsson and Wolfgang Herbst, *The "Sign" of the Last Days—When?* (Atlanta: Commentary Press, 1987), 183.
7. *WT*, 1 Mar. 1993, 5.
8. *WTR*, 15 Feb. 1904, 3327.
9. Ibid.
10. *Free Minds Journal*, Nov.-Dec. 1992, 10.
11. J. David Singer and Melvin Small, *The Wages of War 1816-1945: A Statistical Handbook* (New York: John Wiley & Sons, 1972), 201.
12. John Mueller, *Retreat From Doomsday* (New York: Basic Books, Inc., 1989), 3.
13. Ernest J. Wilson III and Ted R. Gurr, "Fewer Nations Are Making War," *Los Angeles Times*, M2.
14. *WT*, 15 Sept. 1924, 277.
15. *WT*, 1 May 1933, 141. "Call to mind that since 1914 there have been more disastrous earthquakes than in any other time of the world's history" (*WT*, 15 Feb. 1935, 60).
16. *From Paradise Lost to Paradise Regained* (1958), 183.
17. *Awake!*, 22 Feb. 1977, 11. The same approach has been made with other specific sources: "The *New Encyclopaedia Britannica* (1987) lists 63 'Major historical earthquakes' spanning the past 1,700 years. Of this total, 27, or 43 percent, have struck since 1914." Two other sources are listed: *Terra Non Firma* and *The World Book Encyclopedia*, which "lists 37 'Major Earthquakes' from 526 forward. Of this list, 65 % have occurred since 1914" (*WT*, 15 Oct. 1988, 3).
18. *You Can Live Forever in Paradise on Earth*, 151. According to *Jehovah's Witnesses—Proclaimers of God's Kingdom* (1993), 62,428,231 copies of the *Paradise* book had been distributed (594).
19. Jonsson and Herbst, 46.
20. Ibid., 72.
21. Ibid., 82, 84.
22. Ibid., 87.
23. Ibid., 46-87, 237-48.
24. *WT*, 15 May, 1983, 6.

25. Jonsson and Herbst, 241.

26. Ibid., 242.

27. *WT*, 15 May, 1983, 6. Brackets in original.

28. Jonsson and Herbst, 71. The *Il Piccolo* material has appeared in many Watch Tower publications: *WT*, 15 June 1979, 11; *Happiness—How to Find It* (1980), 148; *Awake!*, 8 Oct. 1980, 20-21; *"Let Your Kingdom Come"* (1981), 113; *Awake!*, 8 Apr. 1982, 13; *WT* 15 Apr. 1982, 9; *WT*, 15 Apr. 1982, 9; *WT*, 15 May 1983, 6.

29. Jonsson and Herbst, 72.

30. Ibid., 62.

31. *You Can Live Forever in Paradise on Earth*, 151.

32. *Catalog of Significant Earthquakes 2150 B.C.-1991 A.D.* (Sept. 1992). Published by the National Geophysical Data Center. Available from the National Geophysical Data Center, 325 Broadway, Dept. ORD, Boulder, Colorado 80303-3328 (FAX 303-497-6513).

33. *Reasoning From the Scriptures*, 236.

34. The *Catalog* "list includes all events that meet at least *one* of the following criteria: Moderate damage (approximately $1 million or more), ten or more deaths, magnitude of 7.5 or greater, intensity X or greater (for events lacking magnitude)" (1).

35. *Reasoning From the Scriptures*, 236.

36. Jonsson and Herbst, 78.

37. Ibid., 79, Appendix A.

38. Ibid., 245-46.

39. Ibid., 246.

40. *WT*, 15 May 1983, 7.

41. Jonsson and Herbst, 64.

42. Ibid.

43. Ibid.

44. Ibid., 65, see footnotes 34, 35. *The Catalog of Significant Earthquakes 2150 B.C.–1991 A.D.*, page 150, lists figures from three sources, which are given here in chronological order of publication: 555,237 (1977), 240,000 (1979), 242,000 (1979, 1988). Herbst and Jonsson explain how the higher figures came about: "A report from Hong Kong first erroneously set the death figure at 655,237, from which the Western estimates of 650,000-800,000 were derived. When finally, the Chinese authorities, who at first kept all information about the catastrophe secret, released information about the earthquake, they put the total at 242,000" (65, note 34). The 800,000 death figure was still used in the January 15, 1987, *Watchtower* which identifies the 1976 earthquake as "one of the most lethal earthquakes on record" (21). Of related interest—The 1556 A.D. earthquake that shook Kansu Province in China "killed more than **820,000 persons recorded by name**. Nobody knows how many were killed whose names were not recorded" (J. Tuzo Wilson, "Mao's Almanac 3,000 Years of Killer Earthquakes," *Saturday Review*, 19 Feb. 1972, 60).

45. *WT*, 15 July 1991, 5.

46. Charles F. Richter, "Earthquakes," *Natural History*, Dec. 1969, 44.

47. Steven A. Austin, "Earthquakes in These Last Days," *Impact #198* (Dec. 1989), iv.

48. Steven A. Austin, "Twentieth Century Earthquakes," *Impact # 295* (Jan. 1998), ii-iii.

49. Steve Dutch, "Famous Earthquakes," in *Magill's Survey of Science*, vol. 1, ed. by Frank N. Magill (Pasadena, Calif.: Salem Press 1990), 481-82.

50. *Catalog of Significant Earthquakes*, 5-6.

51. *WT*, 15 Jan. 1987, 21.

52. *Awake!*, 22 Apr. 1995, 7.

53. In Italy, the years 1903, 1905, 1906, 1907, 1908 and 1909 also experienced earthquakes rated at XII on the Modified Mercali Intensity Scale: "Damage total. Waves seen on ground surfaces. Line of sight and level distorted. Objects thrown upward into the air" (*Catalog of Significant Earthquakes 2150 B.C.- 1991 A.D.*, 2).

54. Ibid., under countries listed alphabetically.

55. Ibid.

56. *WT*, 15 Sept. 1998, 7.

57. The Kingston, Jamaica earthquake occurred on January 14, 1907. It was 6.5 magnitude and about 1,000 people died. A 7.8 magnitude quake occurred in 1899 (*Catalog of Significant Earthquakes 2150 B.C.–1991*, 201).

58. *Harvest Gleanings, vol. 1* (Chicago: Chicago Bible Students, n.d.), 397-98.

59. Ibid., 400.

60. Jay Robert Nash, *Darkest Hours* (Wallaby edition; New York: Pocket Books, 1977), 732-34.

61. Ibid., 262.

62. Ibid., 268.

63. Ibid., 262.

64. Ibid.

65. Ibid., 114.

66. *WT*, 15 Apr. 1983, 3. This statement in the 1983 *Watchtower* contradicts what had been claimed in earlier Watch Tower publications. *From Paradise Lost to Paradise Regained* (1958) states: "Shortly after World War I China had the **biggest famine it ever had**—15,000 died every day and 30,000,000 were effected" (181). The book, *You Can Live Forever in Paradise on Earth* (1982) agrees: "Following World War I came the **greatest famine in all history**. In northern China alone 15,000 died *every day* from starvation" (150). But as Jonsson and Herbst point out: "The 15,000 a day may seem impressive at first glance—until it is learned that the situation was soon relieved by government and private philanthropic efforts. According to the best obtainable information half a million (500,000) perished in the famine" (Jonsson and Herbst, 17).

67. *WTR*, 1 May, 1995, 1805.

68. *WTR*, 15 Feb. 1897, 2105.

69. Nash, 262-63.

70. Josue' de Castro, *The Geopolitics of Hunger* (New York: Monthly Review Press, 1977), 53.

71. Bruce F. Johnston, "Famine," *Collier's Encyclopedia*, vol. 9 (New York: P. F. Collier, 1997), 552.

72. *WTR*, 15 Nov. 1901, 2906.

73. *WTR*, 1 July 1911, 4846.

74. Jonsson and Herbst. The quotations are taken from chapters 2 and 4: "Famine—Is It Worse Today?" and "Pestilences—Past and Present," which should be read to see how the conclusions are determined.

75. Ibid., 18.

76. Ibid., 32.

77. Ibid., 37.

78. Ibid., 42.

79. Ibid., 123.

80. David Beckmann and Arthur Simon, *Grace at the Table: Ending Hunger in God's World* (Downers Grove, Ill.: InterVarsity Press, 1999), 4.

17.

"The Sign" of Christ's Presence
in 1914 and "the Last Days"
—Continued

5. Increasing Lawlessness—Matthew 24:12

In an article in the May 1882 *Watch Tower*, J. C. Sunderlin reports that "a late secular paper of some note said that crimes were *becoming* so frequent that they, in their weekly issue, could only make a *statement* of them, not having room for particulars."[1] He then comments: "It is a *fact*, not an *assumption*, but a solemn fact, that we are *now* living in a time when crime and *corruption* have assumed prodigious proportions.... Even all the machinery of church and state seems to be so rotten that many are exclaiming, without knowing that their utterances are the **fulfilling of the spirit of prophecy**: 'I don't know what we are coming to!'"[2]

The *Watch Tower* of September 15, 1903, under the heading, "Lawlessness on the Increase," quotes the *Jewish Exponent*:

> "The earth was filled with violence" (Gen. 6:11). Are these words less true today than they were in the days of which the Bible speaks? Mob violence, race hatred, the subjugation of weaker nations—these are accepted almost as matters of course by a large section of humanity. Each outbreak of lawless violence furnishes the fuel to kindle anew the flames of passion and of hatred, until respect for law and authority is derisively mocked at and whole communities bow in helpless impotence before the cruel, brutal instincts of the unbridled mob....

The *Watch Tower* comments:

> The Apostle foretold that evil men and seducers would wax worse and worse, and that disobedience to parents, headiness, boastfulness, and love of pleasure more than love of God, would mark nominal Christian sentiment in the end of this age.... The Scriptures clearly indicate that the result will be world-wide anarchy—lawlessness.[3]

It is obvious according to the *Watch Tower* that this part of the composite sign was being fulfilled long before 1914.

6. Ruining of the Earth—Revelation 11:18

"But the nations became wrathful, and your own wrath came, and the appointed time for the dead to be judged, and to give [their] reward to your slaves the prophets and to the holy ones and to those fearing your name, the small and the great, **and to bring to ruin those ruining the earth**" (*NWT*).

Earlier lists of the Witnesses' "signs" of the "last days" did not include "those ruining the earth" as one of them. For example, the book *"Make Sure of All Things"* (1953) lists 39 features which comprise "the sign."[4] The October 15, 1961, *Watchtower* presents 17, citing 2 Timothy 3:1-5 but not Revelation 11:18 as a sign.[5]

But in more recent Watchtower publications, the subject of global pollution has frequently been featured citing Revelation 11:18.[6] The book *You Can Live Forever in Paradise on Earth* (1982) presents "ruining the earth" as one of the events of "the sign" of the "last days" and of Christ's presence.[7] The March 1, 1993, *Watchtower* claims: "Although Jesus did not specifically mention this in his prophecy, Revelation 11:18 indicates that prior to the coming destruction, man would be 'ruining the earth.' The evidence that this ruining is taking place is abundant."[8]

But this "sign" is different—"one feature is unique to the time in which we live—that of 'ruining the earth.' (Rev. 11:18) Global pollution is ruining the air we breathe, the water we drink and the soil in which our food grows.... But it is Jehovah who will stop polluters in order to save the earth for his divine purpose."[9] This interpretation of Revelation 11:18, with graphic presentations of global ruination, impresses the readers of Watch Tower publications. But is this verse being properly interpreted?

A Greek-English Lexicon of the New Testament, by Arndt and Gingrich, defines the word *diaphtheiro* in this context: "*destroy* persons and nations ... Rev. 11:18a.... *ruin* in the moral sense ... the earth (i.e., its people) Rev. 11:18b; 19:2....'[10] The *Theological Dictionary of the New Testament* places its usage in this verse under "*Moral and Religious Sense....* Rev. 11:18 refers to those who corrupt or seduce the human race (cf. the harlot 19:2)."[11] Joseph Henry Thayer's *A Greek-English Lexicon of the New Testament* agrees: "*To change for the worse, to corrupt*: minds, morals; ... [the earth], i.e. the men that inhabit the earth, Rev. xi. 18."[12] And in his commentary on Revelation, Patristic scholar Henry Barclay Swete writes: "Paganism was 'destroying'—the lapse into the present is significant—'the earth' by corrupting the fountains of moral life, as well as by the physical horrors of the amphitheatre and the tyrannies of imperialism; and this moral reference is probably uppermost."[13]

This understanding of "earth," which relates it to the **corrupting of mankind** rather than to the physical earth, is also **in agreement with past Watch Tower publications**. For example, Russell commenting on "them which destroy [or corrupt] the earth," writes: "Those that give forth a corrupting influence and that refuse to come into harmony with righteousness during the thousand years will be destroyed from amongst the people."[14] *The Finished Mystery* (1917) interprets this part of the verse: "**And shouldest destroy them.**—The Papal and Protestant Sects. **Which destroy the earth.**—Corrupt the earth, Greek—Rev. 19:2 ["**Which did corrupt the earth with her fornication.**—Her illicit union with worldly governments" 19:2].[15]

Rutherford explains this verse in his commentary on Revelation, in the first volume of *Light* (1930): "Jehovah by his prophet tells of the ruling classes on earth, under Satan the invisible ruler, who have defiled the earth because they have transgressed his law, changed his ordinances, and broken his everlasting covenant (Isa. 24:5). These wicked ruling factors have **so corrupted the earth, that is to say, the organization of men on earth**, that God will destroy the wicked organization."[16] In the second volume of *Vindication* (1932), he writes: "The **disturbers and polluters of mankind** will be destroyed and, as it is written: '[Thou] shouldest destroy them which destroy the earth' (Rev. 11:18)."[17]

Russell also saw the passage that includes verse 18 as **being fulfilled before 1914**: "Thus, the events of the 'great day of God Almighty' are transpiring before our eyes.... Even now the 'trump of God' the 'Seventh Trumpet' is sounding, and the events it introduces (Rev. 11:15-18) are visible to the eyes of the understanding of such as have had their eyes anointed ... and whose senses are exercised by reason of use."[18]

And finally, *Revelation—Its Grand Climax At Hand!* (1988), commenting on Revelation 8:7, says: "**In the Bible, the word 'earth' often refers to mankind** (Genesis 11:1; Psalm 96:1). Since the second plague is on the sea, which also has to do with mankind, **'the earth' must refer to the seemingly stable human society** that Satan has built up and that is due to be destroyed."[19]

In the light of the foregoing discussion, it can be concluded that Watch Tower writers have manufactured a "sign" using Revelation 11:18, and that the verse cannot be interpreted to support the Witnesses' 1914 date.

7. Love Cooling Off—Matt. 24:12

"The love of the greater number will cool off" (*NWT*). Matthew 24:12 was seen as being fulfilled according to the *Watch Towers* of June 15, 1896, and October 15, 1912: "It would seem that the testing of those who have come into the 'harvest' light is to be specially severe and prolonged. The test of endurance is one of the severest; but we have the assurance, though 'the love of many shall wax cold, because iniquity shall abound,' yet 'he that shall endure unto the end, the same shall be saved (Matt. 24:12, 13)."[20] "Our Lord forewarns us that in the end of the Gospel age, many who have a love for Christ will allow their love to grow cold because of the iniquity and sin in the world (Matt. 24:12). It will be a test for such to decide whether they will partake of the worldly spirit. **We see this testing in operation now.**" Many Christians will fail, "their faith and zeal are not sufficient to endure the test."[21]

8. Fearful Sights—Luke 21:11, [25-26]

Luke 21:11 is sometimes joined with verses 25 and 26 in Watch Tower publications, as in the October 1, 1988, *Watchtower*: "There will be fearful sights and from heaven great signs.... Also there will be signs in sun and moon and stars, and on earth anguish of nations, not knowing the way out because of the roaring of the sea and its agitation, while men faint out of fear and expectation of the things coming upon the inhabited earth."[22] These verses are then explained:

> World War I introduced terrible new weapons. From the **heavens**, airplanes and airships rained down bombs and bullets. Even more terrifying was the destruction that rained down on helpless civilians in World War II, including that of two atom bombs.
>
> The **sea** also became the scene of new horrors. When World War I started, submarines were considered very insignificant, but by the end of World War II, they had sunk over ten thousand vessels.... Man has also reached into the region of "**sun moon and stars**." Ballistic missiles ... spacecraft ... satellites.... Meanwhile, as foretold, "men become faint out of fear and expectation of the things coming upon the inhabited earth." Crime, terrorism., economic collapse, chemical pollution, and radiation poisoning from nuclear power plants, together with the mounting threat of nuclear war, are all causes of "fear."[23]

This interpretation, in terms of modern technology, fits well with the Watch Tower attempt to support the 1914 date, but can it be accepted as a legitimate understanding? The answer is no. Why? The May 15, 1896, *Watch Tower* gives the Luke 21 passage a different interpretation, which views it as being fulfilled **before** 1914:

> Verses 25–31 ... **point to events near the close of Gentile Times** [1914], and mention the signs of the close of the Gospel age, and connected with the revealing of the Son of Man in glory. The signs in the sun, moon and stars were to give a general idea as to the time when the kingdom

would be nigh. We will not here particularize respecting these signs, but will mention them: The remarkable darkening of the sun and moon, May 19, 1780; and the notable falling of the stars or meteoric shower on the morning of Nov. 13th, 1833. While we believe also in a symbolic fulfillment of the darkening of the sun and falling of the stars, yet we cannot overlook the literal fulfillment, and hence expect, in harmony with Verses 32, 33, that some of the generation which saw the falling stars will continue to live until God's kingdom shall be fully established.[24]

The February 15, 1935, *Watchtower* again explains more fully the fulfillment of the "signs in the sun, and in the moon, and in the stars" and the "sea" in Luke 21:25,26 in a radically different way from the 1988 *Watchtower* article—not in terms of advanced military and other technology. Rutherford explains:

The sun and moon and the stars give light to men on earth. So the light of God shines upon and about them that love and serve him. Those of God's organization on earth are sure of God's light and favor both day and night; and it is in the light which God gives from heaven that they are able to discern the two great "signs" in the heavens, namely, Jehovah's organization (as symbolized by his "woman) and Satan's organization (as symbolized by a "great red dragon")…. "Nations," in this scripture, clearly refers to the organized governments of the earth; and all these governments are now in perplexity and distress, not knowing what to do. They are in fear and trepidation of losing their power…. The "sea" represents the ungodly peoples of earth, alienated from God, and that mother, nourish, bear up and support the visible part of Satan's organization. All these things further testify that the world reached its end and began to pass away in the year 1914….[25]

The March 28, 1945, *Consolation* gives a radically different interpretation of Luke 21:25,26:

The sun is a symbolic expression used to represent the main light in the Devil's exalted organization, whereas the moon and stars are symbolic of lesser lights **which try to lighten up the darkness of Satan's world.** But those exalted elements of human society to which the people look up for light on the situation and to guide their way and beam upon them with prosperity are showing signs of complete inability to create a brighter, safer, more prosperous world. And the demon powers, Satan and his wicked angels, have been shaken out of heaven by the power of the Messianic King…. The distress of nations has not subsided … but is now accentuated by the resumption of total warfare since 1939. The nations in distress are more shown to be in perplexity, not knowing what to do…. The "sea" of ungodly peoples of this earth roars and rages. All the foregoing things testify that the world reached its end in 1914….[26]

The February 15, 1994, *Watchtower,* however, presents an "adjustment" in which Luke 21:25-28 **will not be fulfilled until the end of this present system**: "We can look forward to the start of the great tribulation, *then* the sign of the Son of man…."[27] Luke 21:26 has often been featured as a separate sign in Watch Tower publications ("men become faint out of fear" *NWT).*[28] This verse was also viewed by Russell and Society writers as **already fulfilled in the years before 1914**.

…Today [1879] every civilized nation is in dread, and Nihilism, Communism and Socialism, are household words, and we see "men's hearts failing for fear and for looking after those things *coming* on the earth, for the powers of heaven (governments) shall be shaken." Luke xxi. 26.[29] A great and very general storm is even now [1891] in progress.... The effect already is to cause the hearts of the great and rich and mighty (ecclesiastically and socially) to fail for fear and for looking forward to those things coming upon the earth—society. (Luke 21:26)[30] ...Increasingly [1894], there is, deep down in men's hearts, even in the theaters and sporting grounds, a feeling of unrest which cannot be better described than by the prophetic words of our Master: "Men's hearts failing them for fear...."[31] There will surely be great disappointment, sorrow, pain, trouble and anguish throughout Christendom in that "day of trouble." Already [1906], as our Master predicted, men's hearts are failing them for fear and for looking after the things that are coming upon the earth (Luke 21:25-28)....[32]

9. **Inordinate Love of Money—2 Timothy 3:2**

10. **Disobedience to Parents—2 Timothy 3:2**

11. **Loving Pleasures More Than God—2 Timothy 3:4**

12. **Love of Self Dominates—2 Timothy 3:2**

13. **General Lack of Natural Affection—2 Timothy 3:3**

14. **People Not Open to Any Agreement—2 Timothy 3:3**

15. **Self-Control Lacking at All Levels of Society—2 Timothy 3:3**

16. **Widespread Loss of Love of Goodness—2 Timothy 3:3**

17. **Many Hypocritically Claiming to be Christian—2 Timothy 3:5**
Signs 9–17 are all found in 2 Timothy 3:2-5 and will be examined together.

But know this, that in the last days critical times hard to deal with will be here. For men will be lovers of themselves, lovers of money, self-assuming, haughty, blasphemers, disobedient to parents, unthankful, disloyal, having no natural affection, not open to any agreement, slanderers, without self-control, fierce, without love of goodness, betrayers, headstrong, puffed up [with pride], lovers of pleasures rather than lovers of God, having a form of godly devotion but proving false to its power; and from these turn away (*NWT*).

Second Timothy 3:2-5 was viewed by Russell and his followers **as being fulfilled during the nineteenth century and before 1914** according to the *Watch Tower.* Many statements could be cited. Some examples follow.

Zion's Watch Tower of April 1882 argues: "Already to any who have eyes to see, the outward signs are multiplying. Day by day we see all about us increased proof of our position. Compare 2 Tim. 3:1-7 with the days we live in, and see if the picture is not a faithful one. But such things have always been, says some one. True, to a certain extent, in accordance with verse 13; but **are we not reaching a climax in wickedness?**"[33]

The article "INCREASE IN CRIME" (1886) quotes 2 Timothy 3:1-5, and then observes: "...It is a day of increase of crime and of decrease of vital interest in godly things, as ably summed up in the last statement of the apostle quoted above; outwardly there is a form of piety—actually it is merely a benevolence and morality inspired by the increase of general intelligence."[34]

The article, "PERILOUS TIMES AT HAND" (1891), quotes 2 Timothy 3:1, and then states: "Realizing that we are **now living in the very times referred to by the Apostle,** some may inquire, How can this be?" Verses 2-5 are further quoted and explained in the treatment.[35]

In her report on the condition of the church (1894), Mrs. C. T. Russell writes: "We were forewarned by God of the very conditions that **now** surround us; and that such conditions, while they were quite prominent in the harvest of the Jewish age and beginning of the Gospel age, would more especially characterize this harvest period; for 'in the last days' many will have a form of godliness, but deny the power thereof, and such deceptions will make the 'perilous times' of this 'evil day' (2 Tim. 3:1,5)."[36]

In 1896, the *Watch Tower* exhorted: "In view of the general prevalence of the proud, boastful, self-seeking and combative spirit (2 Tim. 3:1-5), let us who are seeking to walk close to the Lord, remember and continually practice the Apostle's injunction, 'So far as lieth in you, live peaceably with all men.'"[37]

In the *Watch Tower* of May 1, 1899, the heading, "IN THE LAST TIMES PERILOUS TIMES SHALL COME," is followed by the quotation of 2 Timothy 3:1-5. The lengthy discussion of the passage is introduced with the statement: "Claiming, as we do, that we are **now** living in the closing days of the Gospel age, it is quite proper that we should look about us to see whether or not present conditions correspond to the Apostle's inspired descriptions of what must be expected in the last days of this age."[38] After discussing the vices characterizing the "last days," the article transitions to outside confirmation: "It would be difficult to imagine a more striking corroboration of these facts than is furnished by the recent proclamation of a Fast day by the Governor of the State of New Hampshire" dated April 6, 1899.[39] This is followed by further outside evidence and the conclusion: "Having satisfied ourselves respecting the fulfillment of the Apostle's charges against 'Christendom' and having found his **predictions fully corroborated by facts well witnessed to**, the question arises, Can the Lord's truly consecrated people learn any further valuable lessons and what are they?"[40]

After a lengthy quote from the *New York Times*, the April 1, 1904, *Watch Tower* states: "We prefer now and again to quote expressions like the foregoing from men of national repute rather than make the statements ourselves.... But how well the facts do correspond to the predictions of the Bible respecting the characteristics of nominal Christendom **of our day**! The fulfillment is—remarkable!" Second Timothy 3:2-5 is then quoted.[41]

Under the title "PERILOUS TIMES SHALL COME," 2 Timothy 3:1 is quoted. Later in the article is the following: "The Apostle tells us that in the dawning of this new dispensation and the closing of the Gospel age, men shall be trucebreakers—violent. He proceeds with the entire list (2 Tim. 3:1-5). **This description is prophetic, we believe, of the time in which we are living.**"[42]

If these *Watch Tower* articles claimed that 2 Timothy 3:1-5 was fulfilled in the decades **before** 1914, it is difficult to see how the passage can be used to prove that this world has been in the "last days" only **since** 1914.

18. Excessive Eating and Drinking By Some—Luke 21:34

"But pay attention to yourselves that YOUR hearts never become weighted down with overeating and heavy drinking and anxieties of life, and suddenly that day be instantly upon YOU as a snare" (*NWT*). After Luke 21:34-36 is quoted, the fulfillment is affirmed in the December 1883 *Zion's Watch Tower*:

> One of the strongest evidences which we have of the truth of these prophecies spoken in connection with these words is, that **at the very time when they are being fulfilled by rapidly suc-**

ceeding events, at the very time when his people should be lifting up their heads knowing that their 'redemption draweth nigh,' at the very point where expectations should be on tip-toe, we find many who have been enlightened, *so busied* with a multitude of *other* things that they cannot attend to preparation for the coming kingdom.[43]

19. Ridiculers Reject the Sign—2 Peter 3:3,4

"For YOU know this first, that in the last days there will come ridiculers with their ridicule, proceeding according to their own desires and saying: 'Where is this promised presence of his?'" (*NWT*).

While this reference is currently applied by Witnesses to the "time of the end" beginning in 1914, it was applied by Russell to those who scoffed about the presence of Christ during, according to his view, 1874-1914: "The scoffing described is on the very subject here noticed, and such as we hear and shall hear from professed Christians, whenever the subject of the Lord's presence and harvest work, etc. is presented."[44]

20. Many False Prophets are Active—Matthew 24:5, 11; Mark 13:6

Matthew 24:11: "And many false prophets will arise and mislead many" (*NWT*). In a June 1885 *Watch Tower* article, Matthew 24:11, 24-25 and Deuteronomy 13:1-3 are initially quoted, and later it is stated: "Standing where we do to-day, in 'The Time of the End,' and looking back, we are able to discern many false Christs and false prophets, and can see how Jesus' words have proved true, that many have been deceived thereby."[45] On the next page the passage is given a present application.[46]

Pastor Russell used Matthew 24:23-25 in dealing with the subject of false Christs and false teachers and affirmed its contemporary fulfillment: "But in the prophecy under consideration our Lord warns us of danger from false Christs 'then'—**that is now** [1897]."[47]

21. Preaching of the Good News of God's Established Kingdom —Matthew 24:14; Mark 13:10

Matthew 24:14: "And this good news of the kingdom will be preached in all the inhabited earth for a witness to all nations, and then the end will come" (*NWT*).

The Witnesses currently quote their own publications to indicate that they have covered the earth with their witnessing and thereby are fulfilling Matthew 24:14. In 1879, Russell proclaimed that the fulfillment had already been realized in the **nineteenth century**: "This witness **has already been given**.... Not that all earth's myriads had received it.... Yet it has fulfilled the text—it has been a *witness* to every *nation*."[48] In the April 1882 *Watch Tower*, J. C. Sunderlin quotes Matthew 24:14 and asks, "Has that been done?" His answer, "Yes."[49]

In his comments on Matthew 24:14 in *The Divine Plan of the Ages* (1886), Russell writes:

> The text says nothing about how the testimony will be received. This witness **has already been given**. In 1861 the reports of the Bible Societies showed that the Gospel had been published in every language of earth, though not all of earth's millions had received it. No, not one half of the fourteen hundred millions living have ever heard the name of Jesus. Yet the condition of the text is fulfilled: the gospel has been preached in all the world for a *witness*—to every *nation*.[50]

In 1897 Russell again affirmed the fulfillment of Matthew 24:14: "This *witness* **has already been given**: the world of the Lord, the gospel of the Kingdom, has been published to every nation of earth. Each individual has not heard it; but that is not the statement of the prophecy. It was to be, and has been, a national proclamation. And *the end has come!*"[51] And in *Millions Now Living Will Never Die* (1920), Rutherford states that the witness of Matthew 24:14 "**has already been done**, and we are at the end of the old order and the new one is coming in."[52] This teaching would be changed that same year.[53]

22. Persecution of True Christians—Matthew 24:9; Luke 21:12

Jesus: "YOU will be objects of hatred by all the nations on account of my name" (Matt. 24:9 *NWT*). In Russell's *The Day of Vengeance* (1897), a section in the chapter about the Olivet Discourse is headed, "THE HISTORY OF EIGHTEEN CENTURIES BRIEFLY FORETOLD." Matthew 24:6-13, Mark 13:7-13, and Luke 21:9-19 are cited. After Matthew 24:9-13 is quoted, Russell comments: "In the light of history would it be possible to portray the course of God's true Church in fewer words? Surely not.... 'Whosoever will live godly shall suffer persecution,' is the Apostle's declaration; and whoever has not shared it has every reason to doubt his relationship as a son."[54] Under the title, "Persecution Rightly Received," it is reported:

> Sectarian leaders in our day [1902] have not the power to imprison those toward whom they feel enmity; nevertheless, having the same spirit as their prototypes, they manifest it to the extent of their ability. For instance; during the 'volunteer' service in Allegheny—in which the brethren and sisters quietly and pleasantly tendered tracts and booklets free to Christian people on Sunday—some of the modern Pharisees and Sadducees were envious, and manifested their envy.... Some of the preachers *commanded* their congregations not to take the pamphlets, and heaped abuse and scandalous epithets.... A committee of preachers waited upon the city officials and endeavored to have their cooperation—to secure the arrest and imprisonment of the brethren and sisters unless they would cease to preach this 'Gospel of the kingdom'....[55]

In 1911, persecution was seen as the dedicated Christian's expected life experience throughout history, including the present:

> Similarly, **all down through this Gospel age**, those who have been burning and shining lights in the world have been hated and persecuted chiefly (almost exclusively) by those who had some light.... Thus was fulfilled our Lord's testimony, "If they hated me they will also hate you"; "Whosoever will live godly in Christ Jesus shall suffer persecution." (John 15:18; 1 John 3:13; 2 Tim. 3:12.). The **Lord's followers in the present time are called upon to suffer persecution** for righteousness' sake...."[56]

And finally, in 1913: "The persecutions of today are different from those of any other period of history. Many faithful followers of the Lord are reproved and slandered for their loyalty to the word of God. Our Lord's words, however, warrant us in expecting that those who are faithful to him will be evil spoken of, even as he was."[57]

23. Cry of Peace and Security to Climax the Last Days—1 Thessalonians 5:3

"Whenever it is that they are saying: 'Peace and security!' then sudden destruction is to be instantly upon them..." (*NWT*). In 1915, when Russell was asked if Jeremiah 6:14 and 1 Thessalonians 5:3 "*apply now, or do they refer to Armageddon?*," he answered: "We think that this saying of 'Peace! Peace!' **has been going on for some years**. The Church systems and everybody have been claiming, ever since the first Peace Conference at The Hague [1899], that war had come to an end, that we were living in the time of peace, that we were having the time of peace that the Bible tells us about. They thought this was true; but those of us who had a better knowledge of the Bible knew it was not true."[58]

24. People Take No Note of Danger—Matthew 24:39

"And they took no note ["knew not" *KJV*] until the flood came and swept them all away..." (*NWT*). In *The Time is At Hand* (1889), Russell comments on Matthew 24:37 and 39:

> The point of comparison is stated clearly, and is readily seen if we read critically: The people, except the members of Noah's family, were *ignorant* of the coming storm, and *unbelieving* as to the testimony of Noah and his family, and hence they "*knew not*"; and this is the point of comparison. *So* shall also the PRESENCE [since 1874] of the Son of man be. None but those of the family of God will believe here: others will "know not," until society, as at present organized, begins to melt with the fervent heat of the time of trouble now impending.[59]

The April 1, 1905, *Watch Tower* observes:

> How strange the scene appears, and yet it is no more strange than at present. Again we are in the days of the Son of man—again the doctors of law, doctors of divinity and chief priests and scribes and learned professors and prominent church people, professing faithfulness to the Lord and praying continually, "Thy kingdom come, thy will be done on earth as it is done in heaven," are blind to the fact of our Lord's second coming, to the fact that we are now living "in the days of the Son of man."—Matt. 24:37-39[60]

Some Additional Signs

The December 1, 1954, *Watchtower* lists only 14 signs, but three of these are not included in the 24 above. They are briefly examined here because the 14 are introduced with the claim: "The 'time of the end' has come. The sign of the 'last days' is visible evidence. **Never before in history, prior to 1914, have all these things occurred at once upon one generation.**"[61]

Formation of the League of Nations and United Nations—Rev. 13:14, 15; 17:11

This claimed sign would appear to present a problem for a pre-1914 fulfillment because the League and UN were not functioning until 1920 and 1945, respectively. But it should be remembered that Rutherford viewed the Hague World Court, which came into existence in 1899, as a fulfillment of prophecy. In his commentary on Revelation 17, he quotes verse 11 and gives his interpretation: "'And the beast that was, and is not, even he is the eighth, and is of the seven, and goeth into perdition.' The eighth 'beast' came into existence in 1899 as 'The Hague World Court.' It is a 'royal-colored beast' because made up of rulers of the world. In 1914 it went into the pit and 'was not,' and came out after the war ... in the form of the League of Nations."[62]

In the November 15, 1896, *Watch Tower*, Russell presented a fulfillment, but a different interpretation:

> To our understanding the present Italian government is the seventh head of the "beast" (Rev. 17:9-11) which has continued "a short space," represented in the present monarch and his father Victor Immanuel. According to this prophecy Rome will never have another head—the *eighth condition* will be the beast without a head—either a republic or anarchy. If a republic, we shall shortly expect anarchy, "perdition." All the signs of our time corroborate prophecy and bid us lift up our heads and rejoice that our redemption is nigh.[63]

Nations Perplexed—Luke 21:25

The following observation is made in the May 1882 *Watch Tower*: "No sane man today, unless he is trying to sustain a creed, fails to see (recognize) that thrones stand unsteady, and that throughout the world there is a feeling of *distrust* among all classes; there is '*perplexity*.' Luke 21:25. Verily, the foundations of the world do *shake*."[64]

Sleepy Condition of the World Despite the Sign—1 Thess. 5:2, 6

The following quotations are in the January 1881 and August 15, 1902, *Watch Towers*: "The Church is not to blame for not seeing before; how can one be expected to see in the night anything more than the outlines of the landscape; but now the day dawns, 'let us not sleep, as do others,' 1 Thes. v. 6."[65] "The Apostle's exhortation [1 Thess. 5:6] ... is well worthy of being continually borne in mind by all who would make their calling and election sure to a place in the glorious priesthood of the future—'Let us watch and be sober.'"[66]

Conclusion

The foregoing review (chapters 16 and 17) of the claimed features of the composite sign for 1914, advanced by the Jehovah's Witnesses and their publications, shows that these do not support their prophetic scheme.

Notes

1. *WTR*, May 1882, 352.
2. Ibid., 353.
3. *WTR*, 15 Sept. 1903, 3241-42.
4. *"Make Sure of All Things"* (1953), 337-44.
5. *WT*, 15 Oct. 1961, 626-32.
6. For example, *Awake!*: 22 Sept. 1979, 4-10; 22 Nov. 1980, 5-13; 22 Nov. 1981, 3-12; 8 Apr. 1988, 11-12; 22 Jan. 1993, 3-11; 22 Mar. 1993, 8; 22 Oct. 1993, 11; 22 June 1995, 11; 8 Jan. 1996, 3-14; 8 Sept. 1996, 32; 8 Jan. 1997, 10; 22 Mar. 1997, 13; 22 Aug. 1997, 11; 8 May 1998, 13; 8 Oct. 1999, 31. *WT*: 1 July 1990, 3-6; 1 Apr. 1991, 6-7; 15 July, 1983, 7; 1 Mar. 1993, 5-6; 1 Apr. 1997, 8; 15 June 1998, 4. *Revelation—Its Grand Climax at Hand!* (1988), 173-75. *Knowledge That Leads to Everlasting Life* (1995), 105.
7. *You Can Live Forever in Paradise on Earth* (1982), 153. The *Watch Tower Publications Index 1930-1985*, under "Signs," "ruining the earth" lists only this entry.
8. *WT*, 1 Mar. 1993, 5.
9. *1984 Yearbook* (1983), 4-5. "Greedy men have always been willing to ruin the earth for selfish gain, but never before this generation have they had the power to do so. Now, since 1914, modern technology has put that power into their hands, and they are misusing it. They are ruining the earth" (*Awake!*, 22 Mar. 1993, 8).
10. William F. Arndt and F. Wilbur Gingrich, *A Greek-English Lexicon of the New Testament* (Chicago: University of Chicago Press, 1957), 189.
11. Geoffrey W. Bromiley, ed., *The Theological Dictionary of the New Testament* (Grand Rapids: Wm. B. Eerdmans, 1985), 1260.
12. Joseph Henry Thayer, *A Greek-English Lexicon of the New Testament* (4th ed.; Edinburgh: T & T Clark, 1901), 143.

13. Henry Barclay Swete, *The Apocalypse of St. John. The Greek Text with Introduction Notes and Indices* (3rd ed., 1909; Grand Rapids: Wm. B. Eerdmans, 1954), 144.

14. *WTR*, 1 Nov. 1914, 5567 (Brackets in original).

15. Clayton J. Woodworth and George H. Fisher, *The Finished Mystery* (1917), 182, 289.

16. Rutherford, *Light I* (1930), 227.

17. Rutherford, *Vindication II* (1932), 186. Brackets in original.

18. *WTR*, Mar. 1886, 834. With a 30-year adjustment, this was carried over from Second Adventism: "... In 1844 when the trumpet of the seventh angel began to sound...." (Damsteegt, 216; see also: 43, 123, 131, 139).

19. *Revelation—Its Grand Climax At Hand!* (1988), 133.

20. *WTR*, 15 June 1896, 1995.

21. *WTR*, 15 Oct. 1912, 5118.

22. *WT*, 1 Oct. 1988, 6.

23. Ibid., 6-7.

24. *WTR*, 15 May 1896, 1983.

25. *WT*, 15 Feb. 1935, 61.

26. *Cons.* 28 Mar. 1945, 17-18.

27. *WT*, 15 Feb. 1994, 21. See this issue for more details.

28. *"Make Sure of All things"* (1953), 340; *Reasoning from the Scriptures* (1985), 237; *WT*, 15 Oct. 1988, 3; *WT*, 1 Nov. 1988, 5; *WT*, 15 Nov. 1988, 3.

29. *WTR*, Sept. 1879, 26.

30. *WTR*, July 1891, 1305.

31. *WTR*, 1 July 1894, 1675.

32. *WTR*, 1 May 1906, 3771.

33. *WTR*, Apr. 1882, 341.

34. *WTR*, Apr. 1886, 846.

35. *WTR*, Sept. 1891, 1319.

36. *WTR*, 11 June 1894, 1664.

37. *WTR*, 1 Apr. 1896, 1954.

38. *WTR*, 1 May 1899, 2459.

39. Ibid., 2461.

40. Ibid., 2463.

41. *WTR*, 1 Apr. 1904, 3343.

42. *WTR*, 15 Feb. 1912, 4976.

43. *WTR*, Dec. 1883, 565.

44. Russell, *The Time Is at Hand* (1889), 167.

45. *WTR*, June 1885, 766.

46. Ibid., 767.

47. Russell, *The Day of Vengeance* (1897), 580-81.

48. *WTR*, July 1879, 4.

49. *WTR*, April 1882, 342.

50. Russell, *The Divine Plan of the Ages* (1886), 91-92.

51. Russell, *The Day of Vengeance*, 568.

52. Rutherford, *Millions Now Living Will Never Die* (1920), 57.

53. Rutherford's view stated in the *Millions* book would change as the new order was not realized: "In 1920 ... Bible Students came to a correct understanding of our Lord's prophecy contained in Matthew 24:14. Then they realized that 'this gospel' ... was not a gospel of a kingdom yet to come but a gospel to the effect that the Messianic King has begun his reign over the earth..." (*WT*, 1 Dec. 1928, 365). "The latter part of A.D. 1919 marks the beginning of the work of Jehovah's witnesses after the interference of the World War. By ... 1922 their service work was organized and under way, and it was then that, as Jesus foretold and commanded, 'this gospel of the kingdom' was being preached.... Jehovah's witnesses, received from the hand of God's angel the message of the kingdom gospel..." (*WT*, 1 Nov. 1935, 331). The December 1, 1968, *Watchtower* states: "It has been in particular since 1919 that this good news has been preached" (715). And the December 15, 1967, *Watchtower* explains: "Jesus prophecy in Mark 13:10 ... has not been undergoing fulfillment during the past nineteen centuries. It is only since the second decade of our twentieth century that this prophecy has been undergoing fulfillment" (754).

54. Russell, *The Day of Vengeance*, 566-67.

55. *WTR*, 1 Feb. 1902, 2947.

56. *WTR*, 1 May 1911, 4813.

57. *WTR*, 1 Feb. 1913, 5173.

58. L. W. Jones, ed., *What Pastor Russell Said* (1917 ed. reprint, Chicago Bible Students), 529.

59. Russell, *The Time Is at Hand*, 161.

60. *WTR*, 1 Apr. 1905, 3538.

61. *WT*, 1 Dec. 1954, 712. The Article, "The 'Time of the End,'" lists these signs: 1. World wars; 2. Widespread food shortages; 3. Unusual number of earthquakes; 4. Sore pestilence and disease; 5. Persecution of Christians; 6. Many forsaking of Christianity; 7. Formation of the League of Nations and United Nations; 8. Nations perplexed; 9. Increased lawlessness; 10. Sleepy condition of the world despite the sign; 11. Moral breakdown in public and private life; 12. Widespread juvenile delinquency; 13. People overly engaging in everyday affairs of life; 14. World-wide preaching of the established kingdom as good news (712).

62. Rutherford, *Light II* (1930), 104-05.

63. *WTR*, 15 Nov. 1896, 2062.

64. *WTR*, May 1882, 353.

65. *WTR*, Jan. 1881, 179.

66. *WTR*, 15 Aug. 1902, 3056. See also: *WTR*, 15 June 1913, 5256-57.

18.

Selected Quotations from
Watch Tower Publications
for the Years 1915-1919

Watch Tower materials published during these years confidently predicted a number of events and the scenario that would ultimately lead to the establishment of Messiah's Kingdom: the Golden Age. These should be noted by the reader. Were **any** of them realized at that time or in the decades that followed?

1915

(Sometime during the war): "The **present great war in Europe is the beginning of the Armageddon of the Scriptures**. (Rev. 16:16-20.) It will eventuate in the complete overthrow of all the systems of error which have so long oppressed the people of God and deluded the world.... We believe the present war cannot last much longer until revolution shall break out" (Russell, *Pastor Russell's Sermons*, 676).[1]

"**This war, and the anarchy of Armageddon, which will follow it**, will prove conclusively the need of Divine interposition in human affairs.... When the war is ended, these nations, sorrowful and famine-stricken, will be greatly angered at their rulers. Then will come the determination for something like Socialism. This the governments will endeavor to put down, and to some extent they will succeed. **Then will follow the great explosion—the Armageddon of the Scriptures**. Then will be the Time of Trouble, immediately preceding the Messianic Kingdom, which will inaugurate the long-promised Peace on Earth" (*Bible Student's Monthly*, volume 6, No. 5, in *Harvest Gleanings, I*, 676).

"We pointed out that according to the Scriptures the 2520 years of Gentile dominion ended in September, 1914; and **that the war is the one predicted in the Scriptures as associated with the great day of God Almighty**—'the day of vengeance of our God'" (*WTR*, 1 Jan. 1915, 5601).

"The **Battle of Armageddon, to which this war is leading**, will be a great contest between right and wrong, and will signify the complete and everlasting overthrow of the wrong, and the permanent establishment of Messiah's righteous kingdom for the blessing of the world.... Our sympathies are broad enough to cover all engaged in the dreadful strife, as our hope is broad enough and deep enough to include all in the great blessings which our Master and his Millennial kingdom **are about to bring to the world**" (*WTR*, 1 Apr. 1915, 5659).

"**Some of our dear readers very commendably arranged their affairs some time ago so as to give their entire time to the harvest work, not anticipating the prolongation of the harvest**—the gleaning work, the burning of the tares, the threshing of the wheat, etc. Moreover, **many of them used in the harvest work**

nearly all of their surplus of this world's goods—striving to lay up treasure in heaven. Some of these dear brethren and sisters have nearly or quite gone to the limit of their possibilities, as far as present arrangements are concerned. They are, properly, looking about them to see the leadings of the Lord's providence in respect to their future operations" (*WTR*, 15 Apr. 1915, 5669).

"...For God's own time has come for lifting the veil of ignorance and darkness which for so long he has permitted Satan to put before our eyes. To our understanding the present war is pictured in the Bible, as due to begin in 1914. It is a great 'wind.' Following the great **war**, the Bible teaches, a great earthquake—**social revolution**—will take place. In connection with that earthquake will come an exaltation of religious sects, Catholic and Protestant, on the side of the kings and princes—political, social, financial, religious. Next will come the **downfall of all present religious systems**. Speedily the symbolic 'fire' of the Bible will consume the earth—**anarchy**. Following the anarchy **quickly will come the long-promised kingdom of God**, for which Christians have prayed..." (*WTR*, 1 June 1915, 5697).

"The things of the present order are **soon to pass away**—its banking institutions, its great monetary affairs, its stocks and bonds, its politics, its great religious systems, indeed, the entire social fabric. The whole arrangement is **now about to be melted down**. An entirely new order is **about to come in**" (*WTR*, Aug. 1, 1915, 5735).

"Many Bible Students are thoroughly convinced that the 2,520 years from Zedekiah's day to October, 1914, ended there—that that date marked the end of God's lease of world power to the Gentile nations. They are convinced that the **present war** is the result, and that **its ultimate conclusion will be the complete overthrow of all the kingdoms of the world and the full establishment of Messiah's kingdom in the control of earth**" (*WTR*, 15 Sept. 1915, 5772).

"For the past forty years Pastor Russell has been pointing out Scriptural proof showing that the great International wars would be upon the earth in 1914, just exactly as they have come, and that **shortly thereafter Messiah's Kingdom would be established**. His teachings have emphasized the nearness of the Kingdom of Messiah" (Rutherford, *A Great Battle in the Ecclesiastical Heavens* [New York: Rutherford, 1915], 38).

1916

Viewing Elijah as a type of the Christ class, Body of Christ, Russell writes: "During this harvest of the age the Lord, through his Word, has seemed to send his people to four different points of time—**1874, 1878, 1881 and 1914. At each of these points of time the watching saints who realized that the end of the age was upon the church have thought that the 'change' might come.** They watched for it. When they came to each of these points, the Lord said, 'Go to another place'" (*WTR*, 1 Feb. 1916, 5845).

"...**The present great war in Europe will, according to prophecy, so utterly wreck all the participating nations that they will have no strength for further combat,** no gold reserves, called war-chests, for military purposes. War-smitten, bankrupted, discouraged, the nations will be many years in repairing the terrible losses they are now inflicting upon each other. Moreover, the Bible assures us that with the crisis of their trouble, coming through revolution and anarchy, the **world will be saved from its own madness by the establishment of Messiah's kingdom**" (*WTR*, 15 Feb. 1916, 5852).

"**The long foretold time of trouble, such as never was and never will be again (Daniel 12:1; Matthew 24:21, 22), has begun.** Daily the heat of human passion is growing more intense. In view of this approaching dissolution, **now at the very door**, what should be our attitude of heart?" (*WTR*, 1 Mar. 1916, 5864).

"We believe that Gentile Times have ended, and that **God is now allowing the Gentile Governments to destroy themselves**, in order to prepare the way for Messiah's kingdom" (*WTR*, 15 Apr. 1916, 5888).

"The thought that the **Church would all be gathered to glory before October, 1914**, certainly did have a very stimulating and sanctifying effect upon thousands, all of whom accordingly can **praise the Lord— even for the mistake**.... Our mistake was evidently not in respect to the ending of the Times of the Gentiles; we drew a false conclusion, however, **not authorized by the Word of the Lord**" (Russell, *The Time Is at Hand* (1889), 1 Oct. 1916, Author's Foreword, iv).

"The 'Gentile Times' prove that the present governments must all be **overturned about the close of A.D. 1915**..." (ibid., 242).

Under the title, "The Harvest is Not Ended": "Some of us were quite strongly convinced that the harvest would be ended by now, but our expectations must not be allowed to weigh against the facts. The fact is that the harvest work is going grandly on; it is not ended by any means. As far as our present judgment goes, it would appear that there is a considerable harvest work yet to be done.... It still seems clear to us that the prophetic period known as **the Times of the Gentiles ended chronologically** in October, 1914.... We see no reason for doubting therefore, that the Times of the Gentiles ended in October 1914; and that **a few more years will witness their utter collapse and the full establishment of God's kingdom** in the hands of Messiah" (*WTR*, 1 Sept. 1916, 5950).

"In the meantime, our eyes of understanding should discern clearly the **Battle of the Great Day of God Almighty [Armageddon] now in progress**; and our faith, guiding our eyes of understanding through the Word, should enable us to see the glorious outcome—Messiah's kingdom" (ibid., 5951).

"Evidently, the 'door' is not yet shut, although we anticipate that before a very long time—perhaps **a year or two or three—the full number of the Elect will be completed**, and all will have gone beyond the Veil and the door will be shut" (Russell, *Thy Kingdom Come* (1891), 1 Oct. 1916, Author's Foreword, i-ii).

———————

In the author's Foreword to *Thy Kingdom Come* (Oct. 1, 1916), Russell claimed:

> This volume was written in 1890 and has since passed through many editions in many languages, and still more editions are in prospect.... The light of Truth is shining so clearly and the Divine Plan is so manifest that **scarcely a word of the Volume would need to be changed if it were written today—26 years later**" (i).

Even a cursory examination of the contents shows such a statement to be wrong. For example, the predictions for 1914 in Studies V and VI, "The Time of Harvest" and "The Work of Harvest" (121-226), were not fulfilled. Study VIII, "The Restoration of Israel" (243-300) also failed to be realized, and the last chapter, on the Great Pyramid of Egypt (311-76) was later rejected when the Pyramid was discredited in 1928 by Watch Tower president Rutherford.

Some additional examples of teachings found in *Thy Kingdom Come* include: The 2,300 days of Daniel 8 were symbolic and fulfilled in 1846 (105-108), the "Time of the end" was a 115-year period—1799-1914 (121-22). "The End" or "Harvest" was 1874-1914 and "this brief period is the most momentous and eventful period of the entire age" (121). Christ returned invisibly in 1874 (125, 127, 129) The 6,000-year chronology ran out in 1874 (128). "And, with the end of A.D. 1914, what God calls Babylon, and what men call Christendom, will have passed away, as already shown from prophecy" (153). Babylon was cast off in 1878 (189). The "high calling" ended in 1881 (219). "That the deliverance of the saints must take place **some time before** [changed to **very soon after**] 1914 is manifest.... Just how long before [changed to **after**] 1914 the last living members of the body of Christ will be glorified, we are not directly informed..." (228). "...In the spring of 1878 all the holy apostles and other 'overcomers' of the Gospel age who slept in Jesus were raised spirit beings..." (234) and "the Kingdom began to be *set up*, or brought into power..." (235).

"The time is fast approaching when God will speak peace to Israel and comfort them and fully turn away their blindness" (249) beginning in 1878 (278). "Thus we see remarkable indications of God's returning favor to Israel [specific events are mentioned].... And how evidently it is all of God!" (286).

1917

"The **evidence points strongly to the fact that the world is now nearing the great earthquake, the great revolution, to be followed shortly by the fire of anarchy.**" And after quoting Psalm 107:25-29: "Thus the Lord describes the passing away of the present order, preparatory to the establishment of the Kingdom of Righteousness under the Prince of Peace" (*WTR*, 1 Jan. 1917, 5).

"The *Pittsburgh Press* is numbered among the great newspapers that apparently see some things which will follow in the wake of the great European conflict, which now threatens to engulf all nations and **to lead up to the 'Battle of Armageddon' of Scripture**. As God's people observe increasing signs of the presence of our invisible King, preparatory to the establishment of his kingdom on earth, they rejoice at each evidence of the world's recognition that mankind is passing through the 'fire' of purification, which shall burn until the last vestige of evil and selfishness shall have been consumed and God's will is wrought on earth as completely as it is done among the heavenly hosts" (WTR, 15 Mar. 1917, 6056).

"In view of the present conditions, we suggest to the friends of the truth that it would be well to begin the practice of economy along the lines suggested by the above food expert, and to lay in a supply of plain foods, such as corn meal. ... **We see that the present unrighteous institutions of the earth are going down in the worst time of trouble the world as ever known**, and that this marks the hour of deliverance for the last members of the Body of Christ and the early establishment of Messiah's Kingdom, which will bring peace and comfort, happiness and plenty, health and joy to every one who loves righteousness and will do righteously.... The fall of 'Babylon' and all systems of unrighteousness, which **soon must take place**, will make way for the deliverance of the people from the thraldom in which they have been held for centuries" (*WTR*, 15 Apr. 1917, 6072).

"...We have some recommendations to offer to our readers. While we are not certain that all the dire calamities of the day of the Lord will befall the earth within the **next eleven months, nevertheless there seems to be a sufficient possibility of this to warrant us in making certain provisions against the distress of that time**—in the interest of our families, our friends and our neighbors. We recommend to those having clean, dry cellars or other places suitable and well ventilated, to lay in a good stock of life's necessities..." (*WTR*, 1 July 1917, 6108).

"Forty days after Christ's resurrection His ascension occurred. This confirms the hope of the Church's glorification (a year for a day) after the awakening of the sleeping saints in the Spring of 1878. The seven days before the Deluge may represent seven years, from **1914 to 1921, in the midst of which 'week of years' the last members of the Messiah pass beyond the veil**. The Great Company class shall be cut off at its end—the fact that we see the first half of this week so distinctly marked would lead us to expect **three and one-half years more** of witnessing by the Great Company class.... Our proposition is that **the glorification of the Little Flock in the Spring of 1918 A.D.** will be half way ... between the close of the Gentile Times and the close of the Heavenly Way, A.D. 1921" (Clayton J. Woodworth and George H. Fisher, *The Finished Mystery*, 64).

"Some of the Scriptures, which, when understood in their connections and significance, prove that the **Lord's Second Advent occurred in the fall of 1874** are as follows: [after almost 3 pages of "proofs"] ... and **these are but 88 of the proofs** hastily collected" (Ibid., 68, 71).

"The vision of the prophet Ezekiel depicts the embryonic and established Kingdom of God on earth, civil and religious, spiritual and earthly.... **The Time of the establishment of the Kingdom in power** is indicated as 'in the fourteenth year after the city (Christendom) was smitten—or thirteen years after 1918, viz., in **1931**. Ezek. 40:1" (Ibid., 569).

"The 15th verse of that same chapter [Rev. 14] refers to the Great Pyramid, the measurements of which confirm the Bible teaching that 1878 marked the beginning of the harvest of the Gospel Age. The parallel, therefore, would establish definitely that **the Harvest would close forty years thereafter; to wit, in the spring of A.D. 1918**. If this be true, and the evidence is very conclusive that it is true, then **we have only a few months in which to labor** before the great night settles down when no man can work" (*WTR*, 1 Oct. 1917, 6149).

"**There will be no slip-up. Abraham inherits the land by faith** (as its reward); **God's oath makes it certain**. 'The gifts and calling of God are without repentance.' (Romans 11:29) The promise respecting the land is as **absolute and unconditional** as the promise respecting the spiritual seed. 'To the end that the promise might be sure to all the seed.'—Romans 4:16.... As he began his sojourn in the land in the year 2,045 B.C., it follows that the 3,960 years begin to count from 2,035 B.C. 2,035 plus 1,925 equals 3,960. Accordingly Abraham should enter upon the actual possession of his promised inheritance in the year **1925 A.D.**" (*WTR*, 15 Oct. 1917, 6157).

"He [Russell] **proved by Bible chronology the presence of the Lord from 1874 on**, and demonstrated that 1914 would mark the end of the Gentile period and the beginning of the great international conflict. Time and events have proven the correctness of his deductions from the Scriptures, showing **he possessed heavenly wisdom**" (*WTR*, 1 Nov. 1917, 6159).

"So the Christian today has the privilege of standing in the **very dawn of the morning**, when the light of the kingdom is breaking upon the earth and soon will shine forth in its resplendent glory: 'The day' that 'is at hand' is the thousand-year day of Christ..." (*WTR*, 1 Dec. 1917, 6175).

1918

"What will the year 1918 bring forth?... The Christian looks for the year to bring the full consummation of the church's hopes" (*WTR*, 1 Jan. 1918, 6191).

"**The tangible evidence that the present order is passing away, and that soon the kingdom of God will be fully established, is overwhelming**. Such proof causes the true saints to look up and lift their heads with rejoicing" (ibid., 6193).

"Surely the child of God can plainly see that **the end of all things of the present order is at hand**" (ibid., 6194).

"How appropriate, therefore, the text for the year—'The end of all things is at hand; be ye therefore sober and watch unto prayer....' That we are at the end of the Gospel age, we all agree. We are at the end of the harvest period of that age. **The end of Satan's dominion is also here, and the beginning of the Millennial age**" (*WTR*, 15 Jan. 1918, 6201).

"We recognize in the **present great war one that is different from any other war ever before known, to wit: That it marks the end of the world—that is to say, the end of the present evil order of things**— and is purging the nations and preparing the way for the kingdom of God for which followers of the Great Master, Christ Jesus, have prayed for many centuries; and that for forty years this Association has held and taught that the year 1914 would mark the beginning of this great international conflict which the prophets of the Lord foretold must take place, immediately preceding the establishment of the everlasting kingdom of righteousness" (ibid., 6203).

"We believe that **the end of the harvest is here** and that the kingdom of heaven is at hand. And if so, then shortly after the great time of trouble ends, restitution blessings will begin" (*WTR*, 1 Apr. 1919, 6231).

"For many years the Lord's people have wondered whether or not each convention might be the last. Each one has always proved to be the last for some of the dear friends; but abundant evidence, not only for the Lord's Word, but also from corroborative occurrences pressing in upon us from all sides, seems to lend more basis for the hope that this **might be the last in this vicinity, before the great convention beyond the vail**" (ibid., 6233).

"Several times during the harvest, during the progress of what seemed plagues to Christendom, the Lord has permitted his people to think that they were about to go. Brother **Russell expected the church to go beyond the vail in 1878, 1881, 1910 and 1914**—just as with Elijah, who went with Elisha to four different places before he was actually taken" (*WTR*, 15 Apr. 1918, 6237).

"Zion's Triumph Near": "With bated breath and joyful heart the watchers in Zion behold the closing of the harvest. Next the dark night, followed shortly by the glorious sunburst of everlasting happiness. Wonderful is the present privilege of the faithful watchers. The graduating test is now upon the church.... During the past forty years the harvest of the age has been in progress. That the harvest began in 1878, there is ample and convincing proof. **The end of the harvest is due in the spring of 1918**" (*WTR*, 1 May 1918, 6243).

"Brother Russell stated that the **work of the harvest would end in the summer of 1918**, that the door would close and the dark night would settle down" (*WTR*, 1 July 1918, 6288).

"In the clear light of unfolding time-prophecy, we see that we are now living at the very end of the reign of sin and death; that the night of sorrow, pain and tears is almost over; that **the glorification of the last members of the Christ body is very soon to be completed**" (*WTR*, 1 Aug. 1918, 6300).

1919

"...**We are standing upon the very threshold of the Messianic Kingdom**, and that soon the Lord shall be pleased to take us home, if we have developed his spirit and proven faithful to him and to his cause through all circumstances and conditions.... We shall shortly have the blessed privilege of being ushered into the eternal glories of immortality" (*WTR*, 15 Jan. 1919, 6380).

In a letter by J. F. Rutherford: "Brother Russell's last expression concerning the **harvest** was that it **would end in the spring of 1918**. We believed this; and believing it, we felt that the Seventh Volume must go out before the harvest closed.... The spring of 1918 came; and the evidences began to increase that **the harvest was closing**.... Rejoice now, Beloved; **the work of harvesting the church is done. The dark night is coming rapidly on, and soon we will be home.** There may be a little more work for the faithful to do in calling the world's attention to the message and in aiding the Elisha class" (*WTR*, 15 Feb. 1919, 6392).

"THE IMPORTANCE of assembling ourselves together, as the Lord's people and in the spirit of the Master, cannot be overstated, especially as we see **the end of the earthly journey of the church draw near**" (*WT*, 1 Aug. 1919, 235).

A letter from Bible Student in England: "I am one of those who, since coming into the truth, have been led to expect an **early glorification of the little flock—1910, 1911, 1912. All my temporal affairs were arranged with a view to October 1914.** Each time the Lord has seemed to be saying: 'Thou must prophesy again,' etc." (*WT*, 15 Sept. 1919, 287).

In the introductory issue of *The Golden Age* magazine: "Its purpose is to explain in the light of Divine wisdom the true meaning of the great phenomena of the present day and to prove to thinking minds by evidence incontrovertible and convincing that the time of a greater blessing to mankind is **now at hand**. Like a voice in the wilderness of confusion, **its mission is to announce the incoming of the Golden Age**" (*GA*, 1 Oct. 1919, 3).

It was reported that J. F. Rutherford, speaking at the Cedar Point convention, "said that Bible prophecy is fulfilled and the **reconstruction period for blessing humankind is at hand**" (*WT*, 1 Oct. 1919, 294).

"...**We confidently believe that the end of the journey of the church is at hand and within a short time all its members will be removed from the earth**; that the time of trouble now on the world will then cease and the Sun of Righteousness, rising with healing in its beams, will bring comfort and peace and blessings to the people" (ibid., 294-95).

"We submit that the evidence is conclusive to the reasonable mind who believes in the Scriptures, that **the world has ended; that the old order is passing away and the new is coming in**; and if that be true, then this must mark the dawning of a new and better day; it must mark the beginning days of the Golden Age..." (*GA*, 12 Nov. 1919, 127).

Notes

1. *Pastor Russell's Sermons* (1917) was published by the People's Pulpit Association, which was formed in 1909 when the Watch Tower Bible and Tract Society headquarters were moved from Pittsburgh to Brooklyn, New York. It is now known as the Watchtower Bible and Tract Society of New York, Inc.

19.

The Laodicean Messenger and Period of the Church

Under a photograph of his tombstone, *Jehovah's Witnesses—Proclaimers of God's Kingdom* states that C. T. Russell died on October 31, 1916. The inscription reads: "**Charles T. Russell ... The Laodicean Messenger.**"[1] The tombstone inscription is in agreement with *The Finished Mystery* (1917), which claims that "the *special messenger to the last Age of the Church* was Charles T. Russell."[2] This book, it is claimed, "brings together all that **the messenger of the Laodicean Church** has written concerning Babylon....[3]

As to time: "**The Laodicean period of the Church extends from the fall of 1874 to the spring of 1918**, three and one-half years of preparation, and forty years of harvest."[4] The 1926 edition of *The Finished Mystery* changed the statement: "The Laodicean period of the Church **extends from the fall of 1874 to the demise of the last spirit-begotten one**. One by one the last members of the Body are now passing."[5] With this change of the text the "Laodicean period of the Church" has already been extended over eight decades! There were still 8,661 Memorial partakers (spirit begotten) in 2000.[6]

But what about Russell as The Laodicean Messenger? The September 15, 1922, *Watch Tower* explains: "Those who have left the truth and taken him [Dr. Bullinger] as guide of necessity must give up the truth respecting the Lord's return: There could be no return in 1874, therefore there has been no harvesting, and it follows that Brother Russell was altogether mistaken in is work, and that the church **has been misled respecting Russell's position as the Lord's messenger to Laodicea**."[7]

It would appear that the Watch Tower Society itself joined those who "left the truth." Compare the preceding *Watch Tower* statement with the following from the November 1, 1928, issue:

> The "angel" or **messenger of the Laodicean church could not be an individual** [Russell].... The messenger, therefore, must be the faithful and zealous body members who have the testimony of Jesus Christ and who are putting forth their best efforts to give a witness on earth according to God's commandments.... Understanding then that the **Laodicean period began about 1919** [not 1874?], it was after that date that many came to a knowledge of truth and made a consecration to do God's will.[8]

This is another good example of the Watch Tower Society's moving from affirmation of doctrine to change or denial.

Notes

1. *Jehovah's Witnesses—Proclaimers of God's Kingdom* (1993), 64.
2. Clayton J. Woodworth and George H. Fisher, *The Finished Mystery* (1917), 53.
3. *WTR*, 15 Feb. 1918, 6212.
4. *The Finished Mystery*, 58.
5. Ibid. (1926 ed.).
6. *WT*, 1 Jan. 2001, 21.
7. *WT*, 15 Sept. 1922, 280.
8. *WT*, 1 Nov. 1928, 324.

20.

The Elijah and Elisha Types

Pastor Russell and those who followed him in Watch Tower leadership often interpreted Old Testament accounts as having prophetic significance. The "Elijah motif" was already found during the mid-nineteenth century in Second Adventism.[1] Among the applications of the Elijah type was the view that he represented the remnant church ("little flock"), and "Elijah's ascension to heaven" was to be the "remnant's" experience—to "be translated without tasting death."[2]

The book *Three Worlds* (1877), published by N. H. Barbour and C. T. Russell, includes an explanation of Elijah as a type of the Church: "Why should *Elijah* be translated? *he* was no better than his fathers (1 Kings 19:4). Because being a typical character he represents the body of Christ in all its humiliation and final victory."[3] The "final victory" was pictured by Elijah's being taken "into heaven by a whirlwind" (2 Kings 2:1). When would this be realized by the church? "...Deliverance may come any time between this [Feb. 14 and April 6, 1875—both already past] and the end of the 'harvest,' in 1878."[4] When the prediction for 1878 failed, other dates were set with similar expectations (1881, 1910 and 1914). "When October 1914 passed without the expected change to heavenly life, brother Russell knew that there would be serious searchings of heart."[5] "As the years 1914 and then 1915 passed, those spirit-anointed Christians waited eagerly for the fulfillment of their heavenly hope. At the same time, they were encouraged to keep busy in the Lord's service. Even though they viewed their remaining time in the flesh as very brief...."[6]

The teaching of Elijah as a type of the glorification of the church continued to appear in Russell's writings until his death. Reflecting his belief that this event was very near, Russell wrote and spoke on the Elijah type as much as on any other subject during the last sixteen months of his life.[7] For example, in 1915 he wrote: "We believe that the taking away of Elijah in the chariot of fire ... is about to be fulfilled as respects the church of Christ in the flesh. Soon they shall be no more in the flesh; for the Lord will take them, will glorify them with himself."[8] It was further stated: "While we are certain that Elijah typed the church of God in the flesh, we may not be quite so positive that Elisha was also a type and represented a secondary class of God's people, referred to in the Bible sometimes as the 'foolish virgin' class, sometimes as the servants of the bride class ... sometimes as a great company...."[9] And in 1916, he explained:

> ...**The taking up of Elijah into heaven, typically represents the final passing of the church from the earthly conditions to the heavenly....** As Jordan was the last point to which Elijah was directed, so 1915 is the last point to which the church has been directed. As Elijah went on, not knowing any further place, so the true church is going on without any definite time-point before it. Soon the chariot of fire will separate the Elijah class from the Elisha class. The fiery chariot seems to mean severe trials or persecutions. A little later, the Elijah class will be taken up in a

whirlwind ... apparently used to symbolize the great time of anarchy. The lesson possibly is that the Lord's faithful of the Elijah class will be amongst the first in civilized lands to suffer some kind of violence through lawlessness and anarchy.[10]

After Russell's death, his teaching was cited: "Time and again the church has been told through the channel [Russell] which the Lord chose as his mouthpiece during the church's last experience that Elijah is a type of the overcoming church and that Elisha probably represents in a measure the great company class."[11]

The Society's administrative staff was arrested and charged for sedition under the American Espionage Act. On June 21, 1918, they were sentenced to prison. With this, according to the Witnesses' account, "the preaching of the good news came to a virtual standstill. Was this the time when they would at last be united with the Lord in heavenly glory?"[12] Rutherford penned the following in a letter on the night before his removal to the Atlanta penitentiary: "Brother Russell's last expression concerning the harvest was that it would end in the spring of 1918.... Rejoice now, Beloved; the **work of harvesting the church is done. The dark night is coming rapidly on, and soon we shall be home. There may be a little more work for the faithful to do** in calling the world's attention to the message and in aiding the Elisha class."[13] The war ended, however, and Rutherford and his associates were released from prison on March 26, 1919. There was still more work to be done—**much more!**[14]

Rutherford's "New" Light

A study of other Watch Tower "types" reveals that these were often reinterpreted as needed.[15] In 1919, Rutherford was confronted with a serious problem. According to Russell's teaching and as continued after his death, the harvest of the Gospel age would close "in the spring A.D. of 1918."[16] But it was obvious that this did not happen. With the previous interpretations and predictions in mind, how could the work be revived? The answer became clear: the Elijah and Elisha types must be reinterpreted. This was accomplished in a two-part article in the *Watch Tower*. **In place of the expected glorification of the church**, as the Elijah type had been interpreted, the Bible Students read the *Watch Tower* magazine where, according to *Jehovah's Witnesses—Proclaimers of God's Kingdom*, "heartwarming Scriptural encouragement was given. 'Blessed are the Fearless' was the subject featured in the *Watch Tower* issue of August 1 and 15, 1919. It warned against fear of man, drew attention to Gideon's courageous 300 warriors who were alert and willing to serve in whatever way the Lord directed and against overwhelming odds, and commended Elisha's fearless reliance on Jehovah."[17]

This review is significant, not in what it reveals about these *Watch Tower* issues, but in what it **omits**. Note what is emphasized concerning these **same** articles in the July 15, 1940, *Watchtower*: "At the Cedar Point convention in 1919, and in *The Watchtower*, many scriptures were produced supporting the conclusion that the **Elijah work ended in the fiery trouble of 1918 and that now the Elisha work of God's remnant must begin**. It was a voice from heaven, because it was Jehovah's voice through his Word."[18] The December 1, 1940, *Watchtower* reported: "The keynote address of that convention was 'Blessed are the Fearless,'" **particularly disclosing the distinction between the end of the Elijah work of the church and the beginning of the Elisha work** of God's organization.[19]

The two "Blessed are the Fearless" *Watch Tower* articles presented a **reinterpretation** of the Elijah and Elisha types, which was introduced by the claim of advancing light on prophecy: "...The faithful Christian is enabled, by reason of the illumination of the holy Spirit, to see and have some appreciation of fulfilled prophecy." Consideration is given to the "prophets Elijah and Elisha from the viewpoint of type and antitype."[20] "Elijah typed a class of persons; and **the fiery chariot and whirlwind might not be the last earthly experiences of the persons composing that class**.... The taking away of Elijah in the whirlwind **might represent a marked point in the church's career**, and yet many of the persons composing the church might remain in the flesh for a time after having that antitypical experience."[21]

What is now meant by Elijah being taken away by a whirlwind?

> In the spring of 1918, the Watch Tower Bible and Tract Society was bearing a fiery message, a message due at that time. At the same time there was great trouble. **There ended the work that Elijah pictured,** and the taking away of Elijah indicates such ending. This does not mean the taking away of individuals, but it would mean the cessation by the Lord's people for a time at least of **certain work pictured by Elijah.** Elisha standing by the Jordan would indicate a period of time, however short or long, lapsing until Elisha would take up the mantle—the message borne by Elijah—and use it according to the Lord's direction.[22]

Russell's view that Elisha was a type of the great company class (previously cited) was reviewed and rejected by Rutherford:

> It would hardly seem reasonable, then, for us to conclude that Elisha merely because of the deeds above recorded, would typify the great company class.... If Elisha, then, was a type, whom did he picture? Our answer to that question is that we believe he as a type of the little flock; that Elijah typed the little flock up until a certain stage of the work done and performed by the followers of Jesus; to wit, up to the time the fiery trial came upon the church in 1918, at which time the mantle, that is, the message of truth, particularly represented in 'The Finished Mystery,' was thrown down and the remaining work to be done by the church in the flesh is pictured by Elisha....[23]

After arguing in support of his position, Rutherford concludes:

> ...Therefore, that the Prophets **Elijah and Elisha both typify the same class, towit, the little flock;** that where the Elijah picture ended the Elisha picture began, and in the antitype two parts of the same character of work done by the same class of people are shown....[24] If, therefore, our conclusion is correct, that **Elisha pictures the church during the last of her earthly experiences,** it means that there must yet be another smiting of the waters with the mantle of truth, and that during such smiting it must be expected that the 'beast' will use all the power against the church that the Lord will permit it to use.[25]

Rutherford's interpretation, claiming a "new light" from Jehovah, saw the conclusion of the Elijah work in 1918 and the beginning of the Elisha phase from then on. This was published after that time, and those who accepted the "new light" were enlightened and specially blessed, and those who did not were censured. Some examples, of many, are cited here.

1920

"In the spring of 1918 the war, pictured by the whirlwind, was [at] its height. The fiery experiences of the church which came then as a result of an assault upon the Society and its work marked the separation of the Elijah and Elisha work, Elijah being taken away and Elisha left; i.e., **the Elijah part of the worked ceased here, to be followed by the Elisha work,** which work must be done by the truly consecrated, the saintly class.[26]

1922

"...The Elijah work was done from 1874 forward, ending in 1918."[27]

1925

"We understand it was **in 1918 that the Elijah work ceased, and that in 1919 the Elisha work began**; and those who discerned this fact, and appreciated the privilege of boldly declaring the message of the King and advertising his kingdom, **received a double portion of the spirit**; that is to say, their joy in the Lord was greatly increased."[28]

1926

"True to his promise **greater light has come to the church of God since 1918.** It is upon the pathway of those justified ones who have been awake and desirous of walking in the light that the greater light has been shining and continues to shine. **It was in the year 1919 that the Lord permitted the church to see for the first time that Elijah pictured the work of the church prior to 1918 and the Elijah pictured the work of the church thereafter.**"[29]

1928

"**While still some may doubt** that we have passed from the Elijah phase of the church's activity into that of Elisha, and that the Lord has in very fact poured forth a double portion of the spirit upon his people, **those who are abiding in the secret place of the Most High and who are 'walking in the light as he is in the light' are in no doubt about the point.**"[30]

1930

"Those who have seen and appreciated these **great truths from the Lord** have rejoiced, while those who have not discerned the difference between the Elijah and Elisha work of the church, and the blessed truths revealed in connection therewith, continue to complain, and many have entirely gone into outer darkness."[31]

"At the Cedar Point convention in 1919, and in *The Watch Tower*, **many scriptures were produced** supporting the conclusion that the Elijah work ended in the fiery trouble of 1918 and that now **the Elisha work of the church must begin. It was a voice from heaven, because it was Jehovah's voice.**"[32]

1933

In a letter in *The Watchtower* which had been sent in answer to a Society representative's questions, Rutherford writes: "The **Elijah work ended in 1918.** Any attempt to carry on the Elijah work thereafter would be an **attempt to revive a dead thing, and hence out of harmony with the Lord.**"[33]

1937

"It was **in 1919 that the 'faithful servant' class began to see the significance of the Elisha work.** The 'servant' more fully saw in 1922 the meaning thereof... In that year the faithful ... went forward to do the Elisha work in advertising the King and the Kingdom."[34]

1940

"The keynote address of that convention [Cedar Point, Ohio] was 'Blessed Are the Fearless,' particularly disclosing the distinction between the end of the Elijah work of the church and the beginning of the Elisha work of God's organization."[35]

1943

"John's course, in fact, foreshadowed the **'Elijah work,' from 1878 to 1918,** of Jehovah's witnesses.... First after the Lord came to the temple in 1918 and after the Elijah work was forcibly stopped that year and then the 'Elisha work,' its successor, was opened in 1919, the general house-to-house witnessing began in the real sense."[36]

1945

"Elijah and his work foreshadowed the work done by faithful men on earth under the direction of Christ Jesus, God's Elect Servant, for the period of time **from about A.D. 1878 to the year 1918**. Elijah was taken away in a whirlwind, and Elisha succeeded him in the office of prophet and servant of God."[37]

1954

"Such a work was prosecuted in a particular way from *1878 to 1918*, though similar work still continues with greater intensity, and is known as the **'Elisha' work**, and this goes on until Armageddon, when Jehovah 'smites the earth with a curse.'"[38]

Which is it, Elisha or Elijah?

Compare the following two quotations that deal with the same event, the first published in 1940 and the second in 1961. "At the Cedar Point convention in 1919, and in *The Watch Tower*, many scriptures were produced supporting the conclusion that **the Elijah work ended in the fiery trouble of 1918 and that now the Elisha work of God's remnant must begin**. It was a voice from heaven, because it was Jehovah's voice through his Word."[39]

"...But in the quiet of the first post-war year, A.D. 1919, came the 'calm, low voice' from the quiet pages of God's written Word, pages further illuminated with the light of recent fulfillment of prophecies. **Back to work**, inside of Christendom, yes, outside of Christendom! That was Jehovah's commission to the **Elijah class**."[40]

This contradiction is typical of how Witness publications make former interpretations of specific dates, types, etc., agree with subsequently held views.

Post-Rutherford "New" Light

The new view that **the Elijah work ended in 1918** was announced by Rutherford in 1919 and was consistently promoted for over four decades. As cited above, it was claimed that the interpretation was supported by "many scriptures" and disclosed by Jehovah. Rutherford had argued that to continue the Elijah work after 1918 "would be an attempt to revive a dead thing, and hence out of harmony with the Lord." In spite of these and other claims, "new" light brought an "adjustment."

In 1961, the new position was first articulated: "In modern fulfillment, the **Elijah work was not finished in 1918**, and the Elijah class was not taken off the scene."[41] When did the "Elijah work" end? When Rutherford died on January 8, 1942, "it appears that there the Elijah work passed, to be succeeded by the Elisha work."[42]

The August 15, 1965, *Watchtower* explains the new transition date as Elijah's experience is interpreted:

> ...Elijah ascended to the heavens in a windstorm after being separated from Elisha by a fiery war chariot and horses. That prophetically pictured the end of the work by the Elijah class and the continuation of the same work, only intensified, by the Elisha class. The historical **events occurring early in the war year of 1942 marked the fulfillment of this changeover**. Just prior to that time, in the midst of World War II, it seemed as if the witness work might be coming to an end.[43]

The April 15, 1971, *Watchtower* also deletes the former "Elijah work" dates (1878-1918): "But as to mod-crn times, after World War I and **since the year 1919 a work like that of Elijah** has been carried on by Jehovah's Christian witnesses."[44]

Elijah and Elisha as types are used by M. James Penton to illustrate the following statement: "...It must be noted that frequently the interpretations of Watch Tower types have **changed whenever the society has found it useful or necessary to make such changes**."[45] And, concerning this example and others, he concludes:

> At this point, then, it can hardly be said that Jehovah's Witnesses have anything that can be described as a systematic method of hermeneutics or biblical interpretation. If they have anything it is tradition and nothing more. And that tradition allows them to be arbitrary in using the Scriptures to explain what is wanted in terms of Witness doctrine or the notions of the dominant figures on the governing body.[46]

Notes

1. P. Gerhard Damsteegt, *Foundations of the Seventh-Day Adventist Message and Mission* (Grand Rapids: Wm. B. Eerdmans, 1977), 250-54.
2. Ibid., 252.
3. N. H. Barbour and C. T. Russell, *Three Worlds* (Rochester, N.Y. 1877), 122. See "Elijah the Prophet," 120-24. Concerning its production, Russell writes: "... As I was enabled to give some time and thought to its preparation it was issued by us both jointly. both names appearing on its title page—though it was mainly written by Mr. Barbour" *(WTR,* 15 July 1906, 3822).
4. Ibid., 124.
5. *Jehovah's Witnesses—Proclaimers of God's Kingdom* (1993), 636.
6. Ibid., 211.
7. Paul S. L. Johnson, *Elijah and Elisha* (Philadelphia: Paul S. L. Johnson, 1938), 67.
8. *WTR,* 15 Sept. 1915, 5771.
9. Ibid., 5771-72.
10. *WTR,* 1 Jan. 1916, 5824.
11. *WTR,* 15 Feb. 1918, 6213.
12. *Proclaimers,* 211.
13. *WTR,* 15 Feb. 1919, 6392.
14. *Proclaimers,* 75-76, 654.
15. M. James Penton, *Apocalypse Delayed* (2nd ed.; Toronto: University of Toronto Press, 1997), 179.
16. *WTR,* 1 Oct. 1917, 6149; *WTR,* 15 Feb. 1919, 6392.
17. *Proclaimers,* 563.
18. *WT,* 15 July 1940, 223.
19. *WT,* 1 Dec. 1940, 357.
20. *WT,* 15 Aug. 1919, 243.
21. Ibid., 245.
22. Ibid., 248.
23. Ibid., 246.
24. Ibid., 248-49.
25. Ibid., 249.

26. *WT*, 1 July 1920, 198.

27. *WT*, 1 Nov. 1922, 334.

28. *WT*, 1 Feb. 1925, 38.

29. *WT*, 15 Apr. 1926, 117.

30. *1929 Year Book* (1928), 100.

31. Rutherford, *Light I* (1930), 64.

32. Ibid., 212.

33. *WT*, 15 May 1933, 154.

34. *WT*, 1 Feb. 1937, 44.

35. *WT*, 1 Dec. 1940, 357.

36. *WT*, 15 June 1943, 183.

37. *WT*, 1 Mar. 1945, 76.

38. *WT*, 1 Mar. 1954, 150.

39. *WT*, 15 July 1940, 223.

40. *"Let Your Name Be Sanctified"* (1961), 318.

41. Ibid.

42. Ibid., 336.

43. *WT*, 15 Aug. 1965, 494-95. "**In 1942 the change came.** In the throes of World War II, with the change in administrations of the second and third presidents of the Watch Tower Bible and Tract Society, the Elijah work passed away, having realized its purpose to Jehovah's praise" (*WT*, 1 Oct. 1967, 595).

44. *WT*, 15 Apr. 1971, 239.

45. Penton, 179.

46. Ibid.

21.

The Finished Mystery (1917)

In Watch Tower publications, *The Finished Mystery*, volume seven of *Studies in the Scriptures*, is obviously viewed as a significant book. Its publication is included among the "Noteworthy Events" in the history of the Jehovah's Witnesses.[1] A number of references to *The Finished Mystery* and events surrounding it are found in the two Witness histories: *Jehovah's Witnesses in the Divine Purpose* (1959) and *Jehovah's Witnesses—Proclaimers of God's Kingdom* (1993).[2]

Pastor Russell hoped to write the volume himself, but was unable to do so before his death. Headquarters associates Clayton J. Woodworth and George H. Fisher were then assigned to prepare the "commentary on Revelation, The Song of Solomon, and Ezekiel. In part, it was based on what Russell had written about these Bible books, and other comments and explanations were added."[3] When the book was released on July 17, 1917, it resulted in conflict within the movement.[4]

The Watch Tower's *Revelation—Its Grand Climax At Hand!* (1988) claims that *The Finished Mystery* is "a powerful commentary on Revelation and Ezekiel."[5] However, Raymond Franz, former Governing Body member, states, "A review of its contents forces one to wonder if the writer of those words had even read the book or given it any serious consideration. I sincerely doubt that the organization today would consider reprinting a single chapter, in fact any portion whatsoever of that book. It would prove painfully embarrassing."[6]

As to its contents, the above mentioned Watch Tower histories state that *The Finished Mystery* attacked the clergy with references "that were very cutting."[7] It "was a stinging exposure of these false shepherds,"[8] and "roundly exposed the hypocrisy of Christendom's clergy,"[9] who were furious over their exposure.[10] Further information is given concerning the "remarkable distribution" of the *Finished Mystery* and the persecution experienced by many of the Bible Students as a result.[11] The focus of these two Witness reviews diverts attention from much of the book's contents and the numerous ridiculous statements and false prophecies found in it.

Without citing specific teachings in *The Finished Mystery* or in other Watch Tower materials that needed clarification, the *Proclaimers* history states that "continued study of the Scriptures, along with fulfillment of divine prophecy, has in many instances made it possible to express Bible teachings with greater clarity."[12] There is no mention in the Witness histories of the claim that *The Finished Mystery* was the subject of and the fulfillment of prophecy,[13] or that it was to be "the **last and final serving** at our Father's table...."[14] This last statement was included in a letter to the *Watch Tower*, and it is in agreement with a letter Rutherford wrote to the brethren the night before his removal to Atlanta Penitentiary, which was also published in the *Watch Tower*.

Brother Russell's last expression concerning the harvest was that it would end in the spring of 1918. We believed this; and believing it, we felt that **the Seventh Volume must go out before the harvest closed....** Rejoice now, Beloved; the work of harvesting the church is done. The dark night is coming rapidly on, and soon we shall be home. There may be a little more work for the faithful to do in calling the world's attention to the message and in aiding the Elisha class.[15]

Further Claims

There were additional claims made for *The Finished Mystery* that were published in the *Watch Tower*. Here are several:

> The great symbolic earthquake cannot occur until the Seventh Volume of SCRIPTURE STUD-IES is published. All signs indicate that this earthquake is near. The Seventh Volume has been published.... **Ezekiel's prophecy, heretofore a sealed book, is now made clear** in the closing hours of the harvest. It confirms the Lord's promise of the 'faithful and wise Servant,' and identifies him.[16]

> It is something marvelous to us, and a mighty confirmation of faith to see the **God-given interpretation of Revelation and Ezekiel in the Seventh Volume** of STUDIES IN THE SCRIPTURES already in process of fulfillment before our very eyes.[17]

> Brother Russell had promised the Seventh Volume. The **Scriptures show that it must be published.**[18] ...We are pleased to set forth a few positive evidences that **none other than the Lord himself has served us with the truth of Ezekiel and Revelation,** which at the same time constitute the last plague upon Babylon. Let us not say: "Why should we accept it as present truth?" Rather let us say: "Why should I not **accept it as meat in due season from the Lord?**" Is not the Watch Tower Bible and Tract Society the **one and only channel which the Lord has used** in dispensing his truth continually since the beginning of the harvest period?[19]

Colporteurs were to tell prospective buyers:

> For a long time order-loving people, Bible readers and Christians have desired to understand the prophecies of Revelation and Ezekiel. I have here a work recently published by the BIBLE SOCIETY of Brooklyn, New York which is **the first and only book that makes clear every part of Revelation and Ezekiel.**[20]

In view of the above claims published during his presidency, Judge Rutherford apparently had a short memory as he later wrote the Preface to his own commentary on Revelation (1930):

> All who love God, his beloved Son, and his kingdom, have been eager to understand The Revelation. Students have prayerfully and earnestly sought the meaning thereof. **Prior to 1930 there never was a satisfactory explanation of The Revelation published,** the manifest reason being it was not God's due time for his servants to have an understanding thereof.... **It now seems clear that it is God's due time** for his servants to understand that great prophecy so long clothed in mystery.[21]

The identical claim is found in Rutherford's Preface to his commentary on Ezekiel (1931): "During the centuries that prophecy [Ezekiel] has been a mystery sealed to all who have sought to unlock it. **God's due time has come for the prophecy to be understood.**"[22] Compare both of these claims with those in the *Watch Tower* cited above concerning *The Finished Mystery*.

Gleanings from *The Finished Mystery*

The Finished Mystery, stated to be "a posthumous publication of Pastor Russell," applies the events formerly scheduled to come in 1914 and before to the period of 1918-1925. When some of the explanations given in the 1917 first edition did not transpire as predicted, a later edition (the edition cited here is 1926) altered the statements and dates. Statements from this volume, with changes noted, are given with occasional comments. The quotations cited are only a small sampling from its almost 600 pages.[23]

The *Finished Mystery* uses bold print in Scripture citations, and additional bold print has been added for emphasis.

"William Miller, in the year 1829, was privileged to see approximately the correct date for ... the beginning of the Time of the End (1799 A. D.). Morton Edgar, author of *Pyramid Passages*, has found foreshown in the Great Pyramid of Egypt abundant evidence of the accuracy of the Bible chronology of Pastor Russell [which dated Adam's creation at 4127]..." (60).

"**The chronology as it appears in the STUDIES IN THE SCRIPTURES is accurate**" (61).

"...The Spring of **1918 will bring upon Christendom a spasm of anguish** greater even than that experienced in the Fall of 1914.... It is possible that **A.D. 1980** may have something of special interest for Fleshly Israel, but certainly not for us..." ["It is possible that A.D. 1980 marks the regathering of all of Fleshly Israel from their captivity in death"—1918 ed.] (62).

"The awakening of the sleeping saints, A.D. 1878, was just half way ... between the beginning of the Times of Restitution in 1874 and the close of the High Calling in 1881. **Our proposition is that the glorification of the Little Flock in the Spring of 1918 A.D. will be half way ... between the close of the Gentile Times and the close of the Heavenly Way, A.D. 1921.** The three days' (three years—1918-21) fruitless search for Elijah (2 Kings 2:17-18) is a confirmation of this view. We shall wait to see ... **The time is not long; but if we have to go on for fifty years, why should we care?**" (64-65).

"...The Lord's Second Advent occurred in the fall of 1874..." (68).

"Rev. 3:20. **Behold, I stand at the door**. Some of the Scriptures, which, when understood in their connections and significance, **prove that the Lord's Second Advent occurred in the Fall of 1874** are as follows: [Isa. 40:2; Jer. 16:18; Zech. 9:12; Num. 9:11; Gen. 25:24; Acts 7:23, 30, 36; Dan. 12:12; Lev. 25:9; 2 Chron. 36:21; Isa. 19:19,20; 1 Pet. 3:21; Ezra 1:1; Ezra 6:15; Ezra 7:6-8; Neh. 2:1]....

Besides the above Scriptures, time-proofs of the Lord's return are the fulfillments of the promised signs: [these are presented on two pages] "...**And these are but 88 of the proofs hastily collected**" (68-71).

"No doubt **Satan *believed* the Millennial Kingdom was due to be set up in 1915**.... There is evidence that the establishment of the **Kingdom in Palestine will probably be in 1925**, ten years later than we once calculated" (128).

"Rev. 8:1.... **There was silence.... In heaven.... About the space of half an hour**. On the scale of a year for a day this would mean but **a week...**" (143).

Compare this interpretation with Rev. 17:12: "**One hour with the beast**—The 'one hour' in this verse (17:12) may signify **one year**, or thereabouts" (269)].

"Rev. 8:3. **And another angel.**—Not the 'voice of the Lord,'... but the corporate body—the WATCH TOWER BIBLE AND TRACT SOCIETY, which Pastor Russell formed to finish his work. This verse shows that, **though Pastor Russell has passed beyond the veil, he is still managing every feature of the Harvest**

work" (144).[24]

In Revelation 9:11, "**the angel of the [bottomless pit] ABYSS ... Whose name in the Hebrew tongue is Abaddon ... But in the Greek tongue hath his name Apollyon,**" is interpreted as "'The prince of the power of the air'—Eph. 2:2.... That is, Destroyer. But in plain English his name is **Satan, the Devil**" (159).

This identification is quite significant, because this same angel was later identified as **Jesus**! "In Hebrew his name is Abaddon, meaning 'Destruction'; and in the Greek it is Apollyon, meaning 'Destroyer.' All this plainly identifies the 'angel' as picturing **Jesus Christ, the Son of Jehovah God**" (*"Then Is Finished the Mystery of God,"* 232). "As 'angel of the abyss' and 'Destroyer,' **Jesus** had truly released a plaguing woe on Christendom" (*Revelation—Its Grand Climax At Hand!*, 148).

"9:18.... **And [by] the smoke.** Smoke is a symbol of confusion. The following is an extract from an article on the brain written by a well-known physician and alienist.... A study of the foregoing leads to the conclusion that all **modern church organizations were founded by bald-headed men**, and the smoke being unable to find the way out through their scalps naturally had to come out of their mouths!" (165-66).

"10:3. **And cried with a loud voice.** Pastor Russell was the voice used—Rev. 7:2.... **And when,** In 1881 A.D. **He had cried.** With the first great cry, '*Food for Thinking Christians*,' 1,400,000 copies given away, *free*. **Seven thunders.** Seven volumes of 'STUDIES IN THE SCRIPTURES'—Rev. 8:5. **Uttered their voices.** Were foreseen as necessary to the complete statement of the Plan, and the fulfillment of this and other Scriptures" (167).

"11:11... We therefore expect three and a half years of proscription of the Truth, **from the spring of 1918 to the fall of 1921. This will give the Great Company splendid opportunities for martyrdom** and allow another three and a half years, to the spring of 1925, for the world to think the matter over, by which time, doubtless, they will be quite ready to listen to the voice that speaketh from Heaven" [The words after the first sentence were deleted in the 1926 ed., which then reads: "But it is well to remember that prophecy is not given with a view to satisfying curiosity, but with a view to enabling the Lord's people to identify events as they transpire. **For this reason any advance view of dates is liable to be blurred, and the experience of the church has abundantly shown this to be so.** But this fact would be no adequate reason for indifference toward chronology"] (177).

"11:19.... **The Ark**—The repository of the sacred and hidden things of Revelation and Ezekiel. **Of [His] THE testament of God**—The Secret—'The Finished Mystery'" (182).

"12:7.... **Michael**—'Who as God,' the Pope. **And his angels**—The Bishops" (188).

"14:20. "**And the winepress**—The **Seventh Volume** of *Scripture Studies*, the work that will squeeze the juice out of the 'Abominations of the Earth.'" [These words are replaced by: "The facts on which the Seventh Volume of *Scripture Studies* is founded, which bring to light the spirit of ecclesiasticism," 1926 ed.] (229).

"15:1.... **Seven angels**—The seven volumes of *Studies in the Scriptures*. **Having the seven last plagues**— The seven volumes of *Studies in the Scriptures* together constitute the third and last woe poured out upon papacy" (231).

"15:6. **And the Seven angels came out of the Temple**—The seven volumes of *Scripture Studies*, emerged, all in harmony with the teachings of the Tabernacle, from which they proceeded" (235).

"**And having their breasts girded with golden girdles**— ...The *Scripture Studies* are servants of the Church—righteous servants, clad in the Lord's robe" (236).

"16:20. **And every island fled away**—Even the **republics will disappear in the fall of 1920** ["in the time of anarchy," 1926 ed.].

And the mountains were not found—Every kingdom of earth will pass away, be swallowed up in anarchy" (258).

"16:21... The three days in which Pharaoh's host pursued the Israelites into the wilderness represent the three years from **1917 to 1920 at which time all of Pharaoh's messengers will be swallowed up in the sea of anarchy**. The wheels will come off their chariots—organizations" (258).

"17:10.... "**And the other.... Is not yet come**— But is due to make its appearance with the close of the war, some time about October 1st, 1917" (1917 ed.). ["But is due to make its appearance with the close of the war, probably early in the year 1918" (1918 ed.) "But is due to make its appearance after the close of the war, probably early in the year 1918." (1926 ed.)] (268).

And when he cometh, he must continue a short space—"From the summer or fall of 1917 to the spring or summer of 1918" (1917 ed.) ["Probably from the fall of 1917 to the spring or summer of 1918" (1918 ed.—The words have been dropped in the 1926 ed.] (268).

"18:19. **And they cast dust on their [heads] HEAD**—Did a certain amount of mudslinging" ["Expressed their grief by dust-throwing" (1926 ed.)] (286).

"19:15.... **And He treadeth the winepress of the fierceness and wrath of THE ANGER of Almighty God**—The Lord assumes an interest in and responsibility for the complete series of STUDIES IN THE SCRIPTURES, the last one of which especially represents the winepress feature (Rev. 14:18-20), but it would be unreasonable to expect that the Lord would miraculously use imperfect tools to do an absolutely perfect work and each must use his judgment as to the value of the interpretations in this book" (295).

"19:17. **And I saw [an] ANOTHER angel.**"—The Elijah class after the publication of Volume Seven, *Studies in the Scriptures*" (295).

"[Ezek.] 1:1. **Now it came to pass in the thirtieth year ... that the heavens were opened, and I saw visions of God....** In the early seventies Charles Taze Russell found himself engaged in commerce, but earnestly studying the Word of God, and in striving to teach what he had found therein. **In fulfillment of the Divine promise the Heavenly things were opened to him** (Matt. 3:16), and he saw the significance of the visions, prophecies, given in olden times by the Almighty" (367).

"7:1-6.... There will be no chance of escaping from destruction, though the nations—as in cases of Germany, the Allies and the United States—earnestly seek in vain for some way of securing peace. The trouble is due to the dawning of the Day of Christ, the Millennium. **It is the Day of Vengeance, which began in the world war of 1914 and which will break like a furious morning storm in 1918**" (404).

"21:14.... Pastor Russell was to give expression to the final wrath of God.... The Sword of the Spirit was to be wielded by Pastor Russell twice three times, in his six volumes of *Studies in the Scriptures*" (465-66).

"21:15.... The point of the sword against ecclesiasticism, revealing its true nature and imminent fall, is the present exposition of the prophecies of Revelation and Ezekiel.... How gladly the clergy would have destroyed these two books of the Bible, had they known what they taught!" (466).

"24:25, 26.... Also, in the **year 1918, when God destroys** ["begins to destroy," 1926 ed.] **the churches wholesale and the church members by millions**, it shall be that any that escape shall come to the works of Pastor Russell to learn the meaning of the downfall of 'Christianity'" (485).

"26:2.... This system and its adherents will manifest their essentially non-Christian nature when Christendom (Jerusalem) **falls at the hands of the revolutionists in 1918**" (489).

"31:15.... In the year **1918, when Christendom shall** ["begin to," 1926 ed.] **go down as a system to oblivion**, (Sheol) to be succeeded by revolutionary republics, God will cause mourning" (513).

33:21, 22. Ezekiel's dumbness in this chapter of Ezekiel and the restoration of his speech represents Pastor Russell. "Pastor Russell's voice was stilled in death on October 31, 1916. If an application of Ezekiel's period of dumbness is valid here as a time feature, the tidings, the realization that **Christendom is smitten by the onslaughts of revolution, might be expected to flash throughout the world on or about April 27, 1918....** Pastor Russell, though dead, shall again speak through this, the seventh volume of his *Studies in the Scriptures...*" (530).

"35:15.... As the fleshly-minded apostates from Christianity, siding with the radicals and revolutionaries, will rejoice at the inheritance of **desolation that will be Christendom's after 1918**, so will God do to the successful revolutionary movement; it shall be utterly desolated, 'even all of it.' **Not one vestige of it shall survive the ravages of world-wide all-embracing anarchy, in** ["in the end of the time of trouble," 1926 ed.] **the fall of 1920.** (Rev. 11:7-13)" (542).

"The Time of the establishment of the Kingdom in power is indicated as 'in the fourteenth year after that the city (Christendom) was smitten'—or **fourteen years after 1918, viz., in 1932** ["or **thirteen years after 1918, viz in 1931**," 1926 ed.]—Ezek.40:1" (569).

The June 1, 1920, *Watch Tower*, under the heading, "Seventh Volume Corrections," presents about four pages of revisions to *The Finished Mystery* with the following introductory statement:

> We have found the explanations of the Seventh Volume helpful, and are convinced that they contain meat now due to the household of faith, and that this meat came from the Father's storehouse. However, this food was arranged and placed upon the table by imperfect servants and contains some blemishes which it is the purpose of the following notes to correct.[25]

In 1919, Rutherford wrote that he was thankful to God and "Christ Jesus for the privilege of having a part in publishing" *The Finished Mystery* "which the people in the **centuries to come will read with deep interest and profit** and will give God the glory."[26] But, according to *God's Kingdom of a Thousand Years Has Approached* (1973): "Later in the year 1927 any remaining stocks of the six volumes of the six volumes of *Studies in the Scriptures* by Russell and of *The Finished Mystery* were disposed of among the public"[27]—never to be reprinted by the Watchtower Society—and difficult to find today.[28]

In more recent years, the Watchtower's book *Revelation—Its Grand Climax At Hand!* (1988), also ignored the claims made for *The Finished Mystery* and stated concerning it: "In time, though, this book proved to be unsatisfactory as an explanation of Revelation. The remnant of Christ's brothers had to wait a while longer, until the visions started to be fulfilled, for an accurate understanding of that inspired record."[29] And as already reviewed, Rutherford produced his own "due time" commentaries on Revelation and Ezekiel in five volumes.[30] These too have in turn been superseded by others after Rutherford's death.[31]

In conclusion, the Dawn Bible Students' booklet, *When Pastor Russell Died*, is quoted:

> The story of the "Seventh Volume" would not be complete should we fail to mention that in a remarkably short time after it was published it was virtually rejected by the publishers. It is well nigh impossible to believe, yet true, that whereas **when this book was first published those who did not accept it were condemned and disfellowshipped, within a few years those who did accept it were disfellowshipped.**[32]

Notes

1. *Jehovah's Witnesses—Proclaimers of God's Kingdom* (1993), 719.
2. *Jehovah's Witnesses in the Divine Purpose* (1959), 32, 70-71, 73-75, 77-79, 90-92, 98, 100. *Proclaimers*, 66-70, 88, 148, 211, 423-24, 647-52, 719.
3. Ibid., 67.
4. See the above Witnesses' histories. See also M. James Penton, *Apocalypse Delayed* (2nd ed.; Toronto: University of Toronto Press, 1997), 50-52, 55.

5. *Revelation—Its Grand Climax At Hand!* (1988), 165.

6. Raymond Franz, *In Search of Christian Freedom* (Atlanta: Commentary Press, 1991), 142.

7. *Proclaimers*, 69.

8. *Jehovah's Witnesses in the Divine Purpose*, 73.

9. *Proclaimers*, 647.

10. Ibid., 423.

11. Ibid., 69-70, 211, 423-24, 647-51.

12. Ibid., 148. "In 1917 a study of Revelation was published in the book *The Finished Mystery*. But 'the Lord's day,' referred to in Revelation 1:10, was just beginning back then; much of what was foretold had not yet occurred and was not clearly understood. However, developments during the years that followed cast greater light on the meaning of that part of the Bible, and these events had a profound effect on the very illuminating study of Revelation that was published in 1930 in the two volumes entitled *Light*" (Ibid., 148). Subsequent studies on Revelation were published.

13. *The Finished Mystery* (1917), Preface, 5. See *The Finished Mystery* text quoted in this study and the *Watch Tower* quotes below.

14. *WTR*, 1 Dec. 1917, 6180.

15. *WTR*, 15 Feb. 1918, 6392.

16. *WTR*, 15 Nov. 1917, 6170.

17. *WTR*, 15 Dec. 1917, 6188.

18. *WTR*, 15 Feb. 1919, 6392.

19. *WTR*, 1 Apr. 1919, 6414.

20. *WTR*, 1 Oct. 1917, 6150.

21. Rutherford, *Light I* (1930), 5-6.

22. Rutherford, *Vindication I* (1931), 5.

23. In his *In Search of Christian Freedom*, Raymond Franz discusses *The Finished Mystery* and includes photo-copies from the book (136-45).

24. The November 1, 1917, *Watch Tower* also viewed Russell as influencing the work on earth: "Hence our dear Pastor, now in glory, is without doubt, manifesting a keen interest in the harvest work, and is permitted by the Lord to exercise some strong influence thereupon. (Revelation 14:17) It is not unreasonable to conclude that he has been privileged to do, in connection with the harvest work, things which he could not do while with us.... We recognize that he [the Lord] would privilege the saints beyond the veil to have a part in the work on this side..." (*WTR*, 6161). In Rutherford's rejection of this view he writes: "No one of the temple company will be so foolish as to conclude that some brother (or brethren) at one time amongst them, and who has died and gone to heaven, is now instructing the saints on earth and directing them as to their work" (*Jehovah* [1934], 191).

    It appears that the earlier view has been revived. Commenting on Revelation 7:13-14: "This suggests that resurrected [1918] ones of the 24-elders group [the 144,000, anointed] may be involved in the communicating of divine truths today" (*Revelation—Its Grand Climax At Hand!* [1988], p. 125).

25. *WT*, 1 June 1920, 169.

26. *WTR*, 15 Feb. 1919, 6392.

27. *God's Kingdom of a Thousand Years Has Approached* (1973), 347.

28. According to ex-Witness David Reed, "Few JWs can read this volume without becoming quite upset over the teachings found in it. For that reason it has been removed from the libraries of most of their kingdom halls" (*Jehovah's Witness Literature: A Critical Guide to Watchtower Publications* [Grand Rapids:

Baker Books, 1993], 58-59). Witness Inc. (P.O. Box 597, Clayton, CA 94517), has reprinted the 1917 edition (first printing, 75,000 ed.) of *The Finished Mystery* in an 8½" x 11" format.

29. *Revelation—Its Grand Climax At Hand!*, 159.

30. *Light I* and *II* (1930), *Vindication I* (1931), *II*, *III* (1932).

31. On Revelation: *"Babylon the Great Has Fallen!" God's Kingdom Rules!* (1963); *"Then Is Finished the Mystery of God"* (1969); *Revelation—Its Grand Climax At Hand!* (1988). On Ezekiel: *"The Nations Shall Know That I Am Jehovah"* (1971).

32. *When Pastor Russell Died* (East Rutherford, N.J.: Dawn Bible Students Assoc., n.d.), 7. This is also verified in the *Epiphany Bible Students Assn. Journal*: "... It is not more than 10 or 15 years after its appearance in 1917 that 'The Finished Mystery'... was placed on the list of forbidden things—in contrast to the ruling of 1917. Those who didn't accept the book in 1917 were disfellowshipped—but any one caught reading and accepting its teachings at the later date was also disfellowshipped" (1 Oct. 1975, 6; 1 Aug. 1971, 2; 1 Aug. 1978, 2).

22.

Selected Quotations from Watch Tower Publications for the Years 1920-1929

1920

"In fact, **we stand today at the portals of the Golden Age**. Just beyond the distress that is now upon mankind, by the eye of faith we see the incoming blessings" (*GA*, 14 Apr. 1920, 477).

"Since my [Rutherford's] release from jail and my recovery from a great illness resulting from imprisonment, I have spoken to thousands of people on the timely and up-to-date subject: 'Millions Now Living Will Never Die,' and made glad many hearts. By the Lord's grace we purpose to continue to make proclamation of **His message; because we are convinced beyond a doubt that within five years** the people will awaken to the fact that they are entering the period of the greatest blessings man has ever dreamed could come to the world" (*GA*, 9 June 1920, 591).

"**Suppose we should be wrong in the chronology and that the kingdom will not be fully set up in 1925. Suppose that we were ten years off**, and that it would be 1935 before restitution blessings began. Without a doubt there are now millions of people on the earth who will be living fifteen years from now; and we could with equal confidence say that 'Millions Now Living Will Never Die.' **Whether it be 1925 or 1935, restitution blessings must soon begin...**" (*WT*, 15 Oct. 1920, 310).

1921

"Just how long the remaining members of the church will be this side of the vail of course we do not know; but all the evidence points to the fact that **it cannot be a great while**. The King of glory is not only present, but he is putting his kingdom in order and **soon all the members of the kingdom class must be with him in glory**" (*WT*, 1 Jan. 1921, 8).

"*Do these things appeal to you?* Unending human life; perpetual health ... no more sickness, disease, or pestilence; no more ignorance or superstition; no more sorrow; no more tears! *No, we are not trifling*: these things and more are absolutely sure, because promised by the Word of God. The world has already ended, in the Bible and only proper sense of that term; and the antitypical Jubilee, earth's times of restitution, its springtime, begins to count in 1926. *When that time comes*, **all the above blessings will not come instantaneously, but will come speedily on those who live through the next five or six years of trouble**" (*GA*, 19 Jan. 1921, back cover).

"Twelve hundred and sixty years from A.D. 539 brings us to 1799, another proof that **1799 definitely**

marks the beginning of 'the time of the end'" (Rutherford, *The Harp of God* [1921 ed.], 230).

"Counting three and a half years from 1874, the time of his presence, brings us to 1878. During the presence of the Lord from 1874 to **1878** he was making preparation for the harvest of the age. **The Jewish harvest covered a period of forty years**, ending in A.D. 73. **We should expect, then, the general harvest of the gospel age to end in 1918**" (ibid., 236). The 1928 edition rewords this section and changes the length of the harvest period: ...From the time of the beginning of the Jewish harvest until Pentecost was fifty days; and carrying out the Biblical rule of a day for a year, **it would not be unreasonable to conclude that the harvest of the Christian era would cover a period of fifty years**" (241).

"In 1844 the telegraph was invented and later the telephone.... This great increase of knowledge and the tremendous running to and fro of the people in various parts of the earth is without question a fulfillment of prophecy testifying as to 'the time of the end.' These physical facts can not be disputed and are sufficient to **convince any reasonable mind that we have been in the 'time of the end' since 1799**" (ibid. [1921 ed.], 234).

"The proof cited herein shows that the old world (social and political order) ended and began to pass away in 1914, and that **this will be completed in a few years** and righteousness fully established" (ibid., 333). (The 1928 edition has the same statement except that the parenthetical statement has been changed to "the Devil's organization," and the material is on p. 339.)

"Hence these faithful men [Abraham, Isaac, Jacob and the other faithful prophets described by the apostle Paul in Hebrews 11] may be expected on earth **within the next few years**. They will constitute the legal representatives of the Christ in the earth" (ibid., 340). The 1928 edition drops the words "within the next few years" and reads, "Hence these faithful men may be expected on earth at the inauguration of the new covenant" (346).

"The **British empire is now tottering** at every corner, and **her existence is only a matter of a few years at most.** When the Lord is ready to establish His kingdom in Palestine it will be fully established; and the Jews will be the chief ones in it, the British notwithstanding" (*GA*, 31 Aug. 1921, 714).

"The remaining kingdoms are going to pieces. Shortly God's kingdom will be established, His *favor return to the Jews* regathered in Palestine, and the Lord Himself, through His chosen ones, will rule the earth" (ibid., 715).

"The message 'Millions Now Living Will Never Die' is not only a judgment against Satan, the father of lies, and his empire, but it contains a message of good cheer and comfort to those who mourn. It is a message of glad tidings, which **must now be preached to all nations as a witness before the final end**.... The time is short" (*WT*, 1 Sept. 1921, 265).

"*The Watchtower* has **consistently** presented evidence to honest-hearted students of Bible prophecy that **Jesus' presence in heavenly Kingdom power began in 1914**" (WT, 15 Jan. 1993, 5).

1922

"The **indisputable facts**, therefore, show that the 'time of the end' began in 1799; **that the Lord's second presence began in 1874**; that the harvest followed thereafter and greater light has come upon the Word of God" (*WT*, 1 Mar. 1922, 73).

"...The year 1925 marks the date when all shall see His mighty power demonstrated in the **resurrection of the ancient worthies**, and the time when 'millions now living will never die'" (*GA*, 1 Mar. 1922, 350).

"We have no **doubt whatever** in regard to the chronology relating to the dates of **1874**, 1914, 1918, and

1925" (*WT*, 15 May 1922, 147).

Under the subheading "STAMPED WITH GOD'S APPROVAL": "Thus it was **in 1844, in 1874, in 1878 as well as in 1914 and 1918. Looking back we can now easily see that those dates were clearly indicated in Scripture** and doubtless intended by the Lord to encourage his people, as they did, as well as to be a means of testing and sifting when all that some expected did not come to pass" (ibid., 150).

"And it was in **1878, then, that the process of setting up the kingdom began. There our Lord raised the sleeping saints** from the tomb and joined them to himself, while his members upon the earth continued the work of making ready the remaining members of the body and of giving world-wide witness of the coming change of dispensation" (*WT*, 1 June 1922, 174).

"The date **1925 is even more distinctly indicated by the Scriptures** because it is fixed by the law God gave to Israel. Viewing the present situation in Europe, one wonders how it will be possible to hold back the explosion much longer; and that **even before 1925 the great crisis will be reached and probably passed**" (*WT*, 1 Sept. 1922, 262).

"No one can properly understand the work of God at this present time who does not realize that **since 1874, the time of the Lord's return in power**, there has been a complete change in God's operations" (*WT*, 15 Sept. 1922, 278).

"Many earnest students of the Word of God contend that we are today living in the period of time in which the gospel aged is closing and the **Millennial age dawning**" (*GA*, 25 Oct. 1922, 62).

"...There is now **impending and about to fall** upon the nations of the earth, according to the words of Christ Jesus, a great time of 'tribulation such as was not since the beginning of the world to this time, no, nor ever shall be' [again], and it is this **impending** trouble that the rulers and mighty men of earth see coming" (*WT*, 1 Nov. 1922, 324-25. Brackets in original).

"Bible prophecy shows that the Lord was due to appear for the second time in the year **1874. Fulfilled prophecy shows beyond a doubt that he did appear in 1874.** Fulfilled prophecy is otherwise designated the physical facts; and these facts are indisputable" (ibid., 333).

"According to **all the Scriptural evidence, Jesus was due to make his second appearance in 1874.** Since then, fulfilled prophecy furnishes the evidence conclusively showing his presence" (*WT*, 1 Dec. 1922, 375).

"Surely the prophecies are sufficiently emphatic in foretelling an unprecedented convulsion, now imminent, and Pastor Russell certainly taught that **the late war was merely a prelude to Armageddon**" (*GA*, 6 Dec. 1922, 149).

1923

"Some are inclined to become doubtful about 1925; hence they are growing lukewarm. But, beloved of the Lord, **what difference does it make whether the things expected to transpire in 1925 do transpire of not?** God will not change his plans. He made his plans long ago. He has made no mistakes" (*WT*, 1 Feb. 1923, 35).

"By proof is meant the physical facts in fulfillment of prophetic utterances by the Lord or some of his inspired witnesses. This proof shows that the **Lord has been present since 1874**, and that he has been conducting and is still conducting a harvest work..." (*WT*, 1 Mar. 1923, 67).

"Besides the United States and Canada, there are many other countries, in Europe, Asia, and Africa, where we must help to send the message to the people while **there remains a short time for proclaiming the message before the final end.**... The day of deliverance is **at hand!**" (*WT*, 1 Apr. 1923, 102).

"*Question:* Did the order go forth eight months ago to the Pilgrims to cease taking about 1925? Have we more reason, or as much, to believe the kingdom will be established in 1925 than Noah had to believe that there would be a flood? *Answer:* ... There was never at any time any intimation to the Pilgrim brethren that they should cease talking about 1925.... Our thought is that **1925 is definitely settled by the Scriptures**, marking the end of the typical jubilees. Just exactly what will happen at that time no one can tell to a certainty; **but we expect such a climax** in the affairs of the world that the people will begin to realize the presence of the Lord in his kingdom power.... As to Noah, the Christian now has much more upon which to base his faith than Noah had (so far as the Scriptures reveal) upon which to base his faith in a coming deluge" (*WT*, 1 Apr. 1923, 106).

"The dissolving of Satan's empire began in the World War; and there is no possible restoration of any crumbling kingdom, but rather the crushing, disintegrating process continues until all shall cease to function. The **Scriptures seem to limit this transition period to eleven years, from 1914 to and including 1925**. At this time the Lord Jesus is invisibly present bringing to naught the wisdom of the 'wise' men of earth..." (*GA*, 6 June 1923, 563).

"The church is nearing the end of her earthly career. The fullness of the gentiles has practically come in, and the heavenly body of Christ will soon be completed" (*WT*, 1 Sept. 1923, 259).

"The greatest crisis of the ages is upon the nations of earth" (*GA*, 26 Sept. 1923, 806). "...**All the nations are marching to the great battle of Armageddon**, and there they shall fall to rise no more as unrighteous nations" (ibid., 807). "**IS THERE no possible way to avert the battle of Armageddon? Five years ago it was possible; now it is impossible**" (ibid., 808).

Ad for *Millions Now Living Will Never Die*: "Bible proof that Christ's kingdom is **about to be established** and that death will cease" (*GA*, 21 Nov. 1923, back cover).

1924

"**Surely there is not the slightest room for doubt in the mind of a truly consecrated child of God that the Lord Jesus is present and has been since 1874** ... that most of the saints have now been gathered.... Do not all the physical facts about us indicate **just exactly what we expected** during the concluding hours of the church's earthly pilgrimage?" (*WT*, 1 Jan. 1924, 5).

"Americans are beginning to wonder who will be their next President. Many of our readers are not especially interested in this subject; for they believe the Lord's kingdom is at the doors and will be a visible reality in the earth **some time during the term of the next presidential administration**" (*GA*, 2 Jan. 1924, 203).

"Prophecy indicates that 1925-1926 will see the greater part of the ousting completed. All the world's statesmen are dreading the next few years" (W. E. Van Amburgh, *The Way to Paradise*, 171).

"When you take up a more advanced study of the Bible, you will find that the year **1925 A.D. is particularly marked in prophecy**" (ibid., 220).

"What a privilege to be living just at this time and to see **the ending of the old and the coming in of the new!** Of all the times in earth's history, today is the most wonderful" (ibid., 227).

"1914 marked the beginning of God's wrath upon the nations of earth, composing Satan's government, and marked the beginning of sorrows upon these nations, as stated by Jesus. This must continue until a great climax is reached, resulting in the overthrow of Satan's power and the complete establishment of the new government. **These things are now in progress**" (Rutherford, *A Desirable Government*, 23-24).

"How rejoiced we are to have the knowledge that the Millennial reign of Jesus Christ with righteousness and truth is **so near at hand...**" (*GA*, 30 Jan. 1924, 283).

"It is true that we hold that the **saints who slept were raised in 1878**; also that since 1881 those who enter the high calling take the places that were vacated by some who were consecrated to the Lord at that time. As to the glorification of the church in 1918 ... **we expect the full glorification of the church in about two years**" (*GA*, 13 Feb. 1924, 313).

"The actual end of the jubilees brought about the destruction of literal Babylon; and the end of the seventy cycles (as indicated by seventy jubilees), **in the fall of 1925, will surely bring the deathblow to symbolic Babylon** [Christendom]" (*WT*, 15 May 1924, 159).

"**All these evidences are so patent that we cannot be mistaken as to what they mean.** They mean this: The old order is passing out; the new order is coming in; Messiah's kingdom is **at the door**; and the time for Him to begin His reign is here.... I am happy to tell you that we are **standing at the very portals** of a new and glorious time of relief for mankind" (*GA*, 18 June 1924, 601).

"We are living now in the most wonderful time of man's history to date. We are witnessing the transition period from a bad condition to a happy condition. We are standing at the **portals of the Golden Age**" (*GA*, 2 July 1924, 637).

"It will not do to say that 1925 is approaching and the work will not be finished during that year, and that therefore one can slack up for awhile and take on the work again some time later. Who knows that the work of the Church this side of the vail may not be completed in 1925?... **Suppose the Lord should say to his people in 1925 words to the effect that several years more will be required to give witness to the nations before all the body members shall be changed into glorious spirit beings? .... The year 1925 is a date definitely and clearly marked in the Scriptures, even more clearly than that of 1914...**" (*WT*, 15 July 1924, 211).

"Assured of the fact that we are standing now in the presence of the Lord at the beginning of his reign, and certain of the fact that the kingdom of heaven **is at hand**, and that we are **standing at the portals** of the Golden Age, **it is with confidence that we announce that millions now living will never die...**" (*WT*, 15 Sept. 1924, 281).

"Pastor Russell adhered closely to the teachings of the Scriptures. **He believed and taught that we are living in the time of the second presence of our Lord, and that this presence dates from 1874; that since that time we have been living in the 'time of the end,'** the 'end of the age,' during which the Lord has been conducting his great harvest work..." ("Biography," Russell, *The Divine Plan of the Ages* [1924-1927 eds.], 6-7).

1925

"The year 1925 is here. With great expectation Christians have looked forward to this year. Many have confidently expected that all members of the body of Christ will be changed to heavenly glory during the year. **This may be accomplished. It may not be.** In his own due time God will accomplish his purposes concerning his own people" (*WT*, 1 Jan. 1925, 3).

"Briefly summing up, **the Millennial reign of Christ is at the door; yea, it has already begun....** In the early part of the reign of Christ the faithful prophets of old—Abraham, Isaac, Jacob, and others—will be resurrected as perfect human beings, and made princes, or rulers on earth.... **The day, therefore, is not far distant when Abraham will stand on Mount Zion and, by means of the radio or even some more improved instrument, speak with authority....** Seeing, then, that we are at the very beginning of this wonderful time, with confidence it can be said: '**Millions now living will never die**'" (*GA*, 14 Jan. 1925, 254).

"Bible Students know that **the number seven often has peculiar significance in the Scriptures....** It was on the seventeenth of July, 1917, that 'The Finished Mystery' was distributed to the Bethel Family; and it was on that day that trouble at Bethel came to a head, and continued until many who had been very active in the service for years withdrew from further activities in connection with the SOCIETY. **July 17th, 1917, was therefore a marked date**"(*WT*, 15 Feb. 1925, 54).

"No doubt Mr. Miller was correct in locating 1844 as a Bible date. But he expected too much. 1874 was also easily located. 1878 was also a marked date, and one which caused Brother Russell a severe trial until he corrected his expectations.... **Many can remember how 'absolutely sure' some were about 1914.** No doubt the Lord was pleased with the zeal manifested by his servants; but did they have a Scriptural basis for all they expected to come to pass that year? **Let us be cautious, therefore, about predicting particulars**" (ibid., 57).

"From 1878 forward Jesus was gathering together his consecrated followers; and these, with the hope of an early birth of the new nation or government, have struggled on for the cause of righteousness, holding fast to the precious truths. **They expected this birth in 1910 and at other dates, but particularly in 1914.** In that year the Lord took his power and began his reign" (*WT*, 1 Mar. 1925, 69).

"The new nation is born. Its glory shall fill the whole earth. **The kingdom of heaven is here. The day of deliverance is in sight.** Let this good news be heralded to the peoples of earth. Victory is with our King. Faithful now to the end of the war; and we shall forever bask in the sunshine of his love, where there is full-ness of joy and pleasures for evermore" (ibid., 74).

"The Truth that THE GOLDEN AGE stands for is that **Christ Jesus returned to earth in 1874**, and that his kingdom is in the process of construction before our very eyes" (*GA*, 25 Mar. 1925, 407).[1]

"**That we are nearing the time of a great and final battle of the forces of darkness against the Lord is testified to by many Scriptures.**... It is the great battle of God Almighty" (*WT*, 15 July 1925, 215).

"The speaker [Rutherford] then demonstrated the fact that all forward-looking men are expecting the col-lapse of our present civilization. He quoted excerpts to this end, especially some from the pen of Mr. W. G. Shepherd, the noted war correspondent, to show that even now the great powers of Europe are preparing for chemical warfare on a colossal scale. He declared that by airplane raids the great cities of the world could be destroyed in a night; and that no flesh could possibly escape from the rain of poison gases which would fall upon the helpless inhabitants of the world's centers of commerce. But it was not his wish, he said, to frighten his audience, but **to forewarn them of Christendom's doom.**... Old Testament Scriptures were then read to show that terrible as the impending disaster will be, yet it will not last long; that millions will survive the catastrophe; and that upon the ruins of the old order of human civilization will be erected the glorious Messianic kingdom..." (*GA*, 12 Aug. 1925, 721).[2]

"**It is to be expected that Satan will try to inject into the minds of the consecrated the thought that 1925 should see an end of the work**, and that therefore it would be needless for them to do more.... Diligence now and to the end seems absolutely essential to victory" (*WT*, 1 Sept. 1925, 262).

"SIR ARTHUR CONAN DOYLE, spiritist, is widely quoted as saying that the denizens of the spirit world have repeatedly announced lately that a great catastrophe is impending.... **It is possible that the demons have some advance notice of what is to happen soon**" (*GA*, 2 Dec. 1925, 131).

"That there is a a great and terrible time of trouble **impending and immediately about to fall is true beyond a question of a doubt**, and there is no power on earth that can now avert it.... The world today **stands at the portals** of a tribulation such as man has never before known" (*WT*, 15 Dec. 1925, 372).

"No power aside from Jehovah's can now avert Armageddon, and he will not. The Devil's organization must fall to make way for the kingdom of righteousness" (ibid., 376).

1926

"Mankind is now at a period of the greatest crisis in their experiences. Their deliverance from despotic and unrighteous power is **near at hand**" (*WT*, 15 July 1926, 213).

"All the nations and kingdoms of earth are **rapidly marching** to the great battle of God Almighty" (ibid., 216).

"The hosts are **marching toward Armageddon now**. Are you in the ranks? If so, on what side? Armageddon shall mark the use of the winepress which shall completely crush out the vine and the fruit of the earth" (*WT*, 1 Sept. 1926, 262).

"The treading of the winepress is **near at hand**; because the day of God's wrath has come" (ibid., 263).

"...The day of deliverance **is here**" (*1927 Year Book*, 14 Sept.). "**Very soon** he will triumph in Armageddon's conflict..." (18 Oct.).

"The literature of the SOCIETY **once plainly set forth that 1914 would mark the complete glorification of the church**. Many set their hearts upon that date. The time passed, and the church was not yet glorified. Then THE WATCH TOWER began to set forth the truth as to where the mistake in calculation had been made, and that 1914 was in truth and in fact a correct chronological date, but that **the mistake was as to what would transpire at that date**" (*WT*, 1 Oct. 1926, 294).

"Earth's Greatest Conflict is Near," Rutherford's address at Madison Square Garden: "Why should I say that the day of earth's greatest conflict **is near**? Because prophecies fulfilled and the physical facts show conclusively that **it is near**. The World War and attending conditions from 1914 to 1918 prove the end of the world and the beginning of God's kingdom" (*GA*, 17 Nov. 1926, 106).

"In the great time of trouble **just ahead** millions of people will die.... **It can now be confidently stated that there are millions now living who will never die!**" (ibid., 107).

1927

"Twelve hundred and sixty years from A.D. 539 brings us to 1799, which is another proof that **1799 definitely marks the beginning of 'the time of the end.'** This also shows that it is from the date of 539 A.D. that the other prophetic days of Daniel must be counted" (Rutherford, *Creation* (100,000 ed.), 315).

"**'The time of the end' embraces a period from 1799 A.D.** to the time of the complete overthrow of Satan's empire and the establishment of the kingdom of Messiah" (ibid., 319).

"**For many years Bible Students have held that the resurrection of the apostles and other faithful saints who slept in Jesus occurred in the spring of 1878**" (*WT*, 15 May 1927, 150).

"**It seems impossible to find anything in these parallel events to indicate the resurrection of the sleeping saints in 1878....** The known facts that apply to 1878 relate only to the beginning of God's favor to the Jews and seem to have no reference to the church.... **There is nothing to indicate that Jesus Christ took his power and began his reign in 1878**" (ibid., 151).

"The New World **at the Door**." "...We are right **at the very doorstep** of the new world, the world to come" (*GA*, 10 Aug. 1927, 733).

"The overwhelming weight of evidence therefore shows that we **stand now almost in the shadow of Armageddon**" (*WT*, 15 Nov. 1927, 343).

"Undoubtedly the World War ceased that the witness might be given; and when it is given, it may be expected that the Battle of Armageddon will follow" (ibid., 344).

"There is **no Scriptural evidence to warrant the conclusion that the sleeping saints were resurrected in 1878**" (ibid., 350).

"That great time of trouble expressed as the battle of the great day of God Almighty is yet future; it is near at hand; it **is impending and soon will fall upon the nations of the earth.... The day of God's vengeance is at hand.** All the evidence from the Scriptures and outside thereof testifies to this fact. The forces are hastening to Armageddon" (*WT*, 15 Dec. 1927, 377).

1928

"...Satan has been expelled from heaven ... **all the forces are now gathering for Armageddon....** To this [faithful servant] class the Lord gives commandment to proclaim the great message of God's truth to the nations of earth as a witness and then Armageddon shall quickly follow and that shall be the final trouble upon earth" (*WT*, 1 Jan. 1928, 4).

"The kingdom is sure; the days of oppression and of every hurtful thing are nearly run. The day of deliverance **is at hand**. This is the gospel of the kingdom which the servants of the Lord sing before the nations, and to the honor of Jehovah's name" (*WT*, 15 Aug. 1928, 255).

"Jehovah's prophecies and the physical facts marking the fulfillment thereof show to his anointed that the great battle of **Armageddon is rapidly approaching**" (*WT*, 1 Oct. 1928, 291).

1929

"Doubtless there will be millions living on earth when the judgment begins. There is a great deal of evidence showing that **the judgment will begin within a very short time**" (Rutherford, *Judgment*, 44).

"The revelation of the book of Job to God's people is another evidence that we are **rapidly approaching** the great battle of Almighty God and, after it, the blessings of God's kingdom on earth" (Rutherford, *Life*, 297).

"Satan knows that **shortly** he must fight the Lord, and therefore he prepares for the conflict" (Rutherford, *Prophecy*, 266).

"According to the Scriptures, we are living in the last days, which means the last days of Satan's reign and the permission of evil. The Scriptures show that even now Christ has begun to set up his kingdom, and that **very soon** its blessings will be apparent to all. It is a special pleasure to announce that the **next few years will witness the full establishment of that kingdom** which is to be the desire of all nations" (*WT*, 1 Oct. 1929, 302).

═══════════

"Jehovah's Witnesses have **consistently shown** from the Scriptures that **the year 1914 marked the beginning of this world's time of the end** and that 'the day of judgment and of destruction of the ungodly men' has drawn near" (*WT*, 15 Aug. 1993, 9).

═══════════

"**For a long while it has been understood that 'the time of the end' began with 1799 A.D. and continued until 1914...**"[3] (*WT*, 1 Dec. 1929, 355).

"...It is easy to be seen that the definitely fixed 'time of the end' was and is 1914 A.D. Nothing came to pass in 1799 that corresponds so well with these prophecies as did 1914" (ibid., 357).

"'**The time of the end' is, both by facts and by the Scriptures, definitely fixed at, to wit, 1914 A.D**" (ibid., 360).

Notes

1. In an unpublished study based on primary sources, Duane Magnani concludes: "The record shows that when Russell said Jesus was 'present,' he meant that **literally**—Jesus was **here**—on earth.... Russell's doctrine of the 'invisible' presence would make no sense, if he believed Jesus was still in heaven. Why mention his **invisibility** at all. Obviously, the word invisible would only have significance if Jesus was **here**." For documentation see: *Three Worlds* (1877), 8, 40, 105-08; *WTR*, July 1879, 4; *WTR*, Mar. 1885, 735 (quoted in chapter 4); *WT*, 1 Oct. 1919, 301; Russell, *Thy Kingdom Come* (1891), 234 (quoted in chapter 5); *The Bible Students Monthly*, Vol. 6, No. 1, 1 (quoted in chapter 7 under 1914).

2. Quoted by Ken Raines in "The Next War," *JW Research Journal*, Spring, 1995, 16. In his article, Raines writes: "A little known 'prophecy' of the Watchtower Society during the Rutherford period concerned

what they believed the 'next war' would be like and how it would be fought. This started in 1923 or so when they were pointing to 1925 as the date when the kingdom of God would be established on the earth. Before Paradise was to begin, the battle of Armageddon would occur. A [final] war would precede and lead up to it. The Society believed this 'next war' would be fought in the air with unmanned electrical airplanes dropping chemical weapons or germ bombs" (ibid. Brackets in original.). The May 1, 1925, *Watch Tower* also gives excerpts from Shepherd's article (132-33).

3. See, for example: *WTR*, Aug. 1879, 24 (which has 1798); *WTR*, 1 Nov. 1914, 5565; Russell, *Thy Kingdom Come* (1891), 23); Rutherford, *The Harp of God* (1921), 234; Rutherford, *Creation* (1927), 319. Later editions of the *Harp* book (1928, 1937, 1940) continued to have the 1799 date (*JW Research Journal*, Spring 1994, 20).

23.

The Cedar Point Convention,
September 5-13, 1922

*J*ehovah's *Witnesses—Proclaimers of God's Kingdom* makes a number of references to the September 5-13, 1922, convention at Cedar Point, Ohio, which is also identified as one of the "Noteworthy Events" in Witness history.[1] One of these references states that the Bible Students were "stirred by evidence of the fulfillment of Bible prophecy," and that the "climax of the convention" came on September 8 in Rutherford's discourse, "The Kingdom."[2]

What were some of the "fulfilled" prophecies and other significant insights presented at Cedar Point, reviewing just this one discourse? The November 1, 1922, *Watch Tower* reproduced Rutherford's talk. Here are some excerpts:

Bible prophecy shows that **the Lord was due to appear for the second time in the year 1874. Fulfilled prophecy shows beyond a doubt that he did appear in 1874.** Fulfilled prophecy is otherwise designated the physical facts; and **these facts are indisputable**.... Jesus himself declared that in the time of his presence he would conduct a **harvest** of his people, during which he would gather unto himself the true and loyal ones. **For some years this work has been in operation and is nearing its completion.** He stated that during his presence he would have **one who would fill the office of a faithful and wise servant** [Russell],[3] through whom the Lord would bring to his people meat in due season. All **the facts show that these prophecies have been fulfilled**.... Since he has been **present from 1874**, it follows, from the facts as we now see them, that the period from **1874 to 1914 is the day of preparation**. This in no wise militates against the thought that **'the time of the end' is from 1799 until 1914**.[4]

The physical facts, then, clearly show that the day of preparation was from 1874 forward; and that the **Elijah work was done from 1874 forward, ending in 1918**.[5] ... Prior to 1878 the nominal church had grown mighty in the earth. In **1878 God's favor was withdrawn from the nominal systems**.[6] ... Prophecy can be better understood when fulfilled. [In 1919] they came to a knowledge of the fact that the **Elijah work had ended**, and that now the work pictured by **Elisha must begin**.[7]

The kingdom of heaven is at hand; the King reigns; Satan's empire is falling; **millions now living will never die** [because of expectations for 1925]. Do you believe it?[8] **Do you believe that**

the King of glory is present, and has been since 1874? Do you believe that during that time he has conducted his harvest work? **Do you believe that he has had during that time a faithful and wise servant** [Russell] through whom he directed his work and the feeding of the household of faith?[9]

How are these interpretations of fulfilled prophecy and insights viewed today?

Notes

1. *Jehovah's Witnesses—Proclaimers of God's Kingdom* (1993), 72, 77-78, 138, 246, 260, 265, 678, 720.
2. Ibid., 77, 678. The fulfillment of the 1,335 days of Daniel 12:12 are seen as beginning in September of 1922 (*WT*, 1 Nov. 1993, 11).
3. "All the 'feet members' who are now engaged in proclaiming this precious message received their enlightenment by partaking of the 'food' which the Lord sent through his chosen servant. THE WATCH TOWER **unhesitatingly proclaims Brother Russell as 'that faithful and wise servant'**" (*WT*, 15 Feb. 1917, 6049).
4. *WT*, 1 Nov. 1922, 333.
5. Ibid., 334.
6. Ibid., 335.
7. Ibid., 336.
8. It is significant that the *1975 Yearbook* quotes this paragraph using only the words: "Do you believe it?" followed by an ellipsis (131).
9. *WT*, 1 Nov. 1922, 337.

24.

1925 and the "Millions Now Living Will Never Die" Fiasco

Judge Rutherford's *Millions Now Living Will Never Die* (1920) booklet (sometimes referred to as a book) and the "Millions Campaign," a public-speaking lecture program, which began on September 25, 1920,[1] have often been mentioned in Watch Tower publications since that time. The attention-getting slogan, or its equivalent, has even appeared in Society literature in more recent years.[2] But not until a few years ago were readers of Watch Tower Society publications informed "that the *prime foundation* and the *whole strength* of the claim that 'Millions Now Living Will Never Die' rested on the predictions about 1925, predictions that proved utterly false."[3]

For example, *Jehovah's Witnesses in the Divine Purpose* (1959) is typical in its coverage of the subject, in that it makes no reference to the 1925 focus of the campaign or the "book."[4] This history does make statements mentioning 1925, but they are not connected with the "Millions" failure: "From 1922 through 1925 Jehovah God helped his people to wait or endure, carrying on his kingdom preaching on a worldwide scale.... The year 1925 especially proved to be a year of great trial to many of Jehovah's people" as many left the organization.[5] The reader is not told why the defections took place.

The *Jehovah's Witnesses—Proclaimers of God's Kingdom* (1993) history gives significant space to the discussion of the "Millions" message and the 1925 expectations.[6] "What an exciting message they proclaimed— 'Millions now living will never die!'" The *Proclaimers* book goes on to recount how it was the topic of speeches beginning in 1918 and then in printed form in 1920. And "from 1920 through 1925, that same subject was featured again and again around the world in public meetings in all areas where speakers were available and in upwards of 30 languages."[7] Great efforts were made to publicize the message and booklet through advertisements in *The Golden Age*, handbill distribution, newspaper notices, and billboards.[8] As a result, "There have been very few statements at any time that have made a greater impact on the public mind than that confident declaration 'Millions Now Living Will Never Die.'"[9] "So extensive was the campaign that the slogan has been remembered through the years."[10] The *Proclaimers* book contains the most open acknowledgment of the 1925 "Millions" failure. For example, it quotes from pages 89 and 90 of *Millions Now Living Will Never Die*: "We may confidently expect that 1925 will mark the return [from the dead] of Abraham, Isaac, Jacob, and the faithful prophets of old ... to the condition of human perfection."[11] It also admits, "some hoped that anointed Christians might receive their heavenly reward that year. The year 1925 came and went. Some abandoned their hope." Then, rather than conceding that this was an example of false prophecy, a Bible Student is quoted: "'Our family ... came to appreciate that unrealized hopes are not unique to our day. The apostles themselves had similar misplaced expectations....'—Compare Acts 1:6,7."[12] It must be pointed out, however, that the apostles did not set forth and promote a false date or expectations as false prophets. In fact, the reference cited here condemns what the "Millions" date-setting and speculations represent: "When, now, they had assembled, they were asking him: 'Lord, are you restoring the kingdom to Israel at this time?' He said to them: 'It does not belong to YOU to get knowledge of the times or seasons which the Father has placed in his own jurisdiction'" (*NWT*). Simply stated, "Don't speculate on such things!"[13] Rutherford not only promoted the 1925 date, which failed, but even attributed the source of the message to God, and claimed that it was the correct Scriptural understanding. This will be documented below.

The *Proclaimers* book also explains that the Bible Students "thought that the time of restitution was very near"[14] and how the 1925 date was calculated.[15] They believed that the glorification of the church and the resurrection of the "pre-Christian servants of God" to serve "on earth as princely representatives of the heavenly kingdom" would take place in 1925. This "would mean that mankind had entered an era in which death would cease to exist," and the realization of the slogan, "millions now living will never die." "What a happy prospect! Though mistaken, they eagerly shared it with others."[16] In essence, they "eagerly shared" what became a **proven false prophecy!**

And, in reference to the 1925 failure, the *Proclaimers* book quotes a Bible Student, and then states, "They recognized a mistake had been made ... **some** expectations had not been fulfilled, but that did not mean that Bible chronology was of no value."[17] It would appear that the real mistake was to believe those who were the source of the false message. As to the statement, "some expectations had not been fulfilled"—to be accurate, **none** of the predicted expectations had been fulfilled for 1925—and other dates could be added which would illustrate the same point (1881, 1914, 1918, 1975).

One additional observation in reference to the *Proclaimer's* book should be made. It omits one important subject in the contents of the "Millions" message and *Millions Now Living Will Never Die*. There is no mention of the coverage given to God's favor returning to Israel, Zionism, and the return of the Jews to Palestine. This is found in almost 17 pages (22-38) of the 107 pages in the body of Rutherford's booklet. Many additional references are found in the "Bible Citations in Substantiation" section (108-24), compiled by C. J. Woodworth.[18]

Watch Tower Publications and 1925

What were Watch Tower followers (and those to whom they were ministering) reading and being told as they looked forward to 1925? The following quotes, in chronological order, provide an answer.

An article in the June 2, 1919, *New York Times* was headlined: "NEW DATE FOR MILLENNIUM. Russellites Now See it Coming on Earth in 1925." It went on to report that A. H. Macmillan, a Society representative, spoke at the closing session of the International Bible Students Association convention at the Academy of Music, Brooklyn. "The speaker said he wanted to warn all the sinners to prepare for the millennium, which was to arrive in 1925. 'Moses and Abraham will be here then,' he declared, 'and we shall be associated with the holy ancients when the Kingdom of God is upon the earth. These ancients will help to restore man to a proper civilized condition.'"[19]

The November 12, 1919, *Golden Age* confidently states: "We submit that **the evidence is conclusive to the reasonable mind who believes in the Scriptures**, that the world has ended; that the old order is passing away and that the new is coming in; and if that be true, then this must mark the dawning of a new and better day; it must mark the beginning days of the Golden Age...."[20]

Rutherford's New York Hippodrome meeting on March 21, 1920, is described as "one of the most successful meetings ever held by International Bible Students":

We trust that much good was done and that many hearts were comforted by the good message of God's Word to the effect that the **long night of sin and death is about over** and that the glorious light of the Millennial morning is about to usher in the Sun of Righteousness with healing in his beams, that all flesh will not be destroyed, even in the fiercest phase of the time of trouble, but that some flesh will be saved and that, hence, "Millions Now Living Will Never Die."[21]

In his lecture Rutherford ventured to assert:

To many of you it may sound presumptuous for me to announce with boldness as we have done in this case, that millions of people now living on this earth will never die; but when you have heard the evidence and carefully considered it, I do not believe you will call me presumptuous.... Now I am going to give you another date. The year 1914 stands out today emblazoned on the escutcheon of history as a date that can no longer be questioned by any one. **And just so sure as we are here this afternoon you will see that another date will stand out just as prominently.** And what date is that? I am not a prophet, but **I reach this conclusion from a careful examination of the prophecies**, and my only purpose in calling it to your attention today is that in this hour of stress, in this hour of suffering, in this hour of turmoil on the earth the people might turn their minds with hope to a day in the near future in which all the ills of humankind shall begin to be treated with divine remedy—**and the date if you please is nineteen hundred twenty-five.**[22]

The following excerpt is from a statement Rutherford prepared for the *Brooklyn Eagle*:

...I have spoken to thousands of people on the timely and up-to-date subject: "Millions Now Living Will Never Die," and made glad many hearts. By the Lord's grace we purpose to continue to make proclamation of **His message; because we are convinced beyond a doubt that within five years the people will awaken to the fact that they are entering the period of the greatest blessings man has ever dreamed could come to the world.**[23]

The October 15, 1920, *Watch Tower* announced the **new "gospel"** for this period: "**Surely the words of the Master are now in course of fulfillment: 'This gospel ["The World Has Ended: Millions Now Living Will Never Die"]** shall be preached in all the world for a witness, and then shall the end come.' The Master's inspiring words thrill the heart of the Christian and spur him on with greater zeal to give the witness now" [brackets in original].[24]

In the report on the 1920 European tour, it was explained that in Athens, Greece, arrangements had been made for a wider distribution of the *Millions* book, after which it was stated: "**We feel quite sure that it is the Lord's will** that this message should now go to all the nations of Christendom as **a final witness before the final end of the present order.**"[25]

The Annual Report for 1920, under the heading, "The Message of the Hour," discusses the publication of the *Millions* book, along with the great demand for it, its translation into 17 languages and its unprecedented distribution.[26] How was this to be explained?

There is no explanation for this except that this message is the one **the Lord desires now to go to the people as a witness before the final and complete end**; and that he will have it thus carried to all nations **as a witness before the end comes.** Everywhere the friends are realizing the privilege of giving out this message. ... **The Lord is affording a wonderful opportunity** for all the consecrated now to devote their talents of time, energy, money, etc., **in the publication and proclamation of this message.**[27]

The back cover of *The Golden Age* of March 16, 1921, in advertising the *Millions* book, asks: "Do you know that we are now in the death-throes of the old and in the birth-pangs of the new order of things, and that those who survive the difficulties of the **next few years will be able to begin work on their everlasting homes?**"

Concerning the "millions" witness, the September 1, 1921, *Watch Tower* asserts: "It is a message of glad tidings, **which must now be preached to all nations as a witness before the final end,**"[28] and the October 15 issue claims that "**the Lord** has placed in the hands of his people the comforting message that 'millions now living will never die,' because his kingdom is here."[29]

When Rutherford's book, *The Harp of God,* was first published in 1921, it bore a subtitle: "*Proof Conclusive that* Millions now Living will never Die." This was retained in the 1925 printing, but deleted in the 1928 edition.

Rutherford gave his "world famous" message to a reported 7,000 at the New York Hippodrome on December 11, 1921. The January 4, 1922, *Golden Age* reported: "New York City has had another tremendous witness to the incoming of Messiah's kingdom."[30] In the conclusion to his lecture, Rutherford stated: "Every thinking person can see that a great climax is at hand. The **Scriptures clearly indicate** that that climax is the fall of Satan's empire and the full establishment of the Messianic Kingdom. **This climax being reached by 1925.... Therefore it can be confidently said at this time that MILLIONS NOW LIVING WILL NEVER DIE.**"[31]

For followers, the propagation of the "Millions" message became a test of their faith and loyalty to the organization and to God. Note what is stated in the April 1, 1922, *Watch Tower*:

> We are now at the inauguration of the kingdom. There is a message for us as members of his body, and as his ambassadors, to deliver. **A few of the friends have raised objection to the repeated use of the message "Millions Now Living Will Never Die,"** because, say they, it is made to appear that we can talk about nothing else. **This objection is without merit....** [After quoting Matthew 24:14] *This gospel* means the specific good news that the old world has ended, the kingdom of heaven is here, and millions now living will never die. **His messengers must give this witness throughout the world; otherwise he will provide other messengers.**[32]

In their book, *The Desolations of the Sanctuary* (1930), Bible Students Emil and Otto Sadlack personally observed that "those who had scruples about using this theme and chose a different one for a lecture, had to bear with the reproach from the Pilgrim brother giving the lecture.... Yes, those who did not joyfully and painstakingly colabor in the proclamation of this kingdom gospel (?) were suspected and set aside."[33]

Again, the crucial importance of the "Millions" message is claimed in *The Golden Age* of July 5, 1922: "This King of right and truth is now present. **He has authorized** the battlecry of freedom, **the message which He promised would go forth preceding the final destruction of Satan's kingdom.** His victorious army are now proclaiming **that message: 'Millions Now Living Will Never Die.'**"[34]

Some continued to question the message, as the February 1, 1923, *Watch Tower* observed: "Some are inclined to be doubtful concerning 1925; hence they are growing lukewarm. But, beloved of the Lord, **what difference does it make whether the things expected to transpire in 1925 do transpire or not? God will not change his plans.**"[35] What is this—doublethink? What are the implications of such reasoning? What had been claimed for the message?

Was 1925 now to be deemphasized? The following was published in the April 1, 1923, *Watch Tower*:

> *Question*: **Did the order go forth eight months ago to the Pilgrims to cease talking about 1925?** Have we more reason, or as much, to believe the kingdom will be established in 1925 than Noah had to believe that there would be a flood?

> *Answer*: It is surprising how reports get abroad. There was never at any time an intimation to the Pilgrim brethren that they should cease talking about 1925.... **Our thought is, that 1925 is definitely settled by the Scriptures**, marking the end of the typical jubilees. Just exactly what will happen at that time no one can tell to a certainty; but **we expect such a climax in the affairs of the world that the people will begin to realize the presence of the Lord and his kingdom power**.... As to Noah, the Christian now has much more upon which to base his faith than Noah had (so far as the Scriptures reveal) upon which to base his faith in a coming deluge.[36]

"Judge Rutherford at Madison Square Garden," headlined the November 7, 1923, *Golden Age*. "Judge Rutherford, during August, gave his celebrated lecture on 'All Nations Marching to Armageddon, but Millions Now Living Will Never Die' to record-breaking crowds in Tacoma and Los Angeles." He also spoke on the same subject to about 14,000 at Madison Square Garden on October 21.[37] He told his audience that a change of dispensation was then taking place: "...We are now passing out from under the machinations of the human family's arch enemy, the devil, into the glorious reign of righteousness, truth, peace, happiness, and life everlasting, under Christ. **The thing now impending is the battle of Armageddon, which will wipe the old order from the slate.**"[38]

The "Millions" theme continued to be emphasized: "**The evidence is now [1924] conclusive that we have come to the end of the old world and to the beginning of Messiah's kingdom**; hence the time for the world's blessings is about due.... Because we have come to that time in the development of the divine plan, **it can now be confidently stated** that millions living on earth will never die."[39]

In 1924, *The Way to Paradise* by Watch Tower Society corporate secretary and treasurer W. E. Van Amburgh was published, with an Introduction by Rutherford.[40] Affirming the significance of 1925, Van Amburgh instructs his readers: "When you take up a more advanced study of the Bible, you will find that the year **1925 A.D. is particularly marked in prophecy.**"[41] In his discussion Van Amburgh predicts: "It would be very reasonable to expect to see some beginning of God's favor returning to the Jewish people, as a part of the world, shortly after that date [October 1, 1925].... We should, therefore, expect shortly after 1925 to see the awakening of" those mentioned in Hebrews, chapter 11.[42]

The *Golden Age* of January 14, 1925, affirms: "Briefly summing up, the Millennial reign of Christ is at the door; yea, it is already begun.... Seeing, then, that we are at the very beginning of this wonderful time, with confidence it can be said: 'Millions now living will never die.'"[43]

The first *Watch Tower* issue for 1925, with the lead article titled, "Work For the Anointed," was less affirming:

> The year 1925 is here. With great expectation Christians have looked forward to this year. Many have confidently expected that all members of the body of Christ will be changed to heavenly glory during the year. **This may be accomplished. It may not be. In his own due time God will accomplish his purposes concerning his own people.** Christians should not be so deeply concerned about what may *transpire* during this year that they would fail to joyfully *do* what the

Lord would have them to do....[44] There is much to do during the year. Let us not be overburdened about just when we are going home. Let us think constantly upon the faithful performance of the duties now at hand in order that in his due time we may go home.[45]

Statements in various issues of the *Watch Tower* in 1925 and early in 1926 shifted attention away from literal fulfillment in 1925 and made it unimportant. Blame for unrealized expectations for that year was placed on Satan and the out-of-control speculations of the Bible Students.

"We find the date 1925-1926 clearly indicated in the prophetic outline, and the Lord has not lifted the curtain sufficiently for us to see distinctly beyond. **We feel sure that he will set his seal upon that date as clearly as he did upon 1914....** Let us learn from experiences of the past not to be too positive about details...."[46]

What about 1925 and the setting of dates? The August 15, 1925, *Watch Tower* instructs the reader: "**Time is no more. By that is meant that no longer are we to deeply concern ourselves about time.** The Lord is in his temple. The King and his kingdom are here. **Whether all the church is taken beyond the vail in 1925 or not is a matter of little moment.**"[47] And in the very next issue, the Bible Students are told: "**It is to be expected that Satan will try to inject into the minds of the consecrated the thought that 1925 should see an end of the work**, and that therefore it would be needless for them to do more. This conclusion is warranted by the words of the Master. Referring to these very perilous times in the end, Jesus said: 'If it were possible they would deceive the very elect.'"[48]

The February 15, 1925, *Watch Tower* is another example of the Society's preparation to escape blame for unfulfilled expectations for 1925:

> **It seems to be a weakness of many Bible students** that if they locate a future date in the Bible, immediately they center as many prophecies upon the date as possible. This has been the cause of many siftings in the past. **As far as we recall, all the dates foreseen were correct. The difficulty was that the friends inflated their imaginations beyond reason**; and that when their imaginations burst asunder, they were inclined to throw away everything.[49]

Two questions should be asked. Was it **Satan** who injected into the minds "the thought that 1925 should see the end to the work"? Was it true that "the difficulty was that the friends inflated their imaginations beyond reason" about what was to be expected in 1925? The answers are to be found in the review of Watch Tower publications.

1. Who wrote concerning the "Millions" message: "We feel quite sure that it is the Lord's will that this message should now go to all the nations of Christendom as a **final witness before the final end of the present order**"?[50]

2. Who wrote that "the jubilee cycles show that **1925 will mark the complete passing of the old order and the inauguration of Messiah's kingdom**; that shortly thereafter will begin the resurrection..."?[51]

3. Who wrote that "there is evidence that the establishment of the Kingdom in Palestine will probably be in 1925, ten years later than we once calculated,"[52] and in commenting on Jeremiah 25:11-12 explained it as "a reference to the seventy jubilees that must pass over Israel before they really enter the promised land ... in the spring of 1925 A.D."?[53]

4. Who wrote that "**we may confidently expect** that 1925 will mark the return of Abraham, Isaac, Jacob and the faithful prophets of old ... to the condition of human perfection"?[54] or, "Accordingly Abraham should enter upon the actual possession of his promised inheritance in the year 1925 A.D."?[55]

5. Why had the Bible Students looked to 1925 as the year for the glorification of the church? The

Proclaimers book says: "On the basis of what was said there [*Millions Now Living Will Never Die*], many hoped that perhaps the remaining ones of the little flock would receive their heavenly reward by 1925."[56] While wrong, it should be remembered that "Russell expected the church to go beyond the vail [be glorified] in 1878, 1881, 1910 and 1914...."[57] In 1919, it was said that "**within a short time** all its members will be removed from the earth,"[58] and in 1923 the followers were told that "the church is nearing the end of her earthly career"[59] And finally, if the resurrection of the ancient worthies took place in 1925 as Rutherford had predicted (see 4 above), in agreement with previous statements, the church must be glorified **before** that event. In 1921, Rutherford had stated: "**Following the glorification of the church** and the making of the new covenant, Abraham, Isaac, Jacob, David, Barak, Jeptha, and the prophets ... the Lord has promised shall be brought forth from the tomb, being given a better resurrection."[60] The source of the Bible Students' expectations is not difficult to identify.

In conclusion, it is obvious that the wrong individuals were blamed—in all the examples cited above, wrong conclusions and inflated imaginations emanated from the Watch Tower leadership and publications—but no admission of fault or apology by Rutherford can be found in these publications.[61]

The Post-1925 Message

Although 1925 had passed, the July 15 and August 15, 1926, *Watch Towers* continued the message: "God's kingdom is here; therefore with confidence it can be announced that MILLIONS NOW LIVING WILL NEVER DIE!"[62] "Has not 'the servant,' the church, during the past few years been telling the people that millions of them shall get life and shall never die if they obey the Lord? Our slogan has been, and is, MILLIONS NOW LIVING WILL NEVER DIE!"[63]

In his study on the Jehovah's Witnesses, Herbert H. Stroup comments on the continuing importance of the *Millions Now Living Will Never Die* motto, even in the 1930s: "The theme of the booklet was so rich an energizer of his followers and so compelling an idea in itself that even as late as 1932 [or even later] Mr. Rutherford was still delivering talks upon it. In that year he declared that the religious work of the Witnesses was 'coming to a conclusion,' that the end was 'only a short time away,' and that **the end was 'much less than the length of a generation.'**"[64]

Stroup's statement is confirmed by the following short quotations from Watch Tower publications: "Because the world is just at the portals of that time of blessing under the kingdom of God, it can now be confidently said that millions now living will never die" (1932).[65] In Rutherford's "World Control" broadcast from Los Angeles on March 25, 1934, he claimed that his message was "not the message of any man, but the message from God's Word delivered according to his will." After explaining "why a change of world control must shortly come to pass"—he concludes: "Hence it can be truly said, 'Millions now living will never die'"[66] "Those millions now [1937] living who will survive Armageddon and never die will begin then to receive the material benefits of God's kingdom under Christ."[67]

In the light of the focus of *Millions Now Living Will Never Die* on 1925 and the **obvious failure of all of the predictions made for that year**, it is surprising that one could still write the following in the July 27, 1938, *Consolation* concerning the book: "**The book contains full, ample evidence of the validity of the title and its truth**. It is supported by an array of not less the 473 scriptures bearing directly upon the subject."[68] Also consider what was published in 1984. In his testimony, "Jehovah Has Dealt Rewardingly With Me," Karl F. Klein, a member of the Governing Body since 1974, recalled the 1925 message and failure. Speaking of Rutherford, "Regarding his misguided statements as to what we could expect in 1925, he once confessed to us at Bethel, 'I made an ass of myself.'"[69] What about God and the Scriptures as the supposed source of the message? Surprisingly, this confession was later used as an example of Rutherford's **humility**, worthy of emulation![70] What had he done to all those who believed in and propagated the false message?

"Birth of the Nation"

Rutherford's "Birth of the Nation" article, published in the March 1, 1925, *Watch Tower,* is viewed by Joseph Zygmunt and other non-Witness observers as an attempt early in the year to prepare for the failure of the 1925 predictions—to divert attention "by a dramatic announcement that an important prophecy bearing directly upon the movement had been fulfilled...."[71] In summary, Rutherford explained that the birth of the nation (God's Kingdom) had taken place in 1914, Satan and his host had been cast out of heaven, and in 1918 he began "to persecute the members of the church on earth." Society officers were imprisoned, and after their release on March 26, 1919, the Church "fled into the wilderness for 1260 literal days ... at the end of which period the remnant of the Church on earth makes a bold proclamation of its allegiance to the King and his kingdom, and announces its determination to begin and press the fight against Satan's empire until it is excluded from the earth."[72] "The more complete establishment of the Kingdom awaited a fuller confrontation between the new nation and its King, on the one hand, and Satan and his forces on the other."[73]

"The Birth of the Nation" article is described by Witness writers as a "brilliant flash of Bible understanding"[74] and as "dramatic,"[75] and it is listed among the "Noteworthy Events" of Jehovah's Witness history.[76] Why was it so identified? The *Proclaimers* book explains: "It presented an **enlightened understanding** of Revelation chapter 12 that **some found difficult to accept**."[77] Why? "For one thing, it was a **striking departure** from what had been published in *The Finished Mystery*"[78]—which volume, it should be remembered, was claimed to include the "God-given interpretation of Revelation....'"[79]

To call this a "striking departure" is too weak—more accurate would be **a shocking contradiction**, as the following illustrates: The heading for chapter 12 of Revelation in *The Finished Mystery* (1917) is "**The Birth of Antichrist**,"[80] while Rutherford's "Birth of the Nation" article explained it as **the birth of God's kingdom** in 1914,[81] or, as expressed in *"Then Is Finished the Mystery of God"* (1969): "**The Heavenly Birth of God's Messianic Kingdom**."[82] And in the more recent, *Revelation—Its Grand Climax at Hand!* (1988), it is "**God's Kingdom is Born!**"[83] Little wonder some found the new interpretation "difficult to accept."

Although Rutherford's article begins with the statement, "What is here published is not dogmatically stated. Trusting in the Lord for guidance, it is submitted for the prayerful and careful consecration of the anointed ones'"[84]—this would not be the case. In a letter to Rutherford, published in the June 1, 1925, *Watch Tower,* Board member J. A. Bohnet writes:

> ..."Birth of the Nation" is surely convincing and perfectly satisfactory to my mind.... The TOWER article is **indisputably correct**. Unquestionably **this interpretation may prove to be a sifting medium**, but the really earnest and sincere ones of the faith will stand firm and receive in this further manifestation of the love of God in giving this additional evidence that the SOCIETY is his honored servant and mouthpiece.... **Only the deflecting ones will disagree** with the interpretation and antagonize the thoughts set forth in this article, and **Satan** will unquestionably use all such to upset the minds of the unstable....[85]

It is obvious that Bohnet's letter was intended to intimidate and to discredit any who would disagree with Rutherford's "new light" which was "not dogmatically stated." One excerpt from the "Birth of the Nation" article would indicate that it was an effort to continue the dramatic mood of the Millions campaign, but **without a definite future date for fulfillment**: "The new nation is born. Its glory shall fill the whole earth. The kingdom of heaven is here. **The day of deliverance is in sight**. Let this good news be heralded to the peoples of the earth. Victory is with our King. Faithful now to the end of the war; and we shall forever bask in the sunshine of his love, where there is fullness of joy and pleasures for evermore."[86]

The Impact of 1925 on Lives

How did the predictions for 1925 impact the lives of many of the Bible Students? "According to reports still circulated by persons who were then members of the Bible Student community, many gave up their businesses, jobs, and even sold their homes in the expectation that they would soon be living in an earthly paradise.... Numerous Bible Student farmers in both Canada and the United States refused to seed their spring crops and mocked their co-religionists who did."[87]

Obviously many persons were induced by the "Millions" message to become followers of the movement. Many examples of this could be given, but the following should suffice. On Sunday morning (May 31, 1925) at the convention in Magdeburg, Germany, Rutherford "asked all in the audience who had received the truth since 1922 to rise. The result was astounding. Fully two-thirds of that great audience stood up...."[88] On the other hand, many thousands would later leave the organization because of the 1925 failure and a growing displeasure with Rutherford.[89]

The Experience of William J. Schnell

What was it like to be personally involved in promoting the "Millions" message and to later cope with its failure? What would convince a person to remain in the movement after this? One of those involved, William J. Schnell, wrote of his experiences. Schnell began association with the Bible Students in 1921. He recounts how, after the failure of 1914, new dates were promoted by the leadership. When he joined, attention had been switched to 1925 through the "Millions Campaign" and *Millions Now Living Will Never Die*. He was heavily involved with the sale of the booklet, selling thousands of copies. He explains:

> They kept that new date prominently before us and all the people, as the year when the Kingdom would come with the re-appearance on earth of the Old Testament worthies or the princes amid Bible Students. **This expectation was fanned by every publication of the Organization of that time** and it left a deep imprint upon our minds. In fact, it virtually made irrational crack-pots out of many of us. For example, I well remember that in the fall of 1924 my father offered to buy me a much needed suit of cloths. I asked him not to do it since it was only a few months to 1925, and with it would come the Kingdom.[90]

> When 1925 came and Abraham, Isaac and Jacob did not show, I was disappointed. But clever explanations by Judge Rutherford ... in May 1925, assuaged my misgivings. He told us that night among other things, **"Boys, you do not want to go to heaven now when the Lord has so much work for us to do.** Let us print books and go with them into the highways and byways and: advertise, advertise, advertise, the King and kingdom until the end shall come." **He talked two hours that night and when he was through, he had talked us foolish ones out of going to heaven.**[91]

Even while the expectations for 1925 were strongly promoted, something was not right, as Schnell relates: "However, at that time some of the mature among the Bible Students began to catch on and to notice the discrepancy in the Society's statements about 1925 being the beginning evidence for the Kingdom and the end of the present wicked world, and evidence of the Society's increasing activities of buying land, buildings, ordering printing presses, all making for expansion! The two just did not go together."[92]

Yet Schnell would not leave the movement until, as he states, "One Sunday evening in 1953 I inobtrusively walked out of the Kingdom Hall never to return."[93]

Conclusion

The title of this chapter, "1925 and the 'Millions Now Living Will Never Die' Fiasco," is appropriate. Yet the Witnesses' *Proclaimers* book, after discussing other failed interpretations of prophecy and concluding with 1925, states: "Some expectations had not been fulfilled...."[94] Actually, as stated earlier, none of the expectations were fulfilled! It was indeed a **fiasco**—a complete failure. And Scripturally, it was **false prophecy**! And it should be recalled that Watch Tower publications claimed that this message, which proved to be false, **originated with God and was authorized by Him!**[95]

Notes

1. *Jehovah's Witnesses in the Divine Purpose* (1959), 98, 140. Rutherford *Millions Now Living Will Never Die* is identified as a 128-page "book" (ibid., 98). See also *Consolation*, 27 July 1938, 7; Rutherford, *Vindication I* (1931), 110.
2. *WT*, 1 Apr. 1980, 31; *Awake!*, 8 Mar. 1981, 32; 22 Nov. 1981, 32; 22 May 1982, 31. All have: "Many Now Living Will Never Die." The *Awake!* 8 Jan. 1986, 31, and 22 May 1989, 32: have "Millions Now Living Will Never Die." Article: "Millions Now Alive Will Never Die Off Our Earth" (*WT*, 1 Oct. 1983, 8-13).
3. Raymond Franz, *Crisis of Conscience* (Atlanta: Commentary Press, 1983), 175. See also Franz's *In Search of Christian Freedom* (Atlanta: Commentary Press, 1991), 143-45.
4. *Jehovah's Witnesses in the Divine Purpose*, 76-77, 93, 97-98, 100-01, 104, 110, 140, 215.
5. Ibid., 110.
6. Index listings on the booklet or discourse in *Proclaimers*: 78, 163, 259, 425, 426, 632, 719.
7. Ibid., 425.
8. Ibid. Sometimes the entire back cover of *The Golden Age* (19 Jan 1921; 16 and 30 Mar. 1921) carried ads for the message and booklet.
9. *1973 Yearbook* (1972), 109-10.
10. *1975 Yearbook* (1974), 127.
11. *Proclaimers*, 78. Brackets in original.
12. Ibid.
13. In his commentary on these verses, Prof. Richard N. Longenecker explains: "Jesus' answer does, however, lay stress on the fact that the disciples were to revise their thinking about the divine program, leaving to God the matters that are his concern and taking up the things entrusted to them.... The 'times' (*chronoi*) and 'dates' (*kairoi*) refer, it seems to the character of the ages preceding the final consummation of God's redemptive program and to the particular crucial stages of these ages as they draw to a climax (cf. 1 Thess. 5:1). These 'the Father has set by his own authority,' and they are not to be the subject of speculation by believers—a teaching that, sadly, has been all to frequently disregarded" (*The Acts of the Apostles*, in vol. 9 of *The Expositors Bible Commentary* [Grand Rapids: Zondervan, 1981], 256). For further discussion see: B. J. Oropeza, *99 Reasons Why No One Knows When Christ Will Return*. Downers Grove, Ill.: InterVarsity Press, 1994.
14. *Proclaimers*, 163, 632.
15. Ibid., 632. The jubilee system and the 1925 calculation are explained by Rutherford in *Millions Now Living Will Never Die* (1920), 87-88. The booklet has been reprinted by Witness Inc., P.O. Box 597, Clayton, CA 94517.
16. *Proclaimers*, 632.

17. Ibid., 633.
18. Some examples from Woodworth's compilation include: Jer. 15:19-21; 16:19; 24:6, 7; 25:11, 12; 31:34-37; 46:27, 28; 50:4, 5; Ezek. 11:17-19; 20: 33-44; Rom. 10:13-21; 11:26-32.
19. *New York Times*, 2 June 1919, 20.
20. *GA*, 12 Nov. 1919, 127.
21. *WT*, 15 Apr. 1920, 127.
22. Ibid.
23. *GA*, 9 June 1920, 591.
24. *WT*, 15 Oct. 1920, 310.
25. *WT*, 1 Dec. 1920, 356.
26. *WT*, 15 Dec. 1920, 372.
27. Ibid.
28. *WT*, 1 Sept. 1921, 265.
29. *WT*, 15 Oct. 1921, 311.
30. *GA*, 4 Jan. 1922, 212.
31. Ibid., 217.
32. *WT*, 1 Apr. 1922, 111.
33. Emil and Otto Sadlack, *The Desolations of the Sanctuary* (St. Louis: Pastoral Bible Institute, 1930), 226.
34. *GA*, 5 July 1922, 637.
35. *WT*, 1 Feb. 1923, 35.
36. *WT*, 1 Apr. 1923, 106.
37. *GA*, 7 Nov. 1923, 81.
38. Ibid., 83.
39. *GA*, 24 Sept. 1924, 819.
40. Rutherford: "This book is prepared for the express purpose of enabling boys and girls quickly to grasp a knowledge of the new order of things which the Lord is beginning to establish in the earth..." (W. E. Van Amburgh, *The Way to Paradise* (1924), iii).
41. Ibid., 220.
42. Ibid., 224.
43. *GA*, 14 Jan. 1925, 254.
44. *WT*, 1 Jan. 1925, 3.
45. Ibid., 10.
46. *WT*, 15 Feb. 1925, 58.
47. *WT*, 15 Aug. 1925, 247.
48. *WT*, 1 Sept. 1925, 262.
49. *WT*, 15 Feb. 1925, 57.
50. *WT*, 1 Dec. 1920, 356.
51. *GA*, Easter Number, 1921, 367.
52. Clayton J. Woodworth and George H. Fisher, *The Finished Mystery* (1917), 128.
53. Rutherford, *Millions Now Living Will Never Die* (1920), comments by C. J. Woodworth, 117.
54. Ibid., 89-90.
55. *WTR*, 15 Oct. 1917, 6157.
56. *Proclaimers*, 632.
57. *WTR*, 15 Apr. 1918, 6237.

58. *WTR*, 1 Oct. 1919, 295.

59. *WT*, 1 Sept. 1923, 259.

60. Rutherford, *The Harp of God* (1921), 328. The statement in the 1928 edition drops a few words but says the same thing (335). This view was still held in 1925: "Our opinion is that the ancient worthies will not be resurrected until every member of the Church is gone" (*WT*, 15 Jan 1925, 23). In *The Time Is at Hand* (1889), looking forward to 1914, Russell argued that "some time before the end of A.D. 1914 the last member of... 'the body of Christ,' will be glorified with the Head; because every member is to reign with Christ, being a joint-heir with him of the Kingdom, and it cannot be fully 'set up' without every member" (77).

61. M. James Penton, *Apocalypse Delayed* (2nd ed.; Toronto: University of Toronto Press, 1997), 58. Penton writes: "Although Rutherford failed to admit any real fault in the matter in the society's publications, he did give uncharacteristic apologies at IBSA conventions. Evidently, too, he was chagrined.... Yet this did not stop him from continuing to proclaim the end of the world was 'near at hand' and **might be expected within a few years or even a few months**. Neither did the fact that he had prophesied falsely seem to give him second thoughts about the Bible Students' preaching campaign, his ministry, or his desire to maintain and increase his personal powers" (ibid.)

62. *WT*, 15 July 1926, 217.

63. *WT*, 15 Aug. 1926, 248.

64. Herbert H. Stroup, *The Jehovah's Witnesses* (New York: Columbia University Press, 1945), 55.

65. Rutherford, *Good News* (1932), 63.

66. Rutherford, *Righteous Ruler* (1934), 7, 26.

67. *WT*, 15 Mar. 1937, 91.

68. *Cons.*, 27 July 1938, 7.

69. *WT*, 1 Oct. 1984, 24.

70. "...Judge Rutherford, he was at heart a humble man. For example, he once made some dogmatic statements as to what Christians could expect in 1925. When events failed to support his expectations, he humbly told the Brooklyn Bethel family that he had made a fool of himself" (*WT*, 1 Dec. 1993, 18).

71. Joseph Zygmunt, "Jehovah's Witnesses: A Study of Symbolic and Structural Elements in the Development and Institutionalization of a Sectarian Movement," (Ph.D. diss., University of Chicago, 1967), 824.

72. *WT*, 1 Mar. 1925, 73.

73. Zygmunt, 825.

74. *Revelation—Its Grand Climax At Hand!* (1988), 177.

75. *Proclaimers*, 78.

76. Ibid., 720.

77. Ibid., 78.

78. Ibid., 79.

79. *WT*, 15 Dec. 1917, 6188.

80. *The Finished Mystery*, 183.

81. *WT*, 1 Mar. 1925, 69, 73.

82. *"Then Is Finished the Mystery of God"* (1969), 297.

83. *Revelation—Its Grand Climax at Hand!*, 177.

84. *WT*, 1 Mar. 1925, 67.

85. *WT*, 1 June 1925, 175.

86. *WT*, 1 Mar. 1925, 74.

87. Penton, 58.

88. *WT*, 1 Aug. 1925, 233.

89. Penton, 58. See the graph on page 61 in Penton, which shows a world-wide Memorial attendance in 1920 of about 20,000, peaking in 1925 at about 90,000, and declining to the 1920 level by 1928. Robert Crompton concludes that "the loss of members during the years immediately following 1925, then, may represent one of the most significant of the movement's breaks with its early history," and according to information from Bible Student historian James Parkinson, "defections in the wake of 1925 involved not only relative newcomers but also many members of long standing" (*Counting the Days to Armageddon* [Cambridge: James Clarke & Co., 1996], 101, 104). In spite of the evidence, the *Proclaimers* book states: "The year 1925 came and went. Some abandoned their hope. But the **vast majority of the Bible Students remained faithful**" (78).

90. William J. Schnell, *Thirty Years a Watch Tower Slave* (Grand Rapids: Baker Book House, 1956), 33.

91. William J. Schnell, *Christians Awake!* (Grand Rapids: Baker Book House, 1961), 68.

92. Schnell, *Thirty Years*, 33-34. Schnell recounts an experience he had as a member of the movement in the Spring of 1925 in Magdeburg, Germany. A convention was to be held there. Schnell explains, "Three days before the start of this convention Judge Rutherford, Robert Martin, C. C. Binkele and Paul Balzereit met in an important policy meeting held in the Hotel Magdeburger Hof. Jesse Hemery, Vice President of the INTERNATIONAL BIBLE STUDENT ASSOCIATION, was also to be present and was to translate the conversations. Alas, he was delayed. Hence, William J. Schnell, although only 20 years old at the time, being capable of handling both German and English, was pressed into translation services. It developed that the brethren present were cognizant that 1925 would fail and that the repercussions would be tremendous within the ranks of the BIBLE STUDENTS. Robert Martin took the bull by the horns and said, 'I propose we go completely into mass production of books and printed matter and force all brethren who will let themselves be impressed into witnessing with books. **Occupy them and they will forget failures and soon we can use these disappointments like a jilted love who has been left at the church door by the bride-to-be and who finds quickly another love**'" (*The Converted Jehovah's Witness Expositor*, volume X, Special issue, p. 1). The report on the convention Schnell attended is included in the *Watch Tower* (1 Aug. 1925, 233-35) and the names mentioned by Schnell are all included.

93. Schnell, *Thirty Years*, 199.

94. *Proclaimers*, 633.

95. "...This message is the one the **Lord desires** now to go to the people..." (*WT*, 15 Dec. 1920, 372). "...The **Lord has placed** in the hands of his people the comforting message that 'millions now living will never die.'.."(*WT*, 15 Oct. 1921, 311). "**He has authorized** ... the message ... 'Millions Now Living Will Never Die'" (*GA*, 5 July 1922, 637).

25.

Will God Restore the Jews
to Palestine?

Jehovah's Witnesses in the Divine Purpose (1959) makes no mention of the fact that Watch Tower Society presidents C. T. Russell and J. F. Rutherford (until 1932) were strong promoters of Zionism. Since that time, many articles or statements in Watch Tower publications—which disparage Zionism—make no mention of this fact.[1]

This once important doctrine, and its subsequent rejection, is briefly presented in only one place in *Jehovah's Witnesses—Proclaimers of God's Kingdom* (1993). The book explains that

> the Bible Students were well aware of the many prophecies of restoration that were delivered to ancient Israel by God's prophets. (Jer. 30:18; 31:8-10; Amos 9:14, 15; Rom. 11:25, 26) Down till 1932, they understood these to apply to the natural Jews. Thus, they believed God would show Israel favor again, gradually restoring the Jews to Palestine, opening their eyes to the truth regarding Jesus as Ransomer and Messianic King, and using them as an agency for extending blessings to all nations. With this understanding, Brother Russell spoke to large Jewish audiences in New York as well as in Europe on the subject "Zionism in Prophecy," and Brother Rutherford, in 1925, wrote the book *Comfort for the Jews*.
>
> But it gradually became evident that what was taking place in Palestine with regard to the Jews was not the fulfillment of Jehovah's grand restoration prophecies....[2]
>
> What had been taking place in fulfillment of those restoration prophecies pointed in another direction. Jehovah's servants began to realize that it was *spiritual* Israel, "the Israel of God," composed of spirit-anointed Christians, who, in fulfillment of God's purpose, were enjoying peace with God through Jesus Christ. (Gal. 6:16) Now their eyes were opened to discern in God's dealing with such true Christians a marvelous spiritual fulfillment of those restoration promises.[3]

While more candid, the *Proclaimers* history gives an incomplete picture of the importance and significance of the former view and its later rejection. After examining the book's treatment, one ex-Witness author concluded that it "attempts to smooth-over one of the sect's major doctrinal changes."[4]

Part 10 of the serialized treatment of Witness history, published in the May 15, 1955, *Watchtower*, includes a stronger rejection of their former belief: In 1932, "Jehovah's witnesses came to see that such a **'back to Palestine' movement was by the spirit of Jehovah's archfoe, Satan**, who has deceived the entire inhabited earth."[5]

What was taught by Watch Tower Society leaders on the subject, and what claims and efforts were made in promoting the view? What was the significance of the change?

Pastor Russell and Zionism

The return of the Jews to Palestine as a fulfillment of prophecy was a **basic** and **major** part of Russell's theology, appearing in some of his earliest published works and continuing until his death. For example, in *Three Worlds* (1877): "But the great battle does not occur until after the return of the Jews."[6] "The people called out of Babylon must refer to the Jews, we think, because they *are* to be gathered out of all nations, and restored to their own land, while the *saints* are to be taken in the twinkling of an eye, from the mill, the field, and any and every place where they may happen to be."[7]

The July 1878 issue of *Herald of the Morning*, edited by N. H. Barbour (with Russell as an assistant editor), explains: "Just what we are expecting in the next thirty-seven years, is, first, the gathering of the spiritual element of the churches.... Second, the translation or glorification of the chosen bride of Christ. Third, the return of the Jews to Palestine...."[8]

Russell's *Thy Kingdom Come* (1891) devotes a 58-page chapter, "The Restoration of Israel," to his beliefs on prophecy and the Jewish people. Here he states: "That the re-establishment of Israel in the land of Palestine is one of the events to be expected in this Day of the Lord, we are fully assured by the above expression of the Prophet [Amos 9: 11, 14, 15]. **Notice, particularly, that the prophecy cannot be interpreted in any symbolic sense**."[9] Later he concludes: "...**The literalness of the promised return of Israel to their own land, and the rebuilding of Jerusalem upon her heaps, cannot be questioned**...."[10]

In *The Battle of Armageddon* (1897), Russell writes: "The earthly phase of the Kingdom of God when set up will be Israelitish; for such is God's engagement or covenant with Abraham and his natural seed."[11] "It will be the time mentioned by the Prophet when 'a nation shall be born in a day.' (Isa. 66:8.) Israel will be that nation; (1) Spiritual Israel, the 'holy nation'; Fleshly Israel its earthly representative."[12]

It is true, as the *Proclaimers* book states, that "Brother Russell spoke to large Jewish audiences in New York as well as in Europe on the subject 'Zionism in Prophecy,'" or "Zionism the Hope of the World." Russell's message on the Jews took him to England and Scotland, where he spoke to large audiences in London, Manchester, and Glasgow. In the United States, in addition to New York, he also addressed Jewish meetings or spoke on such topics as "Zionism the Hope of the World," in Chicago, Philadelphia, St. Louis, Kansas City, San Francisco and Cincinnati.[13]

A large amount of literature for Jewish audiences was also produced. Russell's sermons were printed in 3,000 newspapers, and "according to his own statistical figures his preaching on the subjects of Judaism and Zionism appeared in 107,000 copies of Anglo-Jewish newspapers and weeklies, and in 650,000 copies of the Yiddish Press. He even considered it worthwhile to publish a Yiddish newspaper of his own, *Di Shtimme*, which aroused interest and echo among the Jews of America. Europe and Russia."[14]

Russell also wrote a number of articles for the *Overland Monthly* magazine (readership 75,000), which began appearing in the February 1909 issue. "The response to the series ['The Divine Program'] was so large that his articles on a variety of subjects continued to appear monthly until his death on October 31, 1916."[15] After the first 12 articles were published, Russell wrote another 12-article series, "God's Chosen People," dealing with Israel—the Jews.[16]

In his *Overland Monthly* article, "Zionism is God's Call," Russell argued:

We agree that there is a spiritual as well as a natural Israel. **But we hold that Christian people have erred in applying all the Scriptures to themselves and in not discerning that a large proportion of the promised coming blessings belong to natural Israel**. Failure to recognize this has worked injury and confusion to the minds of many Christian Bible students. **Appropriating to themselves promises that belong to natural Israel, Christians have been led to turn and twist and spiritualize the Word of the Lord, until they have destroyed much of their own faith in it....**[17]

And now when prophecy shows that God's time has come for remembering and executing his gracious promises to Israel, his first move toward their recovery to his favor comes through Zionism. Not that Zionism was started as a religious movement; quite to the contrary.... Zionism, we believe, is about to take on a new form. Instead of being any longer a movement of race pride and for race protection it seems evident that it will shortly be a religious movement. Back to the prophecies! Back to the Word of God! Back to the promise made to Abraham and repeatedly confirmed![18]

In his sermon, "Zionism, The Hope of the World," "Pastor Russell declared that Christians have inadvertently misappropriated to themselves many of the promises of the Scriptures which are not wholly theirs.... Zionism, amongst the Jews to-day, **we believe the Lord is stirring up, a preparation of natural Israel for the great blessing which so soon will be at their door.**"[19]

On June 5, 1910, Russell spoke at the Brooklyn Academy of Music to an estimated audience of 2,800, where "quite a number of Jews attended" to hear the topic, "Jerusalem." Russell talked with a newspaperman after the meeting: "We pointed out that God's blessings mentioned to Israel from Genesis to Malachi are all earthly and they are shortly to begin to be fulfilled."[20]

On October 9, 1910, Pastor Russell addressed an audience of 4,000 at the New York Hippodrome. It was reported that "by a system of deductions based upon the prophecies of old, the pastor declared that the return of the kingdom of the Jews might occur at so near a period as the year 1914. Persecution would be over and peace and universal happiness would triumph."[21]

The January 1, 1912, *Watch Tower* indicated how important the subject was to Russell:

> The unfulfilled promises to the Jews, spoken of hundreds of times by the prophets of old, and reaffirmed in the writings of the New Testament, attracted Pastor Russell's early attention, and consequently **the time of the restoration of the Jews in Palestine, as a Nation, became a question of almost paramount importance to his mind.**... During the past twenty years, Pastor Russell has written much on Jewish topics and has addressed many Jewish audiences on Biblical Zionism, pointing out the significance of the many unfulfilled promises to them by Jehovah.[22]

Until Russell's death in 1916, additional articles appeared in the *Watch Tower* in which Zionism was identified as the fulfillment of prophecy.[23]

In 1986, David Horowitz, Editor of the *United Israel Bulletin*, published *Pastor Charles Taze Russell: An Early American Christian Zionist*, in recognition of his contribution.[24] The book jacket carries a statement by Benjamin Netanyahu, then Israeli Ambassador to the U.N., and once Prime Minister: "David Horowitz sets the record straight about the beliefs and achievements of Charles Taze Russell. A recognition of Pastor Russell's important role as an early American Christian advocate of Zionism is long overdue. Mr. Horowitz has performed an admirable service in restoring to public knowledge the story of this important Christian Zionist."[25]

Rutherford and the Jews

While the *Proclaimers* book mentions only that "Brother Rutherford, in 1925, wrote the book *Comfort for the Jews*," there is much more to be said concerning his promotion of Zionism. One writer observes: "Until 1930 Rutherford demonstrated a sympathetic and even cordial attitude towards the Jews, and, **to a certain degree, surpassed Russell in his daring prophecies in discussing 'natural' or 'fleshly' Israel.**"[26] Another writes: "If Pastor Russell had been an ardent advocate of the building of the state of Israel, his successor, Joseph Rutherford, was more so. The Watch Tower Society carried on with increasing zeal the advocacy of the return of the Jews to their homeland."[27]

Society publications often carried comments or articles on the subject. For example, the September 1, 1918, *Watch Tower* reminds the reader that "Zionism is a theme of perennial interest to the Lord's people, who for many years have watched with deep sympathy the evidences of the return of divine favor to God's chosen nation. The beloved Seventh Messenger [Pastor Russell] has written much upon this subject in both the SCRIPTURE STUDIES and the columns of this journal."[28]

Under the title, "Zionism Certain to Succeed," it is explained that Rutherford delivered a lecture in Jerusalem "on October 17, 1920, before a large and interested audience of Jews, Arabs and English,"[29] in which he made the following statements:

> **Israel is absolutely certain to be fully established as a nation and the Jews again as a specially favored people of God.** Zionism is a great forward movement in harmony with the divine arrangement, and for that reason the purpose concerning it must be accomplished.[30] **The zealous workers in Zionism today are fulfilling prophecy,** many of them doubtless unwittingly. We believe that if they knew that their very acts have been foretold by the Lord in centuries past such knowledge would inspire them to greater zeal, hope and action.[31] **Zionism is one of the steps in the great divine program.** *God is using this natural means to regather the people of Israel* in fulfillment of His promises made through the mouth of His holy prophet.[32]

The front cover of the August 31, 1921, *Golden Age* declares: "Judge Rutherford answers Mr. Henry Morgenthau's Attack on Zionism." The article's title, "Is Zionism a Stupendous Fallacy?" reflects Morgenthau's attack in his article in the July 1921 *World's Work* magazine.[33] At the outset Rutherford asks the question, "Shall we accept Mr. Morgantheau as final authority? or shall we accept the inspired testimony of the prophets of Jehovah who spoke with authority?"[34] Some brief excerpts from Rutherford's response follow.

> **In due time God raised up Theodor Herzl** to begin to stir up in the minds of Jews a desire to return to Palestine; and gradually, from 1897, Zionism has been growing.[35] Mr. Morganthau says these promises have no reference to the *land* of Palestine. Let those who have faith in the promises of God determine whether they will follow his wisdom or the words of Jehovah through his prophet: "I will set mine eyes upon them for good, and I will bring them again to this *land*; and I will build them, and not pull them down; and I will plant them and not pluck them up...."—Jeremiah 24:6,7.... Any one who has visited Palestine in recent years knows that **this prophecy** [Amos 9:11, 14, 15] **is now actually in course of fulfillment.... That God intends that the Jews shall again inhabit this land and build their homes there, He plainly states through His prophet** [Isaiah 65:21-23]....[36] The kings of the earth have had their day. The remaining kingdoms are going to pieces. Shortly God's kingdom will be established, His *favor return to the Jews* regathered in Palestine, and the Lord Himself, through His chosen ones, will

rule the earth.... **The time has come for the Jews to return to Palestine, and they are return-ing, and fulfilling prophecy**—all of which proves that Zionism, or the securing of a home for the Jewish people in Palestine, is NOT "a stupendous fallacy," but a mighty reality.[37] The day of his deliverance is at hand. **The time for the fulfillment of the words of the prophets has come.** Therefore let the Jews look up and take courage. To them the prophet now says: "Arise, give light, for thy light is come; and the glory of the Lord is shining forth over thee."—Isaiah 60:1, *Leeser.*[38]

Nothing is said in the *Proclaimers* book concerning the **content** of Rutherford's *Comfort for the Jews* (1925). The Publishers' Foreword explains the origin of the book's material: "His lectures to large audiences, which have been broadcast throughout the world, on 'JEWS RETURNING TO PALESTINE,' have created an intense interest. There is a great demand for them in printed form. He has amplified these lectures and now presents them in book form."[39]

A review of *Comfort for the Jews* appeared in the May 19, 1926, *Golden Age.* The reviewer states that cynics might question it, but the message of the book "was foretold by the Prophet Isaiah nearly three thousand years ago; nevertheless we feel fully justified in taking that view of Judge Rutherford's book.... A careful read-ing of the book convinces us it is *epochal.*"[40] "The time set by Jehovah for the blessing of the Jews has come."[41]

> We wish that every Jurist in the world could read Judge Rutherford's book.... We feel that they could have but one opinion of it, and that is that he has proved in most convincing fashion what he started out to prove. Every Christian ought to read it, that he may have part in the work **which the Lord now wishes done**, namely, the comforting of His ancient people, whom He foreknew, and who are beloved for their father's sake.[42]

The reviewer then writes: "After a careful reading of Judge Rutherford's book, we conclude that the best possible review of it is to be found in the words which he has himself made use of in the closing pages"—which the reviewer sees as proven in the book.[43] Some brief excerpts follow:

> It must be apparent to every Jew who has followed the argument herein set forth, **which has been based exclusively upon the Holy Scriptures**, that God intends Israel, the Jews, to have the land of Palestine; that He promised that land to Abraham and to his seed after him, and that He pur-poses to keep that promise.... **The Jews now, in fulfillment of prophecy, are being regathered to Palestine.... The long dark period of Israel's warfare is ended**. The favor of God is being extended to her.... Some one who loves the Lord must speak the message of comfort to the Jews. **The time has come for the prophecy to have its fulfillment**.[44]

Comfort for the Jews was an important book at the time and it "had a wide distribution in Jewish sectors of American cities and was translated into Yiddish for use of Jews not able to speak English."[45] In 1927, *Comfort for the Jews* was republished with the title changed to *Restoration*, and in 1929 several of its chapters were included in the book *Life.*[46]

In a letter to Rutherford, Society board member J. A. Bohnet extols *Comfort for the Jews*:

> I have just read your new book of 712 Scripture citations bearing upon the restoration of Palestine to the Jewish people. **How any Jew can read that book and not be convinced that we have a correct understanding of prophecy relative to the Jewish regathering in Palestine in the very**

near future as God's first people, is beyond my comprehension.... What a research of Bible texts you have put into that work! The subject throughout is handled admirably, forcefully and conclusively. Except the Lord were with you the subject could not have been so delightfully dealt with.[47]

The back covers of *The Golden Age* issues of March 11 and 25, 1925, are headlined, "PALESTINE THE NEW": "Beginning in 1925, the event [new Trans-Atlantic service] proves to be corroborative evidence of the importance the Bible attaches to 1925, touching directly the prophecies regarding Palestine." The issue of July 15, 1925, states:

> Jesus further stated, as an evidence of the end of the world, that God's favor would begin to return to the Jews. You all know that after the Paris Conference in 1919 the Jews began to establish themselves in the homeland of Palestine, and that recently they have dedicated their great university, and that the Jews are rapidly rebuilding Palestine; and **this is one of the best evidences that the new order is at hand.**[48]

Rutherford's *Comfort for the People* (1925) predicts: "The Gentile times ended in 1914, and from that time forward the Jews have been active in Palestine.... We may look with keen expectancy for *some marked manifestation of God's favor in the latter part of 1925*, or shortly thereafter."[49]

The February 15, 1926, *Watch Tower* announced that "a world-wide witness has been arranged for Sunday, February 21st, at which time the classes everywhere have been urged to put forth effort to make a public proclamation of the message: 'PALESTINE FOR THE JEW. WHY?'" On the same page, readers were told: "With the end of 1925 it seems, **according to the Lord's Word**, due time for the message of comfort to be delivered to the Jews. (Isaiah 40:1) It would be expected that the Lord would use the consecrated for this purpose. His Word clearly places this obligation upon the church (Isaiah 40:9)."[50]

Rutherford addressed a large meeting for Jews at the London Convention in May 1926, and "it was interesting to watch the many Jews drinking in the proof that the time has come for them to return to the land of their fathers. The message was really a comfort to them."[51]

An article in the May 1, 1928, *Watch Tower*, titled "Israel's Restoration," again strongly affirms the fulfillment:

> The world has been taught to believe that the advent of Christianity wiped out all previous history so far as it had to do with any particular relationship between God and any nation or individual. **But to say this is wholly to pervert the plan of God as revealed by the Scriptures....**[52] **"Hath God cast away his people whom he foreknew?" He answers the question: "God forbid."** Paul did not say that the Christian becomes a Jew, nor that the Jewish hope was ended because the Christian may have the spirit of the law. ... On the contrary, he shows clearly that when the special calling which brings the church of God into existent and maturity is complete, **God's favor will again come back to his ancient people**. He will restore them not only to his favor, but to their ancient inheritance in the land of Palestine, **in order that he himself may be vindicated** in the eyes of the nations. See Ezekiel 27:28; 38:23.[53]

In chapter eight of his book *Life* (1929), "Bones," Rutherford sees in Zionism the fulfillment of Ezekiel's vision of the dry bones (Ezekiel 37:1-14).[54] He explains:

...**The Lord raised up Theodor Herzl**, a Jew who loved his people and was glad to serve them. Mr. Herzl said that "the miseries of the Jews" were the "propelling force" that induced the formation of the scheme of Zionism. It was this noise and shaking of persecution and agitation that caused the bones, to wit, the Jews, to come together and form the skeleton organization looking to their return to Palestine and to the rebuilding of their homeland. A human skeleton is made up of 206 bones. Zionism was organized into a body at Basel, Switzerland, in 1897; and in that congress, which perfected the organization, there were exactly 206 delegates, the same number as of bones that go to form the human body. **This was not merely an accident, but a physical fact prearranged by the Lord, showing how God looks after the minutest things relative to the recovery of the Jews in bringing them back to himself.** This should arouse the hope of Jews and bring them comfort.[55]

In his book *Prophecy* (1929), Rutherford attacks religious leaders as "false prophets," and states:

Jeremiah prophesied that God would make and inaugurate a new covenant with Israel and that by the terms of that covenant both those dead and those living should have an opportunity for a blessing. If these prophecies have not been fulfilled, and if all possibility of fulfillment is past, then these prophecies are proven false. **The clergy** seize upon such as a basis for denying that God will restore Israel and establish his righteous government on earth through Christ.[56]

And finally, the article "Restoration Foretold," in the September 1, 1931, *Watch Tower* **again affirms what he would refute in 1932**:

God promised to restore Palestine to the Jews. The rebuilding of Palestine is now beginning and is well under way. **This is being done clearly in fulfillment of prophecy uttered as promises from Jehovah.** This alone should command not only the respectful attention but the profoundest interest of every one who believes that Jehovah is God. **It was the great Jehovah, speaking through men who had faith in him, that foretold what we now see transpiring concerning Palestine.** The privilege of living on earth at the time of the fulfillment of these prophecies cannot be overestimated. At once the Jew comes into prominence, and the history of the Jewish people becomes more thrilling than any fiction ever written.[57]

An entire book could be written summarizing the case **made in Watch Tower publications in support of Zionism—the return of the Jews to Palestine**—which was based on Bible prophecy and current history. Hundreds of pages on the subject appeared in these publications.[58]

Rutherford's "New Light" on Israel

After **more than fifty years** of arguing from the Bible and prophecy that the Jews had a special relationship and place in God's divine plan—as cited earlier—**a radically different interpretation** was presented in 1932:

By the publication of Volume 2 of the book *Vindication* that year, Jehovah's Witnesses came to see that such a **"back to Palestine" movement was by the spirit of Jehovah's archfoe, Satan, who has deceived the entire inhabited earth....** Attainment of the correct understanding by such assembled genuine worshipers, in the face of the progress of the worldly Zionist movement, was due to God's real restoration of his spiritual Israel, which began in 1919.[59]

It should be remembered that it was Rutherford who had been the strongest promoter of the "back to Palestine" movement as a literal fulfillment of prophecy, and that both he and Russell argued against the position later taken. Why should one trust Rutherford's new interpretation of the same Scriptures? Recall that his *Comfort For the Jews*, according to insider J. A. Bohnet, had "712 Scripture citations bearing upon the **restoration of Palestine to the Jewish people**." Bohnet then added: "How any Jew can read that book and not be convinced that **we have the correct understanding of prophecy** ... is beyond my comprehension...."[60]

Much could be presented in comparing the contradictions of the two positions, but instead, the radical change of position is well illustrated by the following examples. On October 17, 1920, Rutherford gave a lecture titled, "Zionism Certain to **Succeed**."[61] An article in the March 1, 1958, *Watchtower* was titled: "Why Zionism **Must Fail**." This same article states: "Many Jews and non-Jews see in Zionism the fulfillment of Bible prophecies. Read on to learn **why all such err** and to whom the prophecies apply."[62] Yet in 1921, in answering a critic, Rutherford wrote: "The time has come for the Jews to return to Palestine, and they are returning, and fulfilling prophecy—all of which proves that Zionism, or the securing of a home for the Jewish people in Palestine, is **NOT 'a stupendous fallacy**,' but a mighty reality."[63]

Why the Change?

In assessing the reason for the change in Rutherford's interpretation, Yona Malachy reasoned that "Rutherford saw no great progress made in the realization of the Zionist undertaking. Instead, the world witnessed the rise of the Nazi movement in Europe, the persecution of Jews in Germany, and the Arab disturbances in Palestine. Many despaired of the Zionist hope of establishing a Jewish state. All of this could have influenced Rutherford in taking his negative stand on Jews and Zionism."[64] A change of interpretation was required, and in 1931 Rutherford renamed the movement Jehovah's witnesses.

Malachy further observes: "After the adoption of their new name, the members of the sect claimed that only they fulfilled the prophecy of Isaiah (43:10), 'Ye are My witnesses, saith the Lord, and My servant whom I have chosen.' With this ambitious name, they intended to show the world that they were 'the sole, true and legal apostles of Jehovah on earth.'"[65] They became "Spiritual Israel," and as William J. Schnell, states: "From now on the high Watch Tower Organization claimed the total benefits of the Jewish nation on a spiritual sphere, appropriating to itself all the prophecies given to the Jews. From henceforth, the issues of the *Watchtower* were utilized for **a rewriting of the entire Old Testament into Watch Tower verbiage**, claiming a fulfillment of the Old Testament prophecies in Jehovah's Witnesses."[66] This certainly was a **major** doctrinal change.

Notes

1. See for example: *WT*, 1 Aug. 1939, 239; *Awake!*, 22 July 1949, 7; *WT*, 1 Mar. 1958, 133-36; *Awake!*, 8 Oct. 1959, 25-26; *WT*, 1 June 1968, 326. *Awake!*, 22 May 1976, 20-23.
2. *Jehovah's Witnesses—Proclaimers of God's Kingdom* (1993), 141.
3. Ibid., 141-42.
4. David Reed, *'Proclaimers' Answered Page by Page* (Stoughton, Maine: Comments from the Friends, 1994), 17.
5. *WT*, 15 May 1955, 296.
6. *Three Worlds* (1877), 161. The book was a joint effort by Nelson H. Barbour and C. T. Russell,

Nelson being the primary writer and Russell providing the funds (*Proclaimers*, 47, 135, 575, 619, 718).

7. Ibid., 165.

8. *Herald of the Morning*, July 1878, 2.

9. Russell, *Thy Kingdom Come* (1891), 244.

10. Ibid., 257.

11. Russell, *The Battle of Armageddon* (1897), 624.

12. Ibid., 638-39.

13. *WTR*, 1 Dec. 1910, 4721; 15 Feb. 1911, 4764; 15 July 1911, 4852-53).

14. Yona Malachy, "Jehovah's Witnesses and Their Attitude Toward Judaism and the Idea of the Return to Zion," in *Herzl Year Book*, volume 5, ed. Raphael Patai (New York; Herzl Press, 1963), 188.

15. *What Pastor Russell Wrote for the Overland Monthly* (reprinted by the Chicago Bible Students), title page.

16. Ibid., Table of Contents; Malachy, 184.

17. *Overland Monthly*, 108.

18. Ibid., 111.

19. *Convention Report Sermons* (published by the Chicago Bible Students), 156-57.

20. *WTR*, 15 July 1910, 4649.

21. *Convention Report Sermons*, 135. The Hippodrome meeting is also reported in *WTR*, 15 Oct. 1910, 4700-01.

22. *WTR*, 1 Jan. 1912, 4953.

23. See *WTR*: 1 May 1913, 5234; 15 July 1914, 5503; 1 Nov. 1914, 5568.

24. David Horowitz, *Charles Taze Russell: An Early American Christian Zionist.* New York: Philosophical Library, 1986. 159 pp.

25. The inside book jacket states: "But few realize that Pastor Russell was an early advocate of Zionism and that he predicted the imminent return of the Jewish people to Israel."

26. Malachy, 192-93.

27. Timothy White, *A People For His Name* (New York: Vantage Press, 1967), 194.

28. *WTR*, 1 Sept. 1918, 6315.

29. *GA*, Easter number 1921, 369.

30. Ibid.

31. Ibid., 377.

32. Ibid., 382.

33. *GA*, 31 Aug. 1921, 707.

34. Ibid.

35. Ibid., 711.

36. Ibid., 712.

37. Ibid., 715.

38. Ibid., 716.

39. *Comfort for the Jews* (1925) is not listed in the *Jehovah's Witnesses in the Divine Purpose* index.

40. Ibid., 537.

41. Ibid.

42. Ibid., 538.

43. Ibid.

44. Ibid. The entire quote is found in *Comfort for the Jews*, 125-27.

45. White, 196.

46. The title page of Rutherford's 127-page booklet *Restoration* (1927), states: "A Biblical portrayal of Israel

as God's Chosen People and an account of Zionism in its relation to the Divine Plan." *Comfort for the Jews* also had a soft-cover edition.

47. *WT*, 15 May 1926, 159. J. A. Bohnet was elected as a member of the Board of Directors of the Watch Tower Bible and Tract Society in 1918 (*WTR*, 15 Jan. 1918, 6202; *Proclaimers*, 68). He is also pictured in the *Proclaimers* book and referred to as "J. A. Bohnet, another pilgrim" (79). He was last listed as a pilgrim in the 1929 *Year Book* (67).

48. *GA*, 15 July 1925, 665.

49. Rutherford, *Comfort for the People* (1925), 39.

50. *WT*, 15 Feb. 1926, 50. After the last statement the announcement went on to promote the book *Comfort for the Jews*.

51. *WT*, 15 July 1926, 217.

52. *WT*, 1 May 1928, 137-38.

53. Ibid., 138.

54. *Life* (1929), 171-93.

55. Ibid., 177-78.

56. Rutherford, *Prophecy* (1929), 22-23.

57. *WT*, 1 Sept. 1931, 270-71.

58. For example, there are over 600 pages on the subject in the following books and magazines alone: Russell, *Thy Kingdom Come* (1891, 243-300); Rutherford, *Comfort for the Jews* (1925), republished and retitled, *Restoration* (1927); Rutherford, *Life* (13-227); Russell's series of twelve articles in *Overland Monthly* (63-120), and two articles in *The Golden Age* (Easter Number, 1921, 369-82; 31 Aug. 1921, 707-16).

59. *WT*, 15 May 1955, 296. The *Proclaimers* book identifies this interpretation in *Vindication II* as one of the "noteworthy" events in Jehovah's Witness history (720).

60. *WT*, 15 May 1928, 59.

61. *GA*, Easter number 1921, 369.

62. *WT*, 1 Mar. 1958, 133.

63. *WT*, 31 Aug. 1921, 715.

64. Malachy, 200. "When in 1932 they abandoned Russell's old belief that the Jews had a special relationship with Jehovah, they came to feel that they alone were his *chosen*, his elect" (M. James Penton, *Apocalypse Delayed* [2nd ed.; Tornoto: University of Toronto Press, 1997], 129).

65. Malachy, 199.

66. William J. Schnell, *Thirty Years a Watch Tower Slave* (Grand Rapids: Baker Book House, 1956), 91.

26.

The Great Pyramid of Gizeh:
God's Monument or
"a Monument of Demonism"?

Jehovah's Witnesses—Proclaimers of God's Kingdom includes a brief admission concerning an earlier belief in the Great Pyramid (pyramidology): "For some 35 years, Pastor Russell thought that the Great Pyramid of Gizeh was God's stone witness, corroborating Biblical time periods (Isa. 19:19). But Jehovah's Witnesses have abandoned the idea that an Egyptian pyramid has anything to do with true worship (see 'Watchtower' issues of November 15 and December 1, 1928)."[1] While it is true that the Witnesses no longer accept the Great Pyramid as being of divine origin, the *Proclaimers* statement fails to communicate the significance of the subject in its original promotion. It is also not stated that the Society continued to strongly support the Pyramid **after** Russell's death in 1916, until 1928, and by material distributed even later. What is the history of pyramidology? In greater detail, how was the Great Pyramid viewed by Russell and subsequent Society leadership?

Some Pyramid History

With the publication of John Taylor's *The Great Pyramid: Why Was It Built? And Who Built It?* in 1859, "modern pyramidology was born."[2] Taylor was convinced that the Great Pyramid of Cheops at Gizeh was constructed by an Israeli architect working under divine direction. John Taylor, C. T. Russell, and others who accepted this theory cited a number of Bible passages which they claimed made reference to the Pyramid (e.g., Isa. 19:19-20; Job 38:5-7; Eph. 2:20-21).[3] The Pyramid was viewed as "divinely intended to prophetically reveal a mass of chronological data, a vast stone structure that would, when properly understood, indicate the years, and sometimes the months and very days of the major events in the redemptive program of the world."[4]

The theory became prestigious when the Astronomer-Royal of Scotland and Professor of Astronomy at Edinburgh, Charles Piazzi Smyth, made a personal study of Taylor's theory. Smyth's 664-page book, *Our Inheritance in the Great Pyramid*, first published in 1864, became the foundation of modern pyramidology. In 1865, Smyth made a trip to Egypt to measure the Pyramid himself. The results of his study were published in the three-volume *Life, and Work at the Great Pyramid* (1867) and *On the Antiquity of Intellectual Man* (1868).[5] Russell was well acquainted with Smyth's work.[6]

C. T. Russell, et al.: The Pyramid is God's Monument

Beginning in 1881, a number of statements were printed in Watch Tower materials strongly supporting the divine origin of the Great Pyramid. For example: "We have great respect for *it*, though we do not build our faith *upon it*. It has well been called 'A Miracle in Stone,' and it commends itself to us as a work of God, and not planned by men, for it seems in every respect to be in perfect accord with God's plan as we are finding it written in His Word; and this it is, that causes our respect for *it*."[7] "...The Pyramid *corroborates* scripture...."[8]

Pastor Russell was impressed with Smyth's writing on pyramidology. When *Thy Kingdom Come* (volume 3 of *Studies in the Scriptures*) was published in 1891, the chapter devoted to the Pyramid, "The Testimony of God's Stone Witness and Prophet, the Great Pyramid in Egypt," was prefaced by a letter from Professor Smyth commending Russell's treatment.[9] Russell concluded: "The ancient structure being thus repeatedly referred to in the Scriptures, we cannot doubt that, if questioned, this 'Witness' of the Lord in the land of Egypt will bear such testimony as will honor Jehovah, and fully correspond with his written Word."[10]

In 1883, the reader is told that God "placed the Great Pyramid 'in the midst and in the border of Egypt,' for a *sign*...."[11] And the March 1885 *Watch Tower* claims: "So striking and clear are its teachings that some of the foremost astronomers of the world have unhesitatingly pronounced it to be of Divine origin."[12]

Russell made two trips to visit the Great Pyramid, the first in 1892 and the second in 1910. Concerning his last visit, Russell reported: "We merely reviewed this Great Witness to the Lord of hosts and recalled to mind its testimony...."[13]

Russell's work on the Pyramid caused two brothers in England, John and Morton Edgar, to go to Egypt where they made measurements of their own. The Edgars co-authored two volumes on the subject, and Morton added a third in 1924. The earlier material was advertised in the *Watch Tower*.[14]

The Pyramid is discussed in a short article in the March 15, 1911, *Watch Tower*, which concludes: "No doubt all of our readers have read STUDIES IN THE SCRIPTURES, Vol. III, the last chapter of which describes the Pyramid and sets forth much of the wonderful symbolic teachings shown in its construction. **It shows the Pyramid to be in exact harmony with the Bible.** Indeed, some, after reading this volume, have referred to the Great Pyramid as 'The Bible in Stone.'"[15]

The Great Pyramid was said to support the 1874, 1878, 1881 and 1914 dates Russell had determined by his Bible chronology. Concerning this last date, Russell and "many of the dear friends" were rejoicing over the seven corroborative proofs set forth in the book published by Morton Edgar, which showed "that the close of the year 1914—namely, about October 1914—will mark the closing of the Times of the Gentiles, and the beginning of the Messianic reign."[16]

In Russell's new foreword to *Thy Kingdom Come*, dated October 1, 1916, just one month before his death, he reiterated his faith in the Pyramid: "The Great Pyramid of Egypt discussed in this Volume has not lost any of its interest to the author." While not placing it as equal to the Bible, Russell says, "We do, however, still believe that the structure of this Pyramid, so different from that of all other pyramids, was designed of the Lord and intended to be a Pyramid and a witness in the midst and on the border of Egypt. (Isaiah 19:19.) ... Its wonderful corroboration of the Divine Plan of the Ages is astonishing to everybody who really grasps it."[17]

The Finished Mystery (1917) tells the reader that "Morton Edgar, author of *Pyramid Passages*, has found foreshown in the Great Pyramid of Egypt abundant evidence of the accuracy of the Bible chronology of Pastor Russell and the supplements thereto supplied by Dr. John Edgar, deceased.... Pastor Russell's chronology was written before he ever saw the Pyramid."[18]

The December 15, 1920, *Watch Tower* reports on a visit to the Pyramid. "The object in Egypt which holds such great interest for the Christian is the Great pyramid of Gizeh.... We spent a few days in and about the Pyramid, examining the wonders of its construction and the lessons it teaches in symbol."[19] Then it is stated: "The evidence seems conclusive that this temple, the Sphinx and the pyramid connected with them by the underground passage, as well as all the other pyramids thereabouts, **with the exception of the Great Pyramid, were built under the direction of Satan for the specific purpose of diverting the minds of the people** from the lessons taught by the 'witness unto the Lord,' and to blind them as to God's purpose."[20] "Hence the majority of men today who have ever thought about the subject believe that all the pyramids of Egypt are tombs of the dead, and thus Satan has accomplished his purpose by building the counterfeit and thereby diverting the attention of mankind from the true significance of the Great Pyramid, **which was built under the Lord's supervision.**"[21]

In the June 15, 1922, *Watch Tower,* the Pyramid is again lauded: "In the passages of the Great Pyramid of Gizeh the agreement of one or two measurements with the present-truth chronology might be accidental, but the correspondency of dozens of measurements **proves that the same God designated both pyramid and plan....**"[22]

The March 14, 1923, *Golden Age* claims that "in the course of time Jehovah caused the great Pyramid of Egypt to be builded, which by its geometrical measurements and construction pictures the great divine plan,"[23] and in the *World Distress—Why? The Remedy* (1923) booklet, Rutherford used "Russell's Great Pyramid calculations to buttress his Bible chronology."[24]

The May 21, 1924, *Golden Age* featured a long article in support of the Great Pyramid, "A Bible for the Scientist."[25] A revised version of this same article was reprinted in the December 31, 1924, issue. This time the author's name, W. E. Van Amburgh, was given. Van Amburgh was a prominent Society leader who served as the Society's secretary-treasurer until his death in 1947. The article claims that the Pyramid, the "Scientific Bible," verified the importance of such dates as 1874, 1914 and 1925.[26]

In the book *The Way to Paradise* (1924), with an Introduction by President J. F. Rutherford, author Van Amburgh states that "it is quite probable" that Noah's son Shem [Russell conjectured Melchizedek—*Thy Kingdom Come,* 322] supervised the Pyramid's construction,"[27] and that it "outlines in its own peculiar way the same plan of God that we find in the Bible."[28] The next page features a full-page sketch of the Pyramid's interior features captioned, "GOD'S PLAN WRITTEN IN STONE."[29] On the following page it is claimed that the Pyramid "is so far in advance of the wisdom of that day that no man could have been the architect. **Its harmony with the Bible teachings prove that God designed it**."[30]

The *Watch Tower* of May 15, 1925, says that "the great Pyramid of Egypt, standing as a silent and inanimate witness of the Lord, is a messenger; and its testimony speaks with great eloquence concerning the divine plan."[31] In 1926, the reader is told that "advanced Bible Students believe that the Great Pyramid at Gizeh is the witness to the Lord in the Land of Egypt, mentioned by the Prophet. (Isa. 19:19)"[32]

J. F. Rutherford: The Pyramid Is Satan's Monument

In 1891, Russell predicted a future attack on the Pyramid's testimony: "We thus introduce this 'Witness' because the inspiration of its testimony will doubtless be as much disputed as that of the Scriptures, **by the prince of darkness, the god of this world, and those whom he blinds to the truth.**"[33] But who could have predicted that the human source of this attack would come from the leadership of the Watch Tower Society itself—by a former defender?

The teachings concerning the Great Pyramid were discarded by President Rutherford in a two-part article (totaling 14 pages), "The Altar in Egypt," which appeared in the November 15 and December 1, 1928, *Watch Tower.* In his initial presentation, he makes no specific mention of Russell or any others, including himself, who had promoted the view. "For the past half-century many students of the Word of God have been taught and have believed that the great pyramid of Egypt is that which God through his prophet Isaiah refers to in the text [Isa. 19:19-20] first above quoted."[34]

The Great Pyramid is denounced in the strongest of language. To teach about it "is more than a waste of time. It is diverting the mind away from the Word of God and from his service."[35] "It is certain that the pyramid of Gizeh was not built by Jehovah God; nor was it built at his command."[36] "It is more reasonable to conclude that the great pyramid of Gizeh, as well as the other pyramids thereabout, also the sphinx, were built by the rulers of Egypt and **under the direction of Satan the Devil**."[37] "Then Satan put his knowledge in dead stone, which may be called **Satan's Bible**, and not God's stone witness. In erecting the pyramid, of course, Satan would put in some truth, because that is his method of practicing fraud and deceit."[38] "The Devil himself superintended the building of the pyramid of Gizeh."[39]

"Satan is a wily foe. He resorts to all manner of schemes to draw men away from Jehovah and his service. One of the most subtle schemes Satan has yet adopted to accomplish that purpose has been and is the use of the pyramid of Gizeh. There are those who rely upon the pyramid who claim to be of Christ and his followers."[40] "We now wonder why we ever believed in or devoted any time to the study of the pyramid of Gizeh. Not only will we abandon such a study now, but we will ask God to forgive us for wasting the time that we put in on it and redeem the time by hurrying on to obey his commandments."[41]

Other negative statements by Watch Tower writers, on the Pyramid and those who believe in it, have appeared at other times with such comments as: "nonsense, or worse than nonsense,"[42] an "entanglement" removed "from the paths of Jehovah's people,"[43] "'pyramid' delusion,"[44] "human" philosophy,[45] "a monument of demonism to glorify belief in immortality of the soul or 'survival after death,'"[46] and "not built by those engaging in the true worship of Jehovah God but by those devoted to astrology, a manifestation of Devil religion, and was built in furtherance of such religion."[47] This article also states that "others have developed the hypothesis that it was built under divine inspiration.... Such men as John Taylor of London, Professor Smyth and Dr. Edgar of Scotland advocated the theory that the measurements of the Great Pyramid and particularly the measurements of its internal passageways and chambers, were full of scriptural meaning."[48] A small print footnote on this point says, "Bible Students also held to this thought prior to 1928."[49] It is significant that there is no mention of founder C. T. Russell or J. F. Rutherford, and no hint that **every one of the names** given in the quote were favorably mentioned or quoted in the *Watch Tower* in the past, or that their writings were promoted in Society publications.[50]

One wonders what kind of interpretive method or "due time" enlightenment can produce such diametrically opposite interpretations on the same subject or on the same scripture passages. In this case, the first view was propagated for about 50 years before it was condemned. In fact, each position taken was condemned as Devil-originated! This example is not unique in the history of the Watch Tower movement—in actuality, it is characteristic.

Was "Satan's Bible" Promoted After 1928?

Was literature promoting "Satan's Bible," "a monument to demonism," distributed by the Bible Students (Jehovah's Witnesses) after 1928? The book *God's Kingdom of a Thousand Years Has Approached* (1973) claims that "later in the year 1927 any remaining stocks of the six volumes of *Studies in the Scriptures* by Russell and of *The Finished Mystery* were disposed of among the public."[51] It should be remembered that the third volume of *Studies in the Scriptures* contains Russell's most extensive treatment on the Great Pyramid and that *The Finished Mystery* (1917) recommends Morton and John Edgar's books *Pyramid Passages* to the reader.[52] *The Finished Mystery*, along with the other volumes of *Studies in the Scriptures*, were advertised for sale by the Watch Tower Society in the November 1, 1929, *Watch Tower*.[53] Volume 3 of *Studies*, with an entire chapter in support of the Great Pyramid, was still being sold by the Society in 1944![54]

Notes

1. *Jehovah's Witnesses—Proclaimers of God's Kingdom* (1993), 201.
2. Martin Gardner, *Fads and Fallacies in the Name of Science* (Rev. ed.; New York: Dover Publications, 1957), 174.
3. Ibid., 175. As Russell began his chapter on the Pyramid in *Thy Kingdom Come* (1891), 313, he used Isaiah 19:19-20. The other references cited were also quoted along with many other passages.
4. Wilbur M. Smith, *Egypt in Biblical Prophecy* (Boston: W. A. Wilde, 1957), 210.
5. Gardner, 176.
6. Russell, 311-12; 320-22; *WTR*, 1 Jan. 1912, 4953.
7. *WTR*, May 1881, 224.
8. Ibid., 225.
9. Russell, 312.
10. Ibid., 319.
11. *WTR*, Sept. 1893, 525.
12. *WTR*, Mar. 1885, 737.
13. *WTR*, 1 June 1910, 4621.
14. Gardner, 181; *WTR*, 1 Aug. 1910, 4658; *WTR*, 15 Oct. 1913, 5336.
15. *WTR*, 15 Mar. 1911, 4790.
16. *WTR*, May 1881, 224-25; Russell, 362-67; *WTR*, 15 Oct. 1913, 5336.
17. Russell, *Thy Kingdom Come* (1916 ed.), ii-iii. "We ask, therefore, Could such exactness in matters which concern six thousand years of history on the one hand, and the thousands of inches of Pyramid measurements on the other, be a mere accidental coincidence? Nay; but verily truth is stranger and more wonderful than fiction. 'This is the Lord's doing; it is marvelous in our eyes'" (ibid., 365).
18. Clayton J. Woodworth and George H. Fisher, *The Finished Mystery* (1917), 60.
19. *WT*, 15 Dec. 1920, 377.
20. Ibid.
21. Ibid., 378.
22. *WT*, 15 June 1922, 187.
23. *GA*, 14 Mar. 1923, 356.
24. William J. Whalen, *Armageddon Around the Corner* (New York: John Day Co., 1962), 56.
25. *GA*, 21 May 1924, 518-38.
26. *GA*, 31 Dec. 1924, 205-22. Van Amburgh is often mentioned in the Witness-published histories, *Jehovah's Witnesses in the Divine Purpose* (64, 65, 70, 79, 85) and *Jehovah's Witnesses—Proclaimers of God's Kingdom* (64, 65, 68, 74, 91, 93, 245, 459, 622-24, 652, 653). Van Amburgh attended his first convention in 1900, spoke at Russell's funeral, was named in Russell's will to the five-member *Watch Tower* Editorial Committee, was elected to the seven-member Board of Directors and chosen for the three-member Executive Committee, and was one of the eight Society leaders who were sentenced to prison in 1918.
27. W. E. Van Amburgh, *The Way to Paradise* (1924), 156.
28. Ibid.
29. Ibid., 157.
30. Ibid., 158.
31. *WT*, 15 May 1925, 148.
32. *GA*, 3 Nov. 1926, 71.

33. Russell, 319.

34. *WT*, 15 Nov. 1928, 339.

35. Ibid., 341.

36. Ibid., 343.

37. Ibid., 344.

38. Ibid.

39. Ibid.

40. *WT*, 1 Dec. 1928, 359.

41. Ibid., 361.

42. *GA*, 13 Mar. 1935, 355.

43. *GA*, 10 Apr. 1935, 445.

44. *WT*, 1 May 1935, 142.

45. *WT*, 15 May 1936, 153.

46. *WT*, 15 Nov. 1955, 697.

47. *WT*, 15 May 1956, 300.

48. Ibid., 298.

49. Ibid.

50. Some examples are: **John Taylor**, *Thy Kingdom Come*, 319; **Charles P. Smyth**, *Thy Kingdom Come*, 311-12, 320-321, 337, 338, 342, 369; *WTR*, 1 Nov. 1904: 3451; **Dr. John Edgar**, *WTR*, 15 June 1905: 3574-79, 1 June 1910: 4621; 1 July 1910: 4638; 15 July 1910: 4652; 1 Aug. 1910: 4658; 4953; WT, 1 June 1922: 163; *The Finished Mystery*, 60. In addition, **Joseph A. Seiss**, author of *A Miracle in Stone: or The Great Pyramid of Egypt*, is quoted in *Thy Kingdom Come*, 327-28, 374-75, and an article he wrote and one in which he is quoted, appear in *WTR*, 3612, 3620.

51. *God's Kingdom of a Thousand Years Has Approached* (1973), 347.

52. Woodworth and Fisher, 60.

53. *WT*, 1 Nov. 1929, 322. The advertisement for the books states: "The Society has decided to designate the week beginning November 10 [1929] as a special drive week for the sale of *Studies in the Scriptures*" (ibid.). In a *Special Colporteur Edition Bulletin* (not dated but issued sometime after April 1928), the *Studies in the Scriptures* set was to be promoted with this sales pitch: "Judge Rutherford is recognized as the world's greatest Bible lecturer, and yet he admits that he could not have understood the Bible if he had not used this method (produce booklet showing the set). This series of seven volumes explains every subject from Genesis to Revelation." Then each of the seven volumes is briefly summarized (10).

54. See the photocopy of p. 6 of the February 1, 1944, "Watchtower Cost List," in Duane Magnani's *Bible Students?* (Clayton, Calif.: Witness Inc., 1983), photo #97. The *Kingdom Ministry* for July 1967 lists the deluxe edition of volume 4 of *Studies in the Scriptures* (English) "out of stock in U.S.A."

27.

Beth-Sarim: A Monument
to False Prophecy

Before the publication of *Jehovah's Witnesses—Proclaimers of God's Kingdom* (1993), most Jehovah's Witnesses probably had never heard of Beth-Sarim ("House of the Princes") or seen a photo of the San Diego mansion. The book contains a brief treatment explaining the use and purpose of its construction, refers to the deed, mentions the belief in the pre-Armageddon resurrection of the "princes" ("adjusted in 1950"), and the decision in 1947 to dispose of the property.[1]

An earlier history, *Jehovah's Witnesses in the Divine Purpose* (1959), makes no mention of Beth-Sarim, while a treatment in the *1975 Yearbook* explains the Watch Tower president's poor health and says the house was "for Brother Rutherford's use."[2] Although there were occasional brief references to Beth-Sarim, until the *Proclaimers* book, nothing of significance had appeared in Watch Tower publications since the 1940s.[3] Research reveals that the *Proclaimers* book and the *Yearbook* misled the reader by presenting incomplete information. Commenting on the *Proclaimers* coverage on Beth-Sarim, one reviewer concludes that the "book now provides more information, but still falls short of telling the whole truth,"[4] and another says it presents a "thoroughly sanitized and misleading description of Beth-Sarim."[5]

What made the presentation in the *Proclaimers* book necessary after so many years of ignoring the subject? It can be argued that inclusion of Beth-Sarim was needed because many non-Witness books *did* mention it in their coverage of the Jehovah's Witnesses. Especially significant was the film and video, "Witnesses of Jehovah" (1987), shown thousands of times in the United States and abroad, which caused many viewers to ask Witnesses about it, and they in turn asked questions.[6]

What is the story on Beth-Sarim? Why was it built? Why would reviewers, typical of others, conclude that the *Proclaimers* material on Beth-Sarim is "misleading" and "falls short of telling the whole truth"? Why can it accurately be identified as a monument to false prophecy?

Beth-Sarim

Robert J. Martin, manager of the Watch Tower publishing facilities in Brooklyn, presented the Society's account of acquiring the property and building Beth-Sarim, including a copy of the deed, in the March 19, 1930, *Golden Age*.[7] He explained that as a result of a severe case of pneumonia, Joseph F. Rutherford had only one good lung, a condition which made it very difficult for him to work in Brooklyn during the winter. Because of the mild climate in San Diego, Rutherford had spent the previous four winters there under the care of Dr. Alta G. Eckols, who "repeatedly urged him to spend as much time as possible" there.[8] In 1929, "in company with a few other brethren, we pressed this matter upon him, at that time the Lord having provided the means for the building of the house so that it would not be a burden on the Society. He finally consented that the house might be built only upon the condition that it should be exclusively for the use of the Lord's work, henceforth and for ever...."[9]

In October, Martin went to San Diego to put the title for the two lots purchased by Dr. Albert E. Eckols under his name and to contract for the construction of the house. "A deed was made conveying the title to the house. This deed was written by Brother Rutherford himself." Martin comments, "I am certain there is no other deed to any piece of property like it under the sun."[10]

What made this deed unique? Martin explains that the "loyal ones ... will rejoice when they know that this property **will be for ever** for the Lord's people; that when Brother Rutherford is through with it somebody else in the Lord's work will have it, and **when David and Joseph or some of the other ancient worthies return they will have it.**"[11]

The architect for Beth-Sarim was the renowned Richard S. Requa, who drew "the plans for some of the most beautiful residences in and near San Diego...."[12] The deeds for this unit of Kensington Heights required a minimum building size of 1,500 square feet and a cost of $5,000—"a goodly sum in pre-inflation days."[13] Beth-Sarim was over 5,100 square feet, and in his answer to critics, Robert Martin admits to a building cost approaching $25,000.[14] Judge Rutherford told Walter Salter that he had been offered $75,000 for the residence, a figure also quoted in the *San Diego Sun* published two months after the mansion was occupied.[15] After Rutherford's death, a neighbor described the home as "one of the finest in Kensington Heights."[16] It should also be remembered that he enjoyed the use of several other comfortable living quarters in New York, London, and Magdeburg, Germany (before the Nazis came to power). All are listed in an open letter written by the Watch Tower Canadian branch overseer Walter Salter, Rutherford's friend and associate for twenty years, as he exposes the hypocrisy of Rutherford's luxury lifestyle during the Great Depression.[17] "While his workers plodded from door to door selling his prolific writings, the Judge lived the life of a major industrialist. He spent the winters at Beth-Sarim and traveled by steamship to Europe each summer."[18]

Beth-Sarim Goes Public

Rutherford moved into the 4440 Braeburn Road residence on January 13, 1930. The public was introduced to Beth-Sarim in a front-page article in the March 15, 1930, *San Diego Sun*: "San Diego Mansion—With All Modern Improvements—Awaits Earthly Return of Prophets."[19] It went on to report: "In one of the strangest deeds ever filed in the nation, Rutherford, president of the International Bible Students Association and of the Watch Tower Bible and Tract Society, has put the huge tile-roofed home in fashionable Kensington Heights **in perpetual trust for the ancient kings and prophets of Palestine.**"[20] And later in the article, "Judge Rutherford is intensely proud of the house he has planned and built for David, king of Israel; Samson ... Joseph ... and other equally as famous in the Bible."[21]

On January 9, 1931, the *San Diego Sun* carried another article on Beth-Sarim, "David's House Waits for Owner." When the reporter asked Rutherford how he thought the returned "princes" would look, he responded, "'As perfect men. I interpret that to mean ... that David, Gideon, Barak, Samson, Jepthae, Joseph and Samuel will be sent here to wrench the world from Satan's grasp, clothed in modern garb as we are, and able, with little effort to speak our tongue.' Rutherford pictured the arrival of the biblical delegation perhaps in frock coats, high hats, canes and spats."[22] Rutherford's booklet, *What You Need* (1932), depicted the seven "Ancient Worthies," identified as "Earth's new rulers," in more traditional biblical garb.[23]

The mansion, the article continued, had "the most modern appliances that science has devised" and in a two-car garage "stands a new, yellow 16-cylinder coupe which will be turned over to the rulers along with all the personal property on the place."[24] The Judge did not explain how this coupe could meet the transportation needs of even the seven returned "princes" named in the deed. "To place the value of this automobile in perspective, a new Ford in 1931 cost approximately 600 dollars. A 16-cylinder Cadillac cost between 5400 and 9200 dollars, depending on style. Another V-16 convertible sedan was kept at Brooklyn headquarters, and both cars were used exclusively by Judge Rutherford."[25] Auto historians tell more about the V-16: "Naturally, it was the very rich—and often as not, the famous—who made up the limited clientele of the V-16. Among the owners of the first-generation cars was Al Jolson ... Robert Montgomery ... Marlene Dietrich...."[26]

Rutherford predicted that the return of David and his companions would be the greatest news story in history, and claimed that the testimony of Beth-Sarim had gone all over the world and that thousands had come to see the house. "The seven famous men will not have long to rest at their San Diego estate because they soon will lead the forces of the Lord to vanquish the minions of Satan at the battle of Armageddon, Rutherford believes."[27]

"Beth-Sarim—Much Talked About House"

The Witnesses' July 25, 1931, Columbus, Ohio convention publication, *The Messenger*, carried a significant treatment on Beth-Sarim, including several pictures of the house and grounds. The July 30 issue had a picture of a little girl, captioned "Princess Bonnie." The previous day she had been photographed talking with Judge Rutherford, and many wondered how she had obtained this privilege. Her parents were caretakers at Beth-Sarim where they lived with Bonnie, nearly two, and her younger brother. It was explained:

> Beth-Sarim being "the house of the princes," and, as **we confidently expect, to be occupied and used by some of the princes** in the earth, it seemed quite appropriate that these children who are growing up there should be named in harmony with these scriptures. Hence the little girl is named Princess Bonnie Balko, and the little boy Prince Joseph Barak Balko.... It is hoped that these two little ones may grow up at Beth-Sarim to be with the rulers of the earth and live forever to the glory of Jehovah's name. They have been told, in so far as they can understand, that they may expect these noble men and, when they do appear, to meet them and put themselves completely under their direction.[28]

A letter to "Brother Rutherford" in the August 1, 1931, *Watch Tower* reveals what was believed at the time, "It is thrilling to look forward to the return of the faithful prophets **before** the last members of the remnant pass beyond [changed from the view in 1925]. Surely the Lord guided you to having the **house built in San Diego in preparation for their return**."[29]

Why Was Beth-Sarim Built?

Watch Tower publications have said Beth-Sarim was built for Rutherford's use (currently emphasized), as a testimony of faith in the "princes'" pre-Armageddon resurrection (currently rejected), and for the "princes'" use (currently forgotten). Were these the real or only reasons for its construction? There is evidence for a fourth and more important reason never mentioned in Society publications.

In *Millions Now Living Will Never Die* (1920), Rutherford made a bold prophecy: "Therefore we may **confidently expect that 1925** will mark the return of Abraham, Isaac, Jacob and the faithful prophets of old."[30] But even before 1925 had ended, the *Golden Age* of August 12 adjusted the prophecy, writing that "it is apparent that there are many peoples now on earth who may **confidently hope** to see Abraham, Isaac, Jacob and the other prophets back on earth **within a few years**."[31] The year after the 1925 failure, Rutherford attended a convention in Basel, Switzerland, where he was asked, "Have the ancient worthies returned?" He answered that they had not and that "it would be foolish to make such an announcement." Then changing the wording, "It was stated in the 'Millions' book that we might **reasonably expect** them to return **shortly after 1925**, but this was merely an **expressed opinion**; besides it is still shortly after 1925. There is no good reason why we should expect the ancient worthies to return until the church is complete and the work of the church on earth is done."[32]

When the predictions for the return of the princes and other events in 1925 were not realized, many left the movement, and it has been observed that Rutherford was never the same. He began to "drink to excess," and when drunk "the headquarters staff felt the wrath of his cursing tongue. Old timers say his drinking was covered up, to the degree possible, by associates Frederick W. Franz and Nathan H. Knorr. It was they who showed a brilliance for manipulation. They dealt with Rutherford's further decline into the realm of drunkenness and erratic behavior by encouraging him to build himself a house in California to spend his remaining years 'writing in the sun.'"[33]

Edward J. Ford, Jr., was a Witness for over four decades. He worked on the staff in Bethel headquarters in Brooklyn for a number of years. He recalls conversations with his Witness father and his own contacts with Watch Tower Society leaders. A. H. Macmillan, who served in headquarters under three Watch Tower presidents and was "known to Jehovah's witnesses all over the world,"[34] was a frequent weekend visitor in the Ford home. Although Macmillan was a loyal organization man and supportive of Rutherford, "he was critical of his drunkenness and irrational conduct." Shortly after Rutherford's death, Macmillan told Ford's father that Beth-Sarim was built "for no purpose other than to get the drunken and declining Rutherford out of Brooklyn."[35] This was also confirmed later to him by Society attorney Hayden Covington, who directed the legal department and was elected vice-president after Rutherford's death. Covington "quoted Franz as saying, 'they built the judge a house out in California just to get him out of Bethel.'" He also told him that it was Franz that "concocted the cover story ... saying that the house was for the ancient prophets due back 'any day' in the pre-Armageddon resurrection."[36]

Can Rutherford's alcoholism be confirmed from other sources? Walter Salter writes of his purchases for Rutherford. "... I, at your orders, would purchase cases of whiskey at $60.00 a case, and cases of brandy and other liquors, to say nothing of untold cases of beer. A bottle or two of liquor would not do; it was for THE PRESIDENT and nothing was too good for THE PRESIDENT."[37]

After concluding that Rutherford had a "serious case of alcoholism," M. James Penton writes, "Although Jehovah's Witnesses have done everything possible to hide accounts of the judge's drinking habits, they are simply too notorious to be denied. Former workers at the Watch Tower's New York headquarters recount tales of his inebriation and drunken stupors. Others tell stories of how difficult it sometimes was to get him to the podium to give talks at conventions because of his drunkenness."[38]

His drinking continued at Beth-Sarim where he spent his winters until his death. "... An elderly lady still speaks of how she sold him great quantities of liquor when he came to purchase medicines in her husband's drugstore."[39] In an interview she stated, "We had a liquor department in those days, he was certainly one of our best customers."[40]

More Property for Rutherford and the "Princes"

More property was purchased in 1938 and 1939 and deeded to the Watch Tower Bible and Tract Society. One deed conveying some of this property states, in part:

> To have and to hold in trust ... for the following purposes: ...For the use and benefit of J. F. Rutherford ... and **thereafter for ever** for Abel, Enoch, Noah, Abraham, Moses, Joshua, David, Gideon, Barak, Joseph or any and all of them particu[lar]ly named and identified at the eleventh chapter of Hebrews in the Bible.... The reason for making this Deed in trust is as follows: The

Grantors have full faith and confidence in Jehovah the Almighty God, and in the truthfulness of His Word.... God, according to His promise, will at a **very early date** resurrect said men as perfect human creatures and that the Lord will make them the visible princes or rulers in the earth. This Deed is made as evidence of the faith of the said grantors in said Divine promise that these men **will soon be back on earth** and it is their purpose to prove their faith be deeding this land in trust as herein set forth. The property herein described ... is donated and given as herein stated, to be made part of the property known as BETH-SARIM and the premises built on the lots above described and is made for the same purpose as that recited in the [Beth-Sarim] deed....[41]

Rutherford's Death and Burial

When Rutherford died on January 8, 1942, it was obvious that the predicted "princes" had not yet returned. The *Consolation* of May 27, 1942, reported that "before his death Judge Rutherford made the simple request that his remains be buried somewhere on the hundred-acre estate ... *held in trust for the New Earth's Princes.*"[42] Requests for a permit for interment on the adjacent property below the mansion or on another parcel (Beth-Shan) were denied by the Planning Commission and the Board of Supervisors. A petition for writ of mandate (mandamus) in the County Superior Court to force county officials to issue the permit was also unsuccessful.[43] When Rutherford associate William P. Heath, Jr., spoke before the court, he used the opportunity to promote the current beliefs of the Society, "Further proof that these princes will *shortly* take office upon earth as perfect men is found in the prophecy of Daniel.... Proof is now submitted that we are now living at 'the end of the days,' and we may expect to see Daniel and the other mentioned princes any day now!"[44]

The Unfinished Crypt

When Heath argued for Rutherford's burial on land below Beth-Sarim acquired by Beth-Sarim's Rest, a cemetery corporation of which he was vice-president, he said "that no monument, no structure, no mausoleum would be placed or erected, and that the only grave marker would be a stone beneath an oak tree surrounded by orange and lemon trees."[45]

That this clearly was not the original plan is evidenced by the unfinished concrete crypt measuring approximately 25 feet wide, 8 feet deep, and 12 feet in height built on another location on the hillside property. It can be easily seen from a half mile away. In Heath's extensive arguments before the Planning Commission, the Board of Supervisors, and before the judge in the Superior Court, and the coverage in the May 27, 1942, *Consolation*, the unfinished structure is never once mentioned, while it is noted in the January 13, 1942, *San Diego Union*.[46] According to the official account, Rutherford's body was sent to New York's Woodrow Cemetery, on Staten Island, and the burial took place on April 21st. Shortly after Rutherford's death, A. H. Macmillan told Edward Ford, Sr., that only four people attended the burial. Not one member of Rutherford's immediate family was present, and notable for their absence were Franz and Knorr. Macmillan was greatly disappointed.[47]

What About the "Soon" Return of the Princes?

Predictions concerning the return of the pre-Christian "Ancient Worthies" or "princes" were made long before 1917,[48] the year J. F. Rutherford became president of the Watch Tower Bible and Tract Society. This prophecy—while false—would be propagated worldwide through Rutherford's discourses, his writings, and his promotion of Beth-Sarim, until his death. The prediction that the return of the "princes" would be "any day now," "shortly," or "very shortly" would continue to receive expression for a time after his death. This continued as William P. Heath, Jr., and other Society representatives unsuccessfully attempted to obtain a permit to bury Rutherford's body on its property in San Diego, and through Watch Tower publications.[49] While not stated publicly until 1950, the upcoming "adjustment" of the teaching on the "princes'" imminent pre-Armageddon resurrection can be detected as early as 1945.[50]

Beth-Sarim Sold!

The *New World* (1942) stated that the "faithful men of old may be expected back from the dead any day now. The Scriptures give good reason to believe that it shall be shortly before Armageddon breaks," and that Beth-Sarim was "now held in trust for the occupancy of those princes on their return." It was claimed that "the most recent facts show that the religionists of this doomed world are gnashing their teeth because of the testimony which the 'House of the Princes' bears to the new world."[51] This is an interesting statement in the light of Society President Knorr's August 15, 1947, Assembly announcement concerning the property:

> The audience ... applauded when informed that the Society's board of directors had voted unanimously to dispose of Beth-Sarim, either by outright sale or by rent, because it had fully served its purpose and was **now only serving as a monument** quite expensive to keep; our faith in the return of the men of old time whom the King Christ Jesus will make princes in ALL the earth (not merely in California) is based, not upon that house Beth-Sarim, but upon God's Word of promise.[52]

It is significant that Knorr referred to Beth-Sarim as "now only serving as a monument." It should be remembered that the Great Pyramid of Egypt was promoted by founder C. T. Russell until his death, and Rutherford after him, as designed by God. It was also later identified as a "monument"—"a monument of demonism."[53] It is quite remarkable that the Great Pyramid "monument" was rejected at the end of 1928, using the strongest of language, yet less than a year later, Beth-Sarim, a new "monument"—one which was used to promote false prophecy—was built! And ultimately, with its sale in 1948,[54] its core teachings about the soon return of the "princes" before Armageddon, and their use of Beth-Sarim as their abode, would be rejected.

From the record of history it must be concluded that Beth-Sarim bears a testimony—it is a monument to a false prophet and to false prophecy. Rutherford asked, "How are we to know whether one is a true or a false prophet?" His answer, "If he is a true prophet, his message will come to pass exactly as prophesied. If he is a false prophet, his prophecy will fail to come to pass....—Deut. 18:21, 22."[55]

Notes

1. *Jehovah's Witnesses—Proclaimers of God's Kingdom* (1993), 76.
2. *Jehovah's Witnesses in the Divine Purpose* (1959), 194.
3. *"Let Your Name Be Sanctified"* (1961), 336; *WT*, 1 Nov. 1955, 655; 1 June 1985, 27; 1 Mar. 1992, 27.
4. David A. Reed, *'Proclaimers' Answered Page by Page* (Stoughton, Maine: David A. Reed, 1994), 11.
5. Randall Watters, "Review of the new Watchtower book...," *Free Minds Journal*, Sept.-Oct. 1993, 3.
6. The *Witnesses of Jehovah* video is available postpaid for $22.00 from Good News Defenders, Inc., P.O. Box 8007, La Jolla, CA 92038.
7. *GA*, 19 Mar. 1930, "The Truth About the San Diego House," 405-07.
8. Ibid., 405.

9. Ibid.

10. Ibid. Book 1741, 69-71, San Diego County Recorder.

11. Ibid., 406.

12. *San Diego Union*, 21 Dec. 1986, B-8. Samuel F. Black, *San Diego County California*, vol. II (Chicago: S.J. Clarke Publ. Co., 1913), 215.

13. Thomas H. Baumann, *Kensington-Talmadge 1910-1985* (San Diego: T. H. Baumann, 1984), 12-13.

14. A sale listing dated April 26, 1995, places the size at 5,156 sq. ft. *GA*, Mar. 19, 1930, 406.

15. *San Diego Sun*, 15 Mar. 1930, 1.

16. Minutes of the County Planning Commission, Jan. 24, 1942, 230.

17. Walter Salter, open letter to Hon. J. F. Rutherford, 1 Apr. 1937, 2.

18. Leonard and Marjorie Chretien, *Witnesses of Jehovah* (Eugene, Oreg.: Harvest House, 1988), 46.

19. *San Diego Sun*, 15 Mar. 1930, 1, 3.

20. Ibid., 1.

21. Ibid., 3.

22. *San Diego Sun*, 9 Jan. 1931, 15.

23. Rutherford, *What You Need* (1932), 8. *The Messenger*, 25 July 1931, 8, presents another list of "princes."

24. *San Diego Sun*, 9 Jan. 1931, 15.

25. Chretien, 45-46.

26. *Special Interest Autos* #92, Apr. 1986, 21.

27. *San Diego Sun*, 9 Jan. 1931, 15.

28. *The Messenger*, July 30, 1931, 2.

29. *WT*, 1 Aug. 1931, 239.

30. Rutherford, *Millions Now Living Will Never Die* (1920), 89-90.

31. *GA*, 12 Aug., 1925, 731.

32. *WT*, 1 July 1926, 196.

33. This material is based on telephone interviews with Edward J. Ford, Jr. (pseud.) (Oct.-Dec. 1996), and his manuscript, *The Four Presidents of the Watchtower Society*.

34. President N. H. Knorr, in the Introduction to A. H. Macmillan's book, *Faith on the March* (Englewood Cliffs, N.J.: Prentice-Hall, Inc., 1957).

35. Ford interviews and manuscript.

36. Ibid.

37. Salter, 1.

38. M. James Penton, *Apocalypse Delayed* (2nd ed.; Toronto: University of Toronto Press, 1997), 72.

39. Ibid., 73.

40. Related to Leonard Chretien by Thomas H. Baumann.

41. Signed Feb. 15, 1939, Book 1025, 29-30, San Diego County Recorder.

42. *Cons.*, "San Diego Officials Line Up Against New Earth's Princes," 8 Jan. 1942, 3.

43. Case 106941.

44. *Cons.*, "San Diego Officials," 13.

45. Ibid., 7, quoting the *San Diego Union*, 25 Jan. 1942.

46. *San Diego Union*, 13 Jan. 1942, B-10.

47. Ford interviews and manuscript.

48. In 1904 Pastor Russell taught that the "princes" would be resurrected "about 1914, or shortly there-after..." *(WTR*, 15 Oct. 1904, 3445). In 1881 it was stated that in 1874 "the resurrection of David was

also due..." (*WTR*, Feb. 1881, 188).

49. *Cons.*, 24 Nov. 1941, 17-18; *Cons.*, May 27, 1942, 3-16; *The New World* (1942), 104, 130; *"The Truth Shall Make You Free"* (1943), 358.
50. The adjacent Beth-Shan property, held in trust for the princes use (Book 1075, 42-43), was sold on 29 Mar. 1945, Book 1853, 260-61, San Diego County Recorder.
51. *The New World*, 104.
52. *WT*, 15 Dec. 1947, 382.
53. *WT*, 15 Nov. 1955, 697.
54. Book 2858, 386-89, San Diego County Recorder.
55. *WT*, 15 May 1930, 154.

Pictures of Beth-Sarim, photocopies of deeds, newspaper reports, Watch Tower publications, and other pertinent records are found in the author's book (with Leonard Chretien): *Jehovah's Witnesses—Their Monuments to False Prophecy*. Clayton, Calif.: Witness Inc., 1997. See also: "Beth-Sarim: A Monument to a False Prophet and to False Prophecy," *Christian Research Journal*, Summer 1997, 22-29.

28.

Selected Quotations from Watch Tower Publications for the Years 1930-1939

The decade of the 1930s saw the abandoning of specific date setting, but readers of Watch Tower material were repeatedly assured that the Battle of Armageddon was very near—just "a few remaining months" away in 1935. Rutherford explained the new position for this period:

> There was a measure of disappointment on the part of Jehovah's faithful ones on earth concerning the years 1914, 1918 and 1925, which disappointment lasted for a time. Later the faithful learned that **these dates were definitely fixed in the Scriptures**; and they also **learned to quit fixing dates for the future and predicting what would come to pass on a certain date**, but to rely (and they do rely) upon the Word of God as to the events that must come to pass.[1]

1930

"...There is **now impending and about to fall** upon the nations of the earth, according to the words of Christ Jesus, a great time of 'tribulation such as was not since the beginning of the world to this time, no, nor ever shall be' again, and it is this impending trouble that the rulers and mighty men of earth see coming" (Rutherford, *Light I*, 110).

"*The Watch Tower*, and its companion publications of the Society, **for forty years emphasized the fact that 1914 would witness the establishment of God's kingdom and the complete glorification of the church**.... All of the Lord's people looked forward to 1914 with joyful expectation. When that time came and passed there was much disappointment, chagrin and mourning, and the Lord's people were greatly in reproach. They were ridiculed by the clergy and their allies in particular, and pointed to with scorn, because **they had said so much about 1914, and what would come to pass, and their 'prophecies' had not been fulfilled**" (ibid., 194).

"For the past ten years God has been serving notice on Satan that Armageddon is approaching, and that his kingdom is to be destroyed.... This prophecy **will soon be fulfilled**" (*WT*, 15 July 1930, 219).

"**The second advent of the Lord Jesus Christ dates from about A.D. 1875**, when he began to 'prepare the way before the Lord....' The coming of the Lord to God's temple dates from 1918" (*WT*, 15 Oct. 1930, 308).

"Thus the evidences show that the kingdom *is here*, and that we are now witnessing its first work, namely, the destruction of the old order, so that a new order can be instituted in its place. This glorious message is now going out all over the world.... The kingdom of Christ is already in power, and **soon, very soon now**, everybody will realize it, and soon its blessings will be apparent. But Armageddon *must first come*" (ibid., 317).

"Jehovah has expressed his determination that the issue shall be settled, and **that shortly**; but before doing so, he will cause testimony to be given before the nations and peoples of the world.... That **the giving of such testimony should immediately precede the final determination of the great issue of the battle of Armageddon** is made sure by the words of Jesus Christ, the great Prophet of Jehovah God..." (*WT*, 15 Nov. 1930, 347).

1931

"To be sure, no man can say exactly what day or year Armageddon will be fought, but it is easy to be seen that the conditions amongst the people are such now that **a great crisis is near**" (Rutherford, *Vindication I*, 146).

"God's kingdom has begun to operate. His day of vengeance is here, and Armageddon is at hand and certain to fall upon Christendom, and **that within an early date**. God's judgment is upon Christendom and must shortly be executed" (ibid., 147).

"The day of God's preparation is done. War upon and destruction of Satan's organization is **now about due**" (*WT*, 1 Jan. 1931, 15).

"According to the Scriptural proof, the great battle of Armageddon will **soon be fought**" (*WT*, 15 Jan. 1931, 28).

"**Within a very short time** God will destroy all of Satan's organization, which includes Christendom and all the nations that oppress the people and defame his name" (*The Messenger*, 28 July 1931, 2).

"All observe that at this very time darkness is in the earth and gross darkness upon the people concerning the Word of God, and the whole world is in the very shadow of death because **Armageddon is just ahead**" (Rutherford, *The Kingdom the Hope of the World*, 60).

"The Scriptural proof is that the second presence of the Lord Jesus Christ is invisible and began approximately in the year **eighteen hundred and seventy-eight** (A.D.)" (*WT*, 15 Sept. 1931, 283).

1932

Ad for *The Golden Age*: "The golden age, the age of peace and prosperity, of amity and felicity, of life and health, of everything that is truly desirable, **is at hand, it is even at the doors**, and the purpose of this unique magazine is to announce that happy, happy time" (*GA*, 20 Jan. 1932, 255).

"Let it be known that God's kingdom is the hope of the world and that the day of deliverance **is at hand**. Because the world is just at the portals of that time of blessing under the kingdom of God, **it can now be confidently said that millions now living on the earth will never die**" (Rutherford, *Good News*, 63).

"...Satan has been ousted from heaven and confines his operations at this time to things pertaining to the earth; and that **in the very near future his organization and power will be completely destroyed** in a time of trouble such as the world has never known" (Rutherford, *What You Need*, 17).

"Those of good will now on earth who do see and who are diligent to perform the requirements of Jehovah will be carried through the battle of Armageddon. Millions of such good people are now on earth, and for this reason **it is confidently stated that there are millions now living that will never die**" (ibid., 55).

"God commands his witnesses, therefore, to go and tell the people that their present woe and suffering proceed from the Devil, because he has been cast down to earth, and that he knows that his time for preparation for the final war is **very short**" (*WT*, 15 May 1932, 153).

"From the Word of Jehovah I specifically answer the question 'Can the American government endure?' And that answer is emphatically. No!... The American government has been weighed in the balance and found wanting. **It cannot endure. Together with all other nations, it soon shall fall**" (*GA*, 20 July 1932, 653-54).

1933

"The great battle that is **about to be fought** is called 'the battle of God Almighty' because then is when he will take a hand.... The great battle of the day of God Almighty has not yet begun, but is **near at hand**, as all the evidence shows" (*WT*, 1 Mar. 1933, 72).

"The invisible and visible armies of Satan and of Jehovah God are **assembled now at Armageddon**" (Rutherford, *The Crisis*, 20). "That battle **is near**" (ibid., 23). "The great crisis of the ages **is here**" (ibid., 64).

After quoting Luke 21:25-26: "That means, then, that **we have come to the end of the world** and that God will bring about the **complete change shortly**, and that in his own good way; which means that he will set aside the wicked rule of the world and that the government of nations will pass over into the hands of Christ Jesus, who will rule in righteousness" (Rutherford, *Intolerance*, 49).

Ad in Rutherford's *Preparation*: "The Devil knows he has but that much time ['but a short time'] to get ready for the final battle, Armageddon. (Revelation 12:12) That means there's not much time left for any of us to prepare for the coming of that decisive battle.... Preparation for the battle of battles is feverishly in progress and **will soon reach a climax at Armageddon**" (rear of book).

"The faithful remnant render themselves in full obedience to Jehovah's commandment and his organization instructions, and he is pleased to use them in the temple service and to continue to prepare them for **Armageddon, which is just ahead**" (*WT*, 15 Sept. 1933, 283).

1934

"Notice and warning of the great day of God Almighty, which is **now impending and immediately about to fall**, must be given, and for this purpose Jehovah says to you: 'Ye are my witnesses'" (*WT*, 1 May 1934, 139).

"Armageddon is near" (Rutherford, *Supremacy*, 36). "The American government has been weighed in the balance and found wanting. It cannot endure. Together with all other nations, it shall fall" (ibid., 38).

"**It is not the message of any man**, but the message from God's Word delivered according to his will" (Rutherford, *Righteous Ruler*, 7).

"Satan knows that it is **only a short time until Armageddon**.... The great change from unrighteousness to righteous rule or control of the world is **impending**" (ibid., 14-15).

"The execution of this final judgment must take place now within **a short time**, because the end of the world has been reached..." (Rutherford, *Angels*, 43-44).

"Jehovah having purposed to inaugurate a righteous rule of the world, he is certain to do it. The day of the wicked reign is **nearly at an end**" (*1935 Yearbook*, 162).

1935

"Universal War Near" was a speech given by Rutherford in the Los Angeles Shrine Auditorium on January 13, 1935. The *Golden Age* issue carrying the message states that it "is widely considered the most impressive talk Judge Rutherford has ever given..." (*GA*, Feb. 13, 1935, 291).

In 1918, Rutherford claimed that World War I would end soon so a testimony could be given concerning the Kingdom: "The Scriptural evidence and the physical facts strongly indicate that **such witness work is now almost done, and when it is done the universal war will begin**.... Universal war is absolutely certain to come, and that soon, and no power can stop it.... During the **few remaining months** until the breaking of that universal cataclysm the powers that rule the nations of earth will continue to make treaties and tell the people that by such means they will keep the world peace and bring prosperity" (ibid., 298).

"The present time is really a thrilling time to those who are devoted to the Lord, because they can see the forces getting into battle array and they know that the great fight **must be very near**" (*WT*, 15 Feb. 1935, 56).

"Everything indicates that Armageddon is **very near**" (*GA*, 10 Apr. 1935, 432).

"In the last of these three wonderful books [*Vindication I, II, III*] the Jonadabs (people of good will fore-shadowed by Jonadab) are Scripturally identified as the 'millions now living that will never die.' The destruction of the Devil and all his forces **is imminent**" (ibid., 445).

A letter to Rutherford: "Some of the 'elders' say the battle of Armageddon will be twenty-five years hence; but we are taught of Jehovah through his Word, which you, dear Brother Rutherford have made so *clear*, that it is but **a little way ahead**. The prophecies *prove* it. **We are nearing the midnight hour!**" (*WT*, 15 May 1935, 158).

"When shall Armageddon be fought?... The League of Nations is the desolating abomination spoken of by Daniel the prophet. (Daniel 12:11) Concerning it Jesus said that its coming into view would be an evidence that **Armageddon is just ahead**" (Rutherford, *Government—Hiding the Truth, Why?*, 31).

"A trumpet sound is symbolic of a warning, and in fulfillment of this part of the prophecy Jehovah's witnesses, under the command of the Lord Jesus Christ, now sound the message of the Lord, which message gives warning to the organization that now rules the earth, informing them that the battle of **Armageddon is about to begin**" (Rutherford, *Universal War Near*, 47-48).

"The Scriptures' being fully supported by the physical facts, including the present-day miserable conditions of 'Christendom,' is further proof to the remnant that Armageddon is **near at hand**" (*WT*, 1 July 1935, 203).

"The crisis is here because the end of the Devil's reign is **at hand**. Soon Christ Jesus will destroy all of the Devil's organization visible and invisible, and that includes all who take their stand on the side of the Devil" (*1936 Yearbook*, 29-30).

"Now the remnant have heard Jehovah's words telling of the battle of Armageddon that draws **very near**, and they stand in awe and fear before the Lord" (ibid., 5 Nov.).

1936

"The revelation of the book of Job to God's people is another evidence that **we are rapidly approaching the great battle** of Almighty God and, after it, the blessings of God's kingdom on earth" (*WT*, 15 Jan. 1936, 32).

"The time **is at hand** when the great and final war, the great battle of the great day of God Almighty, will be fought ... the Devil assembles all his forces for that war" (Rutherford, *Choosing, Riches or Ruin?*, 47).

"The day of Armageddon is **rapidly approaching**..." (ibid., 60).

"The kingdom is here and **soon** will destroy all that oppose it. Those who rely upon Jehovah's promises know this to be true.... The day for the destruction of the wicked organization under Satan is **now at hand**" (Rutherford, *Riches*, 358).

"Satan knows that **shortly** he must fight the Lord, and therefore he prepares for the conflict" (*WT*, 1 Aug. 1936, 236).

"**To say that Armageddon is far off is merely expressing the opinion of man**; it is speaking arbitrarily, out of human shortsightedness and without the due consideration of the Scriptures and the present progress of Jehovah's work" (*WT*, 1 Sept. 1936, 270).

"If the Devil knows the shortness of his own time, Jehovah's witnesses should likewise know that their **time is short** to do the work before Armageddon starts" (ibid., 271).

"It is not for them [remnant] to know just how soon the curse will fall, that is to say, just what hour or year Armageddon will take place. They certainly know that it **cannot be far removed** from the present day, because that work marked out for them, and which they are doing, immediately precedes Armageddon" (*WT*, 1 Dec. 1936, 365).

1937

"The question is, Will Great Britain and America become Fascist under the dominating control of the Roman Catholic Hierarchy? The Scriptures and the facts appear to fully support that conclusion" (Rutherford, *Enemies*, 291).

"Those who are diligent to grasp the truths that are placed before them are lifted far above the present sad conditions of this world and see the **incontrovertible proof that the time of deliverance is at hand**" (*WT*, 1 July 1937, 204).

"... 'For the Devil is come down unto you, knowing that he hath but a **short time**.' A short time for what? A short time to prepare for the great battle of God Almighty, the battle of Armageddon, which is **just ahead**" (Rutherford, *Armageddon*, 33-34).

"The **indisputable facts** show that the world's greatest tribulation is **at the door** and that there is only one way of escape" (ibid., 53).

"Jehovah has appointed the day to fully recompense that wicked crowd, and the time for the expression of his wrath appears to be **very near**.... The time of the execution of Jehovah's wrath against the wicked is **near at hand**" (*WT*, 15 Nov. 1937, 339).

1938

"What then is to be expected? The Scriptures answer: God's 'strange work,' that is, his witness work, quickly thereafter to be followed by his 'strange act,' which is Armageddon, the battle of the great day of God Almighty, the worst tribulation that ever came upon the world, and which shall be the last.... **The time limit is up**. God's kingdom is here, and **Armageddon is impending**" (Rutherford, *Face the Facts*, 9).

"Now prove to yourself that the end of evil is at hand, a new and righteous government has begun ruling in the midst of man's enemies, earth shall be made a Paradise, and **millions of people of good will now living will never die!**" (ibid., 62).

"Every thoughtful person senses some great trouble coming upon the world and that it is **impending and about to fall**" (Rutherford, *Warning*, 19).

"To be sure, no man can say precisely what day or year Jehovah's battle at Armageddon will be fought, but it is easy to be seen that now conditions among the people are such as to indicate that **a great crisis is near**" (*WT*, 1 Sept. 1938, 269).

"**Soon it** [League of Nations] **will perish in the battle of Armageddon**, together with all the Devil's institutions..." (**Cons.**, 19 Oct. 1938, 9).

"Did Judge Rutherford make it plain as to what the Lord would do to the Roman Catholic Hierarchy...? He did. Blow by blow, proof by proof, the case against them was presented with so many Bible corroborations that no doubt could remain even in the mind of the pope, if he believed in God, that **destruction of the whole gang was imminent**. This bunch of religionists, whom the Lord hates, are to be destroyed by their erstwhile allies, namely, the radical element represented by the Nazi-Fascist-Communist combine, because God has decreed it so..." (*The Messenger*, Nov. 1938, 10).

"...Mark the words of Jesus, which definitely seem to discourage the bearing of children immediately before or during Armageddon.... It would therefore appear that there is **no reasonable or scriptural injunction to bring children into the world immediately before Armageddon, where we now are**" (*WT*, 1 Nov.

1938, 324).

1939

"When may we expect the Theocratic Government to rule? **Satan's time is up**, and Jehovah has now enthroned Christ Jesus and sent him forth to rule while the enemy still stubbornly holds on and refuses to vacate.... What, then, must quickly follow? The Scriptures answer, Armageddon, the battle of the great day of God Almighty" (Rutherford, *Government and Peace*, 25).

"Q. 42. Why do Jehovah's witnesses now rejoice at the increased opposition by the religionists?... A. They rejoice to suffer for the vindication of God's name ... and the desperate attempt to stop Jehovah's work shows that **Armageddon is near**" (*Model Study 2, Face the Facts*, 40).

"Q. 32. What scriptures show that Armageddon will follow **immediately after the completion of the present witness work?**" (ibid., 46).

"All the evidence, both of the Bible and that of the physical facts which are well known to all persons who try to observe, overwhelmingly proves that the battle of **Armageddon is impending and is very near**" (Rutherford, *Salvation*, 25).

In an ad for Rutherford booklets: "The organization of the world is streamlined for its plunge into destruction at Armageddon, its dead end! You had better GET OFF NOW, before the plunge.... There's **still a little time** in this 'the day of salvation'" (*Salvation*, rear page).

"Their [Jehovah's witnesses] purpose is to do God's will, and His will at this time is that the Day of Vengeance shall be declared throughout the earth, the proclamation that **Armageddon is at the doors**" (*The Messenger*, Aug. 1939, 3).

"Fanatical Fascists and Nazi dictators, with the aid and co-operation of the Roman Catholic Hierarchy at Vatican City are now wrecking continental Europe. **They may for a brief period of time gain control of the British Empire and of America**, and then, God declares, He will act and through Christ Jesus ... will completely destroy all such organizations" (Rutherford, *Fascism or Freedom*, 31).

Concluding Observations

Timothy White, a Jehovah's Witness, thoroughly researched the movement and its publications. His observations concerning Rutherford's writings are pertinent: "Rutherford wrote a tremendous quantity of matter about Armageddon.... Towards the close of his ministry he used to spend about half of each year's *Watchtowers* writing about Armageddon. He seemed to take great relish in describing how completely the wicked would be destroyed."[2] As one reads the details of Rutherford's "expositions" of Scripture, it is obvious that he was **Armageddon obsessed**.[3] But all his predictions failed concerning Armageddon's outbreak, for example, as: "impending," "about to fall," "imminent," "very near," "at the door," and calculated as being a "few" months away.

Notes

1. Rutherford, *Vindication I* (1931), 338-39.
2. Timothy White, *A People For His Name* (New York: Vantage Press, 1967, 234.
3. Ibid., 234-35.

29

The "Man of Sin (Lawlessness)" (2 Thess. 2:3)

Many Watch Tower followers left the movement in the years after Rutherford became the president of the Society. Rutherford himself makes reference to this exodus: "For a time they made progress; and then many became tired and weary in well doing or thought more highly of themselves than they should think or became lawless, while others became offended. These turned away, so that today the larger percentage of those who withdrew from so-called organized Christianity have turned aside and again gone back into the world."[1] Rutherford would later identify those defectors who opposed the Watch Tower Society as a fulfillment of prophecy.

In the September 15, 1930, *Watch Tower* article, "The Man of Sin," Rutherford writes: "For a long time this scripture [2 Thess. 2:3] relating to the 'man of sin' has been interpreted as applying to the **Papal church system**."[2] He then presents several reasons why this view, taught in Watch Tower publications **for over 50 years,**[3] was wrong, and then concludes: "We should look for **a fulfillment at the present time of these prophetic words** written by the apostle."[4] Rutherford explains that the "'man of sin' would first receive the truth concerning the second coming of the Lord and his kingdom and would look for and expect the second coming of the Lord and the setting up of his kingdom; that there would be a disappointment on the part of this class and they would say, 'My Lord delayeth his coming....'" The "man of sin," then, is made up of those who were **former supporters of the Watch Tower Society who had defected and exalted themselves and then vigorously opposed the Society**. They are also identified as the "evil servant" class.[5] "The 'man of sin' was **once in line for the kingdom** but looked forward to enjoying the kingdom wholly for selfish purposes, and he is specifically named 'the son of perdition.'"[6] Rutherford explained: "Long centuries ago he [God] caused Paul to see the coming 'man of sin' and to write a warning to those who should be on the earth in 'the day of Christ,' which is this very day where we now are."[7]

According to more recent Watch Tower publications, the "man of sin" (the "man of lawlessness" class) is represented by the clergy of Christendom: "The foretold 'lawless' one is a composite 'man,' the whole religious clergy of the professed 'Christian' church."[8] "Those who sincerely look into the Bible can readily see that the 'man of lawlessness' class has indeed developed according to the apostle Paul's prophetic words. This composite 'man' is clearly identifiable as the **clergy of Christendom**."[9]

Notes

1. *WT*, 1 Dec. 1927, 355.
2. *WT*, 15 Sept. 1930, 275.
3. *WTR*, "The Antichrist," Dec. 1879, 54-56.
4. *WT*, 15 Sept. 1930, 276.
5. Ibid., 277-78.
6. Ibid., 280.
7. Ibid., 281.
8. *God's Kingdom of 1000 Years Has Approached* (1973), 380. In Rutherford's article on the "Man of Sin," not only did he reject the view that the "man of sin" was the "Papal system" but added, "Nor can it be said that Satan's organization, as an entirety, is the 'man of sin, the son of perdition'" (*WT*, 15 Sept. 1930, 276).
9. *WT*, 15 Apr. 1975, 254.

30.

The Great Multitude
(Company, Crowd)
of Revelation 7:9

The correct interpretation of the "great multitude" (company, crowd)[1] is of major importance, as it relates to one's present relationship to God as well as one's eternal destiny.[2] In the discussion of this subject in the February 15, 1966, *Watchtower*, it is asked: "Who is this 'great crowd'?" The answer: "This was long a mystery. In the very first year [1879] that the magazine *Zion's Watch Tower* was published the attention of readers was called to this 'great multitude.' (Rev. 7:9, AV) But it was thought to be a spiritual class of Christians with a heavenly destiny."[3]

Thirty years later, Russell's teaching on the subject is clear in this question and answer in *What Pastor Russell Said*:

> *Question (1909): Does the Great Company receive life direct from God on the spirit plane?* Answer: Yes, they receive life direct in that they have been begotten of the Holy Spirit, and when they are begotten they are just the same way as the little flock, because we are called in the one hope of our calling. They do not make their calling and election sure, but not being worthy of second death, they therefore receive life on the spirit plane.[4]

This interpretation would continue in the years after Russell's death (1916) as the 1966 *Watchtower* (cited above) states: "In 1930, the book *Light*, in two volumes, gave a verse-for-verse commentary on the book of Revelation, but it still applied the 'great multitude' of Revelation 7:9-17 (*AV*) to a spirit-begotten class of professed Christians who, after a martyr's death at Armageddon, would each 'get life as a spirit creature,' but secondary to the Bride of Christ."[5] Why is this interpretation in *Light* significant? Because of what is claimed for the book. The Preface states:

> **Prior to 1930 there never was a satisfactory explanation of The Revelation published**, the manifest reason being it was not God's due time for his servants to have an understanding thereof.... **It now seems clear that it is God's due time for his servants to understand** that great prophecy so long clothed in mystery. A blessed time is therefore at hand for those who read and understand and obey.[6]

Later, in the text, it is claimed that "in **God's due time he** has sent forth information on the subject [of the great multitude] through *The Watch Tower*."[7] One such *Watch Tower* article is "The Great Multitude," in the January 15, 1927, issue, where Rutherford asks, "Is the great multitude made up of human beings or beings possessing the spirit nature? This question we must determine from the Scriptures." After discussion, it is concluded that "**all the facts and the scriptures** bearing upon the matter under consideration show that those who form the great multitude **constitute a spirit class, born on the spirit plane**."[8]

In the third volume of *Vindication* (1932), Rutherford writes: "Ever and anon **someone advances the conclusion that the 'great multitude' will not be a spiritual class**. The prophecy of Ezekiel shows that **such conclusion is erroneous**. The fact that their position is seven steps higher than the outside shows that **they must be made spirit creatures.... They must be spirit creatures** in order to be in the outer court of the divine structure described by Ezekiel."[9]

Rutherford's statement that the "great multitude" members "must be spirit creatures" is definite—and why not? In the introduction to this *Vindication* volume it is claimed: "That vision of Ezekiel concerning the temple has been a mystery for ages and generations, but **now is due to be understood**. The Scriptures and the physical facts both show that this prophecy was not due to be understood by God's people on earth until the year 1932."[10]

But just **three years later**: "In 1935 **a bright flash of light revealed** that the **great crowd mentioned at Revelation 7:9-17 was not a secondary heavenly class**."[11] Rutherford's "new light" was explained in two articles in the August 1 and 15, 1935, *Watchtower*. The introduction in the first article is typical of other "new light" presentations: "Jehovah makes known his purpose to his creatures when it pleases Him. In his own due time God reveals his secrets according to his pleasure."[12] "Among the Scriptures that could not be understood until the coming of the Lord to the temple is that of Revelation concerning the 'great multitude.'"[13] The former view, "held for many years," is summarized, and the question posed: "Do such conclusions appear to be reasonable and supported by the Word of God?... Are the great multitude, mentioned in Revelation seven, a spirit-begotten class, and will they ultimately attain perfection as spirit creatures? and will they have a place in heaven as servants of the royal house?"[14] After discussion, Rutherford repeats the question and states his conclusion: "The answer must be in the negative. **There is no scripture giving warrant** to the conclusion that the great multitude is a spirit company or will be in the spiritual realm of the kingdom of God.... It appears to be the **Lord's due time** to make these matters concerning the 'great multitude' to be understood...."[15] He even argues that the great multitude "could not come into existence ... prior to 1918."[16]

When these Watch Tower statements and claims made over the years are compared, what contradictory views and conclusions have been articulated as "due time" light based on Scripture! Why is one to be accepted over the other? The challenge that the **1935 "new light" was unscriptural** would come years later, in 1980, from within the Watch Tower Society headquarters.

The "Great Crowd"—Conflict in Brooklyn

In his study, *Where Is the "Great Crowd" Serving God?* ("A discussion of Revelation 7:9-17 in the light of events at the Watchtower Society's headquarters in 1980"), ex-Bethelite Jon Mitchell reports:

> In the spring and early summer of 1980 several long-time members of the Society's headquarters staff (including members of the Writing Department who had researched and written most of the *Aid To Bible Understanding* book) were either dismissed, disfellowshipped or reassigned to another job after lengthy interrogations. One of the first doctrinal matters about which there seemed to be some dispute that became known to other members of the Bethel family pertained to the "great crowd" of Revelation 7:9. **Apparently some were questioning the basis for the Society's teach-**

ing that this is an earthly class instead of a heavenly one as most Bible commentators believe and as the Society itself taught until the year 1935.[17]

In the summary of his study, Mitchell concludes: "The Watchtower Society explains the 'great crowd' of Revelation 7:9-17 to be an earthly class even though they are spoken of as being in God's *naos* [temple] in verse 15 of this chapter.... It is unscriptural to teach that the 'great crowd' could be serving in 'the earthly court of the spiritual temple' of God."[18] In making the point that the "great crowd" is in heaven and not an earthly class, several references (of many) may be cited.[19] In Revelation 7:15 the great crowd "are before the throne of God; and they are rendering him sacred service day and night **in his temple**." Where is "his temple" located? Revelation 11:19 and 14:17 place the temple "in heaven." And Revelation 19:1 sees this "great crowd **in heaven**" (*NWT*). Finally, the Watch Tower book *The Finished Mystery* (1917) also identifies this "great crowd in heaven" in Revelation 19:1 as being the same as the "great crowd" in Revelation 7:9-10.[20]

Notes

1. The terms "multitude," "company," and "crowd" are synonymous. The term "crowd" is from the *NWT*.
2. See *Comments from the Friends*, Spring 1995, 2-4, 8.
3. *WT*, 15 Feb. 1966, 116.
4. L. W. Jones (ed.), *What Pastor Russell Said* (Chicago Bible Students, 1917 reprint), 297.
5. *WT*, 15 Feb. 1966, 118.
6. Rutherford, *Light I* (1930), 5-6.
7. Ibid., 94.
8. *WT*, 15 Jan. 1927, 19-20.
9. Rutherford, *Vindication III* (1932), 204.
10. Ibid., 5.
11. *WT*, 15 May 1995, 20.
12. *WT*, 1 Aug. 1935, 227.
13. Ibid., 228.
14. Ibid.
15. Ibid., 229.
16. Ibid., 233.
17. Jon Mitchell, *Where Is the "Great Crowd" Serving God?*, 1.
18. Ibid., 19. Jon Mitchell was in full-time service for ten years (1971-81) as a Jehovah's Witness, the last five years in Brooklyn headquarters. Much of the research for his *Where Is The "Great Crowd" Serving God?* was done while he was there in 1980 and 1981. The study is available from Biblical Research & Commentary International, P.O. Box 83091, Milwaukee, WI 53223-8391 and Commentary Press, P.O. Box 43532, Atlanta, GA 30336-0532.
19. For additional study and references, see: Mitchell, especially p. 16; Raymond Franz, *In Search of Christian Freedom* (Atlanta: Commentary Press, 1991), 717-20; Ron Rhodes, *Reasoning from the Scriptures with the Jehovah's Witnesses* (Eugene, Oreg.: Harvest House, 1993), chapter 10.
20. Clayton J. Woodworth and George H. Fisher, *The Finished Mystery* (1917), 289. In 1928, Rutherford wrote: "A great number of those who have been less faithful go to make up that unnumbered multitude of Christians who are saved to **life as spirit beings and become servants before the throne of God in heaven. (Rev. 7:9-17)**" (Rutherford, *Reconciliation*, 261).

31.

The "Devil's Calendar"

Jehovah's Witnesses often argue that things identified as of pagan origin ("of the Devil") must be rejected or abandoned regardless of the consequences. An example of this began to appear in the *1935 Year Book*, where a new calendar to replace the Gregorian (in use since the sixteenth century) was published on the page before the daily readings. It is stated that articles in explanation would appear in *The Golden Age*. The calendar for 1935 is identified as "Jehovah's Year of Ransom 1903" (or "The Calendar of Jehovah God").[1] The days of the week and the months are renamed—for example March becomes "Visitment" and Tuesday becomes "Earthday"[2]—and the year consists of only 355 days.

Why such a radical change? Why was a new calendar needed? The March 1, 1935, *Watchtower* explains: "Many persons of the present day have the idea that the calendar generally in use is of divine origin; but in this they are entirely wrong."[3] A brief history of the Gregorian calendar is given, and then the article states:

> According to the Word of God the Gregorian calendar is entirely wrong, and this alone is proof that the making of that calendar and its introduction were not by God's direction but were **done under the influence of Satan**, the enemy of Jehovah. Now, since the coming of the Lord Jesus Christ and his enthronement and his gathering together of his faithful followers, the time seems at hand to more clearly understand God's purposes as expressed in his Word, and this includes the manner of measuring time. **It seems proper and fitting that we should try to ascertain the correct way of measuring time and give publication thereto.**[4]

A full explanation of the new calendar was published in three very detailed articles (totaling 65 pages) in *The Golden Age*, beginning with the March 13, 1935, issue. This new Jehovah's Witness calendar was the creation of the magazine's editor, Clayton J. Woodworth.[5] Some excerpts from the series follow.

"In this series of articles it will be shown that all the foregoing calendars [Jewish, Roman, Greek, Julian, Mohammedan, French Revolution, Gregorian] are **calendars of the Devil**.... Jehovah God is nowhere mentioned in the Gregorian calendar. It would suit Satan well to have Him lost sight of altogether."[6]

"The Devil, of course, was the one who induced the ancestors of the present generation to name all the days of the week after heathen gods and goddesses."[7] "...The calendar of Jehovah God ... it is hoped and believed, will permanently replace, as far as calendars are concerned, the efforts of Satan to hide some of God's beautiful truth, now, since 1918, coming out from his temple in such a refreshing stream."[8]

An ad for the series at the end of the first part states: "Read 'THE SECOND HAND IN THE TIME-PIECE OF GOD,' a series of articles beginning in this issue, and you will **appreciate why a new calendar should be adopted by those who honor the creator.**"[9]

A significant statement concerning the chronology of the new calendar is made in the March 27 installment:

> Would any of the "millions now living" be stumbled by the discovery that they **have a hundred years longer to live than they once thought?** Hardly, Would they be stumbled because they were consecrated with the understanding on their part that **six thousand years of human history ended in 1874?**... Nothing in the Scriptures says that Christ Jesus would have to wait until the beginning of the seventh thousand years of human history before the second advent would occur and the Day of Jehovah begin, in which Christ, as Jehovah's vicegerent, rules in the midst of His enemies.[10]

Russell's borrowed chronology had the 6,000 years run out in 1874, with Adam's creation date as 4128 B.C. The new view presented in the articles dates Adam's creation at 4028 B.C.[11] Another part of Russell's system was being dismantled. It appears that some *Golden Age* readers were bothered by this new date, as the May 1, 1935, *Watchtower* warns the brethren:

> God's people should keep in mind the **"pyramid" delusion** and the speculations that accompanied the study of chronology [published in the Society's materials], and the pitfalls into which these things led many. Do not fall into a similar trap. It is of far more importance to understand our commission and to perform it than to understand at just what time Adam was created. Be reasonable and moderate. Avoid wild speculations as to at what time and in what manner things future come to pass. Be sure that you always are guided by the counsel of the Lord's Word. **The statements in** *The Golden Age* **are not dogmatic, but are worthy of due and careful consideration.**[12]

The first article of the series specifically states that the new calendar material was not like the "pyramid" delusion ("This is no nonsense, or worse than nonsense from the Great Pyramid in Egypt...").[13] The 4028 B.C. creation date would not become official until 1943 with the publication of *"The Truth Shall Make You Free."*[14]

And finally, what about naming one of the months "Jehovah"?

> The month [Jehovah] which is named for Jehovah God takes the place of what, under **the Devil's calendar**, was the first month of the year. In his own expression of His will on the subject, God has made it clear that the first month of the year (*Redemption*) is appropriately named.... Some may wonder whether by calling a month "Jehovah" the name will be brought into common use. It *should* be brought into common use....[15] People who have been writing 'January' all their lives, in honor of the two-faced god of war, should be quite willing now to often write the name of the true and living God. **The due time has come: Jehovah God will not be pushed into a corner any more.** The theologians of the Devil can say nothing....[16]

Conclusion

God had spoken through his organization. The message was clear: it was "due time" to remove the "Devil's calendar" and replace it with the Scripturally proven theocratic "Calendar of Jehovah God." Yet in the years following this new "truth" it has been completely ignored by Jehovah's Witnesses. No one, not even Brooklyn headquarters, uses the "Calendar of Jehovah." It appears that the Witnesses were content to remain disobedient to their own published "truth" and to continue to refer to the "Devil's calendar" in keeping their appointments and planning their lives.

Notes

1. *GA*, 13 Mar. 1935, 380.
2. *1935 Year Book* (1934), 168.
3. *WT*, 1 Mar. 1935, 80.
4. Ibid.
5. M. James Penton, *Apocalypse Delayed* (2nd ed.; Toronto: University of Toronto Press, 1997), 66. Penton describes Woodworth as being "more than a little eccentric." He "denied the germ theory of disease, constantly attacked smallpox vaccination as the filthy custom of injecting animal pus into the human system, and carried on a vendetta against the aluminum industry. Aluminum cookware, according to Woodworth, was poisonous" (ibid.). "Fortunately, Judge Rutherford had the good sense never to allow Woodworth's theocratic calendar to be used" (ibid, 68). An illustration of what Penton refers to is this statement from the May 1, 1929, *Golden Age*: "Thinking people would rather have smallpox than vaccination, because the latter sows the seed of syphilis, cancers, eczema, erysipelas, scrofula, consumption, every leprosy and many other loathsome afflictions. Hence the practice of vaccination is a crime, an outrage and a delusion" (502). Woodworth is prominent in the *Proclaimers* history (650-53). He was one of the compilers/writers of *The Finished Mystery*, one of the eight sentenced to prison in 1918, and he served as editor of *The Golden Age*, renamed *Consolation* (1937) from 1919-1946 (ibid., 634, 652; *Awake!*, 22 Feb. 1952, 25-26).
6. *GA*, 13 Mar. 1935, 356.
7. Ibid., 358.
8. Ibid., 365.
9. Ibid., 383.
10. *GA*, 27 Mar. 1935, 413.
11. *GA*, 13 Mar. 1935, 376.
12. *WT*, 1 May 1935, 142.
13. *GA*, 13 Mar. 1935, 355.
14. *"The Truth Shall Make You Free"* (1943), 152. The 4028 B.C. date was adjusted to 4026 B.C. in *"The Kingdom Is at Hand"* (1944), 171. See *Jehovah's Witnesses—Proclaimers of God's Kingdom* (133, 631-33), for the explanation for the original date and why it was changed.
15. *GA*, 10 Apr. 1935, 446.
16. Ibid., 447.

32.

Face the Facts (1938)

The index of *Jehovah's Witnesses—Proclaimers of God's Kingdom* includes coverage on the 1938 London convention, Rutherford's "Face the Facts" talk in Royal Albert Hall (Sunday, September 10), and the *Face the Facts* booklet in four places.[1] In summary, from these one learns that "more than 10,000 jammed the auditorium" (pictured) "while millions more heard by radio."[2] The message "was carried to some 50 convention cities around the globe," adding about 200,000 more hearers, and almost 1,000 Witnesses marched through the business district of London wearing placards advertising the talk along with "Religion is a Snare and a Racket" signs. Later that week, "to neutralize the hostile reaction of some of the public, signs reading 'Serve God and Christ the King'" were added.[3] Distribution of the *Face the Facts* booklet brought a Haarlem court summons in 1939 "to answer the charge of insulting a group of the Dutch populace."[4] All one is told about the discourse itself is that it was "straightforward."[5]

With a first printing of 10,000,000 copies, distribution of the *Face the Facts* booklet, which also included Rutherford's "Fill the Earth" talk, would reach 12,000,000 worldwide.[6] The October 5, 1938, *Consolation* reported: "Judge Rutherford is back in Brooklyn after delivering the **two greatest discourses, to the greatest audiences in human history**. It is the hand of God," and that "upward of three million people listened to **Jehovah's thrilling ultimatums** delivered through Judge Rutherford, his servant."[7] Of the many cablegrams received commenting on the "Face the Facts" talk, two read, "Grandest message of our time" and "Greatest revelation of truth since Pentecost."[8]

The publisher's statement in the booklet begins: "WHAT ARE THE FACTS? These were not uncovered by some fact-finding body of prejudiced and partial men, but by Almighty God Himself" and advertising for the booklet identifies the contents as "history making addresses."[9]

What was the basic message of Rutherford's "Face the Facts" talk which received such laudatory comments? It "was a daring challenge to the people of the world to recognize the serious condition in which the world found itself and warned the democratic peoples of the **approaching Catholic-Fascist bid for world control**," to be quickly followed by Armageddon.[10]

What were some of the prophetic understandings communicated in Rutherford's speech as recorded in the booklet? "The time limit is up. God's kingdom is here, and **Armageddon is impending**."[11] "When the **totalitarian Catholic combine gains control of the British Isles, which it is certain to do**, then all liberties of the people will be at an end."[12] "The **totalitarian combine is going to get control of England and America**. You cannot prevent it. Do not try. Your safety is on the Lord's side; but **there really will be but a short time that the combine will hold sway**, because it is written in God's Word [quotes 1 Thess. 5:3]."[13]

Jehovah God's kingdom has begun. The end of Satan's world has come. God is now carrying on his "strange work," which consists of his witnesses under the command of the Lord giving testimony of the kingdom to the peoples of earth. **After that work is finished, then immediately follows Armageddon**, which will completely wreck every institution and every part thereof that stands in opposition to the kingdom under Christ. Only the Lord's "other sheep," the Jonadabs, who compose the "great multitude," will survive that great tribulation.[14]

When was Armageddon's destruction to be expected? A previous quote indicated that "Armageddon was impending."

Rutherford's second discourse, "Fill the Earth," is also included in the *Face the Facts* booklet. In it he addresses the "great multitude" who will survive Armageddon. They are told that since the procreation mandate to "fill the earth" given to Adam and Eve would not begin for them until after Armageddon, it would be **right to postpone marriage and childbearing**.[15]

"There are now on earth Jonadabs devoted to the Lord and who doubtless will prove faithful. **Would it be Scripturally proper for them to now marry and to begin to rear children? No**, is the answer, which is supported by the Scriptures."[16]

"It would be far better to be unhampered and without burdens, that they may do the Lord's will now, as the Lord commands, and also be without hindrance during Armageddon."[17]

> Those Jonadabs who now contemplate marriage, it would seem, would do better if they **wait a few years, until the fiery storm of Armageddon is gone**, and to then enter the marital relationship and enjoy the blessings of participating in filling the earth with righteous and perfect children....[18] What should the Jonadabs do now? They should devote themselves wholly to the kingdom interests of Christ, they should see to it that their substance is now used to the glory of God and his kingdom, and therefore should do all within their power to advance the kingdom interest.... **Now the glorious kingdom is here in full sight and will soon be in full operation**, and those who love God will delight now to do all within their power to make known to others the blessings of that kingdom.[19]

How did the Witnesses respond to Rutherford's instructions? According to insider Timothy White,

> This lecture **resulted in a strong communal bias against marriage** among Jehovah's Witnesses, and one who dared to break this tradition was considered **weak in faith**. Marriage was considered to be the **first step in "falling out of the truth" or leaving the Witness movement**. It was even difficult in some places to get marriage solemnized by a Witness ceremony. This strong attitude caused many a young couple to leave the movement to avoid adverse comment, and so the gossipers were justified in their prediction that their faith had weakened. This prejudice continued until the early 1950's when it became clear to the leaders that it was getting extreme.[20]

And finally, said Rutherford: "That 'strange work' is now in progress and soon shall be finished."[21] "**Armageddon is near,** and the conclusion of God's 'strange work' is nearer. We must make haste in doing that work."[22]

Rutherford continued his "Nazi-Fascist-Hierarchy combine" world conquest teaching until his death on January 8, 1942. For example, the *Watchtower* of December 1, 1941, warns the reader: "Mark this in the light of the infallible divine prophecy: that **the totalitarian, arbitrary rule will overrun all the nations of the earth in the very near future. Some makeshift of peace will be made,** and the chief credit for such patched-up peace will be given to the religious element, the Roman Catholic Hierarchy. **The totalitarian rule will be fully in control**, and then will appear THE SIGN. The prophecy of Daniel indicates what shall follow."[23]

Rutherford did not live to see how history again proved his (the Society's) prophetic "insights" a complete failure. When it became evident that Rutherford's scenario of totalitarian victory and rule would not take place and that the Allies would win the war, the September 1, 1944, *Watchtower* presented a new interpretation of Revelation 12:15-17.[24]

Notes

1. *Jehovah's Witnesses—Proclaimers of God's Kingdom* (1993), 80, 267, 447, 682.
2. Ibid., 80.
3. Ibid., 267, 447.
4. Ibid., 682.
5. Ibid. 267.
6. *Jehovah's Witnesses in the Divine Purpose* (1959), 145.
7. *Cons.*, 5 Oct. 1938, 18.
8. Ibid.
9. *WT*, 1 Jan. 1939, 16.
10. *Jehovah's Witnesses in the Divine Purpose*, 145.
11. Rutherford, *Face the Facts* (1938), 9.
12. Ibid, 20.
13. Ibid., 27.
14. Ibid., 28.
15. Ibid., 46-47.
16. Ibid., 46.
17. Ibid., 47.
18. Ibid., 50.
19. Ibid., 50-51.
20. Timothy White, *A People for His Name* (New York: Vantage Press, 1967), 280.
21. *Face the Facts*, 57.
22. Ibid., 58.
23. *WT*, 1 Dec. 1941, 362.
24. *WT*, 1 Sept. 1944, 266-67. The "Nazi-Fascist-Hierarchy combine" would be overcome and lose the war and would be replaced by a revived League of Nations—the United Nations: "Now, according to the unfailing Word of God and all indications of the times, that submerged creature is due to reappear after the global war, in the form of some organization of international cooperation for peace, security and freedom from aggression. It will be hailed as man's last hope. The political forces behind it will exert pressure to have all men worship the Devil's visible organization under this final form of man-rule. Those worshiping it will receive a mark of support and collaboration which will doom them to destruction at Armageddon" (ibid., 267).

33.

Beth-Shan and the Return of the "Princes"

With the publication of *Jehovah's Witnesses—Proclaimers of God's Kingdom* (1993), many Jehovah's Witnesses were for the first time introduced to Beth-Sarim ("House of the Princes") in San Diego. It was identified as the winter residence of Watch Tower Bible and Tract Society president Joseph F. Rutherford.[1] As some reviewers have concluded, the coverage on the mansion in this official Jehovah's Witnesses' history is less than candid.[2] Beth-Sarim, built in 1929 and sold in 1948, is pictured and mentioned a number of times in older Watch Tower publications. An adjacent Society property, known as Beth-Shan ("House of Security"), is mentioned by name only once—in the *Consolation* of May 27, 1942—as a second location for Rutherford's burial. The request for a permit for interment below Beth-Sarim was not approved.[3] The article explains:

> [The] new location for interment was in almost the center of the property known as Beth-Shan, which is roughly 75 acres of canyon and mesa land, adjoining Beth-Sarim but separated by a half-mile width of canyon. This property, also belonging to [the] WATCHTOWER, has one small and one large dwelling upon it and a few out-houses, and consists of some fruit trees and other cultivated patches in aggregate about seven acres, and about 65 acres of unreclaimed brush, either too steep, or rocky, or inaccessible for development.[4]

This request was also denied.

Research reveals that Beth-Shan, in its own way, compares with Beth-Sarim in significance, but it has received little attention. Predictions concerning the return of the "princes," and related teachings sometimes connected with these residences, are important in evaluating the Watch Tower's claim of being God's chosen channel of Biblical understanding. The subjects of Beth-Shan and the "princes" are the focus of the following study.

More Property for the "Princes"

Watch Tower publications and the deed to the property reveal that Beth-Sarim ("House of the Princes") was built and held in trust as a residence for the soon-to-be resurrected "ancient worthies" or "princes."[5] While not generally known, the Beth-Shan house and the property improvements had the same purpose. This is shown by the deed, which transfers the property to the Society.

The Beth-Shan property was purchased on February 3, 1939, by William P. Heath, Jr. He was a Watch

Tower Board of Directors member and Rutherford's confidant and secretary.[6] The deed, dated May 20, 1940, when this property was conveyed to the Watch Tower Bible and Tract Society, reads in part:

> TO HAVE AND TO HOLD IN TRUST FOR THE FOLLOWING PURPOSES, to wit: Whereas the grantor herein W. P. Heath, Jr., was entrusted with the duty and obligation of improving the premises hereinbefore described, and a number of persons who are wholly devoted to the great THEOCRACY under Christ Jesus the King, furnished the money for the purpose of improving said premises, and WHEREAS the said W. P. Heath, Jr., acting in his own behalf and in behalf of other persons so interested in improving said premises, **has erected a house and other improvements** thereon to be used for the purpose hereinafter stated, and WHEREAS the grantor and the other parties interested, and who have contributed towards the improvement of said premises, **thoroughly believe and expect the return of faithful men to earth who are hereafter named, and who according to the Scriptures (Psalm 45:16 and Isaiah 32:1) shall be made the visible rulers on earth, and desire to prepare said property for them.** NOW THEREFORE **this trust is created and the said trustee shall hold the title to said property in trust for the use and benefit of the following named persons, whose names appear in the Bible at the Book of Hebrews,** chapter eleven, verses one to forty, to wit: Abel, Enoch, Noah, Abraham, Isaac, Jacob, Sara, Joseph, Moses, Rahab, Gideon, Barak, Samson, Jephthae, David, Samuel, Until such time as the aforementioned persons return and identify themselves to the legal representatives of the said WATCH TOWER BIBLE & TRACT SOCIETY and by the consent of said Society take possession and control of said premises, the President of the WATCH TOWER BIBLE & TRACT SOCIETY shall have the right and be duty bound to direct the management and use of said premises hereby conveyed and to determine who shall be in possession and have the active management thereof.[7]

Heath and his wife resided in the house mentioned in the deed.

Preparing the Beth-Shan Property

During the construction of the Beth-Shan house and other improvements in 1939, twenty-year-old Fred Eason, while searching for Young's Cave (which was on the property),[8] made his way into the area and unintentionally discovered what was taking place there. The Watch Tower project was being built on the remote mesa accessible only by a steep private driveway, which was gated and guarded. The approach to the driveway was by Mission Valley Road (renamed Montezuma), which was not paved at the time. Being rebuffed by several men on horseback, Eason went up to the top of the isolated mesa from another side (Fairmount Avenue) and observed some of the activity taking place that was so secretive and well-protected. There were a number of workmen building the project. While he did not know it at the time, this would not be his last contact with the property.[9]

In April of 1945, Fred Eason met Bruster Gillies, who had moved to San Diego in 1944 to work for Ryan Aircraft. Gillies was looking for land, and he and his wife Betty bought the Beth-Shan property and adjacent acreage, a total of 250 or more acres.[10] Eason visited the large Watch Tower house shortly after the Gillies' purchase in 1945, and he and "Bud" became good friends and business partners. He recalls, "During this period I became well acquainted with Bud's fabulous home and its amenities. At this time nothing had been changed, everything was original."[11]

In 1962, Eason bought about 30 acres of the property, which included the Watch Tower house and other improvements. Originally he intended to tear the house down as he subdivided and graded the land, but decided the house was worth saving. Its furnishings were top quality and it had fine cabinetry. "It was not a tract house by any stretch of the imagination." It also had a basement, which will be described later.[12]

"A great famine is certain ... in the very near future"

The *Watchtower* of November 15, 1941, communicated a warning of impending disaster, "... **A great famine is certain to afflict** the many nations of the earth **in the very near future. The United States is also in line for much suffering**.... The United States is faced with world disaster now impending and about to fall...." At this time it was believed that the war in Europe would lead to Armageddon.[13] This could explain some of the features of the Beth-Shan property. For example, the house had a basement, which is not unusual. But what was unusual was that access to the 10-foot x 20-foot underground room was through a secret trap-door and stairway. No one would know of its existence unless it was shown. It was also lined with shelves for the storage of food and other necessities.

Beth-Shan also had several out buildings: a caretaker's house, a horse barn and stable, a goat barn, and an equipment shed. There was a 4,000-gallon underground tank for diesel fuel, a diesel-powered electric generator, and a workshop. Water was provided by a 425-foot deep well, which was connected to a 2,000-gallon pressure tank, and a 10,000-gallon redwood storage tank. There were two fire hydrants, and water was piped to the house and barns. "They had their own self-sufficiency. They could go for months without city utilities." It is obvious that Beth-Shan was a little-known Witness "Refuge Farm."[14] But there was one feature, that surprised Eason more than anything else.

"FALSE REPORTS"?
"We trust in the Lord for protection"

Under the heading "FALSE REPORTS," the June 1, 1940, *Watchtower* announced that the rumor was untrue that the Society was enlarging Beth-Sarim "as a place of security."[15] And during his testimony before the County Superior Court, April 1-8, 1942, Judge Mundo asked William P. Heath, Jr., "Suppose the Japs were to level that property during an air raid, what would happen then?" Heath answered, "We submit, your honor, that ... we trust in the Lord for protection."[16]

It is obvious that this "false report" concerning Beth-Sarim would accurately relate to what was actually happening on the Beth-Shan part of the Watch Tower's "100-acre estate." And Heath's response, "we trust the Lord for protection," was disingenuous in the light of what was constructed at Beth-Shan shortly after its purchase in February 1939. How so?

The Bomb Shelter

Betty Gillies and Fred Eason each speak of the **bomb shelter, separate from the house**, which had been constructed by the Witnesses on the Beth-Shan property. Fred Eason, who saw it shortly after the Watch Tower sale of the property in 1945, explains that about 250 feet from the house there was a "building that was called the 'goat barn' which was used to stable their goats. To enter the shelter one would go to the small bathroom area at the rear of the building, open the medicine cabinet, and pull a concealed lever inside. A section of the wall would swing open, revealing a stairway down into what can only be identified as a bomb shelter—a room about 30 feet x 15 feet, with a 10-foot-high ceiling. The walls were lined with storage shelves. The cement ceiling of the room was **3 feet thick!**" Someone could go into the bathroom and they would never know the shelter was there. When a house was built on the property in 1967, it was placed on the lot so as to keep the shelter intact, and it still exists today.[17]

The "Princes"

Repeatedly, Watch Tower publications and representatives stressed that according to the Scriptures, the "princes" were due to return shortly, and as already stated, two large residences and their grounds were prepared and held in trust for their use upon their return. The *Consolation* of May 27, 1942, went so far as to claim: "It therefore appears that the return of the princes is a **fundamental teaching of the Scriptures. It is as certain as the truth of God's Word**. Judge Rutherford gave much of his life in endeavoring to bring this vital matter to the people's attention."[18] As it turned out, this so-called "fundamental teaching of the Scriptures ... certain as the truth of God's Word" was "adjusted" a few years later.[19] Watch Tower teachings connected with the resurrection of these Old Testament believers, and statements made promoting Rutherford's burial on the Society's property, provide excellent examples of doctrinal revisionism and demonstrate what happens when human opinion replaces sound interpretation of Scripture.

Prophetic Speculation

What else had been taught concerning the return of these pre-Christian believers? In 1881, it was stated that "prophecies were found which pointed positively to 1874 as the time when Jesus was due to be present, and the resurrection of Daniel [one of the "princes"] was also due...."[20] The prophecy of Daniel's resurrection was still current some **60 years later**, in 1941, when it was stated that "the time for Daniel's resurrection and return to his place, or 'lot,' on earth as one of the princes of the earth is very near. The faithful followers of Christ Jesus now on earth may **look forward with confidence to seeing Daniel among them almost any time**."[21] And in 1947, the reader is told that "we can be sure Daniel will stand in his lot **at no far distant date** by the power of the resurrection."[22] It is now **more than 50 years** since this last statement was made.

In 1904, founder Pastor Russell taught that the "ancient worthies" or "princes" would be resurrected "about 1914, or shortly thereafter...."[23] In 1920, Rutherford changed the date and wrote, "Therefore we may confidently expect that 1925 will make the return of Abraham, Isaac, Jacob and the faithful prophets of old...."[24] But even before 1925 ended, he adjusted the view and predicted that because of fulfilled prophecy, "it is apparent that there are many peoples now on earth who may confidently hope to see Abraham, Isaac, Jacob and the other prophets back on earth within a few years."[25]

In Rutherford's *Harp of God* (1921 ed.), he wrote, "Hence these faithful men may be expected on earth within the next few years,"[26] but the 1928 edition is changed to read, "Hence these faithful men may be expected on earth at the inauguration of the new covenant."[27] In 1928, he wrote that "it may be reasonably concluded that the 'ancient worthies' will be back on earth as perfect men within a comparatively short time."[28] In 1935 Rutherford stated that God's due time for their resurrection "is at hand. The Scriptures give full assurance that those faithful men shall be resurrected soon...."[29]

The March 15, 1937, *Watchtower* predicted "that the faithful prophets will be back on earth ere long and will assume the positions of visible agents of God and his King in the world."[30] In a cover headline, the *Consolation* of November 26, 1941, asks, "Return of the 'Princes': Who will meet earth's new governors?" The article written by Rutherford went on to say that Beth-Sarim was a testimony and predicted, "You may soon meet Abraham, David, and other like faithful men, who shall be here as perfect men acting as governors of the new world."[31]

And in *The New World* (1942), the reader is told that "the Scriptural and physical facts prove that Job is due to be resurrected shortly with those faithful men and to appear on earth with them. These appointed 'princes' of God will take over what the Nazi-Fascist totalitarian dictators desperately try to grab in the earth."[32] **Not one prediction over those many years was realized!**

Predictions on the resurrection of the "ancient worthies" or "princes" were boldly and frequently made during the first years of the 1940s, and all but disappeared by the mid-1940s. In 1950, their return was safely postponed until **after** Armageddon.[33]

Contradictory Teachings on the "Princes"

Beyond the multiple erroneous speculations on the predicted return of the "princes," a brief survey of contradictory teachings concerning them (typical of what characterizes Watch Tower publications on other subjects) is enlightening. These statements taken from Watch Tower publications, or quoting their position, can be easily reviewed in a question and answer format.

1. **Will the "princes" be changed from human to spirit beings?**

   Yes: "...Certain Scriptures seem to teach that the *Ancient Worthies* will not precede, but rank lower than the *Great Company* during the Millennium, but that they will be received to spirit nature and high honors, at its close."[34] "...The Scriptures show, they [the Ancient Worthies] will be changed from human to spirit beings at the end of the Millennium."[35]

   No: "Nor is there any Scriptural reason to conclude that Abraham and the other faithful men of old shall ever be changed from human to spirit creatures, as was once thought."[36]

2. **Will the "princes" be resurrected as perfect, tested men?**

   No: "They will not have perfection of character when they come forth from the grave.... The final test upon which they shall be granted life everlasting will be imposed at the end of the Millennium, not at the beginning."[37]

   Yes: "It is reasonable to expect that these faithful men will be brought forth from the tombs as perfect men, possessing perfect bodies and perfect minds. They were tried and tested before they died."[38]

3. **Will the resurrection "princes" take place only after the Church is glorified?**

   Yes: "I [Russell, 1915] think the Ancient Worthies could not be perfected until the Church has been completed. The Body of Christ must necessarily pass beyond the veil before any of the Ancient Worthies are awakened."[39] "Our opinion is that the ancient worthies will not be resurrected until every member of the Church is gone."[40]

   No: "The Lord in his loving-kindness makes provision, and we may confidently expect that those faithful men of old will be back on the earth before Armageddon ends and while some of the remnant are still on the earth...."[41]

   "From the Scriptures it appears to be absolutely certain that some of the remnant will be on the earth when those faithful men appear, and certainly those who compose the great multitude will also be on the earth, and all of these will meet and greet earth's princes."[42]

   Yes: "Some of the anointed remnant have thought of surviving and living on to welcome back such resurrected faithful ones who died before Pentecost 33 C.E. Will the anointed be thus privileged? This would not be necessary."[43]

4. **Did God's favor return to Israel, and did this indicate the soon return of the "princes"?**

   Yes: "First we shall consider the certainty of the promises that Israel shall be returned to Palestine."[44] "Abraham, Isaac, Jacob, David and the prophets will be brought forth and be made leaders of the people. We may expect their return soon, because the favor of God has begun to return to Israel."[45]

   No: "By the publication of Volume 2 of the book *Vindication* that year [1932], Jehovah's witnesses came to see that such a 'back to Palestine' movement was by the spirit of Jehovah's archfoe, Satan, who has deceived the entire inhabited earth."[46]

5. **Will the "princes" return to Jerusalem when resurrected?**
   Yes: "We should, therefore, expect shortly after 1925 to see the awakening of Abel, Enoch, Noah, Abraham, Isaac, Jacob.... These will form a nucleus of the new kingdom on earth. One of the first things necessary will be to put Jerusalem in condition to be the capital of the world."[47]
   No: "It is confidently expected that in God's due time some of the faithful men mentioned in Hebrews 11 ... will find an abode in that house [Beth-Sarim in San Diego] while carrying on the work the Lord will give them to do."[48]

6. **Will the "princes" be resurrected before Armageddon?**
   Yes: "Other Scriptures show that Abraham, Isaac and Jacob, and all the faithful prophets, resurrected from the dead, will be on earth immediately preceding Armageddon...."[49] "... Hence those faithful men of old may be expected any day now. The Scriptures give good reason to believe that it shall be shortly before Armageddon breaks."[50]
   No: "For years, Jehovah's people thought that faithful men of old times, such as Abraham, Joseph, David, would be resurrected *before* the end of this wicked system of things."[51] "This view was adjusted in 1950, when further study of the Scriptures indicated that those earthly forefathers of Jesus Christ would be resurrected after Armageddon."[52]

7. **Is Psalm 45:16 to be applied to the "princes"?**
   Yes: "In Psalm 45:16 it is written: 'Instead of thy fathers shall be thy children, whom thou mayest make princes in all the earth.'... When he resurrects these faithful men from death ... they will be properly called his 'children.' This prophecy, therefore, shows that Christ the King will make those faithful men the princes or visible rulers in all the earth."[53]
   No: "'Instead of thy fathers shall be thy children, whom thou mayest make princes in all the earth.' Those to be made princes according to this text [Psalm 45:16] were long understood to be the faithful witnesses of ancient times before Christ who were to become the children of Christ the King by being resurrected from the dead."[54] "Jesus' greater interest in princely sons than in forefathers is emphasized by various Bible translations. Here is how some of them render Psalm 45:16: 'Your sons shall step into your fathers' place, and rise to be princes over all the land.... To our great delight, prospective princes are in our very midst."[55]

8. **Are the "princes" of Isaiah 32:1 the same as mentioned in Isaiah 45:16?**
   Yes: "The new earth will consist of righteous men who in times of old proved their integrity toward God and who the Lord shall 'make princes in all the earth,' which princes shall rule in righteousness under the direction of the righteous Lord (Ps. 45:16; Isa. 32:1)."[56]
   No: "Because Isaiah 32:1 mentions princes and connects them with the King of the new world it was thought that these princes were the same as mentioned in Psalm 45:16.... However, from and after 1947 the columns of *The Watchtower* have not been quoting Isaiah 32:1 and applying it in that way."[57]

9. **In addition to "ancient worthies" are there also "modern worthies"?**
   No: "In its issue of January 15, 1920 (pages 21-28) ... *The Watchtower* discussed the question of 'modern worthies' according to the information and facts then available and said *No!* to such a class."[58]
   Yes: "Since they manifest a similarity of faith, there is nothing that Scripturally argues against his tak-

ing as many of these 'other sheep' as he requires and making them 'princes in all the earth.'"[59]

10. Will Beth-Sarim be held for the perpetual use of the Lord's people and the "princes"?
   Yes: "...When David and Joseph or some of the other ancient worthies return they will have it."[60] "The title to that house is in the Society, and is held in trust for the perpetual use of God's faithful ones."[61]
   No: "...The Society's board of directors had voted unanimously to dispose of Beth-Sarim...."[62]

Wrong Again

Watch Tower publications, and William P. Heath, Jr., who stated that he "was in charge of the estate," not only were wrong on their teachings concerning the "princes," but they were also wrong in many additional matters as well. Three examples should suffice.

1. Before the San Diego Planning Commission, on February 28, 1942, Heath argued that the Beth-Shan "property cannot be sold because it is held in trust for the ancient witnesses, Abraham, Isaac, Jacob et al.... As a consequence, it is impossible that this property will ever be sold to anyone else...."[63] The deed conveying this property to its new owners, "B. Allison Gillies and Betty H. Gillies, husband and wife, as joint tenants," is dated March 29, 1945, and ironically the grantors are William P. Heath, Jr., and his wife Bonnie.[64]

2. "The Planning Commission and Board of Supervisors contended that the [Beth-Shan] property could be conveyed and subdivided." Whereas the Witnesses contended that "under the law and the deed it cannot. It therefore became necessary to show that the deed contained a reasonable and legal trust." Heath, who participated in the creation of the trust, "testified as a witness and explained to the court that the trust was for real men and was altogether reasonable and certain of performance."[65] Heath himself, however, initiated the demise of the trust and made the certainty of its performance impossible when it was sold. The property was subdivided, and the prediction made in 1942 by Realtor G. A. Forbes that Beth-Shan was "beautiful residential land with view sites" that "will undoubtedly be developed into high-class homes"[66] was realized.

3. The actions and decisions of the government officials against Rutherford's burial on Society property were viewed as fulfilling Matthew 25:31-46. "This burial, therefore, gives occasion for further separating of the 'sheep' from the 'goats.'"[67] This interpretation is no longer viewed as correct, as the October 15, 1995, *Watchtower* explains that "the parable points to the future when the Son of man will come in his glory.... It will take place after 'the tribulation' mentioned at Matthew 24:29, 30 breaks out and the son of man 'arrives in his glory.'"[68]

What can be said concerning the Watch Tower record? Joseph F. Rutherford, summarized it well, "Jehovah never makes any mistakes. Where the student relies upon man, he is certain to be led into difficulties."[69]

Notes

1. *Jehovah's Witnesses—Proclaimers of God's Kingdom* (1993), 76.
2. David A. Reed, *'Proclaimers' Answered Page by Page* (Stoughton, Maine: David A. Reed, 1994, 11; Randall Watters, "Review of the new Watchtower book...," *Free Minds Journal*, Sept.-Oct, 1993, 3.

3. *Cons.*, 27 May 1942, 6-8.
4. Ibid., 9.
5. *GA*, 19 Mar. 1930, 405-07; *Cons.*, 27 May 1942, 3.
6. Book 873, 282-84, San Diego County Recorder.
7. Book 1075, 42-43, San Diego County Recorder.
8. In 1916, W. R. Young began to dig a series of tunnels in the canyon located near the N.E. corner of Montezuma Road and Fairmount Avenue. Details are given in the *San Diego Union's* 1 Aug. 1920 issue. Over the years there were repeated efforts by authorities to close the caves which were viewed as dangerous.
9. Two telephone interviews with Fred Eason, 3 Dec. 1996, and letter dated 12 Dec. 1996.
10. Ibid.
11. Ibid.
12. Ibid.
13. *WT*, 15 Nov. 1941, 343. *WT*, 1 July 1941, 202; *Cons.*, 29 Oct. 1941, 11; *Revelation—Its Grand Climax At Hand!* (1988), 246.
14. Eason interviews and letter. Refuge Farms were places of seclusion where Jehovah's Witnesses would be protected from the soon-coming destruction of Armageddon. The modern Watch Tower Society has not discussed this controversial matter in their official history, *Jehovah's Witnesses—Proclaimers of God's Kingdom*, nor for that matter, even mentioned them in their modern publications. The Society has been successful in burying this interesting piece of history.
15. *WT*, 1 June 1940, 162.
16. *Cons.*, 27 May 1942, 15.
17. Eason interviews and letter. Telephone interview with Betty Gillies 9 Dec. 1996. Aerial photographs of the top of the bomb shelter are included in our book *Jehovah's Witnesses—Their Monuments to False Prophecy* (Clayton, Calif.: Witness Inc., 1997), 76-77.
18. *Cons.*, 27 May 1942, 14.
19. *WT*, 1 Nov. 1950, 414-17.
20. *WTR*, Feb. 1881, 188.
21. *WT*, 15 Sept. 1941, 276.
22. *WT*, 15 Mar. 1947, 88.
23. *WTR*, 15 Oct. 1904, 3445.
24. Rutherford, *Millions Now Living Will Never Die* (1920), 89-90.
25. *GA*, 12 Aug. 1925, 731.
26. Rutherford, *The Harp of God* (1921 ed.), 340.
27. Ibid. (1928 ed.), 346.
28. Rutherford, *Government* (1928), 276.
29. Rutherford, *Who Shall Rule the World?* (1935), 47.
30. *WT*, 15 Mar. 1937, 86.
31. *Cons.* 26 Nov. 1941, 18.
32. *The New World* (1942), 130.
33. *WT*, 1 Nov. 1950, 414-17.
34. Russell, *The New Creation* (1914 ed.), 129.
35. *WT*, 15 Jan. 1925, 23.
36. Rutherford, *Jehovah* (1934), 37.
37. *WT*, 15 Jan. 1925, 23.

38. Rutherford, *Deliverance* (1926; 3.58 million ed.), 324.
39. L. W. Jones, *What Pastor Russell Said* (Chicago Bible Students, 1917), 16.
40. *WT*, 15 Jan. 1925, 23.
41. *WT*, 15 Mar. 1937, 86.
42. Rutherford, *Salvation* (1939), 310.
43. *WT*, 1 Sept. 1989, 20.
44. Rutherford, *Life* (1929), 120.
45. Ibid., 191.
46. *WT*, 15 May 1955, 296.
47. W. E. Van Amburgh, *The Way to Paradise* (1924), 224.
48. *1931 Year Book* (1930), 36.
49. *Cons.* 26 Nov. 1941, 18.
50. *The New World*, 104.
51. *1975 Yearbook* (1974), 213.
52. *Jehovah's Witnesses—Proclaimers of God's Kingdom*, 76.
53. Rutherford, *What You Need* (1932), 8.
54. *WT*, 1 Dec. 1951, 717.
55. *WT*, 1 Sept. 1989, 22.
56. *WT*, 15 Nov. 1938, 339.
57. *WT*, 1 Dec. 1951, 717.
58. *WT*, 1 Nov. 1950, 416.
59. Ibid., 417.
60. *GA*, 19 Mar. 1930, 406.
61. *1931 Year Book* (1930), 36.
62. *WT*, 15 Dec. 1947, 382.
63. Minutes, 28 Feb. 1942, 240.
64. Book 1853, pp. 260-61, San Diego County Recorder.
65. *Cons.*, 27 May 1942, 13.
66. Minutes, 242.
67. *Cons.*, 27 May 1942, 15.
68. *WT*, 15 Oct. 1995, 22-23.
69. Rutherford, *Prophecy* (1929), 67-68.

Pictures of Beth-Shan, photocopies of deeds, newspaper reports, Watch Tower publications, and other pertinent records are found in the author's book (with Leonard Chretien): *Jehovah's Witnesses—Their Monuments to False Prophecy.* Clayton, Calif.: Witness Inc., 1997 (307 pp.). See also: "Beth-Shan and the Return of the 'Princes': The Untold Story." *Christian Research Journal*, Nov.-Dec. 1997, 35-41.

34.

The Olin Moyle Case
and His Observations

Leaving his home in Wisconsin with his wife and son in 1935, Olin Moyle lived in Brooklyn Bethel head-quarters. He served as legal advisor to the organization, without pay, for four years. He had been in the Watch Tower movement for more than twenty years when he first dared to criticize some of Judge Rutherford's policies in a letter of resignation dated July 21, 1939.[1] Peter Moyle explains what happened:

> Because he dared to criticize some matters of policy, my dad was labeled a traitor, a Judas Iscariot, and forced out of the organization. Since the Watchtower Bible & Tract Society (Jehovah's Witnesses) had published certain derogatory remarks in their magazine [*The Watchtower*], Father sued them for libel.... The trial took place in Brooklyn, New York, in 1943 and my dad was awarded $30,000 by the jury. The Watchtower appealed and the amount was reduced to $15,000 but the original verdict was sustained in other respects.[2]

While the entire trial transcript is of interest, one part (Exhibit D) will be cited here.[3] In a survey presentation, Moyle gives 13 examples where positions in Watch Tower Society books, booklets, and *The Watchtower*, all written by Rutherford, were contradicted in his subsequent publications. It should be remembered these all were published as from Jehovah God. Three quotations illustrate this point.

In Rutherford's book *Jehovah* (1934), he writes:

> *The Watchtower* is not the teacher of God's people. *The Watchtower* **merely brings to the attention of God's people that which he has revealed**, and it is the privilege of each and every one of God's children to prove by the Word of God whether these things are from man **or are from the Lord**.[4]

In his book *Riches* (1936), the reader is told:

> The Lord has graciously provided for the publication of his message in the form of books, that the people may be informed of the truth. **On the last pages of this book you will find a list of such publications....** Those books do not contain the opinion of any man.

All sixteen of Rutherford's books from *The Harp of God* (1921) through *Riches* (1936) are listed and pictured.[5]

About six months after Rutherford's death (January 8, 1942), the *Watchtower* reader is told: "During the past twenty years he [God] has equipped them with his **revealed Word in print** in the form of books, booklets, magazines, tracts and leaflets...."[6] Olin Moyle was well aware of the claims made about Watch Tower publications, and his concluding statement clearly indicates that he could not reconcile these oft-repeated claims with the evidence.

Exhibit D [7]
God is not the author of confusion

Ransom
1929   for all   *Life*, 207
1937   not [for all]   *Enemies*, 126

Resurrection
1938   will not take place during 1,000 years   *Face the Facts*, 55
1939   will take place during the 1,000 years   *Salvation*, 355; *WT* Dec. 15, 1939, para. 24

Restitution
1921   for all men   *Harp of God* (old ed.), 330
1934   not for all men   *Jehovah*, 206

Mediator
1928   Church did not need   *Reconciliation*, 171, 172, 161
1934   Church must [have]   *Jehovah*, 206

Redemption of Adam
1929   was redeemed by Jesus   *Life*, 207, 339
1939   was not redeemed by Jesus   *WT*, 1939, 149

Versatile Nebuchadnezzar
1930   Represents Satan   *Light* II, 311-313
1930   Represents God   *WT*, 131, 134, 137

Test of Jesus
1928   Jesus tried and proven at 1st Advent   *Government*, 104
1930   Over at the second Advent   *Light II*, 324

Return of Jesus
Returned 1874   *Prophecy*, 65
Returned 1914   *Vindication I*, 287

Great Company
1933   Spirit begotten   *Preparation*, 164
1936   Lost Spirit begetting   *Riches*, 324

Character Development

1923   Work of God   *WT*, 1923, 184

1927   Became the delusion of Satan   *WT*, 1927, 195, 196, 201.

1925

In 1924, the *WATCH TOWER* proclaimed all would end in 1925. See *WATCH TOWER* 1924, 159.

But in 1926, it was *some others* who anticipated things would end in 1925. See 1926 *WATCH TOWER*, 232.

Ancient Worthies

Tested during the Millennium 1925 *Watch Tower*, 23

Fully tested before the Millennium 1926 *Watch Tower*, 87

Religion

1934   True religion was of God   *Beyond the Grave*, 12

1939   All religion of the devil   *Salvation*, 116

[Moyle's] Conclusion

Isn't it blasphemy to attribute this jumble of contradictions to an all wise God? Are not the WATCHTOWER and its followers being blown about with many conflicting winds of doctrine?

Notes

1. Moyle's letter of resignation and other letters are included in Edmond C. Gruss, *Apostles of Denial* (Nutley, N.J.: Presbyterian and Reformed Publishing Co., 1970), 290-99.
2. Undated open letter, "SINCE GRADUATION ... Where Ye Been Hangin' Out? by Peter Moyle.
3. From a typed copy of the trial transcript examined in the Superior Court, Brooklyn, New York.
4. Rutherford, *Jehovah* (1934), 191; *WT*, 1 May 1934, 131.
5. Rutherford, *Riches* (1936), 353-54.
6. *WT*, 1 July 1942, 203.
7. The exhibit is reproduced here essentially as typed in the original with minor editing for clarity. One entry under "Return of Jesus" was removed: "Will not return" (*Prophecy*, 64).

35.

Selected Quotations from Watch Tower Publications for the Years 1940-1949

The Second World War was initially viewed by the Witnesses as leading to and ending at Armageddon. This interpretation was replaced in 1942 with Knorr's message, "Peace—Can It Last?"—that the war would be followed by a "**very short**" period of peace before Armageddon took place.[1] Many other specific predictions made during this decade did not take place.

1940

Pioneer publishers in Wisconsin, in a letter (resolution) to the Society addressed to Rutherford, wrote: "We realize that **Armageddon is near** and we resolve to 'press the battle to the gate' with greater urgency" (*WT*, 15 Jan. 1940, 30).

"'The year 1940 is certain to be the most important year yet, because **Armageddon is very near**.' It behoves all who love righteousness to put forth every effort to advertise THE THEOCRACY while the privileges are still open" (*Informant*, May 1940, 1).

"Prophecies were written long ago and could not be understood until in course of fulfillment. **Now the Lord has brought about the physical facts and brought them to the attention of men who are devoted to him, and it is easy to be seen what will be the result. Based upon this authority**, I [Rutherford] stated in a public address in Paris more than three years ago that the Nazis and Fascists would overrun France. That has been accomplished. I stated in a public address in Berne, Switzerland, that **the Nazis and Fascists would in time grab Switzerland. Watch for that to be accomplished in the near future. At a public address in London, which was transmitted throughout the British Empire, and was delivered in 1938, I stated that the Nazis and Fascists were bent upon destroying the British Empire, and that would be accomplished.... You may expect totalitarian dictators, acting with the Roman Catholic Hierarchy, to overrun the earth, seize control of almost all the nations, if not all, and rule them for a short season, and then will follow the worst trouble that this earth has ever known.** Based upon divine prophecy, briefly, this will be the result: The big religious institution, the Roman Catholic Hierarchy, acting with dictators, will say: 'We have accomplished our purpose. We are now at peace, and we are safe.' Then the Lord will take a hand. Christ Jesus will lead the forces invisible to human eyes, and there shall result **the battle of Armageddon...**" (Rutherford, *Judge Rutherford Uncovers Fifth Column*, 15-16).

"It is said that Vatican City has stored up more gold and other riches than any other nation or organization. It may be expected that **the various deluded radical elements will swoop down on the Vatican and Hierarchy after they have finished the Jews**" (Rutherford, *Religion*, 315).

"The prophecies of Almighty God, the fulfillment of which now clearly appears from the physical facts, show that **the end of religion has come and with its end the complete downfall of Satan's entire organization**" (ibid., 336).

"The day for final settlement is **near at hand**" (ibid., 338).

"The earnest student of God's Word discerns that the **climax is near** and that soon Jehovah will express his wrath against all enemies of THE THEOCRACY" (*WT*, 15 Aug. 1940, 243).

"The **witness work for THE THEOCRACY appears to be about done in most of the countries of 'Christendom'**.... What, then, does it mean that the THEOCRATIC GOVERNMENT is now suppressed in many nations? It means that **the hour is rapidly approaching when the 'sign' of Armageddon will be clearly revealed** and all who are on the side of Jehovah will see and appreciate it. That 'sign' will be the announcement of 'Peace and Safety.... Shall any of God's people now sigh and cry because they see that the witness work is coming to a close? Not at all" (*WT*, 1 Sept. 1940, 265).

"'The signs of the times' have been and are clear, and next we shall see the sign that **Armageddon is about to begin** and deliverance is very near.... Although the opportunity for world-wide witness work is closing, that will furnish no excuse for any of the consecrated to sleep or be indifferent" (ibid., 266).

"**The Lord has shown us that we have a correct understanding**, and now we see, as the Scriptures declare, the whole world under the sinister influence and power of demons.... The Kingdom is here, the King is enthroned. **Armageddon is just ahead**. The glorious reign of Christ that shall bring blessings to the world will immediately follow. Therefore the grand climax has been reached. Tribulation has fallen upon those who stand by the Lord" (*The Messenger*, Sept. 1940, 6).

"All the evidence now strongly points to the fact that **Armageddon is very near** and that soon we may witness Satan's defeat and the complete vindication of Jehovah's name" (ibid., 8).

1941

"...The wicked persecution of Jehovah's servants is to permit them to prove their own integrity. Seeing this, the faithful ones are not all discouraged, but rather are encouraged. They see the evidence corroborating scriptures that **Armageddon is very near**" (*WT*, 1 Jan. 1941, 11).

"'The Sign' Testimony Period"—"Those looking for the early appearance of 'the sign' for Armageddon to begin will not slack the hand in this final month of the campaign, but rather intensify their efforts, and unquestionably more Theocratic publishers will enter the field. Never have such had a finer offer to make to humankind in danger of Armageddon [*WT* subs., *Religion*, 2 booklets for $1.00]..." (*WT*, 1 Apr. 1941, 98).

"While darkness covers the world, Jehovah continues to turn his light upon his faithful ones, giving them a more wonderful vision of his Word than they ever expected to have while on the earth. This strongly suggests that the battle of **Armageddon is near**" (ibid., 109).

"...The portals of the New World are **swinging open**. Jehovah God will make a sharp and quick work of announcing the Kingdom before the complete end of Satan's wicked world.... The **time is short now till the universal war of Armageddon**, and the privileges are great beyond the description of human words.... The Theocratic Government is at hand. The God-given commission is to now tell the good news to the world" (*WT*, 15 May 1941, 159).

"Today the remnant are declaring the Kingdom message to millions of people on earth, and many of goodwill are forsaking religion and Satan's organization and are seeking the way that leads unto God. Now, before **Armageddon, which is near**, they have the opportunity of wholly devoting themselves to the Lord and entering upon the 'highway,' and, continuing to be faithful, may 'be hid in the day of the Lord's anger' at

Armageddon and thus be of the 'great multitude' of Armageddon survivors" (*WT*, 15 June 1941, 189).

"The fact that in all the nations Jehovah's witnesses are now hated and persecuted is strong circumstantial evidence that **the witness work is about completed** and that **Armageddon is very near**" (*WT*, 1 July 1941, 202).

"If we see, then, the **oncoming storm of Armageddon** and know that Jehovah wants the witness given beforehand, why should we not hasten on?... We are well along in the year 1941. Let everyone now who really loves the Lord abandon religion and put aside selfishness and, moved by the spirit of a loving devotion to Jehovah God and his Theocratic Government under Christ, make the **few remaining months** the greatest witness yet given or possible" (*WT*, 15 July 1941, 222).

"At **Armageddon, which is near**, Christ Jesus, the great King now present, will destroy the wicked, clear them off the earth, and make the way for righteousness and righteous rule to ever thereafter follow. That is the hope of mankind" (*WT*, 1 Aug. 1941, 235).

"'Lightning-War Testimony Period" (October 1941): "The **swift approach** of the real lightening-war of Armageddon behooves all persons of good-will to join in this round-the-world educational campaign before it closes" (*WT*, 1 Sept. 1941, 258).

"[Gen. 24:1-67, the selection of a wife for Isaac by Abraham.] This is at least a suggestion that under THE THEOCRACY men and women will seek the face of the Lord, the King, and beseech him to make the selection of a wife for the husband. **Since Armageddon is near at hand** it would seem wise for those who hope to be of the 'great multitude,' and therefore to fulfill the divine mandate, to **wait upon the Lord and seek his direction and ask him to guide them and make selection of a companion**" (ibid., 264).

"...But the latter date [Final End] is not revealed yet to man. By the circumstances and physical facts now observed the fulfillment of the prophecy strongly indicates that the **FINAL END is very near**.... The fact that the Lord now begins to reveal the meaning of this prophecy [Daniel chapter 11] to his people is strong circumstantial proof that **Daniel may be expected soon to return to the earth**.... Now is the due time for God to reveal to his faithful people the meaning of the prophecy under consideration. That being true, **the time for Daniel's resurrection and return to his place, or 'lot,' on the earth as one of the princes of the earth is very near.** The faithful followers of Christ Jesus now on earth **may look forward with confidence to seeing Daniel among them almost any time**" (*WT*, 15 Sept. 1941, 276).

Rutherford's public message at the St. Louis convention on Saturday, August 9, was "Comfort All That Mourn." "Concerning the good news of The Theocracy he exclaimed: '**Thank God that the message does not proceed from any man!**' (Applause) 'The fulfillment today of Daniel's prophecy and its understanding mean the "end of the days" is here, and 'which is proof that **we may confidently expect Daniel the prophet of God to soon stand amongst the peoples on this earth and many will see him and rejoice.**' (Applause) The audience thrilled again into applause when he added that the Lord's people 'are **looking for those faithful men of God and they will not be surprised when they come**'" (*WT*, Sept. 15, 1941, 286). Hundreds of thousands of *Comfort All that Mourn* booklets were distributed.

On Sunday, August 10, "Children's Day," Rutherford addressed 15,000 children between the ages of 5 and 18: "In the Kingdom the 'great multitude' will look to the Lord to guide them as to selecting each a mate for himself. 'Why, then, should a man who has the prospect before him of being of the great multitude now tie himself up to a stack of bones and a hank of hair?' (Applause) (ibid., 287).... '**You may soon meet Abraham, Daniel and other faithful men of old who shall be here as perfect men.**'... Those resurrected faithful men of old, in the visible rule as princes, will be the 'new earth,' and '**these princes are due now any day!**'" (ibid., 287).

"Concerning the faithful ones of old who shall be resurrected Judge Rutherford commented: 'Soon you will see Barak and Deborah (I got a picture of her in the book), and when you see her you will love her very much. She is a real woman, and will be able to give you girls proper advice, you girls who are looking for a husband. **When you see Daniel, David, Moses and all the prophets, listen to what they have to say**, and they will advise you boys and girls.'" The children were all to receive a copy of the book to study. "'It is your privilege between now and before the day school opens to spend six hours a day in taking the book *Children* to others.' The parents should encourage their children to do this very thing, **if they would have them live**.... Receiving the gift, the marching children clasped it to them, not a toy or plaything for idle pleasure, but the Lord's provided instrument for most effective work in the **remaining months before Armageddon...**" (ibid., 287-88).

Rutherford spoke again, extemporaneously for about 45 minutes. "It is not exactly a new work, but it is putting on a little more steam for **the final roundup**." (ibid., 288).[2]

"**The end of the rule of the totalitarian powers is at hand**. Soon the combined elements of wickedness will put forth their supreme effort in their final endeavor to destroy all who support THE THEOCRACY. They shall fail, and none shall help them, because God has decreed it so. (Daniel 11:45) The Lord God will **literally destroy all of such wicked rule**. Behold the righteous THEOCRATIC GOVERNMENT, by Christ Jesus, taking possession and ruling the world in righteousness. He ... will have complete control from his throne in heaven. **Daniel and other faithful men of old soon shall stand in their lot as the visible governors of the people and the representatives of THE THEOCRACY**" (Rutherford, *Comfort All That Mourn*, 28).

"Should men and women, both of whom are Jonadabs or 'other sheep' of the Lord, now marry before Armageddon and bring forth children? They may choose to do so, but the admonition or advice of the Scriptures appears to be against it" (Rutherford, *Children*, 312).

"That [Noah's experience] would appear to indicate it would be proper that those who will form the 'great multitude' **should wait until after Armageddon to bring children into the world. It is only a few years from the time the 'other sheep' are gathered to the Lord until Armageddon**. That entire period is a time of much tribulation, concluding with the greatest tribulation the world will ever have known" (ibid., 313).

"All the physical facts now indicate the battle of **Armageddon is quite near**, when the real fighting takes place and the enemy will be destroyed. Soon Jehovah God through Christ Jesus will fight against the enemy as he did in times of old, and will completely cut to pieces the enemy, and deliver all those who remain faithful and true to The Theocracy" (*WT*, 15 Oct. 1941, 319).

"...The certainty that evil conditions now everywhere prevalent, and growing worse, will continue but a **relatively short time**, until THE THEOCRACY shall speak at Armageddon and earth's sorrows will be over in one final spasm, the execution of justice by Jehovah's Field Marshal, Christ Jesus" (*Cons.*, 29 Oct. 1941, 3).

"**Meantime the German people are awakening to their horrible predicament**. They no longer laugh as decent men and women were made to laugh, but their faces are white, pinched and filled with forebodings of what the near future will bring and is already hastening to bring them—**Armageddon**, the battle of that great day of God Almighty" (ibid., 11).

"Those persons of good-will who shall form part of the 'great multitude' of Armageddon survivors are now quickly coming forth ere the wintertime of Armageddon sets in on the world, and they will, in increasing numbers, take part with the remnant members in this united Testimony" (*WT*, 1 Nov. 1941, 322).

"While no man yet knows the day nor the hour that Armageddon will begin, 'the signs of the times' show that **Armageddon is very near**; therefore Jehovah bids his faithful servants now on the earth to 'redeem the time' and to 'slack not the hand' in his 'strange work,' the witness work" (ibid., 325).

"Seven years ago *The Watchtower* pointed out that according to the prophecies **the United States would become a dictatorial government; and now the admitted and indisputable facts fully support that con-**

clusion, which conclusion was and is based upon the Word of God. All sober-minded persons, therefore, see that what is now coming to pass was foreknown and foretold by Jehovah..." (*WT*, 1 Dec. 1941, 360).

"Mark this in the light of the infallible divine prophecy: **that the totalitarian, arbitrary rule will over-run all the nations of the earth in the very near future**. Some makeshift peace will be made, and the chief credit for such patched-up peace will be given to the religious element, the Roman Catholic Hierarchy. The totalitarian rule will be fully in control, and then will appear THE SIGN" (ibid., 362).

"That 'beast' of [Rev. 17] verse eight appeared in the form of the League of Nations, and which has now been succeeded by or shortly will be succeeded by **all the nations of the world gone totalitarian**" (*WT*, 15 Dec. 1941, 378).

"And while God has used another means of proclaiming the Theocratic message by continued activity of individuals [where branch offices were closed], the record as herewith published would, on the face of it, show that **the Theocratic witness work on earth is about done**" *(1942 Yearbook, 29)*.

"The Kingdom, or The THEOCRATIC GOVERNMENT, is here, and the peoples of earth shall know that shortly. Within a **very short time** the nations shall know that the final issue is here" (ibid., 30).

1942

Jehovah's Witnesses' president Joseph F. Rutherford died on January 8, 1942, and Nathan H. Knorr became president.

"The **greatest crisis of all time is here**, and it behooves everyone that would live to acquaint himself with present-day truths and hasten to obey the Lord, the rightful King of the world, who is now present and moving into possession of his inheritance" (*WT*, 15 Jan. 1942, 29).

"The doom of 'Christendom' is sealed. **Armageddon is very near**" (*WT*, 1 Feb. 1942, 37).

After quoting Matt. 24:19 and Luke 23:28-30: "This clearly makes it to appear why it is better and wise for those of the Lord's 'other sheep,' and who hope to become of the 'great multitude' that shall survive Armageddon and thereafter be given the divine mandate to 'fill the earth' with a righteous offspring, to **defer matters until after the tribulation and destruction of Armageddon are past**... Now we are **near the FINAL END** of the 'time of the end,' and the nations of 'Christendom' are in the throes of war and turmoil" (ibid., 38).

"What remains yet of God's 'strange work' of witnessing, which immediately precedes that 'strange act,' **is nearing completion**, and, when finished, this grandest privilege on earth will for ever have passed. Jehovah's witnesses, therefore, can ill afford to divide their time and attention between the Lord's active service part of the time and for the rest of the time indulging in the pleasure-mad doings of the nations that forget God.... Faithfulness to duty in the 'strange work' of the Lord is our safeguard, and now, when so near the goal, the vindication of His name and the complete triumph of his Theocracy, we cannot safely or with wisdom let down the barriers to the invasion and control of the demons" (*WT*, 1 Feb. 1942, 39).

"**The time is short**, the opportunity is great, and blessed is he that has a part in it.... Shortly his gathering of all such [those who are of good-will] will be finished, his 'strange work' will be done, and he will bring to pass his 'strange act' of vindication of His name" (ibid., 45).

"The effect of these assemblies [in 1938, 1940, 1941], particularly those in 1941, is to spur the Lord's servants on to greater effort and diligence in connection with the Lord's work of hunting and ingathering of the remainder of his 'other sheep' **before the universal war of Armageddon begins**. They 'put on more steam'" (*WT*, 1 Mar. 1942, 69).

"The Lord's 'other sheep' follow with and after the remnant, and the assembling of the rest of such 'other sheep' continues and the gathering work increases in earnestness as the **'final end' draws near**" (ibid., 70).

"Now, with **Armageddon immediately before us**, it is a matter of life or destruction" (*WT*, 1 May 1942, 139).

"Sound the Lord's merciful warning to those **about to die at Armageddon** if unaided" (ibid., 140).

"The world emergency with **Armageddon at the door** is the very time to most anxiously keep God's law and obey him rather than obey desperate men" (ibid., 140-41).

"Now God's visitation of destruction upon her [Christendom] at **Armageddon draws near**, and the nations are in the greatest distress, and that with increasing perplexity (Luke 21:25). All such are the **sure signs of the FINAL END** as foretold, and Jehovah's faithful witnesses and their companions lift up their heads and rejoice. They sing all the more loudly His praises, because the deliverance of all God's righteous servants draws nigh" (*WT*, 15 May 1942, 157).

"Awaiting New Earth's Princes." "Further proof that these princes will *shortly* take office upon earth as perfect men is found in the prophecy of Daniel.... Proof is now submitted that we are now living at 'the end of the days,' and **we may expect to see Daniel and the other mentioned princes any day now!**" (*Cons.*, 27 May 1942, 13).

"The full setting up of THE THEOCRACY is **at hand**" (ibid., 14).

"The rulers and the people have made the clergy the watchmen over their spiritual interests. Such watchmen, being not of God's appointment, have failed to see the sword of judgment **about to fall at Armageddon** and have not warned the people" (*WT*, 1 June 1942, 163).

"Only those who believe, understand and confidently rely upon God and his Word know what is **soon to come to pass**" (ibid., 173).

"This preaching of the gospel must continue until the great threatening emergency comes to climax. When this preaching of the good news of the Kingdom is completed, and **it shortly will be**, according to all indications, what shall follow? The FINAL END of Satan's ruling organization, and that amidst the greatest trouble of all time..." (ibid., 175).

"Not very much longer shall the people mourn because such stiff-necked wicked ones bear rule. The glorious day of the triumph of Jehovah's THEOCRACY by his Seed, Christ Jesus, **is at hand**..." (*WT*, 15 June 1942, 188).

"The **impending battle of Armageddon** brings destruction to those who refuse or are indifferent to God's way and means of deliverance and who prefer to enjoy or yield to sin in this world. It will be a sudden and decided check in the progress of sin" (*WT*, 15 Aug. 1942, 243).

"The **time is at hand** when the God of righteousness will break the oppressor, destroy the oppression, and set the people of good-will free" (ibid., 253).

On September 20, 1942, N. H. Knorr delivered the discourse "Peace—Can It Last?" at the Cleveland, Ohio Assembly. "Once again we ask the leading question, 'PEACE—Can It Last?' and God's definite answer is, No! **Manmade peace under religion's 'blessing' will be very short lived**, and political kings and rulers **will not long enjoy it**. The record says they 'receive power as kings ONE HOUR with the beast.' 'One hour,' with God, denotes **a very brief time; and suddenly** those ten horns and the beast will go into perdition, not peacefully, but violently, **at the battle of Armageddon**" (*Peace—Can it Last?*, 26).

"The new world of righteousness is **at the doors**. The judgment of the nations of the old world is hastening to its disastrous climax, and the peoples are steadily being pressed to an individual decision and being divided for and against the new world" (*WT*, 15 Oct. 1942, 317).

Ad for *The New World* book: "In these lurid days when the handwriting on the wall is seen dooming the wicked old world **to early destruction** in appalling violence, this book ... is published..." (*WT*, 1 Nov. 1942, 335).

"...The Scriptural and the physical facts prove that **Job is due to be resurrected shortly with these faithful men** and to appear on earth with them. The appointed 'princes' of God will take over what the Nazi-Fascist totalitarian dictators desperately try to grab in the earth" (*The New World*, 130).

1943

"By associating himself with Noah, Shem pictured the 'other sheep' of the Lord who now join with the remnant of the 'body' of Christ, the Greater Noah, as companions in Theocratic service warning of the **impending cataclysm of Armageddon**.... The greater disaster of Armageddon, prefigured by the flood, **is imminent**" (*WT*, 15 Apr. 1943, 126).

"From Adam's creation to the end of 1943 A.D. is 5,971 years. We are therefore **near the end of six thousand years of human history**, with conditions upon us and tremendous events at hand foreshadowed by those of Noah's day" (*"The Truth Shall Make You Free,"* 152).

"Man on earth can no more get rid of these demonic 'heavens' than man can by airplane or rockets or other means get up above the air envelope which is about our earthly globe and in which man breathes" (ibid., 285)

"The **final end of all things of this world is at hand**, and the postwar arrangement will not save them" (*WT*, 1 May 1943, 139).

═══════════

Witness Fred Wilson, whose story appears in the April 15, 1979 *Watchtower*, says of 1943: "At that time many of us believed that **Armageddon was just around the corner**. (Rev. 14:14, 16) So we felt that we should devote more time to the preaching work" (7). Had Wilson and the others read *"The Truth Shall Make You Free"* (1943) where it is stated: "Nevertheless, the appearing of the 'desolating abomination in the holy place' is an **unerring proof** that the unknown day and hour of the beginning of the final war **is dangerously near**" (341)?

═══════════

1944

With the presence of the revived League of Nations (UN): "The cries of 'Peace and safety!' from the mouths of the religious and political rulers will be but the immediate forerunners of a destruction as sudden as the flood of Noah's day" (*"The Kingdom of God is Nigh,"* 28).

"The purpose of Jehovah God still stands, and its vindication is now **very near**" (*WT*, 1 Mar. 1944, 72).

"...These witnesses give warning of the **impending disaster** that shall fall upon the old world at Armageddon. Therefore this is the time of great emergency, because the battle of **Armageddon is very near**. All nations, and particularly the rulers thereof, see something terrible **about to befall** the world..." (*WT*, 1 May 1944, 142).

"Jehovah has as His purpose to create a united world. The time is upon us for Him to do so" (*WT*, 15 May 1944, 147).

"With Satan the Devil and his demons **facing destruction shortly at Armageddon** and bent on dragging as many of humankind as possible down into the destruction with them, it is now a time of great temptation" (*WT*, 15 Aug. 1944, 246).

"JEHOVAH **God is approaching the grand climax of his 'strange work,' which work precedes the battle of Armageddon**. The not distant future, into which the postwar road of mutilated humanity leads, will witness the end of a work that he will never repeat" (*WT*, 15 Oct. 1944, 307).

1945

"Jehovah is now bringing his great mystery to its completion. This means that the blessing of all the families and nations of the earth is **near**" (*WT*, 1 May 1945, 131).

"...Jehovah God has suspended the execution of that sentence [on Satan] until the battle of Armageddon,

now not far distant" (*WT*, 15 June 1945, 189).

"Jehovah has stood for a lot of abuse, for about six thousand years. But he will not forever take it! The long-predicted day for vindicating himself and for vindicating his abused servant has broken over the world. The time for which there was good reason to permit such abuse as a greater test upon worshipers of God has **reached its limit**. Now men who challenge his universal sovereignty and who defame his name must be silenced and brought down to nothing" (*WT*, 1 Sept. 1945, 259).

"The beginning of Jehovah's reign means that the end of the free activity of wickedness is **now in sight**" (*WT*, 15 Oct. 1945, 307).

1946

"Jehovah provides the feast. For nineteen centuries it has been running its course and is **now nearing its climax**. In the remaining time for it, who will take part in it? It is a feast of deliverance and liberty. The present privileges of freedom which it offers are just a foretaste of the 'glorious liberty of the sons of God,' which liberty will be complete in the new world following the battle of Armageddon, **now near**" (*WT*, 1 Mar. 1946, 67).

"We are **very near** the time of that vindication. In this atomic age all nations, under demonic guidance, are pushing ahead to the great battlefield of Armageddon, where Jehovah God will sanctify himself upon them by destroying all who reproach his name and oppose his kingdom" (*WT*, 15 Mar. 1946, 85).

"[Satan] is invisibly bringing about a gathering of all nations on the battlefield of Armageddon for the showdown fight against God's King Christ Jesus over the domination of the world. Hence the work that the Lord God Almighty started nineteen centuries ago is **very near its close**" (*WT*, 15 Nov. 1946, 347).

1947

"All this is cogent proof that the **final end** of the unsatisfying political and religious rulerships of this world **is near** in the final universal war toward which all nations and peoples are surely now marching" (*The Joy of All the People*, 29).

"The weighty obligation rests upon each one of God's consecrated people to put that kingdom first and to proclaim it to all worldly nations for a witness, because the **final end of this world is getting so close**" (*WT*, 15 Nov. 1947, 347).

"Now is not the time to fall to dreaming about past achievements and to drop asleep while relying upon our past exploits in the Lord's service.... Redeem the time during the **fleeting time interval that remains** before the world-destruction at Armageddon!" (*WT*, 15 Dec. 1947, 377).

1948

"Realizing that the world **nears its final end** and that therefore the Memorial celebration will not be very often any more, let us all appreciate our privilege of taking due recognition of this blessed occasion this year of 1948 and what years yet remain. Bear in mind, as **we stand at the portals** of the incoming new world of righteousness, that this is a memorial of the founding of that Glorious new world" (*WT*, 1 Feb. 1948, 44).

"NEARING THE PORTALS OF THE NEW WORLD." "The righteous new world of God's creating is **just ahead** of us now" (*WT*, 1 Sept. 1948, 267).

"The opportunity [of ministry] will close with the battle of Armageddon, **now drawing near**, when this gospel of the Kingdom will have been preached adequately and the final end of this world will have come according to God's due time..." (*WT*, 15 Oct. 1948, 311).

1949

"Here again we have the repeated assurance of God's Word that the overthrow of the wicked world organization **is near**. It is nearer than the modern Babylonians care to think as they scramble now for what they can selfishly seize in fear of otherwise losing all" (*WT*, 1 Oct. 1949, 299).

"It [*Awake!* magazine] answers the rousing call for fearless information, not because we have entered the atomic age, but because the world is fast asleep **near the brink of that universal war** Scripturally called 'Armageddon'..." (*WT*, 15 Oct. 1949, 306).

"...The promised new world **is near** and will last for all time. It means, too, that the accomplished **end of this old world is near**" (*WT*, 1 Nov. 1949, 323).

Two Personal Accounts from the 1940s

Floyd Erwin was influenced by the persistence of his uncle to become a Jehovah's Witness in 1943. He was only 17, but because of the Watchtower-generated urgency of the time, he went into full-time service, spending 150 hours each month teaching what he was learning. A year later, faced with the military draft, as a loyal Witness he chose to go to prison rather than to serve. He was sentenced to five years. After serving nearly two years, he was released on parole for the balance of his term. He explains:

> Finding employment with a prison record was not easy. I didn't get an adequate education because I thought Armageddon was so near that it would be a waste of time. I was having a hard time making ends meet. I had to take any kind of low-paying work I could get. I worked as a laborer, janitor, sales clerk, painter, dug ditches and did other menial work.

> When I first became a Witness I was led to believe that Armageddon (the end of the world) was so near that there was no time for anything except to prepare for it by Watchtower organization directed work. I quickly absorbed the contents of the current Watchtower books at that time: *Children* (1941), *The New World* (1942) and *"The Truth Shall Make You Free"* (1943).

He was much affected by the book *Children* and the story of John and Eunice:

> I was led to believe that we should not get married, have children, get an advanced education, pursue a career, or in any way prepare for continued living in this world, because Armageddon was so near. My dad dropped some insurance policies that were paid several years in advance, thinking Armageddon would nullify the need for them after those few years. Believing in all this I worked diligently for the reward of surviving Armageddon and a happy life, without children, in the new world that would follow. I didn't want to displease Jehovah by having children.

In 1949, Erwin married a Witness girl, but even then "the Society's ideal was to not get married and to stay in full-time service the short time remaining till Armageddon."[3] After marriage, he would remain childless under this influence and would remain so for the rest of his life. He would continue as a Witness for 26 years and serve in many areas of ministry before leaving.[4]

Peter Barnes served as a circuit overseer and was a Jehovah's Witness for 30 years before he left the movement. He gives his account of what he observed in England in the 1940s:

> ...Continual emphasis by Jehovah's Witnesses on date setting has had an adverse effect on their day-to-day living. For example, when I first came into contact with the organization in the late

1940's, British Witness families cheerfully surrendered and cashed in their insurance policies, taking whatever cash might be available instead of allowing the money to accumulate for retirement purposes. They were completely convinced in those days that they would never reach retirement age. During the decade of the 1940's in particular, there was tremendous pressure on young Jehovah's Witnesses not to get married and raise families. This idea was stressed repeatedly at assemblies, conventions and in their literature. The Watchtower leaders felt that it was just not appropriate, nor was it the will of God for young Jehovah's Witnesses to marry and raise families and take on those types of responsibilities because Armageddon and the end of the world and the incoming of the new paradise was so close. They could confidently postpone their marriages in order to enjoy a much superior marriage under much better conditions in the new world.[5]

Notes

1   Knorr, *Peace—Can It Last?* (1942), 26. Knorr's keynote speech was actually written by F. W. Franz and was published as a booklet, *Peace—Can It Last?* (Raymond Franz, *In Search of Christian Freedom* (Atlanta: Commentary Press, 1991), 569).

2. The presentation on the August 6-10, 1941, St. Louis convention in the *Proclaimers* book (86, 88, 220-01, 262), briefly covers Rutherford's "Integrity" talk, but makes no mention of the "eagerly awaited" public discourse, "Comfort All That Mourn," made available for public distribution in booklet form. It identified the "king of the north" and "king of the south" of Daniel chapter 11 as the "Axis powers" and the "British Commonwealth of Nations and supporting nations." It also affirmed the soon appearance of "Daniel and the other faithful men of old as the visible governors of the people and representatives of THE THEOCRACY" (*Comfort All That Mourn*, 11-18, 28). The material I quoted from the report on the convention from the September 15, 1941, *Watchtower* on "Children's Day" was also ignored. The St. Louis convention report is found on pages 283-88 of this issue.

3. *WT*, "Singleness or Marriage in the Postwar World, Which?" 1 Feb. 1947, 35-36.

4. This account is based on interviews and Erwin's written description.

5. Peter Barnes, *Out of Darkness into Light* (San Diego: Equippers, Inc., 1992), 14-15.

36.

"Peace—Can It Last?"
"Peace and Security"
(1 Thess. 5:3)—A Final Sign?

The index of *Jehovah's Witnesses—Proclaimers of God's Kingdom* (1993) lists Society president N. H. Knorr's September 20, 1942, Cleveland, Ohio, Assembly discourse, "Peace—Can It Last?" four times.[1] The address was made available in booklet form after the presentation.[2] The *Proclaimer's* account on the talk states:

> In it he set out powerful evidence from Revelation 17:8 that World War II, which was then raging, **would not lead into Armageddon, as some thought**, but that the war would end and **a period of peace would set in**. There was still work to be done in proclaiming God's Kingdom....[3] Jehovah's Witnesses had already discerned from the Bible, at Revelation 17:8, that the **world peace organization would rise again**, also that it **would fail to bring lasting peace**.[4]

> In the midst of World War II, in 1942, when **some wondered whether the preaching work was perhaps about finished**, the convention public talk delivered by N. H. Knorr, the newly designated president of the Watch Tower Society, was "Peace—Can It Last?" The explanation in that discourse of the symbolic "scarlet-colored wild beast" of Revelation chapter 17 opened up to the view of Jehovah's Witnesses a period following World War II in which there would be opportunity to direct yet more people to God's Kingdom.[5]

Examination reveals that these statements are certainly not candid. (1) Why did "some" or "many" think that World War II would lead to Armageddon? (2) Why did "some" wonder "whether the preaching work was perhaps about finished"? (3) What did Knorr say about the duration of peace in his "Peace—Can It Last?" talk? (4) Was Knorr's interpretation of Revelation 17:8 "due time" light? (5) Did the prediction in 1942 of a revival of the League, as realized in the United Nations, require an enlightened understanding of the Bible?

1. Why did "some" or "many" think that World War II would lead to Armageddon?

The September 1, 1940, *Watchtower* states: "'The signs of the times' have been and are clear, and next we shall see the sign that **Armageddon is about to begin** and deliverance is very near."[6] The time of

Armageddon's outbreak became more definite as the September 15, 1941, *Watchtower* reported that the new book *Children* was distributed at the St. Louis convention that summer "for most effective work in the remaining months before Armageddon."[7] The October 29, 1941, *Consolation* said of Germany's people: "Meantime the German people are awakening to their horrible predicament. They no longer laugh as decent men and women were made to laugh, but their faces are white, pinched and filled with forebodings of **what the near future will bring and is already hastening to bring to them—Armageddon**, the battle of that great day of God Almighty."[8]

2. Why did "some" wonder "whether the preaching work was perhaps about finished"?

The answer again is that this is what they had been told in Society publications! For example, Rutherford's *Universal War Near* (1935), says, "such witness work is now **almost done**...."[9] In the September 1, 1940, *Watchtower,* the Witnesses were told: "The witness work for THE THEOCRACY **appears to be about done** in most of the countries of Christendom."[10] And further: "Shall any of God's people now sigh and cry because they see that the witness work is **coming to a close**? Although the opportunity for worldwide witness **is closing**, that will furnish no excuse for any of the consecrated to sleep or be indifferent...."[11] And the July 1, 1941, *Watchtower* observes: "The fact that in all nations Jehovah's witnesses are now hated and persecuted is strong circumstantial evidence that the witness work **is about completed** and that Armageddon is very near."[12] Similar statements were made in other issues of *The Watchtower*.[13] The *1942 Yearbook* echoes what has already been quoted: "...The record as herewith published would, on the face of it, show that the Theocratic witness work on earth **is about done**."[14]

3. What did Knorr say about the duration of peace in his "Peace—Can It Last?" talk?

The *Proclaimers* book, as quoted above, reported that Knorr's talk indicated that "the war would end and a period of peace would set in." In his presentation, Knorr explained: "Before Armageddon comes the Scriptures show, a peace must come. Hence it is proper that the problems of such peace be now considered."[15] And toward the end of his talk:

> Once again we ask the leading question, "Peace—Can It Last?" and God's definite answer is, No! Manmade peace under religion's "blessing" will be **very short-lived**, and political kings and rulers will **not long enjoy it**. The record says they "receive power as kings ONE HOUR with the beast." "One hour," with God, denotes a **very brief time; and suddenly** those ten horns and the beast will go into perdition, not peacefully, but violently, at the **battle of Armageddon**.[16]

The *Proclaimer's* statement, then, fails to accurately report, and actually hides, what Knorr said—"very short-lived ... very brief time" of peace—then Armageddon. It has now (2001) been almost 56 years since the war ended! An account in the *1975 Yearbook* illustrates this same lapse of accuracy (memory): "Recalling that discourse ["Peace—Can It Last?"], Maria Gibbard comments: 'How accurately the prophecy of Revelation 17 has unfolded, as it was shown that the League would come out of the abyss to an uneasy peace that would not last!"[17] What happened to "**suddenly ... the battle of Armageddon**"?

4. Was Knorr's interpretation of Revelation 17:8 "due time" light?

As already cited, it is claimed that "in 1942, Jehovah's Witnesses had **already discerned from the Bible**, at Revelation 17:8, that the world peace organization would rise again, also that it would fail to bring lasting peace."[18] What is not stated here is that Revelation 17:8 **had already been subjected to two earlier interpretations** taken "from the Bible" and declared to be "due time" light.

***The Finished Mystery* (1917).** As a preface to the interpretation, C. J. Woodworth quotes a letter in which Russell expressed his opinion on the meaning of the passage:

"The Beast that thou sawest was, and is not and shall ascend out of the bottomless pit and go into perdition," we understand to be the Holy Roman Empire—Church and State, united in power from 799-1799. The term "Thou sawest" refers to the thousand-year reign of the Pope, and the term "And is not" refers to the present non-existence of the Empire in power, and the term "And shall ascend from the bottomless pit and again go into perdition," **refers to the re-establishment of the Holy Roman Empire in power and its subsequent destruction**. The statement "When he cometh, he must continue a short space [verse 10]," was understood by Bro. Russell to mean that the beast would rule for only a short time.[19]

Russell had indicated his interpretation was "speculation" until the time when this prophecy was "unsealed." Woodworth then comments: "That time has evidently now come."[20] The "unsealed" commentary follows:

"**The beast that thou sawest**—The Antichrist. **Was**—Exercised actual dominion until 1799 A.D. **And is not**—Has not had a vestige of temporal power since 1870. Since then it has been in oblivion, the "bottomless pit." **And shall ascend out of the [bottomless pit], ABYSS.... And go into perdition**—Be utterly destroyed at the hands of the masses it has so persistently and outrageously deceived.—Rev. 17:11.... **When they behold the beast that was, and is not, and [yet is]** SHALL AGAIN BE PRESENT—The Papal Empire restored [brackets and boldface in original].[21]

Rutherford, *Light II* (1930). Rutherford claimed that Revelation 17 "has long been a mystery.... **Jehovah's due time has come to make it plain**, and he by and through his chief officer, Christ Jesus, now clears away the mystery"[22]:

This "beast" is the satanic organization made up of the ruling classes of the nations of "Christendom," particularly having for its claim and purpose the prevention of war. It came into existence in 1899 [as the Hague World Court]. It then went into the abyss and ceased to function [from 1914-1918]. **After the World War [in 1920] it came out of the abyss or pit and began to function again in the form of the League of Nations.** The [Hague] World Court and the League of Nations are one and the same organization.[23]

Revelation—Its Grand Climax at Hand (1988) summarizes what Knorr said on Revelation 17:8 in his talk:

Clearly identifying the scarlet-colored wild beast of Revelation 17:3 as the League of Nations, President Knorr went on to discuss its stormy career on the basis of the angel's following words to John ... Revelation 17:8a.... "The wild beast ... was." Yes it had existed as the League of Nations from January 10, 1920, onward.... Having failed to keep the peace in the world, the League of Nations virtually plunged into the abyss of inactivity. By 1942 it had become a has-been.... At the New World Theocratic Assembly, President Knorr could declare, in line with prophecy, that "the wild beast ... *is not*." He then asked the question, "Will the League of Nations remain in the pit?" Quoting Revelation 17:8, he answered: "The association of worldly nations will rise again." That is just how it proved to be [in 1945]...."[24]

A comparison of these Watch Tower "due time" interpretations illustrates that a prophecy can be "recycled" to fit whatever the current situation is and whatever the need of the organization happens to be, without regard to the actual meaning of the text.

One additional important point in the interpretation of prophecy made in Knorr's "Peace—Can It Last?" talk should be remembered. He predicted:

> But mark this: **The prophecy shows** that when the "beast" comes out of the abyss at the end of this total war it comes out with the woman "Babylon" on its back, or she climbs upon its back as soon as it gets out. That means that "organized religion," and this time **the religious organization with its headquarters at Vatican City, will ride and exercise guiding influence over the League beast**.... The repeated cries and demands of politicians and religionists for "More religion!" **make certain that religion will ride the peace beast.**[25]

There were attempts to salvage this failure by "various evidences," but, as Timothy White says: "A mere listing of these evidences will show how unconvincing they are."[26]

5. Did the prediction in 1942 of a revival of the League, as realized in the United Nations, require an enlightened understanding of the Bible?

The April 15, 1989, *Watchtower* asks: "Was that Bible-based forecast fulfilled? Truly it was! In 1945 the international 'wild beast' emerged from its abyss of inactivity as the United Nations."[27] But as any informed reader knows, in 1942, or even earlier, it required no special understanding of the Bible to predict that another international organization in place of the League would be organized. The following typical **observations made by secular scholars** should suffice.

> World War II wrought a decided change in American attitudes. It had became clear that support of an international organization was a necessity for a peaceful world as well as in the best national interest, and was not merely the fantasy of dreamers and idealists. As early as December, 1939, the State Department created a Committee on Peace and Reconstruction. Gradually the President veered to the conviction that a general security organization designed to replace the League of Nations would have to be planned and founded.[28]

> It is significant that even though the outbreak of the war had signaled the failure of the League, it was nevertheless **recognized early in the conflict that some kind of international organization must be established to take its place.** When President Roosevelt and Prime Minister Churchill met at their Atlantic rendezvous in 1941, Churchill expressed the desire that by their joint declaration they should give expression to their hope that some form of international organization would be created to provide a greater sense of security after the war.[29]

The July 22, 1951, *Awake!* even explains that what Roosevelt and Churchill "composed that day of August 14, 1941, there on the deck of the American cruiser 'Augusta,' became known as the Atlantic Charter."[30] The article continues: "Nothing short of an international organization exercising authority world-wide could bring the envisioned peace and security, they felt certain. The language of the Atlantic Charter implied that, when the Nazi tyranny should be crushed, some great world alliance would be inevitable."

On January 1, 1942, Roosevelt, Churchill, Litvinov and Soong signed the Declaration by United Nations and the next day twenty-two other national representatives signed the document which "marked the birth of the United Nations."[31]

Months before Knorr's "Peace—Can It Last?" talk (September 20, 1942), newspapers contained reports, statements, and editorials speaking of the need for some kind of a world-wide organization after the war, and some even saw a revival of the League of Nations in the "United Nations." (See the excerpts from articles in the *New York Times*.)[32]

The Peace and Security "Sign"

Knorr's use of "peace and safety" (1 Thess. 5:3), in his "Peace—Can It Last?" talk, was not the first or final use of this theme by the Watch Tower Society. Beginning with Russell, Paul's words, "peace and safety," have often been cited in Society publications as prophetic words **which preceded Armageddon**: "Whenever it is that they are saying: 'Peace and security!' then sudden destruction is to be instantly upon them just as the pang of distress upon a pregnant woman; and they will by no means escape" (*NWT*).

How has this text been viewed by the Watch Tower Society? The May 15, 1984, *Watchtower* explains: "This prophecy makes it clear that, just prior to the end of this system of things, 'peace and security' will be declared in some exceptional way, whether by the United Nations or independently by political and religious leaders. What will follow that declaration? Paul said: 'Then sudden destruction is to be *instantly* upon them.'—1 Thessalonians 5:2,3."[33]

In the beginning of his study on the Society's use of 1 Thessalonians 5:3, ex-Witness elder, Carl Olof Jonsson, states: "...The Society repeatedly during its past history has proclaimed that the period of 'Peace and security' is **immediately at hand**, or even that this period **already has begun**. Each time, however, the 'unmistakable signal' has turned out to be a mistake!"[34] Following his study of the numerous Watchtower references to 1 Thessalonians 5:3, as a sign of the end, Jonsson concludes:

> It might be expected that a movement that has **failed so completely in its predictions** would finally assume a more humble attitude and begin to tone down its prophetic claims. But instead the movement continues, with stubborn presumptuousness, to speak as if it received messages directly for Jehovah himself: "We are confident that Jehovah will keep his people well informed," said *The Watchtower* of May 15, 1987 (p. 19)....[35]

And again, in spite of this record of failure, the *Watchtower* of September 15, 1991, tells its readers: "'The faithful and discreet slave' will continue to publish timely warnings so that Jehovah's servants will not be caught off guard by the coming pretentious proclamation of 'peace and security' by the nations of this old system of things."[36] After surveying the past "peace and security" predictions of the Watch Tower, Raymond Franz concludes: "One would think that—after seven decades of stirring up excitement by statements whose worth proved more short-lived than the peace movements on which they were based—an organization would feel moved to humility."[37] He further observes: "...All the 'timely warnings' of the past **had proved ill-timed, ill-conceived, and ultimately meaningless**. The language employed is consistently a mixture of confident-sounding declarations joined with deliberate indefiniteness and vagueness."[38]

The Use of "Peace and Security (Safety)"

The following is a brief overview of the Watch Tower Society's use of the "Peace and Security (Safety)" prophecy referred to above by Jonsson and Franz.

During World War I, the January 1, 1917, *Watch Tower* predicted:

It may be expected, however, that the warring nations will agree upon some sort of peace terms in the not far distant future. **But such a peace will not be a lasting one; it will be merely temporary.** It may be expected that politicians will from henceforth have much to say about peace; that the ministers of the nominal church systems ... will say "Peace" and will believe that safety has come to them. **There will be, doubtless, a short period of peace; but it will be merely a lull before a greater convulsion.** We base our conclusion upon the Scriptures.... St. Paul, writing of the "day of the Lord," which he declared would come upon the earth as a thief in the night, said: "For when they shall say, Peace and safety, then sudden destruction cometh upon them as travail upon a woman with child; and they shall not escape."—1 Thessalonians 5:3.[39]

Some 18 years later, in his talk, "Universal War Near," given on January 13, 1935, in the Los Angeles Shrine Auditorium, Rutherford stated:

During the **few remaining months until the breaking out of that universal cataclysm** [Armageddon] the powers that rule the nations of the earth will continue to make treaties and tell the people that by such means they will keep the world peace and bring about prosperity.... They will continue to persecute and oppose Jehovah's witnesses who are trying to get the truth to the people. Having laid a strong hand upon the people and completely subdued them, then the dictatorial powers of the nations of the earth will say: "Now we are at peace and safety"; and the scripture replies thereto, at 1 Thessalonians 5:3: "For when they shall say, Peace and safety; then sudden destruction cometh upon them, as travail upon a woman with child; and they shall not escape."[40]

In his book *Enemies* (1937), Rutherford quotes 1 Thessalonians 5:1-3 and warns:

Jehovah is now carrying on his "strange work," which serves to enlighten the people of good will and to show them the only way of escape; and only those who find that way will escape. The old "whore" [Roman Catholic Hierarchy] sitting upon the back of the beast **may soon be expected to say: "Peace and safety**; we have silenced all opponents." Then Jehovah's "strange act" will begin, and sudden destruction comes upon her "as travail upon a woman with child...." The old harlot's triumph will be short, and her destruction complete.[41]

The September 1, 1940, *Watchtower* asks:

What, then, does it mean that The THEOCRATIC GOVERNMENT is now suppressed in many nations? It means that **the hour is rapidly approaching when the "sign" of Armageddon will be clearly revealed** and all who are on the side of Jehovah will see and appreciate it. **That "sign" will be the announcement "Peace and safety"**; which sign cannot fully appear as long as this world-wide witness work of THE THEOCRACY is carried on in the earth. Shall any of God's people now sigh and cry because they see that the witness work is coming to a close? Not at all.[42]

In Knorr's "Peace—Can It Last" talk, given less than a year after Rutherford's death, his interpretation is retained, and it is explained that following the war the "manmade peace under religion's blessing will be **very short-lived,** and political kings and rulers will not long enjoy it"[43]—because Armageddon would follow.

During the opening decades of the "Cold War," following World War II, the 1 Thessalonians 5:3 prophecy "was generally pushed in the background. But early in the 1970's a relaxation, a détente, of the strained relations occurred. This was greeted in the Watchtower publications as an important 'sign,' especially since the society had been stressing for a number of years that 6,000 years since the creation of Adam would expire in 1975."[44]

In large print, the front cover of the October 8, 1972, *Awake!*, asks: "WORLD PEACE COMING—WILL IT LAST?" Inside are a series of nine articles on the theme. Statements indicate a fulfillment soon: "NINETEEN hundred years ago Bible prophecy foretold a time when men would be proclaiming, 'Peace and security!' **That prophecy seems to be rapidly nearing its fulfillment.**"[45] "The major reason the coming world peace set up by human leaders will only be momentary is because Bible prophecy foretells this" in 1 Thessalonians 5:1-3.[46] Because of the fulfillment of other prophecies, "we have basis for conviction that the apostle's prophecy of 'sudden destruction' hard on the heels of a 'peace and security' pronouncement will also **be fulfilled in our day**."[47]

True Peace and Security—From What Source? and *God's Kingdom of a Thousand Years Has Approached*, both published in 1973, added further "proof" to the nearness of the judgment to come. An article in the November 15, 1975, *Watchtower* is one example of many articles that stimulated expectations:

> ...The destructive "day of Jehovah" will come right after men and nations reach the point where they are proclaiming "Peace and security!" (1 Thess. 5:3) **Already there are indications in that direction**. Not only are world leaders more frequently using the words "peace" and "security," but they are also developing a "détente," in which they view more tolerantly the nations that have completely different ideologies and social systems.[48]

Looking at this decade, Jonsson writes: "Despite all the predictions and expectations for the 1970's, the decade passed without either world peace or world destruction."[49]

The November 15, 1981, *Watchtower* declares: "Thus, while the world will be deluded by vain hopes during the coming declaration of 'Peace and security!' Jehovah's servants will not be. Instead, they will take this coming fulfillment of prophecy for what it really is: a final signal that the 'great tribulation' is about to begin."[50] On October 24, 1985, the United Nations declared 1986 as the "International Year of Peace." The October 1, 1985, *Watchtower* cautiously states that the Witnesses would "watch the event with interest," but that Christians "cannot say in advance whether this will prove to be the fulfillment of Paul's words" in 1 Thessalonians 5:3.[51] But as Jonsson observes:

> For safety's sake, however, the Society dusted off one of the books for 1973, *True Peace and Security—From What Source?* and published it again in a new revised edition during the peace year of 1986 (renamed as *True Peace and Security—How Can You Find it?*). Referring to the United Nations declaration of 1986 as the "Year of Peace," the book quoted the prophecy at 1 Thessalonians 5:3 and stated that **"this, no doubt, is a step toward the fulfillment of Paul's above quoted words."** (p. 85) Like all the earlier predictions and expectations, the "peace year" 1986, too, failed to "signal the imminent apocalypse. (*WT*, 15 February 1986, p. 6)"[52]

Moving into the 1990s, Watch Tower publications continued with bold predictions. For example, the April 15, 1991, *Watchtower*, under the subheading, "A Final Signal," asks:

When will all of this [world in turmoil] come to an end? The Bible provides an important clue:

"Whenever it is that they are saying: 'Peace and security!' then sudden destruction is to be instantly upon them"—1 Thessalonians 5:3. Do you appreciate the significance of this warning? World events such as those we have detailed in the previous article show that **rulers and many people are talking about peace and reaching out for it as never before.**[53]

And another example from the September 1, 1991, *Watchtower* states:

The subject of peace and security is especially of interest to Christians because of what the apostle Paul wrote under inspiration to a Christian congregation of the first century. His words are recorded in the Bible at 1 Thessalonians 5:3.... Are the recent apparent moves toward greater world unity and the resulting hopes for peace and security a fulfillment of Paul's prophetic warning?...[54] Hence, while at the moment we cannot say with finally that the present peace and security situation fulfills Paul's words—or to what extent talk of peace and security will yet have to develop—the fact that such talk is now being heard to an unprecedented degree alerts Christians to the need for staying awake at all times.[55]

How, then, can peace and security be achieved?... Almighty God has set a time limit to Satan's activity among mankind. When that time arrives, "sudden destruction" will come upon the world lying in Satan's power (1 Thessalonians 5:3-7). **All evidence leads to the conclusion that this will happen soon.**[56]

From the record just reviewed, can anyone place confidence in the interpretations of such an organization?

Notes

1. *Jehovah's Witnesses—Proclaimers of God's Kingdom* (1993), 92, 95, 193, 262. The talk is only listed once in the *Jehovah's Witnesses in the Divine Purpose* (1959) index (200). Raymond Franz states that Knorr's talk was "written by Fred Franz," his uncle (Raymond Franz, *In Search of Christian Freedom* [Atlanta: Commentary Press, 1991], 569). It was well-known at Bethel that Knorr was not a theologian or Bible scholar.
2. *Jehovah's Witnesses in the Divine Purpose* (1959), 200; *1943 Yearbook*, 68-69). Over 500,000 booklets were distributed after the talk.
3. *Proclaimers*, 95. The title of the talk was arresting, because "at the time, **many** of Jehovah's people expected that the war would escalate into God's war of Armageddon..." (*Revelation—Its Grand Climax At Hand!* [1988], 246).
4. *Proclaimers*, 192-93.
5. Ibid., 262.
6. *WT*, 1 Sept. 1940, 266.
7. *WT*, 15 Sept. 1941, 288.
8. *Cons.*, 29 Oct. 1941, 11.
9. Rutherford, *Universal War Near* (1935), 26.
10. *WT*, 1 Sept. 1940, 265.
11. Ibid., 266.
12. *WT*, 1 July 1941, 202.

13. *WT*, 1 Sept. 1941, 258; *WT*, 1 Feb. 1942, 39, 45.

14. 1942 *Yearbook* (1941), 29.

15. Knorr, *Peace—Can It Last?* (1942), 8.

16. Ibid., 26.

17. *1975 Yearbook* (1974), 203. This period of peace has been longer that any previous one between the major powers (*International Studies Quarterly*, 30 Dec. 1986, 269, cited in Franz, *In Search of Christian Freedom*, 569).

18. *Proclaimers*, 192-93.

19. C. J. Woodworth and George H. Fisher, *The Finished Mystery* (1917), 263.

20. Ibid., 264.

21. Ibid., 265-66.

22. Rutherford, *Light II* (1930), 80.

23. Ibid., 94-95. It is interesting that while Rutherford was in prison, the Editorial Committee wrote concerning the League: "We cannot but admire the high principles embodied in the proposed League of Nations, formulated undoubtedly by those who have no knowledge of the great plan of God. This fact makes all the more wonderful the ideals which they express" (*WT*, 15 Feb. 1919, 6389).

24. *Revelation—Its Grand Climax at Hand* (1988), 247-48.

25. *Peace—Can It Last?*, 22-23.

26. Timothy White, *A People For His Name* (New York: Vantage Press, 1967), 399. See *Awake!*, 22 Feb. 1960, 6-7.

27. *WT*, 15 Apr. 1989, 14.

28. Franz B. Gross, *The United States and the United Nations* (Norman: University of Oklahoma, 1964), 28. Prof. Inis L. Claude, Jr. writes: "The war years were marked by an unprecedented volume of plans and proposals for postwar international agencies.... Official consideration of the problems and possibilities of postwar organization was seriously undertaken, particularly in the United States and Britain. Secretary of State Hull initiated American preparatory work almost immediately after the war began in Europe, and was responsible for the most concentrated and elaborate study of international organization ever conducted by a government" (*Swords Into Plowshares* [3rd ed.; New York: Random House, 1964], 52).

29. Leland M. Goodrich, *The United Nations in a Changing World* (New York: Columbia University Press, 1974), 7.

30. *Awake!*, 22 July 1951, 5.

31. Ibid., 5-6.

32. The following are all taken from *The New York Times*. The signing of the "Declaration by United Nations" by 26 countries was reported in the January 3, 1941, issue (1, 4).

     On February 6, 1941, under the headline "LEAGUE TREASURER SEES ITS REVIVAL," it states: "Victory for England in the war and the revival of the League of Nations on a more practical basis were foreseen yesterday by Seymour Jacklin, for fourteen years treasurer of the League.... Predicting a stronger and more effective League of Nations after the war, in which the United States would be a member, Mr. Jacklin said, 'you could no more suppress the principles for which the League of Nations stand than you could abolish Christianity'" (11).

     Under the headline, "THE LEAGUE: DEAD AND REBORN," an editorial in the January 10, 1942, issue concludes: "The League is dead—and it lives. Though fifty nations failed to make it operative by discussion, twenty-six are now engaged in making it operative by all their armored strength and all their spiritual devotion. Woodrow Wilson's body, like John Brown's, lies moldering in the grave, but his soul is marching on" (14).

Under the headline, "PEACE ASSOCIATION URGED BY STASSEN," it was reported: "A world association of free people, to be founded by the United Nations in the post-war period, was invisioned yesterday by Governor Harold E. Stassen of Minnesota.... 'Our future relationships should be based upon the Atlantic Charter. They might well be implemented by a world association of free people, founded by the United Nations...'" (15 June 1942, 5).

Prof. John B. Condliffe of the University of California Department of Economics addressed the International Chamber of Commerce and is quoted as saying: "When the war ends there will be tremendous problems ... the only organization that can possibly deal with these will be the machinery of collaboration established by the United Nations in the course of the war" (28 Apr. 1942, 13).

Speaking at the National Governors Conference, Governor Harold E. Stassen exhorted "that the United States take the leadership in the 'winning of the peace' as well as the war. Making a clean break with the traditional isolationism of his party in the Middle West, the Midwest leader proposed a post-war 'world association' based upon the United Nations.... Lord Halifax ... expressed interest in Governor Stassen's plan and approval of the general idea of world cooperation for peace after the war based upon the United Nations..." (23 June 1942, 15).

33. *WT*, 15 May 1984, 6.
34. Carl Olof Jonsson, "The Prophecy of 'Peace and Security,'" 2. This is available from Biblical Research and Commentary International, P.O. Box 83091, Milwaukee, WI 53223. I am indebted to Jonsson for his research and writing on the subject of "Peace and security."
35. Ibid., 5.
36. *WT*, 15 Sept. 1991, 16.
37. *In Search of Christian Freedom*, 570.
38. Ibid.
39. *WTR*, 1 Jan. 1917, 6026.
40. *GA*, 13 Feb. 1935, 298.
41. Rutherford, *Enemies*, 293-94.
42. *WT*, 1 Sept. 1940, 265.
43. *Peace Can It Last?*, 26.
44. Jonsson, 3.
45. *Awake!*, 8 Oct. 1972, 9.
46. Ibid., 14.
47. Ibid., 15.
48. *WT*, 15 Nov. 1975, 682.
49. Jonsson, 4.
50. *WT*, 15 Nov. 1981, 15.
51. Jonsson, 4.
52. Ibid. A comparison of the 1973 and 1986 editions shows that the passage of thirteen years produced changes in wording which in some cases made end-time events **more remote in 1986 than they were in 1973!** See chapter 40 of this study under 1973. In his brief review of *True Peace and Security—How Can You Find It?* (1986), David Reed explains how the release of this book communicated hopes for the soon end of this "system of things." How was this accomplished? "A sense of urgency was conveyed by the fact that the book was released at a special talk across the United States on March 9, 1986, rather than at the usual time for book releases during the summer Watchtower conventions" (*Jehovah's Witnesses Literature* [Grand Rapids: Baker Books, 1993], 171).

53. *WT*, 15 Apr. 1991, 7.
54. *WT*, 1 Sept. 1991, 5.
55. Ibid., 6.
56. Ibid., 7.

37.

Selected Quotations from Watch Tower Publications for the Years 1950-1959

1950

"Who Will Share in the Final Witness?" (*WT*, 15 Jan. 1950, 22).

"Who share in giving the final witness concerning Jehovah's kingdom and this world's doom at Armageddon?" (ibid., 23).

"Share in the glorious treasure of giving the final witness now, that you may feed on the fruits of victory. The **time is short**—even Satan knows that!" (ibid., 27).

"**Share in the final witness now or never!**" (ibid., 28).

"Manifestly, if the old world is **soon to go to destruction**, a wise man knows that he cannot spend his time as the world does" (*WT*, 1 Feb. 1950, 36).

"We are urged not to be like them [worldly leaders], especially in these days when catastrophic **Armageddon is so near** and when **what little time remains** counts so much for our salvation and for that of people to whom we preach the message of salvation" (*WT*, 1 May 1950, 138).

"The month of October has been designated 'It Is Nearer than You Think' Testimony period. Do you believe ... that the final end of all wickedness is **very near at hand**, much nearer than the uninformed think?" (*WT*, 15 Sept. 1950, 336).

"He has foreordained a definite time to bring the last vestiges of Satan's world to a violent end; and the **remaining time is very short**" (*WT*, 1 Oct. 1950, 368; 15 Oct. 1950, 400).

"The consummation of the present system of things **has been reached**" (*WT*, 1 Nov. 1950, 419).

1951

"There is no time to lose. This world is weighed in the balances and is found wanting. Her days are numbered. The final day and hour for **Armageddon draws near**." [Quoted Matt. 24:14.] "It is therefore a case of sharing in the final witness **now or never!**" (*WT*, 1 Jan. 1951, 29).

"Counting from the end of the 'appointed times of the nations' in 1914, we are 37 years into the 'time of the end' of this world (Luke 21:24 NW; Dan. 12:4).... We are entering the **most serious and trialsome years of this 'time of the end.'** The final conflict of Armageddon draws near" (*WT*, 15 Mar. 1951, 179).[1]

"We are under a sacred vow to make known the good news that Jehovah through Christ is **about to sweep away** this system of things and set up a system where there will be no more wars and no one will have to sacrifice loved ones to warfare" (*Informant*, June 1951, 2).

"A possible third world war looms large in their [Europeans] minds, yet they utterly fail to see that

Armageddon, the Battle of God Almighty, **is just ahead of them**. Driven by the demons, they fail to see that their all-out armaments race is in fulfillment of prophecy" (*Awake!*, 22 June 1951, 12).

"The actual meaning of these words is, beyond question, that which takes a 'generation' in the ordinary sense, as at Mark 8:12 and Acts 13:36, or for those who are living at the given period.... **This therefore means that from 1914 a generation shall not pass till all is fulfilled**, and amidst a great time of trouble" (*WT*, 1 July 1951, 404).

"The time period allowed for this [kingdom message presentation] since 1914 is **rapidly moving toward its end** with the destruction of this wicked system of things. Hence the remaining time is especially precious to all of Jehovah's servants" (*Informant*, July 1951, 1).

"One of the reasons for the universal war of Armageddon with which the present world will end **in the near future** is mankind's failure to observe this rainbow covenant which requires respect for the blood of living creatures" (*What Has Religion Done for Mankind?*, 81).

In the campaign promoting the above book: "Urgently the warning is given: Mass destruction to befall mankind!... The dark superstitions and beliefs perpetuated by the varied religious systems of earth must be proved false, if sincere-hearted persons are to be saved from **impending destruction**" (*Informant*, Dec. 1951, 1).

"The book brings forcefully home to us that all religion is now on judgment and all that is false **will soon perish** amid the great ruin that it is bringing upon itself" (ibid., 2).

1952

"We still are wondering if we did the right thing in returning to finish high school. Or would it have been better if we entered the full-time ministry.... We know this old system of things **will soon be destroyed at Armageddon**, so why the reasons for attending high school when we could be out warning others?" (*WT*, 15 Feb. 1952, 117).

"The new world is **just ahead** of us" (*WT*, 15 Oct. 1952, 636).

"Now that **we stand on the very crest** looking into the antitypical promised land of the new world..." (*WT*, 1 Dec. 1952, 712).

1953

"After almost six thousand years of human sorrow, suffering and death, at last permanent relief **is near at hand and will be realized within this generation**. A clean, just and healthful new world is immediately before them and they may enter into it" (*"New Heavens and A New Earth,"* 7).

"Yes, the wicked adversary knows he has only **a short period of time now** and he does every possible thing in his power to prevent earth's inhabitants from acknowledging God's kingdom arrangement" (*WT*, 15 Feb. 1953, 119).

"That means that Armageddon is **so near at hand** that it will strike the generation now living" (*After Armageddon—God's New World*, 29).

"Global Enemy Attack at Armageddon.... For years Jehovah's witnesses have been desiring to obtain a detailed Biblical description of the strategy and maneuvers leading to Armageddon. That desire was completely fulfilled ... when F. W. Franz, vice-president of the Watch Tower Society, delivered a most stirring lecture entitled "New World Society Attacked from the Far North."... In no uncertain terms, F. W. Franz sounded the alarm of Armageddon.... **The time of global attack is near** and puts the faith of every one of Jehovah's witnesses to a supreme test. 'Be from now on never relaxing guard,' said Franz. **'Jehovah's witnesses have to know of Armageddon in advance'** that they may be forewarned and forearmed, he showed..." (*Report of the New World Society of Jehovah's Witnesses*, 25 July 1953, 36).

Speaking at the same convention, president N. H. Knorr is summarized: "Because **Armageddon is so close** many will enter the new world without needing to go down into death.... If we hope to enter the new world **just ahead**, we must alter our lives now while this old world yet stands, and bring them in accord with the new-world standards" (ibid., 28 July 1953, 81).

"The sign of the **nearer approach** of the battle of Armageddon is now before our eyes" (*WT*, 15 Sept. 1953, 564).

"We are now **on the threshold of a new world** that will never perish or grow old..." (ibid., 570).

Ex-Witness Stan Thomas reported that when the convention in Yankee Stadium was held in 1953, "the Witnesses were warned to expect an all out attack by Satan's forces (the world) in the near future, an event which would be the spark to ignite Armageddon. As to precisely when this attack was to be expected the Watchtower Society has grown much too wise to officially speculate, but many Witnesses, particularly older ones, felt that 1954 could well be 'The Year.'"[2]

1954

"The **time before Armageddon grows short** and there are still many who are yet to be gathered into Jehovah's new-world society" (*Informant*, Feb. 1954, 1).

"They do not fear government corruption, for they know that while Satan rules corruption is inevitable, but that this **will soon end**" (*WT*, 15 Feb. 1954, 107).

"The **time is close at hand** for Jehovah to punish these Name-destroyers. Terrible destructions are near and immediate action is required of all those who hear the message of true religion and who are for Jehovah and against idolatry" (*WT*, 1 Mar. 1954, 151).

"As Jehovah did then, so now he allows opportunity for flight. Seize it, **now or never!**" (*WT*, 15 July 1954, 446).

"So the time for indecision is past. Decide now. Act now. For **soon**, at Armageddon, a too-busy world, too busy to heed the warning of its own end, will be crushed out of existence. But there is no need for you to die" (*WT*, 15 Aug. 1954, 488).

"For with the **new world, oh so very near**, our fondest hopes, whether heavenly or earthly, will soon be realized to our eternal satisfaction" (ibid., 509).

"The **remaining time is too short** to take chances with our life. The new world is upon us, bringing the old world to its terrible end" (*WT*, 15 Sept. 1954, 553).

"The **remaining time is too short** to permit such losses. Now is the time to be awake, active and consistent in Jehovah's service" (ibid., 555).

"The warning has been sounded! **Sudden death impends!** Flee for your life!" (*WT*, 1 Oct. 1954, 584).

1955

"In the light of the fulfillment of Bible prophecy it is becoming clear that the war of Armageddon is **nearing its breaking-out point**" (*You May Survive Armageddon into God's New World*, 331).

"But why do we say world conquest by God's kingdom 'soon'? We say 'soon,' because the Bible says that the faithful students of God's Word and observers of the fulfillments of its prophecies would be kept informed on God's times and seasons" (*World Conquest Soon—By God's Kingdom*, 27).

"Last week Knorr ... told the Witnesses in convention—to its highly audible delight—that **Armageddon will come 'soon.'** 'Its terrible upheaval,' he assured his audience, '**will take place in my time. I anticipate seeing it**'..." (*Newsweek*, 4 July 1955, 58). Watch Tower president N. H. Knorr died on June 8, 1977.

"With the execution of fiery judgment at the appalling battle of Armageddon **rapidly approaching**, Jehovah the Great Shepherd feels for these sheeplike ones" (*WT*, 15 Nov. 1955, 698).

"In this **short remaining time till Armageddon** it is the due right of the non-Israelite sheep from all nations to come up to the exalted 'house of the God of Jacob' to worship Jehovah there and gain salvation" (*WT*, 15 Nov. 1955, 700).

"As Armageddon **now near** harvesttime comes, then the time of the wine treaders" (*WT*, 1 Dec. 1955, 729).

1956

"Thus, Satan's **time is short**. The destruction of his entire wicked system at Armageddon is **near**" (*WT*, 1 Feb. 1956, 70).

"The **urgency** of the times cannot be emphasized too strongly. The **time is short**, much shorter than when this proclamation began, and there is no time to lose. Armageddon draws on apace. It is now almost forty years since Satan was cast out of heaven down to this earth. The climax of all ages is **fast approaching**" (*WT*, 1 Aug. 1956, 473-74).

"October 1, 1914, is now more than forty-two years ago and the Kingdom's fight at Armageddon is **fast nearing**" (*WT*, 15 Dec. 1956, 756).

1957

"**Soon** the war of Armageddon will finish off the wicked world" (*WT*, 15 Feb. 1957, 112).

"For, strange as it is, this—the fastest-moving generation of all—slumbers as the **climax of Armageddon comes ever closer**" (*WT*, 1 Mar. 1957, 145).

"Satan knows he has but **a short time**, and he is determined to stop the preaching work" (*WT*, 15 Aug. 1957, 499).

"Only a **short time yet remains** in which this preaching work can be accomplished" (ibid., 504).

"Today, **so near the end** of this old world, if we desire to be redeemed and to be shown God's favor by being protected clear through the universal war of Armageddon and kept alive into this new world, we too must walk in integrity toward God, as David did" (*WT*, 15 Dec. 1957, 750).

1958

"The present system of things has been weighed in the balances and found wanting. **Soon** it will be completely destroyed at Armageddon" (*WT*, 15 Apr. 1958, 243).

"This present generation will see the fulfillment of this prophecy. **Shortly** the 'war of the great day of God the Almighty' will bring this wicked system of things to an end" (*WT*, 1 June 1958, 324).

"Fulfillment of Bible prophecy warns that Armageddon is **near**" (*WT*, 15 Oct. 1958, 615).

"This generation of humankind is nearing its normal end.... We know not the day or hour, but the world's end is **near**" (ibid., 637).

"At the 1958 Divine Will International Assembly **amazing advance information** in connection with Daniel's [chapter 11] prophecy was given about **events to occur in the immediate future. Such evidence of spiritual insight is recorded for us in the book** *'Your Will Be Done on Earth.'*[3] Once again the 'faithful and discreet slave' **has been tipped off ahead of time** for the guidance of all lovers of God. Surely one's present security depends on his staying awake with the 'faithful and discreet slave'" (*WT*, 15 July 1960, 444).

What was predicted in *"Your Will Be Done On Earth"* "to occur in the immediate future"? "The **king of the south** [Britain and America (263)] is determined to hold his dominant place on earth to preserve the 'free world,' as he claims. He was urged to begin a preventive war before the **king of the north** [Communist Soviet Union (278)] became too strong..." (297).

"**Down to the 'time of the end' at Armageddon there will be competitive coexistence between the 'two kings.'** In some way the king of the south must act, whether preventively or protectively. In the confused fighting between the 'two kings' as crazed enemies of Jehovah God and his kingdom, the 'kings' will have opportunity and occasion to **try out and use their frightful, deadly weapons of all kinds against each other**" (297).

"How far the **king of the north** will have got when he reaches his 'time of the end' the future alone will tell. But he is **predicted to gain control over the treasures of gold, silver and all the precious things of this commercialized, materialistic world, including oil**" (303).

"The reports that the sanctuary class and the worshipping 'other sheep' announce from house to house and publicly and unpublicly underground disturb the Communist dictatorial power. A **campaign against these Kingdom publishers** becomes more important than the king's aggressive campaign against the king of the south.... The unseen mastermind, the symbolic Gog of Magog, **maneuvers both kings into joining him in a final, full-scale assault** upon Jehovah's 'beauteous land'" (306).

"He meets his end, his Armageddon, at Jehovah's appointed time for it. He has none to help him, not even the king of the south, for this king also is destroyed at Armageddon..." (307).

"Recently, the **political situation regarding the two kings has changed**. The bitter rivalry between the United States and Eastern European countries has cooled. Further, the **Soviet Union has disbanded in 1991 and no longer exists**.... So who is the king of the north now? ... We cannot say..." (*WT*, 1 Nov. 1993, 21).

1959

"For nearly eighty years *The Watchtower* has served sincere watchers faithfully, and it is now 'Announcing Jehovah's Kingdom' as being here and **due soon** to take complete control of earth's rule" (*WT*, 15 Jan. 1959, 64).

"We are **rapidly nearing** the 'war of the great day of God the Almighty' called Armageddon" (*WT*, 1 Apr. 1959, 218).

"It is an active society that zealously proclaims that God's kingdom is now established in the heavens and will **shortly** usher in a new world of righteousness" (ibid., 219).

"Since the nations inescapably face the long-foretold destruction in the 'war of the great day of God the Almighty,' **just ahead**, when is it that God speaks peace to all nations?" (*WT*, 15 Oct. 1959, 622).

Ex-Witness Valerie Tomsett in England explains:

When I was a dedicated Witness, the word Armageddon conjured up terrible, indescribable fear in my heart, for in the 1950s and early 1960s, it was something which was always close at hand.... The thought that Armageddon was just around the corner filled me with blind panic as I was only a teenager when it was being preached. I felt that I had to pack as much into my life as possible because the time was so short. This was exactly what the Watchtower society wanted. They needed to have their members working for dear life on their behalf, trying to get on the "winning side."[4]

In the 1950s, Witnesses bought their possessions with the idea, "Well, so long as it lasts until Armageddon." All plans were short-term. Mistakes did not matter. It would all come right at Armageddon.[5]

Notes

1. In *WT* articles in 1950 (1 Sept., 277 and 1 Nov., 407), it was stated that 1951 would be 37 years after 1914, which was hinted to parallel the 37 years from Christ's death to the destruction of Jerusalem in 70 A.D. (See also *WT*, 15 Mar. 1950, 179; 1 Apr. 1951, 214.)
2. Stan Thomas, *Jehovah's Witnesses and What They Believe* (Grand Rapids: Zondervan Publishing House, 1967), 54.
3. The October 15, 1958, *Watchtower* carried an ad for *"Your Will Be Done on Earth"* which says in part: "It details the activity of the 'king of the north' and "king of the south' in the prophecy of Daniel (chapter 11) and **points with unerring accuracy to their counterparts in today's struggle for world control**.... It contains absolute assurance that God's will *will* be done on earth **in our generation**" (640).
4. Valerie Tomsett, *Watchtower Chaos* (London: Lakeland, 1974), 27.
5. Ibid., 28.

38.

Selected Quotations from Watch Tower Publications for the Years 1960-1969

1960

"Here, then, is a thrilling opportunity! We live now **on the threshold** of the new world of righteousness" (*WT*, 1 May 1960, 281).

"Surely the good news that all these blessings are right **at the door** is cause for singing" (*WT*, 15 May 1960, 312).

"These very facts, however, prove that the time for Jehovah God to vindicate himself by asserting his sovereignty is **near at hand**, for did not Jesus say that at the end of this systems of things there would be an 'increasing of lawlessness'?" (*WT*, 1 July, 1960, 392).

"As with a hurricane, those heeding the warning now being sounded of Armageddon's approach will take steps for safety and survival, for the devastating storm is to **follow shortly**" (*WT*, 15 July 1960, 423).

"Faced as we are with the **impending** destruction of the wicked world at the hands of Jehovah's executioner Christ Jesus, how vital it is to be awake to the responsibilities that rest on those who practice the religion of the Bible!" (*WT*, 1 Sept. 1960, 535).

"... **Soon** this time of the end will reach its climax with the destruction of all wickedness, opening the way for God's everlasting new world" (ibid., 538).

"They [JW] live every day with a keen sense of awareness of the **nearness** of the day of Jehovah's execution of the satanic world" (ibid., 541).

1961

"In this troubled world, tottering so **near the brink** of another total war, and Armageddon, who knows when we shall be able to enjoy further such assemblies! So by all means attend one of the 1961 assemblies" (*WT*, 1 Feb. 1961, 92).

"We are at the portal of a new world. God's kingdom by Jesus Christ will **soon** destroy the kingdoms of this world as foretold by Daniel the prophet" (*WT*, 1 Nov. 1961, 648).

"It is a sign that the great, illustrious, fear-inspiring day of Jehovah **is nearing** and that *now*, in the remaining brief interval, is the time to call upon the name of Jehovah in faith, in order to be saved for everlasting life in His new world" (ibid., 663).

"We are **near** the time of his battle and transcendent victory" (*WT*, 1 Dec. 1961, 726).

1962

"Armageddon, the battle of the great day of God Almighty, is **at the door**.... This worldly generation, therefore, **has not much longer to live**, and the less time it has the more urgent it is that the Witnesses sound the warning and point men to the way of escape" (*WT*, 1 July 1962, 389).

"...The Christian witnesses of Jehovah, is sending out urgent warnings regarding the great storm of Armageddon that is **rapidly approaching**. By calling on the people time and time again the Witnesses are facing up to our urgent times" (ibid., 390).

"Deliverance is **now near** for the faithful remnant of these heirs of God's heavenly kingdom.... God's established kingdom is **at hand**..." (*WT*, 15 Oct. 1962, 622).

1963

"...We are living in the 'last days' of this present world, and a time of final judgment for all living on the earth is **at hand**" (*WT*, 15 Jan. 1963, 41).

"Prove loyal to God and he will prove his faithfulness by concealing you through the world-shaking calamity **just ahead**" (*WT*, 15 Feb. 1963, 104).

"**Shortly** God's people will enter into the great day of Jehovah known as Armageddon" (*WT*, 1 Mar. 1963, 157).

"...Therefore, we have **immediately ahead** of us the most momentous period in the history of mankind; the hour of the execution of God's righteous judgment is **about to strike**, and we are in the day of decision" (*WT*, 15 Nov. 1963, 687).

"Now in her fallen condition she [Babylon the Great] is **approaching** her terrible eternal destruction" (*WT*, 15 Nov. 1963, 702).

1964

"Awake! pledges itself to righteous principles, to exposing hidden foes and subtle dangers, to championing freedom of all, to comforting mourners and strengthening those disheartened by the failures of a delinquent world, reflecting sure hope for the **establishment of God's righteous new order in this generation**" (*Awake!*, 8 Jan. 1964, 2).[1]

"The fallen Great Babylon is now approaching her terrible destruction.... The time is **now short**. To the work, then, all you free messengers of liberation!" (*WT*, 1 Feb. 1964, 85).

"Thus when a Christian realizes that Gog of Magog or Satan the Devil and all his unseen spirit forces are **shortly** going to move against him and all his fellow Christian members of the theocratic society, he comprehends to some degree the awesomeness of this situation" (*WT*, 15 July 1964, 436).

"While we know that the time is **comparatively short**, we do not know just how short. So it will require endurance on our part, a resolve to endure regardless of what we may be called upon to endure and regardless of how long it may yet be until Jehovah calls a halt to the declaration of the good news" (*WT*, 1 Oct. 1964, 607).

1965

"Today there is a Greater Babylon that is **nearing its fall** and horrifying desolation.... Babylon will likewise fall to her complete desolation in the **very near future**..." (*WT*, 15 Jan. 1965, 56).

"To God's servants, then, the swiftly mounting troubles and causes for fear are evidences that **soon now** their work of proclaiming the Kingdom amid the fear-riddled generation will have been completed, and the time for deliverance from the persecutions and galling restrictions of this world's rulers will have arrived" (*WT*, 1 May 1965, 263).

"Even those who do not believe must be told of the **impending** execution of divine judgment" (*WT*, 15 Sept. 1965, 574).

"There is an urgency about our sounding this warning as God's messengers of liberation.... Babylon the Great's fall presages her destruction, even as ancient Babylon was destroyed after she had fallen; only in our day the destruction of Babylon the Great will not be delayed for centuries but only for **a few short years**..." (*WT*, 1 Oct. 1965, 603).

1966

"Exercise your opportunity now to flee from and stay out of Babylon in order to avoid being lastingly crushed in the **fast-approaching** day of her destruction" (*WT*, 15 May 1966, 312).

"**Time is running out!** Running out for what? Running out for the present generation, for the present wicked system of things, for the way things are being done today" (*WT*, 1 June 1966, 325).

"There can be no doubt that the harvesting work is **reaching its climax. Soon** the earth will be reaped of all the sons of the Kingdom, the anointed Kingdom heirs, as well as the great crowd of 'other sheep,' who will get out of Babylon the Great..." (*WT*, 15 June 1966, 376).

"**6,000 Years Completed in 1975.**" "There is another chronological indication that we are **rapidly nearing the closing time** for this wicked system of things. It is the fact that shortly, according to reliable Bible chronology, 6,000 years of human history will come to an end" (*Awake!* 8 Oct. 1966, 19).

"It means that within **relatively few years** we will witness the fulfillment of the remaining prophecies that have to do with the 'time of the end....' What cataclysmic times are **fast approaching! A climax in man's history is at the door!**... Of course, as to the precise day and hour of the end, Jesus noted that knowledge of this was in the province of his heavenly Father alone (Matt 24:36). But when a brief period of years at the most separates us from the great windup of this old system, the vital thing is to stay spiritually awake—Luke 21:34-36.

So how much longer will it be? The answer is: 'not long, for the **end of wickedness is near.**'" (ibid., 20).

W. F. Franz at the 1966 Baltimore assembly: "And don't any of you be specific in saying anything that is going to happen between now and 1975. But the big point of it all is this, dear friends: **Time is short. Time is running out**, no question about that" (*WT*, 15 Oct. 1966, 631).

1967

"True Christians can rejoice because God's kingdom is **near** and deliverance from this system of things **is at hand.**... So with the 'last days' **speedily running out**, positive action is indeed urgent" (*WT*, 15 Mar. 1967, 168).

"Learn what steps to take to flee from Great Babylon and act at once, for her destruction is **alarmingly imminent**" (*WT*, 15 Apr. 1967, 249).

"They tell us what Satan the Devil already knows, namely, that we stand at the **threshold** of Armageddon, that his wicked rule is about to end, that 'God's kingdom come' will **soon** be a reality for the earth. The time is **close at hand**. On God's 'timetable' we are in the closing days of a wicked system of things that will **soon** be gone forever. A glorious new order is **immediately** before us.... The prophecy is sure the **time is short**" (*WT*, 1 May 1967, 262).

"The end, of the approach of which this Kingdom preaching is a trustworthy indication, will come **shortly**" (*WT*, 15 Dec. 1967, 758).

1968

"Proof, all this, that the 'generation' spoken of by Jesus is now close to passing away. **The time is truly**

short!" (*WT*, 15 Jan. 1968, 42).

"**Soon**, God himself will fight the last war that this system of things will ever see" (*WT*, 1 Feb. 1968, 70).

"So, according to God's Word, not only will the nations continue to experience a time of unprecedented distress that will yet grow worse, but in the **very near future** this entire system of things will suffer complete destruction" (*WT*, 1 Mar. 1968, 134).

"...There are only about ninety months left before 6,000 years of man's existence on earth is completed.... The majority of people living today will probably be alive when Armageddon breaks out... (*Kingdom Ministry*, Mar. 1968, 4).

"The seventh day of the Jewish week, the sabbath, would well picture the final 1,000-year reign of God's kingdom under Christ when mankind would be uplifted from 6,000 years of sin and death. (Rev. 20:6) Hence, **when Christians note from God's timetable the approaching end of 6,000 years of human history [in 1975], it fills them with anticipation**" (*WT*, 1 May 1968, 271).

"The immediate future is certain to be filled with climactic events, for this old system is nearing its complete end. **Within a few years at most** the final parts of Bible prophecy relative to the 'last days' will undergo fulfillment, resulting in the liberation of surviving mankind into Christ's glorious 1000-year reign!..." (ibid., 272).

"Does this mean that the year 1975 will bring Armageddon? No one can say with certainty what any particular year will bring" (ibid. 272-73).

"Are we to assume from this study that the battle of Armageddon will be all over by the autumn of 1975, and the long-looked-for thousand-year reign of Christ will begin then? Possibly.... **It may involve only a difference of weeks or months, not years**" (*WT*, 15 Aug. 1968, 499.

"God's Word of truth tells us very clearly that we are **fast approaching** a worldwide change" (*WT*, 15 Sept. 1968, 551).

"How encouraging it is to know that **soon** we will see the end of all the world's troubles! How thrilling it is to know that we have the hope of shortly entering a new system where we can forever enjoy life to the full!" (ibid., 552).

"How fitting it would be for God, following this pattern, to end man's misery [in 1975] after six thousand years of human rule and follow it with His glorious Kingdom rule for a thousand years!... Does this mean that the above evidence positively points to 1975 as the time for the complete end of this system of things? Since the Bible does not specifically state this, no man can say. However, **of this we can be sure: The 1970's will certainly see the most critical times mankind has yet known**" (*Awake!*, 8 Oct. 1968, 14).

"**His time is near**, which is why man's rule is about to give way to God's rule" (*Man's Rule About to Give Way to God's Rule*, 27).

"How glad, then, we can be that God's rule is **now about to give way** to God's rule forevermore!" (ibid., 30).

1969

"Many schools now have student counselors who encourage one to pursue higher education after high school, to pursue a career with a future in this system of things. Do not be influenced by them. Do not let them 'brainwash' you with the Devil's propaganda to get ahead, to make something of yourself in this world. **This world has little time left!**... Make pioneer service, the full-time ministry, with the possibility of Bethel or missionary service your goal. This is a life that offers an everlasting future!" (*WT*, 15 Mar. 1969, 171).

"Whether they recognize it or not the Gentile nations rule today only by God's toleration. Jehovah permits their continuance for **a few years more** so that sheeplike persons from all nations may come out of this system of things before its Armageddon end" (*WT*, 15 May 1969, 302).

"In view of the **short time left** in which to do their work, Jehovah's witnesses do not continue to study the Bible with any who fail to respond to the urgent message within six months. The **nearness of this system's end** compels them to use their time in the most effective way possible" (ibid., 312).

"If you are a young person, you also need to face the fact that **you will never grow old in this present system of things. Why not? Because all the evidence in fulfillment of Bible prophecy indicates that this corrupt system is due to end in a few years**.... Therefore, as a young person, you will never fulfill any career that this system offers. If you are in high school and thinking about a college education, it means at **least four, perhaps even six or eight more years to graduate** into a specialized career. **But where will this system of things be by that time? It will be well on the way toward its finish, if not actually gone!**" (*Awake!* 22 May 1969, 15).

"Of course, there may be a tempting offer of higher education or of going into some field of work that promises material rewards. However, Jehovah God holds out to you young folks many marvelous privileges of service in his organization. Which will you decide to take up? **In view of the short time left, a decision to pursue a career in this system of things is not only unwise but extremely dangerous**. On the other hand, a decision to take advantage of what God offers through his organization opens up excellent opportunities for advancement as well as a rich, meaningful life that will never end" (*Kingdom Ministry*, June 1969, 3).

"People who were only just old enough to understand what was happening to the world in 1914 are now approaching seventy years of age. Yes, the numbers of that generation are dwindling fast, but before they all pass away this system must meet its end in the war of Armageddon. Surely this highlights **what a very short time now remains** to return to Jehovah" (*WT*, 1 July 1969, 395).

"Then act! Do not delay! Do not put it off! **Time is rapidly running out**. Get back into association with Jehovah and with his people. Yes, return to Jehovah *now*, **while there is yet time**" (ibid., 396).

"THE MILLENNIAL PEACE APPROACHING." "When, though, does the Prince of Peace start his government of an endless peace? (*The Approaching Peace of a Thousand Years*, 21).

"More recently earnest researchers of the Holy Bible have made a recheck of its chronology. According to their calculations the six millenniums of mankind's life on earth would end in the mid-seventies [1975]. **Thus the seventh millennium from man's creation by Jehovah God would begin within less than ten years**. Apart from the global change that present-day world conditions indicate is fast getting near, the arrival of the seventh millennium of man's existence on earth suggests a gladsome change for war-stricken humankind" (ibid., 25)

"In order for the Lord Jesus Christ to be, 'Lord even of the sabbath day,' his thousand-year reign would have to be the seventh in a series of thousand-year periods or millenniums (Matthew 12:8, *AV*). Thus it would be a sabbatic reign.... Soon now six millenniums of his [Satan] wicked exploiting of mankind as his slaves will end, within the lifetime of the generation that has witnessed world events since the close of the Gentile Times in 1914 till now.... Would not, then, the end of six millenniums of mankind's laborious enslavement under Satan the Devil be the fitting time for Jehovah God to usher in a Sabbath millennium for all his human creatures? Yes, indeed!" (ibid., 26-27).

"Because it is so late, it is the time of all times for us to keep alert to what is taking place in the world's **speedy approach** to the unavoidable climax, the destruction of Babylon the Great and the war of Armageddon..." (*WT*, 1 Dec. 1969, 733).

Notes

1. Until 1964, the first masthead of *Awake!* in 1946 ended with the words "sure hope for the establishment of a righteous New World." The 1964 statement would be changed in 1975: "Most importantly, '*Awake!*' provides hope, giving you a basis of confidence **in the Creator's promise** of a new order of lasting peace and true security within our generation" (8 Jan. 1975, 2). And in 1982, it was changed again: "Most importantly, this magazine builds confidence in the Creator's promise of a peaceful and secure new order **before the generation that saw the events of 1914 C.E. passes away**" (8 Jan. 1982, 2). The reference to the 1914 generation was dropped in the January 8, 1987, issue and appeared again in the March 8, 1988, *Awake!*. Reflecting the new interpretation of "generation" in the November 1, 1995, *Watchtower*, the November 8, 1995, *Awake!* was again changed: "Most important, this magazine builds confidence in the Creator's promise of a peaceful and secure new world that is **about to replace the present wicked, lawless system of things**" (4).

39.

The "Superior Authorities" ("Higher Powers") of Romans 13:1-7

"Let every soul be in subjection to the superior authorities, for there is no authority except by God; the existing authorities stand placed in their relative positions by God" (*NWT*).

Jehovah's Witnesses—Proclaimers of God's Kingdom discusses the "superior authorities" of Romans 13:1-7 in several places.[1] At one point it is claimed that the Witnesses have experienced the fulfillment of Proverbs 4:18 with increasing light in the understanding of the Bible. Then it is stated: "Viewing matters in the light that was available, they at times had incomplete, even inaccurate, concepts.... As Jehovah has shed more light on his Word by means of his spirit, his servants have been humbly willing to make needed adjustments."[2] The example then given is Romans 13:1-7, where it is explained: "For many years the **Bible Students** had taught that 'the higher powers' (KJ) were Jehovah God and Jesus Christ. Why?" Society president Rutherford's articles in the June 1 and June 15, 1929, *Watch Towers* are explained as the source of this former interpretation.[3]

An informed reader would be surprised by the statement that the **Bible Students** held the view that Jehovah God and Jesus Christ were "the higher powers." If it had been stated that the **Jehovah's Witnesses** had "for many years" taught this, it would be accurate. The **Bible Students** had for "many years" (under Russell and Rutherford until 1929) held that "the higher powers" were in fact the **human governments**. The pre-1929 interpretation is not mentioned here by the *Proclaimers* book at all—but it is mentioned elsewhere, where it is stated that under Russell "they understood that 'the higher powers,' referred to at Romans 13:1-7 (KJ) were the secular rulers."[4] Then, "years later, a careful reanalysis of the scriptures was made, along with its context and its meaning in the light of all the rest of the Bible. As a result, in 1962 it was acknowledged that 'the superior authorities' are the secular rulers, but with the help of the *New World Translation*, the principle of *relative subjection* was clearly discerned."[5]

This explanation of the reversal of the belief held and promoted for over three decades as an example of "progressive understanding" or increasing light is amazing. Why? Materials published **during Russell's time already clearly understood and taught relative subjection**. For example, even the *Proclaimer's* book quotes Russell's *The New Creation* (1904), where he writes that genuine Christians "would naturally be the most sincere in their recognition of the great of this world, and most obedient to the laws and the requirements of law, **except where these would be found in conflict with the heavenly demands and commands**...."[6] And in 1882, the reader of the *Watch Tower* was told: "The church now is commanded to be subject to the powers that be, for 'The powers that be are ordained by God' (Rom. 13:1).... The Church must not resist the powers that be **except in matters of conscience**,"[7] or as expressed in Russell's *The Divine Plan of the Ages* (1886), "except where they conflicted with God's laws...."[8] A more recent attempt to explain the change, published in the May 1, 1996, *Watchtower*, is also deceptive. As author David Reed observes: The "attempted whitewash actually proves the Watchtower Society guilty of a flip-flop on Romans 13:1 *and* guilty of lying to cover it up."[9]

In his study on this point, former insider Raymond Franz concludes, "The claim, then, that in Russell's time there was a deficiency of understanding as to the *relative* nature of subjection to secular authorities is patently false. It simultaneously diverts attention from the basic question of the *identification* of the 'higher powers.'"[10]

How was the pre-1929 position—that the "the higher powers" were human governments—viewed in Society publications over the years, until its reinstatement in 1962? What claims were made for Rutherford's new interpretation? Here are some representative statements.

1931

"Those who profess to be consecrated to God and who hold that 'the higher powers' means the ruling powers of this world **deceive themselves and deceive others**. Many of the elders of the ecclesias or Bible classes insist that 'the higher powers,' described by the apostle in Romans thirteen, means the ruling powers of this world. Being selfish, they have **become blind to the revelation of God's truth**.... They insist on treading softly so far as the Devil and his organization are concerned, and are **led in the way of outer darkness**; and, as the Scriptures declare, **the same fate awaits them that God has provided for the Devil**. They are anti-kingdom-of God" (Rutherford, *Vindication I*, 81).

1932

"Until quite recently God's people understood that this scripture at Romans 13:1, speaking of 'the higher powers,' has reference to worldly ruling powers. Those who have withdrawn from the Society still hold this **wrongful view**. Now, however **the faithful remnant see clearly that this scripture has no reference to any part of Satan's organization** but does apply exclusively to God's arrangement in his organization for his own people. Those who refuse to see **this truth** and who oppose the statement of *The Watchtower* concerning it have seized upon such an excuse for offense and have dropped out and **gone into the dark**" (Rutherford, *Preservation*, 98).

1933

"The time was when even the consecrated believed that the 'higher powers' are the earthly rulers. **The enlightened ones now know that that is not true**..." (*WT*, 15 May 1933, 150).

1934

"**Satan has induced the people to believe that the rulers of this world are ordained of God** and that such rulers constitute the higher powers. **The clergy have been used more than any other class of men to create this improper conclusion** ... by the scripture at Romans 13:1.... The term 'higher powers,' as used in the text quoted, **could not possibly apply to the nations of the earth**..." (Rutherford, *Supremacy*, 48).

"**In 1929 the Lord made clearly to appear to his people** who constitute 'the higher powers,' and since then they have been enabled to see clearly that the faithful ones must **obey Jehovah God and Christ Jesus, who are 'the higher powers,'** and make no compromise with the wicked organization that rules the world, and which powers are not ordained of God" (*WT*, 1 Oct. 1934, 298).

"**In this day only Jehovah's witnesses identify 'the higher powers' properly**. They know and publicly declare that the 'higher powers' consist of Jehovah God and Jesus Christ.... Anyone who holds that a man or company of men or any organization on earth constitutes any part of the 'higher powers' mentioned by the apostle in Romans 13:1 **shows that he does not understand and does not appreciate God's Word**" (*WT*, 15 Nov. 1934, 341).

1936

"'Let every soul be subject unto the higher powers' (Rom. 13:1). **The Devil has caused religionists** to lay hold upon this Scripture text and to induce men to believe that the 'higher powers' are those men who hold the official positions in the government of this world...." (*WT*, 15 Feb. 1936, 55).

1938

"It is not addressed to the nations and people in general, and **has no reference whatsoever to the rulers of the 'state' or nations**.... If the construction placed upon Romans 13:1 by religionists were correct, then it would mean that God is wholly inconsistent because of having different laws under different countries and nations" (*Cons.*, 4 May 1938, 17).

"Prior to 1918 **God's people labored under the delusion** or understanding that the 'higher powers' are made up of the officials of the governments of this world, to whom all must submit, even though that submission might be contrary to God's commandment.... In the June 1929 issue of *The Watchtower* **Jehovah made known to his people clearly and unmistakably** that the 'higher powers' are God and Christ Jesus and that, when any law is made by men or man-made governments which conflicts with God's law, then the covenant people of God must obey God's commandments, and not those of man" (*WT*, 15 July 1938, 211).

1940

"Thus Jehovah delivered the captives from Satan's organization. One noteworthy event was this: that in 1928 **God revealed to his people the truth concerning 'the higher powers,'** showing his faithful people that the 'higher powers' are not the political elements that rule the world, but that Jehovah and Christ Jesus are the Higher Powers" (*WT*, 15 July 1940, 212).

1941

"The scripture at Romans 13:1 has long been applied by **religionists** to the worldly governments of this earth and to the powers thereof. It is manifest, however, that **no such thought was in the apostle Paul's mind** when he wrote the words" (*WT*, 1 Feb. 1941, 44).

1943

The view that the "higher powers" of Romans 13:1 refers to human governments is viewed as a "**perversion of Scripture**." "Such **religious misapplication of Scripture** concerning the 'higher powers' has **long caused the ignorant bondage of professing Christians to worldly officials** at the expense of the interests of God's work and of true freedom.... **In 1929 the clear light broke forth**. That year *The Watchtower* published the Scriptural exposition of Romans chapter 13" (*"The Truth Shall Make You Free,"* 311-12).

"But by publishing *the truth* on Romans 13:1-7, in *The Watchtower* of June, 1929, the remnant were given the freedom of the truth that Jehovah God and Christ Jesus are exclusively 'The Higher Powers,' whom Christians must obey rather than obey men opposed" (*WT*, 1 Oct. 1943, 298).

1946

"He [Jehovah] has pierced the claim of the dragon organization of the Devil that it is the 'higher powers' to which all Christians must be subject. **He has fatally wounded it by the truth now declared** by Jehovah's remnant that Jehovah God and Christ Jesus alone are 'The Higher Powers' whom we must obey.—Rom. 13:1" (*WT*, 15 Jan. 1946, 25).

"From 1928 onward **God's spirit had revealed to them** that 'the higher powers,' to whom every Christian soul must be subject, are not the ruling authorities of this world but are for ever Jehovah God and Christ Jesus..." (ibid., 27).

1950

"**The truth concerning the 'higher powers' as being God and Christ was made clear in 1928 and 1929**, and since then **that pointed truth** has been repeatedly wielded as an important part of the sword of the spirit" (*WT*, 15 June 1950, 182).

"Up till 1928 they, too, had held to the **ecclesiastical interpretation** of Romans 13:1-7 concerning the 'higher authorities.' But that year this scripture was taken under re-examination.... The conclusions arrived at were published in the June 1 and 15, 1929, issue of *The Watchtower*.... Holding to these conclusions ever since **has cost many of Jehovah's Witnesses their personal liberty and even their lives**" (*WT*, 15 Nov. 1950, 441).

1952

"Such **religionists** insist that those rulers are the 'higher powers' mentioned at Romans 13:1-7.... So the 'higher powers' the apostle, mentioned are Jehovah God and Christ Jesus..." (*"Let God Be True"* (1952 ed.), 247-48).

"These last words, 'for there is no authority except by God,' are **proof conclusive** that the 'superior authorities' Paul is speaking of **could no refer to the political powers** of Caesar governments" (*WT*, 15 June 1952, 375).

1959

After the end of World War I, it was realized that the Society "had been held in spiritual bondage too in many ways. There were **many false doctrines and practices that had not been cleaned out of the organization**. Not all of them were recognized at once, but gradually over the years that followed it became evident to what extent the brothers **had been in Babylonish captivity** at that time. **With considerable misunderstanding they had accepted earthly political governments as the 'superior authorities'** that God had ordained according to Romans 13:1; and as a result the Witnesses had been held in fear of man, particularly the civil rulers" (*Jehovah's Witness in the Divine Purpose*, 91).

Progressive Revelation?

Certainly, the quotations from Watch Tower publications cited above, if accepted, would force a rejection of the interpretation that the "higher powers" ("superior authorities") of Romans 13:1 were **secular authorities**. This view is attributed to Satan the Devil, which perverted and misrepresented Scripture, and was advanced by those who were deceived and deluded. The error of this position and the truth that the "higher powers" were God and Christ Jesus were supposedly **revealed by God**.

In spite of this extensive Watch Tower written record, the July 1, 1979, *Watchtower* magazine features the return to **its own thoroughly discredited interpretation as an example of "timely spiritual food"!** There we read: "Yet, over all these years, *The Watchtower* endeavored to provide timely spiritual food. In retrospect, **a notable example** of such 'food at the right time' seems to have been the 1962 *Watchtower* articles clarifying the Christian position of relative subjection to governmental 'superior authorities'—Rom. 13:1-7."[11]

In conclusion, the following statement from *The Watchtower* is made concerning "opposers"—those who left the Witnesses. Would it be appropriate to apply to the Society the principle presented here? Let the reader decide.

It is a serious matter to present God and Christ one way, then find that our understanding of the major teachings and fundamental doctrines of the Scriptures was in error, and **then after that, to go back to the very doctrines that, by years of study, we had thoroughly determined to be in error.** Christians cannot be vacillating—'wishy-washy'—about such fundamental teachings. **What confidence can one put in the sincerity or judgment of such persons?**[12]

Notes

1. *Jehovah's Witnesses—Proclaimers of God's Kingdom* (1993), 145, 147, 190-91, 198, 264. The translation "higher powers" is from the *King James Version*, and "superior authorities" from the Witnesses' *New World Translation*.
2. Ibid., 147.
3. Ibid. The change of doctrine was presented in two articles in the June 1 and 15, 1929, *Watch Tower*. "The instruction of the thirteenth chapter of Romans has long been misapplied" (*WT*, 1 June 1929, 163). After quoting Romans 13:1: "This scripture has been long applied by Christians to the Gentile governments and powers thereof. It is manifest, however, that no such thought was in Paul's mind when he wrote the words" (*WT*, 15 June 1929, 179).
4. *Proclaimers*, 190.
5. Ibid., 147.
6. *Proclaimers*, 190, quoting the *The New Creation*, 590-91. It is significant that the May 1, 1996, *Watchtower* quotes from page 591 of *The New Creation* but ignores this statement (13).
7. *WTR*, June 1882, 362.
8. Russell, *The Divine Plan of the Ages* (1886), 266.
9. *Comments from the Friends*, Summer 1996, 7.
10. *In Search of Christian Freedom* (Atlanta: Commentary Press, 1991), 485. The following statement by Raymond Franz can easily be verified by the reader: "As for recognizing the principle of 'relative subjection,' one can find dozens of Bible commentaries that, when dealing with Romans chapter thirteen, make the point that Christian subjection to secular authorities is always relative, conditional" (ibid., 486).
11. *WT*, 1 July 1979, 8.
12. *WT*, 15 May 1976, 298. According to the May 1, 1996, *Watchtower*, the 1929-1962 interpretation of the "higher powers," while wrong, was used by God: "… It was felt that the higher powers must be Jehovah God and Jesus Christ. This was the understanding Jehovah's servants had during the crucial period before and during World War II and on into the Cold War, with its balance of terror and its military preparedness. Looking back, it must be said that this view of things, exalting as it did the supremacy of Jehovah and his Christ, helped God's people to maintain an uncompromising neutral stand throughout this difficult period" (14). Applying this logic what might be said concerning Watch Tower dates (1925, 1975) which failed or teachings which were wrong (don't get married, don't have children, don't get vaccinated)? Is this the way the God of the Bible leads His people? And it should be remembered that it was claimed that **God** was the source of Rutherford's Romans 13 "new Light."

40.

Selected Quotations
from Watch Tower Publications
for the Years 1970-1979

1970

"These and other prophecies definitely mark this exceptionally violent period since 1914 as the 'time of the end,' the 'last days' of the present system of things. This means that the young people of today who ignore God's purposes and commands **will have a very short future**" (*WT*, 1 Mar. 1970, 142).

"What a fine way for young people to serve their Creator in the **few remaining years** of this present violent system of things!" (ibid., 146).

"In the **few remaining years** of the old system of things they will want to do as the Scriptures admonish: 'Keep proving what you yourselves are'" (ibid., 153).

While saying one can't know for sure exactly how much time is left—6,000 years run out in 1975: "**Only a short time, then, remains** for persons who love righteousness to show God that they want to be in his 'ark' of protection and live to see the blessings of the new system of things" (*WT*, 1 May 1970, 273).

"Who Will Conquer the World in the 1970s?" (Public address at all circuit assemblies during late 1970).[1]

"But all evidence is persuasive that the **climactic end is near**. When it does come, **shortly**, where will it find us?" (*WT*, 15 Dec. 1970, 758).

1971

"The time remaining to proclaim the good news is **very short**" (*WT*, 1 Feb. 1971, 82).

"What, therefore, **lies immediately ahead**? There can be no doubt about it. Demon-inspired woes are certain to increase, and the Bible says that the increased wrath of the ousted Devil will be particularly directed against those 'who observe the commandments of God and have the work of bearing witness to Jesus'" (*WT*, 15 Feb. 1971, 108-9).

"Now we are **at the portals** of God's righteous new system of things (2 Pet. 3:13). **How close the end of this system is!** ... **Very shortly now** we can expect Satan in his final all-out assault against God's people to bring tremendous trials among us" (ibid., 121).

"**Shortly now** the rule of the promised world government in the hands of this Prince of Peace will be manifest in all the earth" (*WT*, 1 Apr. 1971, 198).

"The promised 'times of restoration of all things' are **now upon us**" (*WT*, 15 Apr. 1971, 246).

"Shortly, **within our twentieth century**, the 'battle in the day of Jehovah' will begin against the modern antitype of Jerusalem, Christendom" (*"The Nations Shall Know That I Am Jehovah,"* 216).

"Though **time is short** for the present system of things, Jehovah's witnesses have much to do" (*WT*, 1 Oct. 1971, 605).

"All the nations are now on the march to Har-Magedon! This much can be unerringly said according to the Bible's timetable and according to world events in fulfillment of Bible prophecy. The confrontation with God **is imminent!**" (*WT*, 15 Oct. 1971, 623).

1972

"This deliverance into God's new order is now much nearer than when many of us first saw these predicted things 'start to occur.' Certainly **there is no time to delay** for proving ourselves worthy to experience this much-desired deliverance" (*WT*, 15 Apr. 1972, 240).

"Then, too, there is urgent need for God's ingathering work to be accomplished, for the **time is now short** before the end overtakes this wicked system of things and all who are still part of it" (*WT*, 15 Aug. 1972, 494).

"The Long Waiting in Hope **Soon to End.**" "It is under the feet of this Christ and his faithful followers that Jehovah will 'crush Satan' **shortly**" (*WT*, 15 Oct. 1972, 628, 631).

1973

"It [a Bible drama] certainly made everyone present ask whether he, too, could follow a similar course of full-time service in **the short time remaining**" (*WT*, 1 May 1973, 284).

"They may have prayed for 'God's kingdom to come.' But few realize that the Bible speaks of that kingdom as an actual government, one that **will shortly replace** all present political systems" (*True Peace and Security—From What Source?*, 7). In the 1986 revision of this work the statement **"will shortly replace** all present political systems," was changed to **"will replace"** (*True Peace and Security—How Can You Find It?*, 7).

"Already this separating work has been proceeding for many years. It is now **very near** its conclusion" (1973 ed., 87). The 1986 revision drops the word **"very"** and reads: "It is now **near** its conclusion" (83).

"While there is a genuine urgency in our day **due to the nearness of God's judgment**, our seeking a right standing with him cannot be just for a certain period, nor just to survive the coming 'great tribulation'" (1973 ed., 179). The 1986 revision at this point reads: "If we are to gain a right standing with God, it cannot be just for this period of urgency before his judgment not just to survive the coming 'great tribulation.'" (176).

Tract: "Is Time Running Out For Mankind?" "The generation seeing the start of 'the sign' [world wars, massive famines, disease epidemics, violent crimes, global pollution] in 1914 is now far along in years. **Time is obviously running out!** But what about the great efforts under way by world leaders to bring peace and security world wide? Note carefully 1 Thessalonians 5:3 says: 'Whenever it is that they are saying: "Peace and security!" then sudden destruction is to be instantly upon them.'"

Ex-Witness David A. Reed makes reference to this tract:

> I recall being present at the summer 1973 "Divine Victory" International Assembly of Jehovah's Witnesses when a packet of these tracts was provided for everyone in the audience. They were to be distributed door-to-door worldwide during a ten-day period, from September 21 through 30. I remember President Knorr telling us that breaking a leg would be about the only thing that might excuse us from participation in this vital work. The world's end was close, and it was essen-

tial that every household receive a copy as their official notification of this fact. The *1975 Yearbook* reports that 512,738 people took part in distributing 43,320,048 copies in the United States during September (p. 252).[2]

————————

"In contrast to these faithful servants of old, we are on the **very threshold** of the new system that they 'saw afar off'" (*WT*, 1 Aug. 1973, 477).

"As more persons become convinced that God's kingdom of a thousand years **is close** they feel impelled to tell others about it.... Stimulated by an awareness that **Divine Victory over this wicked system is near**, many more are buying out the time to pioneer" (*Kingdom Ministry*, Nov. 1973, 1).

1974

"According to the Bible's timetable, we are near the end of six thousand years of human history, and Christ's royal reign for the relief and rehabilitation of mankind **is at our doors**" (*WT*, 1 Jan. 1974, 8).

"We are well along in the 'last days,' and the destruction of all wickedness at the hands of Christ is **very near**" (*WT*, 15 Mar. 1974, 165).

"**Right action is necessary now** before that great war breaks out in order to find oneself on the victorious side at Har-Magedon" (*WT*, 15 Apr. 1974, 234).

"Yes, the end of this system is **so very near!** Is that not reason to increase our activity?... Reports are heard of brothers selling their homes and property and planning to finish out the rest of their days in this old system in the pioneer service. Certainly this is a fine way to spend **the short time remaining** before the wicked world's end" (*Kingdom Ministry*, May 1974, 3).[3]

"The generation that saw the beginning of 'these things' in 1914 is now well up in years and, in fact, is near 'passing away.' Therefore, **the time must be close** for the 'great tribulation' and the 'day of wrath' of God and Jesus Christ. What should you do to survive the coming destruction?" (*WT*, 15 June 1974, 359).

"Then F. W. Franz spoke on the urgency of the evangelizing work, with a view to saving as many lives as possible from destruction at the 'great tribulation,' which is now, according to all evidences, **very near at hand**" (*WT*, 1 Nov. 1974, 670).

"Today there is a great crowd of people who are confident that a destruction of even greater magnitude is **now imminent. The evidence is that Jesus' prophecy [Luke 21:20-23] will shortly have a major fulfillment, upon this entire system of things.** This has been a major factor in influencing many couples to **decide not to have children at this time**. They have chosen to remain childless so that they would be less encumbered to carry out the instructions of Jesus Christ to preach the good news of God's kingdom earth wide before the end of this system of things comes.—Matt. 24:14" (*Awake!* 8 Nov. 1974, 11).

"Not one thing only, but many things now taking place concurrently prove that **we are near** the day and hour of that future appearance of the 'sign of the Son of man' to all persons, ever unbelievers" (*WT*, 15 Dec. 1974, 751).

1975

"Hence, are there not clear indications that we definitely must be living in the period of unprecedented fear and trouble foretold by Jesus Christ? Surely! This means that a grand deliverance by means of God's kingdom must be **very near**" (*WT*, 1 Mar. 1975, 140).

"The tribulation of all tribulations is **just ahead**" (*WT*, 1 Oct. 1975, 608).

"Today we have **reached the climax** in this divinely guided course of events that leads to 'one world' under 'one government' over which God is the Universal Sovereign" (*WT*, 15 Oct. 1975, 616).

"Yes, the present fulfilling of 'the sign' means that *soon* God's Kingdom government will bring an end to this unrighteous system of things.... **SOON means within this generation**" (ibid., 635).

"One of those events is now in the process of **reaching its culmination**. It is the preaching of the 'good news' of God's kingdom by his Christ" (*WT*, 15 Nov. 1975, 681).

"Finally, we are one in **awaiting shortly** the dissolution of this moribund old order of things" (*WT*, 15 Dec. 1975, 758).

1976

"The conditions upon earth today, along with the Bible's prophecies, indicate that the time for the creating of a 'new earth' **is at hand**.... What a glorious prospect is **just ahead** for the planet!" (*WT*, 15 Jan. 1976, 36).

"The day **fast approaches** when Jehovah will give the decree to execute the world empire of Babylonish false religion. Her devastation will come quickly, as though 'in one hour'" (*Good News to Make You Happy*, 183-84).

Watchtower front cover: "Hold On—**The Promise Nears Fulfillment!**" The inside has a full page with the same illustration (of smiling people entering an earthly paradise) and the same statement (*WT*, 15 Dec. 1976, 744).

"The fulfillment of this promise [of a "new heavens and a new earth"] is getting nearer and nearer" (ibid., 750).

"...We can be certain that Jehovah's coming to execute judgment upon our opposers and persecutors **will now occur before not very long**" (ibid., 752).

"The 'short period of time' during which Satan the Devil and his demon army are restrained here at the earth is **now nearing its close**" (ibid., 755).

1977

"The thrilling news for our day is that the time for God's kingdom to take over earth's affairs is **fast approaching**" (*WT*, 1 Jan. 1977, 8).

"We are now deep in the twentieth century, with every indication that the present system of things will pass away with this fading generation.... They are very confident that this present wicked system of things **will shortly be replaced** by a new and righteous order—God's kingdom..." (*WT*, 15 Jan. 1977, 45).

"The time for God to end wickedness on the earth must be **soon**, for if present worsening conditions were not called to a halt by the Creator, selfish men would bring an end to humankind on the earth..." (*WT*, 15 Apr. 1977, 236).

"**We know that we are of the 'generation' that saw the start of these things in 1914** at the close of the Gentile Times, and **we believe Jesus' assurance that this same 'generation' of ours will see the finish of these significant things**, all this culminating in the total take-over by the triumphant Kingdom of all human affairs" (*Our Incoming World Government—God's Kingdom*, 156).

1978

"But the time for the 'great tribulation' **grows rapidly nearer**" (*WT*, 1 Jan. 1978, 28).

Front cover of the March 1, 1978, *Watchtower*: "Our Incoming World Government—GOD'S KINGDOM."

"Today in this year of 1978 C.E. the 'war of the great day of God the Almighty' at Har-Magedon **approaches**" (ibid., 31).

"Bible prophecy shows that this happy time [of God's kingdom] is **near at hand**" (*WT*, 15 June 1978, 15).

"Today **we stand on the threshold** of another major event in the history of mankind—the 'great tribulation,' which will reach its climax in 'the war of the great day of God the Almighty' at Har-Magedon" (*WT*, 1 Oct. 1978, 14).

1979

Front cover of the October 15, 1979, *Watchtower*: "TAKE COURAGE! **The Millennium is at Hand.**"

"All the Biblical and historical evidence indicating that we are in the last days of this wicked system of things gives us a firm basis for expecting the millennium of peace to **begin in the near future**" (ibid., 7).

"Today, God's people stand at the **very portals** of the millennium.... May we all 'be courageous and very strong' to survive into that millennium now at hand!" (ibid., 23).

"As God's Word foretold, the Devil is angry, for he knows his **time is short**" (*WT*, 15 Dec. 1979, 21).

Notes

1. The Circuit Assembly program (Oakland, Calif., Dec. 4-6) and advertising flyer with this message title is reproduced in Duane Magnani's *Point/Counterpoint*, volume 1: *False Prophets* (Clayton, Calif.: Witness Inc., 1986), 95.
2. David Reed, *Jehovah's Witness Literature* (Grand Rapids: Baker Books, 1993, 153).
3. Compare this with *WT*, 15 July 1976, 440-41: "Did Jesus mean that we should adjust our financial and secular affairs so that our resources would just carry us to a certain date that we might think marks the end?... This is not the kind of thinking that Jesus advised" (440). It should be noted that this was published *after* the 1975 failure.

41.

The 1975 Fiasco

A short statement in *Jehovah's Witnesses—Proclaimers of God's Kingdom* (1993) summarizes why the year 1975 became significant in 1966: "The Witnesses had long shared the belief that the Thousand Year Reign of Christ would follow after 6,000 years of human history. But when would 6,000 years of human existence end? The book *Life Everlasting—In Freedom of the Sons of God*, released at a series of district conventions [in 1966], pointed to 1975."[1]

On February 10, 1975, Society Vice-President Frederick W. Franz addressed over 20,000 Witnesses in the Los Angeles Sports Arena. Thousands of others were linked by radio hookup to hear the message in other California locations. This was only one of a number of similar meetings held around the world to present the Society's latest information on the significance of 1975. It was obvious from what Franz said that the hopes for 1975 among many Witnesses were very high. "Faced with an anticipated Sept. 5 deadline and growing expectations among many Witnesses," observed *L. A. Times* reporter John Dart, "F. W. Franz, the sect's 81-year-old chief 'theologian,' has put the damper on specific references to the war to end all wars."[2]

In his speech, "Time in Which We Are Now Interested," Franz stated that 6,000 years of human history would definitely end at sundown, September 5, 1975, according to the lunar calendar.[3] He also disclosed what many Witnesses around the world were expecting in 1975:

> Now [in] our inquiries around the world with brothers as to what they're expecting to occur between now and the end of 1975, it is revealed, that some, are very sanguine about matters in the near future, and they're expecting the great tribulation to occur and the destruction of Babylon the Great and the annihilation of all the political systems of this world and then the binding of Satan and his demons and their abyssing to occur before this year is ended—this year 1975. And immediately thereafter the thousand year reign of the Lord Jesus Christ to begin. So they expect a great deal. And they're venting their views to their brothers and sisters in the congregations and raising their expectations very, very high indeed. Well now, we're not saying that by the end of this year 1975 all these things cannot take place. That God cannot bring all these things about! He can! He's almighty. And this omnipotent One can bring this about in a hurry if He wants to do so. But, in view of what the Scriptures inform us, are we warranted in expecting so much to occur by September 5, 1975?...[4]

Franz went on to explain that there was a time interval between Adam's creation and Eve's, and that the sixth creative day ended only after Eve's creation. So while September 5, 1975, would mark the end of 6,000 years of man's existence, it did not mean that mankind would be 6,000 years into the seventh day. This view

294

was also presented in the October 1, 1975, *Watchtower*.[5] If this time interval were one month, then things could terminate in October; if two months, November, and so on. Franz stated, "Well, since that is the case, then we do not necessarily have to insist or even expect that everything is going to be through and over with by September 5 of this year...." Reflecting the urgency that characterized the movement for decades, Franz then cautioned his audience:

> ... After September 5, things could happen, and it looks very likely they're going to happen, according to the way that affairs are going in the world.... So it could come, quickly, within a short time after the terminal day of the lunar year 1975. And we should not jump to wrong decisions on that account and say, well, the time after September 5, 1975, is indefinitely long and **so it will allow for me to realize my human aspirations, getting married and raising a family—kids; or, going to college for a few years and learning engineering and finding a fine position as an engineer ... or some other prominent, fine paying job. No! The time does not allow for that dear friends**.... Evidently there is not much time left....[6]

So, according to Watch Tower speculation communicated by Franz in 1975, Armageddon and the millennial reign of Christ were soon to be realized, so soon that the Witnesses would not have time for the normal pursuits of life which he indicated. History again proved the Society a false prophet.

Randall Watters, ex-Bethel worker and Editor of *Free Minds Journal*, observes:

> Franz seems to be the main figure behind the 1975 date for the end of the world. I personally heard him give the Gilead Missionary Class graduation speech in 1975 where he said to 2000 members of the Bethel family (referring to Armageddon), "We don't know whether it will be weeks or months [away]." **Many Witnesses have argued that THEY never expected the end in 1975, but the Society's president and quite a number at headquarters sure did!** Enough was printed in the *Watchtower* and certain books as well to classify them collectively as a false prophet on 1975 alone, and Franz appears to be the key "prophet" on this ruse.[7]

What About 1975?

In response to questions concerning the 1975 failure, the dedicated Witness today will usually deny that anything definite was predicted or believed, but as Prof. M. James Penton writes:

> Throughout the Witness community circuit and district overseers—frequently the very men who had placed the greatest stress on 1975 as a year of prophetic significance—now often suddenly acted as though the fault for expecting the end in that year had lain with ordinary Jehovah's Witnesses. They held that the society had never said *definitely* that something would happen then, a fact which was quite true. **But they completely ignored the additional fact that Knorr, Franz, and the Watch Tower literature had implied over and over again that year would see the end of the present dispensation of human history**.... Strangely, many Witnesses, particularly those in responsible positions, seemed to suffer from some sort of collective amnesia which caused them to act as though the year 1975 had never held any particular importance to them at all.[8]

Ex-Witnesses Heather and Gary Botting agree: "Many Jehovah's Witnesses have already [in the early 1980s] forgotten the controversy over 1975; indeed many deny that there ever *was* a controversy and refuse to believe that the society ever made *any* predictions. Faithful Witnesses have rearranged their memories, smugly, to accord with the official Party line."[9]

Witness Jim Heidt is quoted in the February 14, 1975, *Los Angeles Times* as saying that "it was only the immature brothers and sisters reading between the lines who felt that Armageddon was definitely predicted for 1975."[10] From the testimonies of former members, it would seem that a great number of Witnesses were "immature" and that they were the ones who contacted potential converts and talked with evangelical Christians. They also seemed to be the ones who were frequently quoted in the news media.

From his own experience as a Witness, Prof. Jerry Bergman said that if a Witness questioned 1975 he was viewed as weak in the faith and not trusting in the organization. In 1973 he was called before the Judicial Committee of his congregation and told not to doubt 1975.[11]

Newspaper Reports and Conversations with Witnesses

What did Witnesses believe and teach concerning 1975, according to newspaper reports and contacts with Witnesses? Here are a few representative articles.

Under the headline, "Witnesses Give World Five Years at the Most," the Religion Editor of the *Arizona Republic* (August 24, 1969) presents an interview with Witness Erroll Burton:

> **Within months, or at the most five years, the end of the world as we have known it will occur** and a thousand-year reign of Jesus will begin. This is the view of the approximately 400,000-member [in the USA] sect calling itself Jehovah's Witnesses. According to Erroll Burton, Paradise Valley Unit of Jehovah's Witnesses, the prediction is based on the estimate that 1975 will mark the end of 6,000 years since the time of Adam and Eve, and that according to scripture, is when Armageddon will occur (Rev. 16:16)....

The March 19, 1970, issue of the English newspaper *Daily Mail* reported the story of how a Witness couple "refused permission for their newly born son to have a life-saving blood transfusion," but that their refusal was overturned by the magistrates at an emergency court hearing, and the transfusion was given. The parents held those responsible for the transfusion as "guilty of a grave sin." The article then went on to state: "The couple, who have been Witnesses for two years, believe that Armageddon—judgment day—will come before 1975. They said: 'If the baby died, he would have been resurrected and reunited with us after Armageddon.'" The *Evening Mail* of May 7, 1971, carried an article on the experiences of former Witnesses, Mr. and Mrs. Herman Goldvag, who had left the movement in 1969. Mrs. Goldvag explained: "We want to prevent other people from going through the misery we have had. Missionaries are working hard in Birmingham to recruit more into the faith before 1975—the expected date of Armageddon."

"Witnesses Take the Plunge for Eternity" was the headline of the article that appeared in the July 25, 1973, *Los Angeles Times*. Reporter Bella Stumbo covered the story of the baptismal service at the five-day Assembly at Dodger Stadium and interviewed some ladies waiting to be baptized: "'But the plain fact is that doomsday is at hand,' said Mrs. McGuire, 26, 'and those who haven't been baptized as Jehovah's Witnesses are going to perish. The occasion,' she elaborated, 'is called Armageddon and it is prophesied in the holy scriptures.' By all the best Witness reckoning, its due in two to three years."

Rev. Frank Triggs of the Cerritos First Assembly of God Church reported that "the leader of a Jehovah's Witness congregation in Southern California was so convinced that Oct. 31, 1974, was the last possible date for Armageddon that he declared he would sell his home for a few dollars on Oct. 30."[12]

John Dart reported that "the Brooklyn-headquartered Watchtower Society, burned by past erroneous prophecies, maintains that it never has said flatly that 1975 was going to be IT," and then concluded, "But in fact the society has left its followers little else to conclude."[13] As with past "erroneous prophecies," the

Witness leadership placed blame for inflated hopes and speculation concerning 1975 on the average Jehovah's Witness. The *Watchtower* of October 15, 1974, claimed that the publications of the Jehovah's Witnesses "have never said that the world's end would come then [1975]," and then added, "Nevertheless, there has been considerable individual speculation on the matter."[14] It is not stated that the source of the "individual speculation" was the Society leaders and its publications.

Contacts with Jehovah's Witnesses during the early 1970s, and with those who have left the movement since that time, verified the importance that was attached to 1975 and their expectation that Armageddon would take place that year, or even before. In 1974, I visited several parts of the United States (California, Nevada, and Hawaii). On three occasions, public school teachers and other observers informed me that Witness parents were so convinced that Armageddon would come during 1975, at the latest, that they removed their children from school. Since that time, many additional examples were related. One former elder and his wife from New York observed that because of 1975, "many Witness kids stopped going to high school."[15]

A significant account dealing with Witness expectations for 1975 appeared in the January 1975 issue of the *Evangelical Times*, published in London. The article, "Will the World End This Year?" was written by Richard E. Cotton (in consultation with ex-Witness George Terry). Cotton had left the Witnesses after eighteen years. Only a portion of the article is reproduced here:

> The year 1975 has dawned, and with it comes the question: Could this be the year of Nemesis, of retribution, for Jehovah's Witnesses? Could it be the year of yet another dashed hope?
>
> To many of the rank and file within the Watchtower Movement, 1975 has meant only one thing—the long awaited year of Divine Wrath. The time of judgment, when God would destroy the wicked and restore this old earth to a paradise state. Eternal life in the restored earth has been the hope of most Jehovah's Witnesses.
>
> For almost ten years, 1975 has hung over the heads of the faithful like a chronological carrot. True, very little has been written about it in official Watchtower publications, but a great deal has been said at grassroot level. And when Witnesses are taught to believe that God is using the Watchtower organisation to the total exclusion of all other churches or bodies (for this is their claim) it only requires a hint of a date to begin a wave of speculation. This is very understandable in a group maintaining that we are living at the very end of the Bible's "time of the end."
>
> A date like 1975 had a fine apocalyptic ring when it was still ten years or so ahead. In 1966, a publication called *Life Everlasting—in Freedom of the Sons of God* announced that independent research into Bible chronology had established that 6,000 years of human history would come to an end in the autumn of 1975. As Jehovah's Witnesses believe that there will be a millennium to complete a divine cycle of 7,000 years, it was clear that the long awaited period would begin around the autumn of 1975.
>
> When the date was made public in 1966, the present writer was a Witness and was able to see what happened. Very little apart from that statement was ever published, but things began to be said and great was the speculation. No doubt many can recall the famous football star who stated on television that the Bible taught that the end would come in 1975. He was so certain of this, viewers were told, that if the expected results did not materialize, he would throw his Bible away.
>
> In the months and years that followed, overseers and visiting speakers of the cult were known to speak to the congregation about the "short time left". Some of the more convinced would total up the number of days to October 1975. When told by indignant householders, "You people are always round at our doors," one full time worker would answer: "We shall not

be calling many more times."

Bible Studies with the unconverted were limited to a certain number of weeks because of the nearness of the end. Some Witnesses never bothered to increase their mortgage repayments as interest rates shot upwards. They were hoping for a permanent settlement on the amount outstanding in 1975. Some were so convinced the world was on its last legs that they speculated the system could not last until 1975.

D.I.Y. fans in the movement were known to remark in the early '70s that the house would not need repainting ever again. There was even the JW in need of surgery who preferred to live with the condition until the healing rays of the Millennium restored all to perfect health.

How many Witnesses, we wonder, will be suffering from loss of memory this year about their expressed hopes of only a year or so back? But these things were said and no amount of forgetting can unsay them.

To add to the fires of speculation, some Witnesses got hold of typed copies of a talk which it was claimed was given by one of the Watchtower Directors in some far away country. This explosive material indicated that soon calamities and even flesh-consuming plagues of a cosmic nature would befall the world of men. Yet members of the Watchtower Movement would be untouched by these manifestations of divine anger.

How sure everyone seemed. Yet now 1975 is here and the dilemma of the Witnesses continues to increase....[16]

I had many revealing conversations with Jehovah's Witnesses during 1975. When one Witness was asked what happened to Armageddon as predicted, the answer given was, "1975 is not over yet!" Another indicated that there was still almost a year available. What would they say now?

Remembering the 1975 Experience

Many who were Witnesses when the 1975 date was first proposed or who went through the 1975 disappointment have written or given accounts of that experience. The following examples are typical of many that could be included.

Eric Grieshaber and his wife Jean resigned from the Jehovah's Witnesses on October 24, 1974. They recall their experiences looking forward to 1975:

As the time for Armageddon drew closer, "the friends" began selling their homes, campers and motorcycles. Many gave up good paying jobs and took janitorial work in order to have more time for service. The year 1973 was an exciting one as we prepared for Armageddon. One of our friends who had left the area wrote and asked permission to stay with us in order to "ride out Armageddon" with the congregation. Two other families that moved to where the "need was greater" came back to our congregation to await Armageddon. We all knew that sometime around October 1, 1974, the last year of mankind's 6,000 years of existence on earth would begin and soon Jesus Christ would take his peaceful rule over the earth.

The sale of one's home was not a unique event. Gerald Sage was raised as a Jehovah's Witnesses and was a dedicated member until he resigned after 53 years. "In 1975, trusting a Witness prediction that the world would end before the year was out, he sold his house in Orange [California] for $37,000 and moved his family into an apartment."[17] According to an article in *The Irish Times*, in 1974, Pamela Gray and her husband Rory joined the Jehovah's Witnesses. "Shortly afterwards they sold their home because they had been told the world would end in 1975. They used their money to preach fulltime and warn others of the impeding doom. Mrs. Gray said many other members sold their homes at the time. The year 1975 came and went but the world stayed. It was the beginning of a period of doubts and questioning within the congregation."[18]

Ken and Gayle Nelson were raised as Jehovah's Witnesses and were active in their beliefs. Ken became an Elder in his congregation at age 20. Ken explains one of the things that caused them to leave the Witnesses:

> ... As an elder from 1963 to 1976, I knew what I had been taught by the Watchtower Society (WT), and what I had taught others during 1975 (Armageddon was supposedly coming that year). I remember the WT sending out special tracts in 1974-75 on which we were to stamp our names and telephone numbers because it would probably be the last time we would ever "work" that neighborhood. Special representatives came to our Kingdom Hall and said **only a few more months remained**. The *"Kingdom Ministry"* pamphlet commended JWs who sold their homes, and planned to finish out the short time left in great preaching activity. My wife and I sold our home, and put the remaining cash in a safety deposit box because we feared the banks were near collapse. Other elders sold their homes as well, and postponed purchases and medical treatments. We increased our preaching time sometimes as much as 75 hours a month during this period. 1975 came and went and nothing happened. We were told it was just a test from God of our faithfulness. I said, "If we can't believe Jehovah God, if He misled us, we should give up now." Does God deceive?[19]

The *Kingdom Ministry* mentioned by Ken Nelson was the May 1974 issue, which stated:

> Yes, the end of this system of things is **so very near!** Is that not reason to increase our activity? In this regard we can learn something from a runner who puts on a final burst of speed near the finish of the race. Look at Jesus, who apparently stepped up his activity during his final days on earth.... By carefully and prayerfully examining our own circumstances, we also may find that we can spend more time and energy in preaching during **this final period before the present system ends**. Many of our brothers and sisters are doing just that.... Reports are heard of brothers selling their homes and property and planning to finish out the rest of their days in this old system in the pioneer service. Certainly this is a fine way to spend the **short time remaining before the wicked world's end**.[20]

But after hopes for 1975 failed, what Nelson and others sacrificially did was no longer viewed in the same way. The July 15, 1976, *Watchtower* counsels these "mistaken" ones:

> It may be that some who have been serving God have planned their lives according to a mistaken view of just what was to happen on a certain date or in a certain year. They may have, for this reason, put off or neglected things that they otherwise would have cared for.... Did Jesus mean that we should adjust our financial and secular affairs so that our resources would just carry us to a certain date that we might think marks the end? If our house is suffering serious deterioration, should we let it go, on the assumption that we would need it only a few months longer? Or, if someone in the family possibly needs special medical care, should we say, "Well, we'll put it off because the time is so near for this system of things to go"? This is not the kind of thinking that Jesus advised.... However, say that you are one who counted heavily on a date, and, commendably, set you attention more strictly on the urgency of the times and the need of the people to

hear. And say you now, temporarily, feel somewhat disappointed; are you really the loser? Are you really hurt? We believe you can say that you have gained and profited by taking this conscientious course. Also, you have been enabled to get a really mature, more reasonable viewpoint—Eph. 5:1-17.[21]

Ex-Witness circuit overseer Donald Nelson, who was baptized in 1952, recalls his experience before 1975:

I remember with some nostalgia the happy days in the Kingdom Hall locally where my wife and I attended. There the Watchtower representatives, the circuit overseers would come by and say, edging forward and whispering confidently into the microphone, "Only thirty-seven months till Armageddon, brothers." And then in succeeding trips, "Only twenty-four months until Armageddon, brothers," and "Only twelve months to Armageddon brothers." Unfortunately, my wife and I left the Society in 1974, which was the year before Armageddon was to hit and demolish the world. So we never did find out how the circuit overseers dealt with "Only one month till Armageddon, brothers," or "Only one month after Armageddon brothers." Because, we had, by this time, found out the lies of the Watchtower chronology and we saw it for what it really was, inane, insane![22]

The "count-down" to Armageddon reported by Nelson was not unique—it was reported in a number of interviews. He also recalled knowing or hearing of those who sold their homes, gave up their education or pursuit of a career, and put off needed medical attention. The prospects for 1975 permeated everything.[23]

Ronald Gardiner was baptized as a Jehovah's Witness on July 27, 1973, at the international convention in Toronto, Ontario, Canada. "It was emphasized at this convention that the remaining time for our wicked system of things before Armageddon was extremely short and that faithful worshippers of Jehovah would be wise to increase their preaching activities from door to door. The speaker then encouraged the listeners to consider full-time service, or 'pioneering.'" Pioneering where the "need was greater" "would involve sacrifices, but I, as a loyal JW, had already sacrificed many things including my education, having decided not to go to the university because Armageddon was fast approaching (in 1975!)."

Ronald became a regular pioneer in a small town in Quebec in February 1974, where he often spent 140-150 hours each month in the work. As a faithful Jehovah's Witness, he was telling people that Armageddon

was near at hand and encouraging others to become Jehovah's Witnesses if they wished to be saved at Armageddon as Jehovah's chosen people. The local oversight in the congregation sincerely believed as other JW's did that Armageddon would occur in 1975. Rumors were continually being circulated amongst the faithful in "Jehovah's Theocratic organization" that strange happenings were just around the corner and the anticipation increased as October 1975 neared.

1975 came and went, and here it is 1978. Another false prophecy of the "faithful and discreet slave" has passed into history.... Jehovah's Witnesses are now denying that they believed 1975 would be the end of the present age. However, the facts are in print for anyone that is interested to see, and who is open-minded enough to examine them.

Ronald writes that a number of Witnesses were shocked by the 1975 failure. He continues:

As 1975 neared its end and a new year began, the organization laid the blame for the 1975 episode on the individual JW's by stating that certain individuals were misinterpreting the publications. This really began to bother me, and I began to read and reread the publications written from 1966 onward. I saw that the Society had definitely taught that 1975 would be the end, and now they were laying the blame on the average Jehovah's Witness. I saw that the average JW is a mere tool in the hands of the Watchtower dictatorship.

Ronald left the Jehovah's Witnesses in February 1977.[24]

Kenneth David Phillips recalls his experiences:

My earliest memory of anything formally religious was when I was about five years of age. My mother, sister and I were visited by a young couple at our home offering "free home Bible studies."... I became an active Jehovah's Witness.... I accepted my early indoctrination with few questions. I was taught that all my friends at school, their families, in fact, everyone who did not join the Watchtower organization and accept the leadership of its governing body, would be destroyed by God at the end of the world. Only JWs who supported the Watchtower without question would survive into the New Order of things. This new order was so close that I was told that I would probably not even finish school before the end came.

This teaching on the nearness of the end began to be intensely promoted to my generation after about 1968, as I entered high school. A book entitled, *Life Everlasting—In the Freedom of the Sons of God*, along with various articles which appeared in the *Watchtower* magazine, began to push the view that the end of the world would come and the millennial reign of Jesus Christ would begin by the year 1975. This information was pushed with great assurance and had a great effect on my outlook concerning the future. We were taught to spend our time "preaching" the good news of God's kingdom from house to house, placing magazines which contained the "Truth," the only correct interpretation of the Bible. We were strongly encouraged to forget education beyond high school, to forego marriage, to wait until the New Order came for these things.... [After 1975 failed] What happened? Did God decide to change the date? At first we thought that maybe he had. God was merciful, we were told. He had given us more time to preach and perhaps save a few more into the kingdom.... The Watchtower told us that the delay would only be a matter of weeks or a few months, but not years.... I do not want to give the impression that the "1975" disappointment was the only difficult issue many faced with the Watchtower. In fact there were many even more critical.... I came to realize that much of what I had been taught was based on half-truths and deception.[25]

Gloria Muscarella, a fifth-generation Witness, was asked, "What started you thinking about the truthfulness of the organization?"

Mom taught me about 1975 since I was 10 years old. She knew it was the date for Armageddon. My grandmother, on the other hand, had been around long enough to be disappointed herself, and she told my mother not to put faith in a date. But my mother and the rest of the family wouldn't listen, especially with all the articles coming out about 1975 and the 7th period of 1000 years of human history that would begin in 1975. So I would say that 1975 was the beginning of a lot of bitterness and anger that began to develop. After 1975 they had special meetings to try and calm down the brothers.... They said we were waiting on the time period between the creation of Adam and the creation of Eve, and this time had to be added on to 1975 to arrive at the end![26]

Grant Lindsey was baptized in 1957, worked in Bethel (1958-61), and later served as congregational overseer and elder. He was active as a Jehovah's Witness until 1975 and attended his last circuit assembly in 1976. He personally could not become enthusiastic about 1975 because of Christ's statement in Matthew 24:36: "Concerning that day and hour nobody knows..." (*NWT*). Because of this he was told: "You don't have the right spirit concerning 1975," and that he was "weak in the faith." He recalled how Jim, a publisher in the congregation, met with the judicial committee after the 1975 failure and asked for an explanation: "How can it be, that before 1975, to promote that date made one 'spiritually mature or strong,' and after the failure such ones were identified as 'spiritually immature' or 'spiritually weak'?"

Lindsey also observed the sacrifices made by many Witnesses looking toward 1975, such as neglecting physical needs and not pursuing an education or even job training. He recalled how shortly before 1975, a well-educated engineer quit his job, sold his home, and moved to another area "where the need was greater," where he lived in a small trailer to finish out the remaining time—which never came.[27]

Vito Potenzieri was baptized in 1967 and became an elder in 1972. He also served in other positions, including temporary circuit overseer. He recalls how almost every meeting, convention, and conversation among the Witnesses focused on 1975, and the statements that the "Time is short," and "Stay alive until 1975" were often made. Vito gave up a good job on Wall Street in 1972 and became a laborer to give him more free time for service. He relates how Witnesses he knew sold their homes, cashed in life insurance policies, put off dental work and operations, gave up professions and college educations, all because of 1975. One Witness he knew told his employer that did not wish to put funds into a retirement account. Vito relates how after 1975, some left the organization, some moved away and were not heard from again, and some even committed suicide.[28]

As a Witness at the time, Ty Sharrer recalls:

> In 1973 our congregation posted a calendar inside the Kingdom Hall showing a countdown until 1975. It presented a Biblical picture which was drawn and colored by my sister-in-law. Several years later she denied ever doing this. Being an Elderette she could use Theocratic Strategy and lie about it. Another weird thing happened that year. Everyone at the Kingdom Hall was given code names to identify each other when the Tribulation began. We were also requested to memorize all the Witnesses' addresses in our congregation.[29]

In their book *Witnesses of Jehovah*, Leonard and Marjorie Chretien write of their post-1975 experiences as Jehovah's Witnesses:

> Of course, when 1975 passed into 1976, there was a great deal of disappointment. Leadership assured us that the end wasn't far off. It was a matter of weeks or months—not years. Most of us were willing to wait another year. But when 1976 passed, everyone could sense the dissension building. Some people had already left and more were thinking about it. And that was the catalyst for members to start questioning other Society policies and doctrine. One might expect that the leadership would finally admit that they were in error concerning 1975. Instead, they did nothing to alleviate these feelings. In fact, in a rather cavalier fashion they dismissed the matter and chastised us for our zeal.[30]

In 1976, the Chretiens attended a meeting in a large new assembly hall in Georgetown, Canada. The speaker was F. W. Franz, who

> gave a convoluted discourse that ultimately led to the point of his visit and talk: He asked the audience in a shrill manner, **"Do you know why nothing happened in 1975?"** After a rather protracted pause he virtually shouted a reply to his question: **"It was because *you* expected something to happen!"** He emphasized his point by waving his hand toward the audience in theatrical style. We looked at each other in amazement, and you could hear a pin drop in that large building holding thousands of Witnesses. Naturally, that didn't set well with us or with most Witnesses. In 1977, for the first time we could remember, there was a slight *decrease* in membership (about 1 percent). Still, we were willing to wait a little longer.[31]

The Chretiens moved to La Jolla, California, and Leonard was appointed an elder at the local Kingdom Hall. "We found that the new congregation was in just as much of an uproar as the one we left in Canada."[32] In 1977, Watch Tower Society representative Harley Miller was sent from Brooklyn to speak to the San Diego area congregations in a Sunday meeting at the Del Mar Fairgrounds. They recount:

> At first when he brought up 1975, it appeared that he was trying to waffle and squirm his way out of the issue. Then suddenly he became very aggressive. In a bombastic manner he told about driving into the Fairgrounds that day and noticing the large palm tree that was prominently planted near the entrance. Pointing with dramatic emphasis toward that tree, he announced, **"Anyone here in the audience who doesn't like what did or did not happen in 1975, I suggest you go out under that palm tree and cry about it."** The statement was shocking, and obviously meant to intimidate people who were used to blind obedience to the organization. But we weren't buying it.... It wasn't so much that we were upset with the date failure; we were disturbed with the way it was handled.... We did not expect grown men to gloss over the truth and twist the fact to the point that many Jehovah's Witnesses began to doubt themselves. Maybe they had misinterpreted the message. Maybe it was their own fault for reading too much into the Watchtower publications.[33]

Having been Witnesses for more than 20 years, leaving the organization was not taken lightly and after a thorough investigation of the Watch Tower Society and its teachings, they concluded: "The organization had misled and misinformed people and changed its mind repeatedly over the years. And it was not willing to tell us the truth now."[34] On August 24, 1982, the Chretiens submitted a letter of disassociation to their local Kingdom Hall.

Raymond Franz, who was a member of the Governing Body from 1971 until 1980, when he resigned, was in a position to see the impact of 1975 on lives:

> I have seen people very greatly harmed by the false urgency surrounding the 1975 predictions, with some undergoing extreme emotional distress, families facing enduring economic strain for years, men who had given up good jobs having bouts with alcoholism due to the difficulty in finding new employment, elderly persons who faced a bleak future due to using insurance or similar funds prematurely, persons whose physical health was seriously damaged due to putting off surgery or other treatment. If the sacrifice had been for truth, for God, for a noble purpose, then it would be worth it. But it was due to a mental concoction originating with one person [F. W.

Franz] and then promulgated by an organization and it ended in nothing, proved a complete fiction. They may try to shrug it off, but the responsibility for all this rests with those who gave birth to the false hopes, who stirred up and excited illusionary expectations.[35]

The erroneous Watch Tower 1975 false date impacted millions of lives. What was the basis for this date? This is investigated in the next chapter.

Notes

1. *Jehovah's Witnesss—Proclaimers of God's Kingdom* (1993), 104.
2. John Dart, "The End is Near ... Maybe," *Los Angeles Times*, 24 Feb. 1975, Part 2, 1.
3. F. W. Franz, Los Angeles Sports Arena, 10 Feb. 1975 (tape recording). To announce that 6,000 years were certain to run out on September 5, 1975, would indicate that the problems of chronology mentioned in the August 15, 1968, *Watchtower* (499-500) and in the article on "Abraham" in *Aid to Bible Understanding* (23, where it is stated that an adjustment would place Adam's creation date as 4027 rather than 4026 B.C.E.) had been solved. I am amazed at the temerity of the Witnesses on such matters when the finest Bible scholars in the world have questioned the entire scheme of dating Adam's creation as being impossible on the basis of the available evidence.
4. Franz tape.
5. *WT*, 1 Oct. 1975, 579. For a discussion of the Adam and Eve time "gap," see the appendix to chapter 5 of my book *Jehovah's Witnesses and Prophetic Speculation* (2nd ed.; Phillipsburg, N.J.: Presbyterian and Reformed Publishing Co., 1972), which was written in December 1975.
6. Franz tape.
7. *Free Minds Journal*, Mar.-Apr. 1993, 6. Brackets in original.
8. M. James Penton, *Apocalypse Delayed* (2nd ed.; Toronto: University of Toronto Press, 1997), 100.
9. Heather and Gary Botting, *The Orwellian World of Jehovah's Witnesses* (Toronto: University of Toronto Press, 1984), 50.
10. Dart, 5.
11. Interview by the author.
12. Dart, 1.
13. Ibid.
14. *WT*, 15 Oct, 1974, 635.
15. Interview with Vito and Annette Potenzieri, May 23, 1998.
16. The *Evangelical Times* address is: Evangelical Times, Elephant and Castle, London, S.E.1.
17. *The* [Orange County] *Register*, 21 June 1984, B4.
18. *The Irish Times*, May 18, 1983.
19. Kenneth Nelson, "From 'Witness' to Witness," *Thoughts... for Jehovah's Witnesses, Ex-Jehovah's Witnesses, & Friends Newsletter*, Sept. 1994, 1.
20. *Kingdom Ministry*, May 1974, 3.
21. *WT*, 15 July 1976, 440-41.
22. Video: *Jehovah's Witnesses—a Non-Prophet Organization* (1995).
23. Interview, May 24, 1998.
24. Ronald Gardiner, *I Was a Jehovah's Witness*, not paginated.
25. Letter to *Free Minds Journal*, Jan.-Feb. 1993, 7-8.

26. *Bethel Ministries*, July-Aug., 1989, 9.

27. Interview, May 23, 1998. The "count-down" to Armageddon, reported by Nelson was not unique—it was reported in every interview with six former Witnesses on May 22-24, 1998.

28. Interview with Vito Potenzieri and his wife Annette, May 23, 1998.

29. "A Personal Memory of the 1975 Fiasco," in "Watchtower & JW FAQ" (Part 5 of 8), p. 8 http://home.sol.no/~jansh/wteng/jwfaq5.htm, accessed 14 Aug. 1998.

30. Leonard and Marjorie Chretien, *Witnesses of Jehovah* (Eugene, Oreg.: Harvest House, 1988), 76.

31. Ibid., 77.

32. Ibid., 77-78.

33. Ibid., 78.

34. Ibid., 84.

35. Raymond Franz, *In Search of Christian Freedom* (Atlanta: Commentary Press, 1991), 567. In his book *Crisis of Conscience* (2nd ed.; Atlanta: Commentary Press, 1992), Franz discusses the 1975 failure and the reluctance of the Watch Tower leadership to deal with the issue. But with serious drops in witnessing activity "there was a vote of 15 to 3 in favor of a statement making at least some acknowledgment of the organization's share in the responsibility for the error. This was published in the March 15, 1980, *Watchtower*" (212). "At best, the organization has never made more than token acknowledgment of the responsibility for the damage produced by its numerous time predictions" (Franz, *In Search*, 477).

42.

The Basis for the 1975 Fiasco

According to *Jehovah's Witnesses—Proclaimers of God's Kingdom*, quoted in the last chapter, "The **Jehovah's Witnesses had long shared the belief** that the Thousand Year Reign of Christ would follow after 6,000 years of human history."[1] This conviction and the calculation that the 6,000 years would end in the year 1975 (according to their study of Bible chronology) were the primary bases for the fiasco.[2] What is the source of this belief in the significance of 6,000 years? How was the theory acquired by C. T. Russell and how was it defended? How is this theory viewed by non-Witness scholars? Is it a creditable view? The following is a brief overview of the subject for which much has been written.

The 6,000 Year Tradition

The view that 6,000 years of human existence would be followed by God's intervention and the end of the present world system can be traced though "pagan, Jewish, Christian and Mohammedan theology."[3] The pagan sources include Chaldean, Egyptian, Etruscan, Median and Persian writings, the Sibylline Oracles, and the philosopher Zoroaster.[4] "A Jewish tradition of the six thousand years, followed by the Sabbath millennium, dates at least from the second century B.C.," and the view is found in the Midrash, the *Cespar Mishna* and *Gemarah*.[5] Within Christianity, the tradition is found at least as early as the *Epistle of Barnabas* (A.D. 70-79) and in many of the Church Fathers' writings.[6]

Many early writers who followed the chronology of the Septuagint concluded that *they* were living in the end of the age. "Elliott in his *Horae Apocalypticae* lists the following dates for the close of the sixth millennium, and the ushering in of the seventh, as set by some of the ancients: Sibylline Oracles, c. A.D. 196 (the earliest); Cyprian, c. 243; Hippolytus, 500; Lactantius, c. 500; Constantius, c. 500; Hilarion, 500; Sulpitius Severus, 581; and Augustine, 650."[7] Nineteenth century author George Peters, adds: "So generally was this theory of the Millenaries held that, adopting the chronology of the Septuagint, at different periods, when it was supposed that the six thousand years were ending, an almost universal belief in the ending of the world was entertained."[8]

The 6,000-year tradition was taught extensively during the Middle Ages and later into the eighteenth century. Writers include Joachim Abbas (?-1212?), Jeane Pierre d'Olive (1248/49-1298), Melanchthon (1487-1560), Joseph Mede (1586-1638), John Bunyan (1628-1688) and Robert Fleming (?-1716).[9]

Many others continued to propagate the view in the nineteenth and twentieth centuries. William M. Alnor devotes a chapter in his book, *Soothsayers of the Second Advent* (1989), to "The 6,000-Year Legend," where he writes: "The theory I call the '6,000-year human history error' is used by almost all of today's date setters and prophecy sensationalists."[10] This includes the Jehovah's Witnesses.

The 6,000 Year Tradition and C. T. Russell

A number of writers held the 6,000-year view during the nineteenth century; among them were William Miller and the Second Adventists. Pastor Russell credited Christopher Bowen of England for first extracting the **correct** 6,000-year chronology and acknowledged this in the October-November 1881 *Zion's Watch Tower*: "We do not here give the time arguments or proofs.... We merely notice here that the Bible chronology, first dug from Scripture by Bowen, of England, **which shows clearly and positively that the 6,000 years from Adam ended in 1873**, and consequently that there the morning of the Millennial day (the seventh thousand) began, in which a variety of things are due."[11] Bowen's chronology had been communicated to Russell by N. H. Barbour in 1876. Barbour had discovered and accepted Bowen's chronology, found in E. B. Elliott's *Horae Apocalypticae*, in 1860.[12]

Russell placed the acceptance of the 6,000-year prophetic scheme in proper perspective when he wrote: "And **though the Bible contains no direct statement that the seventh thousand will be the epoch of Christ's reign**, the great Sabbath Day of restitution to the world, yet the **venerable tradition** is not without reasonable foundation."[13] Russell's admission that "the Bible contains no direct statement" that anything was to happen at the end of 6,000 years, and that the idea was based on "venerable tradition," is just as true today as it was when this statement was published (1889). But one important point might be added: Of the many dates that have been set for the end of 6,000 years and have been connected with specific predicted events, all have failed! "Venerable tradition" does not equal Biblical truth!

The Witnesses and Bible Chronology Defended

From the beginning of the movement, Watch Tower publications have expressed confidence that their chronology was correct. To the uninformed or uncritical reader, the articles and other treatments that have dealt with Bible chronology in these publications, beginning with Russell, appeared impressive and exuded confidence. They were presented as "reliable" and "trustworthy," the result of earnest and independent Bible research.[14] In 1966, the book, *Life Everlasting in Freedom of the Sons of God*, authored by F. W. Franz, affirmed: "According to **this trustworthy Bible chronology** six thousand years from man's creation will end in 1975, and the seventh period of a thousand years of human history will begin in the fall of 1975 C.E."[15] Jehovah's Witnesses knew what this meant. This is clearly explained in the October 8, 1968, *Awake!*: "How fitting it would be for God, following this pattern, to end man's misery after six thousand years of human rule and follow it with his glorious kingdom rule for a thousand years!"[16]

It is significant that the chronology accepted by Russell placed Adam's creation at 4128 B.C., rather than the current date of 4026 B.C.(B.C.E.), and it was verified by elaborate "proofs" and viewed as trustworthy as the following publications illustrate.

In the book *Three Worlds* (1877), the reader is informed that "the mass of evidence which synchronizes with the fact that the six thousand years are already ended, is **absolutely startling**, to one who will take the trouble to investigate," and that "**clear proof can be found** that the six thousand years from Adam are ended."[17]

The November 15, 1904, *Zion's Watch Tower* contains four diagrams submitted by three supporters of Russell's chronology which "serve the one purpose of confirming the Bible chronology" contained in *The Time Is at Hand* "as the **only possible and consistent Bible chronology**, on which alone all the various lines of prophecy are harmonizable.... The lesson of the accompanying diagrams is that no such parallels would be possible **were a single one of our prominent dates altered**."[18]

In *The Finished Mystery* (1917), Russell's chronology is said to be further corroborated by the Great Pyramid of Egypt.[19] The article on "Chronology" in the May 15, 1922, *Watch Tower* begins with the statement: "**We have no doubt whatever in regard to the chronology** relating to the dates 1874, 1914, 1918, and 1925."[20] And the article, "Divinely-Given Chronological Parallelisms (Part I)," in the November 15, 1922, issue, affirms: "It has been shown in a preceding article that the parallel dates of present-truth chronology are proof of divine foreknowledge, and that they demonstrate that **the system is of divine origin**."[21] Russell makes reference to Usher (or Ussher) being "misled by the evident error of I Kings 6:1" which reads "**four** hundred and eightieth year," when it should be "**five** hundred and eightieth year."[22] Later the Witnesses would adjust the "evident error" and accept the first figure. While all the foregoing affirmations concern the chronology accepted and promoted by Russell, the *Proclaimers* book explains that "during the years from 1935 through 1944, a review of the overall framework of Bible chronology revealed that a poor translation of Acts 13:19, 20 in the *King James Version*, along with certain other factors, had thrown off the chronology by over a century."[23] The revised date became 4026 B.C. (B.C.E.).

Creation Chronology as Viewed and Dated by Others

Both Russell and later Watch Tower Society writers mention that many others had attempted to establish Adam's creation date. Russell referred to "**between one and two hundred different systems**,"[24] and the August 15, 1968, *Watchtower* states that "a hundred years ago when a count was taken, no less that **140 different timetables** had been published by **serious scholars**. In such chronologies the calculations as to when Adam was created vary all the way from **3616 B.C.E. to 6174 B.C.E.,** with one wild guess set at 20,000 B.C.E."[25] These quotations, however, do not reflect the full measure of the problem, as the statements which follow demonstrate.

In 1809, years before Russell accepted Bowen's 6,000-year chronology, William Hales published the following:

> Here are upwards of 120 different opinions, and the list might be swelled to **300**, as we are told by *Kennedy*, in his Chronology, p. 350. This specimen, however, is abundantly sufficient to show the disgraceful discordance of chronologers, even in this prime era: the extremes differing from each other, not by *years*, nor by *centuries*, but even by *chiliads*; the first exceeding the last not less than 3268 years!"[26]

In his article on chronology, published in 1858, Joseph Packard writes:

> The uncertainty of ancient chronology and the want of agreement among chronologers have passed into a proverb. Scalinger complains that **no two systems could be found to agree**, and that he rose from the study more doubtful than ever.... We are sorry to damp sanguine hopes of success in the attainment of certainty in this science; but when we remember that Sir Isaac Newton spent a great part of the last thirty years of his life in this study, and wrote over his system *sixteen* [one source says eighteen] times without settling the disputed points.... We have spoken of the want of agreement among chronologists. In proof of it we might mention that there are on record **no less than *three hundred* different opinions** as to the era of the creation, their greatest difference being no less that 3268 years.[27]

Joseph A. Seiss, who was well-known to Russell, after placing Adam's creation at 4131 B.C. and calculating that from Adam's creation to 1878 was 6009 years, cautions:

> **Not much stress is to be laid on these computations**. There are several items in the list which are in dispute between critics and investigators. **Neither does the Bible profess to give a full and**

complete chronology. It has dates and genealogies out of which we can construct a scheme, as above, which may approximate the truth, **but about which we cannot be very certain**. The Septuagint version gives many of these items differently from the Hebrew, and both have their adherents and defenders.... The present state of historical chronology in general, **is very confused, indefinite and uncertain**. With endless study devoted to it, **we are still vastly in the dark**. Authors disagree in regard to the time since the creation of Adam, not only by years and centuries, but by millenniums.[28]

In the second volume of his massive *The Theocratic Kingdom* (1884), George Peters writes: "In this work we have not committed ourselves to the adoption of any chronological reckoning for the simple reason that, owing to several designed chasms in the Bible, **no two chronological tables are alike, although given by able men**."[29]

The Americana article on "Chronology" (1913) states: "One author collects 120 different computations of the true date [of Adam's creation]; another says he has collected over 200; and **300 have been reckoned**; and the **estimates vary over 3,500 years**, from 3,483 to 6,984 years before the Christian era."[30]

I have found many similar observations in Bible dictionaries, commentaries, and other relevant studies. The problem of establishing an absolute chronology has not been solved. The following three expressions on Old Testament chronology, by more recent scholars, are typical.

Noted chronologer Edwin R. Thiele, explains:

> The chronology of the Old Testament **presents many complex and difficult problems**. The data are not always adequate or clear, and at times are almost completely lacking. Because of insufficient data many of the problems are at present beyond solution. Even when the data are abundant the exact meaning is often not immediately apparent, leaving scope for considerable difference of opinion and giving rise to many variant chronological reconstructions. The chronological problem is thus one of the availability of evidence, of correct evaluation and interpretation of that evidence, and of its proper application. Only the most careful study of all the data, both Biblical and extra-biblical, can hope to provide a satisfactory solution.... **Because of the difficulties involved, it must be admitted that the construction of an absolute chronology from Adam to Abraham is not now possible on the basis of the available data**.[31]

Well-known creationist author Henry M. Morris writes:

> The vital question as to exactly *when* the uniquely significant event of Genesis 1:1 took place **cannot be completely settled in the present state of the art of the study of Bible chronology. Although a great number of men have labored diligently in the attempt** to formulate a complete chronology of the Bible, the very fact that they all disagree with each other demonstrates that the problems are serious and the issue still unsettled. A list of the difficulties that hinder this work would include the following, among others:
>
> (1) The uncertainty of accurate copying and transmission of the numbers originally recorded, since the Massoretic, Septuagint, and Samarian texts all disagree in this respect
> (2) The uncertainty as to whether the length of the ancient calendar year was the same as the length of our present year
> (3) The possibility of missing generations in the genealogies of the Old Testament....[32]

And finally, this conclusion from the *Baker Encyclopedia of the Bible* (1988): "Clearly, OT chronology is beset with difficulties. A dogmatic stance seems unwarranted for periods as far separated as the age of Abraham and the career of Ezra."[33]

In spite of these and many similar expressions which could be quoted, in *The Time is at Hand* Russell writes, "The length of time since the creation of man is variously estimated. **Among those who accept the Bible record, there can be little difference of opinion....**"[34] And the January 1, 1975, *Watchtower* claims: "In the Bible an accurate chronology from the creation of man onward is provided."[35] Reflecting these statements, the Watch Tower Society Vice-President F. W. Franz specifically dated the end of the 6,000 years since Adam's creation as **September 5, 1975!**[36] But how credible are these claims?

In researching this book, a number of publications were examined, many of which advanced dates for Adam's creation. Below is a sampling of those mentioned or proposed by various writers. The problem of Old Testament chronology and speculation as to the date of Adam's creation were still subjects of debate even in the twentieth century.[37]

Proposed Dates for Adam's Creation—Dates B.C.

3483, 3616, 3671, 3700, 3734, 3740, 3751, 3754, 3759, 3760, 3761, 3784, 3836, 3849, 3880, 3916, 3928, 3941, 3944, 3947, 3948, 3949, 3950, 3951, 3955, 3958, 3959, 3960, 3961, 3962, 3964, 3966, 3967, 3969, 3970, 3971, 3980, 3983, 3984, 3993, 3996, 3999, 4000, 4001, 4003, 4004, 4005, 4007, 4008, 4019, 4020, 4021, 4025 (WT date), 4026 (WT date), 4028 (WT date), 4040, 4041, 4046, 4051, 4052, 4053, 4058, 4062, 4064, 4073, 4079, 4088, 4090, 4095, 4100, 4103, 4120, 4124, 4125, 4128 (WT date, Bowen), 4129 (WT date), 4131, 4132, 4138, 4140, 4141, 4157, 4161, 4172, 4174, 4184, 4192, 4220, 4231, 4305, 4320, 4359, 4427, 4697, 4698, 4700, 4830, 4832, 4970, 5000, 5049, 5100, 5196, 5198, 5199, 5200, 5201, 5210, 5270, 5296, 5300, 5328, 5336, 5343, 5344, 5351, 5361, 5369, 5394, 5402, 5407, 5409, 5411, 5421, 5426, 5443, 5444, 5469, 5478, 5481, 5487, 5493, 5497, 5500, 5501, 5506, 5507, 5508, 5509, 5515, 5546, 5555, 5556, 5586, 5598, 5608, 5624, 5626, 5634, 5654, 5700, 5708, 5801, 5862, 5872, 5877, 5984, 6000, 6081, 6128, 6138, 6157, 6158, 6174, 6204, 6310, 6484, 6984, 11,013.

Watch Tower Proposed Dates for Adam's Creation—Dates B.C.E.

4129   *Watch Tower Reprints* (1896), 1980.

4128   Russell, *The Time Is at Hand* (1889), 53.

4028   *"The Truth Shall Make You Free"* (1943), 152. Already mentioned in *The Golden Age*, 13 Mar. 1935, 376.

4026   *"The Kingdom Is at Hand"* (1944), 171.

4025   *"New Heavens and a New Earth"* (1953), 364.

4026   *"All Scripture Is Inspired of God and Beneficial"* (1963), 286. *Watchtower*, 1 Oct. 1975, 585. *Insight on the Scriptures I* (1988), 459.

With so many studies "by serious scholars," giving such diverse results, one might legitimately question whether a precise chronology was either **possible or even intended** in Scripture. Can Adam's creation date be determined on the basis of Scripture, as the Witnesses and others have claimed? An examination of the numerous systems and differing results of each would cause the informed and objective researcher to answer negatively. My sentiments are well expressed by Fred Kramer: "In our evaluation of the method of computing chronology on the basis of genealogy, as employed by Ussher and others, we have come to the conclusion that the method is wrong and unsupported by the Scripture itself. We cannot fail to note that the purpose of the genealogies in Scriptures is something far more than the computation of chronology."[38]

Conclusion

Why did the year 1975 become so important in 1966, when a chronology **that agreed with it had already been published in 1963** in *"All Scripture is Inspired of God and Beneficial?"* Why had this publication not stirred the same response? Because this chronology was accompanied by the statement, "**It does no good to use Bible chronology for speculating on dates that are still future in the stream of time—Matt. 24:36.**"[39]

The significance of the 1966 publication was that **chronology was used to speculate on a future date**. Contrary to *"All Scripture Is Inspired of God and Beneficial,"* the emphasis in *Life Everlasting—In Freedom of the Sons of God* was that man's creation and the end of the sixth day were probably parallel to the beginning of the seventh (there was no time gap).[40]

In the report on the "God's Sons of Liberty" District Assemblies, the October 15, 1966, *Watchtower* commented on the response to the release of the new *Life Everlasting* book: "Immediately its contents were examined. It did not take the brothers very long to find the chart beginning on page 31, showing that 6,000 years of man's existence end in 1975. **Discussion of 1975 overshadowed about everything else. 'The new book compels us to realize that Armageddon is, in fact, very close indeed,'** said one conventioner. Surely it was one of the outstanding blessings to be carried home!"[41]

Rather than "one of the outstanding blessings to be carried home," the Society's latest promotion of the 6,000-year theory was the basis of what turned out to be yet another **Watch Tower directed fiasco, this time under F. W. Franz's leadership.**

Notes

1. *Jehovah's Witnesses—Proclaimers of God's Kingdom* (1993), 104.
2. *Life Everlasting in Freedom of the Sons of God* (1966), 29-30; *Awake!*, 8 Oct. 1966, 19; *WT*, 15 Aug. 1968, 499. *Awake!*, 8 Oct. 1968, 14-15.
3. Arnold D. Ehlert, *A Bibliographic History of Dispensationalism* (Grand Rapids: Baker Book House, 1965), 8. Ehlert credits D. T. Taylor "for citing a large part of the literature dealing with the six and seven thousand year tradition ... in his book, *The Voice of the Church.*"
4. Ibid., 8-10.
5. Ibid., 10-11.
6. Ibid., 12-19. Church Fathers cited by Ehlert who espoused the position include: Justin Martyr (c. 100-163/67), Irenaeus (c. 130-?), Hippolytus (3rd. cent.), Cyprian (c. 200-258), Lactantius (c. 260-340), Jerome (c. 349?-420), Hilary, Bishop of Poitiers (c. 300-367), Augustine (354-430), Andrew of Crete (died c. 699) and Ambrose Ansbert (8th cent.). Additional names could be added.
7. Ibid., 19.
8. George N. H. Peters, *The Theocratic Kingdom*, vol. 2 (New York: Funk and Wagnals, 1884), 450.
9. Ehlert, 21.
10. William M. Alnor, *Soothsayers of the Second Advent* (Old Tappan, N.J.: Fleming H. Revell Co., 1989), 99.
11. *WTR*, Oct.-Nov. 1881, 289.
12. Carl Olof Jonsson, *The Gentile Times Reconsidered* (3rd ed.; Atlanta: Commentary Press, 1998), 44, 49.
13. Russell, *The Time Is at Hand* (1889), 39.
14. N. H. Barbour and C. T. Russell, *Three Worlds, and the Harvest of this World* (Rochester, N.Y.: 1877),

67, 186; *WTR*, 15 Nov. 1904, 3459-60.

15. *Life Everlasting in Freedom of the Sons of God*, 29. Robert Crompton writes: "Raymond Franz has pointed out to me in private correspondence that all the Society's books published between 1942 and 1976 were, with few exceptions written by the same man, Fred Franz" (Robert Crompton, *Counting the Days to Armageddon* (Cambridge: James Clarke & Co., 1996), 136. Fred Franz is identified as the author of *Life Everlasting in Freedom of the Sons of God* (152).

16. *Awake!*, 8 Oct. 1968, 14.

17. Barbour and Russell, 67.

18. *WTR*, 15 Nov. 1904, 3459-60.

19. C. J. Woodworth and George H. Fisher, *The Finished Mystery* (1917), 60.

20. *WT*, 15 May 1922, 147.

21. *WT*, 15 Nov. 1922, 355.

22. Russell, *The Time Is at Hand*, 53.

23. *Proclaimers*, 632-33. In his review of the *Proclaimers* book, Randall Watters examines this claim, saying that it "gives the impression that the chronology used by Russell and the Bible Students was thrown off by a factor not under their control, namely, the poor translation of Acts 13:19, 20 in the KJV.... But this factor was only a problem for Christopher Bowen, not for anyone with access to newer Bible translations based on ancient Greek texts that were just coming to light." One such was the *Emphatic Diaglott* (1864), which was familiar to both Barbour and Russell, which carried the alternative rendering in a marginal note. Watters writes that "after the mid-19th century many translations became available using the latest Greek texts ... to render Acts 13:19, 20...." After listing these, he concludes: "So while Christopher Bowen might be excused for publishing an incorrect chronology, there was no such excuse for N. H. Barbour in the early 1870s, and certainly not for the Watchtower Society after 1900. It is quite evident that the only reason the chronology was retained in spite of the availability of correct translations is that it had already become well established doctrine and was seen by Russell as divinely inspired" (Randall Watters, "Notes on the new JW history book, *Jehovah's Witnesses—Proclaimers of God's Kingdom*," 15).

24. *WTR*, Dec. 1883, 561.

25. *WT*, 15 Aug. 1968, 494-95.

26. William Hales, *A New Analysis of Chronology*, Vol. 1 (London: William Hales, 1809), 7.

27. Joseph Packard, "Sacred Chronology," *Bibliotheca Sacra* April 1858, 289-90.

28. Joseph A. Seiss, *The Last Times; or, Thoughts on Momentous Themes* (7th ed.; Louisville, Ky.: Pickett Publishing Co., 1901), 362. The writings of Lutheran minister Joseph Seiss were well known to C. T. Russell. He is quoted in Russell's *Thy Kingdom Come* (1891) (327-28, 374-75). See also two articles in the *Watch Tower* (15 Aug. 1905, 3612-13, 1 Sept. 1905, 3620). Seiss was chief editor of *Prophetic Times*, a paper that was read by Adventists including Russell (Carl Olof Jonsson, *The Gentile Times Reconsidered* [3rd ed.; Atlanta: Commentary Press, 1998], 46). "...Seiss served St. Johns Church in Philadelphia (1858-1874), then the largest English-speaking Lutheran congregation in America. In 1874 Seiss founded the Church of the Holy Communion, Philadelphia, pastoring it thirty years until his death in 1904" ("Seiss, Joseph Augustus (1823-1904)", *Dictionary of Christianity in America* [Downers Grove: InterVarsity Press, 1990], 1070).

29. Peters, 459.

30. Forest Morgan, "Chronology," *The Americana* (New York: Scientific American Compiling Dept, 1913), not paginated.

31. Edwin R. Thiele, "Chronology, Old Testament," *The Zondervan Pictorial Bible Dictionary* (2nd ed.;

Grand Rapids: Zondervan Publishing House, 1963), 166.

32. Henry M. Morris, *The Genesis Record* (Grand Rapids: Baker Book House, 1976), 42-43.

33. "Chronology, Old Testament," *Baker Encyclopedia of the Bible*, vol. 1 (Grand Rapids: Baker Book House, 1988), 458.

34. Russell, *The Time Is at Hand*, 33.

35. *WT*, 1 Jan. 1975, 9.

36. F. W. Franz, Los Angeles Sports Arena, 10 Feb. 1975 (tape recording). According to the February 1, 1955, *Watchtower*, "the fall of the year **1976** would be the end of 6,000 years of human history for mankind..." (95). Raymond Franz relates how, in 1967, Frederick Franz prepared a "Questions from Readers" column which "now argued that the end of 6,000 years would actually *come one year earlier* than had just been published in the new book [*Life Everlasting in Freedom of the Sons of God*], namely that it would come **in 1974 instead of 1975**." The material was never published (Raymond Franz, *Crisis of Conscience* [2nd ed.; Atlanta: Commentary Press, 1992], 61-62).

37. A number of these dates are found in volume 1 of William Hale's *A New Analysis of Chronology* (1809), 3-7. The rest were found in dozens of sources too numerous to list.

38. Fred Kramer, "A Critical Evaluation of the Chronology of Ussher," *Rock Strata and the Bible Record*, ed. Paul A. Zimmerman (St. Louis: Concordia, 1970), 62-63.

39. *"All Scripture Is Inspired of God and Beneficial"* (1963), 286. For further discussion, see: B. J. Oropeza, *99 Reasons Why No One Knows When Christ Will Return*. Downers Grove, Ill.: InterVarsity Press, 1994.

40. In my book, *We Left Jehovah's Witnesses*, it is suggested that the urgency that developed between 1965 and 1966 related to the slowing of the movement's growth. "Bill Cetnar, who worked in Witness headquarters for over eight years, observed that Watchtower leadership became uneasy when growth percentages dipped down (3.2% in 1965; 2.4% in 1966, an increase of only 24,407 active members) and that he expected some important announcement would be made in an effort to stop the trend. That important announcement was the 1975 date. The impact of this date is evident in the yearly reports which followed" ([Phillipsburg, N.J.: Presbyterian and Reformed Publishing Co., 1974], 4-5). This is verified by the statistics in the *Yearbooks* for 1967-1976.

41. *WT*, 15 Oct. 1966, 628-29.

43.

Selected Quotations
from Watch Tower Publications
for the Years 1980-1989

1980

"When, in the **fast approaching 'great tribulation,'** the 'sword' of divine vengeance strikes down all Organized Religion, the people who have not heeded Jehovah's 'watchman,' the Jeremiah class, will seek refuge with the doomed political elements..." (*WT*, 1 Mar. 1980, 24).

"God's kingdom, long prayed for by Christ's disciples, is **now about to come** against all enemy governments for the vindicating of His universal sovereignty" (*WT*, 15 June 1980, 22).

"As we see the things foretold for the 'last days' taking place before our very eyes, we have strong confidence that 'the great tribulation' and the dawning of God's righteous new order are **right at the doors**" (*WT*, 1 Aug. 1980, 22).

"The Bible states: 'The Sovereign Lord Jehovah will not do a thing unless he has revealed his confidential matter to the servants the prophets'—Amos 3:7.... Since Jehovah provides his loyal servants with advance knowledge about this system's end, does this include information that will enable them to discern when the 'great tribulation' actually has begun? Yes. What is that evidence? It has to do with God's execution of judgment against what the Bible calls 'Babylon the Great,'... And already, yes, *right now*, **events are taking place that are preparing the way for that execution!**" (*WT*, 15 Oct. 1980, 17).

"And if the wicked system of this world **survived until the turn of the century, which is highly improbable** in view of world trends and the fulfillment of Bible prophecy, there would still be survivors of the World War I generation. However, the fact that their number is dwindling is one more indication that '**the conclusion of the system of things' is moving fast toward its end**" (ibid., 31).

1981

"The **time is near at hand** when the resurrected Jesus Christ will bring to their end Satan and his wicked world, while preserving God's servants alive forever" (*WT*, 15 May 1981, 29).

"Just as oppressive Nineveh came to nothing, so will all oppressors in the **fast-approaching** 'war of the great day of God Almighty'" (*WT*, 1 Sept. 1981, 31).

"...'The conclusion of the system of things' is **about to reach its climax** at Har-Magedon" (*WT*, 1 Oct. 1981, 24).

1982

Ad for the book *"Let Your Kingdom Come"*: "If you are to continue to live, you will have to submit to this incoming government. Read about the persons who will **shortly be taking over earth's rulership**" (*Awake!*, 22 Feb. 1982, 32).

"**Shortly now** there will be a sudden end to all wickedness and wicked people at Armageddon" (*You Can Live Forever in Paradise on Earth*, 154).

"**Flee While There is Yet Time.**" "**Fleeing now is extremely urgent**. Why? Because the evidence shows that soon the 'disgusting thing' [the United Nations] will desolate also the 'holy place,' the claimed realm of Christendom's churches, marking the start of the 'great tribulation.'... The time for God to execute judgment against Christendom and her 'holy place' **is near**. The desolater is **soon to strike**, ending any further opportunity to flee to Jehovah's protection. Have you already fled to the symbolic 'mountains'? If not, then do not delay. It means your very life" (*WT*, 15 Nov. 1982, 7).

1983

A confidential letter was sent by the Watchtower Society "to all bodies of Elders," dated February 1, 1983, with an announcement to be given to congregations on April 10 or the week after the 10th. They were instructed that a special public talk was to be given on the 10th, entitled "Religion's Time of Judgment," before the release of the new book *Organized to Accomplish Our Ministry*. What is quoted below is from the announcement portion of the material.

"Mankind's state of affairs today forcibly reminds us of the apostle Paul's words at 1 Corinthians 7:29 and 31, that 'the time left is reduced,' and that 'the scene of this world is changing.' Evidence in fulfillment of Bible prophecy clearly indicates that **we are nearing the final end of the present ungodly world** (2 Pet. 3:7, 11, 12). **The ministry has become more urgent than ever before**.... It is evident that Jehovah and his Son is with us. Therefore, the work continues to move on to its **grand climax soon** in vindication of Jehovah's name and word" (ibid., 2-3).

"...It becomes evident that a large number of the 1914 generation are still living today. Of course, their numbers are steadily dwindling, and, therefore, **sometime in the near future, we confidently can expect 'the end' to come**, followed by the time when God's Messianic Kingdom will be the only government ruling the earth" (*WT*, 1 Oct. 1983, 19).

"At the **Brink of Armageddon**..." (*WT*, 1 Nov. 1983, front cover, article, 3).

1984

"He [Jesus] has told us that the 'generation' of 1914—the year that the sign began to be fulfilled—'will by no means pass away until all these things occur.' (Matthew 24:34) **Some of that 'generation' could survive until the end of the century. But there are many indications that 'the end' is much closer than that!**" (*WT*, 1 Mar. 1984, 18-19).

"Just as Jesus' prophecies regarding Jerusalem were fulfilled within the life span of the generation of the year 33 C.E., so his **prophecies regarding 'the time of the end' will be fulfilled within the life span of the generation of 1914**.... The nearness of God's kingdom today spells the end of the present divisive political, religious and commercial system. It means the ushering in of a new government for all obedient mankind.... Yes, you may live to see this promised New Order, along with survivors of the generation of 1914—the generation that will not pass away" (*WT*, 15 May 1984, 7).

"**The countdown that has proceeded for some six millenniums now nears its zero hour.** So close is it that people who were alive in 1914, and who are now well along in years, will not all pass off the scene before the thrilling events marking the vindication of Jehovah's sovereignty come to pass.—Mark 13:30"

(*Survival Into a New Earth*, 184).

1985

"This judgment would be executed **sometime during the life span of people seeing the first evidence of the time period foretold by Jesus**.... Bible chronology and the fulfillment of Bible prophecy provide ample proof that **this time period began in 1914. Thus before the 1914 generation completely dies out, God's judgment must be executed**" (*WT*, 1 May 1985, 4).

1986

"We are, therefore, **rapidly approaching** that glorious time when Christ Jesus will fully take over rulership of earth's affairs and unite all obedient mankind under one government. Yes, there is going to be a **change of rulership soon**" (*WT*, 15 Oct. 1986, 7).

1987

"Remember, the tidal wave bringing conclusive destruction to false religion is on its way. **It can be seen on the horizon**. Where will you be standing when it brings thunderous destruction?" (*WT*, 1 Nov. 1987, 29).

"At this very time, warning is being given to the nations to the effect that **soon** Jehovah will initiate his act of retribution against all parts of Satan's system of things.... Millions of prudent people are heeding this message.... They are getting out of the corrupt political and religious alliance **before it is too late**" (*WT*, 15 Dec. 1987, 25).

1988

"**Now, as never before, 'the time left is reduced.'** Yes, only a limited time remains for Jehovah's people to finish the work he has given them to do.... That work must be accomplished before the end comes. It is, therefore, appropriate for Christians to ask themselves how **getting married or, if married, having children** will affect their share of that vital work" (*WT*, 1 Mar. 1988, 21).

"And, as we keep walking on that narrow road to life, it is likely that Jehovah will not only preserve us alive through the great tribulation but give us eternal life with endless blessings in his new world, now **so very near**" (*WT*, 15 June 1988, 15).

"**A New World Very Near!**" (*WT*, 15 Nov. 1988, 3). "Other Bible prophecies also indicate that the regaining or restoration of Paradise is **very near**, that a new world is on the horizon" (ibid., 5)

1989

"The apostle Paul was spearheading the Christian missionary activity. He was also laying a foundation for a work that would be **completed in our 20th century**" (*WT*, 1 Jan. 1989, 12). Compare this quotation as it appears in the **bound volume** for 1989 and what was stated in the October 1, 1989, issue: "The apostle Paul was spearheading the Christian missionary activity. He was also laying a foundation for a work that would be **completed in our day**" (*WT*, 1 Jan. 1989, 12).

"We have ample reasons to expect that this preaching will be **completed in our time. Does that mean before the turn** of a new month, a new year, a new decade, **a new century**? **No human knows**, for Jesus said that 'even the angels of the heavens' do not know that" (*WT*, 1 Oct. 1989, 31).

"The way is still open for those in all nations 'to attain to repentance,' but there is no time to lose. Peter warned: 'Jehovah's day will come as a thief.' (2 Peter 3:9, 10) God's justice demands that this wicked system **soon be destroyed**" (*WT*, 1 Mar. 1989, 29).

44.

Selected Quotations
from Watch Tower Publications
for the Years 1990-2000

1990

"Have you seen that sign [of Jesus' second presence] as it has developed in every detail? Then have confidence that fulfillment of Jehovah's promise of deliverance is **very near at hand!**" (*WT*, 15 Apr. 1990, 21).

"The spiritual prosperity of Jehovah's Witnesses infuriates Satan the Devil, who will **soon launch and all-out attack against these seemingly defenseless Christians**" (*WT*, 15 May 1990, 6).

"...The present generation will not pass away before Armageddon occurs!" (ibid., 7).

"How glad we are that God will **shortly** 'bring to ruin those ruining the earth'!" (*WT* 1 July 1990, 6).

"By now, more than 70 years after [1914] that battle in the heavens, only '**a short period of time**' remains before the war of Jehovah's great day breaks out..." (ibid., 26).

Article title: "A new world at hand!" (*WT*, 1 Oct. 1990, 6).

1991

"A New World **Very Near!**" "The present-day fulfillments of these and other prophecies prove that we are indeed living in 'the last days.' (2 Timothy 3:1-5) **Just ahead** of us is the 'great tribulation' also foretold by Jesus Christ. Climaxing in 'the war of the great day of God Almighty' at Har-Magedon, it will bring an end to the present wicked system of things" (*WT*, 15 July 1991, 4-5).

"Almighty God has set a time limit to Satan's activity among mankind. When that time limit arrives, 'sudden destruction' will come upon the world lying in Satan's power. (1 Thessalonians 5:3-7) All the evidence leads to the conclusion that this will **happen soon**" (*WT*, 1 Sept. 1991, 7).

1992

"...The worsening conditions on earth that cause so much distress were prophesied in the Bible and are a sign that the coming of the Kingdom **is close**. Yes, the Kingdom of God will **soon** intervene and replace the present political structures" (*WT*, 1 Feb. 1992, 6).

"Just **on the horizon** is God's new world of true freedom" (*WT*, 1 Apr. 1992, 14).

"**Soon** God will rid the globe of wickedness, and humans will enjoy eternal life on a paradise earth" (*WT*, 1 Nov. 1992, 7).

1993

"*The Watchtower* **has consistently presented evidence** to honesthearted students of Bible prophecy **that Jesus' presence in heavenly Kingdom power began in 1914.** Events since that year testify to Jesus' *invisible* presence" (WT, 15 Jan. 1993, 5).

"Jehovah's Witnesses **have consistently shown from the Scriptures that the year 1914 marked the beginning of this world's time of the end** and that 'the day of judgment and of the destruction of the ungodly men' has **drawn near"** (WT, 15 Aug. 1993, 9)

"All evidence, therefore, points to the fact that God's new world is **very near**" (*Awake!*, 22 Oct. 1993, 11).

"We are on the homestretch in the race of life. The **reward is in sight**. May all be determined to endure to the end and thus be among those who will be saved" (*WT*, 1 Nov. 1993, 23).

"...Today we are **at the threshold** of a promised 'new heavens and a new earth'" (*WT*, 1 Dec. 1993, 10).

1994

"Happily, according to Bible prophecies now undergoing fulfillment, we are **at the very threshold** of that new world, in which pain will never cause suffering" (*Awake!*, 22 June 1994, 11).

"The fact that we are now 80 years beyond 1914 indicates that we can **soon expect** the deliverance that God's Kingdom will bring" (*Awake!*, 8 Nov. 1994, 10).

"**Time is fast running out** for this wicked world, and it is imperative for all who want to survive this world's end to learn what is involved in 'obeying the good news' and thus escape destruction" (*WT*, 1 Oct. 1994, 8).

1995

"For untold millions, life in that new world will come by means of the resurrection. Yet, in our day, millions of Jehovah's people—yes, a great crowd that no man can number or limit—will have the unique **privilege of being saved alive through great tribulation. And they will never have to die**" (*WT*, 15 Feb. 1995, 17).

"The nations of the world have been wearied by 50 years of frustrated efforts. **Very soon** they will destroy harlotlike religious organizations. Then Jesus Christ ... and his army of heavenly warriors will dissolve all human governments and put to death all who reject God's sovereignty" (*WT*, 1 Oct. 1995, 7).

"The need to keep awake is more critical than it has ever been. Jehovah has revealed to us 'the things that must **shortly take place**,' and we should respond with an absorbing sense of urgency.... As the time approaches, keep awake, for Jehovah is **about to** bring calamity on all of Satan's system!" (*WT*, 1 Nov. 1995, 20).

1996

"The execution of divine judgment will start with the destruction of Babylon the Great. That harlotlike empire of false religion will be forever blotted out. **That time is very near!**" (*WT*, 1 June 1996, 19).

"So Jesus is the one to fulfill the words of Psalm 72.... What does this mean? It means that freedom from all forms of human oppression **will soon** be a reality" (*WT*, 1 Nov. 1996, 6).

1997

"In the early 1920s, a featured public talk presented by Jehovah's Witnesses was entitled 'Millions Now Living Will Never Die.' This may have reflected over optimism at that time. But today that statement can be made with full confidence. Both the increasing light on Bible prophecy and the anarchy of this dying world cry out that the end of Satan's system is **very, very near!**" (*WT*, 1 Jan. 1997, 11).

"Evidence clearly proves that we are living in the time of the end and that the great day of Jehovah is **near**" (*WT*, 1 Mar. 1997, 19).

"In the **very near future**, Jesus' heavenly government will rule over a righteous new human society, in effect 'a new earth'" (*WT*, 1 July 1997, 7).

"How much time is left remaining we do not know,. Yet, we can say with confidence that 'the end of all things has **drawn close**'" (*WT*, 15 Aug. 1997, 22).

"We should not forget that the day when Jehovah will destroy this system of things as a preliminary to establishing his promised new world is **very near**" (*WT*, 1 Sept. 1997, 19).

"'The day of Jehovah' will **soon** bring an end to the present wicked system of things" (*WT*, 15 Sept. 1997, 20).

1998

"God's New World is Near." "The good news is that such peaceful conditions **will soon be realized earth wide. Why can we be so sure? Because of what Jesus prophesied would occur immediately prior to the world's end** [wars, famines, earthquakes, etc.].... Surely, we are living in 'the last days' of this world! **Soon**, therefore, it will be replaced by God's righteous new world!" (*Awake!*, 22 Feb. 1998, 9).

1999

"...It is clear that **God's judgment against the world must be near** because the world has taken on the characteristics that warranted God's judgment in the past.... All the evidence indicates that **we are now living among the wicked generation of which Jesus said**: 'This generation will by no means pass away until all these things occur' (Matthew 24:34). The world is now filling its 'measure of sin.' 'The clusters of the vine of the earth' are becoming ripe for the harvest" (*WT*, 1 June 1999, 6-7).

"**An Entirely New World Soon.**" "We are now 85 years into the 'last days,' and we are **swiftly nearing the end of this present unsatisfactory system of things**. Soon God's Kingdom, under Christ, 'will crush and put an end to all these kingdoms.'... Ask Jehovah's Witnesses for more information. They will show you from your own copy of the Bible that the critical years of change that marked the 20th century **will soon end** and that you can thereafter enjoy unending blessings!" (*Awake!*, 8 Dec. 1999, 12).

2000

"Yes, we stand at the **very threshold** of the fulfillment of Jehovah's decree against Satan and his entire wicked system" (*WT*, 15 Jan. 2000, 7).

"Jehovah's rocking of the nations at Armageddon is **just ahead**" (ibid., 19)

========

"...We are standing upon the very **threshold** of the Messianic Kingdom, and that soon the Lord shall be pleased to take us home... (*WTR*, 15 Jan. **1919**, 6380).

"We are now on the **threshold** of a new world that will never perish or grow old..." (*WT*, 15 Sept. **1953**, 570).

"Here, then, is a thrilling opportunity! We live now on the **threshold** of the new world of righteousness" (*WT*, 1 May **1960**, 281).

"They tell us what Satan the Devil already knows, namely, that we stand at the **threshold** of Armageddon, that his wicked rule is about to end, that 'God's kingdom come' will soon be a reality for the earth" (*WT*, 1 May **1967**, 262).

"In contrast to those faithful servants of old, we are on the very **threshold** of the new system that they 'saw afar off' (*WT*, 1 Aug. **1973**, 477).

"Today we stand on the **threshold** of another major event in the history of mankind—the 'great tribulation,' which will reach its climax in 'the war of the great day of God the Almighty' at Har-Magedon" (*WT*, 1 Oct. **1978**, 14).

"...Today we are at the **threshold** of a promised 'new heavens and a new earth'" (*WT*, 1 Dec. **1993**, 10).

45.

The Parable of the
Sheep and the Goats

Jehovah's Witnesses—Proclaimers of God's Kingdom (1993) devotes an entire page to the interpretation and fulfillment of the parable of the sheep and the goats in Matthew 25:31-46. It is stated that a new exposition of that parable was "a truly significant step in understanding Jehovah's purpose" for the Bible Students.[1] It is then explained: "It had long been thought that this parable applied during the millennial era, in the time of restitution, and that the final judgment referred to in the parable was the one that would take place at the end of the Millennium. But in 1923, reasons for another view of matters were set forth by J. F. Rutherford, the president of the Watch Tower Society...."[2] But, a little over two years after the *Proclaimers* book was released, another interpretation of the parable was published.[3]

The first view, that the parable had a future fulfillment, was advanced in the August 1884 *Watch Tower* article, "Parable of the Sheep and Goats," which explained: "That this parable refers to the Millennial age is clearly indicated in [Matt. 25] verses 31 and 32.... The scene of this parable, then, is laid after the time of trouble and after the exaltation of the 'little flock' to the throne, when the nations have been subdued, Satan bound (Rev. 20:2) and the authority of Christ's kingdom established."[4]

In the Russell-White debate in 1908, Russell argued, "Note first that this parable does not apply to the present age, but to the millennial age, after the second coming of Christ."[5] After Russell's death in 1916, in agreement with his interpretation, the May 15, 1921, *Watch Tower* explained that the parable of the sheep and goats would be fulfilled after the setting up of the kingdom, when the church is reigning with Christ. Matthew 25:31 is quoted: "When the Son of man shall come in his glory, and all the holy angels with him, then shall he sit upon the throne of his glory." The question was asked, "Who, after proper consideration, will say this is a matter of the past? Who will dispute that this is a description of Messiah's kingdom following the parousia [presence since 1874] and the epiphany [manifestation to the world] of his second advent?"[6] It was further explained that the judgment of the sheep and goats will take place during the entire millennium, and "not until the conclusion of the Millennium will the decision of the Judge be manifested."[7]

This view had been published for over four decades before Rutherford's August 25, 1923, Los Angeles convention talk, "Parable of Sheep and Goats." His presentation is described as "a startling explanation," "an enlightening discourse," and as giving the Bible Students "special illumination for the enlightenment of their understanding."[8] The talk was later published in the October 15, 1923, *Watch Tower*.[9] In his typical fashion, Rutherford argued, "In the Lord's due time, we believe, he will let his consecrated people have an understanding of all his dark sayings.... To understand a prophecy we must wait until it is fulfilled or is in the course of fulfillment."[10] The former interpretation, which "applied the parable to the Millennial reign of Christ and the final judgment of the parable to the end of that reign," was " difficult to harmonize," said Rutherford.[11] "There seems to be a number of legitimate reasons why the parable will not be applicable at the final judgment of the Millennial reign of Christ." Several reasons were then presented.[12] After discussing the subject, Rutherford concluded that Scripture and the physical facts show that the parable had application not to the millennial age or the "separation of the nations; but rather to the separation of two general classes composing the nations of Christendom, one symbolized by goats and the other by sheep."[13] Soon after Rutherford's death, this new interpretation was again attributed to God and its significance stated:

> ...**Jehovah caused other revelations of truth to appear in due time.... In 1923 he caused the first true-to-fact explanation** of the parable of the "sheep and goats," fulfilled at the end of the world, to be published in *The Watchtower.* This showed for the first time that the "sheep" who are now separated from the "goats" are an earthly class of good-will who do good to the remnant of Christ's brethren in contrast with the stubborn opposition by the "goats" to these announcers of God's kingdom.[14]

Rutherford's interpretation of the separation of the people into the "sheep" and "goats" was often included as one of the features of the composite sign of the end. For example, in *"Make Sure of All Things"* (1953), it is listed as feature "28. Separating the People of the Nations into 'Sheep' and 'Goats,'" followed by the quotation of Matthew 25:31-46.[15]

Why did Rutherford make this change? Timothy White suggests: "Although the work was fully in progress, the workers had little idea of what they were supposed to be accomplishing. Even supposing God had commanded a world-wide work at this special time, why? Since the church had all been gathered, and the rest of the world was to wait for the Millennium to be enlightened, what purpose could be gained by a vigorous witness?" The answer: Rutherford's new view of the division of the people—the sheep and the goats. "Russell had applied this parable to the work of dividing the people in the Millennial Age. Rutherford was, then, actually saying that some Millennial work was given to the Bible Students now. With this lecture, another of Russell's teachings was abandoned."[16]

In 1961, it was claimed that "this separating work is nearing its completion as all peoples are identifying themselves either as in support of God's kingdom, or in opposition to it."[17] And the January 1, 1988, *Watchtower* explains: "A person is identified as a 'sheep' or as a 'goat' by the way he responds to the angelic messages. During this 20th century, only Jehovah's Witnesses have cooperated with the angels in this vital work."[18]

The May 15, 1995, *Watchtower* used Rutherford's interpretation as an example of one of Jehovah's "flashes of light," when in 1923 a **"bright light shone** on the parable of the sheep and the goats. It was seen that **this prophecy was to be fulfilled in the present Lord's day, not in the future during the Millennium as previously thought.**"[19]

But just **five months later,** this example of one of Jehovah's "flashes of light" was extinguished with the publication of the October 15, 1995, *Watchtower,* which presented an "adjustment" of Rutherford's earlier interpretation. The view that had been "demonstrated from the Scriptures,"[20] communicated by Jehovah, ministered in cooperation with the angels,[21] and published in Watch Tower Society publications since 1923—over seven decades—was now old "truth" (error). As the article asks: "Does this parable apply when Jesus sat down in kingly power in 1914, as we have long understood?"[22] After consideration of Matthew 25:34 and other passages, it concludes: "Yet nothing indicates that at that time, or for that matter since, Jesus sat to judge people of *all the nations* finally as sheep or goats."[23] "In other words, **the parable points to the future** when the son of man will come in his glory."[24] **"It will take place after 'the tribulation'** mentioned at Matthew 24:29, 30 breaks out and the Son of man 'arrives in his glory.'"[25] The "new" exposition is a partial return to what Russell and the Society taught before 1923: that the parable of the sheep and the goats judgment would see its fulfillment in the future.

Notes

1. *Jehovah's Witnesses—Proclaimers of God's Kingdom* (1993), 163-64.
2. Ibid., 164.
3. *WT*, 15 Oct. 1995, 23-28.
4. *WTR*, Aug. 1884, 654.
5. *Harvest Gleanings I* (Chicago Bible Students), 223.
6. *WT*, 15 May 1921, 155.
7. Ibid.
8. *God's Kingdom of a Thousand Years Has Approached* (1973), 264; *Proclaimers*, 164; *WT*, 15 Feb. 1980, 19.
9. *WT*, 15 Oct. 1923, "The Parable of the Sheep and the Goats," 307-14.
10. Ibid., 307.
11. Ibid.
12. Ibid., 307-08.
13. Ibid., 310.
14. *WT*, 15 Nov. 1943, 342. The February 1, 1938, *Watchtower* also ascribed this interpretation to God: "The **Lord revealed to his people the meaning of the parable** of the sheep and the goats, showing how the 'sheep' only would be spared by Jehovah when his wrath is expressed at Armageddon. All this information came not from or by man, but **by the Lord God**..." (35).
15. Ibid., 341-42. See also: *WT*, 1 May 1952, 276; *WT*, 15 Oct. 1961, 632.
16. Timothy White, *A People for His Name* (New York: Vantage, 1967), 178.
17. *WT*, 15 Oct. 1961, 632.
18. *WT*, 1 Jan. 1988, 16.
19. *WT*, 15 May 1995, 18.
20. *Jehovah's Witnesses in the Divine Purpose* (1959): Rutherford "**demonstrated from the Scriptures** for the first time that in Jesus' illustration of the sheep and goats the sheep referred to a group of persons of good will who are now living on earth before Christ's millennial reign and who are now doing good to Christ's spiritual brothers" (104).
21. *WT*, 1 Jan. 1988, 16. After quoting Matthew 25:31-33: "Yes, all mankind is being scrutinized to see who are the 'sheep' and who are the 'goats.'"... So, clearly, the messages are broadcast by human mouthpieces under angelic direction. A person is identified as a 'sheep' or as a 'goat' by the way he responds to the angelic messengers" (ibid.).
22. *WT*, 15 Oct. 1995, 22.
23. Ibid.
24. Ibid.
25. Ibid., 23.

46.

Speculation on "This Generation" (Matt. 24:34)

For over 100 years, a number of articles and statements have been published by the Watch Tower Society, speculating on the interpretation of the phrase "this generation." This is found in Jesus' prophecy in Matthew 24:34 (also Mark 13:30; Luke 21:32): "Verily I say unto you, **This generation** shall not pass away, till all these things be fulfilled" (KJV). For years, the meaning of "this generation" was important to the message of the nearness of Armageddon and the soon establishment of God's Kingdom. What has been taught over the years?

In 1894, Society founder Russell viewed "the present generation" of **Matthew 23:35-36** as applying to the judgment to come upon the generation of Jesus' time, but also having application to "the closing generation of this Gospel Age"—**ending** in 1914.[1] In his book, *The Day of Vengeance* (retitled *The Battle of Armageddon*) (1897), in the discussion of Matthew 24:32-35, he sees a past fulfillment in part upon Israel in A.D. 70, but also a further fulfillment in the end of the age. As to the meaning of "generation":

> A "generation" might be reckoned as equivalent to a century ... or one hundred and twenty years.... Reckoning a hundred years from 1780, the date of the first sign, the limit would reach to 1880; and, to our understanding, every item predicted had begun to be fulfilled at that date;— the "harvest" or gathering time beginning October 1874; the organization of the Kingdom and the taking by our Lord of his great power as the King in April 1878, and the time of trouble or "day of wrath" which began October 1874 and will end October 1914 ["and will cease about 1915"—1912, 1918 and 1925 eds.]; and the sprouting of the fig tree.... Those who are walking with us in the light of present truth are not looking for things to *come* which are already here, but are waiting for the consummation of matters already in progress. Or, since the Master said, "When you shall see *all* these things," and since "the sign of the Son of Man in heaven," and the budding fig tree, and the gathering of 'the elect' are counted among the signs, **it would not be inconsistent to reckon the 'generation' from 1878 to 1914—36½ years—about the *average of human life today.***[2]

In the February 15, 1927, *Watch Tower,* in answer to the question of what Jesus meant by "this generation" in Matthew 24:34, "generation" is subjected to a different interpretation:

> At the Jordan Jehovah started **a new generation, a new creation, of which Christ Jesus is the**

Head. Jesus selected twelve disciples.... Eleven of these we have every reason to believe constitute a part of that new creation. In 1 Peter 2:9 the apostle, speaking to the church of course, referred to those who are faithful ["you are a chosen generation"]. The irresistible conclusion therefore is that **Jesus referred to the new creation** when he said, "This generation shall not pass until all these things be fulfilled." **This then would be a strong indication that some members of the new creation will be on earth at the time of Armageddon."**[3]

But, it should be noted that such an interpretation of "generation" would be questioned later.[4]

With the non-fulfillment of predictions for 1914 would come the change in the position that 1914 was the **beginning** of the "time of the end" rather than the end. Yet time was short—but it did not turn out that way—and a generation limited to 30-40 years created a problem. So questions and discussions would appear again.

In the September 1, 1952, *Watchtower,* "Questions from Readers" included the following: "Your publications point out that the battle of Armageddon will come in this generation, and that this generation began in A.D. 1914. Scripturally, how long is a generation?" The response was that the Bible "gives no number of years for a generation.... The Bible does speak of a man's days as being threescore and ten or fourscore years; but it assigns no specific number of years to a generation."[5] While the date of Armageddon could not be predicted, the pertinent Scriptures did set a limit. "Some persons living A.D. 1914 when the series of foretold events began will also be living when the series ends with Armageddon.... There are hundreds of millions of persons living now that were living in 1914, and many millions of these persons could yet live a score or more years. Just when the lives of the majority of them will be cut short by Armageddon we cannot say."[6]

In court testimony in 1954, F. W. Franz was asked about the length of a "generation":

Q. What span of time is a generation?
A. We cannot be sure, it is the generation which began to witness the events of 1914.
Q. You mean the human generation?
A. Yes.
Q. Are you using generation in the sense of the lifetime of the individual?
A. The lifetime of an individual. For instance, I witnessed the events of 1914. And I am still alive today, and hope to carry on [Franz b. Sept. 12, 1893, age 21 in Oct. 1914].[7]

The meaning of "generation" was speculated on in a number of Watch Tower publications from the early 1960s on, with some different interpretations. But one thing was certain: "...**Before the 1914 generation completely dies out, God's judgment must be executed."**[8]

How was "generation" understood and explained over the years? Here are some examples.

1962

"The 'generation' of Matthew 24:34 **includes persons alive at the time** that the war in heaven began in 1914. All who were living or who came on the scene around that time are a part of that generation. **Members of that generation** will see the end of this world..." (*Awake!* 22 Sept. 1962, 27).

1966

"It is to be carefully noted that the youngest of those who **saw with understanding** the developing sign of the end of this system of things from its start in 1914 **are now well over sixty years of age!** In fact, the greater part of the adult generation that experienced the start of the 'last days' already passed away in death....

The time left, then, is definitely limited, and it is very short" (*Awake!* 8 Oct. 1966, 18).

1968

"Jesus was obviously speaking about **those who were old enough to witness** *with understanding* what took place when the 'last days' began.... Even if we presume that youngsters **15 years of age** would be perceptive enough to realize the import of what happened in 1914, it would still make the youngest of 'this generation' nearly 70 years old today.... Jesus said that the end of this wicked world would come *before* **that generation passed away in death**" (*Awake!* 8 Oct. 1968, 13-14).

1973

"And, very important for us, it was foretold that such final result would take place *within the lifetime of just one generation*, **the generation that was alive in 1914**. Christ Jesus, the most renowned prophet in human history, was the one foretelling this. His prophecy was twofold.... Jesus had foretold Jerusalem's utter destruction and the scattering of the Jewish nation ... in 70 C.E.... We can be equally sure that, of the **generation alive in 1914, some will see the major fulfillment** of Christ Jesus' prophecy and the destruction with which it culminates..." (*Awake!* 8 Oct. 1973, 19).

1975

"'If one assumes that you must be **10 years old for events to make a lasting impression,**' observed *U.S. News and World Report* recently, 'only 9 per cent of the U.S population today recalls World War I.' Students of Bible prophecy note that Jesus Christ predicted that the 'generation' that saw such a global conflict and what followed 'will by no means pass away until' God's Kingdom rule asserts itself fully over mankind. —Matt. 24:7-14, 30-34" (*Awake!* 8 July 1975, 29).

1978

"Thus, when it comes to the application in our time, the 'generation' logically **would not apply to babies** born during World War I. It applies to Christ's followers and others who were able to observe that war... (*WT*, 1 Oct. 1978, 31).

1980

"What, then, is the 'generation' that 'will by no means pass away until all these things occur?' It does not refer to a time, which some have tried to interpret as 30, 40, 70 or even 120 years, but, rather, **it refers to people, the people living at the 'beginning of pangs of distress'** for this condemned world system. It is the **generation of people who saw the catastrophic events that broke forth in connection with World War I from 1914 onward**.... And if the wicked system of this world survived until the turn of the century, **which is highly improbable in view of world trends and the fulfillment of Bible prophecy**, there would still be survivors of the World War I generation. However, the fact that their number is dwindling is one more indication that '**the conclusion of the system of things' is moving fast toward its end**.... We can be happy, therefore, for Jesus' assurance that there will be survivors of 'the generation of 1914'—that **this generation will not have completely passed away**—when the 'great tribulation' rings down the curtain on this wicked world system" (*WT*, 15 Oct. 1980, 31).

———————————————

Raymond Franz writes that in a Governing Body meeting, the three members of the Chairman's Committee submitted a document dated March 3, 1980, for them to consider. This document proposed that "this generation" should begin to apply not in 1914, but in 1957, "the year when the first Russian Sputnik was launched into outer space." The proposal was not approved.[9]

1982

"...Jesus said: 'This generation will by no means pass away until all things [including the end of this system] occur.' (Matthew 24:34, 14) Which generation did Jesus mean? **He meant the generation of people who were living in 1914.** Those persons yet remaining of that generation are now very old. However, some of them will still be alive to see the end of this wicked system. So of this we can be certain: **Shortly now there will be a sudden end to all wickedness and the wicked people at Armageddon**" (*You Can Live Forever in Paradise on Earth*, 154. Brackets in original).

1984

"1914 The Generation That Will Not Pass Away" (*WT*, May 15, 1984, front cover).

"If Jesus used 'generation' in that sense ["those born around the time of a historic event and all those alive at that time"] and we apply it to 1914, then **the babies of that generation are now 70 years old or older. And others alive in 1914 are in their 80's or 90's, a few even having reached a hundred.** There are still many millions of that generation alive. Some of them 'will by no means pass away until all things occur.' —Luke 21:32" (ibid., 5).

"Is There Enough Time? From a purely human viewpoint, it could appear that these developments could hardly take place before the generation of 1914 disappears from the scene. But fulfillment of all the foretold events affecting the generation of 1914 does not depend on comparatively slow human action. **Jehovah's prophetic word through Christ Jesus is: 'This generation [of 1914] will by no means pass away until all things occur.'** (Luke 21:32) And Jehovah, who is the source of inspired and unfailing prophecy, will bring about the fulfillment of his Son's words in a relatively short time.—Isaiah 46:9, 10; 55:10,11... (ibid., 6-7. Brackets in original).

"Just as Jesus' prophecies regarding Jerusalem were fulfilled within the life span of the generation of the year 33 C.E., **so his prophecies regarding 'the time of the end' will be fulfilled within the life span of the generation of 1914.** (Daniel 12:4) This means that marvelous prospects lie before not only that generation but all those living today.... Yes, you may live to see this promised New Order, along with survivors of the generation of 1914—**the generation that will not pass away**" (ibid., 7).

1985

"Thus judgment would be executed sometime during the life span of people seeing the first evidence of the time period foretold by Jesus.... **Bible chronology and the fulfillment of Bible prophecy provide ample proof that this time period began in 1914. Thus before the 1914 generation completely dies out, God's judgment must be executed**" (*WT*, 1 May 1985, 4).

1987

The *Awake!* of January 8, 1987, removed the masthead concerning the generation of 1914: "...This magazine builds confidence in the **Creator's promise of a peaceful and secure new system before the generation that saw the events of 1914 passes away**" (*Awake!*, 22 Dec. 1986, 2). The *Awake!* of March 8, 1988, restored the words, but substituted the words "new world" for "new system."

1988

Quoting J. A. Bengel: "'The Hebrews ... reckon seventy-five years as one generation.'... Most of the generation of 1914 has passed away. However, there are still millions on earth **who were born in that year or prior to it**.... Jesus' words will come true, 'this generation will not pass away until all these things have happened'" (*Awake!*, 8 Apr. 1988, 14).

1992

"Today, a small percentage of mankind can still recall the dramatic events of 1914. **Will that elderly generation pass away before God saves the earth from ruin? Not according to Bible prophecy.** 'When you see all these things,' Jesus promised, 'know that he is near at the doors. Truly I say to you that *this* generation will by no means pass away until all these things occur.'—Matthew 24:33, 34" (*WT*, 1 May 1992, 3).

"**Before the 1914 generation passes away**, the Kingdom-preaching work will have accomplished its purpose. 'Then,' foretold Jesus, 'there will be great tribulation such as has not occurred since the world's beginning until now, no, nor will occur again. In fact, unless those days were cut short, no flesh would be saved; but on account of the chosen ones those days will be cut short.'—Matthew 24:21, 22" (*WT*, May 1, 1992, 7).

"New Light" on "Generation"

For decades the oft-repeated message was that the "generation of 1914" would see the close of the last days—Armageddon and the establishment of God's Kingdom. What brought about the need for "new light"? Carl Olof Jonsson comments: "As decades went by, leaving 1914 even farther behind, this claim became increasingly difficult to defend. After *80 years* had passed, the claim became virtually preposterous.... A new definition of the phrase 'this generation' was adopted, one that allowed the organization to 'unlink' it from the 1914 date *as a starting point*."[10] The new position, which would be clearly stated in 1995, was anticipated by some observers of the Watch Tower Society.[11]

Keeping in mind the many speculations that have been published in Watch Tower publications for decades, note how the November 1, 1995, *Watchtower* interprets its past record: "Eager to see the end of this evil system, Jehovah's people **have at times speculated** about the time when the 'great tribulation' would break out, **even tying this to calculations of what is the lifetime of a generation since 1914**."[12] Further along, the article asks: "Is anything to be gained, then, **by looking for dates or by speculating** about the literal lifetime of a generation? Far from it."[13] **Such speculation has characterized the movement.**

The new understanding of "this generation" is then stated: "Therefore, in the final fulfillment of Jesus' prophecy today, '**this generation' apparently refers to the peoples of earth who see the sign of Christ's presence but fail to mend their ways**."[14] It should be noted as well that when this interpretation is compared with the 1927 *Watch Tower's* understanding, cited above, "generation" has been degraded, from applying to "the new creation"—**Christ's followers**—to those who "fail to mend their ways"—**unbelievers, the wicked**.

The article continues:

> No human can say when that end will be [Matt. 24:14], but we know that the end of "this generation" of wicked people will come once the witness has been given to God's satisfaction "to the most distant part of the earth."—Acts 1:8.... Does our more precise viewpoint on "this generation" mean that Armageddon is farther way than we had thought? Not at all! Though we at no time have known the "day and hour," Jehovah God has always known it, and he does not change.[15]

The new view is reflected in the comparison of the wording in the last sentence of the October 22, 1995, *Awake!* masthead, with that of the next issue, November 8, 1995:

Most important, this magazine builds confidence in the **Creator's promise** of a peaceful and secure new world **before the generation that saw the events of 1914 passes away.**

Most important, this magazine builds confidence in the Creator's promise of a peaceful and secure new world that is **about to replace** the present wicked, lawless system of things.[16]

In "Questions From Readers" in the June 1, 1997, *Watchtower,* a reader asks about the new interpretation (in the Nov. 1, 1995, issue): "Does this mean that there is some question about whether God's Kingdom was set up in heaven in 1914?" The answer: "That discussion in *The Watchtower* offered no change at all in our fundamental teaching about 1914."[17] The article concludes: "So the recent information in *The Watchtower* about 'this generation' did not change our understanding of what happened in 1914. But it did give us a clearer grasp of Jesus' use of the term 'generation,' helping us to see that **his usage was no basis for calculating—counting from 1914—how close to the end we are.**"[18] This "new light" was delayed for decades while the erroneous "generation of 1914" interpretation was published and heralded around the world.

"A Monumental Change"

John Dart's article, "Witnesses Drop Central Tenet About the 'Generation of 1914,'" was published in the *Los Angeles Times* of October 21, 1995. Dart writes, "The Jehovah's Witnesses have quietly abandoned a prediction that people alive in 1914 would live to see Christ's kingdom on Earth—a major doctrine that lent urgency to the sect's door-to-door warnings that a bloody end of the world is imminent." Robert Johnson, identified as a Witness headquarters spokesman, according to Dart, "minimized the change, saying that **the 1914 timetable 'has not been a cardinal doctrine of faith**.'" This was disputed by ex-Witness Raymond Franz, a Governing Body member from 1971-1980: "'**They've been insisting on this** [the generation of 1914] **as a definite truth for more than 40 years.... This is a monumental change after all this time....**"[19]

In agreement with Raymond Franz, Michael Pendley, who was a Jehovah's Witness for 38 years, affirms:

As most Jehovah's Witnesses know by now, the Watchtower Bible and Tract Society has recently changed key doctrines regarding the generation of 1914, as outlined in the 11/1/95 issue of The Watchtower. **This teaching has long been one of the cornerstones of Jehovah's Witnesses eschatology.** As one of Jehovah's Witnesses, these doctrinal changes have forced me to confront a serious issue of conscience.... **The "new light" on the 1914 generation is not simply "a more precise understanding," it is a major change in doctrine brought about by prophetic failure.**[20]

P.S.

With the understanding of "this generation" published in the November 1, 1995, *Watchtower,* unlinking it from the 1914 date, confusion is produced when one accesses the Jehovah's Witnesses' official website. There one finds the excerpts quoted below from two articles there: "Education for Entering Paradise" and "God's Purpose Soon to Be Realized." These were accessed on June 29, 1999. "'This generation will by no means pass away until all these things occur.' Some, at least, of the generation that saw the 'beginning of the pangs of distress' in 1914 will live to see Paradise restored on earth. (Matthew 24:3-8, 34)"[21]

How long a time period would these last days prove to be? Jesus said regarding the era that would experience the "beginning of pangs of distress" from 1914 onward. "This generation will by no means pass away until all these things occur." (Matthew 24:8, 34-36) Thus, all the features of the last days must take place within the lifetime of one generation, the generation of 1914. So some people who were alive in 1914 will still be alive when this system comes to its end.[22]

Notes

1. *WTR*, 1 Sept. 1894, 1702. The article on "generation" in *Insight on the Scriptures* (1988) vol. 1, sees "generation" in Matthew 23:36 as applying only to Jesus' contemporaries, without a future fulfillment (918).
2. Russell, *The Day of Vengeance* (1897), 604-05.
3. *WT*, 15 Feb. 1927, 62.
4. "Many scriptures confirm that Jesus did not use 'generation' with regard to some small or distinct group, meaning only the Jewish leaders or only his loyal disciples" (*WT*, 1 June 1997, 28; see also *WT*, 1 May 1999, 11). Raymond Franz reports that in 1978, Albert Schroeder, who was a Governing Body member, had suggested "this generation applied to the generation of 'anointed ones,' and that as long as any of these were still living such 'generation' would not have passed away. This understanding was not accepted by the Governing Body" (Raymond Franz, *Crisis of Conscience* [2nd ed.; Atlanta: Commentary Press, 1992], 214).
5. *WT*, 1 Sept. 1952, 542-43.
6. Ibid., 543.
7. Pursuers Proof *Douglas Walsh vs. the Right Honorable James Laytham Clyde, M.P., P.C.*, Scottish Court of Sessions, Nov. 1954 (1958 ed.), 149.
8. *WT*, 1 May 1985, 4.
9. Franz, *Crisis of Conscience*, 218-20.
10. Carl Olof Jonsson, *The Gentile Times Reconsidered* (3rd ed.; Atlanta: Commentary Press, 1998), 2.
11. Randall Watters, "Notes on the Special Lectures Given at the Divine Teaching Conventions (1993-1994) of Jehovah's Witnesses." Randall Watters, "'1914 Generation' Discarded by Watchtower," *Free Minds Journal*, Nov.-Dec. 1995, 2, 5-6. *Reachout Trust Newsletter*, #41, Spring 1995, 9.
12. *WT*, 1 Nov. 1995, 17.
13. Ibid., 19.
14. Ibid.
15. Ibid., 20.
16. *Awake!*, 22 Oct. 1995, 4; 8 Nov. 1995, 4. The former masthead had been carried since the January 8, 1982, issue.
17. *WT*, 1 June 1997, 28.
18. Ibid.
19. John Dart, *Los Angeles Times*, 21 Oct. 1995, B-11.
20. Michael R. Pendley, "A Letter in the Light of 1914," *Watchman Expositor*, Vol. 13, No. 1, 1996, 8.
21. *http://www.watchtower.org/library/lmn/article_11.htm.*
22. *http://www.watchtower.org/library/pr/soon_realized.htm.*

47.

Other Doctrinal Changes

Many doctrinal changes over the years would cause one to question the credibility of the Watch Tower Society, especially its claim of divine insight and direction in the interpretation of Scripture. A small selection of other changes is presented here.

Satan—a.k.a. Lucifer?

Isaiah 14:12-14 has been cited and explained a number of times in Watch Tower publications by Russell and his successors. Verse 12 in the *King James Version* reads: "How art thou fallen from heaven, O Lucifer, son of the morning! *how* are thou cut down to the ground, which didst weaken the nations!" Russell taught that "Lucifer" in the passage was to be understood as one of Satan's names. For example, the August 1, 1894, *Watch Tower* explains: "Previous to his fall into sin he is spoken of as Lucifer, morning star (a glorious being of creation's early morning)."[1] In the May 15, 1916, *Watch Tower*, Russell writes that the devil whose name "was once Lucifer, shining one, was changed to that of Satan, meaning the hater, the accuser. He who was once called, 'Son of the Morning,' became the prince of the 'rulers of darkness.' (Isaiah 14:12-16; Ephesians 6:11,12)."[2] Russell's *Scenario of the Photo-Drama of Creation* (1914), reproduces a slide from the presentation with the caption, "LUCIFER PRINCE OF THE DEMONS."[3]

After Russell's death, Rutherford would continue to identify Lucifer in the same way: "No longer did God permit his creature Lucifer to go by that name which signified a bright, shining one. His name was changed from Lucifer, and thereafter he was known by four names, to wit: Satan, which means adversary or opponent; Devil, which means slanderer; Serpent, which means deceiver; and Dragon, which means devourer."[4] In 1932, Rutherford wrote three articles relating to Lucifer: "Creation of Lucifer and Man," "Rebellion of Lucifer" and "Lucifer and the Tree of Life."[5] And in his book *Religion* (1940), he writes:

> It behoves every person on earth to lay aside prejudice and preconceived opinions and earnestly seek the truth as recorded in God's Word. In doing so it will be found that the chief amongst the demons is Satan, 'that old serpent,' the Devil. When he was one of the trusted officers in the organization of Jehovah God his name was Lucifer, meaning 'bright-shining one,' one with authority. He rebelled against God.... Jehovah changed his name to Dragon, Satan, Serpent, and Devil.[6]

Rutherford died in 1942, but this interpretation would continue through the 1940s. The October 15, 1949, *Watchtower* explains: "In Bible interpretations from the third century onward this name 'Lucifer' has been applied to the Devil. It does apply to him as he is symbolized by Babylon's king."[7]

In "Questions from Readers," in the March 1, 1957, *Watchtower*, it is asked: "Did not Lucifer become Satan the Devil, according to Isaiah 14:12?" After discussion, the answer concludes: "Thus we see that this title **could not** refer to the original perfection, beauty and jewellike brightness that he enjoyed as the covering cherub, which is described by the prophet Ezekiel at Ezekiel 28:14-17, *AS*. It can only be applied in a taunting sense to Satan, and that only from 607 B.C. onward."[8]

And departing further from the earlier view, the writer of *"Babylon the Great Has Fallen!" God's Kingdom Rules!* (1963) explains:

> Lucifer, however, is not the name of the "king of Babylon." Lucifer, as a name, was applied to Satan the Devil by early uninspired religious writers of our Common Era.... Yet the fact that the Latin *Vulgate* and other Bible translations use the name Lucifer in addressing the "king of Babylon" **does not in itself mean or prove that this prophecy applies to Satan the Devil**.... So Isaiah 14:3-20 applies to Satan the Devil only as the earthly king of Babylon symbolizes that wicked spirit or reflects him.[9]

It is significant that the writer of the April 1, 1973, *Watchtower* views the earlier interpretation, one which goes back to the last quarter of the nineteenth century, as incorrect—an example of not "handling the word of the truth aright":

> Jehovah's people, too, need to be cautious in the applying of scriptures so that they correctly present God's Word in their preaching and teaching activity. As an example, take the statement that is sometimes made that one of the names given to Satan the Devil is Lucifer. Reference may be made by some to Isaiah 14:12-14.... The word "Lucifer" ... as here used, is not a personal name or a title, but, rather, a term describing the brilliant position taken by Babylon's dynasty of kings in the line of Nebuchadnezzar. **It would not be correct to say that Satan the Devil is the one called Lucifer as though it were one of his names.... The word Lucifer was not a name given to Satan the Devil**. By "handling the word of the truth aright" we are prepared to speak the clear sayings of God as we have them on the printed pages of the Bible.[10]

It is obvious that Rutherford did not understand that it was wrong to identify Satan as Lucifer when he wrote *Vindication*, his "due time" commentary on Ezekiel. On Ezekiel chapter 28, he discusses the Devil and his fall, applying the name Lucifer to him more than three dozen times![11]

The "Day of the Lord (Jehovah)"—When?

In the September 1879 *Watch Tower*, Russell reminds his readers: "As most of our readers are aware, we believe that the Word of God furnishes us with **indubitable proof that we are *now* living in this 'Day of the Lord'; that it began in 1873, and is a day of 40 years duration**...."[12] The March 1886 issue affirms: "The evidences are increasing on every hand which prove **not that the Day of the Lord is *near*, but that it has come; that we are in it** and that onward 'it hasteneth greatly.'... Thus, **the great events of the 'great day of God Almighty' are transpiring before our eyes**.... Even now the 'trump of God' the 'Seventh Trumpet' is sounding...."[13] The June 15, 1903, *Watch Tower* again views the Day of the Lord as underway: "Already the noise and tumult, which shall thus eventuate in world-wide anarchy, are distinctly heard in every nation; **for the day of the Lord has indeed begun**, and the heat of human passion is growing more and more intense daily, and the great time of trouble is very near."[14]

A new position was taken under Rutherford. The September 15, 1930, *Watch Tower* states: "It was in

1914 that Jehovah placed his Son upon his throne and sent him forth as his representative to rule and to oust Satan the enemy, and therefore **that date marks the beginning of the 'day of Jehovah.'**[15] *Watchtower* articles published in 1935, 1943 and 1953 agree: "The **'day of Jehovah' began in 1914**, when he enthroned his beloved Son and sent him to rule."[16] "At the Kingdom's establishment **in 1914 the long-foretold 'day of Jehovah' began**. It is the 'day of his preparation' for the final conflict of Armageddon."[17] "Most of our readers are familiar with the wealth of Scriptural evidence, frequently discussed in detail in these columns, showing that A.D. **1914 marked the beginning of Jehovah's day**."[18]

The September 15, 1997, *Watchtower* is typical of many other Watch Tower publications which states that "the day of Jehovah" is a future event that is "**near**," "**rapidly**" or "**fast approaching**."[19]

The Resurrection of the People of Old Testament Sodom

The wicked city of Sodom (often Sodom and Gomorrah), which was subjected to the judgment of God (Gen. 19), is referred to as an example of judgment a number of times in the Bible. What did Russell and subsequent Watch Tower publications teach concerning the resurrection of the people of Sodom (and Gomorrah)?

1877, 1879, 1886, 1913, 1934: Resurrection—Yes

Russell: "God proposes to bring them [Sodomites] back to their former estate...."[20]

"Thus Christ's own words teach us that they had not had their full opportunity. 'Remember,' Christ says of the Sodomites, that 'God rained down fire and *destroyed them all.*' So, if their restoration is spoken of, it *implies* their resurrection."[21]

"Thus our Lord teaches that the Sodomites did not have a full opportunity; and he guarantees them such opportunity...."[22]

"As the Sodomites, redeemed by the merit of Jesus' sacrifice, will be awakened from the sleep of death during the Messianic age, and their experiences will be more tolerable than the people of Chorazin and Bethsaida...."[23]

Rutherford: "God has given promise that in his due time the Sodomites and the Jews shall be awakened out of death and given a fair trial under the righteous reign of Christ Jesus."[24]

1952, 1954: Resurrection—No

"Similarly, Sodom did not endure its judgment day, had failed completely, and the Jews knew its fate was sealed."[25]

"He [Jesus] was pinpointing the utter impossibility of ransom for unbelievers or those willfully wicked, because Sodom and Gomorrah were irrevocably condemned and destroyed, beyond any possible recovery."[26]

1965: Resurrection—Yes

"As in the case of Tyre and Sidon, Jesus showed that Sodom, bad as it was, had not got to the state of being unable to repent.... So the spiritual recovery of the dead people of Sodom is not hopeless."[27]

1988: Resurrection—Yes, No
Yes

"Sodom and Gomorrah were everlastingly destroyed as *cities*, but this would not preclude a resurrection for *people* of those cities."[28]

No

"...The Bible uses Sodom/Gomorrah and the Flood as patterns for the destructive end of the present wicked system. It is apparent, then, that those whom God executed in those past judgments experienced irreversible destruction.[29]

"Jude 7 states that those Sodomites underwent 'the judicial punishment of everlasting fire,' meaning eternal destruction"[30]

1982, 1989: Resurrection—Yes, No

When *You Can Live Forever in Paradise Earth* was first published in 1982, it concluded that "Jesus showed that at least some of the unrighteous people of ancient Sodom and Gomorrah will be present on earth during Judgment day. Although they had been very immoral, we can expect that **some of them will be resurrected**." The 1989 revised edition states that "the people of Sodom and of the surrounding cities suffered a destruction from which they will apparently **never be resurrected**."[31]

How could such an interpretation record support the Watch Tower's claim of having Jehovah's guidance in the material printed in its publications?

Nebuchadnezzar's Dream (Dan. 2:31-35)

The Watch Tower's understanding of Daniel 2:31-35 presents a significant example of a revised interpretation of prophecy, with two major changes being made. The earliest position was rejected in 1930, only to be quietly reaffirmed years later.

Beginning with Russell, the Watch Tower interpreted the large metallic image described in Daniel 2 as "the four great empires, Babylon, Medo-Persia, Greece and Rome."[32] "...King Nebuchadnezzar had a dream, which portrayed the Gentile rule of earth during the interregnum of God's kingdom."[33] "From the days of Zedekiah, 606 B.C., to the present time, we have had four distinct kinds of government, and the fourth one modified in a deceptive manner. These kingdoms were (1) Babylonia, (2) Medo-Persia, (3) Greece, and (4) Rome.... The symbolic image which represented all these governments...."[34]

This interpretation held firm until 1930, when "new light" in God's "due time" brought forth a very different view. The previous one, said Rutherford, had been established "more than fifty years ago" by "**some good, honest Christian people who were called Adventists** ... which in substance states that the terrible image that Daniel saw represented the successive world powers.... The *Watch Tower* publications, having no better explanation, practically adopted the foregoing interpretation."[35] But it was "not correct," said Rutherford, for five "good reasons"—the first being, "the true meaning of the terrible image could not be understood by any of those whom Daniel represented until after the coming of the Lord to his temple [in 1918]. The foregoing interpretation having been made long before the coming of the Lord to his temple, it is hardly likely that it would be correct."[36]

The new view was that "the image pictured Satan's organization, of which the wicked one is the head."[37] The interpretation had shifted from a historical to an allegorical understanding, and in 1944 (Rutherford died in 1942), the earlier Watch Tower view was identified as the work of "**religious clergymen**...."[38]

With the condemnation of the earlier position and the strong promotion of Rutherford's "due time" interpretation,[39] it is astonishing to find that in *"Your Will Be Done on Earth"* (1958)[40] and later Watch Tower publications, a return to a view identical to the first—an interpretation which, as quoted earlier, had been identified as "not correct," the creation of "religious clergymen," and as "wrong."

The Parable of the Mustard Seed (Plant) (Matt. 13:31-32)

"Another illustration he set before them, saying: 'The kingdom of the heavens is like a mustard grain, which a man took and planted in his field; which is, in fact, the tiniest of all the seeds, but when it has grown it is the largest of the vegetables and becomes a tree, so that the birds of the heaven come and find lodging among its branches'" (Matt. 13:31-32 *NWT*).

Watch Tower founder C. T. Russell interpreted the man who planted the mustard seed (grain) as **Jesus Christ**.[41] Yet the book *Man's Salvation Out of World Distress at Hand!*, which was released at the "Divine Sovereignty" district assemblies during the summer of 1975,[42] reached a different conclusion: "In the parable, the 'man' that sowed the mustard grain **pictures the 'wicked one,' Satan the Devil**. Outstandingly in the fourth century C.E. Satan the Devil planted or specially cultivated the symbolic 'mustard grain' of contaminated, adulterated, imitation Christianity."[43] This new interpretation should not be surprising because it is claimed that the book, among other things, "provides fresh insights into ... the prophecies and parables of Jesus Christ...."[44]

A short time later, the October 1, 1975, *Watchtower* contained an interpretation in contradiction to that in the *Man's Salvation Out of World Distress at Hand!*: "How **could Jesus as the Sower of the parable** plant the symbolic mustard grain and yet have it become a tree of a foreign kind, the corrupt counterfeit called Christendom?... Jesus Christ, with his prophetic foresight, could foreknow the outcome for the symbolic mustard grain that **he planted** in the first century."[45]

It did not take long for the contradiction to be noted, and in answer to the question as to which was right, the November 1975 *Kingdom Ministry* states that "*The Watchtower* presents the **corrected understanding**" and future printings of the book would be changed.[46]

Vaccination, a Violation of God's Law?

Prof. Jerry Bergman writes that the Watch Tower Society's "vaccination condemnation is another tragic part of their history.... Between 1931 and 1952, Witnesses were instructed to refuse vaccinations for themselves and their children, and some even went to jail for their stand."[47] In 1931, an article in *The Golden Age* claimed: "Vaccination is **a direct violation of the everlasting covenant that God made with Noah** after the flood.... Genesis 9:1-7...."[48] And the April 24, 1935, issue explained why: "...As vaccination is a direct injection of animal matter in the blood stream, vaccination is a direct violation of the holy law of Jehovah God."[49]

In his book *Faith on the March*, with introduction by N. H. Knorr (1957), well-known Jehovah's Witness A. H. Macmillan recounts his experience during World War II of visiting men who were imprisoned under the Selective Service System draft laws: "One of the more serious problems I had to deal with, as I remember, was vaccinations."[50] When the order came from the health department that all the men should be vaccinated, "Some of our boys in one prison in particular considered this the same as blood transfusions, and refused to submit." Because of this, they were placed in solitary confinement. Macmillan convinced the warden to allow him to speak to the men about the vaccination issue in a special meeting.[51] He was asked by one of the Witness leaders what he would do if he were in prison and confronted with a vaccination order. He writes:

> "I was in prison," I reminded them, "and I bared my arm and received the shot. Furthermore, **all of us who visit our foreign branches are vaccinated or we stay at home.** Now vaccination is not anything like blood transfusion. No blood is used in the vaccine. It is serum. **So you would not be violating those Scriptures which forbid taking blood into your system....**" Our discussion lasted about two hours, then **the men decided to submit to vaccination** after making a token resistance. Furthermore they agreed to write a letter of apology for the trouble they had caused through their first stand taken.[52]

What Macmillan stated concerning vaccinations was contrary to Watch Tower teaching at the time, as the following account shows.

In 1951, Brooklyn headquarters Service Department worker Bill Cetnar had received a number of letters "from parents who had asked if it was against God's law to allow their children to have smallpox vaccinations as required by law for admittance into public schools." He knew what was taught, but "did not have confidence in the Society's position on this point." He had an occasion to express his concerns to president Knorr, who replied, "It is not for you to determine policy."[53] Pursuing his doubts, he recounts:

> Later I visited the Lederle Laboratories, which made the smallpox vaccine, and found that my suspicions were correct. Although the Society taught that vaccinations violated God's law because they put animal blood into humans, I found that this was not true. The vaccine was made by a process known as avianization, in which the vaccine was cultured in the developing chick embryo and did not involve blood at all. On my return to headquarters I sent a memo to the president concerning my discovery, but it was never acknowledged.[54]

A short time later, the December 15, 1952, *Watchtower* concluded: "The matter of vaccination is one for the individual that has to face it to decide for himself.... After consideration of the matter, **it does not appear to us to be in violation of the everlasting covenant made with Noah**, as set down in Genesis 9:4, nor contrary to God's related commandment at Leviticus 17:10-14." And after further discussion: "Hence **all objection to vaccination on Scriptural grounds seems to be lacking**."[55] One can only wonder how many were harmed or even died before these conclusions were published.

An article in the August 22, 1965, *Awake!* acknowledges: "There can be little doubt that vaccinations appear to have caused a marked decrease in the number of people contracting contagious diseases."[56] And in the conclusion, it states: "The question as to whether you and your children should be vaccinated is something for personal decision."[57]

The Pleiades, God's Dwelling Place?

"From the 1890's until the 1950's, the Society taught that **God lived in the star system of the Pleiades**."[58] This subject is thoroughly researched by Duane Magnani in his book *The Heavenly Weather Man*.[59]

In *Reconciliation* (1928), Rutherford presents the belief:

> It has been suggested, and with much weight, that **one of the stars of that group [Pleiades] is the dwelling-place of Jehovah** and the place of the highest heavens.... "Canst thou bind the sweet influences of Pleiades, or loose the bands of Orion?"—Job 38:31. The constellation of the Pleiades is a small one compared with others which scientific instruments disclose to the wondering eyes of man. But the greatness in size of other stars or planets is small when compared with the Pleiades in importance, **because the Pleiades is the place of the eternal throne of God**.[60]

It should be noted that Rutherford's foreword to *Reconciliation* claims: "The writer does not give his opinion. No human interpretation of Scripture is advanced. The contents of this book are a statement of the facts as they exist and the citation of the Scriptures in support thereof."

Without referring to it as a long-held Society teaching, the above view on the Pleiades is rejected in the November 15, 1953, *Watchtower*: "Incidentally, Pleiades can no longer be considered the center of the universe and **it would be unwise for us to try to fix God's throne as being at a particular spot in the universe.** Were we to think of the Pleiades as his throne we might improperly view with special veneration that cluster of stars."[61]

Notes

1. *WTR*, 1 Aug 1894, 1686. See also Russell's, *The New Creation* (1904), 609-10.

2. *WTR*, 15 May 1916, 5896. "Lucifer, one of the very highest of spirit beings, became proud and vain in his imagination, and encouraging these evil qualities he lost his exalted position, having become Satan, the adversary of God" (*WTR*, 1 Feb 1916, 5843).

3. Russell, *Scenario of the Photo-Drama of Creation* (1914), 15.

4. *WT*, 15 Feb. 1926, 54.

5. *WT*, 15 May 1932, 155-57; *WT*, 1 June 1932, 170-72; *WT*, 15 July 1932, 221-23.

6. Rutherford, *Religion* (1940), 12-13.

7. *WT*, 15 Oct. 1949, 313.

8. *WT*, 1 Mar. 1957, 159.

9. *"Babylon the Great Has Fallen!" God's Kingdom Rules!* (1963), 314.

10. *WT*, 1 Apr. 1973, 209.

11. Rutherford, *Vindication II* (1932), 87-107. The Introduction states: "Now he [Jehovah] is causing such prophecy to be fulfilled and to be understood" (5). In Rutherford's note to the Witnesses in the book he claims: "It has now pleased him [Jehovah] to give to his anointed an understanding of his prophecy by Ezekiel."

12. *WTR*, Sept. 1879, 26.

13. *WTR*, Mar. 1886, 834.

14. *WTR*, 15 June 1903, 3215.

15. *WT*, 15 Sept. 1930, 275.

16. *WT*, 15 Mar. 1935, 83.

17. *WT*, 15 Dec. 1943, 371.

18. *WT*, 15 Mar. 1953, 178-79.

19. *WT*, 15 Sept. 1997, 16-20.

20. Russell, *The Object and Manner of the Lord's Return* (1877), 25.

21. *WTR*, July 1879, 7.

22. Russell, *The Divine Plan of the Ages* (1886), 110.

23. *WTR*, 15 Nov. 1913, 5351.

24. Rutherford, *His Vengeance* (1934), 38.

25. *WT*, 1 June 1952, 338.

26. *WT*, 1 Feb. 1954, 85.

27. *WT*, 1 Mar. 1965, 139; see also 1 Aug. 1965, 479.

28. *Insight on the Scriptures* (1988), vol. 2, 985.

29. *WT*, 1 June 1988, 31. In "Questions from Readers," it is asked: "Do Jesus' words at Matthew 11:24 mean that those whom Jehovah destroyed by fire in Sodom and Gomorrah will be resurrected?" In answer: "**Prior to 1964, we took these verses to mean that the people of Chorazin, Bethsaida, and Capernaum merited eternal destruction**" (ibid., 30). It is obvious that the writer of this answer either was ignorant of, or chose not to recognize the existence of, the earlier interpretation by Russell and Rutherford, which was taught by God's "channel" for many years (see also *WTR*, 2267, 2623-24, 3348).

30. *Revelation—Its Grand Climax at Hand!* (1988), 273.

31. *You Can Live Forever in Paradise on Earth* (1982), 179.

32. Russell, *The Divine Plan of the Ages*, 252.

33. *WTR*, 1 Sept. 1914, 5526.

34. *WTR*, 15 Apr. 1915, 5673.

35. Rutherford, *Light II* (1930), 295-96.

36. Ibid., 296.

37. Ibid., 310.

38. *The Kingdom Is at Hand* (1944), 179."In these latter years the same God of revelation provides the Scriptural interpretation of the prophetic dream by means of unlocking of the Scriptures and by physical facts in fulfillment of the dream" (ibid. 180).

39. It is a serious matter to change Rutherford's earlier interpretation on this passage because of what was claimed for the *Light* volumes: "God has now given his people an understanding of The Revelation which he gave to Jesus Christ to show unto his servants. The publication of the two books called *Light*, giving the explanation of The Revelation, will greatly anger the Devil and all who have not the spirit of Christ" (*WT*, 15 Sept. 1930, 281). "The conviction is pressed upon me deeply now that no human creature is the author of *Light*. No man could write that book. No man wrote *Light*. It is the manifest power of a living God that gave to us this wonderful revelation of his Word of Truth.... Brother, you were merely the amanuensis in the production of *Light*. Jehovah is its author, even as the book itself declares" (Letter by J. A. Bohnet, to Rutherford, *WT*, 1 Apr. 1931, 111). "This publication of *Light* is manifestly an outstanding event in the history of the church of God upon earth, and therefore in God's organization Zion" (Letter by Jesse Hemery to Rutherford, *WT*, 1 Nov. 1930, 335).

40. *"Your Will Be Done on Earth"* (1958), chapter 8. "But what do the four different beasts of Daniel's dream prefigure historically? ... By means of two heaven-sent dreams the march of world powers from 607 B.C. down to modern times was to be made doubly sure, as by two witnesses" (ibid., 168). Subsequent discussion identifies these world powers as: Babylon, Medo-Persia, Greece and Rome (ibid., 170-74).

41. *WTR*, 15 May 1900, 2634.

42. *WT*, 15 Oct. 1975, 627.

43. *Man's Salvation Out of World Distress at Hand!* (1975), 208.

44. *WT*, 15 Oct. 1975, 627.

45. *WT*, 1 Oct. 1975, 600.

46. *Kingdom Ministry*, Nov. 1975, 4.

47. Jerry Bergman, *Blood Transfusions: A History and Evaluation of the Religious, Biblical, and Medical Objections* (Clayton, Calif.: Witness Inc., 1994), 33. See Bergman for further discussion (32-36, 63-64, 79-84).

48. *GA*, 4 Feb. 1931, 293.

49. *GA*, 24 Apr. 1935, 465.

50. A. H. Macmillan, *Faith on the March* (Englewood Cliffs, N.J.: Prentice-Hall, 1957), 188.

51. Ibid.

52. Ibid., 189.

53. William Cetnar, "An Inside View of the Watchtower Society," in Edmond C. Gruss, *We Left Jehovah's Witnesses* (Phillipsburg: N.J.: Presbyterian and Reformed, 1974), 64.

54. Ibid.

55. *WT*, 15 Dec. 1952, 764.

56. *Awake!*, 22 Aug. 1965, 20.

57. Ibid., 21.

58. Duane Magnani, *The Heavenly Weatherman* (Clayton, Calif.: Witness Inc., 1987), 254.

59. Magnani's study (254-61) also includes photocopies of the Watch Tower sources quoted (262-85).
60. Rutherford, *Reconciliation* (1928), 14.
61. *WT*, 15 Nov. 1953, 703.

48.

Conclusion: What Does the Record Show?

The introductory overview of this study quoted the April 1, 1972, *Watchtower* where it states: "Of course, it is easy to say that this group acts as a 'prophet' of God. It is another thing to prove it. The only way that this can be done is to review the record. What does it show?" This and a number of other claims have been made by the Watch Tower organization. What does the record show?

The more one investigates the interpretations and speculations of C. T. Russell, his Adventist co-workers, J. F. Rutherford, N. H. Knorr, F. W. Franz, and any others responsible for the publications of the Watch Tower Society, the more one sees the magnitude of their errors, follies, fiascoes, and failures. That which was speculated, surmised, suggested, and conjectured was, and still is, often presented as exposition of Scripture, "due time" light, present truth, or God's message for today. There is a record of over 120 years, or even more, if the Second Adventist movement is included—for as has been shown, Russell's Bible Students movement was an offshoot of Millerism.

This chapter (1) quotes statements by former Witnesses and one other informed observer as they comment on the organization's record; (2) reviews some Watch Tower claims and criticisms of others, which are then compared with their own record; (3) examines Watch Tower statements and criteria for the identification of a false prophet; and (4) compares the "good news" of the Jehovah's Witnesses with that of the message of the early Church.

Statements by Others Who Have Examined the Society Record

Walter Salter was Canadian branch overseer and J. F. Rutherford confidante until he was removed from his position in 1936 and disfellowshipped the next year. In his open letter to Society President Rutherford, dated April 1, 1937, he writes:

> It seems strange that after our experiences of 1914 and 1925 **we should still fail to draw a clear cut line of demarcation between deduction and a thus saith the Lord and go on dogmatizing regarding the Lord's presence, dogmatizing about the Lord being at His temple, and dogmatizing concerning what Armageddon will bring about.** But there are "none so blind as those who won't see" and they will go on **prophesying false dreams until events themselves prove the folly thereof.** And this, even though such false teachings bring dishonor to God and His word, for **what is prone to dishonor God's word more in the minds of people than testimony that is made with a declaration that it is based upon God's word when that testi-**

mony is found to be false. One does well to take heed to Deuteronomy **18:21, 22**, which reads: "If thou say in thine heart, how shall we know the word which the Lord hath spoken? When a prophet speaketh in the name of the Lord, if the thing follow not nor come to pass, that is the thing which the Lord hath not spoken, but the prophet hath spoken it presumptuously; thou shalt not be afraid of him." **(An outstanding example, our nonsense concerning what God was going to do in the year 1925.)** And again I quote Jeremiah 23:28-32: "He that hath my word, let him speak my word faithfully.... Behold, **I am against them that prophesy false dreams, saith the Lord**, and do tell them, and cause my people to err by their lies, and by their lightness [and because of their boasting *NWT*]"[1]

In the concluding chapter of *Crisis of Conscience*, Raymond Franz, from past experience, looks into the future:

> **Whatever the changes that come, they will most certainly be heralded as the product of divine direction, and the past doctrines or arrangements that may be discarded will be depicted as "God's will for that time,"** perhaps some kind of "maneuvering" by the heavenly Captain, Christ Jesus, in working toward an end that was ultimately beneficial. **As in the past one hundred years of the organization's history, there is little reason to believe that the changes will be acknowledged for what they are—generallly the result of failing to hold to the Scriptures in the first place, and, in most cases, changes made under the pressure of circumstances, designed to ward off foreseen dilemmas because of a position that has become untenable.** This is not at all the same as corrections that are made by persons who search the Scriptures and, as a result of what they discover there, freely admit that they have been in error and wish to rectify their mistakes.[2]

In a letter to the *JW Research Journal*, ex-Witness Chester Harris writes of his own experience:

> I wanted so much to be right that I became a JW. **I thought for twenty years after that I was right**. When I was first shown some Watchtower blunders and false prophecies I did what most JWs do; I defended the Watchtower. I continued defending it for years after because I sincerely thought that these so-called "false prophecies" were just the Devil's sinister attempts to discredit the Watchtower society. I saw it as intrigue on a cosmic scale; and I could be a player. That meant investigating the most incriminating evidence against the Watchtower. Nothing was too dangerous or too apostate to read. If I couldn't successfully answer any and all allegations against the Society, then I couldn't consider myself a major league player.
>
> **The evidence I read really made me sick to my stomach. I found out that I had frittered away over twenty years selling a sham religion**. During most of those years I had cultivated (with the Watchtower's help) a "holier-than-thou" attitude towards other religions. Now it was my turn to eat dirt. I could do one of two things, I could admit my grave error—or I could entrench myself in error and fight it out. That was unthinkable! I didn't like the alternative; but I had no choice. I did the right thing and abandoned the Watchtower Society.... **The Watchtower Society has been wrong on so many things that we all lost count long ago.** How many frank admissions—I mean *really* frank admissions—can you remember them having made?[3]

Ron Frye, a former circuit overseer and Witness for 33 years, after having researched the organization, writes:

> I *did not want* the Society to be proven false! When I began my research into the doctrine of the faithful and discreet slave early in 1980, I did so with the hope that I would be able to restore my confidence in the Watch Tower Society. **But the more I compared the teachings of the Society with the Scriptures and compared its explanations of its own history with proven historical facts, the more obvious it became that its teachings regarding the spiritual authority of its leaders had no basis in either the Scriptures or history.** Thus I was *forced* intellectually to dismiss the Society's claim that it represents *in any way* the so-called faithful and discreet slave class. At best I concluded that Watch Tower leaders could be no more than a group of sincere religious men who, unfortunately, had taken themselves *far too seriously*, a fact which has led to their presumptuousness.[4]

Frye also makes a significant observation: "...Russell was a man whom, Jehovah's Witnesses still argue, God used to revive the great teachings of Jesus and the apostles. Why, then, do they not study his books today in their congregations if no more than from a historical standpoint? **Because much of it, if not most of it, would be considered *heresy* today!**"[5]

Former Witness, researcher and author Duane Magnani, concludes:

> A reading of the Watchtower Society's history reveals that the Society does not value "truth" in the way it is defined in the dictionary. As one who has read Watchtower publications dating from 1879 to the present, **this author is amazed at the enormous amount of changes in fundamental doctrines over the years. One year a Society doctrine is declared God's "truth"; later it is admitted to be false doctrine.** Older publications are full of "outdated" truth, which the Society considers dangerous to the spiritual health of Jehovah's Witnesses and others.... **A look at these outdated publications uncovers the fact that the Society is an organization that deals in doctrinal speculation, not absolute truth.**[6]
>
> God doesn't make mistakes but the Society does. **A review of their history reveals literally thousands of major doctrinal errors.** One of their key mistakes is in mistaking the very nature of God.... The god of the Watchtower Society is mutable. His changes are expressed in the very doctrinal mistakes we see in Watchtower publications.[7]

Under the heading "The Myth of Progressive Revelation," Prof. James A. Beverly writes:

> **...The idea of progressive revelation is no excuse for error. What Witnesses never face is the enormous corpus of material from Russell and Rutherford that has never been even close to the truth.** Too, these leaders and their current successor advance their teachings in the most dogmatic manner, ready to exercise discipline on those who disagree, and unwilling to recognize that their "truth" might be overturned.... Finally, **progressive revelation is no excuse for extreme doctrinal ambivalence**. Paul warns that "we should no longer be babes, tossed about as by waves and carried hither and thither by every wind of teaching by means of the trickery of men" (Eph. 4:4, *NWT*). **The extent to which the "faithful and discreet slave," the Governing Body, has changed positions on what is really true and beneficial is simply astonishing.**[8]

Beverly supports this last statement by presenting a partial list of 23 doctrines, once taught, which the Watch Tower no longer believes, and a number of other doctrinal changes.[9]

M. James Penton was Professor of History and Religious Studies at the University of Lethbridge in Canada. He was also a fourth-generation Jehovah's Witness who was disfellowshipped in 1981. In the study for his book *Apocalypse Delayed*, he writes: "... As I began to research the history of the movement in the United States in a way that I had not previously done, **I became more and more doubtful of traditional Witness claims to spiritual authority**."[10] He explains further:

> For when they have spoken dogmatically on some doctrine, for example with respect to some eschatological date, they have frequently claimed that they have had proof or definite knowledge which was revealed to them, evidently by the holy spirit acting through them as God's channel. But when their predictions have proved wrong, as time and again they have, Watch Tower writers have fallen back on the idea that progressive revelation[11] can simply mean enhanced knowledge which can, of course, be mistaken, usually about certain details. **In effect, then, the concept of progressive revelation has often been used, whether consciously or not, as a sort of spiritual shell game on the Witness community.** That this has been so can be demonstrated clearly by the way the society has in fact used the concept over the years, **especially with regard to prophetic speculation. Note that most if not all of the major events expected by Russell, Rutherford, and the Watch Tower Society since Rutherford's day have not happened.**[12]

Michael Pendley was a Jehovah's Witness for 38 years. After examining and researching Witness claims, he came away with a number of pertinent questions—many of the same ones raised in the statements above and in this study.

> **As the Society has done on numerous occasions in the past, it has changed doctrine to cover over false prophecy.** These doctrinal changes have raised a number of questions in my mind. **[1]** If God is directing the Watchtower Society by means of His Holy Spirit, how is it possible that key doctrines which were taught for decades are now admitted to have been wrong? **[2]** Why does God allow His chosen channel to teach erroneous doctrine and make false prophecies? **[3]** Why do the teachings of Jehovah's Witnesses undergo constant change so that older publications become out of date? **[4]** Why is the entire history of the Society littered with prophetic failures and doctrinal reversals? **[5]** Does God make mistakes? **[6]** Is God continually learning new things thereby necessitating that He send "New light" to His organization to correct wrong information given in the past? **[7]** Does the Holy Spirit purposely mislead the earthly organization? **Since God is all-knowing and free from any error or deception, I am forced to the conclusion that the Society's teachings do not originate with God but are the product of flawed human reasoning.** The words of Jeremiah concerning false prophets come to mind: "They have prophesied the delusions of their own minds—they have spoken falsely in Jehovah's name."[13]

Watch Tower Claims and Statements and the Record

In spite of the Watch Tower's Society's record as examined in this book, and as summarized in the statements by the informed writers quoted above, in their publications the Jehovah's Witnesses are often not given the whole truth. Also, Watch Tower publications often criticize others for what legitimately applies to them. Here are some typical examples.

1. "Since 1879 it has been published regularly for the benefit of sincere students of the Bible. Over that extended period of time *The Watchtower* **has consistently proved itself dependable**."[14]

   After reviewing the record, has the *Watchtower* "consistently proved itself dependable" from 1879 to 1950 (when this claim was made)—and to the present?

2. "It is true that the Witnesses **have made mistakes** in their understanding of what would occur at the end of certain time periods.... **Matters on which corrections of viewpoint have been needed have been relatively minor** when compared with the vital Bible truths they have discerned and publicized."[15]

   After reviewing the record, is it true that the Witnesses "corrections of viewpoint have been relatively minor..."—by any comparison? What does the record show?

3. **"For over a century, delightful, correct, words of truth covering every aspect of life have been presented in the Watch Tower Society's publications** and widely distributed in many languages. Many families and individuals have thus been able to accumulate in their own homes **a library of reliable reference works that focus on the Bible**."[16]

   After reviewing "over a century" of Watch Tower Society publications, is it accurate to claim that it has always published "**correct, words of truth**" and produced "a library of **reliable reference works** that focus on the Bible"? The present acceptance by a Witness of some of these "correct words of truth" ("old light") would result in his being disfellowshipped.

4. **"There is an additional way, among others, to determine whom Jehovah is using today**. Bible prophecy, history written in advance comes from God. (2 Pet. 1:20,21) He can foresee future conditions with total accuracy and keep his servants abreast of them.... **These things Jehovah has made known to those who obey him as ruler**: 'The Sovereign Lord Jehovah will not do a thing unless he has revealed his confidential matter to his servants the prophets.' (Amos 3:7) **In this century who has been correctly informed about the future?** the clergy? the political leaders? the economic heads? **Or has it been the witnesses of Jehovah?**..."[17] "**Who today deserve our confidence** as they tell of events to come in the very near future?"[18]

   Is it true that in this century the Jehovah's Witnesses have been "**correctly informed about the future**," and because of this, they "deserve our confidence"? After a careful examination, what end time events have been fulfilled as predicted during this entire century? Which have not?

5. "Rather, **the record that the 'faithful and discreet slave' organization has made for the past more than 100 years forces us to the conclusion that Peter expressed when Jesus asked if his apostles also wanted to leave him, namely, 'Whom shall we go away to?'** (John 6:66-69) No question about it. We all need help to understand the Bible, and **we cannot find the Scriptural guidance we need outside the 'faithful and discreet slave' organization**."[19]

   Does the record of the "faithful and discreet slave" show that it is the only reliable source for "Scriptural guidance?"

6. **"At times explanations given by Jehovah's visible organization have shown adjustments, seemingly to previous points of view. But this has not actually been the case.** This might be compared to what is known in navigational circles a 'tacking.' By maneuvering the sails the sailors can cause a ship to go from right to left, back and forth, but all the time making progress toward their destination in spite of contrary winds."[20]

Is it true that the Society's explanations that have been adjusted or clarified **have never gone back "to previous points of view"**? What about the following examples? The "Superior authorities" of Romans 13; "That Servant"; the parable of the Sheep and the Goats; Daniel's image (Dan. 2); and the resurrection of the people of Sodom? Is the "tacking" explanation of Scriptural understanding a valid one? Contrary to their claim, as Raymond Franz correctly observes: "The problem is that shifting of teaching often brings them back virtually to the point where they began."[21] And many times, the interpretations published later were **entirely new ones which contradicted those previously held**.

7. "Consider, too, the fact that Jehovah's organization alone, in all the earth, **is directed by God's holy spirit** or active force (Zech. 4:6).... **Direction by God's spirit** enables Jehovah's servants to have divine light in a world of spiritual darkness. (2 Cor. 4:4)"[22]

If the claim "that Jehovah's organization alone ... is directed by God's holy spirit" is true, how can this claim and the Witnesses' record be reconciled with the following statement in their *Insight on the Scriptures*: "Being 'the spirit of truth,' **God's holy spirit could never be the source of error but would protect Christ's followers from doctrinal falsehoods**"? (Compare 1 John 2:27; 4:1-6.)[23]

8. An objective of the *Watch Tower*, as stated in its very first issue, was "to give the **'meat in due season'** to the 'household of faith'" (Luke 12:42; Gal. 6:10, *Authorized Version*). We are grateful that through these pages it has been possible to direct attention to God's Word and thus provide **spiritual food "at the proper time"** to benefit not only anointed followers of Christ but their associates of the "great crowd" (Matt. 24:45; Rev. 7:4-10).[24]

What is the meaning of "meat in due season" or "spiritual food 'at the proper time'"? According to the December 15, 1916, *Watch Tower*, "'Meat in due season' means the message of the kingdom to the church, **given at the time the Lord intended it should be given**."[25] And further, according to Rutherford, "The Christian's meat in due season **is a proper explanation of the Scriptures as they become due to be understood**."[26] The June 1, 1943, *Watchtower* explains: "The food that the Lord's 'sheep' feed upon and that their feeders must serve to them is the spiritual food provided by the great Life-giver, Jehovah. He gives it through his Good Shepherd Christ Jesus. Jehovah himself is the 'Great Shepherd and Bishop of your souls.' **He sees to it that it is the right food, in due season, and that it is served through his approved visible organization**."[27]

If these explanations are true, why was so much that was **presented as "meat in due season" or "food 'at the proper time'"** not fulfilled as predicted, or was later adjusted or rejected? As one example, *The Finished Mystery* was promoted as "meat in due season": "Let us not say: 'Why should we accept it as present truth?' Rather let us say: 'Why should I not accept it as **meat in due season from the Lord?**'"[28] How are its "meat in due season" interpretations viewed today? See the chapter "The Finished Mystery (1917)" for more details.

9. The December 15, 1988, *Watchtower* is critical of what it views as characterizing Christendom: "The **variety of contradictory interpretations** we find today among so-called Christians is not the fault of the Bible's author, nor is it the fault of Bible writers.... **It is the fault of Bible readers who have failed to follow the leadings of God's spirit in allowing God to interpret his own Word**. They have allowed personal ideas to becloud their view of what the Bible's Author himself says."[29]

How should the multiple contradictory interpretations which characterize the publications of the Jehovah's Witnesses over the years be viewed and explained?

10. While the following statements were made in early *Watch Tower* issues, they express valid principles and are applicable to the Witnesses' doctrine of progressive revelation since that time: "We have sometimes been accused by unbelievers for teaching that the true way to advance light was to displace the *truth* we learned yesterday by *new truth* learned today; but we utterly repudiate the absurd charge. To *grow* in knowledge is to retain the truth we have and add to our stock."[30] "If we were following *a man* undoubtedly it would be different with us; **undoubtedly one human idea would contradict another and that which was light one or two or six years ago would be regarded as darkness now**: But with God there is no variableness, neither shadow of turning, and so it is with *truth*; any knowledge or light coming from God must be like its author. **A new view of truth never can contradict a former truth.** *'New light'* never extinguishes older *'light,'* but adds to it.... So it is with the light of truth; the true increase is by adding to it, not by substituting one for another."[31]

What has characterized the Witnesses' "due time" light? Does not the example, "that which was light one or two or six years ago would be regarded as darkness now," well describe the history of many Watch Tower Society interpretations over the years? Has not "new light" often extinguished "older 'light'"?

11. In criticizing others, the October 8, 1968, *Awake!* concludes: **"True, there have been those in times past who predicted an 'end to the world,' even announcing a specific date.** Some have gathered groups of people with them and fled to the hills or withdrawn into their houses waiting for the end. **Yet, nothing happened. The 'end' did not come. They were guilty of false prophesying. Why? What was missing? Missing was the full assurance of evidence required in fulfillment of Bible prophecy. Missing from such people were God's truths and the evidence that he was guiding and using them.** But what about today? Today we have the evidence required, *all of it*. And it is overwhelming! All the many, many parts of the great sign of the 'last days' are here, together with verifying Bible chronology."[32]

While it is true that the Bible Students or Jehovah's Witnesses of today did not flee to the hills or withdraw to their homes to wait for the end, it is also true that the movement **did set specific times** for "the end of the world" and other important end time events. Such erroneous predictions would make them "guilty of false prophesying." How is this "false prophesying" of others explained? "Missing from such people were God's truths and the evidence that he was guiding and using them" says *Awake!*. Surely the Watch Tower Society cannot escape the implications of its own words.

12. "Eager to see the end of this evil system, Jehovah's people have at times **speculated** about the time when the 'great tribulation' would break out, **even tying this to calculations of what is the lifetime**

of a generation since 1914. However, we 'bring a heart of wisdom in,' not by **speculating** about how many years or days make up a generation...."[33]

While to speculate may be defined as theorizing or conjecturing on the basis of little or no evidence, this certainly is not what was claimed by the Watch Tower Society and the Jehovah's Witnesses for their speculations, which were promoted with assurance worldwide for decades. Setting aside the discussion on the length of a generation, the following was set forth as absolute until "clarified" in 1995: "**Thus before the 1914 generation completely dies out, God's judgment must be executed**."[34]

13. Rutherford asks: "What has been **the Devil's method of contaminating sincere persons at all times?** A. Religious leaders generally have said, '**We are the only ones who can understand the Bible**, and **if you want to know anything about it, ask us**.'"[35]

Many statements could be cited to show that Watch Tower leadership essentially takes such a position, but several should suffice. Society Secretary-Treasurer Grant Suiter gave testimony in the Douglas Walsh trial in Scotland in 1954. The questions and his response follow: "**Q.** Indeed can he [company servant] in the view of Jehovah's Witnesses **have an understanding of the Scriptures apart from the publications of Jehovah's Witnesses? A. No. Q. Only by the publications can he have a right understanding of the Scriptures? A. That is right. Q.** Is that not arrogance? **A.** No."[36]

The following quotations are from the various issues of the *Watchtower*. After urging loyalty to the "faithful and discreet slave," the reader is told: "Let us face **the fact** that no matter how much Bible reading we have done, **we would never have learned the truth on our own**."[37] "We all need help to understand the Bible, and **we cannot find Scriptural guidance we need outside the 'faithful and discreet slave' organization**."[38] "**It is unlikely that someone who simply reads the Bible without taking advantage of divinely provided aids could discern the light**. That is why Jehovah God has provided 'the faithful and discreet slave,' foretold at Matthew 24:45-47."[39] "If we get to thinking that we know better than the organization, we should ask ourselves: 'Where did we learn Bible truth in the first place? **Would we know the way of the truth if it had not been for guidance from the organization?** Really, can we get along without the direction of God's organization?' No, we cannot!"[40]

Conclusion

It is clear that this organization stands convicted even when examined through statements in its own publications.

How Watch Tower Publications Identify a False Prophet

Claiming to have been appointed by God to the prophetic office ("Jeremiah class," "Ezekiel class," "Elijah class," "genuine 'prophet,'" "authentic prophet class," etc.),[41] Watch Tower publications are not reluctant to apply the term "false prophet(s)" to individuals, or whole groups, connected with the financial, political, and especially the religious realms. For example: The August 15, 1919, *Watch Tower* looks at Christendom and concludes: "Surely there is nothing in all history that more clearly fulfills the picture of the **false prophets** [of Baal] **than the majority of the clergy class of our own day**...."[42] In *Prophecy*, discussing "False Prophets," Rutherford writes: "The **clergymen or pastors** of the various churches of modern times claim to be prophets speaking in the name of God.... Put to the divine test, their words are proven false... **They deny the Bible and Bible doctrine**.... Therefore, such men are **false prophets**."[43]

In a radio lecture on "True and False Prophets," Rutherford explains:

A PROPHET is a person who professes to proclaim a message from Jehovah God. The Bible reveals the fact that there are both true and false prophets.... Since the Bible was completed, and "inspiration" is not longer necessary, a true prophet is one who is faithfully proclaiming what is *written* in the Bible.... But it may be asked, **How are we to know whether one is a true or a false prophet?** There are at least three ways by which we can positively decide: (1) If he is a true prophet, **his message will come to pass exactly as prophesied. If he is a false prophet, his prophecy will fail to come to pass.** This rule is laid down by God himself, through Moses as follows: "If thou say in thine heart, How shall we know the word which the Lord hath *not* spoken? When a prophet speaketh in the name of the Lord, if the thing follow not, nor come to pass, that is the thing that the Lord hath not spoken, but the prophet hath spoken it presumptuously."—Deut. 18: 21, 22).... **The true prophet of God *today* will be telling forth what the Bible teaches, and those things that the Bible tells us are soon to come to pass. He will not be sounding forth man-made theories or guesses, either his own or those of others.... The false prophets of our day are the financial, political and clerical prognosticators. They assume to foretell future events; but their dreams or guesses never come true....** In 1914-1918 these same three classes told the world that the great **World War would end all wars and make the world safe for democracy**; and that the young men who died on the field of battle ... would go to heaven. **Their prophecies did not come true. Therefore they are false prophets; and the people should no longer trust them as safe guides....**[44]

In his commentary on Revelation, after quoting the premier of the British Empire, Rutherford writes:

It may well be admitted that the speaker who used those words was sincere, but **we know that his words are not true.**... These two nations [Great Britain and America] acting jointly take the lead of all the nations of the earth to evolve and bring forth plausible schemes and with pleasing and deceptive speech make the people believe that their schemes are just and right. They have been thus prophesying particularly since 1918, and everyone knows that **their prophecies to date have not come to pass; and that alone is strong evidence that they are false prophets.**... They fail to meet a single one of the requirements to prove that they are true prophets—**Deut. 18:21, 22.**[45]

The **false-prophet Anglo-American Empire** admonishes the people to remain quiet and steadfast, always promising that these governments will bring mankind out of danger and make the world a fit place in which to reside. **They prophesy peace, when there is not peace. God says of them that "they are false prophets, following their own selfish desires, and prophecy that which is false"**—Ezek. 13:3,4, 16.[46]

The October 15, 1958, *Watchtower* quotes a California newspaper: "'**Sometime between April 15 and 23, 1957, Armageddon will sweep the world!** Millions of persons will perish in its flames and the land will be scorched.' So prophesied a certain California pastor, Mihran Ask, in January, 1957. Such **false prophets** tend to put the subject of Armageddon in disrepute."[47]

The October 8, 1968, *Awake!* reports: "True, there have been those in times past who **predicted an 'end of the world,'** even announcing a specific date.... **The 'end' did not come. They were guilty of false prophesying.**"[48]

The book *Paradise Restored to Mankind—By Theocracy!* (1972) warns that "Jehovah, the God of the true prophets, will **put all false prophets to shame either by not fulfilling the false prediction of such self-assuming prophets or by having His own prophecies fulfilled in a way opposite to that predicted by the false prophets**. False prophets will try to hide their reason for feeling shame by denying who they really are." The writer goes on to quote Zechariah 13:4-6, where the false prophet says, "I am no prophet."[49]

The September 1, 1979, *Watchtower* explains how God's true prophet and false prophets differ and how false prophets are exposed:

> For nearly 60 years now the Jeremiah class have faithfully spoken forth Jehovah's Word.... **Unlike the clergy class, those of the Jeremiah class have been sent by Jehovah to speak in his name.** Nevertheless, the clergy prophets also claim to speak in his name and, hence, to tell the Bible truth.... **True, the Jeremiah class back up their message by quoting the words, "This is what Jehovah has said."**... How will Jehovah show that such clergy prophets are fakes? **By not fulfilling what they announce to be "an utterance!" or what they presume to speak in his name. He does not back up their falsehood.**[50]

The *Watchtower* article, "Beware of False Prophets!" in the February 1, 1992, issue explains that while prophesying as foretelling was part of the prophet's work,

> in fact, the main thought conveyed by the original Bible language words translated "prophesy" or "prophecy" is **basically to tell forth God's mind on a matter**, or, as the book of Acts puts it, to tell "the magnificent things of God" (Acts 2:11).[51]
>
> As in Jeremiah's day, there exist today **false prophets claiming to represent the God of the Bible; but they too steal God's words by preaching things that distract people from what God, through the Bible, really says**. In what way? Let us answer that question by using, as a touchstone, the fundamental Bible teaching of the Kingdom.[52] **Those who teach that God's kingdom is achieved through political action are false prophets**. They are stealing God's words from the people.[53]

Using the Jehovah's Witnesses' own criteria as quoted above, is this organization a false prophet?

1. **A false prophet will deny the Bible and Bible doctrine and will not "faithfully" proclaim "what is written in the Bible."** The Witnesses affirm that the Bible is God's Word and claim that their teachings are derived from the Bible. Challenging the latter claim cannot be fully done here, but in the conclusion to his book, *Understanding Jehovah's Witnesses* (1991), Robert M. Bowman, Jr., identifies the real problem:

   > The Jehovah's Witnesses confess that the Bible is the inerrant word of God. **Yet, the way they handle Scripture effectively nullifies this confession.** Based on a desire to comprehend God and his dealings with man. **Jehovah's Witnesses twist the Scriptures in the way they translate the Bible as well as in the way they interpret it.** So difficult is it for people who constantly expose themselves to the text of Scripture to continue believing that the Jehovah's Witnesses' doctrinal system is biblical that the Watchtower Society finds it necessary to remind its people in nearly every issue of the

> *Watchtower* magazine to remain trustful and uncritically accepting of everything the "faithful and discreet slave" teaches.[54]

To "faithfully" proclaim "what is written in the Bible" requires more than the proclamation of the Witnesses' teachings that are claimed to be biblical; it **requires accuracy and reliability in what is taught**. This test, the record shows, they have frequently failed.

2. **A false prophet will claim to proclaim a message from God, but his statement is false.** The record shows that the Witnesses have failed this test on a number of occasions, as teachings attributed to God, and identified as "due time" light or "meat in due season" were not fulfilled, were later revised, or were dropped.

3. **The prophecies of a false prophet will fail. They will not "come to pass exactly as prophesied."** That this characterizes Witness history has been documented numerous times in this study. Prof. M. James Penton reminds the reader:

> **No major Christian sectarian movement has been so insistent on prophesying the end of the present world in such definite ways or on such specific dates as have Jehovah's Witnesses,** at least since the Millerites and Second Adventists of the nineteenth century who were the Witnesses' direct millenarian forbears. During the early years of their history, they consistently looked to specific dates—1874, 1878, 1881, 1910, 1914, 1918, 1920, 1925, and others—as having definite eschatological significance.... **When these prophecies failed, they had to be reinterpreted, spiritualized, or, in some cases, ultimately abandoned.**[55]

A false prophet fails the test of Deuteronomy 18:21-22: "And in case you should say in your heart: 'How shall we know the word that Jehovah has not spoken?' when the prophet speaks in the name of Jehovah and the word does not occur or come true, that is the word that Jehovah did not speak. With presumptuousness the prophet spoke it. You must not get frightened at him" (*NWT*).

4. **A false prophet will deny the prophetic office, saying: "I am no prophet."** Raymond Franz comments: "The organization seeks to robe itself in the awesome role of a prophet of God and claim the deference that such a prophetic office merits. Yet, it disclaims the responsibility for accuracy that goes with the office."[56]

5. **In place of sound biblical teachings, the false prophet will set forth "man made theories or guesses, either his own or that of others."** Many of the teachings of the Witnesses fit this mark of a false prophet. If what was published was "not human opinion,"[57] as it was often claimed, those teachings that were changed, or predictions that failed, could not have come from God. Therefore, some of these may be identified as "man-made theories or guesses."

6. **A false prophet will not communicate "the magnificent things of God" (Acts 2:11): "the things about God's kingdom since A.D. 1914, when the Gentile Times ("the appointed times of the nations") ended."**[58] "The magnificent things of God" could not be "the things about God's kingdom since 1914"—for, as it was shown earlier in this study, this teaching is erroneous, and the message being

communicated in the first century could not relate to 1914. Therefore, the Jehovah's Witnesses are proclaiming a false message and are false prophets. What were these "magnificent things of God"? The *Theological Dictionary of the New Testament* comments on the word *megaleion*: "This word, meaning 'greatness,' is used in the plural form 'mighty acts' (Dt. 11:2). In Acts 2:11, *ta megaleia* are the mighty acts of God in the story of Christ."[59]

It is obvious from the Watch Tower's record, from Scripture, and from **their own statements of what characterizes a false prophet,** they cannot escape that same identification. Apparently as a result of being confronted on the issue, various excuses have been published to escape this conclusion.[60]

The "Good News" or a Different Gospel?

Not only is the Watch Tower Society a false prophet organization, but it proclaims a different gospel or "good news" from that proclaimed by Christ and the apostles. This difference is openly acknowledged in the publications distributed by the Jehovah's Witnesses.

How do the Jehovah's Witnesses understand the gospel? The following quotations are all from *The Watchtower.*

"...It is true that the gospel of the kingdom of God and of his Christ was **not preached until after 1918** A.D."[61]

"God's remnant on earth, that is to say, **Jehovah's witnesses, received from the hand of God's angel the message of the kingdom gospel, which they must preach**; as written: 'And I saw another angel fly in the midst of heaven, having the everlasting gospel to preach unto them that dwell on the earth, and to every nation, and kindred, and tongue, and people.' (Rev. 14:6) **'This gospel of the kingdom' has since been preached....**"[62]

"Ever since the end of the Gentile Times in 1914 **something of very present importance has been added to the 'good news' of God that Jesus Christ used to preach....** Namely, the birth of God's Messianic kingdom in the heavens at the end of the Gentile Times in 1914. And after the ensuing war in the invisible heavens and the ouster of Satan the Devil and his demons from heaven and down to earth, **this announcement was sounded forth, to be added to the good news**, as stated in Revelation 12:9-12.... Not before the 'appointed times of the nations' ended in the fall of 1914 could the good news be preached of the newborn, established heavenly kingdom of God and of his Messiah. This, then, must be the good news that Jesus Christ in his prophecy said had to be preached first in all the nations (Mark 13:10)."[63]

"However, from the context of Mark 13:10 it is apparent that **Jesus had in mind a special kind of good news....** It has been in particular since 1919 that this good news has been preached. This good news tells the people that God's kingdom has been established in the heavens, that Satan has been cast out of heaven, God's war of Armageddon is near, that soon the blessings of God's kingdom will make this earth into a paradise and that then even the dead in the memorial tombs will arise."[64]

"But the Kingdom witnessing of Jehovah's Witnesses since 1914 has been **something far different from what Christendom's missionaries have published both before and after 1914.**"[65]

"Let the honest-hearted person compare the kind of preaching of the gospel of the Kingdom done by the religious systems of Christendom during all the centuries with that done by Jehovah's Witnesses since the end of World War I in 1918. **They are not one and the same kind.** That of Jehovah's Witnesses is really 'gospel,' or 'good news,' as of God's heavenly kingdom that was established by the enthronement of his Son Jesus Christ at the end of the Gentile Times in 1914."[66]

"In 'the last days,' **the good news of the Kingdom involves more than it did when Jesus was on earth....** Now that we have reached 'the conclusion of this system of things,' the preaching of the good news of the

Kingdom includes the striking, message that the Kingdom is established in the heavens."[67]

"Truly, our generation is unique in many ways. Nevertheless, one thing stands out as **the most important event of our time, and beside it all other things pale into insignificance**.... According to all the evidence, in the latter part of that year [1914], Jesus received the crown of kingship from the 'Ancient of Days' and began to rule."[68]

"An organization that does not confess God's kingdom before men will not be confessed or acknowledged by God's kingdom in which Jesus serves—Matt. 10:32, 33."[69]

Raymond Franz reports that on November 17, 1979, Society president Fred Franz, among other things, stated: "The **sole purpose of our existence as a Society is to announce the Kingdom established in 1914** and to sound the warning of the fall of Babylon the Great. We have a *special* message to deliver."[70]

From these statements, it is apparent how all-important to the Witnesses this message is. But if it is based on a false foundation, as Carl Olof Jonsson and Wolfgang Herbst state:

> However, **if this enthronement in 1914—demonstrated in this work** [*The "Sign" of the Last Days—When?*] **to be a delusion—is the most distinctive feature of their gospel, the world-wide preaching of it can hardly have anything to do with Jesus' prediction at all.** Moreover, when Jesus spoke of "this" gospel of the kingdom he could only be referring to the gospel he and his apostles were then preaching. Compare Matthew 26:13, where the phrase "this gospel" also occurs. By claiming that Matthew 24:14 was fulfilled on a small scale before 70 A.D., the Watch Tower Society in effect admits this. **Thus Jesus did not have in mind some new, startling gospel to be introduced in this 20th Century. Galatians 1:6-8 actually *condemns* 'new' gospels that becloud or infringe upon the original, genuine "good news" preached in the first century.**[71]

Galatians 1:8-9 (*NWT*) is clear:

> However, even if we or an angel out of heaven were to declare to YOU as good news something beyond what we declared to YOU as good news, let him be accursed. As we have said above, I also now say again, Whoever it is that is declaring to YOU as good news something beyond what YOU accepted, let him be accursed.

The Gospel, or "the good news," is the message that through Christ's death, burial, and resurrection, God has provided the way for sinful man to be redeemed through faith.

> Now I make known to you, brethren, the gospel which I preached to you, which also you received, in which also you stand, by which also you are saved, if you hold fast the word which I preached to you, unless you believed in vain. For I delivered to you as of first importance what I also received, that Christ died for our sins according to the Scriptures, and that He was buried, and that He was raised on the third day according to the Scriptures (1 Cor. 15:1-4 NASB).

Notes

1. Walter Salter, letter to Hon. J. F. Rutherford, 1 Apr. 1937, 3. Salter is mentioned in the Witnesses' *Proclaimers* history as an example of one "who allowed pride to undermine their faith." Among other

things it states that he "began to disagree with the Society's publications"—which is true as his statement clearly shows—but no specifics are given (628). The Salter case was obviously important at the time as material dealing with it appears in various issues of the 1937 and 1939 *Watchtower* and 1937 *Consolation*. Salter responded to charges against him in a letter to W. E. Van Amburgh, secretary-treasurer of the Watch Tower Bible and Tract Society, dated April 3, 1937.

2. Raymond Franz, *Crisis of Conscience* (2nd ed.; Atlanta: Commentary Press, 1992), 344-45.

3. *J. W. Research Journal*, Winter 1996, 3.

4. Ron Frye, "The Watch Tower Society and Spiritual Authority," *The Bible Examiner*, Sept.-Oct. 1982, 30.

5. Ibid., 11.

6. Duane Magnani, *Bible Students: Do Jehovah's Witnesses Really Study the Bible?* (Clayton, Calif.: Witness Inc., 1983), 51.

7. Duane Magnani, *The Heavenly Weather Man* (Clayton, Calif.: Witness Inc., 1987, 178).

8. James A. Beverly, *Crisis of Allegiance* (Burlington, Ontario, Canada: Welsh Publishing Co., 1986), 97-98.

9. Ibid., 98-99.

10. M. James Penton, *Apocalypse Delayed* (2nd ed.; Atlanta: Commentary Press, 1997), xiv.

11. Penton discusses "progressive revelation" (ibid., 165-71) and explains the Witnesses view is "based primarily on a **misapplication of Proverbs 4:18**.... It is usually understood to mean a progressive *organizational understanding* of the Bible through the application of reason, study, and the undefined guidance of the holy spirit. **But at other times it takes on the character of a direct, latter-day revelation...**" (165). As Penton states, Proverbs 4:18 has been misapplied. Proverbs 4:10-19 contrasts the two paths—one of light and the other of darkness: "But the **path of the righteous** ones is like the bright light that is getting lighter and lighter until the day is firmly established. The **way of the wicked ones** is like the gloom; they have not known at what they are stumbling" (*NWT*, vv. 18-19). Those who do not heed the counsel are destined to stumble. Those who hear, have the light ("Jehovah is my Light" [Psa. 27:1]; "Come and let us walk in the light of Jehovah" [Isa. 2:5]; "Your word is a lamp to my foot, And a light to my roadway [path]" [Psa. 119:105]). Proverbs 4:18-19 provides no justification for doctrinal adjustments.

12. Ibid., 165-66.

13. *Watchman Expositor*, vol. 13, No. 1, 1996, 8.

14. *NWT* (1950 ed.), ad in the back.

15. *Reasoning From the Scriptures* (1985), 136. The claim of minor changes in doctrine is stated again in a more recent *Watchtower*: "Today's watchman class has likewise had to **clarify** its views from time to time.... Besides, viewed in context, are not most of the **adjustments** that have occurred **relatively small**? Our basic understanding of the Bible has not changed" (*WT*, Aug. 15, 1997, 16). This statement is simply not true, and as Raymond Franz writes, "...There are very few Watch Tower publications that were published during the first 80 years of the organization's 110-year history that are not considered 'out of date'" (Raymond Franz, *In Search of Christian Freedom* (Atlanta: Commentary Press, 1991), 480).

16. *WT*, 15 Dec. 1990, 26.

17. *WT*, 1 Aug. 1971, 466.

18. Ibid., 467.

19. *WT*, 15 Feb. 1981, 19.

20. *WT*, 1 Dec. 1981, 27.

21. Franz, *Crisis*, 308 fn 8).

22. *WT*, 1 July 1973, 402.

23. "Truth," *Insight on the Scriptures* (1988), vol. 2, 1132.

24. *WT*, 1 July 1979, 7.

25. *WTR*, 15 Dec, 1916, 6023.

26. Rutherford, *The Harp of God* (1921,—early eds.), 237.

27. *WT*, 1 June 1943, 166.

28. *WTR*, 1 Apr. 1919, 6414.

29. *WT*, 15 Dec. 1988, 4.

30. *WTR*, July, 1880, 119.

31. *WTR*, Feb. 1881, 188.

32. *Awake!*, 8 Oct. 1968, 23.

33. *WT*, 1 Nov. 1995, 17.

34. *WT*, 1 May 1985, 4.

35. Rutherford, *Model Study No. 1* (1937), 53.

36. Pursuer's Proof *Douglas Walsh vs. the Right Honorable James Laytham Clyde, M.P., P.C.*, Scottish Court of Sessions, Nov. 1954 (1958 ed.), 503.

37. *WT*, 1 Dec. 1990, 19.

38. *WT*, 15 Feb. 1981, 19.

39. *WT*, 1 May 1992, 31.

40. *WT*, 15 Jan. 1983, 27.

41. *WT*, 1 Oct. 1982, 27; *"The Nations Shall Know that I Am Jehovah"—How?* (1971), *66, 292; "Let Your Name Be Sanctified"* (1961), 334-37.

42. *WT*, 15 Aug. 1919, 244.

43. Rutherford, *Prophecy* (1929), 45-47.

44. *WT*, 15 May 1930, 153-56.

45. Rutherford, *Light II* (1930), 46-47.

46. Ibid., 49.

47. *WT*, 15 Oct. 1958, 613, quoting the *Evening Free Lance* (Hollister, Calif.), 30 Jan. 1957.

48. *Awake!*, 8 Oct. 1968, 23.

49. *Paradise Restored to Mankind—By Theocracy!* (1972), 353-54.

50. *WT*, 1 Sept. 1979, 29-30. "Whom, then, did Jehovah send and who are the ones that **speak in his name**, Christendom's clergy who prophesy oppositely, or the Jeremiah class of today? Future events will identify the truthtellers" (*WT*, 1 Nov. 1979, 25).

51. *WT*, 1 Feb. 1992, 3.

52. Ibid., 4

53. Ibid., 6.

54. Robert M. Bowman, Jr., *Understanding Jehovah's Witnesses: Why They Read the Bible the Way They Do* (Grand Rapids: Baker Book House, 1991), 123.

55. Penton, 3-4.

56. Franz, *In Search*, 425. See the Witness disclaimers in *Awake!*, 22 Mar. 1993, 4.

57. The books and booklets are all by Rutherford: *Reconciliation* (1928), 6; *Government* (1928), 5; *Universal War Near* (1935), 3; *Riches* (1936), 354; *Government and Peace* (1939), 27; *Fascism or Freedom* (1939), 37. *Cons.* 18 May 1938, 31; *WT*, 1 Aug. 1940, 230; *WT*, 1 Jan. 1942, 5; *WT*, 1 July 1958, 406.

58. *WT*, 1 Oct. 1961, 594. To the Witnesses, the Kingdom message is of crucial importance today, because "an organization that does not confess God's kingdom before men will not be confessed or acknowledged by God's kingdom in which Jesus serves—Matt. 10:32, 33" (*WT*, 1 Oct. 1961, 595).

59. Geoffrey W. Bromiley, ed., *The Theological Dictionary of the New Testament* (Grand Rapids: Wm. B. Eerdmans, 1985), 575.

60. In an effort to respond to the false prophet charge, Watch Tower publications have made excuses, such as: "Jehovah's Witnesses do not claim to be inspired prophets. They have made mistakes. Like the apostles of Jesus Christ, they have at times had some wrong expectations" (*Reasoning From the Scriptures* [1985], 136). "Jehovah's Witnesses, in their eagerness for Jesus' second coming, have **suggested** dates that turned out to be incorrect" (*Awake!*, 22 Mar. 1993, 4). Such examples as the prophets Jonah and Nathan, and such references as Luke 19:11, John 21:22-23 and Acts 1:6-7, have been used. A number of these excuses have been examined and answered. See: Bowman, 51-54; Ron Rhodes, *Reasoning from the Scriptures with the Jehovah's Witnesses* (Eugene, Oreg.: Harvest House, 1993), 367-75; and *Comments From the Friends*, Fall 1993 issue. In conclusion: "Although it is true that biblical prophets made mistakes, they did not make such mistakes when they were prophesying. No genuine biblical example of an error in prediction or doctrine can be found in the prophetic teachings of any true prophet of God in the Bible" (Bowman, 53).

61. *WT*, 1 Dec. 1928, 364.

62. *WT*, 1 Nov. 1935, 331.

63. *WT*, 15 Dec. 1967, 753.

64. *WT*, 1 Dec. 1968, 715.

65. *WT*, 1 Oct., 1980, 28.

66. *WT*, 1 May 1981, 17.

67. *WT*, 1 Jan. 1988, 21.

68. Ibid., 10.

69. *WT*, 1 Oct. 1961, 595.

70. Franz, *In Search*, 32-33.

71. Carl Olof Jonsson and Wolfgang Herbst, *The "Sign" of the Last Days—When?* (Atlanta: Commentary Press, 1987), 215-16.

Selected Bibliography

A number of additional sources of helpful information may be found in the endnotes. The inclusion of a book in this selected bibliography **does not indicate endorsement of everything in that publication**.

Barnes, Peter. *Out of Darkness into Light*. San Diego: Equippers Inc., 1992.

Bergman, Jerry. *Jehovah's Witnesses: A Comprehensive and Selectively Annotated Bibliography*. Westport, Conn.: Greenwood Press, 1999. (Contains nearly 10,000 references.)

Bowman, Robert M., Jr. *Understanding Jehovah's Witnesses: Why They Read the Bible the Way They Do*. Grand Rapids: Baker Book House, 1991.

Chretien, Leonard and Marjorie. *Witnesses of Jehovah*. Eugene, Oreg.: Harvest House, 1988.

Crompton, Robert. *Counting the Days to Armageddon: The Jehovah's Witnesses and The Second Presence of Christ*. Cambridge: James Clarke & Co., 1996.

Franz, Raymond. *Crisis of Conscience*. 2nd ed. Atlanta: Commentary Press, 1992.

_____. *In Search of Christian Freedom*. Atlanta: Commentary Press, 1991.

Gruss, Edmond C., with Leonard Chretien. *Jehovah's Witnesses—Their Monuments to False Prophecy*. Clayton, Calif.: Witness Inc., 1997.

Harris, Doug and Bill Browning. *Awake! To the Watchtower*. Rev. ed. 1993. Morden Surrey, UK: Reachout Trust, 1988.

Jonsson, Carl Olof. *The Gentile Times Reconsidered*. 3rd ed. Atlanta: Commentary Press, 1998.

_____, and Wolfgang Herbst. *The "Sign" of the Last Days—When?* (Atlanta; Commentary Press, 1987.

Lingle, Wilbur. *Approaching Jehovah's Witnesses in Love*. Fort Washington, Pa.: Christian Literature Crusade, 1994.

Magnani, Duane. *Bible Students? Do Jehovah's Witnesses Really Study the Bible?—An Analysis*. Clayton, Calif.: Witness, Inc., 1983.

_____, and Arthur Barrett. *Dialogue with Jehovah's Witnesses*, 2 vols. Clayton, Calif.: Witness Inc., 1983.

_____. *Point/Counterpoint: A Refutation of the Jehovah's Witnesses Book: Reasoning from the Scriptures*, vol. 1. *False Prophets*. Clayton, Calif.: Witness Inc., 1986.

_____, with Arthur Barrett. *The Watchtower Files: Dialogue with a Jehovah's Witness*. Minneapolis: Bethany House, 1985.

Penton, M. James. *Apocalypse Delayed: The Story of Jehovah's Witnesses*. 2nd ed. Toronto: University of Toronto Press, 1997.

Reed, David A., ed., complied by Steve Huntoon and John Cornell. *Index of Watchtower Errors 1879-1989*. Grand Rapids: Baker Book House, 1990. (Reed has also published "a mid-1994 supplement to the book *Index of Watchtower Errors: 1879-1989*.")

_____. *Jehovah's Witness Literature: A Critical Guide to Watchtower Publications*. Grand Rapids: Baker Books, 1993.

Rhodes, Ron. *Reasoning from the Scriptures with the Jehovah's Witnesses*. Eugene, Oreg.: Harvest House, 1993.

Watters, Randall. *Thus Saith the Governing Body of Jehovah's Witnesses*. 2nd ed. Manhattan Beach, Calif.: Common Sense Publications, 1996.

White, Timothy. *A People For His Name*. New York: Vantage Press, 1967.

Sources of Information

Some organizations with ministries to Jehovah's Witnesses and materials for Christian training and outreach.

Free Minds Inc. www.freeminds.org
P.O. Box 3818
Manhattan Beach, CA 90266
The Free Minds Inc. website lists more than 100 Watchtower-related websites, plus a number of foreign language sites, and other websites for related information.

Witness Inc. www.witnessinc.com
P.O. Box 597
Clayton, CA 94517

Other Sources of Information

Personal Freedom Outreach www.pfo.org
P.O. Box 26062
St. Louis, MO 63136-0062

Watchman Fellowship www.watchman.org
P.O. Box 13340
Arlington, TX 76094-0340

Christian Research Institute www.equip.org
P.O. Box 7000
Rancho Santa Margarita, CA 92688-7000

Reachout Trust www.reachouttrust.org
24 Ormond Road
Richmond Surrey TW10 6TH
United Kingdom

JW Research Journal www.premier1.net/~raines/journal
P.O. Box 5534
Everett, WA 98206

Printed in the United States
52275LVS00004B/163-172

9 781931 232302